What makes the JobBank series the nation's premier line of employment guides?

With vital employment information on thousands of employers across the nation, the JobBank series is the most comprehensive and authoritative set of career directories available today.

Each book in the series provides information on **dozens of different industries** in a given city or area, with the primary employer listings providing contact information, telephone numbers, addresses, a summary of the firm's business, and in many cases descriptions of the firm's typical professional job categories, the principal educational backgrounds sought, and the fringe benefits offered.

In addition to the **detailed primary employer listings,** JobBank books give telephone numbers and addresses for **thousands of additional employers.**

All of the reference information in the JobBank series is as up-to-date and accurate as possible. Every year, the entire database is thoroughly researched and verified by mail and by telephone. Adams Media Corporation publishes **more local employment guides more often** than any other publisher of career directories.

In addition, the JobBank series features important information about the local job scene -- **forecasts on which industries are the hottest, overviews of local economic trends,** and **lists of regional professional associations,** so you can get your job hunt started off right.

Hundreds of discussions with job hunters show that they prefer information organized geographically, because most people look for jobs in specific areas. The JobBank series offers **30 regional titles**, from Minneapolis to Houston, and from Boston to San Francisco. Jobseekers moving to a particular area can review the local employment data not only for information on the type of industry most common to that region, but also for names of specific companies.

A condensed, but thorough, review of the entire job search process is presented in the chapter **The Basics of Job Winning**, a feature which has received many compliments from career counselors. In addition, each JobBank directory includes a section on **resumes and cover letters** the *New York Times* has acclaimed as "excellent."

The JobBank series gives job hunters the most comprehensive, timely, and accurate career information, organized and indexed to facilitate the job search. An entire career reference library, JobBank books are the consummate employment guides.

Published by Adams Media Corporation
260 Center Street, Holbrook, MA 02343

Manufactured in the United States of America.

Because addresses and telephone numbers of smaller companies change rapidly, we recommend you call each company and verify the information before mailing to the employers listed in this book. Mass mailings are not recommended.

While the publisher has made every reasonable effort to obtain and verify accurate information, occasional errors are inevitable due to the magnitude of the database. Should you discover an error, or if a company is missing, please write the editors at the above address so that we may update future editions.

"This publication is designed to provide accurate and authoritative information with regard to the subject matter covered. It is sold with the understanding that the publisher is not engaged in rendering legal, accounting, or other professional advice. If legal advice or other expert assistance is required, the services of a competent professional person should be sought."

--From a *Declaration of Principles* jointly adopted by a Committee of the American Bar Association and a Committee of Publishers and Associations

The appearance of a listing in the book does not constitute an endorsement from the publisher.

ISBN: 1-55850-673-X

This book is available at quantity discounts for bulk purchases.
For information, call 800/872-5627.

Visit our exciting job and career site at http://www.careercity.com

MORE PRAISE FROM ACROSS THE NATION FOR THE JOBBANK SERIES...

"If you are looking for a job ... before you go to the newspapers and the help-wanted ads, listen to Bob Adams, publisher of *The Metropolitan New York JobBank*."

-Tom Brokaw, *NBC*

"For those graduates whose parents are pacing the floor, conspicuously placing circled want ads around the house and typing up resumes, [*The Carolina JobBank*] answers job-search questions."

-Greensboro News and Record

"A timely book for Chicago job hunters follows books from the same publisher that were well received in New York and Boston ... [*The Chicago JobBank* is] a fine tool for job hunters ..."

-Clarence Peterson, *Chicago Tribune*

"Because our listing is seen by people across the nation, it generates lots of resumes for us. We encourage unsolicited resumes. We'll always be listed [in *The Chicago JobBank*] as long as I'm in this career."

-Tom Fitzpatrick, Director of Human Resources
Merchandise Mart Properties, Inc.

"Job hunters can't afford to waste time. *The Minneapolis-St. Paul JobBank* contains information that used to require hours of research in the library."

-Carmella Zagone
Minneapolis-based Human Resources Administrator

"*The Florida JobBank* is an invaluable job-search reference tool. It provides the most up-to-date information and contact names available for companies in Florida. I should know -- it worked for me!"

-Rhonda Cody, Human Resources Consultant
Aetna Life and Casualty

"*The Boston JobBank* provides a handy map of employment possibilities in Greater Boston. This book can help in the initial steps of a job search by locating major employers, describing their business activities, and for most firms, by naming the contact person and listing typical professional positions. For recent college graduates, as well as experienced professionals, *The Boston JobBank* is an excellent place to begin a job search."

-Juliet F. Brudney, Career Columnist
Boston Globe

"No longer can jobseekers feel secure about finding employment just through want ads. With the tough competition in the job market, particularly in the Boston area, they need much more help. For this reason, *The Boston JobBank* will have a wide and appreciative audience of new graduates, job changers, and people relocating to Boston. It provides a good place to start a search for entry-level professional positions."

-Journal of College Placement

"*The Phoenix JobBank* is a first-class publication. The information provided is useful and current."

-Lyndon Denton
Director of Human Resources and Materials Management
Apache Nitrogen Products, Inc.

"*The Seattle JobBank* is an essential resource for job hunters."

-Gil Lopez, Staffing Team Manager
Battelle Pacific Northwest Laboratories

"I read through the "Basics of Job Winning" and "Resumes" sections [in *The Dallas-Ft. Worth JobBank*] and found them to be very informative, with some positive tips for the job searcher. I believe the strategies outlined will bring success to any determined candidate."

-Camilla Norder, Professional Recruiter
Presbyterian Hospital of Dallas

"Through *The Dallas-Ft. Worth JobBank,* we've been able to attract high-quality candidates for several positions."

-Rob Bertino, Southern States Sales Manager
CompuServe

"Packed with helpful contacts, *The Houston JobBank* empowers its reader to launch an effective, strategic job search in the Houston metropolitan area."

-**Andrew Ceperley, Director**
College of Communication Career Services
The University of Texas at Austin

"[*The Atlanta JobBank* is] one of the best sources for finding a job in Atlanta!"

-Luann Miller, Human Resources Manager
Prudential Preferred Financial Services

"This well-researched, well-edited, job-hunter's aid includes most major businesses and institutional entities in the New York metropolitan area ... [*The Metropolitan New York JobBank* is] highly recommended."

-Cheryl Gregory-Pindell, *Library Journal*

1997 THE San Francisco Bay Area JobBank

Managing Editor: Steven Graber

Series Editor: Jennifer J. Pfalzgraf

Associate Editors: Marcie DiPietro
Andy Richardson

Editorial Assistants: Ted Martin
Matthew P. Moran
Wendy M. Rettman
Michelle Roy
Heidi E. Sampson
Ashlee K. Stokes

Adams Media Corporation
HOLBROOK, MASSACHUSETTS

TABLE OF CONTENTS

INTRODUCTION

HOW TO USE THIS BOOK

Right now, you hold in your hands one of the most effective job-hunting tools available anywhere. In *The San Francisco Bay Area JobBank*, you will find a wide array of valuable information to help you launch or continue a rewarding career. But before you open to the book's employer listings and start calling about current job openings, take a few minutes to learn how best to use the resources presented in *The San Francisco Bay Area JobBank*.

The San Francisco Bay Area JobBank will help you to stand out from other jobseekers. While many people looking for a new job rely solely on newspaper help-wanted ads, this book offers you a much more effective job-search method -- direct contact. The direct contact method has been proven twice as effective as scanning the help-wanted ads. Instead of waiting for employers to come looking for you, you'll be far more effective going to them. While many of your competitors will use trial and error methods in trying to set up interviews, you'll learn not only how to get interviews, but what to expect once you've got them.

In the next few pages, we'll take you through each section of the book so you'll be prepared to get a jump-start on your competition.

The San Francisco Bay Area Job Market: An Overview

To get a feel for the state of the local job scene, read the introductory section called *The San Francisco Bay Area Job Market*. In it, we'll recap the economy's recent performance and the steps that local governments and business leaders are taking to bring new jobs to the area.

Even more importantly, you'll learn where the local economy is headed. What are the prospects for the industries that form the core of the region's economy? Which industries are growing fastest and which ones are laying off? Are there any companies or industries that are especially hot?

To answer these questions for you, we've pored over local business journals and newspapers and interviewed local business leaders and labor analysts. Whether you are new to the area and need a source of regional information, or are a lifelong resident just looking for a fresh start in a new job, you'll find this section to be a concise thumbnail sketch of where the jobs are.

This type of information is potent ammunition to bring into an interview. Showing that you're well versed in current industry trends helps give you an edge over job applicants who haven't done their homework.

Basics of Job Winning

Preparation. Strategy. Time-management. These are three of the most important elements of a successful job search. *Basics of Job Winning* helps you address these and all the other elements needed to find the right job.

One of your first priorities should be to define your personal career objectives. What qualities make a job desirable to you? Creativity? High pay? Prestige? Use *Basics of Job Winning* to weigh these questions. Then use the rest of the chapter to design a strategy to find a job that matches your criteria.

In *Basics of Job Winning,* you'll learn which job-hunting techniques work, and which don't. We've reviewed the pros and cons of mass mailings, help-wanted ads, and direct contact. We'll show you how to develop and approach contacts in your field; how to research a prospective employer; and how to use that information to get an interview and the job.

Also included in *Basics of Job Winning*: interview dress code and etiquette, the "do's and don'ts" of interviewing, sample interview questions, and more. We also deal with some of the unique problems faced by those jobseekers who are currently employed, those who have lost a job, and college students conducting their first job search.

Resumes and Cover Letters

The approach you take to writing your resume and cover letter can often mean the difference between getting an interview and never being noticed. In this section, we discuss different formats, as well as what to put on (and what to leave off) your resume. We review the benefits and drawbacks of professional resume writers, and the importance of a follow-up letter. Also included in this section are sample resumes and cover letters which you can use as models.

CD-ROM Job Search

Jobseekers who are looking for an edge against the competition may want to check out these CD-ROM products.

Online Job Search

The Information Superhighway grows larger every day and offers a multitude of services for the job hunter. This section offers a list of jobseeking sites with employer profiles, company biographies, help wanted advertisements, and more. You can also post your resume on certain sites making them available to nationwide, and in some cases worldwide, employers.

The Employer Listings

Employers are listed alphabetically by industry, and within each industry, by company names. When a company does business under a person's name, like "John Smith & Co.," the company is usually listed by the surname's spelling (in this case "S"). Exceptions occur when a company's name is widely recognized, like "JCPenney" or "Howard Johnson Motor Lodge." In those cases, the company's first name is the key ("J" and "H" respectively).

The San Francisco Bay Area JobBank covers a very wide range of industries. Each company profile is assigned to one of the industry chapters listed below.

Accounting and Management Consulting
Advertising, Marketing, and Public Relations
Aerospace
Apparel and Textiles
Architecture, Construction, and Engineering
Arts and Entertainment/Recreation
Automotive
Banking/Savings and Loans

Biotechnology, Pharmaceuticals, and Scientific R&D
Business Services and Non-Scientific Research
Charities and Social Services
Chemicals/Rubber and Plastics
Communications: Telecommunications and Broadcasting
Computer Hardware, Software, and Services
Educational Services
Electronic/Industrial Electrical Equipment
Environmental and Waste Management Services
Fabricated/Primary Metals and Products
Financial Services
Food and Beverage/Agriculture
Government
Health Care: Services, Equipment, and Products
Hotels and Restaurants
Insurance
Legal Services
Manufacturing: Miscellaneous Consumer
Manufacturing: Miscellaneous Industrial
Mining/Gas/Petroleum/Energy Related
Paper and Wood Products
Printing and Publishing
Real Estate
Retail
Stone, Clay, Glass, and Concrete Products
Transportation
Utilities: Electric/Gas/Water
Miscellaneous Wholesaling

Many of the company listings offer detailed company profiles. In addition to company names, addresses, and phone numbers, these listings also include contact names or hiring departments, and descriptions of each company's products and/or services. Many of these listings also feature a variety of additional information including:

Common positions - A list of job titles that the company commonly fills when it is hiring, organized in alphabetical order from Accountant to X-ray Technician. Note: Keep in mind that *The San Francisco Bay Area JobBank* is a directory of major employers in the area, not a directory of openings currently available. Many of the companies listed will be hiring, others will not. However, since most professional job openings are filled without the placement of help-wanted ads, contacting the employers in this book directly is still a more effective method than browsing the Sunday papers.

Educational backgrounds sought - A list of educational backgrounds that companies seek when hiring.

Benefits - What kind of benefits packages are available from these employers? Here you'll find a broad range of benefits, from the relatively common (medical insurance) to those that are much more rare (health club membership; child daycare assistance).

Special programs - Does the company offer training programs, internships, or apprenticeships? These programs can be important to first time jobseekers and college students looking for practical work experience. Many employer profiles will include information on these programs.

Parent company - If an employer is a subsidiary of a larger company, the name of that parent company will often be listed here. Use this information to supplement your company research before contacting the employer.

Number of employees - The number of workers a company employs.

Companies may also include information on other U.S. locations and any stock exchange the firm may be listed on.

Because so many job openings are with small and mid-sized employers, we've also included the addresses and phone numbers of such employers. While none of these listings include any additional hiring information, many of them do offer rewarding career opportunities. These companies are found under each industry heading. Within each industry, they are organized by the type of product or service offered.

A note on all employer listings that appear in *The San Francisco Bay Area JobBank*: This book is intended as a starting point. It is not intended to replace any effort that you, the jobseeker, should devote to your job hunt. Keep in mind that while a great deal of effort has been put into collecting and verifying the company profiles provided in this book, addresses and contact names change regularly. Inevitably, some contact names listed herein have changed even before you read this. We recommend you contact a company before mailing your resume to ensure nothing has changed.

At the end of each industry section, we have included a directory of other industry-specific resources to help you in your job search. These include: professional and industrial associations, many of which can provide employment advice and job search help; magazines that cover the industry; and additional directories that may supplement the employer listings in this book.

Employment Services

Immediately following the employer listings section of this book are listings of local employment services firms. Many jobseekers supplement their own efforts by contracting "temp" services, headhunters, and other employment search firms to generate potential job opportunities.

This section is a comprehensive listing of such firms, arranged alphabetically under the headings Employment Agencies, Temporary Agencies, and Executive Search Firms. Each listing includes the firm's name, address, telephone number and contact person. Most listings also include the industries the firm specializes in, the type of positions commonly filled, and the number of jobs filled annually.

Index

The San Francisco Bay Area JobBank index is a straight alphabetical listing.

THE SAN FRANCISCO BAY AREA JOB MARKET: AN OVERVIEW

Are you going to San Francisco? You're not alone -- the City by the Bay attracted in the neighborhood of 16 million visitors over the course of 1995, according to the San Francisco Convention & Visitors Bureau. And the beauty and history of the Bay Area ensure that such a figure will only grow larger in the years to come.

But San Francisco is far more than just a nice place to visit. According to *Fortune* magazine, its numerous attributes with respect to location, culture, higher learning, finance, and high-tech industry make San Francisco the nation's No. 1 city for business (November 1995).

That ranking is particularly impressive considering California's recent economic status. It's no secret that the '90s have not been good to California. While the state had avoided the worst of previous recessions on the strength of its mix of fast-growing industries, the recession of the early '90s hit hard. The greatest losses were in construction, led by the collapse of real estate markets and an over-built commercial sector; and manufacturing, due to cutbacks in the defense industry and a slowdown in business equipment spending.

While the worst of the recession took place in Southern California, San Francisco and the Bay Area did not escape unscathed. According to a *San Francisco Business Times* study that analyzed job growth in the 100 largest markets in the U.S. between 1992 and 1994, three of the worst 10 were in the Bay Area -- San Francisco, Oakland, and San Jose. The hardest hit was San Francisco, which lost about 13,000 jobs during that period.

But in 1995, the turnaround began. Rapid growth in industries like communications, multimedia, and computer software development helped launch the recovery. Over the year, unemployment in San Francisco was 5.1 percent, down from 5.7 percent a year earlier. And over the longer term, many analysts believe that the Bay Area may actually be headed for boom times. According to a recent report by the Center for the Continuing Study of the California Economy, the Bay Area's mix of high-tech and export industries make the future look bright.

In addition to those two sectors, the economy is also based on financial services, biomedicine, and (not surprisingly) tourism. Although it falls behind Los Angeles as the West Coast's largest business center, the greater San Francisco metro area still ranks as the fourth-largest consumer market in the nation, behind only Los Angeles, New York, and Chicago.

The Bay Area consists of nine counties: San Francisco, San Mateo, Santa Clara, Alameda, Contra Costa, Solano, Sonoma, Napa, and Marin. The economic and cultural hub of the Bay Area is, of course, San Francisco. It is the financial and business center of Northern California, and many would argue, of the entire West Coast.

To the south lies San Mateo County, which developed as a bedroom community for San Francisco and contains **San Francisco International**

Airport and many business services firms. At the southern end of San Francisco Bay is Santa Clara County, home of **Stanford University**, the city of San Jose, and the high-tech firms of Silicon Valley. Across the Bay lie the counties of Alameda and Contra Costa, where one can find numerous cultural and academic centers, including the **University of California at Berkeley**, as well as many of the region's heavy industrial manufacturers.

The northern counties of Sonoma, Napa, and Marin are mostly suburban and rural areas, although they are also home to the famous winery region, as well as other agricultural industries. Also just north of the Bay is Solano County, one of the fastest growing counties in California. It houses a growing base of biotech and manufacturing employers.

All is not sweetness and light for San Francisco. A recent *Business Journal* study indicates that the city is still near the bottom of the nation's largest metropolitan areas in terms of job growth. It's a negative the city will have to overcome in the next few years in order for its current status as media darling to continue.

Looking at some of the major industries shaping the Bay Area's economy reveals the following:

Banking and Finance

Ever since the Gold Rush of 1849, San Francisco has been an important financial center. Much of this strength is attributable to the presence in the city of such giants as the **Pacific Stock Exchange** and the **Federal Reserve Bank of San Francisco**. Leading financial services firms headquartered here include **Transamerica Corporation**, **Wells Fargo**, and **Fireman's Fund Insurance**.

San Francisco has also long been a center of international finance. More than 60 foreign banks have offices in the city, including **The Bank of Tokyo, Ltd.**, **Bank of California (The Mitsubishi Bank)**, **The Sumitomo Bank of California**, and **Bank of the West (Banque Nationale de Paris)**. This ability to draw international business has become a vital key to the city's economy, especially in the sectors of trade and tourism. According to the *San Francisco Business Times*, **Bank of America** has doubled its trade business from 1993 to 1995, opening an international trade bank that helped that sector grow by 44 percent in 1995. Corporate and international banking accounted for 32 percent of the company's net income that year.

The presence of the Pacific Stock Exchange made securities brokerage an early industry in the city. **Charles Schwab & Co.**, the country's largest discount brokerage firm, is headquartered in San Francisco; **Dean Witter Reynolds** and **Prudential-Bache Securities** are two of the area's other major financial employers.

Transportation and International Trade

Since the completion of the first continental railway in the 1870s and the emergence of Bay Area ports, San Francisco has been a major center of foreign trade. The two major ports serving the area are the **Port of Oakland** and the **Port of San Francisco**. According to the July 1996 issue of the *San Francisco*

Business Times, from the first quarter of 1995 to the first quarter of 1996, trade through the San Francisco Customs District (which includes the ports and airports of San Francisco, Oakland, San Jose, Monterey, Reno, Sacramento, and Fresno) increased by 22.7 percent. That growth is faster than that of Los Angeles, New York, and Detroit by eight, five, and four times, respectively. Those are the nation's three largest customs districts, with San Francisco currently fourth.

One reason: Trade with countries such as Japan has skyrocketed. According to the *Business Times*, Japan has shown a "strong import trend in computers, semiconductors, and manufactured goods." Integrated circuits top the list of imports and exports, and are the fastest-growing commodity traded, as well.

In fact, the Bay Area has traditionally been a strong origin for exports to Pacific Rim countries, as ships make San Francisco their last call before heading overseas. San Francisco's large Asian community and the city's prominence as a financial center also put the region at an advantage. A 1995 *Forbes* article noted that more than 170 Pacific Rim companies have U.S. headquarters in the Bay Area, employing almost 19,000 people.

Computers, Communications, and Electronics

Since the dawn of the computer age, the Bay Area has been at the forefront of high-tech innovation. In addition to well-known companies like **Hewlett-Packard**, **Intel Corporation**, and **Apple Computer**, dozens of other hardware, software, and multimedia firms are headquartered in Santa Clara County's Silicon Valley, a 25-mile stretch from Palo Alto to San Jose that many consider the high-tech capital of the world. Since 1985, high-tech business services in the Bay Area have grown by more than 70 percent.

Today, as much as half of all manufacturing in the region can be classified as high-tech, and business is booming. A recent piece of news comes from **IBM Corporation**, which opened a multimedia production office in San Francisco in mid-1996 in hopes of becoming one of the leading manufacturers of computer games, according to the *Business Times*.

As great as the high-tech opportunities are at some of the larger companies, many of the best job possibilities may be with the legions of lesser-known firms. One such firm, **Cisco Systems**, appeared on *Fortune* magazine's survey of America's fastest growing companies four times in the first half of the '90s. The networking equipment company doubled its sales each year over that period.

In looking at the communications industry, jobseekers do need to use some caution. Take the example of the largest player in the region, **Pacific Telesis Group**. With subsidiaries such as **Pacific Bell** and **Pacific Telesis International**, the company has long been one of the Bay Area's major employers. However, the company has begun phasing out many jobs through automation.

Biotechnology and Health Care

The University of California at San Francisco is the Bay Area's foremost medical research facility and is one of the nation's top health science education facilities. UC Berkeley and Stanford also play a major role in the medical sciences, which include pharmaceutical processes, medical electronics, bioengineering, and agricultural and environmental process technologies.

After **Genentech** was founded in 1976, a flood of new companies, from **Polymer Systems, Inc.** to **XOMA Corporation**, were created soon afterwards. Today, the Bay Area is shaping up to be the next Silicon Valley. According to the San Francisco Chamber of Commerce, the biotech industry could generate $50 billion in sales and create 50,000 jobs by the year 2000. The region is already the biotech capital of the world.

Tourism, Retail, and Restaurants

Tourism is San Francisco's number one business, with over 60,000 jobs directly relying on the money spent by the city's 16 million visitors per year. These visitors are attracted by many things, including: San Francisco's year-round pleasant temperatures, its fabled cable cars, Chinatown, and the spectacular views of San Francisco Bay. The city's cultural life is among the richest in the nation, graced by the world-class **San Francisco Ballet** and **San Francisco Symphony Orchestra**, as well as a host of top-quality restaurants and championship-caliber professional sporting teams.

And according to the Convention & Visitors Bureau, the city's guests spend nearly $5 billion a year in San Francisco, helping to support thousands of local hotels, restaurants, and retailers. The San Francisco Chamber of Commerce has noted that the city's tourists and business travelers spend about $864 million a year on food and beverages alone.

The jewel in San Francisco's retail crown is the Union Square district. Rivaling Manhattan's Fifth Avenue, L.A.'s Rodeo Drive, and even London's Bond Street, Union Square is home to small boutiques and major department stores alike. Also popular: the restaurants and retailers in and around Fisherman's Wharf, which affords views of the famous Golden Gate Bridge and the infamous Alcatraz; and North Beach, whose bars, coffee shops, and Italian restaurants once hosted Jack Kerouac and the rest of the "Beat Generation."

Statewide, California can point to some impressive growth in its economy over the first half of 1996. Its unemployment rate of 7.2 percent in May '96 was down from 7.9 percent in May '95, and was the state's lowest level since January of 1991. Employment increased by over 289,000 jobs from the previous year, according to the California Employment Department. The biggest gains were in services and trade industries, naturally -- but nearly every industry enjoyed job growth over the year, with government and mining the lone exceptions.

In short, all of California appears to be pulling out of the slump which plagued the state in the early '90s -- although it is the Bay Area which has the attention of the business world in early '96. And as long as San Francisco thrives as a computer and biotech leader, a world hub for international trade and finance, and a revered tourist mecca, that distinction is likely to survive as well.

For more information, jobseekers can contact:

California Employment Development Department, Labor Market Information Division, 7000 Franklin Boulevard, Building 1100, Sacramento CA 95823. 916/262-2162. World Wide Web Address: http://www.calmis.cahwnet.gov.

San Francisco Chamber of Commerce, 465 California Street, 9th Floor, San Francisco CA 94104. 415/392-4511.

San Francisco Convention & Visitors Bureau, P.O. Box 429097, San Francisco CA 94142. 415/391-2000.

THE JOB SEARCH

THE BASICS OF JOB WINNING: A CONDENSED REVIEW

This chapter is divided into four sections. The first section explains the fundamentals that every jobseeker should know, especially first-time jobseekers. The following three sections deal with special situations faced by specific types of jobseekers: those who are currently employed, those who have lost a job, and college students.

THE BASICS:

Things Everyone Needs to Know

Career Planning The first step to finding your ideal job is to clearly define your objectives. This is better known as career planning (or life planning if you wish to emphasize the importance of combining the two). Career planning has become a field of study in and of itself.

If you are thinking of choosing or switching careers, we particularly emphasize two things. First, choose a career where you will enjoy most of the day-to-day tasks. This sounds obvious, but most of us have at one point or another been attracted by a glamour industry or a prestigious job title without thinking of the most important consideration: Would we enjoy performing the everyday tasks the position entails?

The second key consideration is that you are not merely choosing a career, but also a lifestyle. Career counselors indicate that one of the most common problems people encounter in job-seeking is that they fail to consider how well-suited they are for a particular position or career. For example, some people, attracted to management consulting by good salaries, early responsibility, and high-level corporate exposure, do not adapt well to the long hours, heavy travel demands, and constant pressure to produce. Be sure to ask yourself how you might adapt to not only the day-to-day duties and working environment that a specific position entails, but also how you might adapt to the demands of that career or industry choice as a whole.

Choosing Your Strategy Assuming that you've established your career objectives, the next step of the job search is to develop a strategy. If you don't take the time to develop a strategy and lay out a plan, you may find yourself going in circles after several weeks of randomly searching for opportunities that always seem just beyond your reach.

The most common job-seeking techniques are:

- following up on help-wanted advertisements
- using employment services
- relying on personal contacts
- contacting employers directly (the Direct Contact method)

Many professionals have been successful in finding better jobs using each one of these approaches. However, the Direct Contact method boasts twice the success rate of the others. So unless you have specific reasons to believe that other strategies would work best for you, Direct Contact should form the foundation of your job search.

If you prefer to use other methods as well, try to expend at least half your effort on Direct Contact, spending the rest on all of the other methods combined. Millions of other jobseekers have already proven that Direct Contact has been twice as effective in obtaining employment, so why not benefit from their experience?

Setting Your Schedule

With your strategy in mind, the next step is to work out the details of your search. The most important detail is setting up a schedule. Of course, since job searches aren't something most people do regularly, it may be hard to estimate how long each step will take. Nonetheless, it is important to have a plan so that you can monitor your progress.

When outlining your job search schedule, have a realistic time frame in mind. If you will be job-searching full-time, your search could take at least two months or more. If you can only devote part-time effort, it will probably take at least four months.

You probably know a few currently employed people who seem to spend their whole lives searching for a better job in their spare time. Don't be one of them. If you are presently working and don't feel like devoting a lot of energy to job-seeking right now, then wait. Focus on enjoying your present position, performing your best on the job, and storing up energy for when you are really ready to begin your job search.

> **The first step in beginning your job search is to clearly define your objectives.**

Those of you who are currently unemployed should remember that job-hunting is tough work physically and emotionally. It is also intellectually demanding work that requires you to be at your best. So don't tire yourself out by working on your job campaign around the clock. At the same time, be sure to discipline yourself. The most logical way to manage your time while looking for a job is to keep your regular working hours.

If you are searching full-time and have decided to choose several different contact methods, we recommend that you divide up each week, designating some time for each method. By trying several approaches at once, you can evaluate how promising each seems and alter your schedule accordingly. But be careful -- don't judge the success of a particular technique just by the sheer number of interviews you obtain. Positions advertised in the newspaper, for instance, are likely to generate many more interviews per opening than positions that are filled without being advertised.

If you are searching part-time and decide to try several different contact methods, we recommend that you try them sequentially. You simply won't have enough time to put a meaningful amount of effort into more than one method at once. Estimate the length of your job search, and then allocate so many weeks or months for each contact method, beginning with Direct Contact.

And remember that all schedules are meant to be broken. The purpose of setting a schedule is not to rush you to your goal but to help you periodically evaluate how you're progressing.

The Direct Contact Method

Once you have scheduled your time, you are ready to begin your search in earnest. If you decide to begin with the Direct Contact method, the first step is to develop a checklist for categorizing the types of firms for which you'd like to work. You might categorize firms by product line, size, customer type (such as industrial or consumer), growth prospects, or geographical location. Your list of important criteria might be very short. If it is, good! The shorter it is, the easier it will be to locate a company that is right for you.

Now you will want to use this *JobBank* book to assemble your list of potential employers. Choose firms where *you* are most likely to be able to find a job. Try matching your skills with those that a specific job demands. Consider where your skills might be in demand, the degree of competition for employment, and the employment outlook at each company.

Separate your prospect list into three groups. The first 25 percent will be your primary target group, the next 25 percent will be your secondary group, and the remaining names you can keep in reserve.

After you form your prospect list, begin work on your resume. Refer to the Resumes and Cover Letters section following this chapter to get ideas.

Once your resume is complete, begin researching your first batch of prospective employers. You will want to determine whether you would be happy working at the firms you are researching and to get a better idea of what their employment needs might be. You also need to obtain enough information to sound highly informed about the company during phone conversations and in mail correspondence. But don't go all out on your research yet! You probably won't be able to arrange interviews with some of these firms, so save your big research effort until you start to arrange interviews. Nevertheless, you should plan to spend several hours researching each firm. Do your research in batches to save time and energy. Start with this book, and find out what you can about each of the firms in your primary target group. Contact any pertinent professional associations that may be able to help you learn more about an employer. Read industry

The more you know about a company, the more likely you are to catch an interviewer's eye. (You'll also face fewer surprises once you get the job!)

publications looking for articles on the firm. (Addresses of associations and names of important publications are listed after each industrial section of employer listings in this book.) Then try additional resources at your local library. Keep organized, and maintain a folder on each firm.

If you discover something that really disturbs you about the firm (they are about to close their only local office), or if you discover that your chances of getting a job there are practically nil (they have just instituted a hiring freeze), then cross them off your prospect list. If possible, supplement your research efforts by contacting individuals who know the firm well. Ideally you should make an informal contact with someone at that particular firm, but often a direct competitor, or a major supplier or customer, will be able to supply you with just as much information. At the very least, try to obtain whatever printed information the company has available -- not just annual reports, but product brochures and any other printed materials that the firm may have to offer, either about its operations or about career opportunities.

DEVELOPING YOUR CONTACTS: NETWORKING

Some career counselors feel that the best route to a better job is through somebody you already know or through somebody to whom you can be introduced. These counselors recommend that you build your contact base beyond your current acquaintances by asking each one to introduce you, or refer you, to additional people in your field of interest.

The theory goes like this: You might start with 15 personal contacts, each of whom introduces you to three additional people, for a total of 45 additional contacts. Then each of these people introduces you to three additional people, which adds 135 additional contacts. Theoretically, you will soon know every person in the industry.

Of course, developing your personal contacts does not work quite as smoothly as the theory suggests because some people will not be able to introduce you to anyone. The further you stray from your initial contact base, the weaker your references may be. So, if you do try developing your own contacts, try to begin with as many people that you know personally as you can. Dig into your personal phone book and your holiday greeting card list and locate old classmates from school. Be particularly sure to approach people who perform your personal business such as your lawyer, accountant, banker, doctor, stockbroker, and insurance agent. These people develop a very broad contact base due to the nature of their professions.

Getting the Interview

Now it is time to arrange an interview, time to make the Direct Contact. If you have read many books on job-searching, you may have noticed that most of these books tell you to avoid the personnel office like the plague. It is said that the personnel office never hires people; they screen candidates. Unfortunately, this is often the case. If you can identify the appropriate manager with the authority to hire you, you should try to contact that person directly. However, this will take a lot of time in each case, and often you'll be bounced back to personnel despite your efforts. So we suggest that initially you begin your Direct Contact campaign through personnel offices. If it seems that the firms on your prospect list do little hiring through personnel, you might consider some alternative courses of action.

The three obvious means of initiating Direct Contact are:

- Showing up unannounced
- Mail (postal or electronic)
- Phone calls

Cross out the first one right away. You should never show up to seek a professional position without an appointment. Even if you are somehow lucky enough to obtain an interview, you will appear so unprofessional that you will not be seriously considered.

Mail contact seems to be a good choice if you have not been in the job market for a while. You can take your time to prepare a letter, say exactly what you want, and of course include your resume. Remember that employers receive many resumes every day. Don't be surprised if you do not get a response to your inquiry, and don't spend weeks waiting for responses that may never come. If you do send a letter, follow it up (or precede it) with a phone call. This will increase your impact, and because of the initial research you did, will underscore both your familiarity with and your interest in the firm.

Another alternative is to make a "cover call." Your cover call should be just like your cover letter: concise. Your first statement should interest the employer in you. Then try to subtly mention your familiarity with the firm. Don't be overbearing; keep your introduction to three sentences or less. Be pleasant, self-confident, and relaxed. This will greatly increase the chances of the person at the other end of the line developing the conversation. But don't press. If you are asked to follow up with "something in the mail," this signals the conversation's natural end. Don't try to prolong the conversation once it has ended, and don't ask what they want to receive in the mail. Always send your resume and a highly personalized follow-up letter, reminding the addressee of the phone conversation. *Always* include a cover letter if you are asked to send a resume.

Always include a cover letter if you are asked to send a resume.

Unless you are in telephone sales, making smooth and relaxed cover calls will probably not come easily. Practice them on your own, and then with your friends or relatives.

If you obtain an interview as a result of a telephone conversation, be sure to send a thank-you note reiterating the points you made during the

DON'T BOTHER WITH MASS MAILINGS OR BARRAGES OF PHONE CALLS

Direct Contact does not mean burying every firm within a hundred miles with mail and phone calls. Mass mailings rarely work in the job hunt. This also applies to those letters that are personalized -- but dehumanized -- on an automatic typewriter or computer. Don't waste your time or money on such a project; you will fool no one but yourself.

The worst part of sending out mass mailings, or making unplanned phone calls to companies you have not researched, is that you are likely to be remembered as someone with little genuine interest in the firm, who lacks sincerity -- somebody that nobody wants to hire.

HELP WANTED ADVERTISEMENTS

Only a small fraction of professional job openings are advertised. Yet the majority of jobseekers -- and quite a few people not in the job market -- spend a lot of time studying the help wanted ads. As a result, the competition for advertised openings is often very severe.

A moderate-sized employer told us about their experience advertising in the help wanted section of a major Sunday newspaper:

It was a disaster. We had over 500 responses from this relatively small ad in just one week. We have only two phone lines in this office and one was totally knocked out. We'll never advertise for professional help again.

If you insist on following up on help wanted ads, then research a firm before you reply to an ad. Preliminary research might help to separate you from all of the other professionals responding to that ad, many of whom will have only a passing interest in the opportunity. It will also give you insight about a particular firm, to help you determine if it is potentially a good match. That said, your chances of obtaining a job through the want ads are still much smaller than they are with the Direct Contact method.

conversation. You will appear more professional and increase your impact. However, unless specifically requested, don't mail your resume once an interview has been arranged. Take it with you to the interview instead.

Preparing for the Interview

Once the interview has been arranged, begin your in-depth research. You should arrive at an interview knowing the company upside-down and inside-out. You need to know the company's products, types of customers, subsidiaries, parent company, principal locations, rank in the industry, sales and profit trends, type of ownership, size, current plans, and much more. By this time you have probably narrowed your job search to one industry. Even if you haven't, you should still be familiar with the trends in the firm's industry, the firm's principal competitors and their relative performance, and the direction in which the industry leaders are headed.

Dig into every resource you can! Read the company literature, the trade press, the business press, and if the company is public, call your stockbroker (if you have one) and ask for additional information. If possible, speak to someone at the firm before the interview, or if not, speak to someone at a competing firm. The more time you spend, the better. Even if you feel extremely pressed for time, you should set aside several hours for pre-interview research.

You should arrive at an interview knowing the company upside-down and inside-out.

If you have been out of the job market for some time, don't be surprised if you find yourself tense during your first few interviews. It will probably happen every time you re-enter the market, not just when you seek your first job after getting out of school.

Tension is natural during an interview, but knowing you have done a thorough research job should put you more at ease. Make a list of questions that you think might be asked in each interview. Think out your answers carefully and practice them with a friend. Tape record your responses to the problem questions. If you feel particularly unsure of your interviewing skills, arrange your first interviews at firms you are not as interested in. (But remember it is common courtesy to seem enthusiastic about the possibility of working for any firm at which you interview.) Practice again on your own after these first few interviews. Go over the difficult questions that you were asked.

Interview Attire

How important is the proper dress for a job interview? Buying a complete wardrobe of Brooks Brothers pinstripes or Donna Karan suits, donning new wing tips or pumps, and having your hair styled every morning are not enough to guarantee you a career position as an investment banker. But on the other hand, if you can't find a clean, conservative suit or won't take the time to wash your hair, then you are just wasting your time by interviewing at all.

Top personal grooming is as important as finding appropriate clothes for a job interview. Careful grooming indicates both a sense of thoroughness and self-confidence. This is not the time to make a statement -- take out the extra earrings and avoid any garish hair colors not found in nature. Women should not wear excessive makeup, and both men and women should refrain from wearing any perfume or cologne (it only takes a small spritz to leave an allergic interviewer with a fit of sneezing and a bad impression of your meeting). Men should be freshly shaven, even if the interview is late in the day, and men with long hair should have it pulled back and neat.

Men applying for any professional position should wear a suit, preferably in a conservative color such as navy or charcoal gray. It is easy to get away with wearing the same dark suit to consecutive interviews at the same company; just be sure to wear a different shirt and tie for each interview.

Women should also wear a businesslike suit. Professionalism still dictates a suit with a skirt, rather than slacks, as proper interview garb for women. This is usually true even at companies where pants are acceptable attire for female employees. As much as you may disagree with this guideline, the more prudent time to fight this standard is after you land the job.

SKIRT VS. PANTS:
An Interview Dilemma

For those women who are still convinced that pants are acceptable interview attire, listen to the words of one career counselor from a prestigious New England college:

I had a student who told me that since she knew women in her industry often wore pants to work, she was going to wear pants to her interviews. Almost every recruiter commented that her pants were "too casual," and even referred to her as "the one with the pants." The funny thing was that one of the recruiters who commented on her pants had been wearing jeans!

The final selection of candidates for a job opening won't be determined by dress, of course. However, inappropriate dress can quickly eliminate a first-round candidate. So while you shouldn't spend a fortune on a new wardrobe, you should be sure that your clothes are adequate. The key is to dress at least as formally or slightly more formally and more conservatively than the position would suggest.

What to Bring

Be complete. Everyone needs a watch, a pen, and a notepad. Finally, a briefcase or a leather-bound folder (containing extra, *unfolded*, copies of your resume) will help complete the look of professionalism.

Sometimes the interviewer will be running behind schedule. Don't be upset, be sympathetic. There is often pressure to interview a lot of candidates and to quickly fill a demanding position. So be sure to come to your interview with good reading material to keep yourself occupied and relaxed.

The Interview

The very beginning of the interview is the most important part because it determines the tone for the rest of it. Those first few moments are especially crucial. Do you smile when you meet? Do you establish enough eye contact, but not too much? Do you walk into the office with a self-assured and confident stride? Do you shake hands firmly? Do you

BE PREPARED:
Some Common Interview Questions

Tell me about yourself...

Why did you leave your last job?

What excites you in your current job?

Where would you like to be in five years?

How much overtime are you willing to work?

What would your previous/present employer tell me about you?

Tell me about a difficult situation that you faced at your previous/present job.

What are your greatest strengths?

What are your greatest weaknesses?

Describe a work situation where you took initiative and went beyond your normal responsibilities.

Why do you wish to work for this firm?

Why should we hire you?

make small talk easily without being garrulous? It is human nature to judge people by that first impression, so make sure it is a good one. But most of all, try to be yourself.

Often the interviewer will begin, after the small talk, by telling you about the company, the division, the department, or perhaps, the position. Because of your detailed research, the information about the company should be repetitive for you, and the interviewer would probably like nothing better than to avoid this regurgitation of the company biography. So if you can do so tactfully, indicate to the interviewer that you are very familiar with the firm. If he or she seems intent on providing you with background information, despite your hints, then acquiesce.

But be sure to remain attentive. If you can manage to generate a brief discussion of the company or the industry at this point, without being forceful, great. It will help to further build rapport, underscore your interest, and increase your impact.

Soon (if it didn't begin that way) the interviewer will begin the questions, many of which you will have already practiced. This period of the interview usually falls into one of two categories (or somewhere in between): either a structured interview, where the interviewer has a prescribed set of questions to ask; or an unstructured interview, where the interviewer will ask only leading questions to get you to talk about yourself, your experiences, and your goals. Try to sense as quickly as possible in which direction the interviewer wishes to proceed. This will make the interviewer feel more relaxed and in control of the situation.

> **The interviewer's job is to find a reason to turn you down; your job is to not provide that reason.**
>
> -John L. LaFevre, author, *How You Really Get Hired*
>
> Reprinted from the 1989/90 *CPC Annual*, with permission of the National Association of Colleges and Employers (formerly College Placement Council, Inc.), copyright holder.

Remember to keep attuned to the interviewer and make the length of your answers appropriate to the situation. If you are really unsure as to how detailed a response the interviewer is seeking, then ask.

As the interview progresses, the interviewer will probably mention some of the most important responsibilities of the position. If applicable, draw parallels between your experience and the demands of the position as detailed by the interviewer. Describe your past experience in the same manner that you do on your resume: emphasizing results and achievements and not merely describing activities. But don't exaggerate. Be on the level about your abilities.

The first interview is often the toughest, where many candidates are screened out. If you are interviewing for a very competitive position, you will have to make an impression that will last. Focus on a few of your greatest strengths that are relevant to the position. Develop these points carefully, state them again in different words, and then try to summarize them briefly at the end of the interview.

Often the interviewer will pause toward the end and ask if you have any questions. Particularly in a structured interview, this might be the one chance to really show your knowledge of and interest in the firm. Have a list prepared of specific questions that are of real interest to you. Let your questions subtly show your research and your knowledge of the firm's activities. It is wise to have an extensive list of questions, as several of them may be answered during the interview.

Getting a job offer is a lot like getting a marriage proposal. Someone is not going to offer it unless they're pretty sure you're going to accept it.

-Marilyn Hill, Associate Director, Career Center, Carleton College

Do not turn your opportunity to ask questions into an interrogation. Avoid reading directly from your list of questions, and ask questions that you are fairly certain the interviewer can answer (remember how you feel when you cannot answer a question during an interview).

Even if you are unable to determine the salary range beforehand, do not ask about it during the first interview. You can always ask about it later. Above all, don't ask about fringe benefits until you have been offered a position. (Then be sure to get all the details.)

Try not to be negative about anything during the interview (particularly any past employer or any previous job). Be cheerful. Everyone likes to work with someone who seems to be happy.

Don't let a tough question throw you off base. If you don't know the answer to a question, simply say so -- do not apologize. Just smile. Nobody can answer every question -- particularly some of the questions that are asked in job interviews.

Before your first interview, you may be able to determine how many rounds of interviews there usually are for positions at your level. (Of course it may differ quite a bit even within the different levels of one firm.) Usually you can count on attending at least two or three interviews, although some firms are known to give a minimum of six interviews for all professional positions. While you should be more relaxed as you return for subsequent interviews, the pressure will be on. The more prepared you are, the better.

Depending on what information you are able to obtain, you might want to vary your strategy quite a bit from interview to interview. For instance, if the first interview is a screening interview, then be sure a few of your strengths really stand out. On the other hand, if later interviews are primarily with people who are in a position to veto your hiring, but not to push it forward, then you should primarily focus on building rapport as opposed to reiterating and developing your key strengths.

If it looks as though your skills and background do not match the position the interviewer was hoping to fill, ask him or her if there is another division or subsidiary that perhaps could profit from your talents.

After the Interview

Write a follow-up letter immediately after the interview, while it is still fresh in the interviewer's mind (see the sample follow-up letter format found in the Resumes and Cover Letters chapter). Then, if you haven't heard from the interviewer within a week, call to stress your continued interest in the firm, and the position, and request a second interview.

THE BALANCING ACT:
Looking for a New Job While Currently Employed

For those of you who are still employed, job-searching will be particularly tiring because it must be done in addition to your normal work responsibilities. So don't overwork yourself to the point where you show up to interviews looking exhausted and start to slip behind at your current job. On the other hand, don't be tempted to quit your present job! The long hours are worth it. Searching for a job while you have one puts you in a position of strength.

Making Contact

If you're expected to be in your office during the business day, then you have additional problems to deal with. How can you work interviews into the business day? And if you work in an open office, how can you even call to set up interviews? As much as possible you should keep up the effort and the appearances on your present job. So maximize your use of the lunch hour, early mornings, and late afternoons for calling. If you keep trying, you'll be surprised how often you will be able to reach the executive you are trying to contact during your out-of-office hours. You can catch people as early as 8 a.m. and as late as 6 p.m. on frequent occasions.

Scheduling Interviews

Your inability to interview at any time other than lunch just might work to your advantage. If you can, try to set up as many interviews as possible for your lunch hour. This will go a long way to creating a relaxed atmosphere. But be sure the interviews don't stray too far from the agenda on hand.

Lunchtime interviews are much easier to obtain if you have substantial career experience. People with less experience will often find no alternative to taking time off for interviews. If you have to take time off, you have to take time off. But try to do this as little as possible. Try to take the whole day off in order to avoid being blatantly obvious about your job search, and try to schedule two to three interviews for the same day. (It is very difficult to maintain an optimum level of energy at more than three interviews in one day.) Explain to the interviewer why you might have to juggle your interview schedule -- he/she should honor the respect you're

> **Try calling as early as 8 a.m. and as late as 6 p.m. You'll be surprised how often you will be able to reach the executive you want during these times of the day.**

showing your current employer by minimizing your days off and will probably appreciate the fact that another prospective employer is interested in you.

References What do you tell an interviewer who asks for references? Just say that while you are happy to have your former employers contacted, you are trying to keep your job search confidential and would rather that your current employer not be contacted until you have been given a firm offer.

IF YOU'RE FIRED OR LAID OFF:
Picking Yourself Up and Dusting Yourself Off

If you've been fired or laid off, you are not the first and will not be the last to go through this traumatic experience. In today's changing economy, thousands of professionals lose their jobs every year. Even if you were terminated with just cause, do not lose heart. Remember, being fired is not a reflection on you as a person. It is usually a reflection of your company's staffing needs and its perception of your recent job performance and attitude. And if you were not performing up to par or enjoying your work, then you will probably be better off at another company anyway.

Be prepared for the question "Why were you fired?" during job interviews.

A thorough job search could take months, so be sure to negotiate a reasonable severance package, if possible, and determine what benefits, such as health insurance, you are still legally entitled to. Also, register for unemployment compensation immediately. Don't be surprised to find other professionals collecting unemployment compensation -- it is for everyone who has lost their job.

Don't start your job search with a flurry of unplanned activity. Start by choosing a strategy and working out a plan. Now is not the time for major changes in your life. If possible, remain in the same career and in the same geographical location, at least until you have been working again for a while. On the other hand, if the only industry for which you are trained is leaving, or is severely depressed in your area, then you should give prompt consideration to moving or switching careers.

Avoid mentioning you were fired when arranging interviews, but be prepared for the question "Why were you fired?" during an interview. If you were laid off as a result of downsizing, briefly explain, being sure to reinforce that your job loss was not due to performance. If you were in fact fired, be honest, but try to detail the reason as favorably as possible and portray what you have learned from your mistakes. If you are confident one of your past managers will give you a good reference, tell the interviewer to contact that person. Do not to speak negatively of your past employer and try not to sound particularly worried about your status of being temporarily unemployed.

Finally, don't spend too much time reflecting on why you were let go or how you might have avoided it. Think positively, look to the future, and be sure to follow a careful plan during your job search.

THE COLLEGE STUDENT:
How to Conduct Your First Job Search

While you will be able to apply many of the basics covered earlier in this chapter to your job search, there are some situations unique to the college student's job search.

Gaining Experience

Perhaps the biggest problem college students face is lack of experience. Many schools have internship programs designed to give students exposure to the field of their choice, as well as the opportunity to make valuable contacts. Check out your school's career services department to see what internships are available. If your school does not have a formal internship program, or if there are no available internships that appeal to you, try contacting local businesses and offering your services -- often, businesses will be more than willing to have any extra pair of hands (especially if those hands are unpaid!) for a day or two each week. Or try contacting school alumni to see if you can "shadow" them for a few days, and see what their day-to-day duties are like. Either way, try to begin building experience as early as possible in your college career.

What do you do if, for whatever reason, you weren't able to get experience directly related to your desired career? First, look at your previous jobs and see if there's anything you can highlight. Did you supervise or train other employees? Did you reorganize the accounting system, or boost productivity in some way? Accomplishments like these demonstrate leadership, responsibility, and innovation -- qualities that most companies look for in employees. And don't forget volunteer activities and school clubs, which can also showcase these traits.

THE GPA QUESTION

You are interviewing for the job of your dreams. Everything is going well: You've established a good rapport, the interviewer seems impressed with your qualifications, and you're almost positive the job is yours. Then you're asked about your GPA, which is pitifully low. Do you tell the truth and watch your dream job fly out the window?

Never lie about your GPA (they may request your transcript, and no company will hire a liar). You can, however, explain if there is a reason you don't feel your grades reflect your abilities, and mention any other impressive statistics. For example, if you have a high GPA in your major, or in the last few semesters (as opposed to your cumulative college career), you can use that fact to your advantage.

On-Campus Recruiting

Companies will often send recruiters to interview on-site at various colleges. This gives students a chance to get interviews at companies that may not have interviewed them otherwise, particularly if the company schedules "open" interviews, in which the only screening process is who is first in line at the sign-ups. Of course, since many more applicants gain interviews in this format, this also means that many more people are rejected. The on-campus interview is generally a screening interview, to see if it is worth the company's time to invite you in for a second interview. So do everything possible to make yourself stand out from the crowd.

The first step, of course, is to check out any and all information your school's career center has on the company. If the information seems out of date, call the company's headquarters and ask to be sent the latest annual report, or any other printed information.

Many companies will host an informational meeting for interviewees, often the evening before interviews are scheduled to take place. DO NOT MISS THIS MEETING. The recruiter will almost certainly ask if you attended. Make an effort to stay after the meeting and talk with the company's representatives. Not only does this give you an opportunity to find out more information about both the company and the position, it also makes you stand out in the recruiter's mind. If there's a particular company that you had your heart set on, but you weren't able to get an interview with them, attend the information session anyway. You may be able to convince the recruiter to squeeze you into the schedule. (Or you may discover that the company really isn't suited for you after all.)

Try to check out the interview site beforehand. Some colleges may conduct "mock" interviews that take place in one of the standard interview rooms. Or you may be able to convince a career counselor (or even a custodian) to let you sneak a peek during off-hours. Either way, having an idea of the room's setup will help you to mentally prepare.

Be sure to be at least 15 minutes early to the interview. The recruiter may be running ahead of schedule, and might like to take you early. But don't be surprised if previous interviews have run over, resulting in your 30-minute slot being reduced to 20 minutes (or less). Don't complain; just use whatever time you do have as efficiently as possible to showcase the reasons *you* are the ideal candidate.

LAST WORDS

A parting word of advice. Again and again during your job search you will be rejected. You will be rejected when you apply for interviews. You will be rejected after interviews. For every job offer you finally receive, you probably will have been rejected a multitude of times. Don't let rejections slow you down. Keep reminding yourself that the sooner you go out and get started on your job search, and get those rejections flowing in, the closer you will be to obtaining the job you want.

RESUMES AND COVER LETTERS

When filling a position, a recruiter will often have 100-plus applicants, but time to interview only a handful of the most promising ones. As a result, he or she will reject most applicants after only briefly skimming their resumes.

Unless you have phoned and talked to the recruiter -- which you should do whenever you can -- you will be chosen or rejected for an interview entirely on the basis of your resume and cover letter. Your cover letter must catch the recruiter's attention, and your resume must hold it. (But remember -- a resume is no substitute for a job search campaign. *You* must seek a job. Your resume is only one tool.)

RESUME FORMAT:
Mechanics of a First Impression

The Basics

Recruiters dislike long resumes, so unless you have an unusually strong background with many years of experience and a diversity of outstanding achievements, keep your resume length to one page. If you must squeeze in more information than would otherwise fit, try using a smaller typeface or changing the margins.

Keep your resume on standard 8-1/2" x 11" paper. Since recruiters often get resumes in batches of hundreds, a smaller-sized resume may get lost in the pile. Oversized resumes are likely to get crumpled at the edges, and won't fit easily in their files.

First impressions matter, so make sure the recruiter's first impression of your resume is a good one. Print your resume on quality paper that has weight and texture, in a conservative color such as white, ivory, or pale gray. Use matching paper and envelopes for both your resume and cover letter.

Getting it on Paper

Modern photocomposition typesetting gives you the clearest, sharpest image, a wide variety of type styles, and effects such as italics, bold-facing, and book-like justified margins. It is also much too expensive for many jobseekers. And improvements in laser printers mean that a computer-generated resume can look just as impressive as one that has been professionally typeset.

A computer or word processor is the most flexible way to type your resume. This will allow you to make changes almost instantly and to store different drafts on disk. Word processing and desktop publishing systems also offer many different fonts to choose from, each taking up different amounts of space. (It is generally best to stay between 9-point and 12-point font size.) Many other options are also available, such as bold-facing for emphasis, justified margins, and the ability to change and manipulate spacing.

The end result, however, will be largely determined by the quality of the printer you use. You need at least "letter quality" type for your resume. Do not use a "near letter quality" or dot matrix printer. Laser printers will generally provide the best quality.

Household typewriters and office typewriters with nylon or other cloth ribbons are *not* good enough for typing your resume. If you don't have access to a quality word processor, hire a professional who can prepare your resume with a word processor or typesetting machine.

Don't make your copies on an office photocopier. Only the personnel office may see the resume you mail. Everyone else may see only a copy of it, and copies of copies quickly become unreadable. Either print out each copy individually, or take your resume to a professional copy shop, which will generally offer professionally-maintained, extra-high-quality photocopiers and charge fairly reasonable prices.

Proof with Care

Whether you typed it yourself or paid to have it produced professionally, mistakes on resumes are not only embarrassing, but will usually remove you from further consideration (particularly if something obvious such as your name is misspelled). No matter how much you paid someone else to type, write, or typeset your resume, *you* lose if there is a mistake. So proofread it as carefully as possible. Get a friend to help you. Read your draft aloud as your friend checks the proof copy. Then have your friend read aloud while you check. Next, read it letter by letter to check spelling and punctuation.

> **The one piece of advice I give to everyone about their resume is: Show it to people, show it to people, show it to people. Before you ever send out a resume, show it to at least a dozen people.**
>
> -Cate Talbot Ashton,
> Associate Director,
> Career Services,
> Colby College

If you are having it typed or typeset by a resume service or a printer, and you can't bring a friend or take the time during the day to proof it, pay for it and take it home. Proof it there and bring it back later to get it corrected and printed.

If you wrote your resume on a word processing program, also use that program's built-in spell checker to double-check for spelling errors. But keep in mind that a spell checker will not find errors such as "to" for "two" or "wok" for "work." It's important that you still proofread your resume, even after it has been spell-checked.

Types of Resumes

The two most common resume formats are the functional resume and the chronological resume (examples of both types can be found at the end of this chapter). A functional resume focuses on skills and de-emphasizes job titles, employers, etc. A functional resume is best if you have been out of the work force for a long time and/or if you want to highlight specific skills and strengths that your most recent jobs don't necessarily reflect.

Choose a chronological format if you are currently working or were working recently, and if your most recent experiences relate to your desired field. Use reverse chronological order. To a recruiter your last job and your latest schooling are the most important, so put the last first and list the rest going back in time.

Organization

Your name, phone number, and a complete address should be at the top of your resume. Try to make your name stand out by using a slightly larger font size or all capital letters. Be sure to spell out everything -- never abbreviate St. for Street or Rd. for Road. If you are a college student, you should also put your home address and phone number at the top.

Next, list your experience, then your education. If you are a recent graduate, list your education first, unless your experience is more important than your education. (For example, if you have just graduated from a teaching school, have some business experience, and are applying for a job in business, you would list your business experience first.)

Keep everything easy to find. Put the dates of your employment and education on the left of the page. Put the names of the companies you worked for and the schools you attended a few spaces to the right of the dates. Put the city and state, or the city and country, where you studied or worked to the right of the page.

This is just one suggestion that may work for you. The important thing is simply to break up the text in some way that makes your resume visually attractive and easy to scan, so experiment to see which layout works best for your resume. However you set it up, stay consistent. Inconsistencies in fonts, spacing, or tenses will make your resume look sloppy. Also, be sure to use tabs to keep your information vertically lined up, rather than the less precise space bar.

RESUME CONTENT:
Say it with Style

Sell Yourself

You are selling your skills and accomplishments in your resume, so it is important to inventory yourself and know yourself. If you have achieved something, say so. Put it in the best possible light. But avoid subjective statements, such as "I am a hard worker" or "I get along well with my coworkers." Just stick to the facts.

While you shouldn't hold back or be modest, don't exaggerate your achievements to the point of misrepresentation. Be honest. Many companies will immediately drop an applicant from consideration (or fire a current employee) if inaccurate information is discovered on a resume or other application material.

Keep it Brief

Write down the important (and pertinent) things you have done, but do it in as few words as possible. Your resume will be scanned, not read, and short, concise phrases are much more effective than long-winded sentences. Avoid the use of "I" when emphasizing your accomplishments. Instead, use brief phrases beginning with action verbs.

While some technical terms will be unavoidable, you should try to avoid excessive "technicalese." Keep in mind that the first person to see your resume may be a human resources person who won't necessarily know all the jargon -- and how can they be impressed by something they don't understand?

Also, try to keep your paragraphs at six lines or shorter. If you have more than six lines of information about one job or school, put it in two or more paragraphs. The shorter your resume is, the more carefully it will be examined. Remember: Your resume usually has between eight and 45 seconds to catch an employer's eye. So make every second count.

Job Objective

A functional resume may require a job objective to give it focus. One or two sentences describing the job you are seeking can clarify in what capacity your skills will be best put to use.

Examples: An entry-level position in the publishing industry.
A challenging position requiring analytical thought and excellent writing skills.

Don't include a job objective in a chronological resume. Even if you are certain of exactly what type of job you desire, the presence of a job objective might eliminate you from consideration for other positions that a recruiter feels are a better match for your qualifications. But even though you may not put an objective on paper, having a career goal in mind as you write can help give your resume a sense of direction.

Work Experience

Some jobseekers may choose to include both "Relevant Experience" and "Additional Experience" sections. This can be useful, as it allows the jobseeker to place more emphasis on certain experiences and to de-emphasize others.

Emphasize continued experience in a particular job area or continued interest in a particular industry. De-emphasize irrelevant positions. Delete positions that you held for less than four months (unless you are a very recent college grad or still in school). Stress your results, elaborating on how you contributed in your previous jobs. Did you increase sales, reduce costs, improve a product, implement a new program? Were you promoted? Use specific numbers (i.e., quantities, percentages, dollar amounts) whenever possible.

Mention all relevant responsibilities. Be specific, and slant your past accomplishments toward the position that you hope to obtain. For example, do you hope to supervise people? If so, then state how many people, performing what function, you have supervised.

Education

Keep it brief if you have more than two years of career experience. Elaborate more if you have less experience. If you are a recent grad with two or more years of college, you may choose to include any high school activities that are directly relevant to your career. If you've been out of school for awhile, list post-secondary education only.

Mention degrees received and any honors or special awards. Note individual courses or research projects you participated in that might be relevant for employers. For example, if you are an English major applying for a position as a business writer, be sure to mention any business or economics courses.

USE ACTION VERBS

How you write your resume is just as important as *what* you write. The strongest resumes use short phrases beginning with action verbs. Below are a few action verbs you may want to use. (This list is not all-inclusive.)

achieved	developed	integrated	purchased
administered	devised	interpreted	reduced
advised	directed	interviewed	regulated
analyzed	discovered	invented	reorganized
arranged	distributed	launched	represented
assembled	eliminated	maintained	researched
assisted	established	managed	resolved
attained	evaluated	marketed	restored
budgeted	examined	mediated	restructured
built	executed	monitored	revised
calculated	expanded	negotiated	scheduled
collaborated	expedited	obtained	selected
collected	facilitated	operated	served
compiled	formulated	ordered	sold
completed	founded	organized	solved
computed	generated	participated	streamlined
conducted	headed	performed	studied
consolidated	identified	planned	supervised
constructed	implemented	prepared	supplied
consulted	improved	presented	supported
controlled	increased	processed	tested
coordinated	initiated	produced	trained
created	installed	proposed	updated
designed	instituted	provided	upgraded
determined	instructed	published	wrote

Highlight Impressive Skills Be sure to mention any computer skills you may have. You may wish to include a section entitled "Additional Skills" or "Computer Skills," in which you list any software programs you know. An additional skills section is also an ideal place to mention fluency in a foreign language.

Personal Data This section is optional, but if you choose to include it, keep it very brief (two lines maximum). A one-word mention of hobbies such as fishing, chess, baseball, cooking, etc., can give the person who will interview you a good way to open up the conversation. It doesn't hurt to include activities that are unusual (fencing, bungee jumping, snake-charming) or that somehow relate to the position or the company you're applying to (for instance, if you are a member of a professional organization in your industry). Never include information about your age, health, physical characteristics, marital status, or religious affiliation.

References The most that is needed is the sentence, "References available upon request," at the bottom of your resume. If you choose to leave it out, that's fine.

HIRING A RESUME WRITER:
Is it the Right Choice for You?

If you write reasonably well, it is to your advantage to write your own resume. Writing your resume forces you to review your experience and figure out how to explain your accomplishments in clear, brief phrases. This will help you when you explain your work to interviewers.

If you write your resume, everything will be in your own words -- it will sound like you. It will say what you want it to say. If you are a good writer, know yourself well, and have a good idea of which parts of your background employers are looking for, you should be able to write your own resume better than anyone else can. If you decide to write your resume yourself, have as many people review and proofread it as possible. Welcome objective opinions and other perspectives.

> **Those things [marital status, church affiliations, etc.] have no place on a resume. Those are illegal questions, so why even put that information on your resume?**
>
> -Becky Hayes, Career Counselor
> Career Services, Rice University

When to Get Help If you have difficulty writing in "resume style" (which is quite unlike normal written language), if you are unsure of which parts of your background you should emphasize, or if you think your resume would make your case better if it did not follow one of the standard forms outlined either here or in a book on resumes, then you should consider having it professionally written.

There are two reasons even some professional resume writers we know have had their resumes written with the help of fellow professionals. First, they may need the help of someone who can be objective about their background, and second, they may want an experienced sounding board to help focus their thoughts.

If You Hire a Pro

The best way to choose a writer is by reputation -- the recommendation of a friend, a personnel director, your school placement officer, or someone else knowledgeable in the field.

Important questions:

- "How long have you been writing resumes?"
- "If I'm not satisfied with what you write, will you go over it with me and change it?"
- "Do you charge by the hour or a flat rate?"

There is no sure relation between price and quality, except that you are unlikely to get a good writer for less than $50 for an uncomplicated resume and you shouldn't have to pay more than $300 unless your experience is very extensive or complicated. There will be additional charges for printing.

Few resume services will give you a firm price over the phone, simply because some resumes are too complicated and take too long to do for a predetermined price. Some services will quote you a price that applies to almost all of their customers. Once you decide to use a specific writer, you should insist on a firm price quote before engaging their services. Also, find out how expensive minor changes will be.

COVER LETTERS:
Quick, Clear, and Concise

Always mail a cover letter with your resume. In a cover letter you can show an interest in the company that you can't show in a resume. You can also point out one or two skills or accomplishments the company can put to good use.

Make it Personal

The more personal you can get, the better. If someone known to the person you are writing has recommended that you contact the company, get permission to include his/her name in the letter. If you have the name of a person to send the letter to, address it directly to that person (after first calling the company to verify the spelling of the person's name, correct title, and mailing address). Be sure to put the person's name and title on both the letter and the envelope. This will ensure that your letter will get through to the proper person, even if a new person now occupies this position. But even if you don't have a contact name and are simply addressing it to the "Personnel Director" or the "Hiring Partner," definitely send a letter.

Type cover letters in full. Don't try the cheap and easy ways, like using a computer mail merge program, or photocopying the body of your letter and typing in the inside address and salutation. You will give the impression that you are mailing to a host of companies and have no particular interest in any one.

Cover letter do's and don'ts

- *Do* keep your cover letter brief and to the point.
- *Do* be sure it is error-free.
- *Don't* just repeat information verbatim from your resume.
- *Don't* overuse the personal pronoun "I."
- *Don't* send a generic cover letter -- show your personal knowledge of and interest in that particular company.
- *Do* accentuate what you can offer the company, not what you hope to gain from them.

FUNCTIONAL RESUME
(Prepared on a word processor

and laser printed.)

PENELOPE FRANCES PANZ
430 Miller's Crossing
Essex Junction VT 05452
802/555-9354

Objective
A position as a graphic designer commensurate with my acquired skills and expertise.

Summary
Extensive experience in plate making, separations, color matching, background definition, printing, mechanicals, color corrections, and personnel supervision. A highly motivated manager and effective communicator. Proven ability to:

- **Create Commercial Graphics**
- **Produce Embossed Drawings**
- **Color Separate**
- **Control Quality**
- **Resolve Printing Problems**
- **Analyze Customer Satisfaction**

Qualifications

Printing:
Knowledgeable in black and white as well as color printing. Excellent judgment in determining acceptability of color reproduction through comparison with original. Proficient at producing four- or five-color corrections on all media, as well as restyling previously reproduced four-color artwork.

Customer Relations:
Routinely work closely with customers to ensure specifications are met. Capable of striking a balance between technical printing capabilities and need for customer satisfaction through entire production process.

Specialties:
Practiced at creating silk screen overlays for a multitude of processes including velo bind, GBC bind, and perfect bind. Creative design and timely preparation of posters, flyers, and personalized stationery.

Personnel Supervision:
Skillful at fostering atmosphere that encourages highly talented artists to balance high-level creativity with maximum production. Consistently meet or beat production deadlines. Instruct new employees, apprentices, and students in both artistry and technical operations.

Experience
Graphic Arts Professor, University of Vermont, Burlington VT (1987-1993).
Manager, Design Graphics, Barre VT (1993-present).

Education
Massachusetts Conservatory of Art, Ph.D. 1987
University of Massachusetts, B.A. 1984

CHRONOLOGICAL RESUME

(Prepared on a word processor
and laser printed.)

MAURICE DUPETREAUX
412 Maple Court
Seattle, WA 98404
(206) 555-6584

EXPERIENCE

THE CENTER COMPANY — Seattle, WA
Systems Programmer — 1993-present

- Develop and maintain over 100 assembler modules.
- Create screen manager programs, using Assembler and Natural languages, to trace input and output to the VTAM buffer.
- Install and customize Omegamon 695 and 700 on IBM mainframes.
- Develop programs to monitor complete security control blocks, using Assembler and Natural.
- Produce stand-alone IPLs and create backrests on IBM 3380 DASD.

INFO TECH, INC. — Seattle, WA
Technical Manager — 1991-1993

- Designed and managed the implementation of a network providing the legal community with a direct line to Supreme Court cases, using Clipper on IBM 386s.
- Developed a system which catalogued entire library inventory, using Turbo Pascal on IBM AT.
- Used C to create a registration system for university registrar on IBM AT.

EDUCATION

SALEM STATE UNIVERSITY — Salem, OR
B.S. in Computer Science. — 1989
M.S. in Computer Science. — 1991

COMPUTER SKILLS

- Programming Languages: C, C++, Assembler, COBOL, Natural, Turbo Pascal, dBASE III+, and Clipper.
- Software: VTAM, Complete, TSO, JES 2, ACF 2, Omegamon 695 and 700, and Adabas.
- Operating Systems: MVS/XA, MVS/SP, MS-DOS, and VMS.

FUNCTIONAL RESUME

(Prepared on an office-quality typewriter)

LORRAINE AVAKIAN
70 Monback Avenue
Oshkosh, WI 54901
(608) 586-1243

OBJECTIVE:
To contribute over eight years of experience in promotion, communications, and administration to an entry-level position in advertising.

SUMMARY OF QUALIFICATIONS:

- Performed advertising duties for small business.
- Experience in business writing and communications skills.
- General knowledge of office management.
- Demonstrated ability to work well with others, in both supervisory and support staff roles.
- Type 75 words per minute.

SELECTED ACHIEVEMENTS AND RESULTS:

Promotion:
Composing, editing, and proofreading correspondence and PR materials for own catering service. Large-scale mailings.

Communication:
Instruction; curriculum and lesson planning; student evaluation; parent-teacher conferences; development of educational materials. Training and supervising clerks.

Computer Skills:
Proficient in MS Word, Lotus 1-2-3, Excel, and Filemaker Pro.

Administration:
Record-keeping and file maintenance. Data processing and computer operations, accounts receivable, accounts payable, inventory control, and customer relations. Scheduling, office management, and telephone reception.

WORK HISTORY:
Teacher; Self-Employed (owner of catering service); Floor Manager; Administrative Assistant; Accounting Clerk.

EDUCATION:
Beloit College, Beloit, WI, BA in Education, 1987

CHRONOLOGICAL RESUME
(Prepared on a word processor and laser printed)

T. WILLIAM MAGUIRE
16 Charles Street
Marlborough CT 06447
203/555-9641

EDUCATION

Keene State College, Keene NH
Bachelor of Arts in Elementary Education, 1995
- Graduated *magna cum laude*
- English minor
- Kappa Delta Pi member, inducted 1993

EXPERIENCE

September 1995-Present

Elmer T. Thienes Elementary School, Marlborough CT
Part-time Kindergarten Teacher
- Instruct kindergartners in reading, spelling, language arts, and music.
- Participate in the selection of textbooks and learning aids.
- Organize and supervise class field trips and coordinate in-class presentations.

Summers 1993-1995

Keene YMCA, Youth Division, Keene NH
Child-care Counselor
- Oversaw summer program for low-income youth.
- Budgeted and coordinated special events and field trips, working with Program Director to initiate variations in the program.
- Served as Youth Advocate in cooperation with social worker to address the social needs and problems of participants.

Spring 1995

Wheelock Elementary School, Keene NH
Student Teacher
- Taught third-grade class in all elementary subjects.
- Designed and implemented a two-week unit on Native Americans.
- Assisted in revision of third-grade curriculum.

Fall 1994

Child Development Center, Keene NH
Daycare Worker
- Supervised preschool children on the playground and during art activities.
- Created a "Peter Rabbit Corner," where children could quietly look at books or take a voluntary "time-out."

ADDITIONAL INTERESTS

Martial arts, skiing, politics, reading, writing.

GENERAL MODEL FOR A COVER LETTER

Your mailing address
Date

Contact's name
Contact's title
Company
Company's mailing address

Dear Mr./Ms. _________:

Immediately explain why your background makes you the best candidate for the position that you are applying for. Describe what prompted you to write (want ad, article you read about the company, networking contact, etc.). Keep the first paragraph short and hard-hitting.

Detail what you could contribute to this company. Show how your qualifications will benefit this firm. Describe your interest in the corporation. Subtly emphasizing your knowledge about this firm and your familiarity with the industry will set you apart from other candidates. Remember to keep this letter short; few recruiters will read a cover letter longer than half a page.

If possible, your closing paragraph should request specific action on the part of the reader. Include your phone number and the hours when you can be reached. Mention that if you do not hear from the reader by a specific date, you will follow up with a phone call. Lastly, thank the reader for their time, consideration, etc.

Sincerely,

(signature)

Your full name (typed)

Enclosure (use this if there are other materials, such as your resume, that are included in the same envelope)

SAMPLE COVER LETTER

16 Charles Street
Marlborough CT 06447
March 16, 1996

Ms. Lia Marcusson
Assistant Principal
Jonathon Daniels Elementary School
43 Mayflower Drive
Keene NH 03431

Dear Ms. Marcusson:

Janet Newell recently informed me of a possible opening for a third grade teacher at Jonathon Daniels Elementary School. With my experience instructing third-graders, both in schools and in summer programs, I feel I would be an ideal candidate for the position. Please accept this letter and the enclosed resume as my application.

Jonathon Daniels' educational philosophy that every child can learn and succeed interests me, since it mirrors my own. My current position at Elmer T. Thienes Elementary has reinforced this philosophy, heightening my awareness of the different styles and paces of learning and increasing my sensitivity toward special needs children. Furthermore, as a direct result of my student teaching experience at Wheelock Elementary School, I am comfortable, confident, and knowledgeable working with third-graders.

I look forward to discussing the position and my qualifications for it in more detail. I can be reached at 203/555-9641 evenings or 203/555-0248 weekdays. If I do not hear from you before Tuesday of next week, I will call to see if we can schedule a time to meet. Thank you for your time and consideration.

Sincerely,

Bill Maguire

T. William Maguire

Enclosure

GENERAL MODEL FOR A FOLLOW-UP LETTER

Your mailing address
Date

Contact's name
Contact's title
Company
Company's mailing address

Dear Mr./Ms.__________:

Remind the interviewer of the reason (i.e., a specific opening, an informational interview, etc.) you were interviewed, as well as the date. Thank him/her for the interview, and try to personalize your thanks by mentioning some specific aspect of the interview.

Confirm your interest in the organization (and in the opening, if you were interviewing for a particular position). Use specifics to re-emphasize that you have researched the firm in detail and have considered how you would fit into the company and the position. This is a good time to say anything you wish you had said in the initial meeting. Be sure to keep this letter brief; a half-page is plenty.

If appropriate, close with a suggestion for further action, such as a desire to have an additional interview, if possible. Mention your phone number and the hours that you can be reached. Alternatively, you may prefer to mention that you will follow up with a phone call in several days. Once again, thank the person for meeting with you, and state that you would be happy to provide any additional information about your qualifications.

Sincerely,

(signature)

Your full name (typed)

COVER LETTER BLUNDERS TO AVOID

There are certain errors that promise to overshadow a jobseeker's hard work. From typographical mishaps to erroneous employer information, *all* mistakes have a negative impact on the application process. Serious errors will land a cover letter in the wastebasket. Be forewarned: carefully read and reread your work.

The following list outlines some of the most common cover letter mistakes and more importantly, suggests ways to correct them. These examples have been adapted from real-life cover letters gathered during the course of research. Although some of these blunders may seem obvious, they occur far more often than not. Needless to say, none of the inquiries that included these mistakes met with positive results.

① **Unrelated career goals:** Your cover letter should be tailored to the specific position for which you are applying. A hiring manager is only interested in what you can do for the company. Your letter should convey a genuine interest in the position and a long-term pledge to fulfilling its duties. Consider the difference between these two real-life examples:

Example A (wrong way): "While my true goal is to become a professional dancer, I am exploring the option of taking on proofreading work while continuing to train for the Boston Ballet's next audition."

Example B (right way): "I am very interested in this proofreading position, and I am confident of my ability to make a contribution to your staff."

② **Comparisons and clichés:** Avoid obvious comparisons and overused clichés; such expressions distract from the letter's purpose: to highlight the most impressive skills and accomplishments.

Here are a few real-life blunders: "My word processor runs like the wind," "I am a people person," "Teamwork is my middle name," "Your company is known as the crème de la crème of accounting firms," "I am as smart as a whip," "Among the responses you receive for this position, I hope my qualifications make me leader of the pack." Remember to adopt a formal, businesslike writing style.

③ **Wasted space:** Since cover letters are generally only four paragraphs long, every word of every sentence should be directly related to your purpose for writing. In other words, if you are applying for a position as a chemist, include only those skills and experiences most applicable to the field of chemistry. Any other information weakens the application. Some real-life blunders include:

Example: "As my enclosed resume reveals, I possess the technical experience and educational background to succeed as your newest civil engineer. In addition, I am a certified gymnastics instructor who has won several local competitions."

Example: "I am writing in response to your advertisement for an accounting clerk. Currently, I am finishing an associate's degree at Fisher Junior College. My courses have included Medieval Architecture, Film Theory, American History before 1900, and Nutrition."

④ **Form letters:** Mass mailings, in which a general form letter is sent to a large number of employers, are not recommended. This approach does not allow for personalization of each application. Every cover letter you write should be tailored to the position sought and demonstrate both commitment to a specific industry and familiarity with each particular employer. Mass mailings may indicate a lack of interest in joining an organization.

In one real-life mass mailing mishap, the candidate created a form letter with blank spaces where he penned in the employer's name and position for which he was applying. Another applicant who was indecisive about her field of interest created a list of possible positions in her letter. She then circled the most appropriate job description depending on the targeted company. Even if you avoid such obvious faux pas, there are still certain formats and phrases that signal to an employer that a form letter is being used. Play it safe, and avoid mass mailings altogether.

⑤ **Inappropriate stationery:** White and ivory are the only acceptable paper colors for a cover letter. Standard office stationery is recommended; steer clear of transparent typing paper or personal stationery.

In any case, the stationery should not distract from the contents of your cover letter. A cat enthusiast who applied to our company enhanced her letter with several images of her favorite felines. A musician applying for an office position sent a letter decorated with a border of musical notes and instruments. Remember, do not rely on graphics to improve your cover letter; let your qualifications speak for themselves.

⑥ **Erroneous company information:** What company would want to hire a candidate who confuses company's products and services or misquotes recent corporate news? To avoid such errors, be sure to verify the accuracy of any company information mentioned in your cover letter. On the other hand, if you haven't researched a company, do not bluff. Statements like "I know something about your company" or "I am familiar with your products" signal to an employer that you haven't done your homework.

When citing information about a company, be specific. The following is an example of an effective way to use company information in your cover letter. "I have been following Any Corporation's growth for many months and I was excited to learn of your recent acquisition of C&M, Inc."

⑦ **Desperation:** In cover letters, you should sound determined, not desperate. While employers appreciate enthusiasm, they may be turned off by a desperate plea for employment. A fine line often separates the two. Here are a few blunders to avoid: "I am desperately eager to start, as I have been out of work for six months," "Please call today! I'll be waiting by the phone," "I really, really need this job to pay off medical bills." In one letter we came across, the candidate even dramatically enlarged the type of this closing statement, "I AM VERY BADLY IN NEED OF MONEY!"

THE BEST AND WORST WAYS TO FIND A JOB

You may be surprised to learn that some of the most popular job search methods are not successful for the majority of the people who use them. This chapter offers a chance to take a look at the real value of the services and techniques at your disposal.

EMPLOYMENT AGENCIES

Employment agencies are commissioned by employers to find qualified candidates for job openings. However, the agency's main responsibility is to meet the needs of the employer -- not to find a suitable job for the candidate.

This is not to say that employment agencies should be ruled out altogether. There are employment agencies specializing in specific industries that can be useful for experienced professionals. However, employment agencies are not a good choice for entry-level jobseekers. They often try to steer inexperienced candidates in an unwanted direction and frequently place overqualified candidates in clerical positions.

If you decide to register with an agency, your best bet is to find one that is recommended by a friend or associate. Barring that, names of agencies can be found in *The JobBank Guide to Employment Services 1996-1997* (Adams Media Corporation, 1995), found in your local public library. Or you may contact:

National Association of Personnel Services (NAPS)
3133 Mount Vernon Avenue
Alexandria VA 22305
703/684-0180

Be aware that there are an increasing number of bogus employment service firms, usually advertising in newspapers and magazines. These companies promise even inexperienced jobseekers top salaries in exciting careers -- all for a sizable fee. Others use expensive 900 numbers that jobseekers are encouraged to call. Unfortunately, most people find out too late that the jobs they have been promised do not exist.

As a general rule, most legitimate employment agencies will never guarantee a job and will not seek payment until after the candidate has been placed. Even so, every agency you are interested in should be checked out with the local chapter of the Better Business Bureau (BBB). Find out if the agency is licensed and has been in business for a reasonable amount of time. See if any valid complaints have been registered against the agency recently and if the firm has been responsive to these complaints.

If everything checks out with the BBB, call the firm to find out if it specializes in your area of expertise and how it will go about marketing your qualifications. After you have selected a few agencies (three to five is best), send each one a resume with a cover letter. Make a follow-up phone call a week or two later, and try to schedule an interview. Be prepared to take a battery of tests at the interview.

Above all, do not expect too much. Only a small percentage of all professional, managerial, and executive jobs are listed with these agencies, so they are not a terrific source of opportunities. Use them as an addition to your job search campaign, but focus your efforts on other, more promising methods.

EXECUTIVE SEARCH FIRMS

Also known as headhunters, these firms are somewhat similar to professional employment agencies. They seek out and screen candidates for high-paying executive and managerial positions and are paid by the employer. Unlike employment agencies, they typically approach viable candidates directly, rather than waiting for candidates to approach them. Many prefer to deal with already employed candidates and will not accept "blind" inquires from job hunters.

These organizations are not licensed, so if you decide to go with an executive search firm, make sure it has a solid reputation. Names of search firms can be found in *The JobBank Guide to Employment Services* or by contacting the following:

Association of Executive Search Consultants (AESC)
500 5th Avenue
Suite 930
New York NY 10110
212/398-9556

American Management Association (AMA)
Management Services Department
135 West 50th Street
New York NY 10020
212/586-8100

As with employment agencies, do not let an executive search firm become a critical element of your job search campaign -- no matter how encouraging it may sound.

TEMPORARY AGENCIES

Temporary or "temp" agencies can be a viable option. Usually these agencies specialize in clerical and support work but it's becoming increasingly common to find temporary assignments in other areas like accounting or computer programming. Working on temporary assignment will provide you with additional income during your job search and will add experience to your resume. It may also provide valuable business contacts or lead to job opportunities.

Temporary agencies are listed in your local telephone directory. Send a resume and cover letter and call to schedule an interview. Be prepared to take a number of tests at the interview.

NEWSPAPER CLASSIFIED ADS

Contrary to popular belief, newspaper classified ads are *not* a good source of opportunities for job hunters. Few people find jobs, although many spend a tremendous amount of time and effort pouring through newspaper after newspaper.

Only a small percentage of all job openings are advertised in classified ads. Unfortunately, so many applicants respond to these ads that the competition is extremely fierce. Even if your qualifications are good, your chances of getting an interview are not. If you use classified ads as a source for seeking employment, be sure to focus only a small portion of your job search efforts in this direction.

"BLIND" ADS

"Blind" ads are newspaper advertisements that do not identify the employer. Jobseekers are usually instructed to send their resumes to a post office box number. Although they may seem suspicious, "blind" ads can be a source of legitimate job opportunities. A firm may choose to run "blind" advertisements because it does not wish to be deluged with phone calls, or it may be trying to replace someone who has not been terminated yet.

JOB COUNSELING SERVICES

Most states have an employment service (sometimes called the Job Service), which provides career counseling and job placement assistance. Your local city or town may also offer job counseling services. Check your local phone book for the nearest office. Or try writing:

National Board for Certified Counselors
3D Terrace Way
Greensboro NC 27403
910/547-0607

You may also wish to consult *The JobBank Guide to Employment Services*, which lists career counseling services, as well as executive search firms, employment agencies, and temporary help services located throughout the United States.

NONPROFIT AGENCIES

It may be worthwhile to find out what services are provided by nonprofit agencies in the local community. Many of these organizations offer counseling, career development, and job placement services to specific groups such as women and minorities. Also, try contacting the national organizations below for information on career planning, job training, and other employment-related topics.

For Women:

U.S. Department of Labor
Women's Bureau
200 Constitution Avenue NW
Washington DC 20210
202/219-6606

Wider Opportunities for Women
815 15th Street NW
Suite 916
Washington DC 20005
202/638-3143

For Minorities:

NAACP
Attn: Job Services
4805 Mount Hope Drive
Baltimore MD 21215-3197
410/358-8900

National Urban League
Employment Department
500 East 62nd Street
New York NY 10021
212/310-9000

National Urban League
Washington Operations
1111 14th Street NW
6th Floor
Washington DC 20005
202/898-1604

For the Blind:

Job Opportunities for the Blind Program
National Federation for the Blind
1800 Johnson Street
Baltimore MD 21230
800/638-7518

For the Physically Challenged:

President's Committee on Employment of People with Disabilities
1331 F Street NW
Third Floor
Washington DC 20004-1107
202/376-6200

COLLEGE CAREER CENTERS

If you're a recent college graduate, your school's career center is a great place for you to start your job search. Your college career center can help you identify and evaluate your interests, work values, and skills. Most offer workshops on topics like job search strategy, resume writing, letter writing, and effective interviewing, or job fairs for meeting with prospective employers. Yours should also have a career resource library where you can find job leads and an alumni network to help you get started on networking.

Even if you've long since graduated, your college's career center may be able to provide you with valuable networking contacts. You should call to find out if your alma mater offers this or other services to alumni.

ELECTRONIC DATABASES

Electronic databases compile information on jobseekers to be scanned and searched by hiring companies. Databases may be the new wave for jobseekers of the future, but right now they are primarily used by college students and recent graduates, often with limited results.

These services usually charge between $30 and $50 to list a resume for one year. If you decide to go this route, be sure to make it only one small part of your job search plan.

DIRECT CONTACT

One of the best ways to find a job is by direct contact. Direct contact means introducing yourself to potential employers, usually by way of a resume and cover letter, without a prior referral. This type of “cold contact” can be very effective if done the right way. For more information, turn to the chapter entitled "The Basics of Job Winning."

NETWORKING

Another excellent method of finding work is through networking, a strategy that focuses primarily on developing a network of insider contacts. This is a great approach to use even if you do not have any professional contacts. Networking takes many forms; with a little skill and a lot of effort, it can be a very productive tool.

CD-ROM JOB SEARCH

Jobseekers who are looking for any edge they can find may want to check out the following selected CD-ROM products:

ADAMS JOBBANK
260 Center Street
Holbrook MA 02343
800/872-5627
The CD-ROM version of the best-selling *JobBank* series contains 16,000 detailed profiles of companies in all industries, 1,000 executive search firms, and 1,000 employment agencies. For most companies, you will find the name, address, company description, and key contact name. The database also lists commonly held positions and information on benefits for most companies. You can search the database by company name, state, industry, and job title. Calling itself a "total job search package," the CD-ROM also creates personalized resumes and cover letters and offers advice on job interviews, including over 100 sample interview questions and answers. *Adams JobBank* CD-ROM is for Windows® and Windows®95.

AMERICAN BIG BUSINESS DIRECTORY
5711 South 86th Circle
P.O. Box 37347
Omaha NE 68127
800/555-5211
American Big Business Directory has profiles of 160,000 privately and publicly held companies employing more than 100 people. The CD-ROM contains company descriptions which include company type, industry, products, and sales information. Also included are multiple contact names for each company, more than 340,000 in all. You can search the database by industry, SIC code, sales volume, employee size, or zip code.

AMERICAN MANUFACTURER'S DIRECTORY
5711 South 86th Circle
P.O. Box 37347
Omaha NE 68127
800/555-5211
Made by the same company that created *American Big Business Directory*, *American Manufacturer's Directory* lists over 531,000 manufacturing companies of all sizes and industries. The directory contains product and sales information, company size, and a key contact name for each company. The user can search by region, SIC code, sales volume, employee size, or zip code.

BUSINESS AMERICA ON CD-ROM
5711 South 86th Circle
P.O. Box 37347

Omaha NE 68127
800/555-5211
Also from the makers of *American Big Business Directory* and *American Manufacturer's Directory*, this CD-ROM contains information on 10 million U.S. companies. The profiles provide contact information and industry, as well as company size, in terms of both number of employees and sales volume. The profiles also indicate whether a company is public or private, as well as providing information about the company's products. There are a number of different search methods available, including key words, SIC code, geographic location, and number of employees.

CAREER SEARCH - INTEGRATED RESOURCE SYSTEM
21 Highland Circle
Needham MA 02194-3075
617/449-0312
Career Search is a database which contains listings for over 490,000 privately and publicly held companies. It has contact information, including names of human resource professionals or other executives, for companies of virtually all sizes, types, and industries. The extensive database can be searched by industry, company size, or region. This product is updated monthly.

COMPANIES INTERNATIONAL
835 Penobscot Building
645 Griswald Street
Detroit MI 48226
800/877-GALE
Produced by Gale Research Inc., this database is geared toward businesses and job hunters. The CD-ROM is compiled from *Ward's Business Directory* and the *World's Business Directory*, and contains information on more than 300,000 companies worldwide. You can find industry information, contact names, and number of employees. Also included is information on the company's products and revenues. The database can be searched by industry, company products, or geographic location.

CORPTECH DIRECTORY
12 Alfred Street, Suite 200
Woburn MA 01801-1915
800/333-8036
The *CorpTech Directory* on CD-ROM contains detailed descriptions of over 45,000 technology companies. It also lists the names and titles of nearly 155,000 executives -- CEOs, sales managers, R&D managers, and human resource professionals. Home page and e-mail addresses are also available. In addition to contact information, you can find detailed information about each company's products or services and annual sales revenues. The *CorpTech Directory* also lists not only the number of current employees, but also the number of employees twelve months previously. Some companies also list the number of employees they anticipate to have in one year, so you can get an idea of how

much a company expects to grow. You can search the database by type of company, geographic location, or sales revenue. Updated quarterly.

DISCOVERING CAREERS & JOBS PLUS
835 Penobscot Building
645 Griswald Street
Detroit MI 48226
800/877-GALE
A Gale Research Inc. CD-ROM containing both the *DISCovering Careers & Jobs* and *DISCovering Careers & Jobs Plus* software packages. This CD-ROM gives users contact information on more than 30,000 companies, with 5,000 in-depth profiles and 1,000 company-history essays. In addition, the product also provides profiles and application procedures for all major two- and four-year U.S. colleges and universities.

DUN & BRADSTREET MIDDLE MARKET DISC
3 Sylvan Way
Parsippany NJ 07074
800/526-0651
This CD-ROM contains 140,000 private middle market employers. The *Middle Market Disc* allows the user to search for companies by name, geography, industry, company size, and more. You can save certain selections for future use, create a hard copy, generate lists, and compile reports.

DUN & BRADSTREET MILLION DOLLAR DISC
3 Sylvan Way
Parsippany NJ 07074
800/526-0651
This CD-ROM can help locate top executives in a specific field or find employers by location, number of employees, and revenues. The disc consists of companies with either annual sales of over $5 million, or at least 100 employees. The *Million Dollar Disc* is updated four times per year.

DUN & BRADSTREET MILLION DOLLAR DISC PLUS
3 Sylvan Way
Parsippany NJ 07074
800/526-0651
This CD-ROM lists information on over 400,000 companies. Of these, about 90 percent are privately held, but all have at least $3 million in annual sales or at least 50 employees. The *Million Dollar Disc Plus* is a broad directory covering virtually every industry. The directory provides the number of employees, sales volume, name of the parent company, and corporate headquarters or branch locations. This product includes the names and titles of top executives, as well as biographical information, including education and career background. Searches can be done by location, industry, SIC code, executive names, or key words in the executive biographies. This directory is updated quarterly.

**ENCYCLOPEDIA OF ASSOCIATIONS:
NATIONAL ORGANIZATIONS OF THE U.S.**
835 Penobscot Building
645 Griswald Street
Detroit MI 48226
800/877-GALE
This consists of 23,000 national organizations' descriptions and contact information. You can search for data by association name, geographic location, and key words. This CD-ROM is available in both single- and multi-user formats.

GALE BUSINESS RESOURCES CD-ROM
835 Penobscot Building
645 Griswald Street
Detroit MI 48226
800/877-GALE
This contains statistics on over 200,000 businesses nationwide. You can search by company name, products, market share, and more. The CD-ROM contains detailed profiles on certain industries and covers the major companies in each industry. This product is available in both single- and multi-user formats.

GALE'S CAREER GUIDANCE SYSTEM
835 Penobscot Building
645 Griswald Street
Detroit MI 48226
800/877-GALE
This CD-ROM provides contact information, as well as the names of key personnel, for more than 210,000 potential employers. You can choose from among 250 job categories and 1,200 job titles for a more personalized search. The database can also be searched by SIC code. This annually updated directory also includes the full text of two federal government publications, the *Dictionary of Occupational Titles* and also the *Occupational Outlook Handbook.*

HARRIS INFOSOURCE INTERNATIONAL
2057 Aurora Road
Twinsburg OH 44087
800/888-5900
This directory of manufacturers profiles more than 300,000 companies. Although the majority of the companies listed are located in the United States, the directory also provides listings for some companies overseas. Besides contact information, you can find out the number of employees, plant size, and sales revenue. The database also contains the names and titles of over 600,000 top executives. This CD-ROM is updated annually and can be purchased in smaller regional or state editions.

HOOVER'S COMPANY AND INDUSTRY DATABASE ON CD-ROM
6448 Highway 290-E
Suite E-104
Austin TX 78723
512/454-7778
This CD-ROM contains *Hoover's Handbook of American Businesses*, *Hoover's Handbook of World Businesses*, and *Hoover's Handbook of Emerging Businesses*, as well as listings of various computer companies, media companies, and more. *Hoover's Company and Industry Database* contains 250,000 company profiles in 450 industries. This CD-ROM has three quarterly updates and is available in both single- and multi-user formats.

MARTINDALE-HUBBELL LAW DIRECTORY
121 Clanlon Road
New Providence NJ 07974
800/526-4902
As the name suggests, this is a directory consisting exclusively of the names of law firms and lawyers: over 900,000 in all. In addition to information regarding firms and practices, the database includes the biographies of all individual lawyers in the database. Thus, you can do searches by a variety of criteria, including area of practice, firm name, and law school attended. While it lists some foreign law firms, the database predominantly consists of firms in the U.S.

MOODY'S COMPANY DATA
99 Church Street
New York NY 10007
800/342-5647
Moody's Company Data is a CD-ROM which has detailed listings for over 10,000 publicly traded companies. In addition to information such as industry, company address, and phone and fax numbers, each listing includes the names and titles of its top officers, including the CEO, president, and vice president; company size; number of shareholders; corporate history; subsidiaries; and financial statements. You can conduct searches by region, SIC codes, industry, or earnings. This CD-ROM is updated monthly.

NATIONAL FAX DIRECTORY
835 Penobscot Building
645 Griswald Street
Detroit MI 48226
800/877-GALE
A directory of fax numbers for 250,000 businesses, the *National Fax Directory* gives the user access to 170,000 fax numbers for companies, associations, and government agencies. Information can be obtained alphabetically or by subject. This CD-ROM is updated annually.

STANDARD & POOR'S REGISTER
25 Broadway
New York NY 10004
800/221-5277
The CD-ROM version of this three-volume desk reference provides the same information as its printed companion. The database lists over 55,000 companies, including more than 12,000 public companies. In addition to contact information, which includes the names and titles of over 500,000 executives, you can find out about each company's primary and secondary sources of business, annual revenues, number of employees, parent company, and subsidiaries. When available, the *Standard & Poor's Register* also lists the names of banks, accounting firms, and law firms used by each company. Also, the directory provides biographies of more than 70,000 top executives, which include information such as directorships held and schools attended. There are 55 different search modes available on the database. You can search geographically, by zip code (either three- or five-digit), industry, SIC code, or stock symbol. You can also limit your search to only private or only public companies. This directory is updated quarterly.

WALKER'S CORPORATE DIRECTORY OF U.S. PUBLIC COMPANIES
835 Penobscot Building
645 Griswald Street
Detroit MI 48226
800/877-GALE
A directory of 9,500 publicly held U.S. corporations. The user can access each company's income, earnings per share, assets, stock exchange symbol, and more. Searches on business information are classified by company, SIC code, stock exchange, and more. This CD-ROM also allows the user to print company reports and labels.

ONLINE JOB SEARCH

The Computer Age is upon us and finding a job can be easier than ever thanks to the vast Information Superhighway. The Internet and the World Wide Web have put an end to combing through a maddening mass of Sunday newspapers looking for the perfect job. With the aid of a modem and an Internet service provider, newspapers, employer profiles, industry information, and more can be at your fingertips. You can post your resume and do a nationwide job search in one sitting.

Sometimes the hardest aspect of a search is knowing where and how to begin. One helpful guide to using the Internet for job hunting is Margaret F. Riley's *Employment Opportunities and Job Resources on the Internet*, which can be accessed on the World Wide Web at http://www.jobtrak.com/jobguide. *Catapult* is another great starting point, offering information such as tips on resume building. *Catapult* can be reached at http://www.wm.edu/catapult. An extremely helpful online guide to surfing the Net for employment, *1st Steps In The Hunt* provides job hunting tips and allows the user to connect to other great job sites. This site can be reached at http://interbiznet.com/hunt.

CAREER CITY
http://www.careercity.com
Industries: All
Search Location: Worldwide
One of the most comprehensive and helpful sites on the World Wide Web. *Career City* contains worldwide searches by keyword, location, and industry for thousands of job openings. *Career City* also includes a wealth of beneficial information, including resume, cover letter, and interview tips from Adams career publications and career experts.

THE AT&T COLLEGE NETWORK
http://www.att.com/college
Industries: All
One of the most graphically pleasing and easy-to-use sites, *The AT&T College Network* offers a great deal of jobseeking data. Job listings, research source links, student services, job links, expert advice, and more make this one of the top locales for the college student or job hunting professional.

AMERICA'S JOB BANK
http://www.ajb.dni.us/index.html
Industries: All
Search Location: Nationwide
Offers a vast database, with over 250,000 employment opportunities.

THE BOSTON GLOBE HELP WANTEDS
http://www.globe.com/helpwanted/job/hwjob.html
Industries: All
Search Location: Boston and surrounding areas
Offers the help-wanted section of the *The Boston Globe* online. This site allows the browser to search for employment using the last two Sunday editions of *The Boston Globe*. You can search by industry and part-time or full-time employment. Another useful feature on this site is searching for internships. You can post your interests and availability for an internship, while companies have the opportunity to search for interns and the credentials that they are seeking. There is also a resume and cover letter development section, as well as interview tips.

THE BOSTON HERALD'S JOB FIND
http://www.bostonherald.com/jobfind
Industries: All
Search Location: New England and surrounding areas
This job hunter's site offers corporate profiles, career news, online resumes, and a job search.

BUSINESS-TO-BUSINESS MARKETING EXCHANGE
http://www.mba.wfu.edu/b2b.html
Industries: Marketing
A site offering job listings and contact names for professionals in the marketing field.

CAREER MAGAZINE
http://www.careermag.com/careermag
Industries: All
Career Magazine offers employer profiles, a directory of career consultants, a directory of executive recruiters, a resume bank, job openings, a career forum, and news and articles, including information from *The Wall Street Journal*'s *National Business Employment Weekly.*

CAREER MOSAIC
http://www.careermosaic.com
Industries: All
Produced by Bernard Hodes Advertising, this is currently one of the hottest job search sites. *Career Mosaic* contains an online job fair, a career resource center, resume posting, and a forum for college jobseekers. Surfing this site can prove fruitful, as this is one of the choice spots for businesses to post job openings.

CAREERPATH
http://www.careerpath.com
Industries: All
Search Location: Nationwide

An enormous site that you can visit to scan employment advertisements from seven of the nation's top newspapers. *CareerPath* consists of the complete Sunday want ad sections for the *Boston Globe*, *Chicago Tribune*, *Los Angeles Times*, *Philadelphia Inquirer*, *San Jose Mercury News*, *South Florida Sun-Sentinel*, and *Washington Post.* You can search these advertisements by newspaper, job category, and other keywords.

CAREERWEB
http://www.cweb.com
Industries: All
Search Location: Worldwide
This site offers a database containing worldwide employers and franchisers. You can search by job, state, country, company, or keyword. *CareerWEB* allows the user to search its library of employment publications and posts listings from the *Wall Street Journal*'s *National Business Employment Weekly.* "Jobmatch" allows you to fill out a form with your credentials and *CareerWEB* will match them with an employer seeking your qualifications. *CareerWEB* will also soon have a forum called the "Career Fair," which will allow users to chat with representatives from top corporations.

CHRONICLE OF HIGHER EDUCATION
http://chronicle.merit.edu/.ads/.links.html
Industries: Education
Search Location: Nationwide
This site provides job listings from the weekly published higher education newspaper *The Chronicle of Higher Education.* Listings are updated every Tuesday. You can seek information by geographic location or keywords.

COLLEGE GRAD JOB HUNTER
http://www.collegegrad.com
Industries: All
A good site for recent college graduates offering interviewing tips, resume development and posting, job search preparation, and entry-level job opportunities. You can search for entry-level positions by keywords.

DIRECT MARKETING WORLD'S JOB CENTER
http://www.dmworld.com
Industries: All
Search Location: Direct marketing
Posts professional job openings for the direct marketing industry. This site also provides a career reference library.

EMPLOYMENT EDGE
http://sensemedia.net/employment.edge
Industries: Accounting, auditing, engineering, legal, management, and computer programming

This site offers career fair calendars, salary guides, job search tips, resume posting, and more. You can browse through the employment database using keywords.

ENTRY LEVEL JOB SEEKER ASSISTANT
http://www.utsi.edu:70/students
Industries: All
A directory for jobseekers who have never had a full-time, permanent position in their field or who have not yet been in the professional workforce for a year.

FEDERAL JOBS CENTRAL
http://www.fedjobs.com
Industries: Government
This resourceful site has only one drawback: Its services require a fee. Many jobseekers cannot afford to shell out cash for this service, but it just may be worth the monetary loss. *Federal Jobs Central* offers a subscription to a 64-page biweekly publication containing over 3,500 job listings; online listings that are accessible by occupation, salary, and location; and a service that pairs you with the precise job you are seeking.

FEDERAL JOBS DIGEST
http://www.jobsfed.com
Industries: Government
One of the best sites for jobseekers hoping to work for the government, this site offers federal jobs in fields such as engineering, medical, administration, management, secretarial, computer services, and law enforcement.

FEDWORLD
http://www.fedworld.gov
Industries: Government
Search Location: Nationwide
Provides employment information on approximately 3,000 federal government job opportunities, organized by state.

FLEET HOUSE CAREER MATCH
http://www.fleethouse.com/career
Industries: Engineering and information technology
Search Location: United States, Canada, Europe, and Asia
A joint effort from Fleet House Information Management Solutions and Wood and Associates, this site offers a low-cost service that matches employees with employers. Subscribers can post resumes and inquire about firms.

4WORK
http://www.4work.com
Industries: All
Search Location: Worldwide

This site lists worldwide *Fortune* 500 corporations. You can search through businesses by location, company, position, or keyword. You can also locate certain internship and volunteer opportunities.

HELP WANTED-USA
http://www.webcom.com/-career/hwusa.html
Industries: All
Search Location: Nationwide
A division of Gonyea & Associates, Inc., this nationwide network of employer listings allows you to search by state, industry, or keyword. *Help Wanted-USA* also offers a resume bank.

HOSPITALITY NET VIRTUAL JOB EXCHANGE
http://www.hospitalitynet.nl/job
Industries: Hospitality and lodging
Even though this site is just over a year old, it offers jobseeking hospitality professionals a chance to get ahead of the competition. This site has intership and job opportunities. It allows you to post your qualifications for other employers to search. *Hospitality Net Virtual Job Exchange* is still growing, but even in its early stages, it has much to offer.

INTELLIMATCH
http://www.intellimatch.com
Industries: All
Search Location: Worldwide
A service which matches jobseekers and employers. You can use *IntelliMatch* to create your resume, which you can then either print out or post on a worldwide database. This site also allows you to post your resume confidentially. The listings of hot jobs and the online career center include companies such as Hewlett-Packard, Mitsubishi, Oracle, Pitney Bowes, Silicon Graphics, and more.

THE INTERNET FASHION EXHANGE
http://www.fashionexch.com
Industries: Fashion and retail
Search location: Worldwide
An excellent place for those interested in apparel and retail. The extensive search engine allows you to search by job title, location, salary, product line, industry, and whether you want a permanent, temporary, or freelance position. This site is a rare find for the professional in this industry. *The Internet Fashion Exchange* also offers career and human resources services such as recruiting and outplacement firms that place fashion and retail professionals.

JOB SOURCE
http://jobsource.com
Industries: All
Search location: Nationwide

Every profession can benefit from a trip to this expansive site. *Job Source* offers a job search using keywords, industry, or location. It also has employer profiles (alphabetically), a resume generator, employer of the week, and a career center offering articles, links, and various job-hunting resources.

JOB TRAK
http://www.jobtrak.com
Industries: All
College students and recent graduates will enjoy this site designed just for them. Used by over 200,000 employers, this site has over 2,100 new job openings posted each day. There are career fairs, job search suggestions, resumes online, job listings, top recruiters, and a guide to graduate schools. This site works with hundreds of college and university career centers and provides a search for both students and alumni to search their alma mater for job opportunities.

JOB WEB
http://www.jobweb.com
Industries: All
The *Job Web* offers a surplus of jobseeking options, such as career planning resources, job searches, industry information, and the opportunity to have your job search questions answered by human resource and career service professionals. You can peruse the company directory, job postings, internships, federal government positions, and more. The *Job Web* search engine allows Web surfers to comb through listings by keyword, state, and location.

KAPLAN'S CAREER CENTER
http://www.kaplan.com/career
Industries: All
Kaplan's Career Center is a great place to start or enhance your job search. This site offers trade advice with fellow job hunters, career links, career counselors, resume and interview tips, and an amusing interview game online.

MARKETING CLASSIFIEDS ON THE INTERNET
http://www.marketingjobs.com
Industries: Marketing, sales, and advertising
Search Location: Nationwide
This is a marketing industry site offering job listings by state, resume posting, discussions with other marketing professionals, links to other career sites, and company home pages.

MEDSEARCH AMERICA
http://www.medsearch.com
Industries: Medical
A huge site geared for the medical professional and a definite "must see" for professionals seeking positions in this area, *Medsearch America* offers job searches, career forums, resume posting, recruiters' sites, listings of professional

associations, and employer profiles. Precise and extensive searches can be done by job category, association or company name, keyword, or location.

THE MONSTER BOARD
http://www.monster.com
Industries: All
Search Location: Worldwide
ADION's dazzling graphics and over 55,000 job listings from 1,500 hot companies are found on *The Monster Board.* Whether you are going on a "Career Safari" or admiring the "Corporate Sphere," this is likely to be an enjoyable job search. The "Career Safari" offers an exhaustive career search, online resume posting, and employer profiles. The "Corporate Sphere" contains human resource information and employment success stories. Jobseekers specify keyword searches by skill, job title, or criteria. Over 300 employer profiles are available, as well as information on job fairs and helpful job-hunting tips.

THE NATIONAL MULTIMEDIA ASSOCIATION OF AMERICA'S (NMAA) JOB BANKER
http://www.nmaa.org/jobbank.html
Industries: All
At this site you can search by keyword, location, duration, commitment, and industry. If you only want to be placed for 6 months or if you simply desire to be a part-time worker in your field, NMAA's search engine will accommodate your request.

NONPROFIT JOBNET
http://www.nando.net/philant/philant.html
Industries: Nonprofit
The *Philanthropy Journal*'s site lists jobs in nonprofit associations and philanthropic occupations.

ONLINE CAREER CENTER
http://www.occ.com
Industries: All
Search Location: Nationwide
Internet surfers can find resume databases, job fair listings, electronic books and directories, and employment opportunities from over 300 United States companies. As one of the most sizzling sites on the Web, this is a prime area for you to post a resume.

STUDENTCENTER
http://www.studentcenter.com
Industries: All
A great resource for graduates or current college students, *StudentCenter* allows the surfer to browse a database of over 35,000 companies and 1,000 industries.

This highly informative site offers internship opportunities, career advice, tips on resume and cover letter building, resume construction, and a student forum.

UNEMPLOYED RADIO DJ'S
http://www.icnet.net/users/wwhite/urdjhome.htm
Industries: Broadcasting
Absolutely anyone wanting to gain a job in the broadcasting industry should at least visit this site for its links to trade magazines, radio stations, major record labels, and job postings. *Unemployed Radio DJ's* does not yet have a search engine to narrow the user's job search, but this site should not be overlooked.

VIRTUAL JOB FAIR
http://www.vjf.com
Industries: All
Search Location: Nationwide
This site offers job searches, a resume center, high-technology careers, career resources, and more. *Virtual Job Fair* allows you to search by job title, industry, location, or company.

YAHOO'S BUSINESS EMPLOYMENT
http://www.yahoo.com/Business/Employment
Industries: Business
This location uses the Yahoo search engine to connect to top business job sites.

ZDNET JOB DATABASE
http://www.zdnet.com/~zdi/jobs/jobs.html
Industries: High-Tech
Search Location: Nationwide
Ziff-Davis Interactive and ADION, in partnership with The Monster Board, offer this nationwide job search directory which allows you to search by state, industry, and position.

PRIMARY EMPLOYERS

ACCOUNTING AND MANAGEMENT CONSULTING

As the number of accounting graduates drops and the economy strengthens, all types of accounting professionals will benefit. According to the Bureau of Labor Statistics, the number of accounting jobs may grow by as much as 40 percent by the year 2005. A recent survey conducted by Robert Half International found that the best opportunities for accountants were in the financial, insurance, and real estate sector, followed by the retail and wholesale industries.

Even faster growth is projected for the management consulting industry, where the number of jobs is expected to grow almost three times faster than the rate for all industries. The increasing complexity of business will contribute to industry growth. Among other things, today's managers must worry about rapid technological innovations, changes in government regulations, growing environmental concerns, continuing reduction of trade barriers, and globalization of markets. Because it has become difficult to keep abreast of these changing conditions, corporations, institutions, and governments will increasingly need the aid of well-trained, well-informed management consulting professionals.

ALEXANDER & ALEXANDER CONSULTING GROUP
WESTERN CONSULTING RESOURCE CENTER

525 Market Street, Suite 700, San Francisco CA 94105. 415/222-7200. **Contact:** Human Resources. **Description:** Alexander & Alexander Consulting Group is an international human resource consulting and benefits brokerage firm, providing integrated advisory and support services in retirement planning, health care management, organizational effectiveness, compensation, human resource related communications and information technologies. Alexander & Alexander's organizational effectiveness services include advisory and support services in compensation, strategy development, organizational design, business process redesign, human resource development, management training and development, organizational communications, and information technology applications. Strategic health care services include advisory and support services in traditional group health and welfare programs, strategic health planning, strategic health care management, quality assurance, flexible benefits and compensation, financial management, data management, vendor oversight, and communications. Strategic retirement planning and education services include consulting and support services in core actuarial applications, retirement health and welfare benefits, funding and investment strategy, recordkeeping and administration, employee sensing and communications, personalized retirement modeling, holistic lifestyle and family planning, and database information and proprietary studies. Information technologies services include human resource information systems development (information management strategies, systems, databases, software, and technology advisement) and human resource systems applications (human resource planning, recordkeeping, communication and education). **Parent company:** The Alexander Consulting Group.

THE ALEXANDER CONSULTING GROUP
2540 North First Street, Suite 400, San Jose CA 95131. 408/954-0900. **Contact:** Human Resources. **Description:** The Alexander Consulting Group is an international human resource consulting and benefits brokerage firm, providing integrated advisory and support services in retirement planning, health care management, organizational effectiveness, compensation, human resource related communications and information technologies. ACG's organizational effectiveness services include advisory and support services in compensation, strategy development, organizational design, business process redesign, human resource development, management training and development, organizational communications, and information technology applications. Strategic health care services include advisory and support services in traditional group health and welfare programs, strategic health planning, strategic health care management, quality assurance, flexible benefits and compensation, financial management, data management, vendor oversight, and communications. Strategic retirement planning and education services include consulting and support services in core actuarial applications, retirement health and welfare benefits, funding and investment strategy, recordkeeping and administration, employee sensing and communications, personalized retirement modeling, holistic lifestyle and family planning, and database information and proprietary studies. Information technologies services include human resource information systems development (information management strategies, systems, databases, software, and technology advisement) and human resource systems applications (human resource planning, recordkeeping, communication, and education). **Subsidiaries include:** Alexander & Alexander Consulting Group.

ARTHUR ANDERSEN & COMPANY
One Market Plaza, Spear Street Tower, #3500, San Francisco CA 94105. 415/546-8200. **Fax:** 415/543-1827. **Contact:** Director of Recruiting. **Description:** One of the six largest certified public accounting firms in the world. Organized in 1913, Arthur Andersen & Company has offices in 40 countries. The firm operates in the following divisions: Audit (offering assignments in all types of businesses and industries); and Tax (offering assignments involving consultation and compliance in all areas of taxation including income, real estate, trust, and gift taxation). **Common positions include:** Accountant/Auditor. **Educational backgrounds include:** Accounting; Business Administration; Computer Science; Economics; Engineering; Finance; Mathematics. **Benefits:** Dental Insurance; Disability Coverage; Life Insurance; Medical Insurance; Pension Plan; Profit Sharing. **Corporate headquarters location:** Chicago IL. **Operations at this facility include:** Regional Headquarters.

BDO SEIDMAN
One Sansome Street, Suite 1100, San Francisco CA 94104-4430. 415/397-7900. **Contact:** Samuel A. Vitoski, National Director of Recruiting. **Description:** A public accounting and consulting firm. **Other U.S. locations:** Chicago IL; Boston MA.

BAIN & COMPANY
One Embarcadero Center, Suite 3600, San Francisco CA 94111. 415/434-1022. **Contact:** Kathleen McCarthy, Recruiting Manager. **Description:** An international management consulting firm that helps major companies in a wide range of manufacturing and service industries achieve competitiveness and profitability. Founded in 1973. **Corporate headquarters location:** Boston MA.

BENSON & NEFF
180 Montgomery Street, Suite 1900, San Francisco CA 94104. 415/705-5615. **Contact:** Thomas J. Parry, Director of Personnel. **Description:** A certified public accounting firm offering accounting, auditing, tax, computer, and other consulting services to a diversified clientele. **Common positions include:** Accountant/Auditor. **Educational backgrounds include:** Accounting. **Benefits:** Disability Coverage; Life Insurance; Medical Insurance; Pension Plan. **Corporate headquarters location:** This Location. **Operations at this facility include:** Service.

BOOZ-ALLEN & HAMILTON INC.
101 California Street, Suite 3300, San Francisco CA 94111. 415/391-1900. **Contact:** Human Resources. **Description:** A diversified, international, management consulting organization, offering services in both the commercial and public sectors. Areas of expertise include technology, strategy and planning, social research, and many other technical fields. Specific services include: corporate strategy and long-range planning, organization design, human resources management, financial management and control; acquisitions and divestiture, information systems and automation, manufacturing, inventory, and distribution control, qualitative and quantitative market research; attitudinal and demographic trend research, marketing strategy and positioning; venture management; transportation and environmental systems, technology research, new products and process development, government programs, and regulatory compliance. Booz-Allen's staff includes 185 partners and 1,600 professionals nationally. The company operates 15 regional offices in the United States and eight in Europe, North Africa, and Latin America, all offering a full range of services. **Corporate headquarters location:** New York NY.

COOPERS & LYBRAND
333 Market Street, 21st Floor, San Francisco CA 94105. 415/957-3000. **Contact:** Clare Shanahan, Manager, Recruiting. **Description:** One of the Big Six certified public accounting firms, Coopers & Lybrand provides a broad range of services in the areas of accounting and auditing, taxation, management consulting and actuarial, and benefits and compensation consulting. The firm operates over 100 offices in the United States and has 735 foreign offices. **Other U.S. locations:** Oakland CA; Palo Alto CA; San Jose CA. **Number of employees nationwide:** 67,000.

CRAWFORD PIMENTAL & COMPANY, INC.
2150 Trade Zone Boulevard, Suite 200, San Jose CA 95131. 408/942-6888. **Fax:** 408/942-0194. **Contact:** Michele A. Izor, Director. **Description:** A certified public accounting firm. **Common positions include:** Accountant/Auditor. **Educational backgrounds include:** Accounting. **Benefits:** Disability Coverage; Medical Insurance; Pension Plan; Tuition Assistance. **Corporate headquarters location:** This Location. **Operations at this facility include:** Service. **Number of employees at this location:** 25.

DELOITTE & TOUCHE
50 Fremont Street, 31st Floor, San Francisco CA 94105. 415/247-4000. **Contact:** Human Resources. **Description:** Deloitte & Touche is an international firm of certified public accountants, providing professional accounting, auditing, tax, and management consulting services to widely diversified clients. The company has a specialized program consisting of some 25 national industry groups and 50 functional (technical) groups that cross industry lines. Groups are involved in various disciplines, including accounting, auditing, taxation management advisory services, small and growing businesses, mergers

and acquisitions, and computer applications. Deloitte & Touche has international facilities, with more than 500 offices throughout the world.

ERNST & YOUNG
55 Almaden Boulevard, San Jose CA 95113. 408/947-5500. **Contact:** Human Resources Department. **Description:** A certified public accounting firm that also provides its clients with management consulting services. The consulting staff is comprised of more than 1,000 consultants and support staff worldwide involved in such fields as data processing, financial modeling, financial feasibility studies, production planning and inventory management, management sciences, health care planning, human resources, cost accounting and budgeting systems, and others. The company provides services to numerous industries, including health care, financial institutions, insurance, manufacturing, retailing, government, utilities, and transportation. **Number of employees nationwide:** 8,500. **Number of employees worldwide:** 16,000.

ERNST & YOUNG/SAN FRANCISCO
555 California Street, Suite 1700, San Francisco CA 94104. 415/951-3000. **Contact:** Larry Stevenson, Director of Human Resources. **Description:** Provides auditing, tax, and management information services as one of the largest certified public accounting firms. Offices are located in most United States metropolitan areas and in several international locations.

H&R BLOCK
366 West Portal Avenue, San Francisco CA 94127. 415/665-4540. **Contact:** Bernadette Hunley, Manager. **Description:** Primarily engaged in consumer tax preparation, operating more than 9,500 United States offices, and preparing more than 10 million tax returns each year. H&R Block has established offices in over 750 Sears stores in both the United States and Canada. Many offices operate as franchises, and some operate on a seasonal basis. The company is also engaged in a number of other tax-related activities, including group tax programs, executive tax service, tax training schools, and real estate awareness seminars. **Other U.S. locations:** Nationwide.

KPMG PEAT MARWICK LLP
Three Embarcadero Center, San Francisco CA 94111. 415/951-0100. **Fax:** 415/397-1128. **Recorded Jobline:** 415/951-7821. **Contact:** Carrie Low, Recruiting Manager. **Description:** One of the Big Six certified public accounting firms providing auditing, assurance, management consulting, and tax services, with more than 1,900 partners and principals in the United States. KPMG Peat Marwick operates approximately 135 offices in the United States, and approximately 1,100 offices in 131 countries. The firm was founded in 1897. **Common positions include:** Accountant/Auditor; Secretary. **Educational backgrounds include:** Accounting. **Benefits:** Dental Insurance; Disability Coverage; Employee Discounts; Life Insurance; Medical Insurance; Pension Plan; Savings Plan. **Special Programs:** Internships. **Corporate headquarters location:** Montvale NJ. **Operations at this facility include:** Regional Headquarters. **Number of employees at this location:** 1,200.

ARTHUR D. LITTLE, INC.
Four Embarcadero Center, Suite 600, San Francisco CA 94111. 415/981-2500. **Contact:** Human Resources. **Description:** Arthur D. Little's management consulting business serves corporations and institutions worldwide. Founded in 1886, the company now has 34 offices and laboratories around the world. The company offers three programs: management consulting, technology and product development, and environmental,

health, and safety consulting. The company combines technological capabilities and extensive experience in a broad range of industries and markets. The company has developed such business concepts as the High Performance Business, the "Unwritten Rules of the Game", corporate strategic portfolios, the strategic management of technology, and customer-driven planning. **Number of employees nationwide:** 2,500.

PRICE WATERHOUSE
555 California Street, Suite 3600, San Francisco CA 94104. 415/393-8500. **Contact:** Mike Mueller, Director of Recruiting. **Description:** One of the largest public accounting firms in the United States, with offices in 67 cities across the country and more than 290 offices in approximately 90 countries. Positions on the firm's professional staff provide the opportunity to learn the administrative and fiscal policies of companies representing a cross-section of American industry. **Common positions include:** Accountant/Auditor; Tax Specialist. **Educational backgrounds include:** Accounting. **Special Programs:** Internships. **Corporate headquarters location:** New York NY. **Other U.S. locations:** Nationwide. **Listed on:** Privately held.

TENERA, L.P.
1 Market Plaza, Suite 1850, San Francisco CA 94105. 415/536-4744. **Contact:** Human Resources. **Description:** A national consulting firm offering a broad range of products and services. Management Consulting includes strategic planning, organizational effectiveness reviews, management process evaluation, expert witness and litigation support, and integrated resource management. Information Systems and Software offers applications software for maintenance management, operations management, project management, materials management, and general management. Engineering Services include electrical engineering, instrumentation and control engineering, and emergency preparedness services. Government Environmental Services include pre-audit planning and preparation activities, compliance reporting, permitting, quality assurance, and design review for RCRA. Compliance Management, provides support services to the Department of Energy. Self-Assessment services include monitoring and improving self-assessment programs. Operations and Maintenance Support focuses on systems, components, and processes. Strategic Process Management (SPM) includes establishing objectives for the process to be examined; modeling the existing process based on reviews of existing documentation; validating the existing process for efficiency, agreement with industry practice, and conformance with appropriate requirements; identifying opportunities for improvement and carefully assessing the impact on the organization; and revising process procedures to implement client-approved changes.

Note: *Because addresses and telephone numbers of smaller companies can change rapidly, we recommend you call each company to verify the information below before inquiring about job opportunities. Mass mailings are not recommended.*

Additional small employers:

ACCOUNTING, AUDITING, AND BOOKKEEPING SERVICES

The Payroll People
1922 N Helm Ave, Fresno CA 93727-1635. 209/251-9060.

Seiler & Company
1100 Marshall St, Redwood City CA 94063-2029. 415/365-4646.

Grant Thornton CPAs
1 California St Ste 1100, San Francisco CA 94111-5412. 415/986-3900.

Hood & Strong
101 California St Ste 1500,

San Francisco CA 94111-1588. 415/781-0793.

San Filippo and Co.
PO Box 51114, Palo Alto CA 94303. 415/691-1000.

Hemming Morse
160 Bovet Rd Fl 4, San Mateo CA 94402-3107. 415/574-1900.

Vernco Inc.
315 Diablo Rd Ste C 214, Danville CA 94526-3409. 510/820-0221.

Lindquist & Co.
5000 Executive Pkwy Ste 4000 , San Ramon CA 94583-4210. 510/277-9100.

Zenger-Miller
1735 Technology Dr Fl 6, San Jose CA 95110-1354. 408/452-1244.

ASAP Accounting Personnel Service
2107 N 1st St Ste 405, San Jose CA 95131-2026. 408/453-5566.

Grupe Co.
3255 W March Ln Fl 2, Stockton CA 95219-2304. 209/473-6000.

Grant Bennett Pc
1788 Tribute Rd Ste 300, Sacramento CA 95815-4402. 916/922-5109.

Macias & Miranda Certified Public Accountant
2151 River Plaza Dr, Sacramento CA 95833-3881. 916/567-0545.

Northwest Creditors Services Inc.
PO Box 13727, Sacramento CA 95853. 916/851-5000.

Matson & Isom Accountancy Corp.
1360 E Lassen Ave, Chico CA 95973-7823. 916/891-6474.

Frank Rimerman & Co.
2882 Sand Hill Rd, Menlo Park CA 94025-7022. 415/854-3344.

California Society Certified Public Accountants
275 Shoreline Dr, Redwood City CA 94065-1407. 510/926-0189.

Mark Glickman CPA
180 Montgomery, San Francisco CA 94104. 415/705-7788.

Novagradac Fortenbach & Co.
425 Market St, San Francisco CA 94105-2406. 510/356-8006.

Pisenti & Brinker
700 Irwin St Ste 300, San Rafael CA 94901-3300. 415/454-5923.

Pisenti & Brinker
3550 Round Barn Blvd Ste 100 , Santa Rosa CA 95403-0920. 707/542-3343.

Islip & Company CPAs
2410 Fair Oaks Blvd, Sacramento CA 95825-7663. 916/488-1900.

Matson & Isom Accountancy Corp.
1638 Huntoon St, Oroville CA 95965-4902. 916/534-9300.

Concentric Computer Corp.
9099 Soquel Dr, Aptos CA 95003-4033. 408/685-1211.

MANAGEMENT SERVICES

Four Sisters Inns
PO Box 3073, Monterey CA 93942-3073. 408/649-0908.

Aston Hotels & Resorts
85 5th St, San Francisco CA 94103-1812. 415/398-8391.

Intracorp
2300 Contra Costa Blvd Ste 550, Pleasant Hill CA 94523-3973. 510/939-6970.

MCE Corporation
2500 Old Crow Canyon Rd Ste 32, San Ramon CA 94583-1623. 510/837-4111.

Scarbrough Management Corp.
PO Box 1547, San Ramon CA 94583-6547. 510/866-8424.

McCurry Companies
PO Box 838, Sacramento CA 95812-0838. 916/567-9952.

Vanir Construction Management Inc.
555 Capitol Mall Ste 350, Sacramento CA 95814-4503. 916/444-3700.

Xebec Management Services Inc.
777 Campus Commons Rd Ste 200 , Sacramento CA 95825-8309. 916/565-7400.

Eugene Burger Management Corp.
481 Via Hidalgo, Greenbrae CA 94904-1752. 415/461-8660.

Mayta & Jensen
1790 Yosemite Ave, San Francisco CA 94124-2694. 415/822-2200.

Eric F. Anderson Inc.
1066 Beecher St, San Leandro CA 94577-1250. 510/430-8404.

Van Ommeren and Associates
1185 Lombardi Ave, Petaluma CA 94954-4332. 707/762-6326.

Sloat & Associates Inc.
8300 Sierra College Blvd Ste F, Roseville CA 95661-9400. 916/791-7989.

Manufacturers Survey Associates
1331 T St, Sacramento CA 95814-7107. 916/442-1879.

FW Dodge McGraw Hill Construction
1791 Tribute Rd Ste D, Sacramento CA 95815-4403. 916/920-2240.

O'Brien-Kreitzberg
2720 Gateway Oaks Dr, Sacramento CA 95833-3500. 916/567-7877.

Kimpton Group
222 Kearny St, San Francisco CA 94108-4510. 415/397-5572.

Pacific Management
831 Montgomery St, San Francisco CA 94133-5108. 415/392-8260.

American Hotels Inc.
433 Hamilton Ave, Palo Alto CA 94301-1810. 415/321-4106.

Meyer-Trettin Ltd.
26046 Eden Landing Rd, Hayward CA 94545. 510/786-9676.

Restaurants Central
765 Wave St, Monterey CA 93940-1071. 408/649-6690.

Zim's Restaurants
1498 Market St, San Francisco CA 94102-6004. 415/431-3111.

Arete Management
1777 Borel Pl, San Mateo CA 94402. 415/578-1227.

Restaurant Hotel Research
1660 S Amphlett Blvd Ste 245 , San Mateo CA 94402-2508. 415/574-3333.

Ad-Cor Enterprises Inc.
3183 Teddington Dr, San Jose CA 95148-3660. 408/270-5103.

Grace Restaurant Co.
1830 Arden Way, Sacramento CA 95815-5002. 916/922-0220.

BUSINESS CONSULTING SERVICES

Wyatt Watson Worldwide
345 California, Fresno CA 93706. 209/252-3785.

AIS Market Research
4955 E Andersen Ave Ste 134, Fresno CA 93727-1521. 209/252-2727.

Applied Decision Analysis Inc.
2710 Sand Hill Rd, Menlo Park CA 94025-7065. 415/854-7101.

Decision Focus Inc.
650 Castro St Ste 300, Mountain View CA 94041-2057. 415/960-3450.

Unison International
651 Gateway Blvd Ste 880, S San Fran CA 94080-7025. 415/877-0780.

APM Inc.
1 Bush St, San Francisco CA 94104-4425. 415/362-8266.

McKinsey & Co. Inc.
555 California St Ste 4800, San Francisco CA 94104-1779. 415/981-0250.

Towers Perrin
333 Bush St Ste 1600, San Francisco CA 94104-2836. 415/773-3000.

Omega Performance Group
50 Fremont St Ste 1800, San Francisco CA 94105-2235. 415/543-1836.

Comark
90 New Montgomery St Ste 1250 , San Francisco CA 94105-4504. 415/896-0568.

Elrick & Lavidge Inc.
111 Maiden Ln Ste 600, San Francisco CA 94108-5329. 415/434-0536.

Regis McKenna Inc.
1755 Embarcadero Rd, Palo Alto CA 94303-3304. 408/494-2030.

Aguirre International Inc.
411 Borel Ave Ste 406, San Mateo CA 94402-3519. 415/349-1842.

RHR International Company
1350 Old Bayshore Hwy, San Mateo CA 94402. 415/342-9905.

Trammell Crow Co.
1241 E Hillsdale Blvd # 200, Foster City CA 94404-1214. 415/578-8100.

Plangraphics
2300 Clayton Rd, Concord CA 94520-2100. 510/246-8080.

RW Lynch Company Inc.
2333 San Ramon Valley Blvd, San Ramon CA 94583-1613. 510/837-3877.

Roy Jorgensen Associates Inc.
5880 W Las Positas Blvd, Pleasanton CA 94588-8552. 510/463-9340.

Hewitt Associates
1340 Treat Blvd Ste 600, Walnut Creek CA 94596-2972. 510/933-8100.

Development Associates Inc.
1475 N Broadway Ste 200, Walnut Creek CA 94596-4643. 510/935-9711.

Barakat and Chamberlain Inc.
1800 Harrison St, Oakland CA 94612-3429. 510/893-7800.

Lewin Vhi Inc.
100 Tamal Plz, Corte Madera CA 94925-1125. 415/927-5700.

Gerber Business Development Corp.
1310 Redwood Way Ste 200, Petaluma CA 94954-6512. 707/778-2900.

Festival Management Corp.
1901 S Bascom Ave, Campbell CA 95008-2215. 408/371-4700.

New West Industries
601 Walsh Ave, Santa Clara CA 95050-2629. 408/988-2882.

Lee Hecht Harrison Inc.
1740 Tech Dr 400, San Jose CA 95110. 408/453-7722.

Barry Swenson Builder
701 N 1st St, San Jose CA 95112-6303. 408/287-0246.

Sequent Personnel Service Inc.
2107 N 1st St Ste 530, San Jose CA 95131-2028. 408/436-0111.

David M Griffith & Associates
5715 Marconi Ave, Carmichael CA 95608-4474. 916/485-8102.

Xebec Co.
3017 Douglas Blvd, Roseville CA 95661-3848. 916/774-7144.

Applied Risk Management
2000 O St, Sacramento CA 95814-5224. 916/446-6457.

Cordoba Corporation
1201 K St, Sacramento CA 95814-3918. 916/325-0700.

Cooperative Personnel Services
191 Lathrop Way Ste A, Sacramento CA 95815-4217. 916/263-3600.

Fabila Lopez & Associates
6328 Logan St, Sacramento CA 95824-4409. 916/381-7272.

RE Harrington Inc.
831 Mitten Rd, Burlingame CA 94010-1303. 415/692-5221.

Godwins Booke & Dickenson
2595 Bayshore Blvd, Palo Alto CA 94303. 415/496-7400.

Cintas-The Uniform People
777 139th Ave, San Leandro CA 94578-3218. 510/352-6330.

Adminitec Inc.
PO Box 281, Santa Clara CA 95052-0281. 408/246-5837.

Compro Insurance Services Inc.
550 S Winchester Blvd Ste 500 , San Jose CA 95128-2526. 408/236-3000.

Innovations Personnel Service Inc.
345 California St, San Francisco CA 94104-2635. 415/392-4022.

Bent Ericksen & Associates
983 University Ave, Los Gatos CA 95030-2305. 408/354-2869.

Crossroads Personnel Services
4300 Stevens Creek Blvd Ste 11, San Jose CA 95129. 408/778-2889.

Bridgegate Group
2150 North 1st St, San Jose CA 95131-2020. 408/436-2900.

Panagraph Marketing Communications
2445 Capitol St Ste 105, Fresno CA 93721-2224. 209/445-0252.

Electro Diagnostic Imaging
1849 Bayshore Hwy, Burlingame CA 94010-1215. 415/692-7900.

The PPN Company
3 Embarcadero Ctr, San Francisco CA 94111-4003. 415/989-0536.

US Pacrim Group Inc.
1190 Saratoga Ave Ste 210, San Jose CA 95129-3433. 408/236-3226.

The Cilren Company
8048 Archer Ave, Fair Oaks CA 95628-5907. 916/966-8522.

Creative Marketing Design Inc.
8543 Everglade Dr, Sacramento CA 95826-3616. 916/381-0769.

Real Design Labs Inc.
935 Hamilton Ct, Menlo Park CA 94025-1431. 415/688-1850.

Falcon Enterprises
250 E Belmont Ave, Fresno CA 93701-1405. 209/252-2908.

Conference Facilitation Association
652 Bair Island Rd Ste 305, Redwood City CA 94063-2739. 415/364-5241.

A-B Communications
14895 E 14th St, San Leandro CA 94578-2922. 510/839-8787.

Intraspect
3315 Americus Dr, San Jose CA 95148-2804. 408/223-7753.

Medus International
2266-3 Woodside Ln, Sacramento CA 95825. 916/920-8300.

Chico Proam
801 East Ave Ste K3, Chico CA 95926-1250. 916/898-1872.

Rx Net
1931 N Fine Ave, Fresno CA 93727-1510. 209/252-7142.

Heath Consulting Services
577 Airport Blvd, Burlingame CA 94010-2020. 415/342-3213.

Delta One Management Inc.
923 Leneve Pl, El Cerrito CA 94530-2749. 510/527-5455.

David Karp Associates
PO Box 69, Cloverdale CA 95425-0069. 707/894-9363.

Audit Pro Inc.
137 Utah Ave, S San Fran CA 94080-6711. 415/615-9050.

Utility Research
1255 Post St Ste 625, San Francisco CA 94109-6709. 415/673-1081.

Rupert Taylor Real Estate Inc.
16 Park Rd, Burlingame CA 94010-4495. 415/347-9981.

O'Connor Realty Advisors Inc.
525 Market St, San Francisco CA 94105-2708. 415/267-0808.

TRI Realtors
1699 Van Ness Ave, San Francisco CA 94109-3608. 415/474-1750.

Terranomics
455 N Point St, San Francisco CA 94133-1400. 415/474-6100.

Mason-McDuffie Real Estate
2070 Mountain Blvd, Piedmont CA 94611-2816. 510/339-8888.

Seagate Properties Inc.
4000 Civic Center Dr Ste 300, San Rafael CA 94903-4152. 415/492-8771.

Rykoff-Sexton Inc.
1025 Joellis Way, Sacramento CA 95815-3912. 916/927-2211.

Triadigm International
345 California St Ste 1220, San Francisco CA 94104-2621. 415/984-5777.

Ecology & Environment Inc.
160 Spear St Ste 1400, San Francisco CA 94105-1547. 415/777-2811.

Environmental Science Associates
301 Brannan St Ste 200, San Francisco CA 94107-1849. 415/896-5900.

Brown McDaniel Inc.
650 California St Ste 2205, San Francisco CA 94108-2603. 415/397-9500.

EIP Associates
601 Montgomery St Ste 500, San Francisco CA 94111-2608. 415/362-1500.

Peterson Consulting Ltd.
353 Sacramento St Ste 2000, San Francisco CA 94111-3675. 415/956-3654.

The Understanding Business
1160 Battery St Fl 4, San Francisco CA 94111-1212. 415/616-4800.

Resna Industries Inc.
505 Sansome St Ste 501, San Francisco CA 94111-3106. 415/291-9926.

Leigh Fisher Associates
160 Bovet Rd # 300, San Mateo CA 94402-3107. 415/571-7722.

Yellowstone Environmental Services
3160 Crow Canyon Rd, San Ramon CA 94583-1331. 510/867-0322.

Systems Application International
101 Lucas Valley Rd, San Rafael CA 94903-1791. 415/507-7100.

Pacific Environmental Group Inc.
2025 Gateway Pl Ste 440, San Jose CA 95110-1006. 408/441-7500.

International Technology Corp.
2055 Junction Ave, San Jose CA 95131-2105. 408/984-1200.

David E. Miller Urban Plan
2000 Broadway St, Redwood City CA 94063-1802. 415/365-8995.

Telewave Inc.
1155 Terra Bella Ave, Mountain View CA 94043-1831. 415/968-4400.

San Francisco Consulting Group
49 Stevenson St Fl 7, San Francisco CA 94105-2909. 415/777-0721.

Voicepro
4000 Executive Pkwy Ste 140, San Ramon CA 94583-4256. 510/866-8866.

EF&I Services Co.
3350 Scott Blvd Ste 53, Santa Clara CA 95054-3104. 408/970-0602.

Globalnet Telecom Inc.
3298 Monier Cir, Rncho Cordova CA 95742-6804. 916/638-2600.

Price Technical Services Inc.
1600 Sacramento Inn Way Ste 23, Sacramento CA 95815-3457. 916/929-4363.

Universal Network Development Corp.
4705 N Sonora Ave, Fresno CA 93722. 209/275-8505.

Hood Communications
1038 Edwards Rd, Burlingame CA 94010-2318. 415/342-5360.

Walsh Vineyards Management Inc.
870 Napa Valley Corporate Way, Napa CA 94558-6263. 707/258-1500.

Fairfax Lectern
407 San Anselmo Ave, San Anselmo CA 94960-2611. 415/459-2718.

Business Service Systems Inc.
1639 E Shields Ave, Fresno CA 93704. 209/222-0491.

Work Evaluation & Modification Center
6073 North 1st Street, Fresno CA 93710-5444. 209/439-2699.

East Bay Training Academy
1149 MacDonald Ave, Richmond CA 94801-3115. 510/232-0124.

RD Wallace Financial Services
1537 4th Street, San Rafael CA 94901-2737. 415/456-7948.

For more information on career opportunities in accounting and management consulting:

Associations

AMERICAN ACCOUNTING ASSOCIATION
5717 Bessie Drive, Sarasota FL 34233. 941/921-7747. World Wide Web address: http://www.rutgers.edu/accounting/raw/aaa/aaa.htm. An academically-oriented accounting association that offers two quarterly journals, a semi-annual journal, a newsletter, and a wide variety of continuing education programs.

AMERICAN INSTITUTE OF CERTIFIED PUBLIC ACCOUNTANTS
1211 Avenue of the Americas, New York NY 10036. 212/596-6200. A national professional organization for all CPAs. AICPA offers a comprehensive career package to students.

AMERICAN MANAGEMENT ASSOCIATION
Management Information Service, 135 West 50th Street, New York NY 10020. 212/586-8100. Provides a variety of publications, training videos, and courses, as well as an Information Resource Center, which provides management information, and a library service.

ASSOCIATION OF GOVERNMENT ACCOUNTANTS
2200 Mount Vernon Avenue, Alexandria VA 22301. 703/684-6931. World Wide Web address: http://www.rutgers.edu/accounting/raw/aga/home.htm.

ASSOCIATION OF MANAGEMENT CONSULTING FIRMS
521 Fifth Avenue, 35th Floor, New York NY 10175. 212/697-9693. Offers certification programs.

INSTITUTE OF INTERNAL AUDITORS
49 Maitland Avenue, Altamont Springs FL 32701. 407/830-7600. World Wide Web address: http://www.rutgers.edu/accounting. Publishes magazines and newsletters. Provides information on current issues, and professional development and research services.

INSTITUTE OF MANAGEMENT ACCOUNTANTS
Box 433, Montvale NJ 07645-1760. 201/573-9000. World Wide Web address: http://www.rutgers.edu/accounting/raw/ima. Offers a Certified Management Accountant Program, periodicals, seminars, educational programs, a research program, a financial management network, and networking services.

INSTITUTE OF MANAGEMENT CONSULTANTS
521 Fifth Avenue, 35th Floor, New York NY 10175. 212/697-8262. World Wide Web address: http://www.imcusa.org. Offers certification and professional development and a directory of members.

NATIONAL ASSOCIATION OF TAX PRACTITIONERS
720 Association Drive, Appleton WI 54914.

414/749-1040. World Wide Web address: http://www.natptax.com. Offers seminars, research, newsletters, preparer worksheets, state chapters, insurance, and other tax-related services.

NATIONAL BUSINESSWOMEN'S LEADERSHIP ASSOCIATION
6901 West 63rd Street, P.O. Box 2949, Shawnee Mission KS 66201. World Wide Web address: http://www.natsem.com. A professional organization dedicated to advancing the careers of women in management.

NATIONAL SOCIETY OF PUBLIC ACCOUNTANTS
1010 North Fairfax Street, Alexandria VA 22314. 703/549-6400. World Wide Web address: http://www.nspa.org. Offers professional development services, government representation, a variety of publications, practice aids, low-cost group insurance, and annual seminars.

Directories

AICPA DIRECTORY OF ACCOUNTING EDUCATION
American Institute of Certified Public Accountants, 1211 Avenue of the Americas, New York NY 10036. 212/596-6200. $150.00. Only available to AICPA members.

ACCOUNTING FIRMS AND PRACTITIONERS
American Institute of Certified Public Accountants, 1211 Avenue of the Americas, New York NY 10036. 212/596-6200. $150.00.

Magazines

CPA JOURNAL
530 Fifth Avenue, New York NY 10136. 212/719-8300.

CPA LETTER
American Institute of Certified Public Accountants, 1211 Avenue of the Americas, New York NY 10036. 212/596-6200.

JOURNAL OF ACCOUNTANCY
American Institute of Certified Public Accountants, 1211 Avenue of the Americas, New York NY 10036. 212/596-6200.

MANAGEMENT ACCOUNTING
Institute of Management Accounting, 10 Paragon Drive, Montvale NJ 07645. 201/573-9000.

WENDELL'S REPORT FOR CONTROLLERS
Warren, Gorham, and Lamont, Inc., 210 South Street, Boston MA 02111. 617/423-2020.

ADVERTISING, MARKETING, AND PUBLIC RELATIONS

Due to several trends shaping the industry, finding a job in advertising is as tough today as it has ever been. To remain competitive, the industry's largest firms have been downsizing to save money for larger campaigns. On the other hand, smaller agencies are increasingly specializing in fields such as direct marketing and public relations in order to gain a stronger presence in the market. Meanwhile, the growing cable industry has opened the door to new business opportunities, as has the Internet. Increasingly, advertisers are using the information highway to conduct business, as well as to target specific "digital" audiences.

In the public relations field, there has been an explosion in the number and range of consultants in the marketplace. Partially as a result of the recession of the early '90s, many senior executives who were released from their contracts at major firms have launched companies of their own.

BBDO
170 Maiden Lane, 4th Floor, San Francisco CA 94108. 415/274-6200. **Contact:** Rich Silva, Human Resources Coordinator. **Description:** Part of a worldwide network of advertising agencies with related businesses in public relations, direct marketing, sales promotion, graphic arts, and printing. BBDO Worldwide operates 156 offices in 42 countries and 96 cities. The company operates 83 subsidiaries, affiliates, and associates engaged solely in advertising and related operations. **Corporate headquarters location:** New York NY. **Other U.S. locations:** Los Angeles CA; Miami FL; Atlanta GA; Chicago IL; Wellesley MA; Southfield MI. **Parent company:** BBDO Worldwide.

CUNNINGHAM COMMUNICATION, INC.
3945 Freedom Circle, #900, Santa Clara CA 95054. 408/982-0400. **Fax:** 408/982-0403. **Contact:** Lita Unruh, Manager, Recruiting and Training. **Description:** A high-tech public relations agency located in Silicon Valley. **Common positions include:** Management Analyst/Consultant; Public Relations Specialist. **Educational backgrounds include:** Communications; English; Journalism; Marketing. **Benefits:** 401(k); Daycare Assistance; Dental Insurance; Disability Coverage; Employee Discounts; Life Insurance; Medical Insurance; Profit Sharing; Tuition Assistance. **Corporate headquarters location:** This Location. **Other U.S. locations:** Cambridge MA. **Operations at this facility include:** Administration; Service. **Listed on:** Privately held. **Number of employees at this location:** 55. **Number of employees nationwide:** 80.

DATAQUEST INC.
251 River Oaks Parkway, San Jose CA 95134. 408/468-8000. **Contact:** Human Resources. **Description:** A market research company.

FOOTE CONE & BELDING COMMUNICATIONS
1255 Battery Street, San Francisco CA 94111. **Contact:** Sue Poulter, Personnel Director. **Description:** Ranked as one of the largest advertising agencies in the United States, and

among the world's 10 largest, Foote Cone & Belding operates an agency which analyzes the advertising needs of clients, plans and creates advertising for their products and services, and places advertising in various mass-market media. The firm offers such additional services as design and production of merchandising and promotional programs, product research, and package design. The firm operates fully-staffed offices in a number of metropolitan areas. **Corporate headquarters location:** Chicago IL. **Other U.S. locations:** Nationwide. **Listed on:** New York Stock Exchange.

HILL AND KNOWLTON INC.
177 Post Street, Suite 600, San Francisco CA 94108. 415/781-2430. **Contact:** Office Manager. **Description:** One of the largest public relations/public affairs counseling firms in the world, serving more than 1,000 clients throughout the world through more than 60 company offices and through associate arrangements with some 50 leading regional firms worldwide. **Corporate headquarters location:** New York NY. **Other U.S. locations:** Washington DC.

KETCHUM COMMUNICATIONS, INC.
55 Union Street, San Francisco CA 94111. 415/984-6100. **Contact:** Human Resources. **Description:** A communications agency specializing in advertising, public relations, and directory advertising. **Common positions include:** Advertising Account Executive; Food Scientist/Technologist; Media Planner/Specialist; Operations/Production Manager. **Educational backgrounds include:** Art/Design; Business Administration; Communications; Journalism; Liberal Arts; Marketing. **Benefits:** Dental Insurance; Disability Coverage; Life Insurance; Medical Insurance; Profit Sharing; Savings Plan; Tuition Assistance. **Corporate headquarters location:** Pittsburgh PA. **Other U.S. locations:** San Francisco CA; Chicago IL; New York NY. **Operations at this facility include:** Divisional Headquarters.

AUSTIN KNIGHT ADVERTISING
100 Shoreline Highway, Building B, #100, Mill Valley CA 94941. 415/331-5600. **Contact:** Nigel Hartley, Executive Vice President. **Description:** An advertising agency specializing in human resources and employee communications. Austin Knight is a member of the American Association of Advertising Agencies. **Other U.S. locations:** Santa Monica CA; Boston MA.

HAL RINEY & PARTNERS
735 Battery Street, San Francisco CA 94111. 415/981-0950. **Contact:** Human Resources Department. **Description:** An advertising agency.

J. WALTER THOMPSON
4 Embarcadero Center, Suite 900, San Francisco CA 94111. 415/955-2000. **Contact:** Human Resources. **Description:** An advertising agency.

YOUNG & RUBICAM WEST
100 First Street, San Francisco CA 94105. 415/882-0600. **Contact:** Paul Bollwinkel, Human Resources Director. **Description:** An international advertising agency, with 126 agency offices. The company operates through three divisions: Young & Rubicam International; Marsteller Inc., a worldwide leader in business-to-business and consumer advertising, with subsidiary Burson-Marsteller providing public relations services; and Young & Rubicam USA, with 14 consumer advertising agencies operating through four regional groups (except Young & Rubicam Detroit), and five specialized advertising and marketing agencies.

Note: *Because addresses and telephone numbers of smaller companies can change rapidly, we recommend you call each company to verify the information below before inquiring about job opportunities. Mass mailings are not recommended.*

Additional small employers:

PUBLIC RELATIONS SERVICES

Financial Relations Board Inc.
180 Montgomery St Ste 1180, San Francisco CA 94104-4230. 415/986-1591.

Business Wire
44 Montgomery St Ste 3900, San Francisco CA 94104-4812. 415/986-4422.

Hi-Tech Public Relations Inc.
101 Howard St Fl 2, San Francisco CA 94105-1629. 415/904-7000.

McGlinchey and Paul Associates Inc.
1875 S Grant St, San Mateo CA 94402-2666. 415/286-3990.

AG Spanos Public Relations
1341 W Robinhood Dr, Stockton CA 95207-5511. 209/478-3030.

Ian Cornell Companies
PO Box 1011, Fair Oaks CA 95628-1011. 916/965-1805.

Fleishman-Hillard Inc.
555 Capitol Mall, Sacramento CA 95814-4504. 916/441-7606.

Stoorza Ziegaus & Metzger
555 Capitol Mall Ste 600, Sacramento CA 95814-4502. 916/446-6667.

System Sales
27 Terfidia Lane, Milpitas CA 95035-5023. 408/945-9752.

MISC. ADVERTISING SERVICES

Goldberg Moser O'Neill
77 Maiden Ln, San Francisco CA 94108-5414. 415/477-1800.

Saatchi & Saatchi Advertising
1010 Battery St, San Francisco CA 94111-1202. 415/296-6000.

Goodby Silverstein & Partners
921 Front St, San Francisco CA 94111-1426. 415/392-0669.

McCann-Erickson Inc.
201 California Street Floor 7, San Francisco CA 94111-5002. 415/981-2262.

Adland Advertising Incorporated
3000 Steiner St, San Francisco CA 94123-3908. 415/928-1728.

Cohn & Wells
909 Montgomery Street Suite 200, San Francisco CA 94133-4625. 415/788-0525.

MAS Advertising
3157 Corporate Pl, Hayward CA 94545-3915. 510/887-2211.

CKS Partners
10443 Bandley Dr, Cupertino CA 95014-1912. 408/366-5100.

Fisher Graphic Industries
1137 Graphics Dr, Modesto CA 95351-1501. 209/577-0181.

Jeffrey-Scott Advertising Inc.
670 P St, Fresno CA 93721-2704. 209/268-9741.

Evansgroup
530 Bush St, San Francisco CA 94108-3623. 415/398-2669.

Fran Hulse Advertising
99 Osgood Pl, San Francisco CA 94133. 415/391-4224.

Bernard Hodes Advertising
2100 Geng Rd, Palo Alto CA 94303-3317. 415/856-1000.

Delaney Group
2150 Mariner Square Dr, Alameda CA 94501-1069. 510/748-4490.

Fraser Advertising
1180 Quail Valley Run, Oakley CA 94561-3418. 510/625-8624.

Concepts & Strategies
1990 North California Boulevard Suite 830, Walnut Creek CA 94596-3745. 510/933-4496.

RSA
41 Angela Ave, San Anselmo CA 94960-1316. 415/459-0673.

MW Media
60 South Market, San Jose CA 95113. 408/286-4200.

Marquez Advertising Agency
1670 Las Plumas Ave, San Jose CA 95133-1658. 408/272-6963.

Advertising Concepts
3700 Haven Glen Pl,

Sacramento CA 95821-3316. 916/483-9225.

Corcoran Co.
455 University Ave, Sacramento CA 95825-6513. 916/649-1190.

Federal Sign
6805 Sierra Ct # A, Dublin CA 94568-2654. 510/829-9555.

Metropolitan Outdoor Advertising
440 Grand Ave Ste 360, Oakland CA 94610-5012. 510/272-9002.

Gannett Outdoor Co.
1695 Eastshore Hwy, Berkeley CA 94710-1733. 510/527-3350.

Patrick Media Group Inc.
1601 Maritime St, Oakland CA 94607-1037. 510/835-5900.

3M National Advertising Co.
2050 W Fremont St, Stockton CA 95203-1913. 209/466-5021.

Katz-TV & Radio
100 Spear St Ste 1900, San Francisco CA 94105-1529. 415/777-3377.

McGavren Guild
750 Battery St # 3, San Francisco CA 94111-1523. 415/772-2700.

Bay Cable Advertising
39355 California St, Fremont CA 94538-1447. 510/494-8105.

Bay Cable Advertising
20902 Cabot Blvd, Hayward CA 94545-1129. 510/732-7320.

Bay Cable Advertising
1485 Treat Blvd, Walnut Creek CA 94596-2187. 510/746-3800.

Sawyer Ferguson Walker Co.
220 Bush St, San Francisco CA 94104-3502. 415/421-5707.

H&P Co. Inc.
300 Montgomery St, San Francisco CA 94104-1902. 415/693-9132.

CCC Directory Publishers
2515 Santa Clara Ave, Alameda CA 94501-4660. 510/521-6952.

National Directory Services
4136 Grass Valley Hwy, Auburn CA 95602-9194. 916/885-0911.

Tabor Publishing
4513 Montcurve Blvd, Fair Oaks CA 95628-5750. 916/961-2421.

Valley Yellow Pages
800 Howe Ave, Sacramento CA 95825-3911. 916/648-9888.

The Humboldt Beacon
928 Main St, Fortuna CA 95540-2007. 707/725-6166.

Tahoe Daily Tribune
3079 Harrison Ave, S Lake Tahoe CA 96150-7931. 916/541-3880.

Treasure Chest Advertising Co. Inc.
1201 Shore St, W Sacramento CA 95691-3510. 916/371-9500.

Advanced Distributing Company
1900 Point West Way, Sacramento CA 95815-4705. 916/925-7993.

Giltspur-San Francisco
826 Burlway Rd, Burlingame CA 94010-1706. 415/342-3691.

Barrango
360 Swift Ave # 1, S San Francisco CA 94080-6220. 415/871-1931.

Ruszel Woodworks
2980 Bayshore Rd, Benicia CA 94510-1230. 707/745-6979.

Display Solutions
418 Durant Way, Mill Valley CA 94941-4063. 415/381-6070.

Contempo Design West Inc.
212 Railroad Ave, Milpitas CA 95035-4338. 408/956-9555.

Color & Design Exhibits Inc.
1911 Lundy Ave, San Jose CA 95131-1847. 408/432-3220.

Sel-Mor Products Inc.
PO Box 228, Lodi CA 95241-0228. 209/334-1256.

DIRECT MAIL ADVERTISING SERVICES

Snyder Newell Inc.
375 Newhall St, San Francisco CA 94124-1470. 415/826-7170.

Direct Media
1615 Bonanza St Ste 305, Walnut Creek CA 94596-4531. 510/906-1070.

Comac Inc.
565 Sinclair Frontage Rd, Milpitas CA 95035-5413. 408/945-1600.

Advo-System Inc.
3031 Tisch Way, San Jose CA 95128-2541. 408/261-1970.

Val-Pak Bay Area Inc.
4380 Redwood Hwy, San Rafael CA 94903-2110. 415/472-6245.

Dimac Direct
4142 Point Eden Way,

Hayward CA 94545-3737. 510/786-5500.

Pacific Mailing Corp.
8652 Thornton Ave, Newark CA 94560. 510/713-2411.

Computer Targeting Systems
2530 Berryessa Road, San Jose CA 95132. 408/923-8115.

Car Contract & Employment Service
2751 Marine Way, Mountain View CA 94043-1127. 415/961-1119.

For more information on career opportunities in advertising, marketing, and public relations:

Associations

ADVERTISING RESEARCH FOUNDATION
641 Lexington Avenue, New York NY 10022. 212/751-5656. Fax: 212/319-5265. World Wide Web address: http://www.arfsite.org/arf. A nonprofit organization comprised of advertising, marketing, and media research companies. For institutions only.

AMERICAN ASSOCIATION OF ADVERTISING AGENCIES
666 Third Avenue, New York NY 10017. 212/682-2500. Offers educational and enrichment benefits such as publications, videos, and conferences.

AMERICAN MARKETING ASSOCIATION
250 South Wacker Drive, Suite 200, Chicago IL 60606-5819. 312/831-2764. Fax: 312/648-5625. World Wide Web address: http://www.ama.org. An association with nearly 50,000 members worldwide. Offers 25 annual conferences, library and research services, and 25 annual issues of *Marketing News.*

DIRECT MARKETING ASSOCIATION
1120 Avenue of Americas, New York NY 10036-6700. 212/768-7277. World Wide Web address: http://www.the-dma.org. Offers monthly newsletters, seminars, and conferences.

INTERNATIONAL ADVERTISING ASSOCIATION
521 Fifth Avenue, Suite 1807, New York NY 10175. 212/557-1133. Fax: 212/983-0455. E-mail address: IAA@ibnet.com. World Wide Web address: http://www.iaacongress.com. Over 3,600 members in 89 countries. Membership includes: publications; professional development; congresses, symposia, and conferences; annual report and membership directory; and worldwide involvement with governments and other associations. The organization looks to promote the self-regulation of advertising.

LEAGUE OF ADVERTISING AGENCIES
2 South End Avenue #4C, New York NY 10280. 212/945-4991. Seminars available.

MARKETING RESEARCH ASSOCIATION
2189 Silas Deane Highway, Suite #5, Rocky Hill CT 06067. 860/257-4008. Marketing Research Association publishes several magazines and newsletters.

PUBLIC RELATIONS SOCIETY OF AMERICA
33 Irving Place, New York NY 10003. 212/995-2230. World Wide Web address: http://www.prsa.org.

Directories

AAAA ROSTER AND ORGANIZATION
American Association of Advertising Agencies, 666 Third Avenue, 13th Floor, New York NY 10017. 212/682-2500.

DIRECTORY OF MINORITY PUBLIC RELATIONS PROFESSIONALS
Public Relations Society of America, 33 Irving Place, New York NY 10003. 212/995-2230.

O'DWYER'S DIRECTORY OF PUBLIC RELATIONS FIRMS
J. R. O'Dwyer Company, 271 Madison Avenue, Room 600, New York NY 10016. 212/679-2471.

PUBLIC RELATIONS CONSULTANTS DIRECTORY
American Business Directories, Division of American Business Lists, 5711 South 86th Circle, Omaha NE 68127. 402/593-4500.

PUBLIC RELATIONS JOURNAL / REGISTER ISSUE
Public Relations Society of America, 33 Irving Place, New York NY 10003. 212/995-2230.

STANDARD DIRECTORY OF ADVERTISING AGENCIES
Reed Reference Publishing Company, P.O. Box 31, New Providence NJ 07974. 800/521-8110.

Magazines

ADVERTISING AGE
Crain Communications, 740 North Rush Street, Chicago IL 60611. 312/649-5316.

ADWEEK
BPI, 1515 Broadway, 12th Floor, New York NY 10036-8986. 212/536-5336.

BUSINESS MARKETING
Crain Communications, 740 North Rush Street, Chicago IL 60611. 312/649-5260.

JOURNAL OF MARKETING
American Marketing Association, 250 South Wacker Drive, Suite 200, Chicago IL 60606. 312/648-0536.

THE MARKETING NEWS
American Marketing Association, 250 South Wacker Drive, Suite 200, Chicago IL 60606. 312/648-0536.

PR REPORTER
PR Publishing Company, P.O. Box 600, Exeter NH 03833. 603/778-0514.

PUBLIC RELATIONS JOURNAL
Public Relations Society of America, 33 Irving Place, New York NY 10003. 212/995-2230.

PUBLIC RELATIONS NEWS
Phillips Publishing Inc., 1202 Seven Locks Road, Suite 300, Potomac MD 20854. 301/340-1520.

Newsletters

PUBLIC RELATIONS CAREER OPPORTUNITIES
1575 Eye Street NW, Suite 1190, Washington DC 20005. 202/408-7904 Fax: 202/408-7907. World Wide Web address: http://www.entremkt.com/ceo. Contact: James J. Zaniello, Managing Director. Newsletter listing public relations, public affairs, special events, and investor positions nationwide. Available on a subscription basis, published 24 times a year. Company also publishes other newsletters, including *CEO Job Opportunities Update* and *ASAE Career Opportunities* (for the American Society of Association Executives).

AEROSPACE

The aerospace industry, wracked by layoffs throughout the early '90s, has yet to pull out of its tailspin. As ever, the slump is being fueled by declining commercial aircraft orders and further defense cuts. As a result, research and development dollars have been trimmed, and many of the biggest firms in the industry have now merged. As of early 1996, the industry was continuing to shrink -- and is now dominated by fewer, larger companies.

While this consolidation has led to a surge in profits, it also means that rapid downsizing will continue. Some analysts believe that even though the defense industry has cut well over 1 million jobs since the late '80s, the industry still needs to cut its workforce by another 30 percent.

Many companies are trying to shift to commercial production, reducing their dependence on dwindling defense contracts. Even so, defense purchases still support a significant number of aerospace workers. Over the long haul, the industry's focus on advanced technology will mean more professional and technical positions -- with engineers leading the way.

AEROJET
P.O. Box 13222, Sacramento CA 95813-6000. 916/355-4000. **Contact:** Human Resources. **Description:** Engaged in the research, development, testing, and production of liquid propellant rocket engines, solid rocket motors, sounding rockets, defense and aerospace systems, and waterjet propulsion systems. **Common positions include:** Aerospace Engineer; Mechanical Engineer. **Benefits:** Dental Insurance; Disability Coverage; Life Insurance; Medical Insurance; Pension Plan; Savings Plan; Tuition Assistance. **Corporate headquarters location:** This Location. **Parent company:** Gencorp. **Listed on:** New York Stock Exchange.

APPLIED AEROSPACE STRUCTURES CORPORATION
P.O. Box 6189, Stockton CA 95206. 209/982-0160. **Fax:** 209/983-3375. **Contact:** F. Adele Greenman, Human Resources Coordinator. **Description:** Provides design, engineering, and manufacturing services internationally to private and governmental clients in the aerospace industry. **Common positions include:** Accountant/Auditor; Aerospace Engineer; Blue-Collar Worker Supervisor; Buyer; Chemist; Computer Programmer; Cost Estimator; Designer; Draftsperson; Electrician; Environmental Engineer; Financial Analyst; General Manager; Industrial Engineer; Industrial Production Manager; Manufacturing Engineer; Materials Engineer; Mechanical Engineer; Operations/Production Manager; Program Manager; Quality Control Supervisor. **Educational backgrounds include:** Accounting; Engineering; Marketing. **Benefits:** 401(k); Dental Insurance; Disability Coverage; Life Insurance; Medical Insurance; Tuition Assistance. **Special Programs:** Internships. **Corporate headquarters location:** This Location. **Operations at this facility include:** Administration; Manufacturing; Sales. **Listed on:** Privately held. **Number of employees nationwide:** 170.

DEXTER AEROSPACE MATERIALS DIVISION
P.O. Box 312, Pittsburg CA 94565-0031. 510/458-8000. **Contact:** Human Resources. **Description:** Dexter is a diverse manufacturing company whose primary products

include chemical and medical products. The company is involved in molecular biology research items, as well as electronic, automotive, food packaging, and aerospace products. Subsidiaries also produce coatings and wall coverings. This facility produces adhesives and sealants for use in the aerospace industry. **Corporate headquarters location:** Windsor Locks CT. **Parent company:** The Dexter Corporation. **Number of employees nationwide:** 600.

KAISER AEROSPACE & ELECTRONIC CORPORATION
950 Tower Lane, Suite 800, Foster City CA 94404. 415/349-7400. **Contact:** Human Resources. **Description:** Manufactures aircraft equipment.

KAISER ELECTRONICS
2701 Orchard Parkway, Mail Stop 10, San Jose CA 95134. 408/432-3000. **Contact:** Director of Human Resources. **Description:** Designs, develops, and manufactures avionic display systems. **Common positions include:** Aerospace Engineer; Buyer; Chemical Engineer; Electrical/Electronics Engineer; Financial Analyst; Mechanical Engineer. **Educational backgrounds include:** Engineering. **Benefits:** Daycare Assistance; Dental Insurance; Disability Coverage; Life Insurance; Medical Insurance; Pension Plan; Profit Sharing; Savings Plan; Tuition Assistance. **Corporate headquarters location:** Foster City CA. **Parent company:** Kaiser Aerospace & Electronics. **Operations at this facility include:** Administration; Manufacturing; Research and Development; Service. **Number of employees at this location:** 800.

LOCKHEED MARTIN MISSILES & SPACE COMPANY INC.
P.O. Box 3504, Department 27-51, Building 560, Sunnyvale CA 94088-3504. 408/742-9720. **Fax:** 408/742-6194. **Contact:** Personnel Department. **E-mail address:** jobs@LMSC.Lockheed.com. **Description:** One of the major companies of Lockheed Martin, providing government organizations with diversified products and conducting a large number of research projects for these organizations. The company operates in five major areas: Space Systems (develops space technology systems such as rocket systems, Space Shuttle support technology, and other products); Missile Systems (produces fleet ballistic missiles for military applications); Advanced Systems (operates as the research and development organization exploring comprehensive database systems to process the specific needs of other company divisions); and the Austin Division (Austin TX -- responsible for designing and producing military tactical support systems). **Common positions include:** Aerospace Engineer; Chemical Engineer; Computer Programmer; Computer Systems Analyst; Electrical/Electronics Engineer; Environmental Engineer; Materials Engineer; Mathematician; Metallurgical Engineer; Software Engineer. **Educational backgrounds include:** Computer Science; Engineering. **Benefits:** 401(k); Dental Insurance; Disability Coverage; Life Insurance; Medical Insurance; Pension Plan; Savings Plan; Tuition Assistance. **Special Programs:** Internships. **Corporate headquarters location:** Bethesda MD. **Parent company:** Lockheed Martin. **Operations at this facility include:** Administration; Research and Development. **Listed on:** New York Stock Exchange. **Number of employees at this location:** 12,000. **Number of employees nationwide:** 14,000.

LORAL SPACE SYSTEMS
3825 Fabian Way, Palo Alto CA 94303-4604. 415/852-4000. **Contact:** Human Resources. **Description:** Produces space flight systems and subsystems and related supporting technologies. Overall, Loral is an international high-technology company, which primarily designs, develops, and produces electronic systems and microwave devices used in defense electronics and communications. Loral's vast array of defense

electronics technologies and systems integration expertise are concentrated on the following core activities: electronic combat, training and simulation systems, tactical weapons, command, control, communications, intelligence, systems integration, and telecommunications and space. Among the company's major customers are the U.S. government, including the U.S. Department of Defense (DoD), the National Aeronautics and Space Administration (NASA), Federal Aviation Administration (FAA), and other non-DoD government agencies; international military services; international telecommunications and broadcast service providers; and regional customers. Loral has risen to the top ranks of U.S. defense electronics and government contractors.

NATIONAL AIRMOTIVE CORPORATION
7200 Lockheed Street, Oakland CA 94621. 510/613-1008. **Fax:** 510/635-6911. **Contact:** Margaret Lawson, Director of Human Resources. **Description:** Engaged in the repair and sale of turbine engines, parts, and related systems. **Common positions include:** Accountant/Auditor; Buyer; Computer Operator; Cost Estimator; Credit Manager; Customer Service Representative; Electrical/Electronics Engineer; Electrician; Employment Interviewer; Financial Manager; Human Resources Specialist; Industrial Engineer; Machinist; Manufacturing Engineer; Mechanic; Payroll Clerk; Purchasing Agent and Manager; Quality Control Supervisor; Services Sales Representative; Sheet-Metal Worker; Stock Clerk; Systems Analyst; Technical Writer/Editor; Transportation/Traffic Specialist; Typist/Word Processor; Welder. **Educational backgrounds include:** Accounting; Aviation; Business Administration; Computer Science; Engineering; Finance. **Benefits:** 401(k); Dental Insurance; Disability Coverage; Employee Discounts; Life Insurance; Medical Insurance; Pension Plan; Profit Sharing; Savings Plan; Tuition Assistance. **Corporate headquarters location:** This Location. **Parent company:** First Aviation Services, Inc. **Operations at this facility include:** Administration; Manufacturing; Sales; Service. **Number of employees at this location:** 375.

OEA AEROSPACE
P.O. Box KK, Fairfield CA 94533. 707/422-1880. **Contact:** Mal Castro, Human Resource/Security Administrator. **Description:** Produces explosive devices and systems for the aerospace industry. **Common positions include:** Aerospace Engineer; Computer Programmer; Manufacturing Supervisor; Mechanical Engineer; Production Coordinator; Production Operator; Supervisor; Technical Writer/Editor. **Educational backgrounds include:** Business Administration; Engineering. **Benefits:** 401(k); Dental Insurance; Disability Coverage; Life Insurance; Medical Insurance; Profit Sharing; Tuition Assistance. **Corporate headquarters location:** This Location. **Operations at this facility include:** Administration; Manufacturing; Research and Development. **Listed on:** New York Stock Exchange.

QUANTIC INDUSTRIES, INC.
990 Commercial Street, San Carlos CA 94070. 415/595-1100. **Contact:** Carol Bledsoe, Personnel Administrator. **Description:** Produces sophisticated aerospace equipment such as satellite guidance systems and aerospace ordnance devices.

WYMAN-GORDON COMPANY
PRECISION FOUNDERS DIVISION
414 Hester Street, San Leandro CA 94577. 510/568-6400. **Fax:** 510/632-0949. **Contact:** Lana Gossett, Human Resources Manager. **Description:** A manufacturer of high-technology, high-integrity, investment castings for the aerospace industry. **Common positions include:** Accountant/Auditor; Aerospace Engineer; Blue-Collar Worker

Supervisor; Buyer; Ceramics Engineer; Chemical Engineer; Computer Programmer; Customer Service Representative; Electrician; General Manager; Human Resources Specialist; Industrial Engineer; Management Trainee; Materials Engineer; Mechanical Engineer; Metallurgical Engineer; Operations/Production Manager; Purchasing Agent and Manager; Quality Control Supervisor. **Educational backgrounds include:** Accounting; Engineering. **Benefits:** 401(k); Dental Insurance; Disability Coverage; Employee Discounts; Life Insurance; Medical Insurance; Pension Plan; Profit Sharing; Savings Plan; Tuition Assistance. **Corporate headquarters location:** Groton CT. **Other U.S. locations:** Tilton NH; Carson City NV. **Subsidiaries include:** Wyman-Gordon Investment Castings, Inc. **Operations at this facility include:** Administration; Manufacturing; Sales; Service. **Listed on:** NASDAQ. **Number of employees at this location:** 150. **Number of employees nationwide:** 3,000.

For more information on career opportunities in aerospace:

Associations

AIR TRANSPORT ASSOCIATION OF AMERICA
1301 Pennsylvania Avenue NW, Suite 1100, Washington DC 20004. 202/626-4000. World Wide Web address: http://www.air-transport.org. A trade association for the major U.S. airlines.

AMERICAN INSTITUTE OF AERONAUTICS AND ASTRONAUTICS
85 John Street, 4th Floor, New York NY 10038. 212/349-1120. World Wide Web address: http://www.aiaa.org. Membership required. Publishes six journals and books.

FUTURE AVIATION PROFESSIONALS OF AMERICA
4959 Massachusetts Boulevard, Atlanta GA 30337. 770/997-8097. Publishes a monthly newsletter which monitors the job market for flying jobs; a pilot employment guide, outlining what is required to become a pilot; and a directory of aviation employers.

NATIONAL AERONAUTIC ASSOCIATION OF USA
1815 North Fort Myer Drive, Suite 700, Arlington VA 22209. 703/527-0226. World Wide Web address: http://www.naa.ycg.org. Publishes a magazine. Membership required.

PROFESSIONAL AVIATION MAINTENANCE ASSOCIATION
500 NW Plaza, Suite 1016, St. Ann MO 63074. 314/739-2580. World Wide Web address: http://www.pama.org. Members' resumes are distributed to companies who advise the organization of employment opportunities. Many local chapters also provide job referrals. Members have access to the Worldwide Membership Directory.

APPAREL AND TEXTILES

The apparel industry is facing an uncertain future. Women's apparel prices dropped 4.4 percent in 1994, and many experts expect continued deflation through 1996. Consumers have remained disinterested in new fashions and refuse to pay higher prices. Textile and apparel mills are under pressure from the other end of the supply chain as well -- the cost of cotton and other raw materials has remained at close to record highs, with raw cotton prices jumping 35 percent in 1994. As a result, many textile producers have recently reported significant drops in earnings. However, improved consumer confidence, more attractive fashions, and lower prices may prod consumers to buy. This will eventually increase business for mills. Especially hot: sales of men's suits. This trend is expected to continue as men look for upscale casual wear to accommodate more relaxed dress codes. The highest consumer demand in apparel will probably be for lower-priced clothing produced for discount stores.

BYER CALIFORNIA
66 Potrero Avenue, San Francisco CA 94103. 415/626-7844. **Contact:** Personnel Department. **Description:** A manufacturer of women's garments.

FRITZI CALIFORNIA
199 1st Street, San Francisco CA 94105. 415/979-1200. **Contact:** Human Resources Director. **Description:** Designs, produces, and distributes moderately-priced misses, junior, and girls' apparel, sold under a variety of labels. Fritzi offers a wide range of product lines. **Corporate headquarters location:** This Location.

JESSICA McCLINTOCK
1400 16th Street, San Francisco CA 94103. 415/495-3327. **Contact:** Personnel. **Description:** Manufactures women's apparel. Jessica McClintock is best known for its line of formal dresses. **NOTE:** This firm does not accept unsolicited resumes. Please only respond to advertised openings. **Corporate headquarters location:** This Location.

KORET OF CALIFORNIA
611 Mission Street, San Francisco CA 94105. 415/957-2037. **Contact:** Human Resources. **Description:** Manufactures and markets women's apparel. **Common positions include:** Accountant/Auditor; Advertising Clerk; Blue-Collar Worker Supervisor; Buyer; Computer Programmer; Computer Systems Analyst; Credit Manager; Customer Service Representative; Designer; Financial Analyst; Industrial Production Manager; Manufacturer's/Wholesaler's Sales Rep.; Merchandiser; Quality Control Supervisor; Software Engineer; Wholesale and Retail Buyer. **Educational backgrounds include:** Accounting; Art/Design; Business Administration; Communications; Finance; Liberal Arts. **Benefits:** 401(k); Disability Coverage; Employee Discounts; Life Insurance; Medical Insurance; Profit Sharing. **Special Programs:** Internships. **Other U.S. locations:** Chico CA; Los Angeles CA; Napa CA; Miami FL; New York NY; Price UT. **Subsidiaries include:** Koret Canada; Mr. Jax. **Operations at this facility include:** Administration; Sales; Service. **Listed on:** Privately held. **Number of employees nationwide:** 1,200.

LEVI STRAUSS & COMPANY
1155 Battery Street, San Francisco CA 94111. 415/544-6000. **Contact:** Human Resources. **Description:** Designs, manufactures, and markets a diversified line of apparel; primarily jeans and jeans-related products under the brand names Levi's and Brittania. The company also makes the Dockers line of clothing for U.S. markets. Levi Strauss & Company operates 44 manufacturing and warehouse facilities and eight distribution centers in the U.S., and 22 and 19, respectively, overseas. **Common positions include:** Accountant/Auditor; Administrator; Advertising Clerk; Attorney; Blue-Collar Worker Supervisor; Claim Representative; Computer Programmer; Customer Service Representative; Department Manager; Financial Analyst; Human Resources Specialist; Industrial Designer; Industrial Engineer; Manufacturer's/ Wholesaler's Sales Rep.; Marketing Specialist; Operations/Production Manager; Public Relations Specialist; Quality Control Supervisor; Statistician; Systems Analyst. **Educational backgrounds include:** Accounting; Art/Design; Business Administration; Communications; Computer Science; Economics; Engineering; Finance; Marketing. **Benefits:** Dental Insurance; Disability Coverage; Employee Discounts; Life Insurance; Medical Insurance; Pension Plan; Profit Sharing; Savings Plan; Tuition Assistance. **Corporate headquarters location:** This Location.

SALZ LEATHERS INC.
P.O. Box 1840, Santa Cruz CA 95061. 408/423-4470. **Contact:** Alan Smith, Personnel Director. **Description:** Produces a wide variety of leather products and leather tanning services.

TALBOTT INC.
Talbott Studios, Carmel Valley CA 93924-0996. 408/649-6000. **Contact:** Human Resources. **Description:** Produces men's ties and related accessories.

Note: *Because addresses and telephone numbers of smaller companies can change rapidly, we recommend you call each company to verify the information below before inquiring about job opportunities. Mass mailings are not recommended.*

Additional small employers:

APPAREL WHOLESALE

Gap Kids
1689 Arden Way, Sacramento CA 95815-4030. 916/648-3948.

Laurel Burch Inc.
660 3rd St, San Francisco CA 94107-1921. 415/495-1642.

Dress Barn Factory Store
331 Nut Tree Rd, Vacaville CA 95687-3241. 707/451-0128.

Loralie Original Inc.
4350 Caterpillar Rd, Redding CA 96003-1422. 916/244-2351.

Birkenstock Footprint Sandals
8171 Redwood Blvd, Novato CA 94945-1403. 415/892-4200.

Lincoln Shoe Polish Co.
172 Commercial St, Sunnyvale CA 94086-5201. 408/732-5121.

KNITTING MILLS

Chun's Hosiery
818 Jefferson St, Oakland CA 94607-3625. 510/893-0712.

COATED FABRICS

Hexcel Corp. Advanced Compositer
10 Trevarno Rd, Livermore CA 94550. 510/447-1001.

TEXTILE GOODS

United Textile Co.
2225 Grant Ave, San Lorenzo CA 94580-1803. 510/276-2288.

MEN'S AND BOYS' CLOTHING

Ben F. Davis Manufacturing Co.
1663 Mission St, San

Francisco CA 94103-2449. 415/861-3575.

SJ Manufacturing Inc.
148 Townsend St, San Francisco CA 94107-1919. 415/597-7500.

MISC. APPAREL AND ACCESSORIES

Unique Garment Manufacturing
2573 3rd St, San Francisco CA 94107. 415/282-8181.

Linda Apparel Manufacturing Inc.
180 Townsend St, San Francisco CA 94107-1909. 415/882-0868.

For more information on career opportunities in the apparel and textiles industries:

Associations

AMERICAN APPAREL MANUFACTURERS ASSOCIATION
2500 Wilson Boulevard, Suite 301, Arlington VA 22201. 703/524-1864. Publishes numerous magazines, newsletters, and bulletins for the benefit of employees in the apparel manufacturing industry.

AMERICAN TEXTILE MANUFACTURERS INSTITUTE
Office of the Chief Economist, 1801 K Street NW, Suite 900, Washington DC 20006-1301. 202/862-0500. Fax: 202/862-0570. The national trade association for the domestic textile industry. Members are corporations only.

THE FASHION GROUP
597 5th Avenue, 8th Floor, New York NY 10017. 212/593-1715. World Wide Web address: http://www.fgi.org. A nonprofit organization for professional women in the fashion industries (apparel, accessories, beauty, and home). Offers career counseling workshops 18 times per year.

INTERNATIONAL ASSOCIATION OF CLOTHING DESIGNERS
475 Park Avenue South, 17th Floor, New York NY 10016. 212/685-6602.

Directories

AAMA DIRECTORY
American Apparel Manufacturers Association, 2500 Wilson Boulevard, Suite 301, Arlington VA 22201. 703/524-1864. A directory of publications distributed by the American Apparel Manufacturers Association.

APPAREL TRADES BOOK
Dun & Bradstreet Inc., 430 Mountain Avenue, New Providence NJ 07974. 908/665-5000.

FAIRCHILD'S MARKET DIRECTORY OF WOMEN'S AND CHILDREN'S APPAREL
Fairchild Publications, 7 West 34th Street, New York NY 10001. 212/630-4000.

Magazines

ACCESSORIES
Business Journals, 50 Day Street, P.O. Box 5550, Norwalk CT 06856. 203/853-6015.

AMERICA'S TEXTILES
Billiam Publishing, 37 Villa Road, Suite 111, P.O. Box 103, Greenville SC 29615. 864/242-5300.

APPAREL INDUSTRY MAGAZINE
Shore Communications Inc., 6255 Barfield Road, Suite 200, Atlanta GA 30328-4893. 404/252-8831.

BOBBIN
Bobbin Publications, P.O. Box 1986, 1110 Shop Road, Columbia SC 29202. 803/771-7500.

TEXTILE HILIGHTS
American Textile Manufacturers Institute, Office of the Chief Economist, 1801 K Street NW, Suite 900, Washington DC 20006.

WOMEN'S WEAR DAILY (WWD)
Fairchild Publications, 7 West 34th Street, New York NY 10001. 212/630-4000.

ARCHITECTURE, CONSTRUCTION, AND ENGINEERING

The U.S. Department of Labor has estimated 1.2 million new construction jobs from 1992 through 2005, due to the need to replace aging experienced workers. Residential construction will grow slowly, as a result of the expected decline in population growth. Industrial construction, however, will be stronger because of an increase in exports by manufacturers. Heavy construction is growing faster than the industry average, with much activity in highway, bridge, and street construction.

Job prospects for engineers have been good for a number of years, and will continue to improve into the next century. Employers will need more engineers as they increase investment in equipment in order to expand output. In addition, engineers will find work improving the nation's deteriorating infrastructure.

GUY F. ATKINSON COMPANY
1001 Bayhill Drive, Suite 200, San Bruno CA 94066. 415/876-1000. **Contact:** Personnel Director. **Description:** A heavy construction firm with domestic operations in a number of areas.

BECHTEL CORPORATION
P.O. Box 193965, San Francisco CA 94119-3965. 415/768-4449. **Contact:** Employment Department. **Description:** A company operating in the following areas: engineering, construction, financing operations and maintenance, electricity, nuclear fuel, metals, minerals, procurement management, transportation, and pollution control. **Educational backgrounds include:** Computer Science; Engineering; Environmental Science.

BECHTEL NEVADA
P.O. Box 8051, Pleasanton CA 94588. 510/847-1321. **Fax:** 510/847-1012. **Contact:** Ida M. Williams, Human Resources Manager. **Description:** A company operating in the following areas: engineering, construction, financing operations and maintenance, electricity, nuclear fuel, metals, minerals, procurement management, transportation, and pollution control. **Common positions include:** Administrative Services Manager; Computer Programmer; Computer Systems Analyst; Designer; Draftsperson; Electrical/Electronics Engineer; Geologist/Geophysicist; Human Resources Specialist; Mechanical Engineer; Meteorologist; Software Engineer; Technical Writer/Editor. **Educational backgrounds include:** Business Administration; Computer Science; Engineering; Geology; Mathematics; Physics. **Benefits:** 401(k); Dental Insurance; Disability Coverage; Employee Discounts; Life Insurance; Medical Insurance; Pension Plan; Savings Plan; Tuition Assistance. **Other U.S. locations:** Washington DC; NM; Las Vegas NV. **Operations at this facility include:** Administration; Manufacturing; Research and Development; Sales. **Listed on:** American Stock Exchange. **Number of employees at this location:** 87.

CH2M HILL CALIFORNIA INC.
P.O. Box 12681, Oakland CA 94604. 510/251-2426. **Contact:** Human Resources. **Description:** Established in 1946, CH2M Hill is a group of employee-owned companies

operating under the names CH2M Hill, Inc., Industrial Design Corporation, Operations Management International, CH2M Hill International, and CH2M Hill Engineering. The company's objective is to provide planning, engineering design, and operation and construction management services to help clients apply technology, safeguard the environment, and develop infrastructure. The professional staff includes specialists in environmental engineering and waste management, water management, transportation, industrial facilities, and a broad spectrum of infrastructure systems. **Common positions include:** Chemical Engineer; Civil Engineer; Economist/Market Research Analyst; Electrical/Electronics Engineer; Geologist/Geophysicist; Transportation/Traffic Specialist. **Educational backgrounds include:** Chemistry; Economics; Engineering; Geology. **Benefits:** Dental Insurance; Disability Coverage; Life Insurance; Medical Insurance; Pension Plan; Profit Sharing; Tuition Assistance. **Corporate headquarters location:** Denver CO. **Operations at this facility include:** Regional Headquarters.

DILLINGHAM CONSTRUCTION CORPORATION
P.O. Box 1089, Pleasanton CA 94566-0199. 510/463-3300. **Contact:** Employment. **Description:** Engaged in heavy industrial and commercial construction. Dillingham Construction also provides construction management services both domestically and abroad. **Number of employees at this location:** 1,000.

DINWIDDIE CONSTRUCTION COMPANY
275 Battery Street, Suite 300, San Francisco CA 94111. 415/986-2718. **Contact:** Personnel. **Description:** A construction company.

FACTORY MUTUAL ASSOCIATION
P.O. Box 4034, Concord CA 94524. 510/676-1900. **Contact:** Ed Smith, Manager of Operations. **Description:** A loss-control services organization owned by Allendale Insurance, Arkwright, and Protection Mutual Insurance, with 17 district offices strategically located throughout the United States and Canada. Research facilities are located in Norwood MA, and West Gloucester RI. Factory Mutual's primary objective is to help owner/company policyholders to protect their properties and occupancies from damage from fire, wind, flood, and explosion; from boiler, pressure vessel, and machinery accidents; and from many other insured hazards. To accomplish this objective, a wide range of engineering, research, and consulting services are provided primarily in the field of loss control. **Common positions include:** Chemical Engineer; Civil Engineer; Electrical/Electronics Engineer; Fire Science/Protection Engineer; Mechanical Engineer. **Benefits:** Dental Insurance; Disability Coverage; Employee Discounts; Life Insurance; Medical Insurance; Pension Plan; Savings Plan; Tuition Assistance. **Corporate headquarters location:** Norwood MA.

THE FAILURE GROUP, INC.
ENGINEERS AND SCIENTISTS
149 Commonwealth Drive, Menlo Park CA 94025. 415/326-9400. **Contact:** Human Resources. **Description:** The Failure Group, Inc., through its subsidiaries, Failure Analysis Associates, Inc. and PLG Inc., is a technical consulting firm dedicated to the investigation, analysis, and prevention of accidents and failures of an engineering or scientific nature. With 14 domestic and two international offices, this worldwide company of over 275 degreed professionals provides a multi-disciplinary approach to analyze how failures occur. Founded in 1967, Failure Analysis Associates has performed the scientific analysis of thousands of cases, from headline-making multimillion-dollar disasters to small accident investigations and routine risk assessments. The company's expertise is used in areas such as accident reconstruction, biomechanics,

construction/structural engineering, aviation and marine investigations, environmental assessment, materials and product testing, warnings and labeling issues, accident statistic data analysis, and risk prevention/mitigation. PLG Inc. provides consulting services to the energy, space and defense, transportation, and chemical and petroleum industries in the areas of reliability, maintenance, and operational performance assessment. PLG leads the field in analyzing the risk associated with the nuclear power industry and has helped the electric power industry develop and apply tools to meet both regulatory requirements and self-imposed safety and environmental impact goals.

GENSLER & ASSOCIATES/ARCHITECTS
600 California Street, San Francisco CA 94108. 415/433-3700. **Contact:** Corporate Human Resources. **Description:** Gensler & Associates is a firm of architects specializing in providing space planning, graphics, and interior design services on a national basis. **Common positions include:** Accountant/Auditor; Administrative Services Manager; Architect; Computer Programmer; Computer Systems Analyst; Draftsperson; Human Resources Specialist; Librarian. **Educational backgrounds include:** Accounting; Art/Design; Business Administration; Computer Science; Finance; Interior Design; Liberal Arts; Marketing. **Benefits:** Dental Insurance; Disability Coverage; Life Insurance; Medical Insurance; Profit Sharing; Tuition Assistance. **Special Programs:** Internships. **Corporate headquarters location:** This Location. **Other U.S. locations:** Irvine CA; Los Angeles CA; Denver CO; Washington DC; Atlanta GA; Boston MA; Detroit MI; New York NY; Houston TX. **Operations at this facility include:** Administration; Divisional Headquarters; Regional Headquarters; Service. **Listed on:** Privately held. **Number of employees at this location:** 175. **Number of employees nationwide:** 800.

GRANITE CONSTRUCTION INC.
P.O. Box 50085, 585 West Beach Street, Watsonville CA 95076-5125. 408/724-1011. **Fax:** 408/761-7871. **Contact:** Brian Fox, Director, Recruiting. **Description:** A construction company. **Common positions include:** Accountant/Auditor; Civil Engineer; Clerical Supervisor; Computer Programmer; Computer Systems Analyst; Construction Contractor and Manager; Cost Estimator; Mining Engineer; Structural Engineer; Surveyor. **Educational backgrounds include:** Accounting; Construction; Engineering; Management/Planning. **Benefits:** 401(k); Dental Insurance; Disability Coverage; Employee Discounts; Life Insurance; Medical Insurance; Pension Plan; Profit Sharing; Tuition Assistance. **Special Programs:** Internships. **Other U.S. locations:** Nationwide. **Operations at this facility include:** Administration; Divisional Headquarters; Regional Headquarters. **Listed on:** NASDAQ. **Number of employees at this location:** 300. **Number of employees nationwide:** 3,000.

KELLER INDUSTRIES, INC.
1820 Grogan Avenue, Merced CA 95340. 209/383-2221. **Contact:** Personnel. **Description:** Produces aluminum building materials, doors, windows, and other door and sash products.

KIRK-MAYER INC./SUNNYVALE
599 North Mathilda Avenue, Suite 215, Sunnyvale CA 94086. 408/739-1704. **Contact:** Recruiting Department. **Description:** Provides engineering and consulting services to customers in the aerospace, electronics, computer, and other industries. **Corporate headquarters location:** Los Angeles CA.

LATHROP CONSTRUCTION COMPANY
P.O. Box 2005, Benicia CA 94510-0819. 707/746-8000. **Contact:** Olaf Lyssand, Controller. **Description:** A firm specializing in heavy construction. **Corporate headquarters location:** This Location.

PARSONS BRINCKERHOFF INC.
303 Second Street, Suite 700 North, San Francisco CA 94107. 415/243-4600. **Contact:** Teresa Carroll, Human Resources Manager. **Description:** Provides total engineering and construction management services from project conception through completion. Services include the development of major bridges, tunnels, highways, marine facilities, buildings, industrial complexes, and railroads. Numerous domestic and international subsidiaries include: Parsons Brinckerhoff Construction Services; Parsons Brinckerhoff International; and others. There are 21 other U.S. locations. International. **Corporate headquarters location:** New York NY. **Number of employees worldwide:** 1,400.

SWINERTON & WALBERG COMPANY
580 California Street, 12th Floor, San Francisco CA 94104. 415/984-1222. **Fax:** 415/984-1384. **Contact:** Linda Carlson, Personnel Manager. **Description:** Engaged in general contracting, construction management, and industrial mechanical contracting. **Common positions include:** Accountant/Auditor; Administrative Services Manager; Civil Engineer; Computer Programmer; Computer Systems Analyst; Cost Estimator; Mechanical Engineer; Quality Control Supervisor. **Educational backgrounds include:** Accounting; Business Administration; Liberal Arts; Marketing. **Special Programs:** Internships. **Corporate headquarters location:** This Location. **Other U.S. locations:** Los Angeles CA; Denver CO. **Parent company:** Lindgren Holdings. **Operations at this facility include:** Administration; Divisional Headquarters. **Listed on:** Privately held. **Number of employees at this location:** 100. **Number of employees nationwide:** 380.

URS CORPORATION
100 California Street, Suite 500, San Francisco CA 94111. 415/957-5300. **Contact:** Personnel Department. **Description:** An international professional services organization with substantial engineering, training, architectural planning, environmental, and construction management capabilities.

L.E. WENTZ COMPANY
P.O. Box 610, San Carlos CA 94070. 415/592-3950. **Contact:** Bradley W. Wentz, Human Resources. **Description:** Provides general construction services. **Common positions include:** Accountant/Auditor; Branch Manager; Construction Contractor and Manager; Cost Estimator. **Benefits:** 401(k); Dental Insurance; Disability Coverage; Life Insurance; Medical Insurance; Profit Sharing. **Corporate headquarters location:** This Location. **Other U.S. locations:** Los Angeles CA. **Listed on:** Privately held. **Number of employees at this location:** 30.

GEORGE H. WILSON, INC./MECHANICAL CONTRACTORS
P.O. Box 1140, Santa Cruz CA 95061-1140. 408/423-9522. **Contact:** Thomas E. Wilson, Administrative Manager. **Description:** Provides plumbing, heating, air conditioning, and metals fabrication services. **Common positions include:** Industrial Engineer; Mechanical Engineer. **Educational backgrounds include:** Engineering; Liberal Arts. **Benefits:** Dental Insurance; Medical Insurance; Profit Sharing. **Corporate headquarters location:** This Location. **Operations at this facility include:** Administration; Manufacturing.

Note: *Because addresses and telephone numbers of smaller companies can change rapidly, we recommend you call each company to verify the information below before inquiring about job opportunities. Mass mailings are not recommended.*

Additional small employers:

CONSTRUCTION MATERIALS WHOLESALE

Intertile Distributors Inc.
2021 N Fine Ave, Fresno CA 93727-1512. 209/454-5000.

Reed & Graham Inc.
PO Box 5940, San Jose CA 95150-5940. 408/287-1400.

CBS Seal Coating Co.
5650 Arcadia Ave, Loomis CA 95650-8740. 916/652-1032.

Industrial Asphalt Inc.
9800 Del Rd, Roseville CA 95747-9109. 916/773-3968.

Industrial Asphalt Inc.
11825 La Barr Meadows Rd, Grass Valley CA 95949. 916/273-4437.

Marble Palace
6233 Industrial Way, Livermore CA 94550-9281. 510/606-1300.

Cencal Cement Company
2321 W Washington St Ste H, Stockton CA 95203-2948. 209/462-6252.

Ford Construction Co. Inc.
639 E Lockeford St, Lodi CA 95240-2406. 209/333-1116.

WMI Services
42600 Boyce Rd, Fremont CA 94538-3131. 408/288-9449.

PBS Building Systems
1 Annabel Ln, San Ramon CA 94583-1342. 510/277-7120.

PLUMBING, HEATING, AND A/C EQUIPMENT WHOLESALE

Pacific Pipe Co.
PO Box 23711, Oakland CA 94623-0711. 510/452-0122.

Slakey Brothers Inc.
PO Box 15647, Sacramento CA 95852. 916/329-3750.

Slakey Brothers Inc.
1190 Western St, Fairfield CA 94533. 707/427-3990.

PE O'Hair & Co.
120 Lake Blvd E, Redding CA 96003. 916/244-2020.

PE O'Hair & Co.
1102 S Aurora St, Stockton CA 95206. 209/948-8801.

Solar Electric Specialties Co.
PO Box 609, Elk Grove CA 95759-0609. 916/686-4898.

RC Hartnett & Associates Inc.
30852 Huntwood Ave, Hayward CA 94544-7004. 510/471-7200.

Advanced Backflow Protection Services
PO Box 7121, Napa CA 94558-0712. 707/252-9176.

California Concrete Pipe Corp.
2960 S US Highway 99, Stockton CA 95215-8047. 209/466-4212.

Contech Construction Products Inc.
5150 Sunrise Blvd, Fair Oaks CA 95628-4939. 916/863-7107.

Pameco-Western Division
700 Dubuque Ave, S San Fran CA 94080-1803. 415/871-8100.

Air Cold Supply Inc.
5650 E Clinton Ave, Fresno CA 93727-1307. 209/294-7276.

Forster Heating, AC & Sheet Metal
9405 Crater Hill Rd, Auburn CA 95603-9433. 916/888-1163.

MK Associates
PO Box 20457, San Jose CA 95160-0457. 408/268-2949.

ENGINEERING SERVICES

Krazan & Associates Inc.
215 W Dakota Ave, Clovis CA 93612-5608. 209/348-2200.

Gentz Construction Co.
3220 W Belmont Ave, Fresno CA 93722-5905. 209/275-1361.

Lloyd W. Aubry Co. Inc.
1394 Rollins Rd, Burlingame CA 94010-2410. 415/348-9038.

Combustion Power Company
1020 Marsh Rd, Menlo Park CA 94025-1021. 415/324-4744.

Bay Pneumatic Inc.
1460 Obrien Dr, Menlo Park CA 94025-1432. 415/365-1444.

Rambus Inc.
2465 Latham St, Mountain

View CA 94040-1419.
415/903-3800.

Soil Engineering Construction
927 Arguello St, Redwood City CA 94063-1310.
415/367-9595.

Ion Implant Services
1050 Kifer Rd, Sunnyvale CA 94086-5301. 408/732-5555.

Mirage Systems Inc.
232 E Java Dr, Sunnyvale CA 94089-1318. 408/733-3200.

Aptech Engineering Service Inc.
1282 Reamwood Ave, Sunnyvale CA 94089-2233.
408/745-7000.

MP Inc.
1269 Innsbruck Dr, Sunnyvale CA 94089-1317.
408/747-0604.

Peninsula Engineering Group
1150 Morse Ave, Sunnyvale CA 94089-1605. 408/747-1900.

Orbit Semiconductor Inc.
169 W Java Dr, Sunnyvale CA 94089-1016. 408/744-1800.

Flack & Kurtz Consulting Engineers
343 Sansome St Ste 450, San Francisco CA 94104-5601.
415/398-3833.

HJ Degenkolb Associates Inc.
350 Sansome St Ste 500, San Francisco CA 94104-1310.
415/392-6952.

EQE International Inc.
44 Montgomery St Ste 3200, San Francisco CA 94104-4805. 415/989-2000.

Sverdrup Corp.
417 Montgomery St Ste 405, San Francisco CA 94104-1184. 415/392-8927.

ICF Kaiser Engineers
160 Spear St Ste 1380, San Francisco CA 94105-1546.
415/957-0110.

Parsons De Leuw Inc.
120 Howard St Ste 850, San Francisco CA 94105-1622.
415/495-6060.

AWD Technologies Inc.
49 Stevenson St, San Francisco CA 94105-2909.
415/227-0822.

Rutherford & Chekene Consulting
303 2nd St Ste 800, San Francisco CA 94107-1366.
415/495-4222.

Glumac & Assocs Consulting Inc.
275 Battery St Ste 220, San Francisco CA 94111-3330.
415/398-7667.

TY Lin International
825 Battery St, San Francisco CA 94111-1528.
415/291-3700.

Ideo Product Development
151 University Ave, Palo Alto CA 94301-1632.
415/688-3400.

Harris & Associates Inc.
220 Mason Circle, Concord CA 94520-1202. 510/827-4900.

Roy F. Weston Inc.
2300 Clayton Rd Ste 1550, Concord CA 94520-2148.
510/256-0733.

Black & Veatch Engineers & Architects
2300 Clayton Rd Ste 1200, Concord CA 94520-2148.
510/246-8000.

Pacific Mechanical Corp.
2501 Annalisa Dr, Concord CA 94520-1220. 510/827-4940.

Vann Engineering Corp.
PO Box 5728, Concord CA 94524-0728. 510/827-0220.

Majors Engineering Inc.
383 Diablo Rd # 100, Danville CA 94526-3416.
510/820-2423.

SM Technology Inc.
41950 Christy St, Fremont CA 94538-3160. 510/657-4551.

Astrio Corp.
48133 Warm Springs Blvd, Fremont CA 94539-7498.
510/659-9200.

Signet Testing Laboratories
25064 Viking St, Hayward CA 94545-2704. 510/887-8484.

MH Chew & Associates Inc.
1424 Concannon Blvd, Livermore CA 94550-6006.
510/443-5071.

Jacobs Engineering Group Inc.
2530 Arnold Dr Fl 2, Martinez CA 94553-4359.
510/228-9700.

Mittelhauser Corp.
1252 Quarry Ln, Pleasanton CA 94566-4756. 510/416-2900.

SCS Engineers
6761 Sierra Ct Ste D, Dublin CA 94568-2611. 510/829-0661.

Centennial Civil Engineers
5000 Hopyard Rd Ste 100, Pleasanton CA 94588-3349.
510/460-5050.

Transdyn Controls Inc.
5669 Gibraltar Dr, Pleasanton CA 94588-8547. 510/827-2390.

OHM Remediation Services Corp.
5731 W Las Positas Blvd, Pleasanton CA 94588-4084. 510/256-6100.

Sverdrup Corp.
1340 Treat Blvd Ste 100, Walnut Creek CA 94596-2101. 510/256-7500.

Camp Dresser & McKee Inc.
100 Pringle Ave Ste 300, Walnut Creek CA 94596-3580. 510/933-2900.

John Carollo Engineers
2700 Ygnacio Valley Rd Ste 300, Walnut Creek CA 94598-3464. 510/932-1710.

Ransome Co.
PO Box 6849, Oakland CA 94603-0849. 510/430-1900.

JHK and Associates
2000 Powell St Ste 1090, Emeryville CA 94608-1855. 510/428-2550.

DKS Associates
1956 Webster St Ste 300, Oakland CA 94612-2925. 510/763-2061.

Cygna Energy Services
1800 Harrison St Fl 5, Oakland CA 94612-3429. 510/419-4000.

Pacific Electric Motor Co.
1009 66th Ave, Oakland CA 94621-3588. 510/569-7621.

Robert H. Lee & Associates Inc.
1137 N McDowell Blvd, Petaluma CA 94954-1110. 707/765-1660.

S. Levy Inc.
3425 S Bascom Ave, Campbell CA 95008-7308. 408/377-4870.

T&R Communications Inc.
1411 S Milpitas Blvd, Milpitas CA 95035-6828. 408/945-5700.

Hunter Technology Corp.
3305 Kifer Rd, Santa Clara CA 95051-0716. 408/245-5400.

Analytic Design Inc.
2320 Owen St, Santa Clara CA 95054-3210. 408/970-8400.

Menlo Service Corp.
3080 Olcott St Ste 200 A, Santa Clara CA 95054-3218. 408/982-1900.

Meitec America Inc.
4701 Patrick Henry Dr Ste 2501, Santa Clara CA 95054-1819. 408/986-0944.

Radian Technology Inc.
4211 Burton Dr, Santa Clara CA 95054-1512. 408/980-9877.

Sun Circuits Inc.
5124 Calle Del Sol, Santa Clara CA 95054-1009. 408/727-7784.

Alfa-Tech Bouillon
255 W Julian St Ste 602, San Jose CA 95110-2406. 408/283-0331.

Mark Thomas Co. Inc.
90 Archer St, San Jose CA 95112-4501. 408/453-5373.

Parsons De Leuw Inc.
100 Pk Ctr Plz Ste 450, San Jose CA 95113. 408/289-8949.

Exsil Inc.
6541 Via Del Oro, San Jose CA 95119. 408/629-3142.

MacKay & Somps
1955 The Alameda, San Jose CA 95126-1433. 408/985-0960.

Eveready Industry Corp.
2085 Zanker Rd, San Jose CA 95131-2107. 408/943-1555.

Olin Interconnect Technologies
544 Industrial Park Dr, Manteca CA 95337-6105. 209/824-4444.

Imbsen and Associates
9833 Horn Rd, Sacramento CA 95827-1945. 916/366-0632.

Nolte and Associates Inc.
1750 Creekside Oaks Drive Suite 200, Sacramento CA 95833-3640. 916/641-1500.

Resource Management International Inc.
PO Box 15516, Sacramento CA 95852-1516. 916/852-1300.

John Carollo Engineers
285 W Bullard Ave, Fresno CA 93704-1706. 209/436-6616.

Boyle Engineering Corporation
1044 E Herndon Ave, Fresno CA 93720-3115. 209/448-8222.

Jacobs Engineering Group Inc.
2525 Natomas Park Dr, Sacramento CA 95833-2933. 916/922-8600.

Air & Water Technologies Corp.
1804 Embarcadero Rd, Palo Alto CA 94303-3308. 415/494-9300.

Woodward-Clyde
10370 Old Placerville Rd, Sacramento CA 95827-2520. 916/368-0988.

CDS Leopold
883 E San Carlos Ave, San Carlos CA 94070-2609. 415/802-6820.

Tracor Aerospace Inc.
18124 Bollinger Canyon Rd, San Ramon CA 94583-1504. 510/837-7201.

FM Industries
25 S Milpitas Blvd, Milpitas CA 95035-5408. 408/262-3326.

Orion Alpha Corp.
2993 Copper Rd, Santa Clara CA 95051-0701. 408/737-0581.

Agrivision Engineering Inc.
2060 E Main St Ste F, Woodland CA 95776-9575. 916/666-1490.

Westin Engineering Inc.
9333 Tech Center Dr, Sacramento CA 95826-2558. 916/362-2400.

SWF Machinery
1324 Academy Ave, Sanger CA 93657-3425. 209/875-2545.

RMC Ripon Manufacturing Co. Inc.
652 S Stockton Ave, Ripon CA 95366-2750. 209/599-2148.

KSI
3080 Raymond St, Santa Clara CA 95054-3430. 408/562-0970.

American Paving Co.
315 N Thorne Ave, Fresno CA 93706-1444. 209/268-9886.

Statewide Excavation Inc.
5408 E Jensen Ave, Fresno CA 93725-1814. 209/227-8537.

California Engineering Contractors Inc.
1110 Terra Bella Ave, Mountain View CA 94043-1832. 415/965-8600.

Ferma Corporation
1265 Montecito Ave Ste 200, Mountain View CA 94043-4506. 415/961-2742.

West Valley Construction Co. Inc.
809 Hurlingame Ave, Redwood City CA 94063-3519. 415/364-9464.

RL Chaides Construction Co. Inc.
42027 Boscell Rd, Fremont CA 94538-3106. 510/656-9000.

Applied Soil Mechanics Inc.
47853 Warm Springs Blvd, Fremont CA 94539-7400. 408/365-8100.

Johnson Western Gunite Co.
940 Doolittle Dr, San Leandro CA 94577-1021. 510/568-8112.

Kulchin-Condon & Associates
PO Box 12368, Oakland CA 94604-2150. 510/534-3400.

JH Fitzmaurice Inc.
2857 Hannah St, Oakland CA 94608-4019. 510/444-7561.

Maggiora & Ghilotti Inc.
555 Du Bois St, San Rafael CA 94901-3965. 415/459-8640.

North Bay Construction Inc.
431 Payran St, Petaluma CA 94952-5908. 707/763-2891.

DSS Company
655 W Clay St, Stockton CA 95206-1722. 209/948-0302.

Teichert & Sons
265 Val Dervin Pkwy, Stockton CA 95206-4001. 209/983-2300.

Parnum Paving Inc.
PO Box 807, Ukiah CA 95482-0807. 707/485-7626.

Cal Sierra Construction Inc.
5904 Van Alstine Ave, Carmichael CA 95608-5327. 916/485-3909.

Balfour Beatty Construction Co.
4993 Golden Foothill Pkwy, El Dorado Hls CA 95762-9642. 916/939-9260.

Jeffries Construction Inc.
3241 Industrial Dr, Yuba City CA 95993-9208. 916/671-6714.

Pedersen & Daly
247 Jackson St, Hayward CA 94544-1949. 510/581-8315.

Alpha Engineering Group Inc.
4637 Chabot Dr, Pleasanton CA 94588-2749. 510/463-8822.

Earth Systems Inc.
2275 E Bayshore Rd, Palo Alto CA 94303-3220. 415/856-6850.

ICF Kaiser Engineers Inc.
11290 Point East Dr, Rancho Cordova CA 95742-6243. 916/852-3700.

BSK & Associates
9845 Horn Rd Ste 190, Sacramento CA 95827-1948. 916/363-1871.

JHK & Associates
1001 G Street, Sacramento CA 95814-0834. 916/447-3171.

Quasar Engineering Inc.
1301 Shoreway Rd Fl 4, Belmont CA 94002-4106. 415/508-6600.

Residuals Management Company
555 Twin Dolphin Dr, Redwood City CA 94065-2102. 415/591-9300.

Hanwa Consulting
790 Lucerne Dr, Sunnyvale CA 94086-3838. 408/737-8905.

STV-Group
231 Sansome St, San Francisco CA 94104-2304. 415/788-7271.

Smith-Emery Geoservices
Hunters Point Shipyard PO Box , San Francisco CA 94188. 415/330-3000.

Aspen Timco Inc.
4562 E 2nd St, Benicia CA 94510-1014. 707/746-4888.

Systems Engineering & Management Co.
5600 Mowry School Rd, Newark CA 94560-5371. 510/659-9745.

Century West Engineering Corp.
7950 Dublin Blvd, Dublin CA 94568-2929. 510/551-7774.

Eldyne Inc.
125 Corporate Pl, Vallejo CA 94590-6968. 707/644-1116.

Affiliated Engineers Inc.
1646 N California Blvd Ste 210, Walnut Creek CA 94596-4113. 510/933-8400.

Erin Engineering & Research Inc.
2175 North California Boulevard Suite 625, Walnut Creek CA 94596-3574. 510/943-7077.

Testing Engineers Inc.
2123 Bering Dr, San Jose CA 95131-2015. 408/451-2420.

Testing Engineers Inc.
2811 Adeline St, Emeryville CA 94608-4409. 510/835-3142.

Hafstad & Associates
784 Montecillo Rd, San Rafael CA 94903-3136. 415/479-4984.

Bechtel Civil Inc.
1754 Technology Dr, San Jose CA 95110-1308. 408/453-1313.

John Carollo Engineers
586 N 1st, San Jose CA 95112. 408/998-3024.

Westin Engineering Inc.
100 Park Center Plz, San Jose CA 95113-2217. 408/971-1000.

Metcalf & Eddy
McClellan Air Force Base, McClellan Afb CA 95652. 916/923-2181.

3D International Inc.
555 Capitol Mall, Sacramento CA 95814-4504. 916/447-7600.

Bryan A. Stirrat & Associates
3780 Rosin Ct, Sacramento CA 95834-1646. 916/568-8300.

ARCHITECTURAL SERVICES

Ehrlich-Rominger Architects
4800 El Camino Real, Los Altos CA 94022-1407. 415/949-1300.

Anshen & Allen
901 Market St Fl 6, San Francisco CA 94103-1729. 415/882-9500.

Skidmore Owings & Merrill
333 Bush St Fl 22, San Francisco CA 94104-2806. 415/981-1555.

Interior Architects Inc.
350 California St Ste 1500, San Francisco CA 94104-1428. 415/434-3305.

Bentley Engineering Co.
180 Howard St Ste 3, San Francisco CA 94105-1614. 415/495-7400.

Stone Marracini & Patterson
1 Market Plz, San Francisco CA 94105-1019. 415/227-0100.

Wallace Roberts & Todd
121 2nd St Fl 7, San Francisco CA 94105-3608. 415/541-0830.

MBT Associates Inc.
185 Berry St Ste 5700, San Francisco CA 94107-1729. 415/896-0800.

ED2 International
1660 Pacific Ave, San Francisco CA 94109-2518. 415/474-1400.

Backen Arrigoni and Ross Inc.
1660 Bush St, San Francisco CA 94109-5308. 415/441-4771.

Esherick Homsey Dodge & Davis
2789 25th St, San Francisco CA 94110-3516. 415/285-9193.

Anderson Debartolo Pan Inc.
444 Market St Ste 2800, San Francisco CA 94111-5332. 415/362-3145.

MBH Architects
1115 Atlantic Ave, Alameda CA 94501-1145. 510/865-8663.

Ratcliff Architects
5856 Doyle St, Emeryville CA 94608-2520. 510/652-1972.

Telfer Chiesa Dunham & Johnson
7599 Redwood Blvd Ste 210, Novato CA 94945-7701. 415/892-5373.

Mansergh & Associates
3355 Benton St, Santa Clara CA 95051-4417. 408/248-0930.

Jordan Knighton Architects
156 Center St, Auburn CA 95603-4713. 916/888-0999.

Stafford King & Associates Architects
1210 G Street, Sacramento CA 95814-1595. 916/443-4829.

Ehrlich-Rominger
2277 Fair Oaks Boulevard Suite 305, Sacramento CA 95825-5533. 916/920-1400.

Nichols Melburg & Rossetto Aia
434 Broadway Street, Chico CA 95928-5323. 916/891-1710.

SURVEYING SERVICES

Nolte & Associates
60 S Market St Ste 600, San Jose CA 95113-2342. 408/287-3400.

GENERAL CONTRACTORS

Saarman Construction
683 McAllister St, San Francisco CA 94102-3111. 415/749-2700.

Webcor Builders Inc.
2755 Campus Dr Ste 175, San Mateo CA 94403-2514. 415/349-2727.

Wooldridge Construction Inc.
395 Taylor Boulevard Suite 120, Pleasant Hill CA 94523-2296. 510/680-7979.

Kaufman & Broad
6379 Clark Ave, Dublin CA 94568-3026. 510/829-4500.

RM Co.
3125 Kerner Blvd, San Rafael CA 94901-5434. 415/457-2668.

Stapleton Construction
40 Redding Way, San Rafael CA 94901-5238. 415/485-1337.

Ravco Construction Co.
540 Heather Way, San Rafael CA 94903-2406. 415/472-4210.

Kurtis Construction
PO Box 3351, San Rafael CA 94912-3351. 415/897-1924.

William F. Fischer Construction
767 De Long Ave, Novato CA 94945-3266. 415/898-0567.

Saunders-Knight Construction
1123 Ferris Dr, Novato CA 94945-1762. 415/897-8962.

Geo Psitas Construction
1612 Vallejo Ave, Novato CA 94945-2322. 415/897-9236.

PR Construction
1421 West Ct, Novato CA 94945-3234. 415/892-2626.

Peter Fraser Construction
12 Kientz Ln, San Anselmo CA 94960-2163. 415/453-0916.

Steve Swezy General Contractor
21 Santa Barbara Ave, San Anselmo CA 94960-1653. 415/459-5088.

LV General Builders
1605 Tully Rd # 2, San Jose CA 95122-2533. 408/251-9711.

James Horn Construction Co.
301 Mitchell Rd, Modesto CA 95354-3913. 209/575-5680.

Suda-Inc.
9918 Kent St, Elk Grove CA 95624-1400. 916/685-1100.

Straight Line Construction
7967 Cavalli Way, Fair Oaks CA 95628-5003. 916/967-4643.

AM Coursey Construction
8771 Petite Creek Dr, Roseville CA 95661-5970. 916/791-3422.

Bighorn Construction
9850 Golden Dr, Orangevale CA 95662-5736. 916/989-5104.

Apandana Construction Inc.
9198 Greenback Ln, Orangevale CA 95662-4770. 916/987-0676.

Martin Worrell & Co.
8930 Golden Gate Ave, Orangevale CA 95662-2216. 916/988-2114.

Sierra General Construction
9430 Drift Way, Orangevale CA 95662-5433. 916/989-4450.

DPR Construction
1451 River Park Dr Ste 210, Sacramento CA 95815-4504. 916/568-3434.

Kruger Construction
PO Box 1066, Fresno CA 93714-1066. 209/292-8101.

Marshall Quality Construction
959 Regina Way, Pacifica CA 94044. 415/355-2294.

David M. Cramer & Associates
617 Veterans Blvd Ste 211,

Redwood City CA 94063-1404. 415/365-7170.

Tom Hacker General Contractor
PO Box 804, San Bruno CA 94066-0804. 415/589-2300.

Robert Smith Construction
41929 Mahoney St, Fremont CA 94538-4114. 510/656-7814.

Miller Construction Company
5465 Farina Ln, Fremont CA 94538-3241. 510/656-7366.

From The Ground Up Construction
247 Folsom Ave, Hayward CA 94544-6506. 510/782-8222.

Grissom Construction
33100 Condor Dr, Union City CA 94587-3146. 510/487-4875.

Gel Construction
3533 Sanddollar Ct, Union City CA 94587-1612. 510/487-1012.

MP Vermeulen Inc.
1495 Francisco Blvd E # L, San Rafael CA 94901-5512. 415/457-3335.

European Craftsmen & Associates
228 Elvia Ct, San Rafael CA 94903-1608. 415/499-1631.

Glagola Construction
188 Almonte Blvd, Mill Valley CA 94941-3571. 415/383-3006.

Sierra Builders
2 Sierra Ave, San Anselmo CA 94960-1801. 415/457-5121.

De Mattei Construction Inc.
1794 The Alameda, San Jose CA 95126-1729. 408/295-7516.

RD Construction
607 Bolton Ct Apt 3, San Jose CA 95129-2056. 408/257-9032.

Homestar
PO Box 53111, San Jose CA 95153-0111. 408/927-0522.

North-West Construction
PO Box 5756, Auburn CA 95604-5756. 916/269-1672.

Weatherite
7344 Pleasant View Dr, Citrus Hts CA 95610-3225. 916/723-3787.

Expert Waterproofing Systems
88 Ross Ave, San Anselmo CA 94960-2818. 415/454-2399.

Lincoln Logs Ltd.
13650 Bowman Rd, Auburn CA 95603-3167. 916/888-3700.

Kings Construction
1445 S Mayfair Ave, Daly City CA 94015-3867. 415/756-2733.

Apex Builders Group
700 Middle Ave, Menlo Park CA 94025-5170. 415/322-1953.

Owens Construction
684 Corona Drive, Pacifica CA 94044-3417. 415/355-7657.

Hilder's Builders
244 Reichling Ave, Pacifica CA 94044-3036. 415/355-2793.

C & M Co.
882 Muender Ave, Sunnyvale CA 94086-5920. 408/733-2578.

AR Construction Co.
315 Rolph St, San Francisco CA 94112-4405. 415/406-1155.

Robert Zlatunich General Contractors
551 6th Ave, San Francisco CA 94118-3816. 415/750-1935.

Building Services Construction
401 Cherry St, San Francisco CA 94118-1621. 415/877-9001.

Appian Construction Co. Inc.
1485 Enea Cir Ste 1330, Concord CA 94520-5228. 510/798-2535.

D&H Construction
7808 Terrace Dr, El Cerrito CA 94530-3023. 510/527-7883.

Scott Hull Construction
PO Box 433, Fairfield CA 94533-0043. 707/425-4538.

JR Construction
43344 Charleston Way, Fremont CA 94538-6103. 510/623-6919.

Brykel Corp.
190 Camino Oruga, Napa CA 94558-6262. 707/224-7797.

Larry Jones Construction
1810 Teresa Ln, Oakley CA 94561-1632. 510/625-6223.

Advanced Design Builders
4673 Alder Dr, Oakley CA 94561-1903. 510/625-3811.

Abrew Repair & Construction
7545 Honey Ct, Dublin CA 94568-1911. 510/828-2177.

Koski Construction Company
PO Box 2650, Dublin CA 94568-0264. 510/833-1937.

Scroggins Construction
987 Kilkare Rd, Sunol CA 94586-9405. 510/862-2458.

Sterling Builders
48 Starling Ct, Walnut Creek CA 94596-2413. 510/938-9643.

Pioneer Development Inc.
1655 N Main St, Walnut Creek CA 94596-4610. 510/944-7015.

Campi Brothers
4016 Walnut Blvd, Walnut Creek CA 94596-5445. 510/944-3515.

Ron Haytack Construction
720 B St, San Rafael CA 94901-3865. 415/454-2232.

Lars Eriksson Construction Co.
16 Grove St, Mill Valley CA 94941-2005. 415/388-7173.

Caletti Construction
PO Box 2641, Mill Valley CA 94942-2641. 415/381-3162.

John Bishop Construction
7517 Redwood Blvd, Novato CA 94945-2433. 415/898-2055.

Matthew Lombardi Construction
169 Los Angeles Blvd, San Anselmo CA 94960-1606. 415/453-4509.

KOR Contracting
119 Brookmead Ct, San Anselmo CA 94960-1471. 415/454-2461.

Grizzly Hill Construction Co.
1501 San Anselmo Ave, San Anselmo CA 94960-1817. 415/459-4018.

RE Nolan & Son
500 Red Hill Ave, San Anselmo CA 94960-2409. 415/454-0140.

Golden Gate Technic
PO Box 1558, San Anselmo CA 94979-1558. 415/456-8750.

Cove Construction
PO Box 2763, San Anselmo CA 94979-2763. 415/453-0515.

LR Free Inc.
1340 Tully Rd, San Jose CA 95122-3055. 408/293-9980.

James Construction
1190 W Hedding St, San Jose CA 95126-1709. 408/984-0173.

Cal-Land Construction
1555 Walkingshaw Way, San Jose CA 95132-1754. 408/258-3682.

Delta General Construction Inc.
1811 Morrill Ave, San Jose CA 95132-1636. 408/251-6313.

Blake's Construction & Roofing
5425 Fraschini Cir, San Jose CA 95136-3010. 408/224-4871.

JR Construction
PO Box 611383, San Jose CA 95161-1383. 408/923-4917.

Golden Gate Fence
PO Box 610578, San Jose CA 95161-0578. 408/272-7400.

The Alden Co.
10416 River Oaks Dr, Stockton CA 95209-4102. 209/478-9021.

Shelton Construction
9865 Lower Sacramento Rd, Stockton CA 95210-3911. 209/957-6564.

Clark & McGrath Construction Inc
7510 Shoreline Dr, Stockton CA 95219-5455. 209/478-2213.

Presley Of Central California
6707 Embarcadero Dr, Stockton CA 95219-3395. 209/956-7000.

Process Construction Inc.
118 E 11th St, Tracy CA 95376-4014. 209/835-4064.

American Canyon Development
1460 Canal St, Auburn CA 95603-2835. 916/823-2418.

Shepherd Construction
PO Box 55, Carmichael CA 95609-0055. 916/635-5085.

Duncan C. McPherson ADC
8080 Madison Ave Ste 200-D, Fair Oaks CA 95628-3759. 916/961-1010.

Lehane Construction Co.
6404 Hazel Ave, Orangevale CA 95662-4026. 916/988-2889.

Construction Dynamics
6751 Hazel Ave, Orangevale CA 95662-3426. 916/987-1442.

RL Skinner Construction Co.
402 Robin Cir, Vacaville CA 95687-7204. 707/447-3341.

Cano Construction
147 Elliot St, Woodland CA 95695-3118. 916/662-1224.

Grove Investment Co.
300 Richards Blvd # 12, Sacramento CA 95814-0200. 916/446-0300.

Visger Construction
5893 Shepard Ave, Sacramento CA 95819-2536. 916/739-8567.

North State Construction Inc.
2740 Fulton Ave Ste 114, Sacramento CA 95821-5108. 916/485-1285.

Hodges & Associates
4317 Rosecrest Way, Sacramento CA 95826-5639. 916/366-0363.

Allen Construction Inc.
5940 Rosebud Ln Ste 1, Sacramento CA 95841-2963. 916/344-2098.

Mark Garcia Associates
5710 Auburn Blvd Ste 9, Sacramento CA 95841-2944. 916/332-5923.

Philips Construction & Consulting
PO Box 60487, Sacramento CA 95860-0487. 916/481-4709.

E-Z Does It Construction Co.
4822 Houghton Ave, Corning CA 96021-9788. 916/824-5187.

Portola Meadows Townhomes
1801 Calle Del Sueno, Livermore CA 94550. 510/371-8377.

GENERAL INDUSTRIAL CONTRACTORS

Sumitomo Construction America Inc.
520 S El Camino Real, San Mateo CA 94402-1726. 415/347-2111.

PMI Corp.
PO Box 1516, Pittsburg CA 94565-0151. 510/432-4080.

Devcon Construction Inc.
555 Los Coches St, Milpitas CA 95035-5469. 408/942-8200.

Morris General Building Co.
PO Box 114, Patterson CA 95363-0114. 8183415135.

Nikor Construction Co.
7475 Murray Dr Ste 8, Stockton CA 95210-5318. 209/957-3440.

Cranston Steel Structures Inc.
1209 Commerce Ave, Woodland CA 95776-5902. 916/662-0966.

Metal Building Development Inc.
2499 S Stockton St, Lodi CA 95240-8819. 209/369-8271.

Country Western Steel Building Sales
22676 N Elliott Rd, Acampo CA 95220-9765. 209/339-4677.

Renovate-It Construction Inc.
623 E Oak St Ste E, Lodi CA 95240-3037. 209/367-8765.

William Hamill & Company
530 Chinquapin Way, Auburn CA 95603-3534. 916/888-0876.

Hodgson Construction Inc.
751 Warrington Ave, Redwood City CA 94063-3585. 415/364-6440.

DPR Construction Inc.
555 Twin Dolphin Dr Ste 260, Redwood City CA 94065-2102. 415/592-4800.

Albert D. Seeno Construction Co.
4021 Port Chicago Hwy, Concord CA 94520-1122. 510/671-7711.

Vanderson Inc.
4174 Technology Dr, Fremont CA 94538-6351. 510/440-7200.

Steiny & Company Inc.
27 Sheridan St, Vallejo CA 94590-6911. 707/552-6900.

Shapell Industries
100 N Milpitas Blvd, Milpitas CA 95035-4401. 408/946-1550.

Ceco Building Systems
12101 E Brandt Rd, Lockeford CA 95237-9708. 209/727-5504.

John F. Otto Inc.
1717 2nd St, Sacramento CA 95814-6214. 916/441-6870.

Campbell Construction Co.
2120 20th St, Sacramento CA 95818-1787. 916/454-5454.

Walsh Construction Company
10365 Old Placerville Rd Ste 2, Sacramento CA 95827-2518. 916/363-6200.

Harbison-Mahony-Higgins Inc.
8589 Thys Ct, Sacramento CA 95828-1099. 916/383-4825.

Codding Construction
6400 Redwood Dr, Rohnert Park CA 94928-2338. 707/584-7550.

ROAD CONSTRUCTION

El Camino Construction Co.
PO Box 7961, Fresno CA 93747-7961. 209/292-2205.

Three Sons Paving Inc.
2294 Vista Del Rio St, Crockett CA 94525-1044. 510/787-7283.

Oliver De Silva Inc.
PO Box 2909, Dublin CA 94568-0909. 510/783-9220.

OC Jones & Sons
1520 4th St, Berkeley CA 94710-1748. 510/526-3424.

Mercer Fraser Co.
77 W 2nd St, Eureka CA 95501-0214. 707/443-6371.

RC Collet Inc.
PO Box 1345, W Sacramento CA 95691-1345. 916/662-9383.

BRIDGE, TUNNEL, AND HIGHWAY CONSTRUCTION

Kewit Pacific Co.
5000 Marsh Dr, Concord CA 94520-5322. 510/686-3030.

Argonaut Constructors Inc.
1236 Central Ave, Santa Rosa CA 95401-4787. 707/542-4862.

HEAVY CONSTRUCTION

WM Lyles
1210 W Olive Ave, Fresno CA 93728-2816. 209/441-1900.

William G. McCullough Co.
2625 E 18th St, Antioch CA 94509-7230. 510/757-1394.

Courtney Company
180 Bales Dr, Walnut Creek CA 94596-6125. 510/944-1448.

Herb McKinley Enterprises
981 E Dudley Rd, French Camp CA 95231-9705. 209/983-0272.

The Boring Business
PO Box 1273, Folsom CA 95763-1273. 916/985-0844.

Emsco General Contractors Inc
9009 Railroad Ave, Oakland CA 94603-1245. 510/562-5454.

PLUMBING, HEATING, AND A/C

Allan Automatic Sprinkler Corp.
439 Eccles Ave, S San Fran CA 94080-1902. 415/952-8383.

Anderson Rowe & Buckley Inc.
2501 Harrison St, San Francisco CA 94110-2797. 415/282-1625.

Amos & Andrews Inc.
PO Box 250, Fairfield CA 94533-0450. 707/422-4844.

Lawson Mechanical Contractors
8995 43rd Ave, Sacramento CA 95828-1118. 916/381-5000.

Can-Am Plumbing Inc.
151 Wyoming St, Pleasanton CA 94566-6277. 510/846-1833.

Solano Mechanical Inc.
1800 Walters Ct, Fairfield CA 94533-2759. 707/428-6244.

Carrier Building Services
1758 Junction Ave Ste B, San Jose CA 95112-1022. 408/436-8530.

Slakey Brothers Inc.
1075 E Bianchi Rd, Stockton CA 95210-3502. 209/474-8201.

ELECTRICAL WORK

Howe Electric Inc.
4682 E Olive Ave # R, Fresno CA 93702-1636. 209/255-8992.

Rex Moore Electrical Contractor
5803 E Harvard Ave, Fresno CA 93727-1366. 209/294-1300.

Rosendin Electric Inc.
440 9th St, San Francisco CA 94103-4411. 415/285-8220.

Metro Electrical Construction
2400 3rd St, San Francisco CA 94107-3111. 415/641-1737.

Pactel Meridian Systems
333 Lakeside Dr, Foster City CA 94404-1147. 415/243-8889.

Schwartz & Lindheim Inc.
500 Independent Rd, Oakland CA 94621-3722. 510/562-1980.

Schwartz & Lindheim Inc.
860 Napa Valley Corporate Way, Napa CA 94558-6281. 707/224-5128.

Collins Electrical Company Inc.
4107 Northgate Blvd, Sacramento CA 95834-1218. 916/567-1100.

Intelligent Technologies & Service
1031 Serpentine Ln, Pleasanton CA 94566-4759. 510/484-3701.

Hess Electric
13393 E Saginaw Way, Sanger CA 93657-9347. 209/875-8407.

AC Electric & Construction
1775 Egbert Ave, San Francisco CA 94124-2518. 415/626-1181.

Mass Electric Co.
2976 Alvarado St, San Leandro CA 94577-5706. 510/483-7094.

MASONRY, STONEWORK, AND PLASTERING

Cal Brik
6905 10th St, Rio Linda CA 95673-2418. 916/991-7221.

Bob Martin Tile
1457 Laguna St, Livermore CA 94550-5233. 510/449-5094.

Benvenuti Tile Inc.
3004 Heirloom Way,

Sacramento CA 95826-4205. 916/364-0234.

ROOFING, SIDING, AND SHEET METAL WORK

Bryant Universal Roofing Inc.
10940 Bigge St, San Leandro CA 94577-1121. 510/568-6911.

Don H. Keefover Roofing
2447 Burlington Pl, Stockton CA 95209-4029. 209/957-5606.

Vander Bend Precision Sheetmetal
1105 Kern Ave, Sunnyvale CA 94086-3908. 408/245-5150.

Performance Metal Products
1709 Junction Ave, San Jose CA 95112-1010. 408/453-7250.

Tag Manufacturing Inc.
912 Olinder Ct, San Jose CA 95122-2619. 408/286-3946.

CONCRETE WORK

Landavazo Concrete Co.
943 Howard St, San Francisco CA 94103-4119. 415/896-1180.

Wagner Construction Company
PO Box 883183, San Francisco CA 94188-3183. 415/822-6082.

West Mont Construction
PO Box 5611, Auburn CA 95604-5611. 916/885-7864.

FRG Construction Co.
1595 Misty Wood Dr, Roseville CA 95747-7909. 916/782-7443.

WATER WELL DRILLING

West Hazmat Drilling Corp.
3233 Fitzgerald Rd, Rncho Cordova CA 95742-6813. 916/638-7276.

MISC. SPECIAL TRADE CONTRACTORS

PDM Strocal Inc.
2324 Navy Dr, Stockton CA 95206-1161. 209/948-4600.

Malcolm Drilling Co. Inc.
200 Oyster Point Blvd, S San Fran CA 94080-1911. 415/952-9052.

Stacy and Witbeck Inc.
290 Toland St, San Francisco CA 94124-1120. 415/285-7570.

West Valley Construction Company Inc.
580 E McGlincey Ln, Campbell CA 95008-4907. 408/371-5510.

KC Equipment
PO Box 1779, Shingle Spgs CA 95682-1779. 916/677-7555.

D&D Management
PO Box 23040, San Jose CA 95153-3040. 408/683-4254.

Penhall Company
696 Walsh Ave, Santa Clara CA 95050-2628. 408/970-9494.

DW Nicholson Corporation
24747 Clawiter Rd, Hayward CA 94545-2225. 510/887-0900.

Halbert Bros Inc.
42800 Boyce Rd, Fremont CA 94538-5108. 510/657-6025.

LVI Environmental Service Inc.
2235 Polvorosa Dr, San Leandro CA 94577-2200. 510/357-5390.

Woodcraft Fence Co.
9147 Elm Ave, Orangevale CA 95662-3525. 916/988-1022.

For more information on career opportunities in architecture, construction, and engineering:

Associations

AACE INTERNATIONAL: THE ASSOCIATION FOR TOTAL COST MANAGEMENT
209 Prairie Avenue, Suite 100, P.O. Box 1557, Morgantown WV 26507-1557. 304/296-8444. 800/858-2678. Toll-free number provides information on scholarships for undergraduates. Fax: 304/291-5728. A membership organization which offers *Cost Engineering,* a monthly magazine; employment referral services; technical reference information and assistance; insurance; and a certification program accredited by the Council of Engineering Specialty Boards.

AMERICAN ASSOCIATION OF ENGINEERING SOCIETIES
1111 19th Street NW, Suite 608, Washington DC 20036-3690. 202/296-2237. World Wide Web address: http://www.asee.org/aaes. A multi-disciplinary organization of professional engineering societies. Publishes reference works, including *Who's Who in Engineering*

Directory of Engineering Societies and Related Organizations, and the *Thesaurus of Engineering and Scientific Terms,* as well as statistical reports from studies conducted by the Engineering Workforce Commission.

AMERICAN CONSULTING ENGINEERS COUNCIL
1015 15th Street NW, Suite 802, Washington DC 20005. 202/347-7474. Fax: 202/898-0068. World Wide Web address: http://www.acec.org. A national organization of more than 5,000 member firms. Offers *Last Word,* a weekly newsletter; *American Consulting Engineer* magazine; life and health insurance programs; books, manuals, video and audiotapes, and contract documents; conferences and seminars; and voluntary peer reviews.

AMERICAN INSTITUTE OF ARCHITECTS
1735 New York Avenue NW, Washington DC 20006. 202/626-7300. Toll-free phone: 800/365-2724. World Wide Web address: http://www.aia.org. Contact toll-free number for brochures.

AMERICAN SOCIETY FOR ENGINEERING EDUCATION
1818 N Street NW, Suite 600, Washington DC 20036. 202/331-3500. World Wide Web address: http://www.asee.org. Promotes engineering education. Publishes monthly magazines.

AMERICAN SOCIETY OF CIVIL ENGINEERS
345 East 47th Street, New York NY 10017. 212/705-7496. Toll-free number: 800/548-2723. World Wide Web address: http://www.asce.org. A membership organization which offers subscriptions to *Civil Engineering* magazine and *ASCE News,* discounts on various other publications, seminars, audio and videotapes, specialty conferences, an annual convention, group insurance programs, and pension plans.

AMERICAN SOCIETY OF HEATING, REFRIGERATING AND AIR CONDITIONING ENGINEERS
1791 Tullie Circle NE, Atlanta GA 30329. 404/636-8400. Fax: 404/321-5478. World Wide Web address: http://www.ashrae.org. A society of 50,000 members which offers handbooks, a monthly journal, a monthly newspaper, discounts on other publications, group insurance, continuing education, and registration discounts for meetings, conferences, seminars, and expositions.

AMERICAN SOCIETY OF LANDSCAPE ARCHITECTS
4401 Connecticut Avenue NW, Washington DC 20008. 202/686-2752. World Wide Web address: http://www.asla.org. Look for Joblink for employment listings.

AMERICAN SOCIETY OF MECHANICAL ENGINEERS
345 East 47th Street, New York NY 10017. 212/705-7722. World Wide Web address: http://www.asme.org. Handles educational materials for certified engineers, as well as scholarships.

AMERICAN SOCIETY OF NAVAL ENGINEERS
1452 Duke Street, Alexandria VA 22314. 703/836-6727. Holds symposiums based on technical papers. Publishes a journal and newsletter bimonthly.

AMERICAN SOCIETY OF PLUMBING ENGINEERS
3617 Thousand Oaks Boulevard, Suite 210, Westlake CA 91362-3694. 805/495-7120. World Wide Web address: http://www.aspehq. Provides technical and educational information.

AMERICAN SOCIETY OF SAFETY ENGINEERS
1800 East Oakton Street, Des Plaines IL 60018-2187. 847/692-4121. Jobline service available at ext. 243. Fax: 847/296-3769. World Wide Web address: http://www.asse.org. A membership organization offering *Professional Safety,* a monthly journal; educational seminars; an annual professional development conference and exposition; technical publications; certification preparation programs; career placement services; and group and liability insurance programs.

ASSOCIATED BUILDERS AND CONTRACTORS
1300 North 17th Street, Rosslyn VA 22209. 703/812-2000. Sponsors annual career fair. Currently in the process of creating a service to find workers for construction companies.

ASSOCIATED GENERAL CONTRACTORS OF AMERICA, INC.
1957 E Street NW, Washington DC 20006. 202/393-2040. A full-service construction

association of subcontractors, specialty contractors, suppliers, equipment manufacturers, and professional firms. Services include government relations, education and training, jobsite services, legal services, and information services.

ILLUMINATING ENGINEERING SOCIETY OF NORTH AMERICA
120 Wall Street, 17th Floor, New York NY 10005-4001. 212/248-5000. An organization for industry professionals involved in the manufacturing, design, specification, and maintenance of lighting systems. Conference held annually. Offers a Technical Knowledge Examination.

JUNIOR ENGINEERING TECHNICAL SOCIETY
1420 King Street, Suite 405, Alexandria VA 22314-2794. 703/548-JETS. Fax: 703/548-0769. E-mail address: jets@nas.edu. A nonprofit, educational society promoting interest in engineering, technology, mathematics, and science. Provides information to high school students and teachers regarding careers in engineering and technology.

NATIONAL ACTION COUNCIL FOR MINORITIES IN ENGINEERING
3 West 35th Street, New York NY 10001. 212/279-2626. Offers scholarship programs for students.

NATIONAL ASSOCIATION OF HOME BUILDERS
1201 15th Street NW, Washington DC 20005. 202/822-0200. World Wide Web address: http://www.nahb.com. A trade association promoting safe and affordable housing. Provides management services and education for members.

NATIONAL ASSOCIATION OF MINORITY ENGINEERING
1133 West Morse Boulevard, Suite 201, Winter Park FL 32789. 407/647-8839.

NATIONAL SOCIETY OF BLACK ENGINEERS
1454 Duke Street, Alexandria VA 22314. 703/549-2207. World Wide Web address: http://www.nsbe.org. A nonprofit organization run by college students.

NATIONAL SOCIETY OF PROFESSIONAL ENGINEERS
1420 King Street, Alexandria VA 22314-2794. 703/684-2800. Call 703/684-2830 for scholarship information for students. Fax: 703/836-4875. World Wide Web address: http://www.nspe.org. A society of over 73,000 engineers. Membership includes the monthly magazine *Engineering Times;* continuing education; scholarships and fellowships; discounts on publications; health and life insurance programs; and employment service programs.

SOCIETY OF FIRE PROTECTION ENGINEERS
One Liberty Square, Boston MA 02109-4825. 617/482-0686. Fax: 617/482-8184. A professional society which offers members reports, newsletters, *Journal of Fire Protecting Engineering,* insurance programs, short courses, symposiums, tutorials, an annual meeting, and engineering seminars.

Directories

DIRECTORY OF ENGINEERING SOCIETIES
American Association of Engineering Societies, 1111 19th Street NW, Suite 608, Washington DC 20036. 202/296-2237. $185.00. Lists other engineering association members, publications, and convention exhibits.

DIRECTORY OF ENGINEERS IN PRIVATE PRACTICE
National Society of Professional Engineers, 1420 King Street, Alexandria VA 22314. 703/684-2800. $50.00. Lists members and companies.

Magazines

THE CAREER ENGINEER
National Society of Black Engineers, 1454 Duke Street, Alexandria VA 22314. 703/549-2207.

CHEMICAL & ENGINEERING NEWS
American Chemical Society, 1155 16th Street NW, Washington DC 20036. 202/872-4600.

COMPUTER-AIDED ENGINEERING
Penton Publishing, 1100 Superior Avenue, Cleveland OH 44114. 216/696-7000.

EDN CAREER NEWS
Cahners Publishing Company, 275 Washington Street, Newton MA 02158. 617/964-3030.

ENGINEERING TIMES
National Society of Professional Engineers, 1420 King Street, Alexandria VA 22314. 703/684-2800.

NAVAL ENGINEERS JOURNAL
American Society of Naval Engineers, 1452 Duke Street, Alexandria VA 22314. 703/836-6727. Subscription: $48.

ARTS AND ENTERTAINMENT/RECREATION

Job opportunities in the entertainment and recreation industries are projected to increase 39 percent through the year 2005, faster than the average for all industries. Higher incomes, growth of leisure time due to a growing population of retirees, and increasing awareness of the health benefits of physical fitness will affect employment growth.

The market for leisure activities is changing. In the past, amusement and recreation services catered to those in their '20s and '30s who had steadily growing incomes. Now that those baby boomers have grown up, companies are targeting adults between 50 and 75 years old.

In Hollywood, the past several years have been marked by mergers: Disney and ABC/Capital Cities, Westinghouse and CBS, Turner Broadcasting and Time Warner, and Seagram and MCA, to name a few of the biggest headline-stealers. And then there's the growing alliance between Hollywood and Silicon Valley. Microsoft, for example, has joined forces with NBC to create an online news station.

ALLIED DIGITAL TECHNOLOGIES CORPORATION
620 Third Street, San Francisco CA 94107-1902. 415/777-1700. **Contact:** Human Resources. **Description:** Allied Digital Technologies Corporation is one of the nation's leading independent multimedia manufacturing companies, offering CD audio and CD-ROM mastering and replication, videocassette and audiocassette duplication, laser video disc recording, off-line and online video editing, motion picture film processing, film-to-tape and tape-to-film transfers and complete finishing, packaging, warehousing, and fulfillment services. The company is the result of the January 1995 merger of HMG Digital Technologies Corporation and Allied Film Laboratory, Inc. Privately held Allied Film, with nine operating divisions in major cities nationwide, was one of the top video duplicators in the U.S. in terms of sales. According to statistics from the Recording Industry Association of America, HMG Digital Technologies Corporation, a publicly held company, was one of the largest independent replicators of music audiocassettes in the U.S., one of the largest duplicators of music videos, and a leading independent replicator of CD audio and CD-ROM optical disc products. Allied Digital Technologies is one of only two independent manufacturers in North America providing audio, video, and CD replication.

AMERICAN RECREATION CENTERS, INC.
P.O. Box 580, Rancho Cordova CA 95670-0580. 916/852-8005. **Contact:** Human Resources. **Description:** American Recreation Centers, Inc. is a publicly-owned business engaged in the operation of bowling and recreation facilities, and in the ownership, operation, and development of real estate property, primarily consisting of commercial facilities such as office buildings, commercial space, and the sale of land for development. The company is gradually phasing out of real estate operations except as it relates to new bowling centers. The company's bowling division operates 29 bowling centers, with 21 in California, six in Texas, and one each in Kentucky and Oklahoma, consisting of a total of 1,144 lanes. American Recreation Centers actively markets its bowling centers throughout the communities it serves and currently has more than

50,000 bowlers involved in its league programs. The company also owns a majority-interest in The Right Start, Inc., one of the nation's leading direct marketers of top-quality products for infants and children through age five, mailing nearly 10 million catalogs a year to new parents throughout the United States. **Corporate headquarters location:** This Location.

BAY MEADOWS OPERATING COMPANY
P.O. Box 5050, San Mateo CA 94402-0050. 415/574-7223. **Contact:** Human Resources. **Description:** Bay Meadows Operating Company operates Bay Meadows Race Track on the San Francisco Peninsula, and California Jockey Club, an equity real estate investment trust whose principal asset is Bay Meadows Race Track. California Jockey Club is one of two publicly traded horse racing real estate investment trusts. The company's real estate assets consist of approximately 175 acres of land, including race track facilities which can accommodate some 25,000 fans and up to 1,550 horses. **Corporate headquarters location:** This Location.

CMX
2230 Martin Avenue, Santa Clara CA 95050. 408/988-2000. **Contact:** Human Resources. **Description:** Designs, develops, manufactures, and markets videotape editing systems. **Listed on:** New York Stock Exchange.

LUCAS DIGITAL LTD.
P.O. Box 2459, San Rafael CA 94912. 415/258-2200. **Recorded Jobline:** 415/258-2100. **Contact:** Human Resources. **Description:** Lucas Digital Ltd. provides services such as visual effects and post production to the film industry.

LUCASFILM LTD.
P.O. Box 2009, San Rafael CA 94912-2009. 415/662-1700. **Contact:** Human Resources. **Description:** LucasFilm Ltd. is a leading film production company.

PHOTO & SOUND COMPANY
2500 Mason Street, San Francisco CA 94133. 415/627-6530. **Contact:** Human Resources. **Description:** Offers audiovisual and multimedia services for conventions and other gatherings. **NOTE:** This company does not accept unsolicited resumes. Please respond only to advertised job listings.

Note: *Because addresses and telephone numbers of smaller companies can change rapidly, we recommend you call each company to verify the information below before inquiring about job opportunities. Mass mailings are not recommended.*

Additional small employers:

ENTERTAINMENT GROUPS

San Francisco Symphony
201 Van Ness Ave, San Francisco CA 94102-4507.

Carmen Arriba's Mariachi Band
PO Box 442, Orinda CA 94563-0442. 510/254-6251.

California Symphony
33 Moraga Way, Orinda CA 94563-3022. 510/253-1535.

DANCE SCHOOLS

San Francisco Ballet School
455 Franklin St, San Francisco CA 94102-4471. 415/861-5600.

MOTION PICTURE AND VIDEO TAPE PRODUCTION AND DISTRIBUTION

Television Associates Incorporated
2410 Charleston Rd, Mountain View CA 94043-1622. 415/967-6040.

Pacific Data Images Inc.
1111 Karlstad Dr, Sunnyvale CA 94089-2117. 408/745-6755.

Skellington Productions Inc.
375 7th St, San Francisco CA 94103-4029. 415/864-2846.

Iconic Interactive Inc.
188 The Embarcadero Ste 750, San Francisco CA 94105-1235. 415/864-3200.

Colossal Pictures
2800 3rd St, San Francisco CA 94107-3528. 415/550-8772.

Preview Media Inc.
747 Front St Ste 3500, San Francisco CA 94111-1945. 415/397-2494.

Saul Zaentz Co.
2600 10th Street, Berkeley CA 94710-2522. 510/549-1528.

Golden Gaters Productions Inc.
400 Tamal Plz, Corte Madera CA 94925-1149. 415/924-7500.

Genigraphics Service Center
2520 Mission College Blvd, Santa Clara CA 95054-1215. 408/970-0380.

Ruth Carranza Productions
PO Box 391025, Mountain View CA 94039-1025. 415/962-8324.

McCune Audio-Visual-Video
2200 Army St, San Francisco CA 94124-1002. 415/641-1111.

Stage Door Music Products
621 1st St, Gilroy CA 95020-5033. 408/848-1554.

Monaco Labs and Video
234 9th St, San Francisco CA 94103-3807. 415/864-5350.

Accom Inc.
1490 Obrien Dr, Menlo Park CA 94025-1432. 415/328-3818.

Alta Group Inc.
535 Race St, San Jose CA 95126-3452. 408/297-2582.

Music Annex Recording Studios
970 Obrien Dr, Menlo Park CA 94025-1407. 415/328-8338.

Pacific Artists Records
246 Esperanza St # A, Bel Tiburon CA 94920-1917. 415/435-2772.

CS Associates
102 E Blithedale Ave, Mill Valley CA 94941-2024. 415/383-6060.

THEATRICAL PRODUCERS AND SERVICES

San Francisco Opera Center
301 Van Ness Ave, San Francisco CA 94102-4509. 415/861-4008.

Alamo Theater Services
3189 Danville Blvd, Alamo CA 94507-1954. 510/820-2001.

Music Matters
PO Box 3773, San Rafael CA 94912-3773. 415/457-0700.

Bernice Street Playhouse
21 Bernice St, San Francisco CA 94103-4320. 415/863-5946.

Marin Academy Theater
5th Av & Cottage Av, San Rafael CA 94901. 415/454-6056.

Stage Lighting Concepts
PO Box 25282, Fresno CA 93729-5282. 209/433-1536.

PROFESSIONAL SPORTS CLUBS AND PROMOTERS

San Francisco Giants Baseball
Candlestick Pk, San Francisco CA 94124. 415/468-3700.

PHYSICAL FITNESS FACILITIES

Nikko Fitness Center
222 Mason St, San Francisco CA 94102-2115. 415/394-1153.

24-Hour Nautilus Fitness Centers
40910 Fremont Blvd, Fremont CA 94538-4375. 510/226-6900.

Spa Fitness Center
2120 Chanticleer Ave, Santa Cruz CA 95062-1834. 408/475-7722.

Spare Time Inc
2399 American River Dr # 2, Sacramento CA 95825-7084. 916/971-8710.

Studio 10 Dance
6190 Bollinger Rd, San Jose CA 95129-3000. 408/446-0103.

International Aerobic Federation
PO Box 10279, San Jose CA 95157-1279. 408/255-5531.

PUBLIC GOLF COURSES

Country Drives Golf Center
3200 Andrade Road, Sunol CA 94586-9481. 510/862-0252.

Mace Meadow Golf & Country Club Inc.
Meadow Drive & Hwy 88,

Pioneer CA 95666. 209/295-7020.

AMUSEMENT AND RECREATION SERVICES

Christie's Fine Art Auctioneers
3516 Sacramento St, San Francisco CA 94118-1847. 415/346-6633.

Maple Hall Comm. Center
1 Alvarado Sq, San Pablo CA 94806. 510/215-3092.

Camanche Recreation Co.
11700 Pattison Rd, Wallace CA 95254. 209/763-5178.

MUSEUMS AND ART GALLERIES

California Academy Of Sciences
Golden Gate Park, San Francisco CA 94118. 415/221-5100.

San Francisco Zoo
Sloat Boulevard At 45th Street, San Francisco CA 94132. 415/753-7080.

Depot Park Museum
270 1st Street West, Sonoma CA 95476-5629. 707/938-1762.

For more information on career opportunities in arts, entertainment, and recreation:

<u>Associations</u>

AMERICAN ASSOCIATION OF MUSEUMS
1225 I Street NW, Suite 200, Washington DC 20005. 202/289-1818. Fax: 202/289-6578. World Wide Web address: http://www.americanmuse.org/aam. Publishes *AVISO,* a monthly newsletter containing employment listings for the entire country.

AMERICAN COUNCIL FOR THE ARTS
1 East 53rd Street, New York NY 10022. 212/223-2787. Fax: 212/980-4857. Visual Artist Information Hotline: 800/232-2789. A nonprofit organization for the literary, visual, and performing arts. Supports K-12 education and promotes public policy through meetings, forums, and seminars.

AMERICAN CRAFTS COUNCIL
72 Spring Street, New York NY 10012. 212/274-0630. World Wide Web address: http://www.mcraft.org. Operates a research library. Publishes *American Crafts* magazine.

AMERICAN DANCE GUILD
31 West 21st Street, New York NY 10010. 212/627-3790. The American Dance Guild holds an annual conference with panels, performances, and workshops. Operates a job listings service (available at a discount to members.)

AMERICAN FEDERATION OF MUSICIANS
1501 Broadway, Suite 600, New York NY 10036. 212/869-1330. Membership required.

AMERICAN FEDERATION OF TELEVISION AND RADIO ARTISTS
260 Madison Avenue, New York NY 10016. 212/532-0800. Membership required.

AMERICAN FILM INSTITUTE
2021 North Western Avenue, Los Angeles CA 90027. 213/856-7706. Toll-free phone: 800/774-4AFI. World Wide Web address: http://www.afionline.org. Membership is required, and includes: a newsletter; members-only discounts on events, seminars, workshops, and exhibits; and two free tickets and discounts at the AFI Theater in Washington, DC.

AMERICAN MUSIC CENTER
30 West 26th Street, Suite 1001, New York NY 10010-2011. 212/366-5260. Fax: 212/366-5265. World Wide Web address: http://www.amc.net/amc. A nonprofit research and information center for contemporary music and jazz. Provides information services and grant programs.

AMERICAN SOCIETY OF COMPOSERS, AUTHORS, AND PUBLISHERS (ASCAP)
One Lincoln Plaza, New York NY 10023. 212/621-6000. Fax: 212/724-9064. World Wide Web address: http://www.ascap.com. A membership association which licenses members' work and pays members royalties. Offers showcases and educational seminars and workshops.

AMERICAN SYMPHONY ORCHESTRA LEAGUE
1156 15th Street NW, Suite 4800, Washington DC 20005. 202/628-0099.

AMERICAN ZOO AND AQUARIUM ASSOCIATION
Oglebay Park, Wheeling WV 26003. 304/242-2160. World Wide Web address: http://www.aza.org. Produces a monthly newspaper.

ASSOCIATION OF INDEPENDENT VIDEO AND FILMMAKERS
625 Broadway, 9th Floor, New York NY 10012. 212/807-1400. World Wide Web address: http://www.virtualfilm.com/aivf.

NATIONAL ARTISTS' EQUITY ASSOCIATION
P.O. Box 28068, Central Station, Washington DC 20038-8068. 202/628-9633. A national, nonprofit organization dedicated to improving economic, health, and legal conditions for visual artists.

NATIONAL DANCE ASSOCIATION
1900 Association Drive, Reston VA 22091. 703/476-3436. Fax: 703/476-9527. Promotes the development and implementation of philosophies and policies in all forms of dance and in dance education at all levels.

NATIONAL ENDOWMENT FOR THE ARTS
1100 Pennsylvania Avenue NW, Washington DC 20506. 202/682-5400. World Wide Web address: http://www.nea.gov.

NATIONAL RECREATION AND PARK ASSOCIATION
2775 South Quincy Street, Suite 300, Arlington VA 22206. 703/820-4940. Fax: 703/671-6772. A national, nonprofit service organization. Offers professional development and training opportunities in recreation, parks, and leisure services. Publishes a newsletter and magazine.

PRODUCERS GUILD OF AMERICA
400 South Beverly Drive, Suite 211, Beverly Hills CA 90212. 310/557-0807. Membership is required, and includes: credit union access; subscription to *P.O.V. Magazine* and the association newsletter; attendance at the organization's annual Golden Laurel Awards and other events; and special screenings of motion pictures at the time of the Academy Awards.

THEATRE COMMUNICATIONS GROUP
355 Lexington Avenue, New York NY 10017. 212/697-5230.

WOMEN'S CAUCUS FOR ART
Moore College of Art, 20th & The Parkway, Philadelphia PA 19103. 215/854-0922. Fax: 215/854-0915. A national organization of professionals in the visual arts. Over 3,700 members. Membership includes an annual conference; participation in juried shows; local chapter meetings and regional conferences; publications including an annual exhibition catalog of honors awards and a quarterly newsletter; and insurance programs.

Directories

ARTIST'S MARKET
Writer's Digest Books, 1507 Dana Avenue, Cincinnati OH 45207. 513/531-2222.

CREATIVE BLACK BOOK
866 3rd Avenue, 3rd Floor, New York NY 10022. 212/254-1330.

PLAYERS GUIDE
165 West 46th Street, New York NY 10036. 212/869-3570.

ROSS REPORTS TELEVISION
Television Index, Inc., 40-29 27th Street, Long Island City NY 11101. 718/937-3990.

Magazines

AMERICAN ARTIST
One Astor Place, 1515 Broadway, New York NY 10036. 212/764-7300. 800/346-0085, ext. 477.

AMERICAN CINEMATOGRAPHER
American Society of Cinematographers, P.O. Box 2230, Hollywood CA 90028. 213/969-4333.

ART BUSINESS NEWS
Myers Publishing Company, 19 Old Kings Highway South, Darien CT 06820. 203/656-3402.

ART DIRECTION
10 East 39th Street, 6th Floor, New York NY 10016. 212/889-6500.

ARTFORUM
65 Bleecker Street, New York NY 10012. 212/475-4000.

ARTWEEK
12 South First Street, Suite 520, San Jose CA 95113. 408/279-2293.

AVISO
American Association of Museums, 1225 I Street NW, Suite 200, Washington DC 20005. 202/289-1818.

BACK STAGE
1515 Broadway, New York NY 10036. 212/764-7300.

BILLBOARD
Billboard Publications, Inc., 1515 Broadway, New York NY 10036. 212/764-7300. A magazine about the music industry.

CASHBOX
157 West 57th Street, Suite 503, New York NY 10019. 212/245-4224.

CRAFTS REPORT
300 Water Street, Wilmington DE 19801. 302/656-2209.

DRAMA-LOGUE
P.O. Box 38771, Los Angeles CA 90038. 213/464-5079.

HOLLYWOOD REPORTER
5055 Wilshire Boulevard, 6th Floor, Los Angeles CA 90036. 213/525-2000.

VARIETY
249 West 17th Street, New York NY 10011. 212/779-1100. 800/323-4345.

WOMEN ARTIST NEWS
300 Riverside Drive, New York NY 10025. 212/666-6990.

AUTOMOTIVE

The automotive industry saw a big turnaround in 1994, with sales of new cars and trucks reaching a six-year high. Unfortunately, the boom didn't last. Rising interest rates in early 1995 put the brakes on auto sales. Although the year can't be classified as truly weak, 1995 sales dropped 2.6 percent off 1994's pace. Rising steel prices have also put pressure on the Big Three automakers to cut costs and boost productivity, so don't look for job opportunities to grow very rapidly in '96. Even so, analysts are predicting a 2 percent sales gain in 1996, spurred in part by dropping interest rates.

Jobseekers should look to auto parts suppliers in addition to the Big Three. While Detroit is using fewer suppliers than in the past, the suppliers that are under contract are being asked to supply more of the finished product. Look for large employers with financial backing and superior skills.

APPLIED TECHNOLOGY
P.O. Box 7012, San Jose CA 95150. 408/365-4747. **Contact:** Human Resources. **Description:** Manufactures industrial trucks, tractors, and trailers.

COOPER ENERGY SERVICES
1351 Harbor Bay Parkway, Suite 1000, Alameda CA 95402. 510/748-7320. **Contact:** Personnel. **Description:** Produces heavy-duty diesel engines.

CUMMINS WEST INC.
1601 Aurora Drive, San Leandro CA 94577. 510/351-6101. **Contact:** Michael Doherty, Vice President of Finance. **Description:** Manufactures in-line and V-type diesel engines from 145 to 1600 horsepower, and replacement parts for these engines. Cummins West also manufactures and markets a broad range of heavy-duty filters and reconditioned diesel engines and parts. This facility is primarily a wholesale dealership. **NOTE:** Send resumes to: 788 Sandoval Way, Hayward CA 94544. **Corporate headquarters location:** Columbus IN. **Listed on:** New York Stock Exchange.

CUSTOM CHROME, INC.
16100 Jacqueline Court, Morgan Hill CA 95037. 408/778-0500. **Fax:** 408/778-7001. **Contact:** Human Resources. **Description:** Custom Chrome, Inc. is the leading independent supplier of aftermarket parts and accessories for Harley-Davidson motorcycles. Custom Chrome distributes its own products, many of which are offered under the brand names Rev Tech, Premium, Dyno Power and C.C. Rider, and products offered by other recognized manufacturers, such as Dunlop, Champion, Hastings and Accel. The company's marketing approach includes an 800-page catalog supported by a national telemarketing program, active participation in numerous trade shows and consumer events, extensive advertising in magazines focused on the Harley-Davidson market, and use of the company's mobile showroom. **Corporate headquarters location:** This Location.

NEW UNITED MOTOR MANUFACTURING COMPANY
45500 Fremont Boulevard, Fremont CA 94538. 510/498-5500. **Contact:** Human Resources Department. **Description:** Manufactures motor vehicle parts.

Note: *Because addresses and telephone numbers of smaller companies can change rapidly, we recommend you call each company to verify the information below before inquiring about job opportunities. Mass mailings are not recommended.*

Additional small employers:

INDUSTRIAL VEHICLES AND MOVING EQUIPMENT

Lantis Corporation
PO Box 80890, Salinas CA 93912-0890. 408/754-6202.

MOTOR VEHICLES AND EQUIPMENT

Utility Truck Bodies Inc.
1530 Wood St, Oakland CA 94607-1500. 510/271-0797.

Friction Inc.
711 S 3rd St, Chowchilla CA 93610-3502. 209/665-5781.

Ford Motor Co.
PO Box 1666, Richmond CA 94802-0666. 510/231-4300.

QB Rebuilders
2325 W Charter Way, Stockton CA 95206-1135. 209/467-0490.

Flowmaster Inc.
2975 Dutton Ave Ste 3, Santa Rosa CA 95407-7800. 707/544-4761.

MGM Brakes International
1184 S Cloverdale Blvd, Cloverdale CA 95425-4412. 707/894-3333.

Super Trapp Industries Inc.
3910 Seaport Blvd, W Sacramento CA 95691-3450. 916/372-5000.

Leer West Inc.
1464 Tanforan Ave, Woodland CA 95776-6109. 916/666-0176.

Ellsworth Harrold Company
1535 Howe Ave, Sacramento CA 95825-3303. 916/922-1535.

Reliance Trailer Manufacturing
7911 Redwood Dr, Cotati CA 94931-3000. 707/795-0081.

MOTOR VEHICLE EQUIPMENT WHOLESALE

Fresno Auto Dealers Auction
278 N Marks Ave, Fresno CA 93706-1136. 209/268-8051.

AB Auto Brokers and Leasing
161 John Glenn Dr, Concord CA 94520-5606. 510/674-8711.

MG Auto Brokers
2821 Howe Ave, Sacramento CA 95821-4537. 916/927-2337.

Fruehauf Trailers
3600 W Capitol Ave, W Sacramento CA 95691-2193. 916/371-6921.

Toyota Motor Distribution Inc.
2451 Bishop Dr, San Ramon CA 94583. 510/830-8300.

Modine Western Inc.
PO Box 2418, Merced CA 95344-0418. 209/383-1311.

Von Housen Auto Parts
10057 Mills Station Rd, Sacramento CA 95827-2203. 916/362-0691.

Automotive Industrial Distributors
2020 Plymouth St, Mountain View CA 94043-1704. 415/969-1276.

Aceomatic Transmission Parts
4590 Pell Dr, Sacramento CA 95838-2153. 916/648-1991.

Accurate Auto Care
3511 1st St, Livermore CA 94550-2201. 510/443-8863.

Reddi Brake Supply Inc.
1273 Industrial Pkwy W, Hayward CA 94544-7025. 510/247-9971.

Reddi Brake Supply Inc.
1585 N 4th St, San Jose CA 95112-4605. 408/453-1644.

Holland Hitch Latin America
425 Chesley Ave, Mountain View CA 94040-4408. 415/390-0337.

Central Chevrolet Co.
4949 Thornton Ave, Fremont CA 94536-6412. 510/793-1340.

Truck Store
25714 Mission Blvd, Hayward CA 94544-2529. 510/886-5464.

Murrell Enterprises
389 Umbarger Rd, San Jose CA 95111-2055. 408/224-4412.

California Auto Center
521 W San Carlos St, San Jose CA 95126-3649. 408/998-5955.

Dick Steinbach's Shop Equipment
3383 Fitzgerald Rd, Rncho

Cordova CA 95742-6820. 916/638-1677.

Cross Equipment Company
9353 Jackson Rd, Sacramento CA 95826-9725. 916/363-5751.

Tire Dealers Warehouse
33377 Transit Ave, Union City CA 94587-2090. 510/489-7600.

Able Tire & Brake
7090 Redwood Blvd, Novato CA 94945-4195. 415/897-4125.

AUTOMOTIVE REPAIR SHOPS

Capitol Collision Repair
3517 Hillcap Ave, San Jose CA 95136-1391. 408/972-0300.

Hansel Autobody
2800 Corby Ave, Santa Rosa CA 95407-7878. 707/525-1488.

Maita Oldsmobile Body Shop
2264 Auburn Blvd, Sacramento CA 95821-1601. 916/927-1804.

Earl Scheib Paint & Body
2431 Fruitridge Rd, Sacramento CA 95822-2243. 916/457-6565.

Carcoa Auto Painting
1729 Fulton Ave, Sacramento CA 95825-2415. 916/488-9800.

Scherba's Auto Stores
S El Camino Rl & E 39th Av, San Mateo CA 94403. 415/341-7478.

Detroit Transmission Products Co.
1709A Rogers Ave, San Jose CA 95112-1108. 408/436-8388.

Boardwalk Auto Center
1 Bair Island Rd, Redwood City CA 94063-2764. 415/364-0100.

Econolube N' Tune
40871 Albrae St, Fremont CA 94538-2482. 510/656-7188.

Del & Joe's Body Shop Inc.
155 Borland Ave, Auburn CA 95603-4995. 916/885-5681.

Jiffy Lube
810 Merchant St, Vacaville CA 95688-6912. 707/446-3035.

Autocare Plus
3531 Sunrise Blvd, Rncho Cordova CA 95742-7320. 916/638-1600.

Sierra Detroit Diesel Allison
855 Stillwater Rd, Broderick CA 95605-1624. 916/372-5078.

Modine Western
1755 E St Ste 110, Fresno CA 93706-2022. 209/442-0436.

Radiator Prince
5320 Old Redwood Hwy, Petaluma CA 94954. 707/795-9633.

Holder's Radiator
PO Box 258, Glencoe CA 95232-0258. 209/293-4097.

Firestone Tire & Service Centers
1379 S Park Victoria Dr, Milpitas CA 95035-6976. 408/945-3911.

For more information on career opportunities in the automotive industry:

Associations

AMERICAN AUTOMOBILE MANUFACTURERS ASSOCIATION
1401 H Street NW, Suite 900, Washington DC 20005. 202/326-5500. Fax: 202/326-5567. A trade association consisting of the Big Three U.S. automakers: Chrysler, Ford, and General Motors. Sponsors research projects, distributes publications, and reviews social and public policies pertaining to the motor vehicle industry and its customers.

ASSOCIATION OF INTERNATIONAL AUTOMOBILE MANUFACTURERS
1001 19th Street North, Suite 1200, Arlington VA 22209. 703/525-7788.

AUTOMOTIVE SERVICE INDUSTRY ASSOCIATION
25 Northwest Point Boulevard, Suite 425, Elk Grove Village IL 60007-1035. 847/228-1310. World Wide Web address: http://www.aftmkt.com. Members are manufacturers and distributors of automobile replacement parts. Sponsors a trade show. Publishes educational guidebooks and training manuals.

AUTOMOTIVE SERVICE ASSOCIATION
1901 Airport Freeway, Suite 100, P.O. Box 929, Bedford TX 76095. 817/283-6205. World Wide Web address: http://www.asashop.org. Works with shops to find workers. Publishes a monthly magazine with classified advertisements.

Directories

AUTOMOTIVE NEWS MARKET DATA BOOK
Crain Communications, Automotive News, 1400 Woodbridge Avenue, Detroit MI 48207-3187. 313/446-6000.

WARD'S AUTOMOTIVE YEARBOOK
Ward's Communications, 3000 Town Center, Suite 2750, Southville MI 48075. 810/357-0800.

Magazines

AUTOMOTIVE INDUSTRIES
Chilton Book Company, 201 King of Prussia Road, Radnor PA 19089. 800/695-1214.

WARD'S AUTO WORLD
Ward's Communications, Inc., 3000 Town Center, Suite 2750, Southville MI 48075.

WARD'S AUTOMOTIVE REPORTS
Ward's Communications, Inc., 3000 Town Center, Suite 2750, Southville MI 48075.

BANKING/SAVINGS AND LOANS

The banking industry has fared well over the past few years. Banks reported record earnings from 1992 to 1995. Low interest rates have decreased the number of bad loans and have increased investment profits. The early '90s were also a good time for banking professionals, who, despite numerous mergers and consolidations throughout the industry, avoided the large layoffs that hit workers in other industries. As a result of rising interest rates in early 1995, times have begun to change. Analysts argue that there are simply too many banks clogging the market. This glut of banks (over 10,000 in the United States as compared to 60 in Canada), the emphasis on multi-branch banking, and the decline in traditional transactions, has forced banks to consolidate and close branches. This has led to shrinking employment with dramatic layoffs of tellers, bank office workers, and managers. This trend will continue to take place into the next century.

AUBURN BANCORP
AUBURN BANK OF COMMERCE, N.A.
P.O. Box 5770, Auburn CA 95604. 916/888-8405. **Contact:** Human Resources. **Description:** Auburn Bancorp and its wholly-owned subsidiary, Auburn Bank of Commerce, N.A. offers a wide range of general commercial banking services. These include personal and business accounts, including money market accounts, NOW accounts, checking accounts, savings accounts and certificates of deposit. The interest paid on time and savings deposits is priced at prevailing market rates. The bank also offers night depository and bank-by-mail services. The bank sells travelers' checks, cashier's checks, and money orders. In addition, it provides note and collection services. The bank does not offer trust or international banking services, but it will arrange for such services through a correspondent bank. On the lending side, the bank engages in a full complement of lending activities, including commercial, consumer/installment, and real estate loans, with particular emphasis on short- and medium-term loans. **Corporate headquarters location:** This Location.

BWC FINANCIAL CORPORATION
P.O. Box 8080, Walnut Creek CA 94596-8080. 510/932-5353. **Contact:** Donna Schneider, Vice President of Human Resources. **Description:** BWC Financial Corporation is a holding company with two subsidiaries: Bank of Walnut Creek and BWC Real Estate. **Corporate headquarters location:** This Location. **Number of employees at this location:** 60.

BANK OF AMERICA
P.O. Box 37000, Unit #10583, San Francisco CA 94137. 415/622-3456. **Contact:** Cheryl Gee, Manager of Corporate College Relations. **Description:** A large banking company and financial services institution. Bank of America is dedicated to affirming diversity through the principles of equal opportunity and affirmative action. **Common positions include:** Accountant/Auditor; Bank Officer/Manager; Computer Programmer; Computer Systems Analyst; Financial Analyst; Securities Sales Representative.

Educational backgrounds include: Accounting; Computer Science; Economics; Finance. **Corporate headquarters location:** This Location. **Annual sales/revenues:** More than $100 million. **Number of employees worldwide:** 90,000.

BANK OF THE WEST
A SUBSIDIARY OF BANQUE NATIONALE DE PARIS
1450 Treat Boulevard, Walnut Creek CA 94596. 510/942-8300. **Toll-free phone:** 800/488-2265. **Contact:** Personnel. **Description:** A banking institution.

BANK OF TOKYO LTD. COMPANY
350 California Street, Fifth Floor, San Francisco CA 94104. 415/705-7270. **Contact:** Personnel. **Description:** A commercial bank offering a wide range of traditional banking services, financial advisory services, international banking services, and trust services. **Corporate headquarters location:** New York NY. **Parent company:** The Bank of Tokyo, Ltd.

BARCLAYS BANK
388 Market Street, Suite 1700, San Francisco CA 94111. 415/765-4700. **Contact:** Human Resources. **Description:** A bank holding company.

BAY BANK OF COMMERCE
P.O. Box 425, San Leandro CA 94577. 510/357-2265. **Contact:** Human Resources. **Description:** A bank which tailors its lending programs to meet customers' individual borrowing needs. SBA loans are available and can be structured for various business needs including working capital, equipment financing, business acquisition, and owner/user commercial real estate construction and purchase. The bank's Construction Lending Division provides residential construction financing for individuals and builders throughout the East Bay. **Parent company:** Bay Commercial Services. **Corporate headquarters location:** This Location. **Number of employees at this location:** 60.

BAY VIEW CAPITAL CORPORATION
2121 South El Camino Real, San Mateo CA 94403. 415/573-7300. **Contact:** Human Resources. **Description:** Bay View Capital Corporation is a savings and loan holding company incorporated in 1989. Its principal business activity is the operation of a savings bank through its wholly-owned subsidiary, Bay View Federal Bank, a Federal Savings Bank. The bank is a federally-chartered capital stock savings bank incorporated in 1911 and a member of the Federal Home Loan Bank of San Francisco. **Common positions include:** Accountant/Auditor; Bank Officer/Manager; Bank Teller; Branch Manager; Customer Service Representative. **Educational backgrounds include:** Accounting; Finance. **Benefits:** 401(k); Daycare Assistance; Dental Insurance; Disability Coverage; Employee Discounts; Life Insurance; Medical Insurance; Stock Option; Tuition Assistance. **Corporate headquarters location:** This Location. **Parent company:** Bay View Capital Corporation. **Operations at this facility include:** Administration. **Listed on:** NASDAQ; New York Stock Exchange. **Number of employees at this location:** 225. **Number of employees nationwide:** 500.

CALIFORNIA BANCSHARES, INC.
100 Park Place, Suite 140, San Ramon CA 94583. 510/743-4200. **Contact:** Human Resources. **Description:** California Bancshares, Inc. is a bank holding company, having nine banking subsidiaries: Alameda First National Bank; The Bank of Milpitas, N.A.; The Bank of San Ramon Valley; Commercial Bank of Fremont; Community First National Bank; Concord Commercial Bank; Lamorinda National Bank; Modesto

Banking Company and Westside Bank. The company has three nonbanking subsidiaries: CBI Mortgage; Island Bancorp Leasing, Inc.; and LNB Corporation. The banks each provide depository, lending and various specialized services to the business, professional, and consumer sectors of their communities. The banks offer installment note collection, issue cashier's checks, and money orders, sell traveler's checks and provide other customary banking services, except for international banking and trust services. CBI Mortgage engages primarily in the origination and servicing of real estate loans for investors. Island Bancorp Leasing is engaged primarily in the leasing of imported automobiles, but is currently inactive. LNB Corporation serves as a third-party trustee for deeds of trust originated by the banks.

CALIFORNIA COMMERCE BANK
111 West St. John Street, San Jose CA 95113. 408/286-2660. **Contact:** Personnel. **Description:** A full-service commercial bank. **Common positions include:** Bank Officer/Manager; Branch Manager; Credit Manager; Customer Service Representative; Department Manager. **Educational backgrounds include:** Accounting; Business Administration; Finance; Marketing; Mathematics. **Benefits:** Dental Insurance; Disability Coverage; Life Insurance; Medical Insurance; Pension Plan; Savings Plan; Tuition Assistance. **Corporate headquarters location:** Los Angeles CA. **Operations at this facility include:** Regional Headquarters.

CALIFORNIA FINANCIAL HOLDING COMPANY
501 West Weber Avenue, Stockton CA 95203. 209/948-6870. **Contact:** Human Resources. **Description:** California Financial Holding Company is the corporate parent of Stockton Savings Bank, one of the Central Valley's oldest and largest financial institutions. **Corporate headquarters location:** This Location.

CITICORP/CITIBANK
One Sansome Street, San Francisco CA 94104. 415/627-6000. **Recorded Jobline:** 415/658-4JOB. **Contact:** Citibank Staffing. **Description:** A multinational financial services organization, with a worldwide staff of 85,000 people serving individuals, businesses, governments, and financial institutions in approximately 3,000 locations. **Common positions include:** Bank Officer/Manager; Bank Teller; Branch Manager; Customer Service Representative; Financial Services Sales Rep.; Securities Sales Representative. **Educational backgrounds include:** Accounting; Business Administration; Economics; Finance. **Benefits:** Dental Insurance; Life Insurance; Medical Insurance; Pension Plan; Tuition Assistance. **Corporate headquarters location:** New York NY. **Parent company:** Citicorp. **Operations at this facility include:** Administration; Regional Headquarters; Sales; Service. **Listed on:** New York Stock Exchange.

CIVIC BANCORP
2101 Webster Street, 14th Floor, Oakland CA 94612. 510/836-6500. **Contact:** Human Resources. **Description:** Civic BanCorp is a bank holding company. CivicBank of Commerce is a wholly-owned subsidiary of the company. The bank is a state chartered bank and a member of the Federal Reserve System and FDIC. The bank is a full-service commercial bank dedicated to providing personalized services to independent businesses and professional firms in Alameda and Contra Costa counties. The bank also provides banking services to individuals who are owners, partners, or principals of these businesses or professional practices, and other corporate executives and professionals. The bank offers its clients certain customary banking services, such as checking, savings, and interest-bearing demand; money market and time deposit accounts; commercial,

installment, and real estate loans; safe deposit boxes; automated cash management services; collection services; wire and telephone transfer services; courier services; lockbox services; and account reconciliation. The bank has one operating subsidiary, Pasco Services, Inc., which acts as trustee to perform loan servicing and reconveyance services under deeds of trust held by the bank and other lenders. **Number of employees at this location:** 115.

COMERICA BANK CALIFORNIA
55 Almaden Boulevard, San Jose CA 95113. 408/271-4006. **Fax:** 408/271-4074. **Recorded Jobline:** 800/522-2265x4. **Contact:** Human Resources. **Description:** Comerica Bank California has 31 California offices. Comerica Bank covers markets in the following counties: Santa Clara, Santa Cruz, Monterey, Alameda, San Francisco, Los Angeles, Orange, and San Mateo. **Common positions include:** Accountant/Auditor; Adjuster; Attorney; Bank Officer/Manager; Budget Analyst; Clerical Supervisor; Customer Service Representative; Financial Analyst; Human Resources Specialist; Operations/Production Manager; Purchasing Agent and Manager; Technical Writer/Editor. **Educational backgrounds include:** Accounting; Business Administration; Communications; Economics; Finance; Marketing. **Benefits:** 401(k); Dental Insurance; Disability Coverage; Employee Discounts; Life Insurance; Medical Insurance; Pension Plan; Profit Sharing; Savings Plan; Tuition Assistance. **Corporate headquarters location:** San Jose CA. **Other U.S. locations:** FL; IL; MI; TX. **Parent company:** Comerica Bank, Inc., the parent company, is a $33 billion bank holding company headquartered in Detroit that operates banking affiliates in Michigan, Texas, California, Illinois, and Florida. Comerica, Inc. is a diversified financial services provider, offering a whole range of financial products and services for businesses and individuals through more than 400 offices nationwide. The five core business markets Comerica covers are corporate banking, consumer banking, private banking, institutional trust and investment management, and international finance and trade services. Including subsidiaries, Comerica Inc. has operations in 16 states and two Canadian provinces. Comerica's global financial services operations serve customers worldwide. **Operations at this facility include:** Administration; Divisional Headquarters; Regional Headquarters; Sales; Service. **Listed on:** New York Stock Exchange. **Number of employees at this location:** 1,000. **Number of employees nationwide:** 14,000.

**DELTA NATIONAL BANK
ADMINISTRATIVE OFFICE**
611 North Main Street, Manteca CA 95336. 209/824-4050. **Fax:** 209/823-1104. **Contact:** Human Resources. **Description:** Delta National Bancorp was incorporated in 1981 for the purpose of serving as a bank holding company. The company's wholly-owned subsidiary, Delta National Bank, operates as a commercial bank in the cities of Manteca, Riverbank, Denair, and Modesto CA. **Parent company:** Delta National Bancorp.

EUREKA BANK
950 Tower Lane, Suite 600, Foster City CA 94404. 415/358-6100. **Contact:** Peggy Hiraoka, Personnel Director. **Description:** Administrative offices for an area savings and loan institution. **Corporate headquarters location:** This Location.

FEDERAL HOME LOAN BANK OF SAN FRANCISCO
P.O. Box 7948, San Francisco CA 94120. 415/616-1000. **Contact:** Human Resources Administrator. **Description:** Serves as the central bank and regulating agency to more than 200 savings and loan associations in California, Arizona, and Nevada.

FEDERAL RESERVE BANK OF SAN FRANCISCO
P.O. Box 7702, San Francisco CA 94120. 415/974-2000. **Contact:** Personnel Department. **Description:** One of 12 regional Federal Reserve banks that, along with the Federal Reserve Board of Governors in Washington DC, and the Federal Open Market Committee (FOMC), comprise the Federal Reserve System, the nation's central bank. As the nation's central bank, the Federal Reserve is charged with three major responsibilities: monetary policy, banking supervision and regulation, and processing payments.

FIRST COMMERCIAL BANCORP, INC.
P.O. Box 591, 2450 Venture Oaks Way, Sacramento CA 95833. 916/646-0554. **Contact:** Human Resources. **Description:** First Commercial Bancorp, Inc. is a bank holding company. The company's sole subsidiary, First Commercial Bank, commenced operations in 1979. The bank conducts a general banking business through its eight branch offices with two locations in Sacramento, two in Roseville, and one each in Santa Rosa, San Francisco, Concord, and Campbell CA. **Corporate headquarters location:** This Location.

FIRST FINANCIAL BANCORP
Call Box 3009, 701 South Ham Lane, Lodi CA 95241-1913. 209/367-2000. **Contact:** Human Resources. **Description:** First Financial Bancorp is a banking holding company with Bank of Lodi, N.A. as its sole subsidiary. As a full-service commercial bank, it provides a full complement of depository accounts including checking, interest-bearing checking, negotiable orders of withdrawal, money market and passbook savings. A full range of lending activities are provided, with a particular emphasis on providing the agricultural, business, and professional communities with short-term commercial loans at interest rates tied to prevailing rates in the current money market. In particular, Bank of Lodi's lending focuses on light-industrial, manufacturing, and agricultural concerns and professional organizations in the city of Lodi and its surrounding area. It also offers a full line of residential mortgage products and engages in limited consumer lending activities. **Corporate headquarters location:** This Location. **Number of employees at this location:** 70.

FIRST NATIONWIDE BANK
135 Main Street, San Francisco CA 94105. 415/904-1100. **Contact:** Human Resources. **Description:** A federal savings bank. **Common positions include:** Accountant/Auditor; Bank Officer/Manager; Clerical Supervisor; Computer Programmer; Computer Systems Analyst; Credit Manager; Customer Service Representative; Underwriter/Assistant Underwriter. **Educational backgrounds include:** Accounting; Business Administration; Computer Science; Marketing. **Benefits:** 401(k); Daycare Assistance; Dental Insurance; Disability Coverage; Employee Discounts; Life Insurance; Medical Insurance; Profit Sharing; Tuition Assistance. **Corporate headquarters location:** This Location. **Other U.S. locations:** Sacramento CA. **Operations at this facility include:** Administration; Regional Headquarters; Service. **Listed on:** Privately held. **Number of employees at this location:** 350. **Number of employees nationwide:** 3,500.

FIRST REPUBLIC BANCORP INC.
388 Market Street, San Francisco CA 94111. 415/392-1400. **Contact:** Human Resources. **Description:** First Republic Bancorp is a leading banking and mortgage banking institution with growing operations in four major urban markets -- San Francisco, Los Angeles, San Diego, and Las Vegas. The company is financially strong,

customer service-oriented, and narrowly focused on core lending and savings businesses. **Corporate headquarters location:** This Location.

HOME FEDERAL FINANCIAL CORPORATION
26 O'Farrell Street, San Francisco CA 94108. 415/982-4560. **Contact:** Gail Mejeur, Director of Human Resources. **Description:** A savings and loan banking institution. **Common positions include:** Accountant/Auditor; Administrative Services Manager; Bank Officer/Manager; Branch Manager; Financial Analyst; Human Resources Specialist; Underwriter/Assistant Underwriter. **Educational backgrounds include:** Accounting; Business Administration; Finance; Real Estate. **Benefits:** 401(k); Dental Insurance; Disability Coverage; Life Insurance; Medical Insurance. **Corporate headquarters location:** This Location. **Operations at this facility include:** Administration; Divisional Headquarters; Sales; Service. **Number of employees at this location:** 80. **Number of employees nationwide:** 200.

REDWOOD BANCORP
735 Montgomery Street, San Francisco CA 94111. 415/788-3700. **Fax:** 415/391-9090. **Contact:** Sue Allen, Assistant Vice President. **Description:** A bank holding company. Redwood Bank offers full banking services at four area facilities. **Common positions include:** Bank Officer/Manager; Customer Service Representative. **Educational backgrounds include:** Business Administration; Finance. **Benefits:** 401(k); Dental Insurance; Disability Coverage; Life Insurance; Medical Insurance; Profit Sharing. **Corporate headquarters location:** This Location. **Operations at this facility include:** Administration. **Listed on:** Privately held. **Number of employees at this location:** 40.

SUMITOMO BANK OF CALIFORNIA
320 California Street, 3rd Floor, San Francisco CA 94104. 415/445-8000. **Contact:** Mr. Mas Miyakoda, Personnel. **Description:** Operates a full-service bank with several area branches. **Operations at this facility include:** Administration.

UNION BANK OF CALIFORNIA
400 California Street, 10th Floor, San Francisco CA 94104. 415/765-2142. **Contact:** Maureen Mack, Human Resources Manager. **Description:** Union Bank is a full-service commercial bank providing a broad range of financial services including retail and small business banking; middle market banking; real estate finance; corporate banking; trade finance, with a focus on the Pacific Rim; and financial management and trust services. **Common positions include:** Bank Officer/Manager; Credit Manager; Lender. **Benefits:** 401(k); Dental Insurance; Disability Coverage; Employee Discounts; Life Insurance; Medical Insurance; Savings Plan; Tuition Assistance.

UNION BANK/SAN FRANCISCO
350 California Street, San Francisco CA 94104. 415/705-7427. **Fax:** 415/705-7088. **Contact:** Corporate Staffing. **Description:** Union Bank is a full-service commercial bank providing a broad mix of financial services including retail and small business banking, middle market banking, real estate finance, corporate banking, trade finance (with a focus on the Pacific Rim), and financial management and trust services. **Common positions include:** Bank Officer/Manager; Branch Manager; Credit Clerk and Authorizer; Customer Service Representative; Financial Analyst; Financial Services Sales Rep.; Management Trainee; Paralegal; Securities Sales Representative; Services Sales Representative. **Educational backgrounds include:** Economics; Finance; Marketing. **Benefits:** 401(k); Dental Insurance; Disability Coverage; Employee Discounts; Life Insurance; Medical Insurance; Pension Plan; Profit Sharing; Savings

Plan; Tuition Assistance. **Corporate headquarters location:** This Location. **Subsidiaries include:** U.S. Investment Services, Inc. **Operations at this facility include:** Administration; Divisional Headquarters; Regional Headquarters; Sales; Service. **Listed on:** NASDAQ. **Number of employees at this location:** 350. **Number of employees nationwide:** 7,000.

WELLS FARGO BANK
420 Montgomery Street, 11th Floor, MAC#0101-118, San Francisco CA 94163. 415/396-3849. **Contact:** Recruitment Services. **Description:** Wells Fargo is a subsidiary of one of the largest bank holding companies in the United States. **Common positions include:** Accountant/Auditor; Bank Officer/Manager; Branch Manager; Computer Programmer; Credit Manager; Customer Service Representative; Financial Analyst; General Manager; Human Resources Specialist; Management Trainee; Marketing Specialist; Operations/Production Manager; Services Sales Representative; Systems Analyst. **Educational backgrounds include:** Accounting; Business Administration; Computer Science; Economics; Engineering; Finance; Liberal Arts; Marketing; Mathematics. **Benefits:** Daycare Assistance; Dental Insurance; Disability Coverage; Employee Discounts; Life Insurance; Medical Insurance; Pension Plan; Profit Sharing; Savings Plan; Stock Option; Tuition Assistance. **Special Programs:** Internships. **Corporate headquarters location:** This Location. **Parent company:** Wells Fargo and Company. **Listed on:** Frankfurt Stock Exchange; London Stock Exchange; New York Stock Exchange. **Number of employees nationwide:** 19,600.

WORLD SAVINGS & LOAN ASSOCIATION
GOLDEN WEST FINANCIAL
1901 Harrison Street, Fourth Floor, Oakland CA 94612. 510/446-3050. **Contact:** Suzun Almquist, Human Resources. **Description:** One of the largest savings and loan associations in the United States. **Common positions include:** Accountant/Auditor; Administrator; Advertising Clerk; Bank Officer/Manager; Branch Manager; Computer Programmer; Credit Manager; Customer Service Representative; Department Manager; Financial Analyst; General Manager; Human Resources Specialist; Insurance Agent/Broker; Management Trainee; Marketing Specialist; Purchasing Agent and Manager; Systems Analyst; Technical Writer/Editor; Transportation/Traffic Specialist. **Educational backgrounds include:** Accounting; Business Administration; Computer Science; Economics; Finance; Marketing. **Benefits:** Dental Insurance; Disability Coverage; Employee Discounts; Life Insurance; Medical Insurance; Pension Plan; Savings Plan; Tuition Assistance. **Corporate headquarters location:** This Location. **Other U.S. locations:** Sacramento CA; San Francisco CA; Walnut Creek CA; CO; KS. **Operations at this facility include:** Administration; Service. **Listed on:** New York Stock Exchange.

***Note:** Because addresses and telephone numbers of smaller companies can change rapidly, we recommend you call each company to verify the information below before inquiring about job opportunities. Mass mailings are not recommended.*

Additional small employers:

COMMERCIAL BANKS

Glendale Federal Bank
1330 E Shaw Ave, Fresno CA 93710. 209/438-3531.

Glendale Federal Bank
201 N Main Street, Sebastopol CA 95472. 707/823-8561.

Bank One Fresno N.A.
1315 Van Ness Ave, Fresno CA 93721-1713. 209/443-5554.

Western Financial Savings Bank
160 E El Camino Real, Mountain View CA 94040-2725. 415/967-8931.

University Bank & Trust Co.
250 Lytton Ave, Palo Alto CA 94301-1427. 415/327-0210.

Bank Of California
491 S El Camino Real, San Mateo CA 94402-1727. 415/548-9031.

East-West Federal Bank FSB
1650 Tiburon Blvd, Tiburon CA 94920-2512. 415/435-9161.

Bank Of Santa Clara
2027 El Camino Real, Santa Clara CA 95050-4067. 408/249-5900.

Silicon Valley Bank
3000 Lakeside Dr, Santa Clara CA 95054-2895. 408/980-0766.

Pacific Coast Farm Credit
595 Auto Center Dr, Watsonville CA 95076-3727. 408/728-2249.

Western Financial Savings Bank
7337 Pacific Ave, Stockton CA 95207-1924. 209/951-5641.

Placer Savings Bank
305 Railroad Ave, Nevada City CA 95959-2854. 916/265-5868.

Placer Savings Bank
1224 Broadway Ste A, Placerville CA 95667-5899. 916/626-3470.

Western Sierra National Bank
1450 Broadway, Placerville CA 95667-5904. 916/622-1010.

First Interstate Bank Of CA
190 E Monte Vista Ave, Vacaville CA 95688-2809. 707/446-1575.

First Interstate Bank Of CA
3205 W Hammer Ln, Stockton CA 95209-2751. 209/952-7701.

First Interstate Bank Of CA
PO Box 981, Petaluma CA 94953-0981. 707/763-0923.

First Interstate Bank Of CA
1380 Hilltop Dr, Redding CA 96003-3805. 916/223-6400.

Placer Savings Bank
8595 Auburn Folsom Rd, Granite Bay CA 95746-6201. 916/791-1173.

Tri Counties Bank
15 Independence Cir, Chico CA 95973-0251. 916/898-0300.

Bank Of Canton Of California
555 Montgomery St, San Francisco CA 94111-2541. 415/362-4100.

Mid-Peninsula Bank
420 Cowper St, Palo Alto CA 94301-1504. 415/323-5150.

Great Western Bank
5050 Broadway, Oakland CA 94611-4618. 510/452-6606.

Great Western Bank
437 Corte Madera Town Ctr, Corte Madera CA 94925-1215. 510/452-6663.

Bank Of Petaluma
100 Petaluma Blvd S Ste A, Petaluma CA 94952-2983. 707/765-2222.

San Benito Bank
300 Tres Pinos Rd, Hollister CA 95023-5578. 408/637-2265.

Coast Commercial Bank
PO Box 1818, Santa Cruz CA 95061-1818. 408/458-4520.

Central Sierra Bank
373 W Saint Charles St, San Andreas CA 95249-9618. 209/754-1883.

County Bank
1160 W Olive Ave Ste A, Merced CA 95348-1958. 209/725-2200.

US Bank of California
304 F St, Davis CA 95616-4118. 916/756-7283.

US Bank of California
115 Main St, Woodland CA 95695-3125. 916/662-9615.

US Bank Of California
22953 Twain Harte Dr, Twain Harte CA 95383-9628. 209/586-3277.

US Bank Of California
735 5th St, Eureka CA 95501-1101. 707/445-3051.

US Bank Of California
525 McBean Park Dr, Lincoln CA 95648-1840. 916/645-8989.

US Bank Of California
600 Market St, Colusa CA 95932-2441. 916/458-5858.

US Bank Of California
11111 Olson Dr, Rancho Cordova CA 95670-5644. 916/638-9812.

US Bank Of California
1110 Dana Dr, Redding CA 96003-4083. 916/223-3700.

Great Western Bank
501 Broadway, Sonoma CA 95476-6650. 707/996-1081.

San Francisco Federal Savings & Loan
5610 Sunrise Blvd, Citrus Hts CA 95610-7602. 916/965-7613.

San Francisco Federal Savings & Loan
2717 Marconi Ave, Sacramento CA 95821-4913. 916/973-0785.

San Francisco Federal Savings & Loan
9601 Greenback Ln, Folsom CA 95630-2088. 916/988-1590.

Continental Pacific Bank
555 Mason St Ste 280, Vacaville CA 95688-4612. 707/448-1200.

Business & Professional Bank
PO Box 1050, Woodland CA 95776-1050. 916/661-1333.

Sacramento Commercial Bank
525 J Street, Sacramento CA 95814-2383. 916/443-4700.

Commerce Security Bank
1545 River Park Drive Suite 200, Sacramento CA 95815-4600. 916/922-9500.

Feather River State Bank
777 Colusa Ave, Yuba City CA 95991-3734. 916/671-2265.

North Valley Bank
1327 South Street, Redding CA 96001-1979. 916/243-8600.

SAVINGS INSTITUTIONS

California Savings & Loan
800 Market St, San Francisco CA 94102-3001. 415/986-3600.

Continental Savings Bank Of America
250 Montgomery St, San Francisco CA 94104-3401. 415/398-6080.

Continental Savings Bank of America
801 Franklin Street, Oakland CA 94607-4252. 510/452-1886.

Old Stone Bank Of CA FSB
24970 Hesperian Boulevard, Hayward CA 94545-2420. 510/887-6000.

American Savings Bank FA
1502 Redwood Highway Suite C-49, Corte Madera CA 94925-1224. 415/927-3701.

American Savings Bank FA
2915 Stevens Creek Blvd, Santa Clara CA 95050-6708. 408/261-7500.

California Thrift & Loan
3158 Auto Center Circle Suite B-1 , Stockton CA 95212-2839. 209/957-3671.

El Dorado Savings Bank
1332 Oak Court, Arnold CA 95223. 209/795-4414.

Sacramento Savings Bank
5999 Madison Ave, Carmichael CA 95608-0519. 916/969-2222.

Sacramento Savings Bank
8859 Madison Avenue, Fair Oaks CA 95628-3907. 916/966-9111.

CREDIT UNIONS

American Electric Association Credit Union
505 North Mathilda Avenue, Sunnyvale CA 94086-3505. 408/720-0374.

San Francisco City Employment Credit Union
770 Golden Gate Ave, San Francisco CA 94102-3120. 415/775-5377.

Kaiperm Walnut Creek Federal Credit Union
1425 S Main St, Walnut Creek CA 94596-5318. 510/295-5626.

Patelco Credit Union
1009 Alamo Dr, Vacaville CA 95687-5603. 707/453-0127.

Pacific IBM Employee Federal Credit Union
5615 Chesbro Ave, San Jose CA 95123-3000. 408/972-5222.

Coast Central Credit Union
1814 Main Street, Fortuna CA 95540-2797. 707/725-6195.

Travis Federal Credit Union
11 Cernon Street, Vacaville CA 95688-2803. 707/451-5100.

Yolo Federal Credit Union
815 Harbor Boulevard, West Sacramento CA 95691-2201. 916/668-2724.

Schools Federal Credit Union
5210 Madison Ave, Sacramento CA 95841-3004. 916/334-2420.

Sierra Central Credit Union
Yuba St, Herlong CA 96113. 916/827-2191.

Sierra Central Credit Union
820 Plaza Way, Yuba City CA 95991-3299. 916/671-3000.

OFFICES OF BANK HOLDING COMPANIES

Pacific Capital Bancorp
1001 S Main St, Salinas CA 93901-2302. 408/757-4900.

Fremont Bancorporation
39150 Fremont Blvd,

Fremont CA 94538-1316. 510/795-5702.

Northbay Financial Corporation
20 Petaluma Blvd S, Petaluma CA 94952-3031. 707/792-7400.

North Valley Bancorp
880 E Cypress Ave, Redding CA 96002. 916/221-8400.

Truckee River Bank
10181 Truckee Tahoe Airport Road, Truckee CA 96160. 916/582-3000.

For more information on career opportunities in the banking/savings and loans industry:

__Associations__

AMERICA'S COMMUNITY BANKERS
900 19th Street NW, Suite 400, Washington DC 20006. 202/857-3100. A trade association representing the expanded thrift industry. Members are institutions (not individuals).

AMERICAN BANKERS ASSOCIATION
1120 Connecticut Avenue NW, Washington DC 20036. 202/663-5221. World Wide Web address: http://www.aba.com/aba. Provides banking education and training services, sponsors industry programs and conventions, and publishes articles, newsletters, and the ABA Service Member Directory.

__Directories__

AMERICAN BANK DIRECTORY
Thomson Financial Publications, 6195 Crooked Creek Road, Norcross GA 30092. 770/448-1011.

AMERICAN SAVINGS DIRECTORY
McFadden Business Publications, 6195 Crooked Creek Road, Norcross GA 30092. 770/448-1011.

BUSINESS WEEK/TOP 200 BANKING INSTITUTIONS ISSUE
McGraw-Hill, Inc., 1221 Avenue of the Americas, 39th Floor, New York NY 10020. 212/512-4776.

MOODY'S BANK AND FINANCE MANUAL
Moody's Investors Service, Inc., 99 Church Street, First Floor, New York NY 10007. 212/553-0300.

POLK'S BANK DIRECTORY
R.L. Polk & Co., P.O. Box 305100, Nashville TN 37320-5100. 615/889-3350.

RANKING THE BANKS/THE TOP NUMBERS
American Banker, Inc., 1 State Street Plaza, New York NY 10004. 212/943-6700.

__Magazines__

ABA BANKING JOURNAL
American Bankers Association, 1120 Connecticut Avenue NW, Washington DC 20036. 202/663-5221.

BANK ADMINISTRATION
1 North Franklin, Chicago IL 60606. 800/323-8552.

BANKERS MAGAZINE
Warren, Gorham & Lamont, Park Square Building, 31 St. James Avenue, Boston MA 02116-4112. 617/423-2020.

JOURNAL OF COMMERCIAL BANK LENDING
Robert Morris Associates, P.O. Box 8500 S-1140, Philadelphia PA 19178. 215/851-9100.

BIOTECHNOLOGY, PHARMACEUTICALS, AND SCIENTIFIC R&D

During the early '90s, the pharmaceutical industry was characterized by a mass of mergers and acquisitions, with drug companies concentrating on cutting costs to boost profit margins.

While more mergers may be on the way, most of the big staff cuts are history, and profitability is up. Even so, industry watchers don't expect the arrival of many big-selling new products in the near future, and many companies have slashed research and development budgets. According to the Pharmaceutical Research and Manufacturers of America, the 8 percent growth in R&D spending was the lowest in 20 years.

As more drug patents continue to expire, the impact will be felt by large pharmaceutical companies. There will be a negative impact on their sales growth. Conversely, the expired patents mean more opportunities for generic drug manufacturers, who should continue to gain market share through 1996.

ABAXIS, INC.
1320 Chesapeake Terrace, Sunnyvale CA 94089. 408/734-0200. **Contact:** Gina Czerwinski, Human Resources. **Description:** Since commencing operations in 1989, Abaxis, Inc. has been a development stage company engaged in research and development. Activities focus on commercialization of the Piccolo System, which consists of a small whole-blood analyzer and blood chemistry reagent rotors. Near patient blood testing has grown rapidly due to physician demand for more rapid diagnostic information. Earlier diagnoses are necessary to improve the efficiency and reduce the cost of medical care. The company also completed development of a nine-test reagent rotor for sale to veterinarians, called the Primary Health Profile. Abaxis system is well-suited for their needs because of its simplicity and its ability to perform a panel of tests on a small quantity of whole blood. **Corporate headquarters location:** This Location. **Number of employees at this location:** 75.

ADVANCED POLYMER SYSTEMS INC.
3696 Haven Avenue, Redwood City CA 94063. 415/366-2626. **Contact:** Shelly Howell, Human Resources Administrator. **Description:** Advanced Polymer Systems is a leader in polymer-based delivery systems and related technologies for use in pharmaceuticals, over-the-counter drugs, toiletries, and select specialty applications. In addition to building its own portfolio, Advanced Polymer is working in collaboration with major corporations to develop and supply specialized delivery systems to enhance their products, primarily in the field of dermatology. **Common positions include:** Chemical Engineer; Chemist. **Educational backgrounds include:** Chemistry. **Benefits:** 401(k); Dental Insurance; Disability Coverage; Life Insurance; Medical Insurance; Tuition Assistance. **Corporate headquarters location:** This Location. **Other U.S. locations:** Greenwich CT; Lafayette LA. **Operations at this facility include:** Administration; Research and Development; Sales. **Listed on:** NASDAQ. **Number of employees at this location:** 45.

ALZA CORPORATION

P.O. Box 10950, Palo Alto CA 94303-0802. 415/494-5000. **Fax:** 415/494-5151. **Recorded Jobline:** 415/494-5319. **Contact:** Darlene Markovitch, Human Resources Director. **Description:** Alza Corporation, founded in 1968, develops, manufactures, and markets therapeutic systems for both humans and animals. Major products include transdermal drug-delivery patches and OROS drug delivery technology. Products are used for the treatment of angina, chronic pain, respiratory diseases, motion sickness, and periodontal disease, as well as nicotine withdrawal. **Common positions include:** Accountant/Auditor; Attorney; Biological Scientist/Biochemist; Biomedical Engineer; Buyer; Chemical Engineer; Chemist; Clinical Lab Technician; Computer Programmer; Designer; Economist/Market Research Analyst; Financial Analyst; Industrial Engineer; Industrial Production Manager; Insurance Agent/Broker; Librarian; Library Technician; Materials Engineer; Mechanical Engineer; Physician Assistant; Public Relations Specialist; Quality Control Supervisor; Registered Nurse; Statistician. **Educational backgrounds include:** Biology; Chemistry; Engineering; Health Care. **Benefits:** 401(k); Dental Insurance; Disability Coverage; Employee Discounts; Life Insurance; Medical Insurance; Pension Plan; Profit Sharing; Tuition Assistance. **Special Programs:** Internships. **Corporate headquarters location:** This Location. **Other U.S. locations:** Vacaville CA; Minneapolis MN. **Operations at this facility include:** Administration; Divisional Headquarters; Manufacturing; Research and Development. **Listed on:** New York Stock Exchange. **Number of employees at this location:** 1,000. **Number of employees nationwide:** 1,370.

APPLIED IMMUNE SCIENCES, INC.

5301 Patrick Henry Drive, Santa Clara CA 95054. 408/492-9200. **Fax:** 408/980-5888. **Contact:** Human Resources. **Description:** Applied Immune Sciences, Inc. (AIS) develops, manufactures, and delivers cell and gene therapy products designed to enhance and restore the immune system in immune-related conditions such as bone marrow transplantation, cancer, autoimmune, and infectious diseases. AIS' core technologies include patented cell isolation devices, gene transfer systems, and cell processing techniques. AIS isolates specific immune cells from a patient's or donor's bone marrow or peripheral blood, allowing the cells to be purified, treated, numerically expanded, or genetically modified. After processing, the cells are infused into a patient in an attempt to provide therapeutic benefit. **Corporate headquarters location:** This Location. **Number of employees at this location:** 140.

ARRIS PHARMACEUTICAL CORPORATION

385 Oyster Point Boulevard, Suite 3, South San Francisco CA 94080. 415/829-1000. **Contact:** Human Resources. **Description:** Arris Pharmaceutical Corporation is a development stage corporation engaged in the discovery and development of synthetic small molecule therapeutics that modulate the activity of medically important proteins. Arris' approach to drug discovery uses proprietary artificial intelligence technology to correlate data from both compound library screening and structure-based drug analysis to generate a predictive model of drug activity. The company believes that this approach will substantially shorten the development cycle and increase the likelihood of discovering and optimizing promising compounds. Arris has focused its initial product development programs on oral cytosine and growth factor mimetics and mast cell-mediated inflammation. **Corporate headquarters location:** This Location. **Number of employees at this location:** 60.

ATHENA NEUROSCIENCES, INC.
800F Gateway Boulevard, South San Francisco CA 94080. 415/877-0900. **Fax:** 415/877-8370. **Contact:** Human Resources. **Description:** Athena Neurosciences, Inc. is a research-based pharmaceutical company committed to the field of neurology. The goal of the company is to become a leader in the discovery, development, and marketing of therapeutic and diagnostic products for patients with neurological diseases and disorders. Athena's principal research efforts are directed toward the discovery of products to diagnose and treat Alzheimer's disease and for the treatment of degenerative brain diseases such as multiple sclerosis. **Corporate headquarters location:** This Location.

AXION, INC.
395 Oyster Point Boulevard, Suite 405, South San Francisco CA 94080. 415/952-8400. **Contact:** Human Resources. **Description:** Axion distributes cancer pharmaceuticals and related products to oncology physicians. **Listed on:** Privately held. **Number of employees at this location:** 60.

BECTON DICKINSON IMMUNOCYTOMETRY SYSTEMS
2350 Qume Drive, San Jose CA 95131. 408/432-9475. **Contact:** Craig Andersen, Manager of Staffing and Salary Administration. **Description:** A manufacturer of products for use in cell analysis and immune monitoring. The product line includes monoclonal antibody reagents, flow cytometry instrumentation, and accessories for a variety of applications to the basic research, clinical research, and clinical markets. **Common positions include:** Accountant/Auditor; Biological Scientist/Biochemist; Biomedical Engineer; Budget Analyst; Buyer; Chemist; Computer Programmer; Computer Systems Analyst; Customer Service Representative; Designer; Draftsperson; Economist/Market Research Analyst; Editor; Electrical/Electronics Engineer; Electrician; Financial Analyst; Industrial Engineer; Mechanical Engineer; Purchasing Agent and Manager; Quality Control Supervisor; Scientist; Software Engineer; Statistician; Technical Writer/Editor. **Educational backgrounds include:** Biology; Chemistry; Computer Science; Engineering. **Benefits:** 401(k); Daycare Assistance; Dental Insurance; Disability Coverage; Life Insurance; Medical Insurance; Pension Plan; Savings Plan; Tuition Assistance. **Corporate headquarters location:** Franklin Lakes NJ. **Other U.S. locations:** Mansfield MA. **Operations at this facility include:** Divisional Headquarters; Manufacturing; Research and Development; Sales; Service. **Listed on:** New York Stock Exchange. **Number of employees at this location:** 500. **Number of employees nationwide:** 600.

BIOCIRCUITS CORPORATION
1324 Chesapeake Terrace, Sunnyvale CA 94089-1100. 408/745-1961. **Fax:** 408/752-8792. **Contact:** Human Resources. **Description:** Biocircuits is developing new immunodiagnostic testing systems. The company believes that its initial system will be the first commercially available product which will permit a physician to perform a menu of immunodiagnostic tests at the point of patient care. In addition, the company plans to develop automated immunodiagnostic testing systems for clinical laboratories. The company believes that its system, if successfully developed, will significantly reduce the cost of immunodiagnostic testing and provide test results more rapidly than current testing procedures. **Common positions include:** Biological Scientist/Biochemist; Chemist; Electrical/Electronics Engineer; Mechanical Engineer; MIS Specialist; Software Engineer. **Benefits:** 401(k); Dental Insurance; Disability Coverage; Life Insurance; Medical Insurance; Savings Plan; Tuition Assistance. **Corporate headquarters location:** This Location. **Operations at this facility include:** Administration; Manufacturing; Research and Development; Sales; Service. **Listed on:**

NASDAQ. **Annual sales/revenues:** Less than $5 million. **Number of employees at this location:** 80.

CALGENE, INC.
1920 Fifth Street, Davis CA 95616. 916/753-6313. **Fax:** 916/753-1510. **Contact:** Human Resources. **Description:** Calgene is a biotechnology company that is developing a portfolio of genetically engineered plants and plant products for the food, seed, and oleochemical industries. The company's research and business efforts are focused in three core crop areas: fresh market tomato, edible and industrial plant oils, and cotton. Calgene scientists have genetically engineered tomato varieties with a gene which delays softening and reduces spoilage in order to enable the company to provide vine-ripened tomatoes with improved taste. Calgene is developing genetically-engineered grapeseed oils that are intended to have a broad range of food and industrial applications. Calgene's cotton genetic engineering program focuses on reducing farmers' growing costs through the development of herbicide-resistant and insect-resistant cotton varieties. **Corporate headquarters location:** This Location.

CELL GENESYS, INC.
322 Lakeside Drive, Foster City CA 94404. 415/358-9600. **Contact:** Human Resources. **Description:** Cell Genesys is genetically engineering the human immune system to create innovative therapies for serious diseases. Using gene therapy technology to produce human T-cell therapies and transgenic technology to produce human monoclonal antibodies, the company is developing new approaches to the treatment of viral infection, cancer, and other diseases. Cell Genesys' lead program, anti-HIV T-cell gene therapy for AIDS, is currently in human clinical testing. Human monoclonal antibodies are being developed through the company's Xenotech joint venture. **Corporate headquarters location:** This Location.

CELTRIX PHARMACEUTICALS INC.
3055 Patrick Henry Drive, Santa Clara CA 95054-1815. 408/988-2500. **Fax:** 408/450-4700. **Contact:** Human Resources. **Description:** Celtrix is a biopharmaceutical company with a full pipeline of product candidates focused on the treatment of degenerative diseases associated with aging or autoimmune conditions. The company's mission is to improve the quality of life by providing innovative, cost-effective therapeutics. The most advanced product candidate is BetaKine, used for the treatment of potentially blinding ophthalmic diseases. BetaKine has doubled the success of existing macular hole therapy and has demonstrated potential for treating currently untreatable age-related macular degeneration. Other product development programs show promise for the treatment of chronic dermal ulcers, localized tissue damage, and systemic, degenerative diseases such as multiple sclerosis, and osteoporosis. **Corporate headquarters location:** This Location.

CHIRON CORPORATION
4560 Horton Street, Emeryville CA 94608. 510/655-8730. **Contact:** Human Resources. **Description:** A biotechnology company that focuses on the development of products in four key area: diagnostics, vaccines, therapeutics, and ophthalmics. **Number of employees nationwide:** 1,867.

CHOLESTECH CORPORATION
3347 Investment Boulevard, Hayward CA 94545. 510/732-7200. **Fax:** 510/732-7227. **Contact:** Human Resources. **Description:** The company is engaged in designing, developing, and manufacturing diagnostic point-of-care systems capable of performing

numerous diagnostic tests, using very small quantities of whole blood. The company began marketing its first lipid tests, TC (total cholesterol) and HDL (high density lipoprotein), to the United States in the summer of 1991. Since that time, the company has introduced two additional tests: the TC and HDL Panel, and the Lipid Profile. **Corporate headquarters location:** This Location. **Number of employees at this location:** 90.

CIBAGENEVA PHARMACEUTICAL COMPANY
One Lagoon Drive, Suite 145, Redwood City CA 94065. 415/610-7800. **Contact:** Human Resources. **Description:** CibaGeneva Pharmaceutical Company is a pharmaceuticals manufacturer.

COLLAGEN CORPORATION
2500 Faber Place, Palo Alto CA 94303. 415/856-0200. **Contact:** Human Resources Department. **Description:** Collagen Corporation was founded in 1975 by a biochemist and three physicians affiliated with Stanford University, who pioneered the commercial development of injectable collagen. Today, Collagen Corporation is a world leader in the development of collagen-based biomaterials. The mission of Collagen Corporation is to develop, manufacture, and market, on a worldwide basis, high-quality biocompatible products for the treatment of defective, diseased, traumatized, or aging human tissues. Collagen Corporation seeks to enhance, expand, and protect its technology -- the science of collagen -- and to develop new applications in human medical markets worldwide that take full advantage of the biophysical activities of novel biomaterials and matrix proteins, especially collagen. **Corporate headquarters location:** This Location.

COR THERAPEUTICS, INC.
256 East Grand Avenue, South San Francisco CA 94080. 415/244-6800. **Fax:** 415/244-9208. **Contact:** Human Resources Department. **Description:** COR Therapeutics, Inc. is dedicated to the discovery, development, and commercialization of novel pharmaceutical products for the treatment and prevention of severe cardiovascular diseases. Since the founding of COR in 1988, its research has focused on advancing the basic understanding of the molecular and cellular mechanisms underlying the development of cardiovascular diseases. This targeted scientific strategy, when combined with the company's multidisciplinary approach to drug discovery and design, has resulted in the identification of novel molecules with the potential to treat a range of cardiovascular disorders, including complications associated with coronary angioplasty, unstable angina, acute myocardial infarction, stroke, and deep vein thrombosis. **Corporate headquarters location:** This Location.

CYGNUS THERAPEUTIC SYSTEMS
400 Penobscot Drive, Redwood City CA 94063. 415/369-4300. **Contact:** Human Resources. **Description:** Cygnus Therapeutic Systems is a leader in the development and manufacturing of advanced drug delivery systems which control the release of drugs over extended periods of time at predetermined rates. The products have the potential to help prevent illness, improve the effectiveness of therapies, and reduce health care costs. The company has developed a core set of technologies to design and develop products primarily focused on four major markets: hormone replacement, glucose monitoring, consumer products, and smoking cessation. The goal is to become the recognized leader in every market in which Cygnus competes. **Corporate headquarters location:** This Location.

ENVIRON CORPORATION
5820 Shellmound Street, Suite 700, Emeryville CA 94608. 510/655-7400. **Fax:** 510/655-9517. **Contact:** Human Resources. **Description:** A multidisciplinary environmental and health sciences consulting firm that provides a broad range of services relating to the presence of hazardous substances in the environment, consumer products, and the workplace. Services provided by ENVIRON are concentrated in the assessment and management of chemical risk and are characterized by engagements supporting private sector clients with complex, potentially high-liability concerns. **Corporate headquarters location:** Arlington VA. **Other U.S. locations:** Emeryville CA; Irvine CA; Novato CA; Princeton NJ; Houston TX. **Parent company:** Applied Bioscience International Inc. (Arlington VA).

ENVIRON CORPORATION
Golden Gate Plaza, 101 Rowland Way, Novato CA 94945-5010. 415/899-0700. **Fax:** 415/899-0707. **Contact:** Human Resources. **Description:** A multidisciplinary environmental and health sciences consulting firm that provides a broad range of services relating to the presence of hazardous substances in the environment, consumer products, and the workplace. Services provided by ENVIRON are concentrated in the assessment and management of chemical risk and are characterized by engagements supporting private sector clients with complex, potentially high-liability concerns. **Corporate headquarters location:** Arlington VA. **Other U.S. locations:** Emeryville CA; Irvine CA; Princeton NJ; Houston TX. **Parent company:** Applied Bioscience International Inc. (Arlington VA).

ESCAGENETICS CORPORATION
830 Bransten Road, San Carlos CA 94070-3305. 415/595-5335. **Contact:** Human Resources. **Description:** Historically, Escagenetics business has emphasized the use of plant biotechnology in combination with advanced breeding methods to develop and produce improved planting materials, crops, and natural food ingredients. More recently, through its majority-owned subsidiary, PHYTOpharmaceuticals, Inc., the company has focused its efforts on proprietary research and development, using its plant tissue culture technology for the production of a promising anti-cancer drug called taxol. The company has produced taxol in the laboratory and has formed collaborations for the scale-up to commercial quantities.

GENELABS TECHNOLOGIES, INC.
505 Penobscot Drive, Redwood City CA 94063. 415/369-9500. **Contact:** Human Resources. **Description:** Genelabs is a health care products company focused on the discovery, development, and commercialization of products for the treatment, prevention, and diagnosis of viral and severely debilitating or life-threatening diseases. The company operates through its biopharmaceutical division as well as through its diagnostic division. Genelabs Diagnostics develops and provides high-quality and cost-effective diagnostic products and services to clinical laboratories and physicians' offices worldwide. Genelab's initial focus is on the European and the rapidly growing Asian markets.

GENENTECH INC.
460 Point San Bruno Boulevard, South San Francisco CA 94080. 415/225-1000. **Contact:** Human Resources. **Description:** Genentech Inc. discovers, develops, manufactures, and markets human pharmaceuticals.

GILEAD SCIENCES
353 Lakeside Drive, Foster City CA 94404. 415/574-3000. **Contact:** Human Resources. **Description:** Gilead Sciences is a leader in the discovery and development of a new class of human therapeutics based on nucleotides, the building blocks of DNA and RNA. The company's research and development efforts encompass three interrelated programs: small molecules, aptamers, and code blockers. These research programs use nucleotides in unique ways to create potential treatments for a broad range of diseases. Gilead's small molecule product candidates are single nucleotides designed to treat viral infection by interfering with the replication of viral genes in infected cells. These research programs are focused on potential human therapeutics for certain types of viral infections, vascular disease, inflammatory disease, and cancer. Gilead has multiple, ongoing clinical development programs, which include human clinical trials of several of its small molecule compounds as potential treatments for serious viral diseases.

GLYCOMED INC.
860 Atlantic Avenue, Alameda CA 94501. 510/523-5555. **Contact:** Human Resources. **Description:** Glycomed Inc. is a leader in the discovery and development of a new class of pharmaceuticals based on complex carbohydrates. The company's drug discovery strategy is to create biologically-active small molecules for therapeutic use. Glycomed is using its unique carbohydrate technologies to commercialize products for the treatment of important diseases such as cancer.

ERNEST ORLANDO LAWRENCE BERKELEY NATIONAL LABORATORY
One Cyclotron Road, MS 938A, Berkeley CA 94720. 510/486-7950. **Fax:** 510/486-5870. **Recorded Jobline:** 510/486-4226. **Contact:** Human Resources. **E-mail address:** employment@LBL.gov. **World Wide Web address:** http://www.LBL.gov. **Description:** A multi-program national research facility operated by the University of California for the Department of Energy. Its fundamental mission is to provide national scientific leadership and technological innovation to support the DOE's objectives. The oldest of the nine national laboratories, LBL's major activities include the Advanced Light Source, Human Genome Center, California Institute for Energy Efficiency, and the Center for Advanced Materials. **Common positions include:** Biological Scientist/Biochemist; Chemical Engineer; Chemist; Computer Programmer; Computer Systems Analyst; Electrical/Electronics Engineer; Environmental Engineer; Geologist/Geophysicist; Mathematician; Mechanical Engineer; Physicist/Astronomer; Science Technologist. **Educational backgrounds include:** Biology; Chemistry; Computer Science; Engineering; Mathematics; Physics. **Benefits:** 401(k); Dental Insurance; Disability Coverage; Employee Discounts; Life Insurance; Mass Transit Available; Medical Insurance; Pension Plan; Savings Plan; Telecommuting; Tuition Assistance. **Special Programs:** Internships. **Corporate headquarters location:** This Location. **Operations at this facility include:** Administration; Research and Development. **Number of employees at this location:** 3,000.

LAWRENCE LIVERMORE NATIONAL LABORATORY
P.O. Box 808, L-725, Livermore CA 94551. 510/422-9367. **Contact:** Gay Spivey, Recruiting Coordinator. **Description:** Engaged in basic and applied research. The laboratory's work centers around six major programs: weapon studies; magnetic fusion energy; laser isotope separation; laser fusion energy; energy and resources; and biomedical, environmental, and atmospheric sciences. **Common positions include:** Biological Scientist/Biochemist; Environmental Scientist. **Educational backgrounds include:** Biology; Mathematics. **Benefits:** 401(k); Dental Insurance; Disability Coverage; Employee Discounts; Life Insurance; Medical Insurance; Pension Plan;

Savings Plan; Tuition Assistance; Vision Insurance. **Operations at this facility include:** Research and Development. **Number of employees nationwide:** 8,000.

MOLECULAR DYNAMICS
928 East Arques Avenue, Sunnyvale CA 94086-4520. 408/773-1222. **Contact:** Human Resources. **Description:** Molecular Dynamics develops, manufactures, markets, and supports innovative systems that increase data quality and throughput in life science research laboratories. Integrated systems from Molecular Dynamics comprise instrumentation, software, and reagents, giving researchers the ability to bypass or automate the most time-consuming steps on the path between laboratory samples and experimental results. Vistra Systems, an alliance between Amersham Life Science and Molecular Dynamics, brings a new level of productivity to the world's laboratories. This alliance allows the development of integrated hardware, software, and reagents for even greater laboratory efficiency and automation. Molecular Dynamics has sales and service professionals in 29 countries.

PERKIN-ELMER APPLIED BIOSYSTEMS
850 Lincoln Centre Drive, Foster City CA 94404. 415/570-6667. **Contact:** Employment. **Description:** A supplier of systems and tools for biotechnology research. **Common positions include:** Chemical Engineer; Chemist; Customer Service Representative; Electrical/Electronics Engineer; Manufacturer's/Wholesaler's Sales Rep.; Mechanical Engineer; Technical Writer/Editor. **Educational backgrounds include:** Biology; Chemistry; Engineering. **Benefits:** Dental Insurance; Disability Coverage; Employee Discounts; Life Insurance; Medical Insurance; Pension Plan; Stock Option; Tuition Assistance. **Corporate headquarters location:** This Location. **Other U.S. locations:** Pomona CA; San Jose CA. **Operations at this facility include:** Administration; Manufacturing; Research and Development; Sales; Service. **Listed on:** New York Stock Exchange. **Number of employees nationwide:** 900.

PHARMCHEM LABORATORIES INC.
1505-A O'Brien Drive, Menlo Park CA 94025. 415/328-6200. **Fax:** 415/688-1123. **Contact:** Mike Splane, Director of Human Resources. **Description:** A forensic drug testing laboratory. **Common positions include:** Laboratory Technician. **Educational backgrounds include:** Biology; Chemistry. **Benefits:** 401(k); Dental Insurance; Employee Discounts; Life Insurance; Medical Insurance; Savings Plan; Tuition Assistance. **Special Programs:** Internships. **Corporate headquarters location:** This Location. **Operations at this facility include:** Administration; Regional Headquarters; Research and Development; Sales; Service. **Listed on:** NASDAQ. **Number of employees at this location:** 260.

SRI INTERNATIONAL
333 Ravenswood Avenue, Menlo Park CA 94025. 415/326-6200. **Contact:** Personnel. **Description:** A multi-disciplinary research, development, and consulting organization engaged in government and private industry research. **Common positions include:** Biological Scientist/Biochemist; Biomedical Engineer; Chemical Engineer; Chemist; Economist/Market Research Analyst; Electrical/Electronics Engineer; Financial Analyst; Human Resources Specialist; Mechanical Engineer; Physicist/Astronomer; Systems Analyst; Technical Writer/Editor. **Educational backgrounds include:** Biology; Business Administration; Chemistry; Communications; Computer Science; Economics; Engineering; Finance; Mathematics; Physics. **Benefits:** Dental Insurance; Disability Coverage; Employee Discounts; Life Insurance; Medical Insurance; Pension Plan; Tuition Assistance. **Corporate headquarters location:** This Location.

SANDIA NATIONAL LABORATORIES
P.O. Box 969, Livermore CA 94551. 510/294-3000. **Contact:** Human Resources. **Description:** A scientific research company.

SCIOS INC.
2450 Bay Shore Parkway, Mountain View CA 94043. 415/966-1550. **Contact:** Human Resources. **Description:** Researches, develops, and manufactures pharmaceuticals.

SMITHKLINE BEECHAM CLINICAL LABORATORIES
6511 Golden Gate Drive, Dublin CA 94568-2907. 510/828-2500. **Contact:** Human Resources. **Description:** The largest clinical laboratory in North America, providing a broad range of clinical laboratory services to more than 50,000 health care clients and to industry. The company offers and performs 1,500 tests on blood, urine, and other bodily fluids and tissues to provide information for health and well-being. SmithKline Clinical Laboratories was among the first to receive certification from the U.S. Government's National Institute on Drug Abuse and performs more drug tests than any other company in the industry. The company operates 24 laboratories throughout the U.S., as well as an additional 300 testing sites and specimen collection centers to support these labs. Labs are staffed by certified technologists, including more than 200 physicians and Ph.D.'s. The company performs more than 56 million tests a year. Clients include physicians, hospitals, clinics, dialysis centers, and pharmaceutical companies. **Parent company:** SmithKline Beecham Corporation is a health care company engaged in the research, development, manufacture, and marketing of ethical pharmaceuticals, animal health products, ethical and proprietary medicines and eye care products. In addition to SmithKline Beecham Clinical Laboratories, the company's principal divisions include SmithKline Beecham Pharmaceuticals, SmithKline Beecham Animal Health, and SmithKline Beecham Consumer Healthcare. The company is also engaged in many other aspects of the health care field, including the production of medical instruments and electronic instruments used in the health care field. SmithKline Beecham Corporation manufactures proprietary medicines through its subsidiary, Menley & James Laboratories, including such nationally known products as Contac Cold Capsules, Sine-Off sinus medicine, Love cosmetics, and Sea & Ski outdoor products.

SMITHKLINE DIAGNOSTICS
225 Baypointe Parkway, San Jose CA 95134. 408/435-2660. **Contact:** Human Resources. **Description:** A human therapeutics and diagnostics company. **Number of employees at this location:** 75.

SOMATIX THERAPY CORPORATION
950 Marina Village Parkway, Alameda CA 94501. 510/748-3000. **Fax:** 510/814-8002. **Contact:** Cecilia Vitug, Senior Human Resources Representative. **Description:** A leader in the field of gene therapy. Somatix Therapy Corporation's mission is to research, develop, and commercialize proprietary processes for genetic modification of cells and their use in the treatment of human diseases. The company's strategic assets include its proprietary broad-based gene transfer technology and product development programs focused on cancer and neural diseases. **Common positions include:** Biological Scientist/Biochemist; Research Assistant. **Educational backgrounds include:** Science. **Benefits:** 401(k); Dental Insurance; Disability Coverage; Employee Discounts; Life Insurance; Medical Insurance; Tuition Assistance. **Operations at this facility include:** Administration; Manufacturing; Research and Development. **Listed on:** NASDAQ. **Number of employees at this location:** 125.

STANFORD LINEAR ACCELERATOR CENTER
2575 Sand Hill Road, Menlo Park CA 94025. 415/926-3300. **Recorded Jobline:** 415/926-2353. **Contact:** Human Resources. **Description:** A non-commercial research center.

VEHRING DIAGNOSTICS, INC.
P.O. Box 49013, San Jose CA 95161-9013. 408/239-2000. **Contact:** Professional Employment. **Description:** Engaged in medical diagnostics. The company develops, manufactures, and markets tests to diagnose infectious diseases and to detect and quantify clinically significant substances in patients' bodily fluids. **Common positions include:** Biological Scientist/Biochemist; Biomedical Engineer; Chemist; Microbiologist; Physicist/Astronomer.

Note: *Because addresses and telephone numbers of smaller companies can change rapidly, we recommend you call each company to verify the information below before inquiring about job opportunities. Mass mailings are not recommended.*

Additional small employers:

MEDICAL AND DENTAL LABORATORIES

Chowchilla District Memorial Hospital
1104 Ventura Ave, Chowchilla CA 93610-2244. 209/665-3781.

Pathlab-Unilab
295 O'Connor Dr, San Jose CA 95128-1624. 408/295-0392.

Pathlab-Unilab
115 N Jackson Ave, San Jose CA 95116-1924. 408/259-6806.

Pathlab-Unilab
100 O'Connor Dr, San Jose CA 95128-1638. 408/293-5406.

Pathlab-Unilab
967 Mabury Rd, San Jose CA 95133-1025. 408/288-9850.

Pathlab-Unilab
1828 El Camino Real, Burlingame CA 94010-3103. 415/692-6712.

Contra Costa MRI
2051 Contra Costa Blvd, Pleasant Hill CA 94523-3301. 510/674-1986.

Meris Laboratories Inc.
5525 Dewey Dr, Fair Oaks CA 95628-3129. 916/961-3972.

Meris Laboratories Inc.
2844 Summit St, Oakland CA 94609-3637. 510/839-8186.

Meris Laboratories Inc.
1999 Mowry Ave, Fremont CA 94538-1723. 510/794-0684.

Spectra Laboratories
48818 Kato Rd, Fremont CA 94538-7364. 510/623-6900.

ETM Electromatic Inc.
35451 Dumbarton Ct, Newark CA 94560-1100. 510/797-1100.

Rossmoor Clinical Laboratory
1220 Rossmoor Pkwy, Walnut Creek CA 94595-2501. 510/988-7540.

Nichols Institute
3012 Summit St, Oakland CA 94609-3409. 510/835-4940.

Marin Mobile Outpatient Services Inc
5 Bon Air Rd, Larkspur CA 94939-1127. 415/924-0755.

Puls Imagery
124 Pine St, San Anselmo CA 94960-2602. 415/454-6935.

Metwest Clinical Laboratories
2516 Samaritan Dr, San Jose CA 95124-4108. 408/356-9154.

Bloss Memorial Health Care District
1691 3rd St, Atwater CA 95301-3692. 209/358-8201.

Physicians' Clinical Laboratory
7618 Auburn Blvd, Citrus Hts CA 95610-2215. 916/726-3380.

Physicians' Clinical Laboratory
1 Scripps Dr, Sacramento CA 95825-6206. 916/929-5359.

Physicians' Clinical Lab
1101 Smith Ln # D, Roseville CA 95661-4103. 916/783-4452.

Physicians' Clinical Lab
9727 Elk Grove-Florin Rd # 110, Elk Grove CA 95624-2265. 916/685-3254.

Marshall Diagnostic Center
3105 Cedar Ravine Rd, Placerville CA 95667-6561. 916/626-2669.

Moss Landing Marine Lab
893 Blanco Cir, Salinas CA 93901-4455. 408/755-8650.

Peninsula Diagnostic Service Ltd.
1875 Trousdale Dr, Burlingame CA 94010-4509. 415/697-7006.

Alameda Imaging Inc.
2236 Mariner Square Dr, Alameda CA 94501-1071. 510/522-4146.

Mercy General Hospital
3941 J St, Sacramento CA 95819-3628. 916/733-6930.

Redding Physicians Center
1441 Liberty St, Redding CA 96001-0848. 916/244-4817.

DIAGNOSTIC SUBSTANCES

Bio Source International
887 Mitten Rd, Burlingame CA 94010. 415/692-4015.

Cooper Development Co.
2420 Sand Hill Rd, Menlo Park CA 94025-6942. 415/233-2727.

Sugen Inc.
515 Galveston Dr, Redwood City CA 94063-4720. 415/306-7700.

Clontech Laboratories Inc.
1020 E Meadow Cir, Palo Alto CA 94303-4230. 415/424-8222.

Bio Genex Laboratories
4600 Norris Canyon Rd #200, San Ramon CA 94583-1320. 510/275-0550.

MEDICINAL CHEMICALS AND BOTANICAL PRODUCTS

Rainbow Light Nutri Systems
207 McPherson St, Santa Cruz CA 95060-5820. 408/429-9089.

PHARMACEUTICAL PREPARATIONS

Matrix Pharmaceutical Inc.
1430 Obrien Dr, Menlo Park CA 94025. 415/326-6100.

Shaman Pharmaceuticals
213 E Grand Ave, S San Fran CA 94080-4812. 415/952-7070.

In-Site Vision Inc.
965 Atlantic Ave, Alameda CA 94501. 510/865-8800.

Natural Formulas Inc.
2125 American Ave, Hayward CA 94545-1803. 510/785-0461.

Oclassen Pharmaceuticals
100 Pelican Way, San Rafael CA 94901. 415/258-4500.

Nasco West
1524 Princeton Ave, Modesto CA 95350-5728. 209/529-6957.

Baxter Microscan
2040 Enterprise Blvd, W Sacramento CA 95691-3427. 916/374-3108.

BIOLOGICAL PRODUCTS

Peninsula Laboratories Inc.
611 Taylor Way Ste 2, Belmont CA 94002-4041. 415/592-5392.

Anergen Inc.
301 Penobscot Dr, Redwood City CA 94063-4700. 415/361-8901.

Adeza Biomedical Corp.
1240 Elko Dr, Sunnyvale CA 94089-2212. 408/745-0975.

Baxter Hyland Biotech Inc.
1978 W Winton Ave, Hayward CA 94545-1206. 510/786-9744.

Berkeley Antibody Co. Inc.
4131 Lakeside Dr Ste B, Richmond CA 94806-1965. 510/222-4940.

For more information on career opportunities in biotechnology, pharmaceuticals, and scientific R&D:

<u>Associations</u>

AMERICAN ASSOCIATION FOR CLINICAL CHEMISTRY
2101 L Street NW, Suite 202, Washington DC 20037-1526. 202/857-0717. Toll-free phone: 800/892-1400. World Wide Web address: http://www.aacc.org. International scientific/medical society of individuals involved with clinical chemistry and other clinical lab science-related disciplines.

AMERICAN ASSOCIATION OF COLLEGES OF PHARMACY
1426 Prince Street, Alexandria VA 22314-2841. 703/739-2330. World Wide Web

address: http://www.aacp.org. An organization composed of all U.S. pharmacy colleges and over 2,000 school administrators and faculty members. Career publications include *Shall I Study Pharmacy?*, *Pharmacy: A Caring Profession*, and *A Graduate Degree in the Pharmaceutical Sciences: An Option For You?*

AMERICAN COLLEGE OF CLINICAL PHARMACY (ACCP)
3101 Broadway, Suite 380, Kansas City MO 64111. 816/531-2177. Operates ClinNet jobline at 412/648-7893 for both members and nonmembers, for a fee.

AMERICAN PHARMACEUTICAL ASSOCIATION
2215 Constitution Avenue NW, Washington DC 20037. 202/628-4410. Operates a resume referral service for all members.

AMERICAN SOCIETY FOR BIOCHEMISTRY AND MOLECULAR BIOLOGY
9650 Rockville Pike, Bethesda MD 20814-3996. 301/530-7145. World Wide Web address: http://www.saseb.org/asbmb/asbmb.html. A nonprofit scientific and educational organization whose primary scientific activities are in the publication of the *Journal of Biological Chemistry* and holding an annual scientific meeting. Also publishes a career brochure entitled *Unlocking Life's Secrets: Biochemistry and Molecular Biology.*

AMERICAN SOCIETY OF HEALTH SYSTEM PHARMACISTS
7272 Wisconsin Avenue, Bethesda MD 20814. 301/657-3000. World Wide Web address: http://www.ashp.com/pub/ashp/index.html. Provides pharmaceutical education. Offers a service for jobseekers for a fee.

BIOMEDICAL RESEARCH INSTITUTE
355 K Street, Chula Vista CA 91911-1209. 619/427-9940. Fax: 619/427-2634. A nonprofit organization which promotes scientific research and education and provides annual scholarships to students. Maintains a national Institutional Review Board.

BIOTECHNOLOGY INDUSTRY ORGANIZATION
1625 K Street NW, Suite 1100, Washington DC 20006-1604. 202/857-0244. Fax: 202/857-0237. World Wide Web address: http://www.bio.org. Represents agriculture, biomedical, diagnostic, food, energy, and environmental companies.

NATIONAL PHARMACEUTICAL COUNCIL
1894 Preston White Drive, Reston VA 22091. 703/620-6390. Fax: 703/476-0904. An organization of research-based pharmaceutical companies. Fax requests to the attention of Pat Adams, Vice President of Finance and Administration.

Directories

DRUG TOPICS RED BOOK
Medical Economics Company, 5 Paragon Drive, Montvale, NJ 07645. 201/358-7200.

Magazines

DRUG TOPICS
Medical Economics Company, 5 Paragon Drive, Montvale NJ 07645. 201/358-7200.

PHARMACEUTICAL ENGINEERING
International Society of Pharmaceutical Engineers, 3816 West Linebaugh Avenue, Suite 412, Tampa FL 33624. 813/960-2105.

BUSINESS SERVICES AND NON-SCIENTIFIC RESEARCH

The business services sector, which includes 16 of the 20 fastest growing industries, covers a broad spectrum of careers, including everything from adjustment and collection services to data processing companies. While the job outlook varies upon which service is being discussed, in general, the business services sector is among the fastest-growing in the nation. Increasingly, American companies are "outsourcing" functions like data processing to outside firms. Often large organizations will go so far as to hand over the management of their entire data center to an outside service provider. This trend is expected to boost opportunities for those who work for data processing services.

Other types of services that benefit from this trend include security firms and personnel services firms. Many businesses are using temporary workers instead of hiring new permanent staffers, thus avoiding the much higher overhead costs such as health insurance. Companies that supply these temporary workers, as well as those that place permanent workers, are among the fastest-growing in the nation. While one-third of the jobs available are administrative support occupations, there is a growing trend toward specialization which will open up more positions for highly skilled workers, such as engineers or managers.

AMERICAN BUILDING MAINTENANCE INDUSTRIES/SAN FRANCISCO
50 Freemont, San Francisco CA 94105. 415/597-4500. **Contact:** Human Resources. **Description:** A national contract maintenance firm providing janitorial, maintenance, and building management products and services in more than 60 metropolitan areas in the United States and Canada. **Corporate headquarters location:** This Location.

AUTOMATIC DATA PROCESSING
3300 Olcott Street, Santa Clara CA 95052. 408/988-6565. **Contact:** Maureen Singer, Human Resources Director. **Description:** Engaged in payroll processing services, including unemployment claims management, and local, state, and federal tax filing. **Common positions include:** Customer Service Representative. **Benefits:** Dental Insurance; Disability Coverage; Life Insurance; Medical Insurance; Pension Plan; Stock Option; Tuition Assistance. **Corporate headquarters location:** Roseland NJ. **Operations at this facility include:** Sales; Service. **Listed on:** New York Stock Exchange. **Number of employees at this location:** 500. **Number of employees nationwide:** 20,000.

C&T MANAGEMENT SERVICES, INC.
625 3rd Street, San Francisco CA 94107. 415/536-DPAS. **Fax:** 415/536-3700. **Contact:** Rula Adranly, Director of Human Resources. **E-mail address:** DPAS@netcom.com. **Description:** Offers a wide range of data processing, database management, and imaging and scanning services. **Common positions include:** Accountant/Auditor; Blue-Collar Worker Supervisor; Branch Manager; Clerical Supervisor; Computer Programmer; Customer Service Representative; Data Entry Clerk; Department Manager; General

Manager; Human Resources Specialist; Services Sales Representative; Systems Analyst. **Educational backgrounds include:** Accounting; Business Administration; Computer Science; Marketing. **Benefits:** Dental Insurance; Disability Coverage; Life Insurance; Medical Insurance; Profit Sharing. **Corporate headquarters location:** This Location.

COPART, INC.
5500 East 2nd Street, 2nd Floor, Benicia CA 94510. 707/644-4468. **Contact:** Human Resources. **Description:** Copart auctions salvage vehicles as a service to vehicle suppliers, principally major insurance companies. Salvage vehicles are those deemed a total loss for insurance or other business purposes and recovered stolen vehicles. Copart services numerous vehicle suppliers, including many of the largest insurance, financial and rental car companies in the country. **Corporate headquarters location:** This Location.

JETRO SAN FRANCISCO
235 Pine Street, Suite 1700, San Francisco CA 94104. 415/392-1333. **Contact:** Human Resources. **Description:** A nonprofit organization which helps businesses export to Japan. This location also has a Japanese resource center that is open to the public.

LEWIS & TAYLOR
440 Bryant Street, San Francisco CA 94107. 415/781-3496. **Contact:** Oneda Turner, Personnel Director. **Description:** Provides building maintenance services throughout the area.

LOOMIS ARMORED INC.
One Kaiser Plaza, Suite 945, Oakland CA 94612-3610. 510/452-1100. **Contact:** Human Resources. **Description:** An armored car service.

MAJOR LEGAL SERVICES
180 Howard Street, San Francisco CA 94105-1660. 415/905-1449. **Fax:** 415/356-4109. **Contact:** Sheldon Silverman, Human Resources Manager. **Description:** A secretarial and court reporting service with 14 locations statewide. **Common positions include:** Computer Programmer; Customer Service Representative; Operations/Production Manager. **Educational backgrounds include:** Business Administration. **Benefits:** Dental Insurance; Disability Coverage; Life Insurance; Medical Insurance; Tuition Assistance. **Corporate headquarters location:** This Location. **Operations at this facility include:** Administration; Divisional Headquarters; Sales; Service. **Number of employees at this location:** 200. **Number of employees nationwide:** 275.

PINKERTON SECURITY COMPANY
731 Market Street, Suite 410, San Francisco CA 94103. 415/543-2100. **Contact:** Personnel Manager. **Description:** Operating for more than 130 years, Pinkerton Security is the oldest and one of the largest non-governmental security services organizations in the world today. The company's principal business is providing high-quality security, investigative, and consulting services to a multitude of commercial, industrial, institutional, governmental, and residential clients. Pinkerton Security operates from 129 offices in the United States, Canada, and Great Britain. Major services include industrial and nuclear plant security, institutional security, commercial and residential building security, retail security, construction security, patrol and inspection services, community security, sports and special events services, K-9 patrol services, courier services, inventory services, investigation services, security consultation, and equipment

evaluation. **Common positions include:** Security Officer. **Other U.S. locations:** Encino CA; Santa Ana CA. **Number of employees worldwide:** 35,000.

UNDERWRITERS LABORATORIES INC.
1655 Scott Boulevard, Santa Clara CA 95050. 408/985-2400. **Contact:** Human Resources. **Description:** An independent, nonprofit corporation established to help reduce or prevent bodily injury, loss of life, and property damage. Underwriters Laboratories accomplishes its objectives by scientific investigation of various materials, devices, equipment, constructions, methods, and systems, and by the publication of standards, classifications, specifications, and other information. Engineering functions are divided between six departments: Electrical; Burglary Protection and Signaling; Casualty and Chemical Hazards; Fire Protection; Heating, Air-Conditioning, and Refrigeration; and Marine. The company also provides a factory inspection service through offices throughout the United States and in 54 other countries. **Number of employees worldwide:** 2,600.

UNITED FOOD & COMMERCIAL WORKERS INTERNATIONAL
P.O. Box 4324, Vallejo CA 94590. 707/643-8611. **Contact:** Personnel. **Description:** An organization for food and commercial workers.

Note: *Because addresses and telephone numbers of smaller companies can change rapidly, we recommend you call each company to verify the information below before inquiring about job opportunities. Mass mailings are not recommended.*

Additional small employers:

ADJUSTMENT AND COLLECTION SERVICES

Payco Gen American Credits Inc.
5933 Coronado Blvd, Pleasanton CA 94588-8518. 510/460-8592.

Transworld Systems Inc.
1155 Ellis St, San Francisco CA 94109-7656. 415/563-6226.

Transworld Systems Inc.
5880 Commerce Blvd, Rohnert Park CA 94928-1644. 707/584-4225.

Collection Bureau of San Jose
299 Stockton St, San Francisco CA 94108-5316. 415/391-5388.

Collections Unlimited
27591 Mandarin Ave, Hayward CA 94544-5013. 510/785-2279.

Creditors Trade Association Inc.
650 University Ave, Sacramento CA 95825-6726. 916/927-5445.

Foothill Collection Service Inc.
5301 Madison Ave, Sacramento CA 95841-3146. 916/338-6789.

CREDIT REPORTING SERVICES

Equifax Credit Information Service
2665 N Air Fresno Dr Ste 101 , Fresno CA 93727-1548. 209/456-7777.

Trans Union Corporation
1390 Willow Pass Rd, Concord CA 94520-5200. 510/689-1912.

ADA Credit Service
2670 S White Rd, San Jose CA 95148-2071. 408/223-7155.

Credco Inc.
5345 Madison Ave, Sacramento CA 95841-3141. 916/334-0626.

American Financial Consumer Service
5250 Claremont Ave, Stockton CA 95207-5700. 209/472-3621.

Credit Unlimited
10578 Partridge Rd, Grass Valley CA 95945-7412. 916/274-0128.

SECRETARIAL AND COURT REPORTING SERVICES

Sherwood Executive Center
5250 Claremont Ave, Stockton CA 95207-5700. 209/478-6600.

Business Office Services
3700 Delta Fair Blvd Ste 212, Antioch CA 94509-4074. 510/757-1555.

Morf Organization
384 Bel Marin Keys Blvd, Novato CA 94949-5638. 415/883-3600.

CLEANING AND MAINTENANCE SERVICES

Your Pest Control
4240 Ralph Ln N, Fresno CA 93727-7154. 209/291-4008.

Terminix International
Redwood City, Mountain View CA 94043. 415/369-2603.

Tallon Termite & Pest Control
30073 Ahern Ave, Union City CA 94587-1234. 510/429-7200.

Clark Pest Control
2986 Coloma St, Placerville CA 95667-4441. 916/622-7844.

Western Exterminator Co.
Placer County, Placerville CA 95667. 916/622-6141.

MISC. EQUIPMENT RENTAL AND LEASING

Clementina Ltd.
1657 Rollins Rd, Burlingame CA 94010-2385. 415/692-9920.

DETECTIVE, GUARD, AND ARMORED CAR SERVICES

International Security Service Inc.
1101 San Antonio Rd Ste 418, Mountain View CA 94043-1008. 415/968-0120.

Allied Security Inc.
519 17th St # 410, Oakland CA 94612-1503. 510/839-4041.

Allied Security Inc.
1900 McCarthy Blvd Ste 302, Milpitas CA 95035-7440. 408/954-8274.

Guardsmark Inc.
2151 River Plaza Dr Ste 170, Sacramento CA 95833-3881. 916/565-2950.

Guardsmark Inc.
3031 Tisch Way Ste 306, San Jose CA 95128-2530. 408/241-1493.

RG Professional Security Inc.
3830 Watt Ave Ste 7, Sacramento CA 95821-2669. 916/361-8133.

Armored Transport Inc.
1333 8th St, Oakland CA 94607-2100. 510/451-1333.

Burns International Security Service
1913 N Gateway Blvd, Fresno CA 93727-1605. 209/252-9740.

Curtis Security Services
2503 San Pablo Ave, Pinole CA 94564-1308. 510/741-8111.

Grupe Patrol Services
3255 W March Ln Fl 4, Stockton CA 95219-2304. 209/957-3333.

Hart Security Service
PO Box 15085, Mather CA 95655. 916/635-2865.

Wells Fargo Guard Services
1401 El Camino Ave Ste 110, Sacramento CA 95815-2744. 916/447-7288.

Rosevear Investigations
6636 Commerce Blvd Ste 21, Rohnert Park CA 94928-2410. 707/585-6126.

Don White Investigations
PO Box 991567, Redding CA 96099-1567. 916/244-0782.

West Coast Investigative Service
PO Box 720052, Redding CA 96099-7052. 916/357-3173.

MISC. BUSINESS SERVICES

Document Copy Service
717 Market St Ste 308, San Francisco CA 94103-2109. 415/543-0750.

American Telemarketing Inc.
32 Ponderey Place, Concord CA 94521-2349. 510/674-4274.

Golden Gate Auto Auction
6700 Stevenson Blvd, Fremont CA 94538-2467. 510/657-5660.

California Translation International
1904 Olympic Boulevard Suite 12, Walnut Creek CA 94596-5023. 510/947-3520.

Machiraju & Associates
4010 Moorpark Ave Ste 105, San Jose CA 95117-1842. 408/247-8007.

B&T Home Inspection Service
4736 Minnesota Ave, Fair Oaks CA 95628-5805. 916/863-1882.

Ken Mason Lais General Contractors
5250 Date Ave Ste G, Sacramento CA 95841-2564. 916/349-0339.

GES Exposition Services
2128 N 1st St, San Jose CA 95131-2006. 408/436-4914.

Calvin Lau Designs
27 Maiden Ln Ste 201, San

Francisco CA 94108-5415. 415/398-7487.

Andary Design
170 Maiden Ln, San Francisco CA 94108-5328. 415/433-4431.

Cowan Design
4000 Moorpark Ave, San Jose CA 95117-1859. 408/248-1622.

Adagio Interiors
3201 Greentree Way, San Jose CA 95117-3027. 408/246-3902.

Beverly A. Williams Interiors
2525 Ontario Drive, San Jose CA 95124. 408/559-3525.

Fitch & Associates
1501 F Street, Sacramento CA 95814-1608. 916/447-5777.

Donna Berry ASID & Associates
2394 Fair Oaks Blvd, Sacramento CA 95825-4738. 916/486-8658.

Brandt Money Handling Products
134 Wolfe Grade, Kentfield CA 94904. 415/461-0278.

Brandt Inc. Field Service Division
3400 De La Cruz Blvd, Santa Clara CA 95054-2609. 408/727-2119.

Telecheck
3851 N Freeway Blvd, Sacramento CA 95834-1928. 916/565-2190.

Rodney's Answering Service
3480 Carpenter Rd, Stockton CA 95215-8100. 209/466-2122.

Attune International Inc.
111 Anza Blvd, Burlingame CA 94010-1932. 415/344-3515.

Lumberjack Productions
840 Folsom Ave, Hayward CA 94544-6409. 510/887-6563.

The Art of Ears
21087 Cabot Boulevard Suite 6, Hayward CA 94545-1147. 510/887-4612.

San Jo Rae Enterprises
PO Box 23836, San Jose CA 95153-3836. 408/226-5525.

Association For Retarded Citizens
1849 Industrial Way, Sanger CA 93657-9501. 209/875-2905.

Mail It Quick
230 Skyline Plz, Daly City CA 94015-3825. 415/755-1303.

Postal Plus
1685 Branham Ln, San Jose CA 95118-5212. 408/266-3230.

Low Cost Legal Center
4010 Moorpark Ave, San Jose CA 95117-4101. 408/248-8665.

First Bay Legal
562 6th Ave, San Francisco CA 94118-3836. 415/668-7899.

Automobile Appraisal Association
1010 Hurley Way, Sacramento CA 95825-3215. 916/484-6116.

Auto Appraisal Service
4918 Brewster Ave, San Jose CA 95124-5447. 408/371-2962.

Northern California Appraisal
2670 S White Rd, San Jose CA 95148-2071. 408/238-4642.

Helen Smotherman HIS Appraisal
5445 Elsinore Way, Fair Oaks CA 95628-3207. 916/489-1870.

Philip H. Cooper & Associates Inc.
455 Capitol Mall Ste 701, Sacramento CA 95814-4405. 916/325-4960.

The Iremonger Co.
400 Lincoln Ave, Alameda CA 94501-3236. 510/865-8661.

Export International Inc.
2645 Mercantile Dr, Rncho Cordova CA 95742-6521. 916/635-0133.

Real Reel Images
PO Box 566, Pacifica CA 94044-0566. 415/355-8897.

United States Holographics
936 Detroit Ave, Concord CA 94518-2517. 510/687-3800.

Quest Seven
4168 Bay St, Fremont CA 94538-4205. 510/651-7326.

CFC Network
1715 E St, Fresno CA 93706-2021. 209/486-4040.

Arrow Delivery & Courier Service
2550 Wyandotte St, Mountain View CA 94043-2315. 415/969-2888.

Executive Courier Network
1124 Chess Dr, Foster City CA 94404-1103. 415/518-0733.

DVC Courier
7567 Amador Valley Blvd, Dublin CA 94568-2441. 510/833-0777.

Trans-Box Systems Inc.
211 Lathrop Way, Sacramento CA 95815-4222. 916/921-9011.

PDA
265 Cheswick Ct, Alameda CA 94502. 510/521-6251.

Banshee Development Inc.
36 Harold Ave, San Jose CA 95117-1026. 408/246-2699.

Advanced Business Concepts
PO Box 36047, San Jose CA 95158-6047. 408/295-2968.

Chamber Business Incubator
1550 W Fremont St, Stockton CA 95203-2643. 209/547-2966.

Professional Office Services
6455 Almaden Expy Ste 205, San Jose CA 95120-2801. 408/997-8587.

Crane Pro Services-Kone
2957 Teagarden St, San Leandro CA 94577-5718.

Hugo Arenas & Associates
795 4th Ave, Redwood City CA 94063. 415/363-0337.

MDR CAD Services
1730 Franklin St, Oakland CA 94612. 510/839-1552.

CAD Design Concepts
458 S Henry Ave, San Jose CA 95117. 408/249-5288.

Harrington Construction
PO Box 6323, Folsom CA 95763-6323. 916/351-9425.

Hadley Auto Transport
3800 Industrial Way, Benicia CA 94510. 707/745-4995.

Bi-Rite Auto Transport Services
29901 Industrial Pkwy Sw, Hayward CA 94544-6901. 510/732-0983.

Auto Driveaway Co.
3275 Stevens Creek Blvd, San Jose CA 95117-1108. 408/984-4999.

Collegeville Rural Fire District
13225 E Mariposa Rd, Stockton CA 95215-9651. 209/462-3883.

AAA Baricade Co.
2004 Piccoli Rd Ste 8, Stockton CA 95215-2330. 209/477-1450.

Fund Development Associates
2012 H St, Sacramento CA 95814-3100. 916/441-6800.

RGIS Inventory Specialist
2889 Cohasset Rd, Chico CA 95973-0991. 916/898-1015.

Aquifier Plant Watering Systems
1026 Clayton St, San Francisco CA 94117-4415. 415/681-3966.

Capital Relocation Services
7840 Madison Ave Ste 145, Fair Oaks CA 95628-3518. 916/863-1277.

Ellen Co.
1033 Pacific Ave, San Francisco CA 94133-4209. 415/776-4799.

A-1 Pool Service
1909 Hackett Ave, Mountain View CA 94043-4359. 415/969-2582.

Langford's Mastic Service
1303 Antonio Ln, San Jose CA 95117-3602. 408/378-8208.

MVP Pool Service
782 Cypress Ave, San Jose CA 95117-2114. 408/244-1801.

Paradise Pool Service
9116 Sandalwood Ct, Stockton CA 95210-1517. 209/473-2134.

Clean Swim Pool Service
PO Box 41841, Sacramento CA 95841-0841. 916/334-5862.

Quality Plus Water Systems
4010 Moorpark Ave, San Jose CA 95117-4101. 408/241-3211.

Aquarium & Pond Maintenance Co.
373 Richmond Ave, San Jose CA 95128. 408/295-5643.

For more information on career opportunities in miscellaneous business services and non-scientific research:

Associations

AMERICAN SOCIETY OF APPRAISERS
P.O. Box 17265, Washington DC 20041. 703/478-2228. Toll-free number: 800/ASA-VALU. Fax: 703/742-8471. An international, nonprofit, independent appraisal organization.

EQUIPMENT LEASING ASSOCIATION OF AMERICA
1300 17th Street, Suite 1010, North Arlington VA 22209. 703/527-8655. World Wide Web address: http://www.elaonline.com.

NATIONAL ASSOCIATION OF PERSONNEL SERVICES
3133 Mt. Vernon Avenue, Alexandria VA 22305. 703/684-0180. Fax: 703/684-0071. Provides federal legislative protection, education, certification, and business products and services to its member employment service agencies.

CHARITIES AND SOCIAL SERVICES

The outlook for social service workers is better than average. In fact, opportunities for qualified applicants are expected to be excellent, partly due to the rapid turnover in the industry as a result of lower wages offered.

Note: Because of the high turnover rate and the continuous need for social services, the outlook for this industry has remained constant over the past few years.

AMERICAN CANCER SOCIETY
1710 Webster Street, Suite 210, Oakland CA 94612-3448. 510/893-7900. **Contact:** Human Resources. **Description:** A nonprofit cancer research organization which helps fund cancer research, public education, and direct help to patients, such as transportation to treatment and rehabilitation services.

AMERICAN RED CROSS
2731 North First Street, San Jose CA 95134-2029. 408/292-6242. **Contact:** Human Resources. **Description:** A humanitarian organization that aids disaster victims, gathers blood for distribution in crisis situations, and provides a variety of other social services. These services include training individuals to respond to emergencies, educating them on various diseases, and raising funds for other charitable organizations.

BOY SCOUTS OF AMERICA
970 West Julian, San Jose CA 95126. 408/280-5088. **Contact:** Human Resources. **Description:** Western regional office of the national scouting organization for young adults. The Boy Scouts of America has 340 local councils nationwide.

CATHOLIC CHARITIES
1000 Gravenstein Highway North, Sebastopol CA 95472-2814. 707/829-8424. **Contact:** Human Resources. **Description:** A network of private social service organizations which provides food, shelter, and clothing to more than 10 million poor and homeless people annually.

SAN JOSE JOB CORPS CENTER
3485 East Hills Drive, San Jose CA 95127. 408/254-5627. **Fax:** 408/254-5663. **Contact:** Human Resources Department. **Description:** Offers vocational and educational training for youths. **Common positions include:** Advisor; Counselor; Driver; Food and Beverage Service Worker; Licensed Practical Nurse; Maintenance Worker; Recreation Worker; Teacher. **Corporate headquarters location:** Rochester NY. **Number of employees at this location:** 200.

SIERRA CLUB
730 Polk Street, San Francisco CA 94109. 415/776-2211. **Recorded Jobline:** 415/978-9085. **Contact:** Human Resources Department. **Description:** A national, volunteer-based, environmental nonprofit company chiefly concerned with the maintenance and preservation of national natural resources, wildlife, and wildlands. **NOTE:** Applications are only accepted for available positions. **Common positions include:** Accountant/Auditor; Administrative Worker/Clerk; Computer Operator; Editor; Fundraising Specialist; Production Coordinator; Researcher. **Educational backgrounds**

include: Business Administration; Communications; Computer Science; Environmental Science; Journalism; Liberal Arts; Political Science. **Benefits:** Dental Insurance; Disability Coverage; Employee Discounts; Life Insurance; Medical Insurance; Pension Plan; Spending Account. **Corporate headquarters location:** This Location. **Operations at this facility include:** Administration; Communications; Publishing; Service.

THE UNITED WAY
50 California Street, Suite 200, San Francisco CA 94111-4696. 415/772-4300. **Contact:** Human Resources. **Description:** Through a vast network of volunteers and local charities, the United Way helps to meet the health and human-care needs of millions of people. The United Way includes approximately 1,900 community-based organizations.

Note: Because addresses and telephone numbers of smaller companies can change rapidly, we recommend you call each company to verify the information below before inquiring about job opportunities. Mass mailings are not recommended.

Additional small employers:

JOB TRAINING AND VOCATIONAL REHABILITATION SERVICES

Private Industry Council San Francisco
745 Franklin St # 400, San Francisco CA 94102-3228. 415/621-6853.

The Arc San Francisco
1500 Howard St, San Francisco CA 94103-2525. 415/255-7200.

Jewish Vocational Services
77 Geary St # 401, San Francisco CA 94108-5723. 415/391-3595.

Utility Workshop
598 Potrero Ave, San Francisco CA 94110-1432. 415/863-2620.

Cerebral Palsy Center
4500 Lincoln Ave, Oakland CA 94602-2532. 510/531-3323.

Hope Rehabilitation Services
4351 Lafayette St, Santa Clara CA 95054-1701. 408/748-2850.

Cooley Associates Counseling & Consultants
331 Hemsted Dr, Redding CA 96002-0910. 916/223-2208.

MISC. SOCIAL SERVICES

San Francisco Aids Foundation
25 Van Ness Ave Ste 660, San Francisco CA 94102-6033. 415/864-5855.

Catholic Charities of San Francisco County
814 Mission St # 6, San Francisco CA 94103-3018. 415/864-7400.

Golden Gate Regional Center
120 Howard St Fl 3, San Francisco CA 94105-1696. 415/546-9222.

Association For Retarded Citizens
4321 Ingot St, Fremont CA 94538-6455. 510/490-7777.

Economic Social Opportunities
1445 Oakland Rd, San Jose CA 95112. 408/971-0888.

City Team Ministries
2302 Zanker Rd Ofc, San Jose CA 95131-1137. 408/998-4770.

Catholic Charities AIDS/HIV Service
2350 Pacheco St, Concord CA 94520-2018. 510/825-8193.

Fresno County Economic Opportunities Commission
3120 W Nielsen Ave, Fresno CA 93706-1139. 209/486-6594.

American Cancer Society
4930 E Yale Ave, Fresno CA 93727-1517. 209/452-9770.

Progress Foundation
368 Fell St, San Francisco CA 94102-5144. 415/861-0828.

Rap Inc.
2730 Bryant St, San Francisco CA 94110-4226. 415/282-9984.

Shelter Network San Mateo County
319 Villa Ter, San Mateo CA 94401-2218. 415/340-8814.

Xanthos Inc.
1335 Park Ave, Alameda CA 94501-4511. 510/522-8363.

East Bay Regional Center
1800 Sutter St, Concord CA 94520-2563. 510/798-3001.

Contra Costa Special Olympics
1070 Concord Ave Ste 165, Concord CA 94520-5608. 510/602-1555.

Center For Counseling Education & Crisis Service
157 Main St, Pleasanton CA 94566-7320. 510/462-5544.

Adolescent Family Life Program
990 Broadway St, Vallejo CA 94590. 707/647-0470.

Fourteenth Street Medical Group Inc.
1124 E 14th St, Oakland CA 94606-4331. 510/533-0700.

East Bay Perinatal Council
654 13th St, Oakland CA 94612-1241. 510/452-3441.

Neighborhood House N Richmond
1442 York St, Richmond CA 94801-1847. 510/235-2643.

Neighborhood House
208 23rd St, Richmond CA 94804-1830. 510/233-1270.

Youth Advocates Inc.
4340 Redwood Hwy, San Rafael CA 94903-2104. 415/507-1590.

Cedars Development Foundation Marin
Bolinas Av & Upper Rd, Ross CA 94957. 415/454-5310.

Community Companions Inc.
11065 Monterey Hwy, Gilroy CA 95020. 408/848-1566.

The Bridge
15850 Concord Cir, Morgan Hill CA 95037-5451. 408/779-2113.

Children's Placement Service
210 High St, Santa Cruz CA 95060-3760. 408/457-8019.

Palomares Group Homes
1525 Seabright Ave, Santa Cruz CA 95062-2528. 408/457-1404.

Head Start
15 Madison St, Watsonville CA 95076. 408/724-3885.

Planned Parenthood
1691 The Alameda, San Jose CA 95126. 408/287-7532.

Valley Rehabilitation Industries
1103 N Aurora St, Stockton CA 95202. 209/948-2065.

American Friends Service Committee
445 W Weber Ave, Stockton CA 95203. 209/465-4265.

World Relief Corporation
829 Rosemarie Ln, Stockton CA 95207. 209/952-1414.

Heifer Project International
3906 Don Pedro Rd, Ceres CA 95307. 209/537-8996.

Community Hospice Inc.
601 McHenry Ave Ste C, Modesto CA 95350-5443. 209/577-0615.

Senior Center
490 N Harold St, Fort Bragg CA 95437-3331. 707/964-0443.

Social Advocates For Youth
670 W Napa St, Sonoma CA 95476-6437. 707/996-7991.

Arc Senior Services
3642 Taylor Rd, Loomis CA 95650-9998. 916/652-9218.

Association For Retarded Citizens
219 Estates Dr, Roseville CA 95678-2311. 916/783-5700.

Solano County-Headstart
66 Vine St, Vacaville CA 95688-9301. 707/446-6791.

International Rescue Committee
3000 T St Ste 204, Sacramento CA 95816-7052. 916/739-0122.

Sacramento Association For The Retarded
2100 21st St, Sacramento CA 95818-1708. 916/452-4743.

MV Transportation
4141 Power Inn Rd, Sacramento CA 95826-4335. 916/456-9600.

Walden Environment Inc.
3336 Bradshaw Rd, Sacramento CA 95827-2615. 916/366-1656.

For more information on career opportunities in charities and social services:

<u>Associations</u>

AMERICAN COUNCIL OF THE BLIND
1155 15th Street NW, Suite 720, Washington DC 20005. 202/467-5081. World Wide Web address: http://www.acb.org. Membership. Offers an annual conference, a monthly magazine, and scholarships.

CATHOLIC CHARITIES USA
1731 King Street, Suite 200, Alexandria VA 22314. 703/549-1390. Membership.

FAMILY SERVICE ASSOCIATION OF AMERICA
11700 West Lake Park Drive, Park Place, Milwaukee WI 53224. 414/359-1040. Membership.

NATIONAL COUNCIL ON FAMILY RELATIONS
3989 Central Avenue NE, Suite 550, Minneapolis MN 55421. 612/781-9331. Fax: 612/781-9348. Membership. Publishes two quarterly journals. Offers an annual conference and newsletters.

NATIONAL FEDERATION OF SOCIETIES FOR CLINICAL SOCIAL WORK, INC.
P.O. Box 3740, Arlington VA 22203. 703/522-3866. A lobbying organization. Offers newsletters and a conference every two years to membership organizations.

NATIONAL FEDERATION OF THE BLIND
1800 Johnson Street, Baltimore MD 21230. 410/659-9314. World Wide Web address: http://www.nfb.org. Membership of 50,000 in 600 local chapters. Publishes a monthly magazine.

NATIONAL MULTIPLE SCLEROSIS SOCIETY
733 Third Avenue, New York NY 10017. 212/986-3240. Toll-free: 800/344-4867. World Wide Web address: http://www.nmss.org. Publishes a quarterly magazine.

NATIONAL ORGANIZATION FOR HUMAN SERVICE EDUCATION
Brookdale Community College, Newman Springs Road, Lyncroft NJ 07738. 908/842-1900, ext. 546.

CHEMICALS/RUBBER AND PLASTICS

First the good news: Overall growth in the chemical industry is on the upswing. Chemical products and services are currently in high demand, thus creating a need for more workers, and recent price increases are holding steady.

Now the bad news: Costs for pollution reduction are rising. Factories are running at 85 percent capacity, and if companies increase spending on plant and equipment, an oversupply could result if economic growth slows too quickly.

Growth prospects for the domestic synthetic rubber industry remain mixed, reflecting the industry's dependence on tire manufacturing. The tire industry shows signs of stabilizing after undergoing a period characterized by massive restructuring, the effects of recession in the domestic market, and consistently high levels of imports.

In the plastics industry, greater reliance on computer-aided design and manufacturing is expected in the last half of the 1990s, as production is streamlined. These measures will be aimed at strengthening the industry's competitiveness in the areas of quality control and improved client relations.

ALLIEDSIGNAL, INC.
3500 Garrett Drive, Santa Clara CA 95054. 408/562-0300. **Contact:** Human Resources. **Description:** Manufactures industrial chemicals. **Parent company:** AlliedSignal Corporation serves a broad spectrum of industries through more than 40 strategic businesses, which are grouped into three sectors: Aerospace, Automotive, and Engineered Materials.

BOC GASES
2389 Lincoln Avenue, Hayward CA 94545. 510/786-2611. **Contact:** Jill Clark, Regional Sales Manager. **Description:** A manufacturer of industrial gases, electronic gases, medical gases, and cryogenic equipment. This facility primarily produces industrial specialty gases. **Common positions include:** Manufacturer's/Wholesaler's Sales Rep.; Mechanical Engineer. **Educational backgrounds include:** Chemistry; Engineering; Marketing. **Benefits:** Dental Insurance; Disability Coverage; Life Insurance; Medical Insurance; Pension Plan; Profit Sharing; Savings Plan; Tuition Assistance. **Corporate headquarters location:** Murray Hill NJ. **Operations at this facility include:** Administration; Regional Headquarters.

BIO-RAD LABORATORIES
1000 Alfred Noble Drive, Hercules CA 94547. 510/724-7000. **Contact:** Dick Anderson, Human Resources Manager. **Description:** Develops, manufactures, and markets diagnostic test kits, specialty chemicals, and related equipment used for separating complex mixtures. The company also produces sophisticated analytical instrumentation used to detect and measure chemical components in minute quantities, as well as products for electron microscopy. **Common positions include:** Accountant/Auditor; Advertising Clerk; Biological Scientist/Biochemist; Biomedical Engineer; Buyer; Chemical Engineer; Chemist; Computer Programmer; Customer Service Representative; Department Manager; Electrical/Electronics Engineer; Financial Analyst; General

Manager; Human Resources Specialist; Mechanical Engineer; Medical Records Technician; Medical Technologist; Operations/Production Manager; Purchasing Agent and Manager; Quality Control Supervisor; Systems Analyst; Transportation/Traffic Specialist. **Educational backgrounds include:** Accounting; Biology; Business Administration; Chemistry; Computer Science; Engineering; Finance; Marketing; Mathematics. **Benefits:** Dental Insurance; Disability Coverage; Life Insurance; Medical Insurance; Pension Plan; Profit Sharing; Savings Plan; Tuition Assistance. **Corporate headquarters location:** This Location. **Operations at this facility include:** Administration; Divisional Headquarters; Manufacturing; Research and Development; Service. **Listed on:** American Stock Exchange.

BURKE INDUSTRIES
2250 South 10th Street, San Jose CA 95112. 408/297-3500. **Contact:** Anne Howe, Personnel Director. **Description:** Burke Industries is a producer of natural and synthetic rubber products.

DEXTER CORPORATION
PACKAGING PRODUCTS DIVISION
31500 Hayman Street, Hayward CA 94544-7120. 510/471-7171. **Contact:** Human Resources. **Description:** Dexter is a diverse manufacturing company whose primary products include chemical and medical products. The company is also involved in molecular biology research items, as well as electronic, automotive, food packaging, and aerospace products. Subsidiaries of Dexter Corporation produce coatings and wall coverings.

DUNN-EDWARDS CORPORATION
2201 Junipero Serra, Davis City CA 94015. 415/992-9660. **Contact:** Human Resources Department. **Description:** Dunn-Edwards Corporation is a manufacturer and seller of paint.

FLINT INK
750 Gilman Street, Berkeley CA 94710. 510/525-1188. **Contact:** Human Resources. **Description:** Manufactures printing and other inks.

HOLTZ RUBBER
P.O. Box 241002, Lodi CA 95241. 209/368-7171. **Contact:** Personnel. **Description:** Produces a wide range of molded, extruded, and hand-fabricated rubber products, tires, and related items.

ICI AMERICAS
1200 South 47th Street, Richmond CA 94804. 510/231-1000. **Contact:** Human Resources. **Description:** A chemical manufacturing plant, wholly-owned by Imperial Chemical Industries plc of London England is one of the top four chemical companies in the world. Products include a broad line of pharmaceuticals, agricultural chemicals, plastics, polyester films, paints, specialty chemicals, dyes and colorants, advanced materials/composites, fibers, security devices, and aerospace components. This facility produces industrial inorganic chemicals.

KELLY-MOORE PAINT COMPANY
987 Commercial Street, San Carlos CA 94070. 415/592-8337. **Contact:** Ms. Samme Ripley, Human Resources. **Description:** Manufactures a wide variety of interior and exterior paints. **Corporate headquarters location:** This Location.

RO-LAB AMERICAN RUBBER COMPANY INC.
P.O. Box 450, Tracy CA 95376. 209/836-0965. **Contact:** John Dodge, Vice President. **Description:** Produces a wide range of rubber products, gaskets, and seals for mechanical and industrial uses.

ROCHESTER MIDLAND CORPORATION
1905 Dennison Street, Oakland CA 94606-5208. 510/535-1700. **Contact:** Human Resources. **Description:** A chemical company.

SANDOZ AGRO, INC.
975 California Avenue, Palo Alto CA 94304. 415/857-1130. **Contact:** Human Resources. **Description:** Engaged in the production and marketing of industrial agricultural chemicals. **Common positions include:** Biological Scientist/Biochemist; Chemist. **Corporate headquarters location:** Des Plaines IL. **Parent company:** Sandoz, Inc. **Operations at this facility include:** Research and Development.

THE SHERWIN-WILLIAMS COMPANY INC.
WEST AREA OFFICE
1450 Sherwin Avenue, Emeryville CA 94608. 510/420-7232. **Contact:** Roy Haney, Human Resources Manager. **Description:** This location is a support office for area stores, and primarily manufactures emulsion paints. Overall, Sherwin-Williams operates internationally in six segments: Retail Stores, Coatings, Chemicals, Packaging Products, Specialty Products, and International. Products include Sherwin-Williams, Dutch Boy, Martin Seymour, Baltimore, and Kem paints, as well as such related packaging products as paint cans, sprays, and labels. The Sherwin-Williams labeled architectural and industrial coatings are sold through approximately 2,000 co-owned specialty paint and wall covering stores located in 48 states. Coatings are produced for original equipment manufacturers in various industries, as well as for the automobile aftermarket, the industrial maintenance market, and the traffic paint market. **Common positions include:** Accountant/Auditor; Administrative Worker/Clerk; Blue-Collar Worker Supervisor; Buyer; Chemist; Customer Service Representative; Department Manager; Electrical/Electronics Engineer; Financial Analyst; General Manager; Human Resources Specialist; Manufacturer's/Wholesaler's Sales Rep.; Mechanical Engineer; Operations/Production Manager; Quality Control Supervisor. **Educational backgrounds include:** Accounting; Business Administration; Chemistry; Communications; Engineering; Finance; Liberal Arts; Marketing; Mathematics. **Benefits:** Dental Insurance; Disability Coverage; Employee Discounts; Life Insurance; Medical Insurance; Pension Plan; Profit Sharing; Savings Plan; Tuition Assistance. **Special Programs:** Internships. **Corporate headquarters location:** Cleveland OH. **Operations at this facility include:** Administration; Manufacturing; Research and Development; Sales; Service. **Listed on:** New York Stock Exchange.

UNITED TECHNOLOGIES CORPORATION
CHEMICAL SYSTEMS DIVISION
P.O. Box 49028, San Jose CA 95161-9028. 408/779-9121. **Fax:** 408/776-5789. **Contact:** Barbara A. Cyr, Senior Human Resources Representative. **Description:** Chemicals division of the diversified industrial company. Overall, United Technologies Corporation provides high-technology products and support services to customers in the aerospace, building, military, and automotive industries worldwide. Products include large jet engines, temperature control systems, elevators and escalators, helicopters, and flight systems. The company markets its products under a variety of brand names including Carrier, Hamilton Standard, Otis, Pratt & Whitney, and Sikorsky. Production

facilities are located in the U.S., Latin America, Mexico, Canada, Australia, Europe, and Asia. **Common positions include:** Accountant/Auditor; Aerospace Engineer; Budget Analyst; Buyer; Ceramics Engineer; Chemical Engineer; Computer Systems Analyst; Draftsperson; Electrical/Electronics Engineer; Electrician; Financial Analyst; Geologist/Geophysicist; Human Resources Specialist; Materials Engineer; Mechanical Engineer; Metallurgical Engineer; Science Technologist; Structural Engineer. **Educational backgrounds include:** Accounting; Chemistry; Computer Science; Economics; Engineering; Finance; Mathematics. **Benefits:** 401(k); Dental Insurance; Disability Coverage; Employee Discounts; Life Insurance; Medical Insurance; Pension Plan; Savings Plan; Tuition Assistance. **Special Programs:** Internships. **Corporate headquarters location:** West Palm FL. **Operations at this facility include:** Administration; Manufacturing; Regional Headquarters; Research and Development. **Listed on:** New York Stock Exchange. **Number of employees at this location:** 1,100.

WESTEC PLASTICS CORPORATION
2044 Concourse Drive, San Jose CA 95131. 408/432-6161. **Contact:** Personnel Department. **Description:** Engaged in plastic injection molding for a variety of original equipment manufacturers.

ZEP MANUFACTURING COMPANY
297 Corzin Avenue, Santa Clara CA 95051. 408/739-3656. **Contact:** Human Resources. **Description:** A manufacturer of specialty chemical products such as soaps, waxes, disinfectants, detergents, and insecticides. There are 42 branches nationwide. The company also operates in 15 foreign countries.

Note: *Because addresses and telephone numbers of smaller companies can change rapidly, we recommend you call each company to verify the information below before inquiring about job opportunities. Mass mailings are not recommended.*

Additional small employers:

ALKALIES AND CHLORINE

All Pure Chemical Co.
PO Box 268, Tracy CA 95378-0268. 209/835-5423.

INDUSTRIAL INORGANIC CHEMICALS

Garratt-Callahan Co.
111 Rollins Rd, Millbrae CA 94030-3114. 415/697-5811.

Imperial West Chemical Co. Inc.
2151 Wilbur Ave, Antioch CA 94509-8509. 510/757-8230.

Criterion Catalyst Co. Lp
2850 Willow Pass Rd, Pittsburg CA 94565-3237. 510/458-7200.

General Chemical Corp.
PO Box 1712, Richmond CA 94802-0712. 510/232-7193.

AGRICULTURAL CHEMICALS

Grace Sierra Horticultural
1001 Yosemite Dr, Milpitas CA 95035. 408/263-8080.

Moyer Products Inc.
PO Box 5434, Fresno CA 93755-5434. 209/226-4664.

ADHESIVES AND SEALANTS

Henkel Adhesives Corp.
25817 Clawiter Rd, Hayward CA 94545-3217. 510/786-3700.

INDUSTRIAL ORGANIC CHEMICALS

EI Du Pont De Nemours
PO Box 310, Antioch CA 94509-0903. 510/757-1210.

CHEMICALS AND CHEMICAL PREPARATIONS

Morton International Inc.
7380 Morton Ave, Newark CA 94560-4200. 510/797-2281.

Asbury Graphite Inc.
2855 Franklin Canyon Rd, Rodeo CA 94572-2116. 510/799-3636.

TIRES AND INNER TUBES

Thompson Aerospace
160 Beacon St, San Francisco CA 94131-2628. 415/589-3030.

RUBBER PRODUCTS

O'Neill Inc.
2090 Evans Ave, San Francisco CA 94124-1023. 415/826-9091.

Performance Elastomers Division
326 E Warren Ave, Fremont CA 94539-7966. 510/651-2022.

Boyd Corporation
6630 Owens Dr, Pleasanton CA 94588-3334. 510/463-2760.

PW Pipe
PO Box 386, Cameron Park CA 95682. 916/677-2286.

UNSUPPORTED PLASTICS PRODUCTS

Kennerley-Spratling Inc.
2116 Farallon Dr, San Leandro CA 94577-6604. 510/351-8230.

PLASTICS PRODUCTS

Apache Plastics LP
2050 East Fremont St, Stockton CA 95205. 209/466-4356.

Carlon Lamson & Sessions
PO Box 2027, Woodland CA 95776-2027. 916/666-1683.

Harrington Industrial Plastics
4680 Pell Drive, Sacramento CA 95838. 916/920-5392.

Tap Plastics Inc. Packaging
2323 C Street, Sacramento CA 95816-3023. 916/442-7940.

Wade Manufacturing Company
2851 E Florence Ave, Fresno CA 93721-3407. 209/485-7170.

Dow Chemical Co. Continental Operations
4787 East Date Avenue, Fresno CA 93725-2102. 209/488-7600.

Trans Western Polymers Inc.
6645 Las Positas Rd, Livermore CA 94550-0207. 510/449-7800.

American Poly-Therm Company
PO Box 100, Lincoln CA 95648-0100. 916/645-3900.

CHEMICALS AND ALLIED PRODUCTS WHOLESALE

Helena Chemical Company
2589 North Air Fresno Drive, Fresno CA 93727-1554. 209/453-9385.

Baychem
234 Marshall St, Redwood City CA 94063-1550. 415/369-5102.

LDR
274 Harbor Way, South San Francisco CA 94080-6816. 415/872-1400.

Altar Gases & Equipment
4000 Executive Parkway Suite 520, San Ramon CA 94583-4256. 510/277-2100.

Dow Chemical USA
1676 North California Boulevard, Walnut Creek CA 94596. 510/930-6400.

Brulin Corporation
2775 Giant Road, Richmond CA 94806. 510/233-9012.

Great Western Chemical
520 Zephyr Street, Stockton CA 95206-4201. 209/982-5781.

Atochem North America
1144 Boole Road, Applegate CA 95703. 916/878-0570.

Mock Resources Northwest
6601 Koll Center Parkway, Pleasanton CA 94566-3112. 510/426-7176.

Air Products and Chemicals Inc.
151 North Sunrise Avenue, Roseville CA 95661-2924. 916/786-9100.

Airco Gas and Gear
1397 Colusa Highway, Yuba City CA 95993-9092. 916/673-8591.

Better Living Products
5357 Calderwood Ln, San Jose CA 95118-2903. 408/264-9279.

Descale-It Products Company
401 Wainwright Ave, San Jose CA 95128-2164. 408/279-0635.

Austin Powder Co.
3872 Bithell Ln, Suisun City CA 94585-9736. 707/429-8502.

ETI Explosives Products
2901 State Highway 16, Plymouth CA 95669-9723. 209/245-6977.

For more information on career opportunities in the chemicals/rubber and plastics industries:

Associations

AMERICAN ASSOCIATION FOR CLINICAL CHEMISTRY
2101 L Street NW, Suite 202, Washington DC 20037-1526. 202/857-0717 or 800/892-1400. International scientific/medical society of individuals involved with clinical chemistry and other clinical labscience-related disciplines.

AMERICAN CHEMICAL SOCIETY
Career Services, 1155 16th Street NW, Washington DC 20036. 202/872-4600. World Wide Web address: http://www.acs.org.

AMERICAN INSTITUTE OF CHEMICAL ENGINEERS
345 East 47th Street, New York NY 10017. 212/705-7338 or 800/242-4363. World Wide Web address: http://www.aiche.org. Provides leadership in advancing the chemical engineering profession as it meets the needs of society.

AMERICAN INSTITUTE OF CHEMISTS, INC.
7315 Wisconsin Avenue, Suite 502 E, Bethesda MD 20814. 301/652-2447. A professional organization supporting the social, economic, and career objectives of the individual scientist.

CHEMICAL MANAGEMENT & RESOURCES ASSOCIATION
60 Bay Street, Suite 702, Staten Island NY 10301. 718/876-8800. Fax: 718/720-4666. Engaged in marketing, marketing research, business development, and planning for the chemical and allied process industries. Provides technical meetings, educational programs, and publications to members.

CHEMICAL MANUFACTURERS ASSOCIATION
2501 M Street NW, Washington DC 20037. 202/887-1100. World Wide Web address: http://www.cmahq.com. A trade association that develops and implements programs and services and advocates public policy that benefits the industry and society.

THE ELECTROCHEMICAL SOCIETY
10 South Main Street, Pennington NJ 08534-2896. An international educational society dealing with electrochemical issues. Also publishes monthly journals.

SOAP AND DETERGENT ASSOCIATION
475 Park Avenue South, 27th Floor, New York NY 10016. 212/725-1262. A trade association and research center.

SOCIETY OF PLASTICS ENGINEERS
14 Fairfield Drive, P.O. Box 403, Brookfield CT 06804-0403. 203/775-0471. World Wide Web address: http://www.bbsnet.com/spe. Dedicated to helping members attain higher professional status through increased scientific, engineering, and technical knowledge.

THE SOCIETY OF THE PLASTICS INDUSTRY, INC.
1275 K Street NW, Suite 400, Washington DC 20005. 202/371-5200. Promotes the development of the plastics industry and enhances public understanding of its contributions while meeting the needs of society.

Directories

CHEMICAL INDUSTRY DIRECTORY
State Mutual Book and Periodical Service, Order Department, 17th Floor, 521 5th Avenue, New York NY 10175. 516/537-1104.

CHEMICALS DIRECTORY
Cahners Publishing, 275 Washington Street, Newton MA 02158. 617/964-3030.

DIRECTORY OF CHEMICAL ENGINEERING CONSULTANTS
American Institute of Chemical Engineering, 345 East 47th Street, New York NY 10017. 212/705-7338.

DIRECTORY OF CHEMICAL PRODUCERS
SRI International, 333 Ravenswood Avenue, Menlo Park CA 94025. 415/326-6200.

Magazines

CHEMICAL & ENGINEERING NEWS
American Chemical Society, 1155 16th Street NW, Washington DC 20036. 202/872-4600.

CHEMICAL MARKETING REPORTER
Schnell Publishing Company, 80 Brot Street,

23rd Floor, New York NY 10004. 212/248-4177.

CHEMICAL PROCESSING
Putnam Publishing Company, 301 East Erie Street, Chicago IL 60611. 312/644-2020.

CHEMICAL WEEK
888 7th Avenue, 26th Floor, New York NY 10106. 212/621-4900.

COMMUNICATIONS: TELECOMMUNICATIONS AND BROADCASTING

The telecommunications and broadcasting industries are poised on the edge of a revolution. At long last, Congress has deregulated the telecommunications industry, allowing long-distance carriers, local phone companies, and cable TV operators to get into each other's businesses. For the first time, consumers will be able to choose their local phone company, and that company will probably also provide them with their cable hookups.

Business in the telecommunications industry has been booming even without deregulation. The industry continues to break new ground and reach more customers, especially in wireless phone service. However, the industry has been shaken by recent layoffs at AT&T.

In broadcasting, competition is high, especially for high-profile positions such as newscasters and DJs. In television, the hottest industry is cable. Cable companies are rapidly expanding, and opportunities for technical workers are growing. In radio, syndicated radio shows are tearing up the airwaves. Larger stations with more money, more experience, and bigger names are producing shows which smaller stations are picking up to save money. This increase in syndication will lead to continued competition in the radio industry.

ACCUGRAPH CORPORATION
4155-F El Camino Way, Palo Alto CA 94306. 415/857-1629. **Contact:** Human Resources. **Description:** Accugraph Corporation develops and supports computer-based software products and manages graphic information, focusing primarily on applications in the areas of telecommunications, facilities management, and computer network management. Accugraph's products originally served the needs of engineers, architects, planners, and manufacturers for computer-aided design and computer-aided manufacturing software applications. The company's business has since evolved to also serve high-growth markets such as telecommunications, computer network management, and facilities management. The company produces and markets its proprietary software products for operation on third-party platforms. The integrated systems which are created are used by the company's customers to automate telecommunications applications and provide related services to manage computer networks and for facilities management. The company's largest customers, segmented by application, are Northern Telecom (telecommunications), BellSouth (computer network management), and Hewlett-Packard (worldwide facilities management). **Corporate headquarters location:** El Paso TX.

AIR TOUCH COMMUNICATIONS
2785 Mitchell Drive, MS 9-1, Walnut Creek CA 94598. 510/210-3547. **Contact:** Robert Graves, Technical Recruiter. **Description:** Air Touch Communications provides cellular telephone and paging services. **Common positions include:** Computer Engineer; Electrical/Electronics Engineer; Software Engineer; Telecommunications Analyst. **Parent company:** PacTel Corporation. **Other area locations:** 2999 Oak Road, Walnut Creek CA 94596.

AIR TOUCH COMMUNICATIONS
2999 Oak Road, Walnut Creek CA 94596. **Contact:** Human Resources Department. **Description:** Air Touch Communications provides cellular telephone and paging services. **Parent company:** PacTel Corporation.

ALLIED TELESIS, INC.
950 Kiser Road, Sunnyvale CA 94086. 415/964-2771. **Contact:** Human Resources. **Description:** Allied Telesis, Inc. manufactures connectors and repeaters for communications networks. **Common positions include:** Computer Programmer; Network Engineer.

APPLIED SIGNAL TECHNOLOGY
400 West California Avenue, Sunnyvale CA 94086. 408/749-1888. **Fax:** 408/738-1928. **Contact:** Human Resources. **Description:** Applied Signal Technology designs, develops, manufactures, and markets signal reconnaissance equipment to collect and process telecommunications signals. The equipment is purchased by the U.S. government for foreign signal reconnaissance. **Common positions include:** Communications Engineer; Electrical/Electronics Engineer; Mechanical Engineer; Nurse; Telecommunications Analyst.

ASCEND COMMUNICATIONS, INC.
1275 Harbor Bay Parkway, Alameda CA 94502. 510/769-6001. **Fax:** 510/814-2300. **Contact:** Human Resources. **Description:** Ascend Communications, Inc. develops, manufactures, markets, sells, and supports a broad range of high-speed digital wide area network access products that enable its customers to build videoconferencing networks; remote LAN access networks that provide remote offices, telecommuters, and mobile computer users access to corporate backbone networks; and voice, video, and data integrated access networks. These products establish high-speed switched digital connections whose bandwidth, duration, and destination can be adjusted to suit user application needs. The company has three bandwidth-on-demand product families, each of which is focused on a major application segment: multiband products for videoconferencing access, pipeline products for remote LAN access, and MAX products for voice, video, and data integrated access. These products support a wide variety of application interfaces, cabling systems, switched digital services, and digital access line types. This wide range of connectivity and interoperability options significantly increases the number of corporate sites that can benefit from bandwidth-on-demand networking. **Corporate headquarters location:** This Location. **Number of employees at this location:** 80.

ASPECT TELECOMMUNICATIONS CORPORATION
1730 Fox Drive, San Jose CA 95131. 408/441-2200. **Fax:** 408/441-2260. **Contact:** Human Resources. **Description:** Aspect Telecommunications Corporation develops, manufactures, and supports call transaction processing systems, intelligent call control, and management systems that can improve customer service and reduce operating costs for firms handling high volumes of telephone sales or inquiries. **Common positions include:** Accountant/Auditor; Electrical/Electronics Engineer; Financial Analyst; Telecommunications Analyst.

AYDIN CORPORATION WEST
30 Great Oaks Boulevard, San Jose CA 95119. 408/629-0100. **Fax:** 408/224-5592. **Contact:** Human Resources Department. **Description:** Aydin Corporation West manufactures broadcasting equipment.

CALIFORNIA MICROWAVE, INC.
555 Twin Dolphin Drive, Redwood City CA 94605. 408/732-4000. **Contact:** Personnel. **Description:** California Microwave, Inc. designs, develops, manufactures, and markets electronic communications equipment and systems for commercial and defense applications. Customers of California Microwave include telecommunications and satellite common carriers, the U.S. government, private service networks, and foreign governments. **Common positions include:** Accountant/Auditor; Administrator; Buyer; Computer Programmer; Customer Service Representative; Department Manager; Draftsperson; Electrical/ Electronics Engineer; Financial Analyst; General Manager; Human Resources Specialist; Marketing Specialist; Mechanical Engineer; Operations/Production Manager; Quality Control Supervisor; Sales Representative; Technical Writer/Editor. **Educational backgrounds include:** Accounting; Business Administration; Communications; Computer Science; Economics; Engineering; Finance; Marketing; Mathematics; Physics. **Benefits:** Dental Insurance; Disability Coverage; Employee Discounts; Life Insurance; Medical Insurance; Profit Sharing; Savings Plan; Tuition Assistance. **Corporate headquarters location:** This Location. **Operations at this facility include:** Administration; Manufacturing; Research and Development; Sales; Service.

CAPITAL CITIES/ABC
KGO-TV
900 Front Street, San Francisco CA 94111. 415/954-7778. **Contact:** Kathryn Cox, KGO-TV Personnel Representative. **Description:** This location is the San Francisco affiliate of the major television company. Capital Cities/ABC operates TV and radio stations, provides warehousing services, and owns advertising agencies. **Benefits:** Dental Insurance; Disability Coverage; Employee Discounts; Life Insurance; Medical Insurance; Pension Plan; Profit Sharing; Savings Plan; Tuition Assistance. **Corporate headquarters location:** New York NY.

CENTIGRAM COMMUNICATIONS CORPORATION
91 East Tasman Drive, San Jose CA 95134. 408/944-0250. **Fax:** 408/428-3732. **Contact:** Human Resources Department. **Description:** Centigram Communications Corporation designs, manufactures, and markets communications systems which enable users to access and interact with a broad range of information in a variety of formats -- including voice, text, data, e-mail, and facsimile -- from a touch-tone telephone. Centigram Communications' applications, such as voice messaging, facsimile store-and-forward, and interactive voice response, are integrated on the company's Adaptive Information Processing platform, a communication server that is based on industry-standard hardware and software. **Common positions include:** Computer Programmer; Computer Systems Analyst; Electrical/Electronics Engineer; Software Engineer. **Educational backgrounds include:** Engineering. **Benefits:** 401(k); Dental Insurance; Disability Coverage; Life Insurance; Medical Insurance; Pension Plan; Profit Sharing; Savings Plan; Tuition Assistance. **Corporate headquarters location:** This Location. **Operations at this facility include:** Administration; Divisional Headquarters; Manufacturing; Research and Development; Sales. **Listed on:** NASDAQ. **Number of employees at this location:** 400.

CIDCO INC.
220 Cochrane Circle, Morgan Hill CA 95037. 408/779-1162. **Fax:** 408/779-3106. **Contact:** Human Resources. **Description:** CIDCO Inc. designs, develops, and markets subscriber telephone equipment that supports intelligent network services being introduced by telephone operating companies. The company's first area of focus has been

Caller ID, a service that allows subscribers to view the telephone number and name of the calling party before the call is answered. The company's Caller ID products connect directly into subscriber's telephone lines, receive complex network signaling and display call information on a liquid crystal display. The company has developed or is currently developing several new products for existing and future telephone services, including a family of intelligent feature telephones. **Corporate headquarters location:** This Location.

COMPRESSION LABS, INC.
2860 Junction Avenue, San Jose CA 95134. 408/435-3000. **Contact:** Human Resources Department. **Description:** Compression Labs, Inc. (CLI) is a recognized leader in video communications. As a pioneer of compressed digital video technology, Compression Labs, Inc. manufactures and markets a wide variety of video communications products that allow people at different locations to see and interact with one another in a natural, intuitive manner. CLI's Videoconferencing Products Group supplies group systems and desktop solutions to organizations in the industries of business, government, and education. The company's installed base totals more than 10,000 systems, representing more than 20 percent of the worldwide market. CLI's Broadcast Products Group provides a broad range of digital video systems for the entertainment, business television, and distance learning markets. These systems include encoders and decoders for applications such as direct broadcast satellite, video-on-demand, and cable television program distribution. **Corporate headquarters location:** This Location.

DANTEL, INC.
P.O. Box 55013, Fresno CA 93747-5013. 209/292-1111. **Fax:** 209/292-9355. **Contact:** Stephanie Thiessen, Human Resources Manager. **Description:** Dantel, Inc. is a telecommunications equipment manufacturer. **Common positions include:** Accountant/Auditor; Blue-Collar Worker Supervisor; Buyer; Computer Programmer; Computer Systems Analyst; Customer Service Representative; Draftsperson; Electrical/Electronics Engineer; Financial Analyst; Manufacturer's/Wholesaler's Sales Rep.; Mechanical Engineer; Operations/Production Manager; Purchasing Agent and Manager; Quality Control Supervisor; Software Engineer; Technical Writer/Editor; Wholesale and Retail Buyer. **Educational backgrounds include:** Accounting; Business Administration; Computer Science; Engineering; Finance; Marketing. **Benefits:** 401(k); Dental Insurance; EAP; Employee Discounts; Life Insurance; Medical Insurance; Tuition Assistance; Vision Insurance. **Corporate headquarters location:** This Location. **Operations at this facility include:** Administration; Manufacturing; Research and Development; Sales; Service. **Listed on:** Privately held. **Number of employees at this location:** 150.

DIGITAL LINK CORPORATION
217 Humboldt Court, Sunnyvale CA 94089. 408/745-6200. **Fax:** 408/745-6250. **Contact:** Human Resources. **Description:** Digital Link was founded in May 1985 to develop, manufacture, and market high-speed digital access products for the WAN (wide area networks) marketplace. The company provides DSU/CSU (Digital Service Units/Channel Service Units) and inverse multiplexer products; and SMDS (Switched Multimegabit Data Service), ATM, and its Encore family of enhanced T1/E1 and Prelude access products. The multiplexer takes low-speed inputs and concentrates them onto one high-speed T1 line; the inverse multiplexer reverses the process. The Encore family presents the user with T1 access solutions, including a T1/E1 port for digitized voice or video, enabling efficient line utilization. The company markets its products primarily through a direct sales force, value-added resellers, and original equipment manufacturers.

In addition to six sales offices in the United States, the company has two international offices in the United Kingdom and Germany. **Corporate headquarters location:** This Location.

DIGITAL MICROWAVE CORPORATION
170 Rose Orchard Way, San Jose CA 95134. 408/943-0777. **Fax:** 408/944-1678. **Contact:** Human Resources. **Description:** Digital Microwave Corporation designs, manufactures, and markets advanced, high-performance digital microwave radios and other short- and medium-haul communications products for use in cellular telephone systems, private networks, and other wireless telecommunications applications worldwide. Digital Microwave Corporation's products are capable of transmitting and receiving multiple digital lines, carrying voice, data, and video signals, up to a total capacity of 45 megabits per second. The company's comprehensive family of technologically advanced transmission products is designed to be highly reliable, and easily installed and maintained. The company has regional sales and service headquarters in the United Kingdom, Singapore, and San Jose, with additional sales offices in Asia, Europe, Latin America, and North America. **Corporate headquarters location:** This Location.

EXECUTONE INFORMATION SYSTEMS, INC.
850 Dubuque Avenue, South San Francisco CA 94080-1804. 415/952-2000. **Contact:** Human Resources. **Description:** Executone Information Systems, Inc. designs, manufactures, and supports voice processing and health care communications systems, including call center management, telephone systems, locator systems, videoconferencing, health care communications, and network and data services. Brand names include EXECUTONE, INFOSTAR, IDS, LIFESAVER, and INFOSTAR/ILS. Products are marketed throughout the country via a network of direct sales, service offices, and independent distributors, located nationwide. Foreign sales and service offices are located in Argentina, Brazil, Canada, Dominican Republic, Hong Kong, Indonesia, Israel, Japan, Mexico, Singapore, Thailand, United Kingdom, Uruguay, and Venezuela. **Corporate headquarters location:** Milford CT. **Number of employees nationwide:** 2,400.

FIRST PACIFIC NETWORKS
871 Fox Lane, San Jose CA 95131. 408/943-7600. **Fax:** 408/943-7666. **Contact:** Human Resources. **Description:** First Pacific Networks, Inc. supplies equipment for two-way communications over hybrid fiber/coaxial cable networks. FPN is currently marketing two products: the FPN1000 System, which integrates telephony services into cable television-type networks. The North American version of the FPN1000 is being marketed as a way for cable operators to generate new revenues from their networks. It is also being offered to telephone companies who are interested in using broadband solutions to serve their customers. The international version of the product, the FPN1000i, is being marketed as a cost-effective way to provide digital telephone systems to small business customers. Using this integrated approach, these network operators can position themselves to provide a full range of telecommunications services, including video and data communications without building separate networks. PowerView is a wide-area communications system that enables electric utilities to reduce costs on power generation, transmission, and distribution facilities. This is achieved by offering a real-time, two-way data exchange with residential and small business customers allowing them to automatically take advantage of more attractive off-peak rates. PowerView can

also lower a utility's operational costs through customer-controlled load management, automated distribution operations, and improved customer service. Like the FPN1000, PowerView operates using cable television-like networks. PowerView is being marketed chiefly to electric utilities in the U.S. Both products consist of three main components: a microprocessor-based device that resides at the home or business, providing access to the cable network; and two products at the headend, central office, or utility substation that provide communications access and monitoring between the cable network and other networks, such as the public-switched telephone network or a private computer network. **Common positions include:** Design Engineer; Hardware Engineer; Software Engineer. **Educational backgrounds include:** Engineering. **Benefits:** 401(k); Dental Insurance; Disability Coverage; Life Insurance; Medical Insurance; Savings Plan; Stock Purchase. **Corporate headquarters location:** This Location. **Operations at this facility include:** Administration; Research and Development; Sales; Service. **Listed on:** NASDAQ. **Annual sales/revenues:** $5 - $10 million. **Number of employees at this location:** 135. **Number of employees nationwide:** 140.

FORE SYSTEMS
2115 O'Nell Drive, San Jose CA 95134-2134. 408/955-9000. **Fax:** 408/955-9500. **Contact:** Human Resources. **Description:** Founded in 1987, Fore Systems (which formerly operated under the name ATLANTEC Corporation) develops, manufactures, and markets a family of high-bandwidth intelligent switching hubs that enable users to optimize their existing investments in Ethernet and Fiber Distributed Data Interface (FDDI) technology. The company's flagship product, the PowerHub Intelligent Switching Hub, employs a unique Shared Memory Architecture to provide an innovative approach to reducing the bandwidth. The PowerHub family offers users as many as 240 independent Ethernet channels which can be used to segment a single Ethernet into smaller groups of users, or to deliver a full 10 megabits per second (Mbps) of bandwidth to a high-performance user or server. This capability offers users an exponential increase in bandwidth over solutions which share a single 10 Mbps channel among multiple users. The PowerHub can also provide up to sixteen 100 Mbps FDDI connections, 100 Mbps Ethernet connections, full-duplex Ethernet support, and ATM connections for bandwidth-hungry servers, workstations, and other enterprise bridges and routers. **Corporate headquarters location:** This Location. **Number of employees at this location:** 70.

FRIDEN NEOPOST
30955 Huntwood Avenue, Hayward CA 94544. 510/489-6800. **Contact:** Human Resources. **Description:** Friden Neopost is engaged in the manufacture and sale (both directly and indirectly) of electronic mailing systems and related mailing equipment. **Common positions include:** Accountant/Auditor; Administrator; Buyer; Computer Programmer; Credit Manager; Customer Service Representative; Department Manager; Draftsperson; General Manager; Human Resources Specialist; Management Trainee; Manufacturer's/Wholesaler's Sales Rep.; Marketing Specialist; Purchasing Agent and Manager; Quality Control Supervisor; Systems Analyst; Technical Writer/Editor; Transportation/Traffic Specialist. **Educational backgrounds include:** Accounting; Business Administration; Computer Science; Engineering; Finance; Liberal Arts; Marketing. **Benefits:** 401(k); Dental Insurance; Disability Coverage; Employee Discounts; Life Insurance; Medical Insurance; Tuition Assistance. **Corporate headquarters location:** This Location. **Parent company:** Neopost NA (France); ITT (New York). **Operations at this facility include:** Administration; Research and Development; Sales; Service.

GLOBAL VILLAGE COMMUNICATION, INC.

1144 East Arques Avenue, Sunnyvale CA 94086. 408/523-1000. **Fax:** 408/523-2407. **Contact:** Human Resources. **E-mail address:** careers@globalvillage.com. **World Wide Web address:** http://www.globalvillage.com. **Description:** Global Village Communication, Inc. is a leading supplier of integrated communication solutions for personal computer uses. A long-time leader in the Macintosh arena, Global Village Communication acquired SofNet, Inc. in 1994, a leading PC software manufacturer. The company introduced a cross-platform "plug-and-play" Internet service for small businesses in 1995. Global Village Communication, U.K. Ltd. was the result of a 1996 acquisition and offers complete Windows-based ISDN solutions. **Benefits:** 401(k); Dental Insurance; Disability Coverage; Employee Discounts; Life Insurance; Medical Insurance; Tuition Assistance; Vision Insurance. **Corporate headquarters location:** This Location. **Other U.S. locations:** Marietta GA; Richardson TX. **Operations at this facility include:** Administration; Research and Development; Sales; Service. **Listed on:** NASDAQ. **Annual sales/revenues:** More than $100 million. **Number of employees at this location:** 180. **Number of employees nationwide:** 200. **Number of employees worldwide:** 250.

THE GRASS VALLEY GROUP INC.

P.O. Box 1114, Grass Valley CA 95945. 916/478-3000. **Fax:** 916/478-3808. **Contact:** Workforce Planning Manager. **Description:** The Grass Valley Group Inc. is a manufacturer of television broadcasting line equipment, terminal equipment, and video switching systems and related products. **Corporate headquarters location:** This Location.

KNIGHT-RIDDER, INC.
DIALOG INFORMATION SERVICES INC.

2440 El Camino Real, Mountain View CA 94040. 415/254-8017. **Contact:** Human Resources. **Description:** An international online information vendor. Offering online access to more than 300 databases containing over 80 million records, Dialog Information Services Inc. is one of the largest of its kind in the world. Knight-Ridder, a major newspaper publishing company, owns 28 dailies in 15 states, and three non-dailies in suburban areas. The company also produces niche publications such as *Myrtle Beach's Golf*, *CubaNews* newsletter in Miami and *Northland Outdoors* in Grand Forks. The larger papers include the *Miami Herald*, *Philadelphia Inquirer*, *Philadelphia Daily News*, *Detroit Free Press*, and *San Jose Mercury News*. Knight-Ridder, Inc. also has interests in the information distribution market through Business Information Services, with subsidiaries Knight-Ridder Information, Inc., Knight-Ridder Financial, and Technimetrics. Dialog online information retrieval serves the business, scientific, technology, medical, education, and medical communities in more than 100 countries. Knight-Ridder Financial provides real-time financial news and pricing information through primary products MoneyCenter, Digital Datafeed, ProfitCenter, and TradeCenter. Knight-Ridder also has interests in cable television and other businesses. TKR Cable, a 50-50 joint venture with Liberty Media Corporation, serves 344,000 basic subscribers in New Jersey and New York and manages Kentucky systems with 277,000 subscribers. Through TKR Cable Partners, Knight-Ridder owns a 15 percent share of TCI/TKR L.P. cable systems with 867,000 subscribers in five states. Other interests include partial ownership of the Seattle Times Company, two paper mills, a newspaper advertising sales company, and SCI Holdings. In 1993, Knight-Ridder acquired Technimetrics, Inc., a diversified data management company specializing in the design, production, and maintenance of worldwide financial database systems. **Common**

positions include: Accountant/Auditor; Computer Programmer; Customer Service Representative; Financial Analyst; Librarian; Services Sales Representative; Software Engineer; Technical Writer/Editor. **Educational backgrounds include:** Accounting; Biology; Business Administration; Chemistry; Communications; Computer Science; Finance; Library Science; Marketing; Mathematics. **Benefits:** Credit Union; Dental Insurance; Life Insurance; Medical Insurance; Pension Plan; Profit Sharing; Savings Plan; Tuition Assistance. **Corporate headquarters location:** This Location. **Operations at this facility include:** Administration; Research and Development; Sales; Service.

MFS INTELENET, INC.
2678 Bishop Drive, Suite 200, San Ramon CA 95483. 510/824-2000. **Contact:** Human Resources. **Description:** MFS Intelenet, Inc. provides telecommunication management services.

MICROTEL INTERNATIONAL, INC.
2040 Fortune Drive, Suite 102, San Jose CA 95131. 408/435-8520. **Contact:** Human Resources. **Description:** MicroTel International designs, manufactures, and markets electronic telecommunications test equipment and data communications equipment. The company's customers include AT&T, the Regional Bell Operating Companies, interconnect carriers, independent telephone operating companies, private communications networks, banks, brokerage firms, and government agencies. **Corporate headquarters location:** This Location.

NORTHERN TELECOM, INC.
2305 Camino Ramon, P.O. Box 5070, San Ramon CA 94583-1356. 510/867-2000. **Contact:** Human Resources Department. **Description:** Northern Telecom, Inc. designs, develops, manufactures, markets, sells, installs, and services central office switching equipment, integrated business systems, terminals transmission equipment, cable and outside plant products, and other telecommunications products and services. **Corporate headquarters location:** Research Triangle Park NC. **Other U.S. locations:** Stone Mountain GA; Morton Grove IL; Nashville TN. **Number of employees nationwide:** 30,000.

OCTEL COMMUNICATIONS
1001 Murphy Ranch Road, Milpitas CA 95035-7912. 408/321-2000. **Fax:** 408/321-9823. **Contact:** Human Resources. **Description:** Octel Communications makes and markets voice information processing systems that allow users to access, manage, and integrate multiple forms of information -- voice, image, and data -- across the telephone network in a single call from any touchtone phone in the world. **Common positions include:** Accountant/Auditor; Computer Programmer; Computer Systems Analyst; Customer Service Representative; Electrical/Electronics Engineer; Financial Analyst; Human Resources Specialist; Purchasing Agent and Manager; Software Engineer; Technical Writer/Editor. **Educational backgrounds include:** Accounting; Business Administration; Computer Science; Engineering; Marketing. **Benefits:** 401(k); Daycare Assistance; Dental Insurance; Disability Coverage; Employee Discounts; Life Insurance; Medical Insurance; Profit Sharing; Tuition Assistance. **Special Programs:** Internships. **Corporate headquarters location:** This Location. **Subsidiaries include:** Octel Network Services and Rhetorex. **Other U.S. locations:** Nationwide. **Operations at this facility include:** Administration; Manufacturing; Research and Development. **Listed on:** NASDAQ. **Number of employees at this location:** 1,000. **Number of employees nationwide:** 2,750.

PACIFIC BELL
666 Folsom Street, Room 925, San Francisco CA 94105. 510/867-6609. **Contact:** Employment. **Description:** Pacific Bell offers complete and varied telephone and telecommunications services in California. **Common positions include:** Computer Programmer; Computer Scientist; Customer Service Representative; General Manager; Marketing Specialist; Operations/Production Manager; Services Sales Representative. **Benefits:** Daycare Assistance; Dental Insurance; Disability Coverage; Employee Discounts; Life Insurance; Medical Insurance; Pension Plan; Profit Sharing; Savings Plan; Tuition Assistance. **Special Programs:** Internships. **Corporate headquarters location:** This Location. **Parent company:** Pacific Telesis Group (San Francisco CA). **Listed on:** New York Stock Exchange.

PACIFIC TELESIS GROUP
130 Kearny Street, San Francisco CA 94108. 415/394-3000. **Contact:** Human Resources Department. **Description:** Pacific Telesis Group is engaged in telecommunications and related businesses in the United States and overseas through its various subsidiaries. Pacific Bell and Nevada Bell provide local telephone service and network access to toll and long-distance services. They serve consumers, businesses, and interexchange and exchange carriers. Pacific Bell Directory produces print directories and offers Yellow Pages advertising and related marketing services in California and Nevada. PacTel Cellular and PacTel Paging own, build, and operate cellular telephone and paging systems in California as well as in other states. PacTel Cable manages investments in the home entertainment industry, including cable television operations in the United Kingdom. Pacific Telesis International conducts business activities directly and through affiliates in such markets as Germany, Thailand, the United Kingdom, Japan, and South Korea. The company's offerings include wireless communications, value-added networks, and international long-distance telecommunications. PacTel Business Systems sells, services, and finances key telephones systems, small PBXs, microcomputers, and local area networks for small- and medium-sized businesses and branch offices of large corporations. PacTel Properties maintains a portfolio of commercial and industrial properties primarily in the Los Angeles and San Francisco areas. **Corporate headquarters location:** This Location.

POST-NEWSWEEK CABLE, INC.
3242 Airway Drive, Santa Rosa CA 95403. 707/575-1320. **Fax:** 707/575-1374. **Contact:** Human Resources. **Description:** Post-Newsweek Cable, Inc. functions as a multiple-system cable television operator. **Parent company:** The Washington Post Company.

TCI
222 Caspian Drive, Sunnyvale CA 94089. 408/747-6100. **Contact:** Sheila Mele, Personnel Director. **Description:** TCI manages cable television communications. The Cable Communications Division has more than 1.6 million subscribers. **Common positions include:** Blue-Collar Worker Supervisor; Buyer; Civil Engineer; Customer Service Representative; Draftsperson; Electrical/Electronics Engineer; Mechanical Engineer. **Educational backgrounds include:** Engineering. **Benefits:** Dental Insurance; Disability Coverage; EAP; Life Insurance; Medical Insurance; Profit Sharing; Tuition Assistance; Vision Insurance. **Operations at this facility include:** Manufacturing. **Listed on:** NASDAQ. **Number of employees at this location:** 160. **Number of employees nationwide:** 3,100.

***Note:** Because addresses and telephone numbers of smaller companies can change rapidly, we recommend you call each company to verify the information below before inquiring about job opportunities. Mass mailings are not recommended.*

Additional small employers:

COMMUNICATIONS EQUIPMENT

Centillion Networks Inc.
359 Ravendale Dr, Mountain View CA 94043-5217. 415/969-6700.

David Systems
615 Tasman Drive, Sunnyvale CA 94089. 408/541-6000.

Coastcom
1151 Harbor Bay Parkway, Alameda CA 94502-6511. 510/523-6000.

TCSI Corp.
2121 Allston Way, Berkeley CA 94704-1301. 510/649-3700.

Ilex Systems Inc.
1988 Tarob Court, Milpitas CA 95035-6824. 408/945-0294.

Cidco Inc.
220 Cochrane Circle, Morgan Hill CA 95037-2803. 408/779-1162.

Synchronous Communications Inc.
77 Las Colinas Lane, San Jose CA 95119. 408/943-0222.

Madge Network Inc.
2310 North 1st Street, San Jose CA 95131-1011. 408/955-0700.

Telesensory Corporation
PO Box 7455, Mountain View CA 94039-7455. 415/960-0920.

Interactive Network Inc.
1991 Landings Drive, Mountain View CA 94043-0800. 415/960-1000.

Abekas Video Systems
101 Galveston Drive, Redwood City CA 94063-4795. 415/369-5111.

Chaparral Communications
2450 North 1st Street, San Jose CA 95131-1000. 408/435-1530.

SP Telecom
60 Spear St Ste 700, San Francisco CA 94105-1513. 415/905-4000.

P-Com Inc.
3175 Winchester Boulevard, Campbell CA 95008-6557. 408/866-3666.

Larscom Inc.
4600 Patrick Henry Drive, Santa Clara CA 95054-1817. 408/988-6600.

Scantronic USA Inc.
4772 Frontier Way #A, Stockton CA 95215-9672. 209/941-2944.

TELEPHONE COMMUNICATIONS

Cellular Telephone Co.
577 Airport Blvd, Burlingame CA 94010-2020. 415/871-9500.

Cellular Telephone Co.
200 Pringle Ave Ste 100, Walnut Creek CA 94596-3570. 510/256-6868.

Eagle Communications
1509 Grass Valley Hwy, Auburn CA 95603-2806. 916/889-1957.

Airsignal
1750 Howe Ave Ste 600, Sacramento CA 95825-3370. 916/565-0378.

Phoenix Network Inc.
550 California St, San Francisco CA 94104-1006. 415/399-3300.

Phoenix Network
599 N Mathilda Ave, Sunnyvale CA 94086-3507. 408/735-7004.

Phoenix Network
185 Berry St, San Francisco CA 94107-1729. 415/957-9516.

Phoenix Network
3550 Stevens Creek Blvd, San Jose CA 95117-1031. 408/296-8690.

MCI Telecommunications Inc.
201 Spear St Ste 6, San Francisco CA 94105-1630. 415/978-1100.

AT&T
3221 Ramos Cir, Sacramento CA 95827-2501. 916/361-5200.

AT&T
4440 Rosewood Dr Ste 4530, Pleasanton CA 94588-3050. 510/460-2020.

Sprint Communications
150 Spear St, San Francisco CA 94105-1535. 415/357-5500.

LDDS-Metromedia
411 Pacific St, Monterey CA 93940-2726. 408/462-1503.

California Page Inc.
10805 Saddle Rd, Monterey

CA 93940-6609. 408/375-1854.

Intelliglobe Telecom
1121 San Antonio Rd, Mountain View CA 94043-1002. 415/988-9200.

IDB Communications
450 Mission St, San Francisco CA 94105-2505. 415/281-7400.

France Telecom Inc.
455 Market St Ste 1440, San Francisco CA 94105-2442. 415/597-6550.

Fax International
605 Market St, San Francisco CA 94105-3219. 510/975-3910.

Cherry Communications
555 Howard St, San Francisco CA 94105-3014. 415/541-0166.

MAQ Marketing
440 Brannan St, San Francisco CA 94107-1713. 415/974-6875.

GFEA International Group
1355 6th St, San Francisco CA 94107-2215. 415/487-0231.

Bright Telecom
185 Berry St # 3503, San Francisco CA 94107-1729. 415/243-3200.

Inter Globe Communications
353 Sacramento St, San Francisco CA 94111-3620. 415/956-1234.

Zanne-Cann Co.
PO Box 803, Fairfield CA 94533-0080. 707/426-5705.

Allcity Paging
3423 Investment Blvd, Hayward CA 94545-3802. 510/293-5800.

Worldconnect Communications
1811 Santa Rita Rd Ste 130, Pleasanton CA 94566-4741. 510/462-9045.

Tele-Canadian Inc.
1811 Santa Rita Rd, Pleasanton CA 94566-4746. 510/417-0228.

Darwin Communications Systems
1811 Santa Rita Rd, Pleasanton CA 94566-4746. 510/462-5063.

Cal Tech International Telecom Corp.
4900 Hopyard Rd, Pleasanton CA 94588-3344. 510/463-4811.

Co-Net Communications Inc.
1850 Mount Diablo Boulevard, Walnut Creek CA 94596-4428. 510/939-1999.

European Telcom
2033 N Main St Ste 390 A, Walnut Creek CA 94596-3727. 510/934-2153.

Toll Call Inc.
1990 N California Blvd, Walnut Creek CA 94596-3742. 510/935-9343.

TCG
Regional Office
201 N Civic Dr, Walnut Creek CA 94596-3800. 510/279-5100.

Lanier Worldwide Inc.
2255 Martin Ave, Santa Clara CA 95050-2709. 408/453-5844.

National Telephone & Communications Area Sales
1737 North 1st Street, San Jose CA 95112-4505. 408/441-6580.

National Telephone & Communications
PO Box 2008, Los Gatos CA 95031-2008. 408/395-4682.

Direct Line Telephone Co.
71 S 15th St, San Jose CA 95112-2026. 408/998-2500.

Asia Pacific
432 Oakshire Ave, Modesto CA 95354-1711. 209/524-7355.

Excel Telecommunications
7840 Madison Ave, Fair Oaks CA 95628-3518. 916/863-6068.

Cyberlink Inc.
735 Sunrise Ave, Roseville CA 95661-4568. 916/783-9935.

Russell Independant
11344 Coloma Rd, Gold River CA 95670-4457. 916/631-9143.

Express Tel
2755 Campus Dr Ste 100, San Mateo CA 94403-2514. 415/571-0800.

Express Tel
11025 Trade Center Dr, Rncho Cordova CA 95670-6131. 916/638-0300.

Gary D. Cox & Associates
11344 Coloma Rd, Rncho Cordova CA 95670-4457. 916/631-9322.

Telegration Inc.
1006 4th St, Sacramento CA 95814-3314. 916/325-4700.

A & B Design
140 San Lazaro Ave, Sunnyvale CA 94086-5209. 408/749-8037.

Telekol
2732 Camino Segura, Pleasanton CA 94566-5887. 510/485-0446.

Boston Technology Inc.
19799 San Ramon Valley Blvd, San Ramon CA 94583-3140. 510/803-2140.

Voice Message Center
525 Bollinger Canyon Way, San Ramon CA 94583-4934. 510/735-5500.

Voice Message Center
2920 Camino Diablo, Walnut Creek CA 94596-3936. 510/943-5475.

Telephony Integration
99 N 6th St, San Jose CA 95112-5423. 408/298-8966.

ADA International Enterprises
PO Box 26192, San Jose CA 95159-6192. 408/294-3176.

Teletask Inc.
4159 Natoma Ave, Fair Oaks CA 95628-7658. 916/863-2200.

Wireless Connections
260 S Sunnyvale Ave # 9, Sunnyvale CA 94086-6244. 408/245-8144.

Halestone Enterprises
1457 W San Carlos St Apt D, San Jose CA 95126-3275. 408/297-3787.

Red Dog Telecommunications
6447 Little River Ct, Citrus Heights CA 95621-4749. 916/331-4948.

SD&W Promotions
4279 Niblick Way, Fair Oaks CA 95628-6731. 916/961-5276.

Veronica J. Miles Phone Communications
4488 San Juan Ave, Fair Oaks CA 95628-5612. 916/967-5809.

C&H Communications
10200 Van Parker Ln, Galt CA 95632-8884. 209/745-2294.

Pattel
11867 Point Rock Way, Rancho Cordova CA 95670-8371. 916/858-1200.

Cly Gen Communications
2137 Winafred St, Sacramento CA 95825-0135. 916/921-5477.

SJS Communications
372 Aquapher Way, Sacramento CA 95831-3701. 916/399-1502.

TELEGRAPH AND OTHER MESSAGE COMMUNICATIONS

HQ Business Centers
980 9th St, Sacramento CA 95814-2719. 916/449-9900.

RADIO BROADCASTING STATIONS

KMPH FM
5087 E McKinley Ave, Fresno CA 93727-1965. 209/255-5600.

KCEA FM
555 Middlefield Rd, Atherton CA 94027-3400. 415/321-6049.

KSFH FM
1885 Miramonte Ave, Mountain View CA 94040-4029. 415/968-1213.

KNBR AM
55 Hawthorne St, San Francisco CA 94105-3906. 415/995-6800.

KFRC FM 99.7
500 Washington St, San Francisco CA 94111-2919. 415/391-9970.

KSFO AM
900 Front Street, San Francisco CA 94111. 415/398-5600.

KSAN FM
750 Battery St Ste 200, San Francisco CA 94111-1524. 415/291-0202.

KCBS AM
1 Embarcadero Ctr, San Francisco CA 94111-3607. 415/765-4000.

KYCY
500 Washington St, San Francisco CA 94111-2919. 415/391-9330.

KOFY AM
2500 Marin St, San Francisco CA 94124-1015. 415/821-2020.

Henry Broadcasting Co.
2277 Jerrold Ave, San Francisco CA 94124-1011. 415/285-1133.

KMEL Radio
55 Francisco St Ste 400, San Francisco CA 94133-2113. 415/391-1061.

Douglas Broadcasting Inc.
499 Hamilton Ave Ste 140, Palo Alto CA 94301-1810. 415/324-5888.

KCSM FM
1700 W Hillsdale Blvd, San Mateo CA 94402-3757. 415/574-6427.

KECG FM
540 Ashbury Ave, El Cerrito CA 94530-3221. 510/525-0234.

KCEQ FM
1200 Pleasant Hill Rd, Lafayette CA 94549-2623. 510/935-2600.

Alliance Broadcasting Ltd. Partnership
2175 N California Blvd, Walnut Creek CA 94596-3579. 510/256-4690.

KRE AM & KBLX FM Inner City
601 Ashby Ave, Berkeley

CA 94710-2801. 510/848-7713.

KLIV AM
750 Story Rd, San Jose CA 95122-2604. 408/293-8030.

KBRG
2905 S King Rd, San Jose CA 95122-1518. 408/274-1170.

United Broadcasting Co.
PO Box 6616, San Jose CA 95150-6616. 408/370-7377.

KHOP
3401 Dale Rd, Modesto CA 95356-0502. 209/572-0104.

KTUO FM
430 N Washington St, Sonora CA 95370-5526. 209/532-5511.

KZSA FM
4050 Flying C Rd Ste 17, Cameron Park CA 95682-9608. 916/676-5996.

Fuller Jeffrey Broadcasting Co.
8842 Quail Lane, Roseville CA 95746-8800. 916/448-1450.

TELEVISION BROADCASTING STATIONS

KFSN TV
1777 G St, Fresno CA 93706-1688. 209/442-1170.

KJEO
4880 N 1st St, Fresno CA 93726-0514. 209/222-2411.

KSEE
5035 E McKinley Ave, Fresno CA 93727-1964. 209/454-2424.

KSBW
238 John St, Salinas CA 93901-3339. 408/758-8888.

KCBA
1550 Moffett Street, Salinas CA 93905-3342. 408/422-3500.

KSMS TV
67 Garden Ct, Monterey CA 93940-5302. 408/373-6767.

KCCN TV
2200 Garden Rd, Monterey CA 93940-5329. 408/649-0460.

KRONP TV Chronicle Broadcasting
1001 Van Ness Ave, San Francisco CA 94109-6913. 415/441-4444.

KMTP TV
1311 Sutter St Ste 200, San Francisco CA 94109-5415. 415/882-5566.

KPIX TV
855 Battery St, San Francisco CA 94111-1503. 415/362-5550.

John Blair Communications Inc.
505 Sansome St, San Francisco CA 94111-3106. 415/434-2393.

D&R Radio
750 Battery St Ste 340, San Francisco CA 94111-1525. 415/772-2735.

ABC National Television Sales
900 Front St, San Francisco CA 94111-1427. 415/954-7810.

Caballero Spanish Media
750 Battery St Ste 340, San Francisco CA 94111-1525. 415/772-2740.

KDTV
2200 Palou Ave, San Francisco CA 94124-1505. 415/641-1400.

KTEH Channel 54
100 Skyport Dr, San Jose CA 95110-1301. 408/437-5454.

KNTV
645 Pk Ave, San Jose CA 95110. 408/286-1111.

KDTV Channel 14
1530 Oakland Rd Ste 150, San Jose CA 95112-1241. 408/437-1414.

KSTS Channel 48
2349 Bering Dr, San Jose CA 95131-1125. 408/435-8848.

KBVU
PO Box 4159, Modesto CA 95352-4159. 209/523-0777.

KIEM TV
5650 S Broadway St, Eureka CA 95503-6996. 707/443-3123.

KOVR Channel 13
2713 Kovr Dr, Broderick CA 95605-1600. 916/374-1313.

Kelly Broadcasting Co.
3 Television Cir, Sacramento CA 95814-0750. 916/446-3333.

KRBK TV
500 Media Pl, Sacramento CA 95815. 916/929-0300.

KXTV Inc.
400 Broadway, Sacramento CA 95818-2041. 916/441-2345.

KTXL
4655 Fruitridge Rd, Sacramento CA 95820-5201. 916/454-4422.

KCPM
180 E 4th St, Chico CA 95928-5412. 916/893-2424.

KRCR TV
755 Auditorium Dr, Redding CA 96001-0920. 916/243-7777.

Roslin Radio & Television Sales
390 Swift Ave, South San

Francisco CA 94080-6221. 415/794-9150.

Health Club TV Radio
750 Bay St, San Francisco CA 94109-1321. 415/563-0559.

CBS Group W Televison Sales
855 Battery St, San Francisco CA 94111-1503. 415/765-8605.

Outtalk Magazine
PO Box 883544, San Francisco CA 94188-3544. 415/974-5766.

KSBT
133 Eastmont Mall Lower, Oakland CA 94605-2428. 510/261-1919.

KTVU TV News Tipline
2 Jack London Sq, Oakland CA 94607-3727. 510/839-2222.

KGO TV South Bay News Bureau
1735 Technology Dr, San Jose CA 95110-1313. 408/441-1566.

KCRA TV Channel 3
6 S El Dorado St, Stockton CA 95202. 209/948-5272.

KCSO TV Channel 19
2842 Iowa Ave, Modesto CA 95358-9453. 209/578-1900.

KUCA TV Channel 58
58 Television Circle, Sacramento CA 95814-0750. 916/447-5858.

KPWB TV 31
500 Media Pl, Sacramento CA 95815-3733. 916/925-3100.

Broadcast Services International
2618 J Street, Sacramento CA 95816-4313. 916/446-3594.

CABLE/PAY TELEVISION SERVICES

Intermedia Partners LP
235 Montgomery Street Suite 420, San Francisco CA 94104-2907. 415/616-4800.

Viacom Cablevision
6640 Sierra Lane, Dublin CA 94568-2622. 510/828-8520.

For more information on career opportunities in the communications industries:

Associations

ACADEMY OF TELEVISION ARTS & SCIENCES
5220 Lankershim Boulevard, North Hollywood CA 91601. 818/754-2800.

AMERICAN WOMEN IN RADIO AND TELEVISION, INC.
1650 Tysons Boulevard, Suite 200, McLean VA 22102. 703/506-3290. A national, nonprofit professional organization of women and men who work in electronic media and related fields. Services include *News and Views,* a fax newsletter transmitted biweekly to members; Careerline, a national listing of job openings available to members only; and the AWRT Foundation.

INTERACTIVE SERVICES ASSOCIATION
8403 Colesville Road, Suite 865, Silver Springs MD 20910. 301/495-4955. World Wide Web address: http://www.isa.net.

INTERNATIONAL TELEVISION ASSOCIATION
6311 North O'Connor Road, Suite 230, Irving TX 75309. 214/869-1112. World Wide Web address: http://www.itva.org.

NATIONAL ASSOCIATION OF BROADCASTERS
1771 N Street NW, Washington DC 20036. 202/429-5300, ext. 5490. Fax: 202/429-5343. Provides employment information.

NATIONAL CABLE TELEVISION ASSOCIATION
1724 Massachusetts Avenue NW, Washington DC 20036-1969. 202/775-3651. Fax: 202/775-3695. A trade association. Publications include *Cable Television Developments, Secure Signals, Kids and Cable, Linking Up, Only on Cable,* and *Producers' Sourcebook: A Guide to Program Buyers.*

PROMAX INTERNATIONAL
2029 Century Park East, Suite 555, Los Angeles CA 90028. 310/788-7600. Fax: 310/788-7616. Ask for the jobline.

U.S. TELEPHONE ASSOCIATION
1401 H Street NW, Suite 600, Washington DC 20005-2136. 202/326-7300. World Wide Web address: http://www.usta.org.

Magazines

BROADCASTING AND CABLE
Broadcasting Publications Inc., 1705 DeSales

Street NW, Washington DC 20036. 202/659-2340.

ELECTRONIC MEDIA
Crain Communications, 220 East 42nd Street, New York NY 10017. 212/210-0100.

COMPUTER HARDWARE, SOFTWARE, AND SERVICES

Hardware and software: Companies are starting to invest more in corporate technology after several years of lean spending. Network servers have been the hot business product recently, and that trend should continue through 1997. Expect the boom in big machines -- parallel computers, mainframes, and minicomputers -- to support a growing interest in online databases, accessing the Internet, and e-mail. PCs will remain the strongest part of the hardware market. The composition of the software industry is shrinking with many firms merging or acquiring others. Despite consolidation in the industry, and despite the crisis at Apple Computer, the overall number of software jobs is still rising.

What's hot on the market? Although it still accounts for a tiny percentage of software sales, Internet-related software -- and World Wide Web browsing software in particular -- is quickly transforming the industry. Analysts predict that sales of Internet software will double every year through at least 2000, and by then sales could hit $4 billion a year.

Services: Computer services professionals perform three activities: systems integration, custom programming, and consulting/training. Consulting and integration are the fastest-growing segments in computing due to the demand for networking. With more computer power available, more computer support will be needed.

ACCUGRAPH CORPORATION

4155-F El Camino Way, Palo Alto CA 94306. 415/857-1629. **Contact:** Human Resources. **Description:** Develops and supports computer-based software products and manages graphic information, focusing primarily on applications in the areas of telecommunications, facilities management, and computer network management. Accugraph's products originally served the needs of engineers, architects, planners and manufacturers for computer-aided design and computer-aided manufacturing software applications. The company's business has since evolved to also serve high-growth markets such as telecommunications, computer network management, and facilities management. The company produces and markets its proprietary software products for operation on third-party platforms. The integrated systems which are created are used by the company's customers to automate telecommunications applications and provide related services to manage computer networks and for facilities management. The company's largest customers, segmented by application, are Northern Telecom (telecommunications), BellSouth (computer network management), and Hewlett-Packard (worldwide facilities management).

ACTEL CORPORATION

955 East Arques Avenue, Sunnyvale CA 94086-4521. 408/739-1010. **Contact:** Michelle Begun, Vice President of Human Resources. **Description:** Manufactures integrated

circuits and develops software. Actel is a world leader in high-performance field programmable gate arrays. Actel is also the home of antifuse technology, arguably the most efficient technology in logic integration today. **Common positions include:** Computer-Aided Designer; Design Engineer; Manufacturing Engineer; Marketing Specialist; Software Engineer; Systems Analyst; Test Engineer. **Number of employees at this location:** 190.

ADAPTEC, INC.
691 South Milpitas Boulevard, Milpitas CA 95035. 408/945-8600. **Contact:** Human Resources. **World Wide Web address:** http://www.adaptec.com. **Description:** Adaptec is a supplier of high-performance intelligent subsystems and associated software. The company also produces VLSI circuits used to control the flow of data between a microcomputer's central processing unit (CPU) and its peripherals, including storage devices, laser printers, and network file servers. Products, mostly based on Small Computer System Interface (SCSI) Technology, include host adaptors, proprietary VLSI circuits, and software-based development systems. The company's I/O solutions allow advanced computer applications, like multimedia, disk arrays, and high-speed/high resolution printing. The company's key products, called IOware, speed the transfer of data from one part of the computer system to another. **Number of employees nationwide:** 1,300.

ADOBE SYSTEMS, INC.
1585 Charleston Road, Mountain View CA 94043. 415/961-4400. **Contact:** Susan Hall, Human Resources Representative. **World Wide Web address:** http://www.adobe.com. **Description:** Adobe develops, markets, and supports computer software products and technologies for Apple Macintosh, Windows, and OS/2 compatibles that enable users to create, display, print, and communicate electronic documents. The company licenses its technology to major computer and publishing suppliers, and markets application software products and typeface products for authoring and editing visually rich documents, including digital and video output. The company distributes its products through a network of original equipment manufacturer customers, distributors and dealers, value-added resellers, and system integrators. The company has operations in the Americas, Europe, and the Pacific Rim. In 1994, the company acquired the Aldus Corporation. Aldus focused on three lines of business: applications for the professional print publishing, graphics and prepress markets; applications for the general consumer market; and applications for the interactive publishing market. **Common positions include:** Electrical/Electronics Engineer; Graphic Artist; Software Engineer. **Corporate headquarters location:** This Location.

ALLDATA CORPORATION
9412 Big Horn Boulevard, Elk Grove CA 95758-1100. 916/684-5200. **Contact:** Department of Interest. **Description:** Provides computer consulting services. **Common positions include:** Accountant/Auditor; Electrical/Electronics Engineer; Financial Analyst; Mechanical Engineer; Software Engineer. **Number of employees at this location:** 290.

ALTERA CORPORATION
2610 Orchard Parkway, San Jose CA 95134-2020. 408/894-7000. **Fax:** 408/435-5065. **Contact:** Human Resources. **Description:** Designs, develops, and markets programmable logic integrated circuits and associated computer engineering development software and hardware. The company's semiconductor products, which are known as Erasable Programmable Logic Devices (EPLDs) and Flexible Logic Element

Matrix (FLEM) devices, are standard logic chips that customers configure for specific end-use applications using the company's proprietary software. The company's customers enjoy the benefits of low development costs, short lead times, and standard product inventories when compared to application specific integrated circuits (ASICs) and high-density and low-power consumption when compared to Transistor Logic (TTL). **Common positions include:** Accountant/Auditor; Automotive Engineer; Computer Programmer; Design Engineer; Manager of Information Systems; Mechanical Engineer; Research Technician; Sales Representative.

AMDAHL CORPORATION
1250 East Arques Avenue, Sunnyvale CA 94088. 408/746-6000. **Contact:** Lisa Carter, Staffing Consultant. **E-mail address:** jobs@amdahl.com. **Description:** Designs, develops, manufactures, markets, and services large-scale, high-performance, general purpose computer systems, both hardware and software. Customers are primarily in large corporations, government agencies, and large universities with high-volume data-processing requirements. Amdahl markets more than 470 different systems. **Common positions include:** Accountant/Auditor; Computer Programmer; Computer Systems Analyst; Customer Service Representative; Financial Analyst; Human Resources Specialist; Mechanical Engineer; Software Engineer; Technical Writer/Editor; Transportation/Traffic Specialist. **Educational backgrounds include:** Accounting; Business Administration; Communications; Computer Science; Engineering; Finance; Liberal Arts; Marketing. **Benefits:** 401(k); Daycare Assistance; Dental Insurance; Disability Coverage; Employee Discounts; Life Insurance; Medical Insurance; Pension Plan; Profit Sharing; Savings Plan; Tuition Assistance. **Special Programs:** Internships. **Corporate headquarters location:** This Location. **Other U.S. locations:** IL; NY; TX. **Operations at this facility include:** Administration; Manufacturing; Regional Headquarters; Research and Development; Sales; Service. **Listed on:** NASDAQ. **Number of employees at this location:** 3,500.

ANALYSTS INTERNATIONAL CORPORATION (AiC)
1850 Gateway Boulevard, Suite 120, Concord CA 94520-3277. 510/687-5522. **Contact:** Human Resources. **Description:** AiC is an international computer consulting firm with 2,700 employees worldwide. The company assists clients in developing systems in a variety of industries using different programming languages and software. This involves systems analysis, design, and development. **Corporate headquarters location:** Minneapolis MN.

APPLE COMPUTER, INC.
One Infinite Loop, MS 75-2CE, Cupertino CA 95014. 408/862-7080. **Fax:** 408/974-5691. **Recorded Jobline:** 408/974-9500. **Contact:** Employment Department. **Description:** Develops, manufactures, and markets personal computer systems. The company's desktop publishing and communications products are marketed internationally. **NOTE:** The jobline number in Sacramento is 916/314-2675. **Common positions include:** Computer Engineer; Computer Programmer; Marketing Specialist; Software Engineer. **Educational backgrounds include:** Business Administration; Computer Science; Finance. **Special Programs:** Internships. **Corporate headquarters location:** This Location. **Other U.S. locations:** Sacramento CA; Fountain CO; Austin TX. **Listed on:** NASDAQ.

APPLE COMPUTER, INC.
1 Bush Street, 10th Floor, San Francisco CA 94104-4425. **Toll-free phone:** 800/462-

7753. **Contact:** Human Resources. **Description:** Develops, manufactures, and markets personal computer systems. The company's desktop publishing and communications products are marketed internationally. **Corporate headquarters location:** Cupertino CA.

ASANTE TECHNOLOGIES
821 Fox Lane, San Jose CA 95131. 408/435-8401. **Fax:** 408/894-9150. **Contact:** B. Young, Human Resources Director. **E-mail address:** hr@asante.com. **World Wide Web address:** http://www.asante.com. **Description:** Designs, develops, and manufactures ethernet and fast ethernet networking systems. **Common positions include:** Design Engineer; Electrical/Electronics Engineer; Manufacturing Engineer; Software Engineer. **Educational backgrounds include:** Computer Science; Engineering. **Benefits:** 401(k); Dental Insurance; Disability Coverage; Life Insurance; Medical Insurance; Telecommuting; Tuition Assistance. **Operations at this facility include:** Administration; Research and Development; Sales; Service. **Listed on:** NASDAQ. **Annual sales/revenues:** $51 million - $100 million. **Number of employees at this location:** 170. **Number of employees nationwide:** 195.

ASTEA INTERNATIONAL INC.
100 South Ellsworth Avenue, 9th Floor, San Mateo CA 94401. 415/696-3260. **Fax:** 415/696-3265. **Contact:** Human Resources. **Description:** Develops, markets, and supports a variety of applications for client/server and host-based environments that permit organizations of various sizes across a wide range of industries to automate and integrate field service and customer support functions. Astea also offers a full range of consulting services, training, and customer support. **Other locations:** Australia, France, Germany, the Netherlands, New Zealand, United Kingdom, and Israel. **Benefits:** 401(k); Bonus Award/Plan; Profit Sharing; Stock Option. **Corporate headquarters location:** Chalfont PA. **Other U.S. locations:** Bedford MA. **Listed on:** NASDAQ. **Number of employees nationwide:** 200.

AUSPEX SYSTEMS, INC.
5200 Great America Parkway, Santa Clara CA 95054-1139. 408/492-0900. **Contact:** Leesa Gidaro, Senior Recruiter. **E-mail address:** employment@auspex.com. **World Wide Web address:** http://www.auspex.com. **Description:** Auspex Systems, Inc. is a leading provider of a family of high-performance network data servers that are optimized to move large amounts of data quickly and reliably from central information repositories to users' workstations. The Auspex network data server product line offers a cost-effective solution for client/server environments that require high reliability, a scaleable architecture, fast response times, and large storage capacities up to 900 gigabytes per server. Founded in 1987. **Common positions include:** Budget Analyst; Credit Manager; Manufacturing Engineer; Marketing Specialist; Mechanical Engineer; Sales Representative; Software Engineer. **Educational backgrounds include:** Computer Science. **Corporate headquarters location:** This Location. **Other locations:** Worldwide. **Operations at this facility include:** Administration; Manufacturing; Research and Development; Sales; Service. **Listed on:** NASDAQ. **Stock exchange symbol:** ASPX. **Annual sales/revenues:** More than $100 million. **Number of employees worldwide:** 500.

AUTODESK, INC.
111 McInnis Parkway, San Rafael CA 94903. 415/507-5000. **Contact:** Steve McMahon, Vice President of Human Resources. **Description:** Designs, develops, markets, and

supports a line of computer-aided design (CAD), engineering, and animation software products for desktop computers and workstations. **Common positions include:** Computer Programmer; Quality Control Supervisor; Systems Analyst. **Educational backgrounds include:** Computer Science. **Benefits:** Dental Insurance; Disability Coverage; Life Insurance; Medical Insurance; Pension Plan; Tuition Assistance. **Corporate headquarters location:** This Location. **Operations at this facility include:** Administration; Divisional Headquarters; Manufacturing; Regional Headquarters; Research and Development; Sales; Service. **Number of employees nationwide:** 1,800.

BARRA, INC.
1995 University Avenue, Suite 400, Berkeley CA 94704. 510/548-5442. **Contact:** Human Resources. **Description:** Develops, markets, and supports application software and information services used to analyze and manage portfolios of equity, fixed income, and other financial instruments. The company serves more than 750 clients in 30 countries, including many of the world's largest portfolio managers, fund sponsors, pension and investment consultants, brokers/dealers, and master trustees. **Common positions include:** Computer Systems Analyst; Customer Service Representative; Economist/Market Research Analyst; Electrical/Electronics Engineer; Human Resources Specialist; Mathematician; Payroll Clerk; Quality Control Supervisor; Receptionist; Services Sales Representative; Software Engineer; Statistician. **Educational backgrounds include:** Computer Science; Economics; Engineering; Finance; Mathematics; Physics. **Benefits:** Daycare Assistance; Dental Insurance; Disability Coverage; Employee Discounts; Home Loan Assistance; Life Insurance; Medical Insurance; Pension Plan; Profit Sharing; Savings Plan; Tuition Assistance. **Corporate headquarters location:** This Location. **Other U.S. locations:** NY. **Operations at this facility include:** Administration; Regional Headquarters; Research and Development; Sales; Service. **Number of employees at this location:** 260. **Number of employees nationwide:** 300.

BELL MICROPRODUCTS INC.
1941 Ringwood Avenue, San Jose CA 95131. 408/451-9400. **Contact:** Human Resources. **Description:** Founded in 1987, Bell Microproducts Inc. markets and distributes a select group of semiconductor and computer products to original equipment manufacturers and value-added resellers. Semiconductor products include memory, logic microprocessors, peripheral, and specialty components. Computer products include disk, tape and optical drives and subsystems, drive controllers, computers, and board-level products. The company also provides a variety of manufacturing and value-added services to its customers, including the supply of board-level products to customer specifications on a turnkey basis, as well as certain types of components and subsystem testing services, systems integration and disk drive formatting and testing, and the packaging of electronic component kits to customer specifications. **Corporate headquarters location:** This Location.

BLYTH HOLDINGS INC.
989 East Hillsdale Boulevard, Suite 400, Foster City CA 94404. 415/571-0222. **Contact:** Human Resources. **Description:** Blyth Holdings Inc., through its subsidiary Blyth Software, develops, markets, and supports software products for the development and deployment of applications for accessing multi-user databases in workgroup and enterprise-wide client/server computing environments. The company's OMNIS family of products is used by corporations, system integrators, small businesses, and independent consultants to deliver custom information management applications for a wide range of

uses including financial management, decision support, executive information, sales and marketing, and multimedia authoring systems. In addition to these products, Blyth provides consulting, technical support, and training to help plan, analyze, implement, and maintain applications software based on the company's technology. **Corporate headquarters location:** This Location.

BOOLE & BABBAGE, INC.
3131 Zanker Road, San Jose CA 95134. 408/526-3000. **Contact:** Human Resources. **Description:** Developers of automation software. **Common positions include:** Computer Programmer; Software Engineer.

BORLAND INTERNATIONAL
100 Borland Way, Scotts Valley CA 95066. 408/431-1000. **Contact:** Human Resources. **Description:** Borland International designs and markets computer software products for both businesses and software developers. **Common positions include:** Customer Service Representative; Manager of Information Systems; Public Relations Specialist; Quality Control Supervisor; Software Engineer; Technical Writer/Editor; Technician. **Number of employees nationwide:** 1,900.

BRODERBUND SOFTWARE, INC.
500 Redwood Boulevard, Novato CA 94948. 415/382-4400. **Contact:** Human Resources. **Description:** Broderbund develops, publishes, and markets personal computer software for the home, school, and small business markets. Products are offered primarily in two consumer software categories: personal productivity and education. Since its founding in 1980, the company has sold more than 15 million units of consumer software. **Common positions include:** Computer Engineer; Computer Programmer; Design Engineer; Software Engineer. **Number of employees at this location:** 340.

CADENCE DESIGN SYSTEMS, INC.
555 River Oaks Parkway, San Jose CA 95134. 408/943-1234. **Fax:** 408/955-0820. **Contact:** Elie Barbarito, Staffing Representative. **Description:** A producer of electronic design automation software. **Common positions include:** Design Engineer; Electrical/Electronics Engineer. **Benefits:** 401(k); Dental Insurance; Disability Coverage; Life Insurance; Medical Insurance; Tuition Assistance. **Special Programs:** Internships. **Corporate headquarters location:** This Location. **Operations at this facility include:** Research and Development; Sales. **Listed on:** New York Stock Exchange.

CAERE CORPORATION
100 Cooper Court, Los Gatos CA 95030-3321. 408/395-7000. **Contact:** Human Resources. **Description:** Develops and markets information recognition software. **Common positions include:** Computer Programmer; Software Engineer.

CENTURA SOFTWARE
1060 Marsh Road, Menlo Park CA 94025. 415/321-9500. **Fax:** 415/321-5471. **Contact:** Katherine Lowe, Staffing Specialist. **Description:** Engaged in software development for local area networks and database management systems. Services include support, consulting, and training, including interactive video training. **Common positions include:** Software Engineer; Technical Support Representative. **Educational backgrounds include:** Computer Science; Engineering. **Benefits:** 401(k); Dental Insurance; Disability Coverage; Employee Discounts; Flexible Benefits; Life Insurance;

Medical Insurance. **Corporate headquarters location:** This Location. **Other U.S. locations:** Los Angeles CA; Washington DC; Atlanta GA; Chicago IL; New York NY; Dallas TX. **Operations at this facility include:** Administration; Research and Development; Sales; Service. **Listed on:** NASDAQ. **Number of employees at this location:** 270. **Number of employees nationwide:** 300.

CISCO SYSTEMS, INC.
1700 West Tasman, San Jose CA 95134. 415/326-1941. **Contact:** Human Resources. **Description:** Cisco Systems, Inc., develops, manufactures, markets, and supports high-performance internetworking systems that enable customers to build large-scale integrated computer networks. Its products connect and manage communications among local and wide area networks that employ a variety of protocols, media interfaces, network topologies, and cable systems. **Number of employees at this location:** 880.

CLARIS CORPORATION
A SUBSIDIARY OF APPLE COMPUTER
5201 Patrick Henry Drive, Santa Clara CA 95052. 408/987-7000. **Contact:** Human Resources. **Description:** Claris is engaged in software development and sales. Claris is the developer of ClarisWorks 3.0, a software product that combines word processing, spreadsheet, charting, graphics, database, drawing, and painting functions.

COGNEX CORPORATION
1949 Landings Drive, Mountain View CA 94043. 415/969-4812. **Contact:** Human Resources. **Description:** Cognex Corporation designs, develops, manufactures, and markets machine vision systems used to automate a wide range of manufacturing processes, replacing human vision. Sophisticated pattern recognition software and high-speed, special purpose computers, when connected to video cameras, interpret video images and generate information about them. Cognex machine vision systems are used in the electronics, semiconductor, pharmaceutical, health care, aerospace, automotive, packaging, and graphic arts industries to gauge, guide, inspect, and identify products in manufacturing operations. United States offices are located in California and Illinois; international branches can be found in France, Germany, Japan, Singapore, and the United Kingdom. **NOTE:** Send resumes to: Human Resources, One Vision Drive, Natick MA 01760. **Benefits:** 401(k); Stock Option. **Corporate headquarters location:** Natick MA. **Listed on:** NASDAQ. **Number of employees nationwide:** 175.

COMMUNICATION INTELLIGENCE CORPORATION
275 Shoreline Drive, Suite 520, Redwood Shores CA 94065. 415/802-7888. **Fax:** 415/802-7777. **Contact:** Human Resources. **Description:** Communication Intelligence Corporation develops, markets, and licenses handwriting recognition technology and related technologies for the emerging pen-based computer market. The company has created a natural input recognition system which allows a computer to recognize hand-printed character input. **Corporate headquarters location:** This Location.

COMPUTER ASSOCIATES
1201 Marina Village Parkway, Alameda CA 94501. 510/769-1400. **Contact:** Human Resources. **Description:** Manufactures computer equipment.

COMPUTER ASSOCIATES
2880 Scott Boulevard, Santa Clara CA 95050. 408/562-8800. **Contact:** Human Resources. **Description:** Provides computer systems design and integration services. **Common positions include:** Computer Engineer; Electrical/Electronics Engineer.

COMPUTER CURRICULUM CORPORATION
1287 Lawrence Station Road, Sunnyvale CA 94089. 408/541-3308. **Contact:** Human Resources. **Description:** Engaged in the programming of educational software. **Common positions include:** Accountant/Auditor; Administrative Services Manager; Attorney; Budget Analyst; Buyer; Claim Representative; Clerical Supervisor; Computer Programmer; Computer Systems Analyst; Credit Manager; Electrician; Financial Analyst; Human Resources Specialist; Human Service Worker; Librarian; Mathematician; Services Sales Representative; Software Engineer; Statistician; Technical Writer/Editor. **Educational backgrounds include:** Accounting; Art/Design; Business Administration; Communications; Computer Science; Engineering; Finance; Liberal Arts; Marketing; Mathematics. **Benefits:** 401(k); Dental Insurance; Disability Coverage; Employee Discounts; Life Insurance; Medical Insurance; Savings Plan; Tuition Assistance. **Special Programs:** Internships. **Corporate headquarters location:** This Location. **Operations at this facility include:** Administration; Divisional Headquarters; Regional Headquarters; Research and Development; Sales; Service. **Listed on:** NASDAQ. **Number of employees at this location:** 400. **Number of employees nationwide:** 600.

COMPUTER IDENTICS CORPORATION
1641 North First Street, Suite 225, San Jose CA 95112. 408/437-2460. **Contact:** Human Resources. **Description:** Computer Identics Corporation is dedicated to providing data collection integrators with complete solutions, including scanning components, networking, software tools, and support services. Customers are primarily involved in materials handling and factory automation environments, and include systems integrators, original equipment manufacturers, value-added resellers, and end users performing in-house system integration. Products and related services fall into four major categories: omnidirectional scanning systems, intelligent fixed position line scanners, data collection terminals, and networking products. Computer Identics' foreign subsidiaries are located in Canada, Belgium, England, France, and Germany. **Benefits:** 401(k). **Corporate headquarters location:** Canton MA. **Other U.S. locations:** Mission Viejo CA; West Hartford CT; Roswell GA; Schaumburg IL; Southfield MI; Raleigh NC; Cincinnati OH; Irving TX. **Listed on:** NASDAQ.

CONCURRENT COMPUTER CORPORATION
1900 McCarthy Boulevard, Milpitas CA 95035. 408/432-6111. **Contact:** Human Resources. **Description:** A nationwide manufacturer of computer peripherals.

CONSILIUM, INC.
485 Clyde Avenue, Mountain View CA 94043. 415/691-6100. **Contact:** Human Resources. **Description:** Consilium, Inc. is the world's leading supplier of integrated manufacturing execution systems software and services. For more than 15 years, the company has been helping world class manufacturers achieve best practices in their manufacturing operations through better visibility and control of the plant floor. Consilium has helped 50,000 users in 20 countries solve critical business problems by providing solutions that optimize manufacturing performance. The company's WorkStream and FlowStream product lines provide real-time access to critical information about the production process, enabling manufacturers to identify and implement best practices in cost, quality, service, and speed. **Corporate headquarters location:** This Location.

CONTROL DATA
1306 Orleans Drive, Sunnyvale CA 94089. 408/541-4200. **Contact:** Human Resources. **E-mail address:** info@cdc.com. **Description:** Control Data helps business and government integrate the complex networks and applications required to compete in today's electronic marketplace. The company helps its customers implement business solutions by providing a range of services that include design consulting, program management, application development, network integration, and life cycle support. Control Data relies on a worldwide cadre of computer professionals to provide the consulting services required to define, develop, install, and maintain its networked solutions. These consultants select hardware and software components from Control Data's growing family of open systems technology partners and suppliers, and assemble them into custom solutions for clients. An independent company since 1992, Control Data is pursuing systems integration opportunities with two network infrastructure solutions: message integration (designing and building messaging solutions for large corporations and government institutions that want widely dispersed users and applications to exchange information) and product data management (Control Data consultants use the workflow, product configuration, and imaging capabilities of the Metaphase concurrent engineering software to help manufacturers track design and tooling data from initial sketches on a CAD terminal to the final checkout on the assembly line floor, even when these facilities are located on different continents. The Computer Products Group is a supplier of computer systems and services in engineering, scientific, and other technical markets. **NOTE:** Send resumes to: 4201 Lexington Avenue North, Arden Hills MN 55126. **Common positions include:** Computer Programmer; Technical Writer/Editor. **Educational backgrounds include:** Computer Science; Mathematics. **Benefits:** Dental Insurance; Disability Coverage; Employee Discounts; Life Insurance; Medical Insurance; Pension Plan; Profit Sharing; Savings Plan; Tuition Assistance. **Special Programs:** Internships. **Corporate headquarters location:** Minneapolis MN. **Operations at this facility include:** Divisional Headquarters; Research and Development; Sales. **Listed on:** New York Stock Exchange.

CORNERSTONE IMAGING, INC.
1710 Fortune Drive, San Jose CA 95131. 408/435-8900. **Contact:** Human Resources. **Description:** Cornerstone Imaging, Inc. is a technology and market leader in image display products for large-scale production document imaging processing systems. The company's products, which are based on proprietary silicon and software, improve the scanning and display of digitally stored images. **Corporate headquarters location:** This Location. **Number of employees at this location:** 98.

DATA TECHNOLOGY CORPORATION (DTC)
1515 Centre Pointe Drive, Milpitas CA 95035. 408/942-4000. **Contact:** Page Frechette, Manager of Staffing. **Description:** Develops and manufactures computer peripherals such as printers, disk drives, terminals, controllers, and supplies. Products are marketed to both original equipment manufacturers and distributors. **Common positions include:** Computer Programmer; Editor; Electrical/Electronics Engineer; Systems Analyst; Technical Writer/Editor. **Educational backgrounds include:** Computer Science; Engineering. **Benefits:** Dental Insurance; Disability Coverage; Employee Discounts; Life Insurance; Medical Insurance; Profit Sharing; Savings Plan; Tuition Assistance; Vision Insurance. **Corporate headquarters location:** This Location. **Listed on:** New York Stock Exchange.

DIGIDESIGN INC.
3401-A Hillview Avenue, Palo Alto CA 94304. 415/842-7900. **Contact:** Human Resources. **Description:** A manufacturer of electronic audio and video equipment for home and auto, public address systems, and music distribution apparatus. Digidesign is engaged in designing, developing, and producing prepackaged software; installing software; and training users.

DIGITAL EQUIPMENT CORPORATION
2575 Augustine Drive, Santa Clara CA 95054. 408/727-0200. **Contact:** Personnel. **Description:** Designs, manufactures, sells, and services computers and associated peripheral equipment and related software supplies. Applications and programs include scientific research, computation, communications, education, data analysis, industrial control time sharing, commercial data processing, graphic arts, word processing, health care, instrumentation, engineering, and simulation. Digital Equipment has operations in 37 foreign countries. This facility produces mini-computers. **Corporate headquarters location:** Maynard MA. **Other U.S. locations:** Oakland CA; San Francisco CA. **Listed on:** New York Stock Exchange.

DIGITAL EQUIPMENT CORPORATION
455 Market Street, 7th Floor, San Francisco CA 94105-2420. 415/882-3600. **Contact:** Human Resources. **Description:** Designs, manufactures, sells, and services computers and associated peripheral equipment and related software supplies. Applications and programs include scientific research, computation, communications, education, data analysis, industrial control time sharing, commercial data processing, graphic arts, word processing, health care, instrumentation, engineering, and simulation. Digital Equipment has operations in 37 foreign countries. **Corporate headquarters location:** Maynard MA.

DIGITAL EQUIPMENT CORPORATION
529 Bryant Street, Palo Alto CA 94301-1704. 415/617-3400. **Contact:** Human Resources. **Description:** Designs, manufactures, sells, and services computers and associated peripheral equipment and related software supplies. Applications and programs include scientific research, computation, communications, education, data analysis, industrial control time sharing, commercial data processing, graphic arts, word processing, health care, instrumentation, engineering, and simulation. Digital Equipment has operations in 37 foreign countries. **Corporate headquarters location:** Maynard MA.

ELECTRONIC ARTS, INC.
1450 Fashion Island Boulevard, San Mateo CA 94404. 415/571-7171. **Contact:** Human Resources. **Description:** Creates, markets, and distributes interactive entertainment software for use primarily on 16-bit computer platforms, including the Sega Genesis and Super Nintendo entertainment systems and floppy disk-based PCs (mostly IBM PCs and compatibles). **Number of employees nationwide:** 910.

ELECTRONIC DATA SYSTEMS CORPORATION
180 Blue Ravine Road, Suite 1A, Folsom CA 95630. 916/351-8938. **Contact:** Staffing. **Description:** Engaged in the management of information technology providing consulting systems development systems integration, and systems management for large-scale and industry specific applications. Founded in 1962, the company pioneered the concept of Facilities Management. **NOTE:** Please contact Pam Craig at 360/697-7558 for employment information.

ELECTRONICS FOR IMAGING, INC.
2855 Campus Drive, San Mateo CA 94403. 415/286-8600. **Fax:** 415/286-8544. **Contact:** Human Resources. **Description:** Electronics for Imaging, Inc. designs and markets products that enable high-quality color printing in short production runs. The company's Fiery Color Servers incorporate hardware and software technologies that transform digital color copiers from the leading copier manufacturers into fast, high-quality color printers. First shipped in 1991, more than 16,000 Fiery Color Servers have been sold and installed in leading corporations, advertising agencies, graphic design studios, and print-for-pay businesses around the world.

EPIC DESIGN TECHNOLOGY, INC.
310 North Mary Avenue, Sunnyvale CA 94086. 408/988-2997. **Contact:** Human Resources. **Description:** EPIC develops, markets, and supports a family of simulation and analysis software tools that helps integrated circuit (IC) designers better manage the timing and power characteristics of IC designs. The company's tools can be used by designers at different stages of IC development to help identify flaws, enhance speed, and reduce power consumption. EPIC's tools are focused on meeting the simulation and static and dynamic analysis requirements of IC designers and reducing the power consumption of complex ICs. The company's three principal products, PathMill, PowerMill, and TimeMill utilize the company's core technologies to enable a designer to address timing and power requirements of an IC. **Corporate headquarters location:** This Location.

EVEREX SYSTEMS INC.
5020 Brandin Court, Fremont CA 94538. 510/498-1111. **Fax:** 510/683-2099. **Contact:** Human Resources. **Description:** Manufactures computer peripheral equipment. **Benefits:** 401(k); Dental Insurance; Disability Coverage; Life Insurance; Medical Insurance. **Corporate headquarters location:** This Location. **Operations at this facility include:** Administration; Manufacturing; Sales; Service. **Listed on:** Privately held. **Number of employees at this location:** 100. **Number of employees nationwide:** 110.

FAIR, ISAAC AND COMPANY
120 North Redwood Drive, San Rafael CA 94903. 415/472-2211. **Contact:** Human Resources Department. **Description:** Fair, Isaac and Company is a leading developer of data management systems and services for the consumer credit, personal lines insurance, and direct marketing industries. The company employs various tools such as database enhancement software, predictive modeling, adaptive control, and systems automation to help its customers "make better decisions through data." Established in 1956, Fair, Isaac and Company pioneered the credit risk scoring technologies now employed by most major U.S. consumer credit grantors. Its rule-based decision management systems, originally developed to screen consumer credit applicants, are now routinely employed in all phases of the credit account cycle: direct mail solicitation (i.e. credit cards and lines of credit), application processing, card reissuance, online credit authorization, and collection. **Common positions include:** Account Executive; Actuary; Client/Server Specialist; Computer Graphics Specialist; Computer Programmer; Computer Systems Analyst; Credit Manager; Customer Service Representative; Economist/Market Research Analyst; Financial Analyst; Human Resources Specialist; Management Analyst/Consultant; Marketing Specialist; Mathematician; Project Manager; Quality Control Supervisor; Recruiter; Software Engineer; Statistician; Technical Writer/Editor. **Educational backgrounds include:** Computer Science; Mathematics; Operations; Statistics. **Benefits:** 401(k); Dental Insurance; Disability Coverage; Life Insurance; Medical Insurance; Pension Plan; Profit Sharing; Savings Plan; Tuition Assistance.

Corporate headquarters location: This Location. **Subsidiaries include:** Dynamark (Minneapolis MN). **Other U.S. locations:** Monterey CA; New Castle DE; Atlanta GA. **Operations at this facility include:** Divisional Headquarters; Research and Development; Sales. **Listed on:** NASDAQ. **Number of employees at this location:** 500. **Number of employees nationwide:** 700.

FAIR, ISAAC AND COMPANY
201 Van Buren Street, Monterey CA 93940. 408/646-9386. **Contact:** Human Resources. **Description:** Fair, Isaac and Company is a leading developer of data management systems and services for the consumer credit, personal lines insurance, and direct marketing industries. The company employs various tools, such as database enhancement software, predictive modeling, adaptive control, and systems automation to help its customers "make better decisions through data." Established in 1956, Fair, Isaac and Company pioneered the credit risk scoring technologies now employed by most major U.S. consumer credit grantors. Its rule-based decision management systems, originally developed to screen consumer credit applicants, are now routinely employed in all phases of the credit account cycle: direct mail solicitation (i.e. credit cards, lines of credit, etc.), application processing, card reissuance, on-line credit authorization, and collection. **Corporate headquarters location:** San Rafael CA. **Subsidiaries include:** Dynamark (Minneapolis MN).

FILENET CORPORATION
100 First Street, Suite 1600, San Francisco CA 94105-2636. 415/957-2700. **Contact:** Human Resources. **Description:** FileNet's customers are among the leaders in their respective industries, consistently employing leading-edge technologies and procedures to compete more effectively, increase productivity, improve customer satisfaction, and achieve higher profitability. FileNet's document-imaging and work flow management solutions help achieve these objectives at more than 900 sites in 39 countries around the world. FileNet has subsidiaries in six European countries. **Corporate headquarters location:** Costa Mesa CA. **Listed on:** NASDAQ. **Number of employees nationwide:** 970.

FIRST IMAGE
2929 Campus Drive, Suite 100, San Mateo CA 94403. 415/345-7272. **Contact:** Personnel. **Description:** Engaged in computer output microfiche production and deliveries. **NOTE:** Personnel matters are handled out of the Atlanta office. Please contact Personnel at: Three Corporate Square, Suite 400, Atlanta GA 30329. 404/321-6730. **Corporate headquarters location:** Atlanta GA.

FIRST IMAGE
1760 Cesar Chavez Boulevard, Suite O, San Francisco CA 94124-1136. 415/285-5771. **Contact:** Human Resources. **Description:** Engaged in computer output microfiche production and deliveries. **NOTE:** Personnel matters are handled out of the Atlanta office. Please contact Personnel at: Three Corporate Square, Suite 400, Atlanta GA 30329. 404/321-6730.

FRAME TECHNOLOGY CORPORATION
333 West San Carlos Street, San Jose CA 95110. 408/975-6000. **Contact:** Human Resources. **Description:** Develops, manufactures, and markets document publishing software that allows users of workstations and personal computers to create and distribute complex, highly-structured documents.

GENERAL MAGIC, INC.
420 North Mary Avenue, Sunnyvale CA 94086. 408/774-4000. **Contact:** Human Resources. **Description:** General Magic, Inc. was founded to develop object-oriented software platform technologies for a new generation of electronic devices, networks, and services. The company has developed two platform technologies called Magic Cap and Telescript. Magic Cap software integrates electronic mail, fax, telephone, and paging capabilities, enables wireless and wireline communications, and provides an intuitive user interface for personal intelligent communicators and other communications devices. Telescript software allows the creation of network platforms by providing a new communications architecture using intelligent mobile software programs that route themselves through networks and perform various tasks on behalf of a user, from carrying messages to executing transactions. The company's technologies are open platforms intended to enable the development of communicating applications and services by independent software vendors, electronic merchants and publishers, and other third parties. The company believes that Magic Cap and Telescript will support the creation of an electronic marketplace in which consumers and business professionals will use various electronic devices to access electronic services which will be available on networks provided by public and private network operators. To promote the emergence of an electronic marketplace based on Magic Cap and Telescript technologies, the company has formed a strategic alliance with multinational consumer electronics, computer, and telecommunications companies including Sony, Motorola, Apple, Fujitsu, Matsushita, Mitsubishi, Northern Telecom, Philips, Oki, Sanyo, and Toshiba; and large network operators such as AT&T, Cable & Wireless, France Telecom, Fujitsu, and Nippon Telegraph and Telephone Corporation.

GEOWORKS
960 Atlantic Avenue, Alameda CA 94501. 510/814-1660. **Contact:** Human Resources. **Description:** Geoworks develops and markets the GEOS operating system, a key enabling technology for the consumer computing device (CCD) market. The company has dedicated years of effort to optimize and evolve GEOS to meet the demands of this diverse market. Working with leading hardware manufacturers, communications providers, and independent software vendors, Geoworks is focused on software for products under $500. The company believes GEOS is a compact and efficient operating system, based on modern, object-oriented design, with multitasking, high-quality imaging, and a patented flexible user interface.

HMT TECHNOLOGY
1055 Page Avenue, Fremont CA 94538. 510/490-3100. **Recorded Jobline:** 510/490-3100x6950. **Contact:** Don Seemann, Human Resources Representative. **Description:** Manufacturers of hard disk drives. **Common positions include:** Accountant/Auditor; Computer Programmer; Computer Systems Analyst; Designer; Electrical/Electronics Engineer; Industrial Engineer; Mechanical Engineer; Science Technologist; Software Engineer. **Educational backgrounds include:** Computer Science; Engineering. **Benefits:** 401(k); Dental Insurance; Disability Coverage; Employee Discounts; Life Insurance; Medical Insurance; Tuition Assistance. **Special Programs:** Internships. **Corporate headquarters location:** This Location. **Parent company:** Hitachi Metals. **Operations at this facility include:** Administration; Manufacturing; Research and Development; Sales; Service. **Number of employees at this location:** 500.

HEWLETT-PACKARD
8000 Foothills Boulevard, Roseville CA 95747. 916/786-8000. **Contact:** Personnel Department. **Description:** Produces business computer systems. Overall, Hewlett-

Packard is engaged in the design and manufacture of measurement and computation products and systems used in business, industry, engineering, science, health care, and education; principal products are integrated instrument and computer systems (including hardware and software), computer systems and peripheral products, and medical electronic equipment and systems.

HEWLETT-PACKARD

1266 Kifer Road, Sunnyvale CA 94086. 408/246-4300. **Contact:** Staffing Department. **Description:** The Test and Measurement Group designs and manufactures analytical and scientific computation products and systems used in business, engineering, science, health care and education. The Integrated Circuits Business Division designs and markets ICs used in Hewlett-Packard and external customer products. Hardware and software engineers collaborate to use the latest technologies in designing state-of-the-art components and products. The Computer Products Organization is responsible for the marketing, sales and support, and distribution of Hewlett-Packard PCs, low-end workstations, printers, calculators, palmtop computers, and related components. **Common positions include:** Computer Programmer; Customer Service Representative; Electrical/Electronics Engineer; Financial Analyst; Hardware Engineer; Marketing Specialist; Software Engineer. **Educational backgrounds include:** Computer Science; Engineering; Finance; Marketing. **Benefits:** Daycare Assistance; Disability Coverage; Employee Discounts; Life Insurance; Medical Insurance; Pension Plan; Profit Sharing; Savings Plan; Tuition Assistance. **Special Programs:** Internships. **Corporate headquarters location:** Palo Alto CA. **Operations at this facility include:** Administration; Manufacturing; Research and Development; Sales; Service. **Listed on:** New York Stock Exchange. **Number of employees nationwide:** 93,100.

HEWLETT-PACKARD
COMMERCIAL SYSTEMS DIVISION

19111 Pruneridge Avenue, Cupertino CA 95014. 408/725-8900. **Contact:** Personnel Department. **Description:** Produces business computer systems for interactive, online data processing, database management, and distributed data processing. Hewlett-Packard is engaged in the design and manufacture of measurement and computation products and systems used in business, industry, engineering, science, health care, and education. Principal products are integrated instrument and computer systems (including hardware and software); computer systems and peripheral products; and medical electronic equipment and systems. **NOTE:** Send resumes to: 1266 Kifer Road, MS/100G, Sunnyvale CA 94086. **Common positions include:** Computer Programmer; Electrical/Electronics Engineer; Financial Analyst; Marketing Specialist. **Educational backgrounds include:** Computer Science; Engineering; Finance; Marketing. **Benefits:** Credit Union; Dental Insurance; Disability Coverage; Employee Discounts; Life Insurance; Medical Insurance; Pension Plan; Profit Sharing; Savings Plan; Tuition Assistance. **Corporate headquarters location:** Palo Alto CA. **Operations at this facility include:** Administration; Divisional Headquarters; Manufacturing; Research and Development; Service. **Listed on:** American Stock Exchange; New York Stock Exchange; Tokyo Stock Exchange.

IBM CORPORATION
STORAGE SYSTEMS DIVISION

5600 Cottle Road, Building 78, San Jose CA 95193. 408/256-1600. **Contact:** Human Resources. **Description:** A worldwide manufacturer and supplier in the area of information technology. Products include data-processing machines and systems, telecommunications systems and products, information distributors, office systems, typewriters, copiers, educational and testing materials, and related supplies and services. IBM operates worldwide through the following groups, each comprised of several operating divisions: Information Systems Group; Information Systems and Technology Group; and Information Systems and Communications Group. **Subsidiaries include:** IBM Credit Corporation; IBM Instruments, Inc.; and IBM World Trade Corporation.

IBM CORPORATION/SAN FRANCISCO
425 Market Street, San Francisco CA 94105. 415/545-2000. **Contact:** Central Employment Office. **Description:** International Business Machines (IBM) is a developer, manufacturer, and marketer of advanced information processing products, including computers and microelectronic technology, software, networking systems and information technology-related services. The company strives to offer value worldwide, through its United States, Canada, Europe/Middle East/Africa, Latin America and Asia Pacific business units, by providing comprehensive and complete product choices. **Corporate headquarters location:** Armonk NY. **Listed on:** New York Stock Exchange.

IKOS SYSTEMS, INC.
19050 Pruneridge Avenue, Cupertino CA 95014. 408/255-4567. **Fax:** 409/366-8699. **Contact:** Human Resources. **Description:** IKOS designs, manufactures, markets, and supports logic simulation software and compatible hardware accelerators. IKOS' simulators are used in the design of Application Specific Integrated Circuits (ASIC) and ASIC-based systems. IKOS supports a direct sales operation in North America, France, and Germany, and a distributor network covering the remainder of Europe and Asia. The company's products are used by designers of electronic systems to determine whether a system design works before incurring the cost and time to build the actual system. **Corporate headquarters location:** This Location.

INFORMATION BUILDERS INC.
224 Airport Parkway, Suite 310, San Jose CA 95110-1022. 408/453-7600. **Contact:** Human Resources. **Description:** A software development firm. Products include FOCUS, EDA, and LEVEL5 software for various platforms. Other services include support and sales.

INFORMIX SOFTWARE, INC.
4100 Bohannon Drive, Menlo Park CA 94025. 415/926-6300. **Fax:** 415/926-6161. **Recorded Jobline:** 415/926-OPEN. **Contact:** Janette Sampson, Human Resources Representative. **Description:** Informix Software, Inc. provides database technology to build, deploy, run, and evolve applications. Informix products include powerful distributed database management systems, robust application development tools, and graphical- and character-based productivity software for delivering information to every significant desktop platform. European headquarters are in London, England and Asian/Pacific headquarters are in Singapore. **Common positions include:** Product Engineer; Software Engineer; Technical Support Representative. **Educational backgrounds include:** Computer Science; Engineering. **Benefits:** 401(k); Dental Insurance; Disability Coverage; Life Insurance; Medical Insurance; Profit Sharing; Tuition Assistance. **Corporate headquarters location:** This Location. **Other U.S. locations:** Lenexa KS; Portland OR. **Operations at this facility include:** Administration; Research and Development; Sales. **Listed on:** NASDAQ. **Number of employees at this location:** 800. **Number of employees nationwide:** 1,300.

INTEGRATED SYSTEMS, INC.
201 Moffett Park Drive, Sunnyvale CA 94089. 408/542-1500. **Fax:** 408/980-0400. **Contact:** Human Resources. **Description:** Integrated Systems, Inc. is a world leader in developing design tool and operating system software for computers embedded in products ranging from everyday consumer goods to industrial and transportation sector capital equipment. Integrated Systems' products offer a complete graphical solution for rapidly designing, simulating, and testing microprocessor-based control systems. The company's real-time operating system environment has gained market share through expediting development of embedded software-based end products. The company also provides embedded and control system application development engineering services. The company focuses on six worldwide embedded systems markets: aerospace, automotive, communications, multimedia/entertainment, office/retail automation, and industrial process control. **Corporate headquarters location:** This Location.

INTELLICORP
1975 El Camino Real West, Suite 101, Mountain View CA 94040-2216. 415/965-5500. **Fax:** 415/965-5647. **Contact:** Human Resources. **Description:** IntelliCorp designs, develops and markets software development tools and provides related training, customer support, and consulting services. IntelliCorp's mission is to provide its customers with object-oriented software tools for the design, development, and delivery of scalable client/server applications. The company's products, Kappa, Kappa-PC, Object Management Workbench (OMW), and KEE are enriched by 12 years of technical leadership in object-oriented development software and knowledge systems applications. IntelliCorp products are marketed through the company's direct sales force and authorized resellers. Headquartered in Mountain View CA, IntelliCorp has approximately 126 employees and offices across the U.S. and Europe.

INTERACTIVE DEVELOPMENT ENVIRONMENTS INC.
595 Market Street, 10th Floor, San Francisco CA 94105. 415/543-0900. **Contact:** Human Resources. **Description:** Develops and markets computer-aided software engineering (CASE) products which allow a network of mini-computers to interact, enabling fully-integrated software environments to exist.

INTERNATIONAL MICROCOMPUTER SOFTWARE, INC. (IMSI)
1895 Francisco Boulevard East, San Rafael CA 94901. 415/257-3000. **Contact:** Human Resources. **Description:** IMSI is a leading developer of productivity software for business and home use. The company has recently established the Living Media division which focuses on CD-ROM multimedia software for learning and education. IMSI's three primary product lines are business, consumer productivity, and multimedia learning software. The majority of IMSI's revenues come from its business software that work with, and extend the functionality of Microsoft Office, as well as operate as stand alone products. IMSI also offers a wide range of productivity for under $50. IMSI is fast becoming a leader in the rapidly emerging market for content-based products for business users and utility software products. Finally, Living Media was formed in 1994 as the consumer multimedia division of IMSI, to address the rapidly-growing home market for educational and learning software. These products educate and entertain users through interactive multimedia presentations, with animation, CD-quality audio, video, graphics, and text.

INTUIT, INC.
P.O. Box 7850, MS-1858, Mountain View CA 94039. 415/944-6000. **Contact:** Human Resources. **Description:** Intuit, Inc. develops and markets personal finance and small

business accounting software and complementary supplies and services for personal computer users. Its principal product is Quicken, which allows users to organize, understand, and manage their personal finances. **Number of employees nationwide:** 500.

JANDEL SCIENTIFIC
2591 Kerner Boulevard, San Rafael CA 94901. 415/453-6700. **Contact:** John J. Osborne, M.D., President. **Description:** Jandel-Scientific is a developer of scientific software.

KOMAG, INC.
275 South Hillview Drive, Milpitas CA 95035. 408/946-2300. **Contact:** Human Resources. **Description:** Komag develops, manufactures, and markets sputtered thin-film media for use in high-capacity, high-performance 5-1/4 inch, 3-1/2 inch and smaller Winchester disk drive storage devices. Komag also makes thin-film recording heads. **Number of employees nationwide:** 3,090.

LSI LOGIC
1551 McCarthy Boulevard, Milpitas CA 95035. 408/433-8000. **Contact:** Personnel Manager. **Description:** LSI Logic is a designer, manufacturer, and marketer of specialized integrated circuits primarily in the desktop, personal computer, networking, and digital video applications markets. The company also provides computer-aided engineering design, technology services, and software design tools to customers in the electronic data processing, telecommunications, and automation industries. **Listed on:** New York Stock Exchange.

THE LEARNING COMPANY
6493 Kaiser Drive, Fremont CA 94555. 510/792-2101. **Contact:** Human Resources Department. **Description:** The Learning Company uses emerging technologies to create a system of highly engaging, easy-to-use, software products that help build important lifelong learning and communications skills. The subject areas and design objectives for The Learning Company's products are developed with input with education and language professionals, purchasers, and end users to ensure that each new product is of the highest quality and matches an identified market need. The Learning Company has developed families of educational software products designed to help build important life-long learning and communication skills in key subject areas that are appropriate for different age groups. Most of The Learning Company's products are available in home editions, and certain products are also available in school editions, which include network, site license, and stand alone configurations. Product families include the Rabbit Family (Ages 3 to 7), The Treasure Family (Ages 6 to 8), The Writing Tools Family (Ages 8 and Up) and The Children's Writing & Publishing Center, and The Foreign Languages Family (Ages 15 and Up). **Number of employees at this location:** 190.

LOCKHEED MARTIN TACTICAL DEFENSE SYSTEMS
3151 Zanker Road, San Jose CA 95134. 408/432-8000. **Fax:** 408/432-7961. **Contact:** Human Resources. **Description:** Lockheed Martin Tactical Defense Systems designs and builds 16-bit and 32-bit technical computing systems used in mil-spec environments. Applications include electronic warfare, signal intelligence, radar, sonar, and imaging where digital signal processing or general purpose computing is required. The company is also involved in systems engineering, software development tools, rugged computer systems, and integrated workstations of commercial architectures for proof-of-concept program phases.

LOGICA, INC.
353 Sacramento Street, Suite 2300, San Francisco CA 94111. 415/288-5200. **Contact:** Human Resources Department. **Description:** Logica, Inc. is a computer industry firm whose business activities include computer programming systems and design, and consulting services, primarily in the banking, insurance, and telecommunications industries.

LOGITECH, INC./PRODUCT SUPPORT
6505 Kaiser Drive, Fremont CA 94555-3615. 510/795-8500. **Fax:** 510/792-8901. **Contact:** Linda Vento, Human Resources Manager. **Description:** Engaged in the design, development, manufacturing, and marketing of computer hardware and software products. Logitech is the worldwide leading manufacturer of computer pointing devices (mice, trackballs, and joysticks) and imaging devices (scanners and cameras) for the PC, MAC, and other platforms. **Common positions include:** Accountant/Auditor; Buyer; Computer Programmer; Computer Systems Analyst; Customer Service Representative; Electrical/Electronics Engineer; Financial Analyst; Manufacturer's/Wholesaler's Sales Rep.; Software Engineer; Technical Support Representative. **Educational backgrounds include:** Accounting; Computer Science; Engineering; Marketing. **Benefits:** 401(k); Dental Insurance; Disability Coverage; Employee Discounts; Life Insurance; Medical Insurance; Tuition Assistance. **Special Programs:** Internships. **Corporate headquarters location:** This Location. **Other U.S. locations:** Framingham MA; Dallas TX. **Parent company:** Logitech International S.A. **Operations at this facility include:** Administration; Research and Development; Sales. **Number of employees at this location:** 350. **Number of employees nationwide:** 350.

LOTUS DEVELOPMENT CORPORATION
One Bush Street, Suite 600, San Francisco CA 94104-4412. 415/421-7013. **Contact:** Human Resources. **Description:** Lotus Development Corporation develops, manufactures, and markets applications software and services that meet the evolving technology and business applications requirements for individuals, work groups, and entire organizations.

MAXTOR CORPORATION
211 River Oaks Parkway, San Jose CA 95134. 408/432-1700. **Contact:** Human Resources Department. **Description:** A large producer of hard disk drives and related electronic data storage equipment for computers, as well as related components for original equipment manufacturers. The company has production plants in Hong Kong and Singapore, 10 U.S. sales offices, and nine sales offices in foreign nations. **Listed on:** NASDAQ.

MICRO LINEAR CORPORATION
2092 Concourse Drive, San Jose CA 95131. 408/433-5200. **Contact:** Human Resources Department. **Description:** Micro Linear designs, develops, and markets high-performance analog and mixed-signal integrated circuits for a broad range of applications within the communications, computer, and industrial markets. The company's products provide highly-integrated systems-level solutions for a variety of applications, including local area networks, mass storage, telecommunications, power management, motor control, and data conversion. The company uses its proprietary design methodology and bipolar, CMOS, and BiCMOS manufacturing processes to produce standard and semi-standard products that enable systems designers to achieve increased levels of systems integration. Micro Linear's approach simplifies system design by reducing the number of required analog and mixed-signal circuits and other passive components in electronic

systems. The company also believes this enables its customers to achieve faster time to market and to design electronic systems that provide significant performance advantages, greater functionality, lower power dissipation, and increased reliability, while reducing system size and cost. Micro Linear targets high-growth applications that require substantial analog and mixed signal content and that derive significant benefits from the use of the company's systems-level expertise. Using its analog and mixed signal design expertise, the company integrates electronic subsystems or several analog building block circuits into a single circuit or chipset. This provides Micro Linear's customers the opportunity to identify and select certain product features that address the technical and time to market requirements of specific customer applications. The combination of highly-integrated circuits with sophisticated systems-level features has enabled Micro Linear to become the sole source supplier for a number of its products.

MICROGRAPHIC TECHNOLOGY CORPORATION

520 Logue Avenue, Mountain View CA 94043. 415/965-3700. **Contact:** Barry Cooper, Personnel. **Description:** Micrographic Technology Corporation manufactures computer peripheral equipment as a division of the national electronics products manufacturing firm.

MICRONICS COMPUTERS, INC.

221 Warren Avenue, Fremont CA 94539. 510/651-2300. **Contact:** Human Resources. **Description:** Micronics Computers supplies high-performance system boards -- which contain the microprocessor and supporting memory components and logic circuitry that form the core of a personal computer -- for high-end IBM compatible PCs sold by original equipment manufacturers and value-added resellers. **Common positions include:** Accountant/Auditor; Buyer; Credit Clerk and Authorizer; Credit Manager; Customer Service Representative; Electrical/Electronics Engineer; Financial Manager; Human Resources Specialist; Manufacturer's/Wholesaler's Sales Rep.; Marketing/Advertising/PR Manager; Payroll Clerk; Purchasing Agent and Manager; Quality Control Supervisor; Receptionist; Software Engineer; Technical Representative. **Educational backgrounds include:** Accounting; Business Administration; Computer Science; Engineering; Finance; Marketing. **Benefits:** Dental Insurance; Disability Coverage; Employee Discounts; Life Insurance; Medical Insurance; Profit Sharing; Savings Plan. **Corporate headquarters location:** This Location. **Parent company:** Softnet (Lake Forest IL). **Operations at this facility include:** Administration; Manufacturing; Research and Development; Sales; Service. **Listed on:** NASDAQ. **Number of employees at this location:** 240.

MICROPOLIS CORPORATION

100 Century Center Court, Suite 410, San Jose CA 95112-4512. 408/441-0333. **Fax:** 408/441-0334. **Contact:** Human Resources. **Description:** Micropolis Corporation is a leading designer and manufacturer of SuperCapacity disk drives, information storage, and video systems. The company's customers are computer system manufacturers, distributors, value-added resellers, and system integrators. Principal products are disk drives and drive arrays with high-capacity, fast-access, high-reliability, and low lifetime cost; and video servers. Micropolis' customers incorporate the company's disk drives into high-performance computer systems for single- and multi-user applications, including computer-aided design and manufacturing systems, workstations, and local area network and video file servers. **Corporate headquarters location:** Chatsworth CA. **Other U.S. locations:** Irvine CA; Larkspur CO; Branford CT; Roswell GA; Des Plaines IL; Salem NH; Plano TX; Charlottesville VA.

MICROSOFT CORPORATION
10000 Torre Avenue, Cupertino CA 95014. 408/777-0314. **Contact:** Human Resources Department. **Description:** Microsoft Corporation designs, sells, and supports a product line of systems and applications microcomputer software for business, home, and professional use. Microsoft also produces related books and hardware products. The company has shown increasing interest in developing applications for interactive television. Software includes spreadsheet, desktop publishing, project management, graphics, word processing, and database applications, as well as operating systems and programming languages.

MOTOROLA COMPUTER GROUP
COMMERCIAL SYSTEMS DIVISION
1150 Kifer Road, Suite 100, Sunnyville CA 94086. 408/749-0510. **Contact:** Nancy Dyal, Recruiter. **Description:** Motorola Computer Group markets and services multi-function computer systems for business applications. **Common positions include:** Computer Programmer; Software Engineer. **Educational backgrounds include:** Accounting; Business Administration; Communications; Computer Science; Engineering; Finance; Marketing. **Benefits:** Dental Insurance; Disability Coverage; Employee Discounts; Life Insurance; Medical Insurance; Profit Sharing; Savings Plan; Tuition Assistance. **Corporate headquarters location:** Schaumburg IL. **Parent company:** Motorola, Inc. **Operations at this facility include:** Divisional Headquarters. **Listed on:** New York Stock Exchange.

MYLEX CORPORATION
34551 Ardenwood Boulevard, Fremont CA 94555. 510/796-6100. **Contact:** Human Resources Department. **Description:** Mylex Corporation designs and manufactures disk array controllers, system boards, and network interface cards, as well as supporting proprietary software and firmware for a wide range of personal computers, workstations and servers. Recognized by OEMs, system integrators, and value-added resellers as a world leader in RAID (Redundant Array of Independent Disks) technology, Mylex believes it is the standard setter for RAID solutions and fully-integrated PCI systems. According to DISK/TREND report, the company has shipped more disk array controllers than all of its worldwide competitors combined. With the introduction of a MicroChannel controller, a dual-connector PCI controller, and an external SCSI controller, Mylex believes that it now offers a RAID solution for virtually every microcomputer-based platform in the industry today. Founded in 1983, Mylex is headquartered in Fremont, California.

NETWORK COMPUTING DEVICES, INC.
350 North Bernardo Avenue, Mountain View CA 94043. 415/694-0650. **Contact:** Human Resources Department. **Description:** Network Computing Devices, Inc. provides desktop information access solutions for network computing environments. The company is a leading worldwide supplier of X Window System terminals and PC-X server software products which integrate Microsoft Windows- and DOS-based PCs into X/UNIX networks. NCD also supplies the Z-Mail family of cross platform electronic-mail and messaging software for open systems environments, as well as Mariner, an Internet access and navigation software tool that provides a unified interface to all Internet resources.

NETWORK GENERAL CORPORATION
4200 Bohannon Drive, Menlo Park CA 94025. 415/473-2000. **Fax:** 415/321-0855. **Contact:** Human Resources Department. **Description:** Network General Corporation

designs, manufactures, markets, and supports software-based analysis and monitoring tools primarily for managing enterprise-wide computer networks. The company's tool line consists of software and network interface cards used with portable PC-compatible computers to monitor and analyze individual local area networks (LANs) or wide area networks (WANs) segments.

NOVELL, INC.
2180 Fortune Drive, San Jose CA 95131. 408/434-2300. **Fax:** 800/688-9931. **Recorded Jobline:** 800/624-4520. **Contact:** Human Resources. **Description:** Novell is a software company that is singularly focused on network software. The company sets and adheres to open standards, develops new tools and systems, works in partnership with other companies, and makes computer networks easy to use and manage. Novell has grown to become the third-largest software company in the world by building software that spans from operating systems, network infrastructure, and services, to network applications and information access products. A $2 billion software company, Novell employs approximately 7,900 worldwide with major development sites in California, Utah, and New Jersey. Novell's leading products include NetWare 4, UnixWare 2, PerfectOffice 3, and GroupWise 4. Novell is built around four business units that develop complementary system software components and applications used to deploy advanced network-based information systems: the NetWare Systems Group; the UNIX Systems Group; the Information Access and Management Group; and the Applications Group.

ORACLE CORPORATION
500 Oracle Parkway, Redwood Shores CA 94065. 415/506-7000. **Contact:** Human Resources Department. **Description:** A computer programming services company. **Common positions include:** Administrative Services Manager; Computer Programmer; Computer Systems Analyst; Economist/Market Research Analyst; Electrical/Electronics Engineer; Purchasing Agent and Manager; Software Engineer. **Educational backgrounds include:** Accounting; Business Administration; Computer Science; Engineering. **Benefits:** 401(k); Dental Insurance; Disability Coverage; Employee Discounts; Life Insurance; Medical Insurance; Profit Sharing; Savings Plan; Tuition Assistance. **Corporate headquarters location:** This Location. **Other U.S. locations:** Nationwide. **Operations at this facility include:** Administration; Sales. **Number of employees nationwide:** 12,000.

ORBIT INTERACTION
131 Hawthorne Drive, Menlo Park CA 94027-2164. 415/325-1960. **Contact:** Human Resources Department. **Description:** Orbit Interaction is involved in user interface analysis and design.

PYRAMID TECHNOLOGY CORPORATION
3860 North First Street, San Jose CA 95134. 408/428-9000. **Fax:** 408/428-7110. **Contact:** Human Resources Department. **Description:** Pyramid Technology Corporation is a computer services company.

QUANTUM CORPORATION
500 McCarthy Boulevard, Milpitas CA 95035. 408/894-4000. **Contact:** Human Resources Department. **Description:** Quantum designs, manufactures, and markets small hard disk drives used in desktop PCs, workstations and notebook computers. The company's primary product line is the ProDrive series of high-performance, 3-1/2 inch hard disk drives. Matsushita-Kotobuki Electronics of Japan manufactures some of

Quantum's drives. **Corporate headquarters location:** This Location. **Number of employees nationwide:** 2,455.

READ-RITE CORPORATION
345 Los Coches Street, Milpitas CA 95035. 408/262-6700. **Contact:** Human Resources Department. **Description:** Read-Rite Corporation is an independent supplier of thin film magnetic recording heads for Winchester disk drives. The company entered the head stack assemblies (HSA) market with the late 1991 acquisition of Conner Peripherals and Maxtor's HSA operations. **Number of employees nationwide:** 2,500.

RECOM TECHNOLOGIES INC.
1245 South Winchester Boulevard, Suite 201, San Jose CA 95128. 408/261-7688. **Contact:** Human Resource Director. **Description:** Designs computer integrated systems and provides engineering services.

ROLM CORPORATION
4900 Old Ironsides Drive, Santa Clara CA 95054. 408/492-2000. **Contact:** Personnel Department. **Description:** A computer firm engaged in the manufacture of business communications systems.

SEI
444 Market Street, Suite 1200, San Francisco CA 94111-5325. 415/989-8960. **Contact:** Human Resources. **Description:** SEI operates primarily in two business markets: trust and banking and fund sponsor/investment advisory. The company invests for clients worldwide in both public and private markets, and also provides investment and business solutions to those in the investment business, who in turn serve their own investor clients. SEI provides direct investment solutions for $50 billion of investable capital and delivers systems and business solutions to organizations investing nearly $1 trillion. SEI is the largest provider of trust systems in the world, claiming over 40 percent of the U.S. trust market. The company's core business is to provide investment accounting software to over 400 banking institution customers.

SEAGATE TECHNOLOGY
P.O. Box 66360, Scotts Valley CA 95067-0360. 408/438-6550. **Contact:** Corporate Employment. **Description:** Seagate is a supplier of disc storage products to original equipment manufacturers. **Common positions include:** Accountant/Auditor; Administrator; Buyer; Chemist; Computer Programmer; Credit Manager; Customer Service Representative; Draftsperson; Electrical/Electronics Engineer; Financial Analyst; Human Resources Specialist; Industrial Engineer; Marketing Specialist; Mechanical Engineer; Quality Control Supervisor; Systems Analyst; Technical Writer/Editor. **Educational backgrounds include:** Accounting; Business Administration; Chemistry; Computer Science; Engineering; Finance; Marketing. **Corporate headquarters location:** This Location.

SEAGATE TECHNOLOGY
3081 Zanker Road, San Jose CA 95134. 408/456-4500. **Contact:** Human Resources Department. **Description:** Seagate Technology is a designer and manufacturer of data storage devices and related products including hard disk drives, tape drives, software, and systems for many different computer-related applications and operating systems. These products include 2.5 and 3.5 inch drives with memory storage capacity between 150 megabytes and one gigabyte. The company sells its products primarily through a sales force to OEMs (original equipment manufacturers) and through non-affiliated

distributors. **Subsidiaries include:** Arcada Holdings, Inc., an information protection and storage management software company serving several operating systems; and Conners Storage Systems. **Listed on:** New York Stock Exchange.

SEQUENT COMPUTER SYSTEMS, INC.
4699 Old Ironsides Drive, Suite 150, Santa Clara CA 95054. 408/970-3640. **Contact:** Human Resources Department. **Description:** Sequent Computer Systems is a leading provider of enterprise architecture and open solutions for large corporations. The company's Enterprise Division provides architectural consulting, professional services, and industry-leading servers that enable customers to migrate successfully from host-based, proprietary computer environments to open, client/server architectures. Working closely with leading hardware and software partners, the Enterprise Division helps customers design and implements enterprise-wide architectures and systems for online transaction processing, decision support, and workgroup computing. Sequent's Platform Division develops -- solely and in partnership with other companies -- high-performance, Intel-based, symmetric multiprocessing servers that run on the UNIX and Microsoft Windows NT operating systems and support enterprise-wide applications and information services. The Platform Division's products are sold by the Enterprise Division and through a variety of indirect channels, including OEM resellers, value-added resellers and distributors. Since the company was founded in 1983, Sequent Computer Systems has installed more than 5,500 large scale systems in 52 countries worldwide.

SIERRA ON-LINE INC.
P.O. Box 485, Coarsegold CA 93614-0485. 209/683-4468. **Contact:** Human Resources Department. **Description:** Sierra On-Line creates, produces, and distributes premium entertainment and educational software for the home, utilizing leading-edge interactive technologies. Sierra's products are designed for IBM compatible and Macintosh systems. Sierra continues to be a market leader in the development and publishing of entertainment software. In 1992, Sierra acquired Bright Star Technology, an educational software publisher. In 1993, they acquired Paris-based Coktel Vision, a leading European publisher of educational software. Sierra On-Line's continuing commitment to being a market leader in education includes releasing network-enabled educational products.

SILICON GRAPHICS
2011 North Shoreline Boulevard, Mountain View CA 94043-1389. 415/960-1980. **Contact:** Human Resources. **Description:** Silicon Graphics makes a family of workstation and server systems that are used by engineers, scientists, and other creative professionals to develop, analyze, and simulate complex, three-dimensional objects. Systems include Onyx, IRIS, Indigo, and Challenge, and all use RISC processors in their circuitry. In 1992, the company acquired MIPS Computer Systems. **Number of employees nationwide:** 3,750.

SOFTWARE TOOLWORKS
88 Roland Way, Novato CA 94945. 415/897-9900. **Fax:** 415/897-2747. **Contact:** Human Resources. **Description:** Develops, publishes, and licenses software for use with PCs and Nintendo. **Number of employees at this location:** 330.

SPECTRA*STAR PRODUCTS
1250 Ninth Street, Berkeley CA 94710. 510/524-3950. **Fax:** 510/524-9954. **Contact:** Human Resources. **Description:** Designs, manufactures, and markets a family of color

printers and presentation hardware and software products for the business and government marketplaces. These products work with PC, PS/2, and Apple Macintosh systems. The company's PostScript color printers include both thermal wax transfer and dye-sublimation printers. The products all use a flexible RISC-based architecture that offers users a range of options and features. In 1984, the company pioneered the electronic presentation marketplace with its introduction of VideoShow. In 1992, the company introduced VideoShow HQ, its third-generation electronic presentation product which positioned the company in the multimedia presentation marketplace. More recently, the company introduced VideoShow PRESENTER, its advanced hand-held remote control product for the PC Windows marketplace. In addition, the company's product line includes a number of other hardware and software presentation products and color printer supplies. Spectra*Star sells its products worldwide through a network of dealers and distributors in the U.S., Canada, Western Europe, Australia, and the Far East. The company's customers cover a broad range of industries and include many *Fortune* 500 companies. The company was founded in 1981 and has headquarters and manufacturing facilities in Berkeley CA and regional field personnel in the United States and Europe.

SPECTRUM HOLOBYTE, INC.
2490 Mariner Square Loop, Suite 100, Alameda CA 94501. 510/814-6370. **Fax:** 510/522-8416. **Recorded Jobline:** 510/814-6400. **Contact:** Human Resources. **Description:** Spectrum Holobyte, Inc. develops and publishes entertainment software for personal computers, including both IBM PCs and Macintoshes. The company also provides software for video game consoles such as those made by Sega and Nintendo and is creating software for next-generation game consoles. Spectrum Holobyte excels in technologies such as 3-D simulation, game artificial intelligence, and networked game-play -- capabilities increasingly critical to PC entertainment software as well as next-generation console software. Over the past decade, the company has published more than 100 software titles for PCs and game consoles, with total sales surpassing 12 million units. Twenty-two of these titles have sold more than 100,000 units each. **Common positions include:** Accountant/Auditor; Attorney; Budget Analyst; Buyer; Computer Programmer; Computer Systems Analyst; Customer Service Representative; Designer; Electrical/Electronics Engineer; Financial Analyst; Human Resources Specialist; Public Relations Specialist; Purchasing Agent and Manager; Quality Control Supervisor; Technical Writer/Editor. **Educational backgrounds include:** Accounting; Art/Design; Business Administration; Communications; Computer Science; Engineering; Finance; Liberal Arts; Marketing; Mathematics. **Benefits:** 401(k); Dental Insurance; Disability Coverage; Employee Discounts; Life Insurance; Medical Insurance; Profit Sharing; Savings Plan; Tuition Assistance. **Corporate headquarters location:** This Location. **Other U.S. locations:** Hunt Valley MD; Seattle WA. **Subsidiaries include:** MicroProse U.S., Hunt Valley MD; and MicroProse Europe, Chipping Sodbury, England. **Operations at this facility include:** Administration; Divisional Headquarters; Research and Development; Sales. **Listed on:** NASDAQ. **Number of employees at this location:** 200. **Number of employees nationwide:** 500.

STERLING SOFTWARE, INC.
FEDERAL SYSTEMS GROUP
Suite 510, Redwood City CA 94065-1417. 415/964-9900. **Fax:** 415/969-3821. **Contact:** Judy Schwartz, Recruiting Manager. **Description:** The Federal Systems Group of Sterling Software provides technical and professional services to the federal government under several multi-year contracts. As one of the largest contractors at the NASA/Ames Research Center, Sterling has been an integral partner in the progress of the center.

Common positions include: Aerospace Engineer; Computer Programmer; Software Engineer. **Educational backgrounds include:** Computer Science; Engineering; Mathematics; Physics. **Benefits:** 401(k); Dental Insurance; Disability Coverage; Life Insurance; Medical Insurance; Tuition Assistance. **Corporate headquarters location:** This Location. **Listed on:** American Stock Exchange. **Number of employees at this location:** 700.

STRUCTURAL DYNAMICS RESEARCH
3945 Freedom Circle, Suite 560, Santa Clara CA 95054-1226. 408/980-0100. **Contact:** Human Resources. **Description:** An international supplier of mechanical computer-aided engineering (MCAE) software and engineering services. Structural Dynamics Research has 55 offices. **Number of employees worldwide:** 1,200.

SUN MICROSYSTEMS INC.
2550 Garcia Avenue, Mountain View CA 94043. 415/336-0470. **Contact:** Human Resources. **Description:** Sun Microsystems produces high-performance computer systems, workstations, servers, CPUs, peripherals, and operating system software. The company developed its own microprocessor called SPARC. Most products are sold to the engineering, scientific, technical, and commercial markets worldwide. **Corporate headquarters location:** This Location. **Listed on:** NASDAQ.

SYBASE, INC.
6475 Christie Avenue, Emeryville CA 94608. 510/922-3500. **Fax:** 510/922-8002. **Contact:** Human Resources. **Description:** Sybase, Inc. develops, markets, and supports a full line of relational database management software products and services for integrated, enterprise-wide information management systems. **Number of employees at this location:** 2,352.

SYMANTEC CORPORATION
10201 Torre Avenue, Cupertino CA 95014-2132. 408/253-9600. **Contact:** Professional Staffing. **E-mail address:** jobs@symantec.com. **Description:** Symantec Corporation is a global organization that develops, manufactures, and markets software products for individuals and businesses around the world. Founded in 1982, the company is a vendor of utility software for stand-alone and networked personal computers. In addition, it offers a wide range of project management products, productivity applications, and development languages and tools. With products available in both U.S. and international versions, Symantec maintains a strong presence. The company is organized into several product groups that are devoted to product marketing, engineering, technical support, quality assurance, and documentation. Finance, sales, and marketing are centralized at this location. **Common positions include:** Software Developer; Software Engineer. **Educational backgrounds include:** Accounting; Computer Science; Engineering; Marketing. **Benefits:** 401(k); Dental Insurance; Disability Coverage; Employee Discounts; Life Insurance; Medical Insurance; Profit Sharing; Tuition Assistance. **Special Programs:** Internships. **Corporate headquarters location:** This Location. **Listed on:** NASDAQ. **Number of employees nationwide:** 1,200.

SYNOPSYS INC.
700 East Middlefield Road, Mountain View CA 94043. 415/962-5000. **Contact:** Human Resources. **Description:** Synopsys develops, markets, and supports high-level design automation (HLDA) software for designers of integrated circuits and electronic systems. Its products offer improved time to market, reduced development time, and reduced

manufacturing costs when compared to earlier generations of electronic design automation (EDA) software. **Number of employees at this location:** 400.

SYQUEST TECHNOLOGY
47071 Bayside Parkway, Fremont CA 94538-6517. 510/226-4000. **Contact:** Human Resources. **Description:** Designs, develops, manufactures, and markets removable cartridge Winchester disk drives and data storage cartridges. **Number of employees nationwide:** 1,100.

SYSTEM INDUSTRIES, INC./MTI
474 Portrero Avenue, Sunnyvale CA 94086. 408/730-1664. **Contact:** Human Resources Manager. **Description:** Manufactures, sells, and services disk and tape drive subsystems for DEC Computers. **Common positions include:** Accountant/Auditor; Administrator; Attorney; Blue-Collar Worker Supervisor; Buyer; Computer Programmer; Credit Manager; Customer Service Representative; Department Manager; Draftsperson; Electrical/Electronics Engineer; Financial Analyst; Human Resources Specialist; Industrial Engineer; Marketing Specialist; Mechanical Engineer; Operations/Production Manager; Public Relations Specialist; Quality Control Supervisor; Services Sales Representative; Systems Analyst; Technical Writer/Editor; Transportation/Traffic Specialist. **Benefits:** Dental Insurance; Disability Coverage; Life Insurance; Medical Insurance; Pension Plan; Tuition Assistance. **Corporate headquarters location:** This Location. **Operations at this facility include:** Administration; Manufacturing; Research and Development; Service. **Listed on:** American Stock Exchange.

SYSTEMSOFT CORPORATION
2350 Mission College Boulevard, Suite 450, Santa Clara CA 95054. 408/988-6756. **Fax:** 408/988-6758. **Contact:** Human Resources. **Description:** SystemSoft Corporation is a supplier of PCMCIA (Personal Computer Memory Card International Association) and other system-level software to the rapidly-growing market of mobile computers, comprised of laptops, notebooks, subnotebooks, and personal computing devices. PCMCIA is a published industry standard which enables personal computers and electronic devices to automatically recognize, install, and configure peripherals (including modems, flash memory, and network cards) incorporated in credit card-sized PCMCIA cards. System-level software provides both a connectivity layer, which facilitates the addition, configuration, and use of peripheral devices, and a hardware adaptation layer, which comprises the communication link between a computer operating system and hardware. **Corporate headquarters location:** Natick MA.

TANDEM COMPUTERS INC.
10600 Ridgeview Court, Cupertino CA 95014. 408/725-6000. **Contact:** Personnel Recruitment. **Description:** Tandem Computers is a designer and producer of networks and fault-tolerant computer systems for the online transaction processing markets. The company also manufactures disk storage devices. Fault-tolerance in the computer market is obtained by backup and component redundancy, and is attractive to the communications, banking, manufacturing, distribution, and transportation industries. Through subsidiary UB Networks, the company provides service, integration, and software for networks. **Corporate headquarters location:** This Location. **Listed on:** New York Stock Exchange.

TANDEM COMPUTERS INC.
444 Market Street, Suite 1450, San Francisco CA 94111. 415/398-9440. **Contact:** Human Resources. **Description:** Tandem Computers is a designer and producer of

networks and fault-tolerant computer systems for the online transaction processing markets. The company also manufactures disk storage devices. Fault-tolerance in the computer market is obtained by backup and component redundancy, and is attractive to the communications, banking, manufacturing, distribution, and transportation industries. Through subsidiary UB Networks, the company provides service, integration, and software for networks.

TELXON CORPORATION
2300 Clayton Road, Suite 1300, Concord CA 94520-2148. 510/682-7044. **Contact:** Human Resources Department. **Description:** Manufactures hand-held microcomputer systems.

3COM CORPORATION
5400 Bayfront Plaza, Santa Clara CA 95052-8145. 408/764-5000. **Contact:** Professional Staffing. **E-mail address:** 3com_resumes@3mail.3com.com. **Description:** 3Com is a billion-dollar *Fortune* 500 company delivering global data networking solutions to organizations around the world. The company designs, manufactures, markets, and supports a broad range of ISO 9000-compliant global data networking solutions including router, hubs, remote access servers, switches, and adapters for Ethernet, Token Ring, and high-speed networks. These products enable computers to communicate at high speeds and share resources such as printers, disk drives, modems and minicomputers. **Common positions include:** Accountant/Auditor; Administrator; Buyer; Computer Systems Analyst; Customer Service Representative; Electrical/Electronics Engineer; Financial Analyst; Human Resources Specialist; Marketing Specialist; Operations/Production Manager; Sales Representative; Software Engineer. **Educational backgrounds include:** Accounting; Business Administration; Computer Science; Engineering; Finance; Marketing. **Benefits:** 401(k); Computer Loans; Dental Insurance; Disability Coverage; Employee Discounts; Life Insurance; Medical Insurance; Pension Plan; Profit Sharing; Savings Plan; Stock Option; Tuition Assistance. **Special Programs:** Internships. **Corporate headquarters location:** This Location. **Other U.S. locations:** North Billerica MA. **Operations at this facility include:** Administration; Divisional Headquarters; Manufacturing; Research and Development; Sales; Service. **Listed on:** NASDAQ. **Number of employees nationwide:** 2,800.

TRIAD SYSTEMS CORPORATION
3055 Triad Drive, Livermore CA 94550. 510/449-0606. **Contact:** Human Resources. **Description:** Manufactures computers.

TRIDENT MICROSYSTEMS
189 North Bernardo Drive, Mountain View CA 94043-5203. 415/691-9211. **Contact:** Human Resources. **Description:** Designs, develops, and markets large-scale integrated circuit graphics products, including graphics controllers for IBM-compatible PC's; flat-panel controllers for notebook PC's; and video processing products for PC's. **Number of employees at this location:** 100.

U.B. NETWORKS, INC.
3900 Freedom Circle, Santa Clara CA 95054. 408/496-0111. **Fax:** 408/970-7353. **Contact:** Staffing Specialists. **E-mail address:** jpeters@ub.com or dfinucan@ub.com. **Description:** Manufactures computer equipment. U.B. Networks was formerly Ungermann-Bass, Inc. **Common positions include:** Accountant/Auditor; Buyer; Computer Systems Analyst; Customer Service Representative; Electrical/Electronics Engineer; Financial Analyst; Human Resources Specialist; Public Relations Specialist;

Software Engineer; Technical Writer/Editor. **Educational backgrounds include:** Computer Science; Engineering; Finance. **Benefits:** 401(k); Daycare Assistance; Dental Insurance; Disability Coverage; Employee Discounts; Life Insurance; Medical Insurance; Tuition Assistance. **Corporate headquarters location:** This Location. **Other U.S. locations:** Andover MA. **Parent company:** Tandem Computers. **Operations at this facility include:** Administration; Divisional Headquarters; Research and Development; Sales; Service. **Listed on:** Privately held. **Number of employees at this location:** 450. **Number of employees nationwide:** 750.

UNISYS CORPORATION
2700 North First Street, San Jose CA 95134-2028. 408/434-2848. **Contact:** Personnel Department. **Description:** Unisys Corporation is a provider of information services, technology, and software. It employs 49,000 people in 100 countries. Unisys specializes in developing business critical solutions based on open information networks. The company's enabling software team creates a variety of software projects which facilitate the building of user applications and the management of distributed systems. The company's platforms group is responsible for UNIX Operating Systems running across a wide range of multiple processor server platforms, including all peripheral and communication drivers. The Unisys commercial parallel processing is engaged in the development of a microkernel-based operating system, I/O device driver development, ATM hardware development, diagnostics, and system architects. The system management group is chartered with the overall management of development programs for UNIX desktop and entry-server products.

UNISYS CORPORATION
7677 Oakport Street, Suite 1200, Oakland CA 94621-1929. 510/613-1300. **Contact:** Human Resources. **Description:** Unisys Corporation is a provider of information services, technology, and software. It employs 49,000 people in 100 countries. Unisys specializes in developing business critical solutions based on open information networks. The company's enabling software team creates a variety of software projects which facilitate the building of user applications and the management of distributed systems. The company's platforms group is responsible for UNIX Operating Systems running across a wide range of multiple processor server platforms, including all peripheral and communication drivers. The Unisys commercial parallel processing is engaged in the development of a microkernel-based operating system, I/O device driver development, ATM hardware development, diagnostics, and system architects. The system management group is chartered with the overall management of development programs for UNIX desktop and entry-server products.

WANG LABORATORIES
160 Spear Street, San Francisco CA 94105-1543. 415/995-9264. **Contact:** Human Resources. **Description:** Wang is a leader in workflow, integrated imaging, document management, and related office software for client/server open systems, and a worldwide provider of integration and support services for office software and networks. Wang's Software Business is a provider of integrated client/server software that enables customers to streamline office information processes, cut costs, and respond more quickly to changes in market dynamics or customer needs. Principal markets for the Software Business are banking, insurance, government, and other enterprises with large-scale business processes. Wang's Solutions Integration Business provides extensive systems integration and other services to the U.S. government. Principal markets are federal agencies, the U.S. Department of Defense, and commercial nonprofit hospitals and medical enterprises. The Customer Services Business provides maintenance and

support services, network integration, installation, training, and other services to customers worldwide. With service delivery operations in more than 130 countries, Wang's Customer Service Business provides maintenance and support services on more than 3,500 products for more than 300 vendors.

WANG LABORATORIES
2484 North Chestnut, Fresno CA 93703. 209/452-8132. **Contact:** Human Resources. **Description:** Wang is a leader in workflow, integrated imaging, document management, and related office software for client/server open systems, and a worldwide provider of integration and support services for office software and networks. Wang's Software Business is a provider of integrated client/server software that enables customers to streamline office information processes, cut costs, and respond more quickly to changes in market dynamics or customer needs. Principal markets for the Software Business are banking, insurance, government and other enterprises with large-scale business processes. Wang's Solutions Integration Business provides extensive systems integration and other services to the U.S. government. Principal markets are federal agencies, the U.S. Department of Defense, and commercial nonprofit hospitals and medical enterprises. The Customer Services Business provides maintenance and support services, network integration, installation, training, and other services to customers worldwide. With service delivery operations in more than 130 countries, Wang's Customer Service Business provides maintenance and support services on more than 3,500 products for more than 300 vendors.

WANG LABORATORIES INC.
910 Bern Court, Suite 140, San Jose CA 95112-1239. 408/467-5560. **Contact:** Human Resources. **Description:** Wang is a leader in workflow, integrated imaging, document management, and related office software for client/server open systems, and a worldwide provider of integration and support services for office software and networks. Wang's Software Business is a provider of integrated client/server software that enables customers to streamline office information processes, cut costs, and respond more quickly to changes in market dynamics or customer needs. Principal markets for the Software Business are banking, insurance, government, and other enterprises with large-scale business processes. Wang's Solutions Integration Business provides extensive systems integration and other services to the U.S. Government. Principal markets are federal agencies, the U.S. Department of Defense, and commercial nonprofit hospitals and medical enterprises. The Customer Services Business provides maintenance and support services, network integration, installation, training, and other services to customers worldwide. With service delivery operations in more than 130 countries, Wang's Customer Service Business provides maintenance and support services on more than 3,500 products for more than 300 vendors.

WESTERN DIGITAL CORPORATION
DRIVE ENGINEERING DIVISION
6201 San Ignacio, San Jose CA 95119. 408/365-1190. **Contact:** Wendy Bronkhorst, Human Resources Representative. **Description:** Western Digital primarily makes small-form factor rigid disk drives for PCs and file servers, and also integrates circuits and board products for graphics, storage control, and systems logic. Prior to March 1988, the company primarily made disk drive controllers, which are now integrated into disk drives. In March 1988, the company acquired Tandy Corporation's disk drive operations and began to make 3.5 inch magnetic disk drives for the IDE (intelligent drive electronics) interface.

WYSE TECHNOLOGY
3471 North 1st Street, San Jose CA 95134. 408/473-1200. **Contact:** Susan Wente, Human Resources. **Description:** Manufactures computer terminals.

XILINX, INC.
2100 Logic Drive, San Jose CA 95124. 408/879-5390. **Fax:** 408/559-4726. **Contact:** Pam Najera, Employment Manager. **E-mail address:** pam@xilinx.com. **Description:** Xilinx, Inc. is the leading supplier of field programmable gate arrays (FPGAs) and related development system software used by electronic systems manufacturers for bringing complex products rapidly to the market. **Common positions include:** Accountant/Auditor; Computer Programmer; Computer Systems Analyst; Customer Service Representative; Electrical/Electronics Engineer; Financial Analyst; Industrial Engineer; Software Engineer; Technical Writer/Editor. **Educational backgrounds include:** Accounting; Computer Science; Engineering. **Benefits:** 401(k); Dental Insurance; Disability Coverage; Life Insurance; Medical Insurance; Profit Sharing; Tuition Assistance. **Special Programs:** Internships. **Corporate headquarters location:** This Location. **Operations at this facility include:** Administration; Divisional Headquarters; Manufacturing; Regional Headquarters; Research and Development; Sales; Service. **Listed on:** NASDAQ. **Number of employees at this location:** 850. **Number of employees nationwide:** 900.

XSOFT
A DIVISION OF XEROX CORPORATION
3400 Hillview Avenue, Palo Alto CA 94304. 415/424-0111. **Contact:** Human Resources. **Description:** XSoft provides software designed to improve the way people create and use documents to capture, manage, and communicate ideas and information. The division develops and markets products that include document management and workflow solutions, office productivity packages, search and retrieval systems, and structured document publishing applications. The division also offers extensive product support, training, and consulting services. **Parent company:** Xerox develops, manufactures, markets, services, and finances information-processing products.

ZYCAD CORPORATION
47100 Bayside Parkway, Fremont CA 94538. 510/623-4400. **Fax:** 510/623-4550. **Contact:** Human Resources. **Description:** Zycad Corporation designs, manufactures, and markets products and services for verification of electronic system and components designs.

Note: *Because addresses and telephone numbers of smaller companies can change rapidly, we recommend you call each company to verify the information below before inquiring about job opportunities. Mass mailings are not recommended.*

Additional small employers:

COMPUTERS AND COMPUTER EQUIPMENT WHOLESALE

Nissei Sangyo America Ltd.
755 Ravendale Dr, Mountain View CA 94043-5219. 415/969-1100.

Lucid Inc.
707 Laurel St, Menlo Park CA 94025-3414. 415/329-8400.

Intergraph Electronics
381 E Evelyn Ave, Mountain View CA 94041-1530. 415/691-9680.

Intertec Diversified Systems
150 Grant Ave, Palo Alto

CA 94306-1929. 415/326-8900.

Experts In Telecommunications & Software
66 Bovet Rd Ste 265, San Mateo CA 94402-3127. 415/345-9100.

Scantron Corp.
1660 S Amphlett Blvd Ste 250 , San Mateo CA 94402-2508. 415/525-3825.

Ncube
919 E Hillsdale Blvd, Foster City CA 94404-2112. 415/593-9000.

Trigem Corp.
45865 N Port Loop E, El Cerrito CA 94530. 408/970-0844.

Asia Source Inc.
48289 Fremont Blvd, Fremont CA 94538-6522. 510/226-8000.

Sherwood
4181 Business Center Dr, Fremont CA 94538-6355. 510/623-8900.

Century Analysis Inc.
114 Center Ave, Pacheco CA 94553-5696. 510/680-7800.

Richard Young Products
32920 Alvarado Niles Rd, #220, Union City CA 94587-3106. 510/429-1700.

Kalleens Computer Products Inc.
PO Box 9127, San Rafael CA 94912. 415/257-1010.

The Oliver Allen Corporation Inc.
80 E Sir Francis Drake Blvd, Larkspur CA 94939-1709. 415/461-4600.

Software Resource Corp.
8 Digital Dr Ste 100, Novato CA 94949-5759. 415/883-8757.

Wolf Computer
105 N Santa Cruz Ave, Los Gatos CA 95030-5918. 408/354-1210.

Tatung Science & Technology
1840 McCarthy Blvd, Milpitas CA 95035-7425. 408/383-0988.

Microware Systems Corp.
2041 Mission College Blvd 151, Santa Clara CA 95054-1553. 408/980-0201.

JSB Corp.
108 Whispering Pines Dr Ste 11, Scotts Valley CA 95066-4785. 408/438-8300.

Mitsui Comtek Corp.
12980 Saratoga Ave Ste B, Saratoga CA 95070-4659. 408/725-8525.

Vitek
2025 Gateway Pl Ste 142, San Jose CA 95110-1005. 408/954-9720.

Fujitsu Computer Products
1741 Junction Ave, San Jose CA 95112-1010. 408/436-5599.

Amtek Electronic Inc.
1150 N 5th St, San Jose CA 95112-4415. 408/971-8787.

C-Net Technology Inc.
2199 Zanker Rd, San Jose CA 95131. 408/954-8000.

PDP Systems
2140 Bering Dr, San Jose CA 95131-2013. 408/944-0301.

JDR Microdevices
3011 Crater Ln, San Jose CA 95132-2305. 408/494-1400.

Law Cypress Distributing Co.
5883 Eden Park Pl, San Jose CA 95138-1800. 408/363-4700.

Videologic Inc.
1001 Bayhill Dr, San Bruno CA 94066-3061. 415/875-0606.

Cellnet Data Systems Inc.
75 Shoreway Rd, San Carlos CA 94070-2705. 415/508-6000.

Inforite Corp.
1670 S Amphlett Blvd #20, San Mateo CA 94402-2510. 415/571-8766.

PC Connections
3480 Investment Blvd, Hayward CA 94545-3811. 510/783-2727.

Edom International Corp.
3010 Scott Blvd, Santa Clara CA 95054. 408/748-6961.

Pionex Inc.
50 W San Fernando St, San Jose CA 95113-2429. 408/271-3850.

Glide-Write
109 Bonaventura Dr, San Jose CA 95134-2106. 408/383-9009.

Diamond Computer Systems Inc.
2880 Junction Ave, San Jose CA 95134. 408/736-2000.

King's Office Products Centers
3230 Jefferson St, Napa CA 94558-3436. 707/253-1234.

Corporate Express Of Northern CA
2550 Zanker Rd, San Jose CA 95131. 408/435-1222.

COMPUTER SOFTWARE, PROGRAMMING, AND SYSTEMS DESIGN

Versant Object Technology
1380 Willow Rd, Menlo

Park CA 94025-1516. 415/329-7500.

Strategic Simulations Inc.
675 Almanor Ave Ste 201, Sunnyvale CA 94086-2930. 408/737-6800.

Strategic Decisions Group
2440 Sand Hill Rd, Menlo Park CA 94025-6900. 415/854-9000.

Intelligenetics Inc.
700 E El Camino Real, Mountain View CA 94040-2800. 415/962-7300.

Proactive Software Inc.
1890 N Shoreline Blvd, Mountain View CA 94043-1320. 415/691-1500.

Metaphor Inc.
1965 Charleston Rd, Mountain View CA 94043-1204. 415/871-6473.

Unison-Tymlabs
675 Almanor Ave Ste 202, Sunnyvale CA 94086-2930. 408/245-3000.

TRW Engineering Center
970 Stewart Dr, Sunnyvale CA 94086-3912. 408/245-5040.

Navigation Technologies
740 E Arques Ave, Sunnyvale CA 94086-3833. 408/737-3200.

HLS Duplication Inc.
520 Almanor Ave, Sunnyvale CA 94086-3533. 408/773-1500.

Silvar-Lisco
703 E Evelyn Ave, Sunnyvale CA 94086-6548. 408/991-6000.

Reach Software Corp.
827 Hermosa Ave, Sunnyvale CA 94086-4105. 408/733-8685.

Microtec Research
PO Box 60337, Sunnyvale CA 94088-0337. 408/980-1300.

Daniel H. Wagner Associates
894 Ross Dr Ste 205, Sunnyvale CA 94089-1443. 408/745-1800.

Space Applications Corp.
1310 Orleans Dr, Sunnyvale CA 94089-1101. 408/744-0990.

System Programming
75 Hawthorne St #2000, San Francisco CA 94105-3919. 415/541-9462.

Tigon Corp.
455 Market St Ste 1050, San Francisco CA 94105-2440. 415/399-8200.

The Indus Group
60 Spear St Floor 9, San Francisco CA 94105-1506. 415/904-5000.

Axiom Information Consulting Inc.
539 Bryant St, San Francisco CA 94107-1237. 415/398-3484.

Computer Resources Group Inc.
275 Battery St Ste 800, San Francisco CA 94111-3332. 415/398-3535.

Legato Systems Inc.
3145 Porter Dr, Palo Alto CA 94304-1224. 415/812-6000.

Marc Analysis Research Corp.
260 Sheridan Ave Ste 309, Palo Alto CA 94306-2010. 415/326-7511.

Scanview Inc.
330 Hatch Dr, Foster City CA 94404-1106. 415/378-6360.

Sungard Shareholder Systems
951 Mariners Island Blvd Ste 5, San Mateo CA 94404-1558. 415/377-3700.

Deltam Systems Inc.
1400 Fashion Island Blvd Ste 3, San Mateo CA 94404-2060. 415/571-0551.

Comdisco Systems Inc.
919 E Hillsdale Blvd, Foster City CA 94404-2112. 415/574-5800.

Micro-MRP Inc.
1065 E Hillsdale Blvd Ste 301 , Foster City CA 94404-1615. 415/345-6000.

Action Technologies Inc.
1301 Marina Village Pkwy # 100, Alameda CA 94501-1058. 510/521-6190.

Wind River Systems Inc.
1010 Atlantic Ave, Alameda CA 94501-1153. 510/748-4100.

Viewstar Corp.
1101 Marina Village Pkwy, Alameda CA 94501-1044. 510/337-2000.

Hotel Information Systems Co.
2300 Clayton Rd Ste 300, Concord CA 94520-2140. 510/602-3000.

Independence Technologies Inc.
42705 Lawrence Pl, Fremont CA 94538-3145. 510/438-2000.

Computer-Aided Systems Inc.
30991 San Clemente St, Hayward CA 94544-7128. 510/429-2800.

Davis Instruments Inc.
3465 Diablo Ave, Hayward CA 94545-2746. 510/732-9229.

Open Vision Technologies
7133 Koll Center Pkwy, Pleasanton CA 94566-3101. 510/426-6400.

Speedware Corp.
3000 Executive Pkwy Ste 11, San Ramon CA 94583-2300. 510/867-3300.

Peoplesoft Inc.
1331 N California Blvd Floor 4, Walnut Creek CA 94596-4537. 510/946-9460.

Scopus Technology Inc.
1900 Powell St Ste 900, Emeryville CA 94608-1819. 510/428-0500.

Berkeley Systems
2095 Rose St, Berkeley CA 94709-1963. 510/540-5535.

SBT Corp.
1401 Los Gamos Rd, San Rafael CA 94903-1848. 415/331-9900.

Island Graphics Corp.
4000 Civic Center Dr, San Rafael CA 94903-4171. 415/491-1000.

Bell Atlantic Health Care
300 Drakes Landing Rd # 1000 , Greenbrae CA 94904-2498. 415/925-0121.

Quadramed Corp.
80 E Sir Francis Drake Blvd, Larkspur CA 94939-1709. 415/461-7725.

The Softad Group
100 Shoreline Hwy Ste B-200, Mill Valley CA 94941-3645. 415/332-4704.

Business Objects Inc.
20813 Stevens Creek Blvd, Cupertino CA 95014-2107. 408/973-9300.

Netmanage Inc.
10725 N De Anza Blvd, Cupertino CA 95014-2030. 408/973-7171.

Quadrex Computer Systems Inc.
170 Knowles Dr Ste 200, Los Gatos CA 95030-1833. 408/866-4510.

Worldtalk Corp.
475 Alberto Way, Los Gatos CA 95032-5418. 408/399-4000.

Aurora Systems
2230 Martin Ave, Santa Clara CA 95050-2704. 408/988-2000.

Anacad Electrical Engineering
4675 Stevens Creek Blvd Ste 20, Santa Clara CA 95051-6759. 408/296-8151.

Buslogic Inc.
4151 Burton Dr, Santa Clara CA 95054-1564. 408/492-9090.

Advantest America Inc.
4301 Great America Pky Ste 500, Santa Clara CA 95054-1236. 408/727-5546.

Fourth Shift Corp.
5201 Great America Pky Ste 320, Santa Clara CA 95054-1127. 408/982-2555.

Smith Dennis & Gaylor
3211 Scott Blvd, Santa Clara CA 95054-3009. 408/727-1870.

Microtec Research Inc.
2350 Mission College Blvd #50, Santa Clara CA 95054-1532. 408/980-1300.

Resumix Inc.
2953 Bunker Hill Ln Floor 3, Santa Clara CA 95054-1131. 408/988-0444.

Inventa Corp.
2620 Augustine Dr Ste 225, Santa Clara CA 95054-2909. 408/987-0220.

Interbase
1600 Green Hills Rd, Scotts Valley CA 95066-4924. 408/431-5428.

Cooperative Solutions Inc.
2125 Hamilton Avenue #100, San Jose CA 95125-5905. 408/377-0300.

Tiburon Systems Inc.
1290 Parkmoor Ave, San Jose CA 95126-3449. 408/293-4400.

Spectral Innovations
1885 Lundy Ave, San Jose CA 95131-1835. 408/955-0366.

Rasna Corp.
2590 North 1st Street Suite 200, San Jose CA 95131-1021. 408/922-6833.

PE Nelson
3833 North 1st Street, San Jose CA 95134-1701. 408/577-2200.

Sherpa Corporation
611 River Oaks Pkwy, San Jose CA 95134-1907. 408/433-0455.

Prodata Inc.
6929 Sunrise Boulevard Suite 105, Citrus Heights CA 95610-3156. 916/969-3064.

Computer Sciences Corp.
3355 Myrtle Ave Ste 265, N Highlands CA 95660-5144. 916/331-6894.

Unify Corporation
3927 Lennane Dr, Sacramento CA 95834-1922. 916/928-6400.

Talis Computer Service Inc.
PO Box 1539, Nevada City CA 95959-1539. 916/265-5777.

Clark Enterprises
5949 E Lansing Way, Fresno CA 93727-7935. 209/292-0650.

Forrester Research Inc.
400 Oyster Point Blvd, S San Fran CA 94080-1904. 415/871-7090.

Melody Desktop Publishing
612 Washington St, San Francisco CA 94111-2106. 415/296-9339.

Interval Research Corp.
1801 Page Mill Rd, Palo Alto CA 94304-1216. 415/354-0900.

Computereyes
1547 3rd Ave, Walnut Creek CA 94596-2604. 510/946-1374.

Business & Professional Consulting
1660 Olympic Blvd, Walnut Creek CA 94596-5137. 510/945-7029.

Innovative Interfaces Inc.
5850 Shellmound St, Emeryville CA 94608-1966. 510/655-6200.

Safari Software Inc.
PO Box 2526, San Rafael CA 94912-2526. 415/456-0348.

Telex Interfaces Inc.
201 Redwood Cir, Petaluma CA 94954. 707/762-4053.

Fanshier & Associates
23890 Summit Rd, Los Gatos CA 95030-9223. 408/353-4365.

Guzik Technical Enterprises
4620 Fortran Dr, San Jose CA 95134-2301. 408/262-5500.

Access
1824 San Simeone Way, Stockton CA 95207-5365. 209/951-3518.

River City Research Group
8700 Bunting Court, Orangevale CA 95662-2424. 916/988-7144.

DKD & Co.
3855 Atherton Rd, Rocklin CA 95765-3715. 916/632-2325.

Jetco Computer Systems
2250 Sandcastle Way, Sacramento CA 95833-3410. 916/922-4526.

Delta Point Inc.
2 Harris Court Ste B 1, Monterey CA 93940-5735. 408/648-4000.

Xiox Corp.
577 Airport Blvd Ste 700, Burlingame CA 94010-2024. 415/375-8188.

Software Associates Inc.
101 1st St, Los Altos CA 94022-2750. 415/367-4994.

Renaissance Software Inc.
175 S San Antonio Rd Ste 210 , Los Altos CA 94022-3749. 415/856-8000.

Addstor Inc.
1040 Marsh Rd, Menlo Park CA 94025-1019. 415/688-0470.

Gupta Corp.
1060 Marsh Rd, Menlo Park CA 94025. 415/321-9500.

Make Systems Inc.
201 San Antonio Cir Ste 225, Mountain View CA 94040-1234. 415/941-9800.

Kaleida Labs Inc.
1055 Joaquin Rd, Mountain View CA 94043-1243. 415/966-0400.

Silicon Valley Research Inc.
300 Ferguson Dr, Mountain View CA 94043-5227. 415/962-3000.

Remedy Corporation
1505 Salado Dr, Mountain View CA 94043-1110. 415/903-5200.

Verity Inc.
1550 Plymouth St, Mountain View CA 94043-1230. 415/960-7600.

Infinity Financial Technical Inc.
2001 Landings Dr, Mountain View CA 94043-0816. 415/940-6100.

Award Software Inc.
777 Middlefield Rd, Mountain View CA 94043. 415/968-4433.

Next Computer Inc.
900 Chesapeake Dr, Redwood City CA 94063-4727. 415/366-0900.

3DO Company
600 Galveston Dr, Redwood City CA 94063-4721. 415/261-3000.

Mercury Interactive Corp.
470 Potrero Ave, Sunnyvale CA 94086-4117. 408/987-0100.

Parcplace-Digitalk Inc.
999 E Arques Ave, Sunnyvale CA 94086-4521. 408/481-9090.

Scitor Corp.
256 Gibraltar Dr, Sunnyvale CA 94089-1324. 408/745-8200.

Geodynamics Corp.
1150 N Fairoaks Ave, Sunnyvale CA 94089-1702. 408/745-1310.

Macromedia Inc.
600 Townsend Street #310 W, San Francisco CA 94103-4945. 415/252-2000.

Worldview Systems Corp.
114 Sansome St Ste 700, San Francisco CA 94104-3816. 415/391-7100.

Accelerated Voice Inc.
25 Stillman St Ste 200, San Francisco CA 94107-1309. 415/543-2773.

The Wallogon Group Inc.
1129 San Antonio Rd, Palo Alto CA 94303-4310. 415/962-7100.

Pillar Corporation
950 Tower Ln Ste 400, Foster City CA 94404-2123. 415/349-6200.

Dynamic Graphics
1015 Atlantic Ave, Alameda CA 94501-1154. 510/522-0700.

Premenos Corp.
1000 Burnett Ave Ste 200, Concord CA 94520-2058. 510/602-2000.

Discopylabs Inc.
48641 Milmont Dr, Fremont CA 94538. 510/651-5100.

Covalent Systems Corp.
47436 Fremont Blvd, Fremont CA 94538-6555. 510/683-3900.

Logistics
48021 Warm Springs Blvd, Fremont CA 94539-7497. 510/656-8000.

Enable Software Inc. Higgins Group
957 Cheryl Ann Cir Apt 13, Hayward CA 94544-4449. 510/865-9805.

Real Time Solutions Inc.
831 Latour Ct Ste D, Napa CA 94558-6260. 707/252-5300.

Maxis
2 Theatre Sq Ste 230, Orinda CA 94563-3346. 510/254-9700.

Viewstar Corp.
5820 Shellmound St, Emeryville CA 94608-1954. 510/652-7827.

Forte Software Inc.
1800 Harrison St # 15, Oakland CA 94612-3429. 510/869-3400.

Pixar
1001 W Cutting Blvd # 200, Richmond CA 94804-2028. 510/236-4000.

Knowledge Data Systems Inc.
80 E Sir Francis Drake Blvd, Larkspur CA 94939-1709. 415/461-5374.

Diversified Data Resources Inc.
7200 Redwood Blvd Ste 222, Novato CA 94945-3247. 415/898-8282.

Word Star International
201 Alameda Del Prado, Novato CA 94949-6657. 415/382-8000.

Contour Software Inc.
700 W Hamilton Ave, Campbell CA 95008-0403. 408/370-1700.

Meta-Software Inc.
1300 White Oaks Rd, Campbell CA 95008-6723. 408/369-5400.

ACI US Inc.
20883 Stevens Creek Blvd, Cupertino CA 95014-2107. 408/252-4444.

XA Systems Corp.
983 University Ave Ste D, Los Gatos CA 95030-2305. 408/395-1800.

Diversified Software Systems Inc.
18630 Sutter Blvd, Morgan Hill CA 95037-2825. 408/778-9914.

ABB Systems Control Co. Inc.
2550 Walsh Ave, Santa Clara CA 95051-1315. 408/988-3200.

Castelle
3255 Scott Blvd Ste 3, Santa Clara CA 95054-3013. 408/496-0474.

Aurum Software Inc.
5201 Great America Pky Ste 238, Santa Clara CA 95054-1126. 408/562-6370.

Silvaco International Inc.
4701 Patrick Henry Dr Ste 3, Santa Clara CA 95054-1819. 408/988-2862.

Veritas Software Corp.
4800 Great America Pky Ste 420, Santa Clara CA 95054-1228. 408/727-1222.

Wings For Learning Inc.
245M Mount Hermon Rd #65, Scotts Valley CA 95066-4007. 408/438-5502.

Meridian Data Inc.
5615 Scotts Valley Dr, Scotts Valley CA 95066-3424. 408/438-3100.

Promis Systems Corp.
1731 Technology Dr Ste 250, San Jose CA 95110-1326. 408/441-9090.

Atwork Corp.
1975 Concourse Drive, San Jose CA 95131. 408/263-1080.

Adept Technology Inc.
150 Rose Orchard Way, San Jose CA 95134-1358. 408/432-0888.

Ascent Logic Corp.
180 Rose Orchard Way # 200, San Jose CA 95134-1358. 408/943-0630.

Exper Vision Inc.
3590 North First St, San Jose CA 95134-1805. 408/428-9444.

Computer Power Software Group
713 Sutter St, Folsom CA 95630-2505. 916/985-4445.

Manzanita Software Systems
2130 Professional Dr, Roseville CA 95661-3738. 916/781-3880.

Mavis Computer Systems Inc.
2976 Alhambra Dr, Cameron Park CA 95682-7600. 916/985-0373.

Bi-Tech Software Inc.
1072 Marauder St, Chico CA 95973-9039. 916/891-5011.

Datalogix International Inc.
533 Airport Blvd, Burlingame CA 94010-2018. 415/375-5855.

HCL America Inc.
330 Potrero Ave, Sunnyvale CA 94086-4113. 408/733-0480.

System Software Alternatives Inc.
1010 W Fremont Ave, Sunnyvale CA 94087-3000. 408/720-0400.

Seer Technology
595 Market St, San Francisco CA 94105-2802. 415/495-7070.

Atomic Software
600 Upland Dr, San Francisco CA 94127-2540. 415/441-7373.

Servio Corp.
2001 Windward Way, San Mateo CA 94404-2473. 415/345-3144.

Odesta Systems Corp.
901 Mariners Island Blvd, San Mateo CA 94404-1592. 415/358-6970.

Computer Aid Structure Technology
46560 Fremont Blvd, Fremont CA 94538-6482. 510/226-8857.

California Management Group Inc.
7000 East Ave, Livermore CA 94550-9516. 510/373-7674.

Health Soft Inc.
1100 Moraga Way, Moraga CA 94556-1146. 510/631-6800.

Wine Country Computing
PO Box 97, Saint Helena CA 94574-0097. 707/965-2522.

Insurnet Inc.
1333 N California Blvd Ste 350, Walnut Creek CA 94596-4527. 510/946-2850.

Insurnet Inc.
1900 Powell St Floor 6, Emeryville CA 94608-1811. 510/652-3771.

Global Dynamics Inc.
1350 Treat Blvd Ste 355, Walnut Creek CA 94596-2151. 510/946-0601.

IA Corp
1900 Powell St Ste 600, Emeryville CA 94608-1816. 510/450-7000.

Lawgic Publishing Co.
999 Andersen Dr Ste 150, San Rafael CA 94901-5366. 408/366-8900.

Alphasoft Marketing
581 Oceana Dr, Dillon Beach CA 94929. 707/878-2640.

Gallivan Associates
PO Box 1726, Novato CA 94948-1726. 415/892-2713.

Ecto
PO Box 458, Novato CA 94948-0458. 415/897-8446.

Greenleaf International
4900 Patrick Henry Dr, Santa Clara CA 95054-1822. 408/653-0222.

Krikware
PO Box 67205, Scotts Valley CA 95067-7205. 408/335-1108.

Electro Mechanical Products Inc.
PO Box 66377, Scotts Valley CA 95067-6377. 408/438-3001.

PFU
226 Airport Pkwy Ste 430, San Jose CA 95110-1027. 408/453-7290.

ICIM
101 Metro Dr, San Jose CA 95110-1314. 408/436-3535.

Deltek Systems Inc.
2001 Gateway Pl Ste 570W, San Jose CA 95110-1013. 408/436-2136.

The CAD Team USA
1731 Technology Dr, San Jose CA 95110-1312. 408/437-1313.

Software Support Inc.
111 W Saint John St Ste 1020 , San Jose CA 95113-1107. 408/294-1772.

Stratus Computers
2065 Hamilton Ave, San Jose CA 95125-5921. 408/559-5300.

Cinnamon Software Inc.
2175 Kruse Dr, San Jose CA 95131-1214. 408/894-9010.

We Compute
7510 Shoreline Dr, Stockton CA 95219-5455. 209/952-3620.

Computer Tutor
7806 Madison Ave, Fair Oaks CA 95628-3517. 916/966-2336.

Electronics Boutique
1689 Arden Way Ste 2004, Sacramento CA 95815-4033. 916/646-9404.

Transamerica Information Management
1860 Howe Ave, Sacramento CA 95825-1073. 916/921-6629.

Syre
Nasa Ames Resarch Ctr Bldg 243, Mountain View CA 94035. 415/964-5851.

Sysorex International Inc.
335 East Midefield Rd, Mountain View CA 94043. 415/967-2200.

Visionary Design Systems
190 Sobrante Way, Sunnyvale CA 94086-4849. 408/524-8800.

Weitek Corp.
1060 E Arques Ave, Sunnyvale CA 94086-4601. 408/738-8400.

Ideographix Inc.
528 Mercury Dr, Sunnyvale CA 94086. 408/739-1290.

David Systems Inc.
701 E Evelyn Ave, Sunnyvale CA 94086-6527. 408/720-8000.

Intouch Group Inc.
333 Bryant St # 300, San Francisco CA 94107-1421. 415/974-5000.

Toner Corporation
27 Maiden Ln Ste 300, San Francisco CA 94108-5415. 415/788-8488.

J. Fran and Associates Inc.
1810 Embarcadero Rd, Palo Alto CA 94303-3308. 415/493-3800.

Business Information Technology Inc.
1800 Sutter St Ste 770, Concord CA 94520-2562. 510/671-0595.

Addtech Group Inc.
41340 Christy St, Fremont CA 94538-3115. 510/623-7583.

Individual Software Inc.
5870 Stoneridge Dr Ste 1, Pleasanton CA 94588-2733. 510/734-6767.

Sonic Solutions
101 Rowland Way, Novato CA 94945-5008. 415/485-4800.

Network Peripherals Inc.
1371 McCarthy Blvd, Milpitas CA 95035-7432. 408/321-7300.

Storage Dimensions Inc.
1656 McCarthy Blvd, Milpitas CA 95035-7417. 408/954-0710.

Ceitronics Inc.
775 Commercial St, San Jose CA 95112. 408/452-5000.

MCR Sharebase Corporation
2055 Logic Dr # A, San Jose CA 95124-3452. 408/369-5500.

Cabletron Systems
174 Component Dr, San Jose CA 95131-1119. 408/383-1550.

Pacific Access Computers
3079 Kilgore Rd, Rncho Cordova CA 95670-6124. 916/635-9300.

SAIC
3800 Watt Ave Ste 210, Sacramento CA 95821-2672. 916/974-8800.

Harbor Bay Telecommunications
1141 Harbor Bay Pkwy Ste 101 , Alameda CA 94502-6576. 510/769-5000.

Eagle Computer Co.
6377 Clark Ave Ste 109, Dublin CA 94568-3034. 510/803-4690.

CRL Network Services
PO Box 236, Mill Valley CA 94942-0236. 415/389-8649.

Quest Media & Supplies Inc.
5822 Roseville Road, McClellan Air Force Base CA 95652. 916/338-7070.

Wavelength
1420 Merkley Avenue, West Sacramento CA 95691-3200. 916/373-0126.

Pen Blueprint Reprographic Centers
1400 W Middlefield Rd, Mountain View CA 94043-3000. 415/967-1966.

Walker Reprographics Inc.
942 Mission St, San Francisco CA 94103-2911. 415/777-9144.

COMPUTER PROCESSING AND DATA PREPARATION SERVICES

Oceanroutes Inc.
680 West Maude Avenue #3, Sunnyvale CA 94086-3518. 408/245-3600.

Massey Data Entry Services
1407 Market Street Fourth Floor, San Francisco CA 94103-1308. 415/543-7206.

The National Data Corp. Cisco Division
44 Montgomery Street Suite 500, San Francisco CA 94104-4607. 415/955-2674.

Ceridian Corp.
One Maritime Plaza Floor 8, San Francisco CA 94111-3404. 415/393-6750.

First Data Resources Inc.
1720 S Amphlett Blvd, San Mateo CA 94402-2702. 415/572-3000.

NCR Information Imaging System
1153-A Triton Dr, Foster City CA 94404. 415/573-8700.

Domor Data Processing
51 Springstowne Ctr, Vallejo CA 94591-5566. 510/828-3928.

West Coast Information Systems Inc.
1901 Olympic Blvd # 30, Walnut Creek CA 94596-5024. 510/930-7700.

ACS Inc.
3001 Tasman Dr, Santa Clara CA 95054-1191. 408/987-4444.

JDR Microdevices Inc.
1224 S Bascom Ave, San Jose CA 95128-3513. 408/947-8881.

GTE Data Services Inc.
7901 Freeport Blvd, Sacramento CA 95832-9701. 916/665-3200.

Faulkner Color Lab Inc.
1200 Folsom St, San Francisco CA 94103-3817. 415/861-2800.

Adolph Gasser Inc.
181 2nd St, San Francisco CA 94105-3894. 415/495-3852.

Management Graphics Inc.
7501 Canyon Meadow Cir, Pleasanton CA 94588-4701. 510/463-8449.

Advanced Imaging Systems
1700 5th St, Berkeley CA 94710-1716. 510/527-2764.

Avcom Systems Inc.
8880 Cal Center Dr, Sacramento CA 95826-3266. 916/368-1846.

Proserv Inc.
4778 Dewey Dr, Fair Oaks CA 95628-4401. 916/961-6696.

Delta Net Inc.
2729 Prospect Park Dr, Rancho Cordova CA 95670-6025. 916/631-1100.

Assured Processing Services
11315 Sunrise Gold Cir, Rancho Cordova CA 95742-6534. 916/638-5886.

Attorneys Diversified Services
1424 21st St, Sacramento CA 95814-5209. 916/441-4396.

MISC. COMPUTER RELATED SERVICES

Knauer Consulting Inc.
100 Bush St Ste 750, San Francisco CA 94104-3910. 415/434-4200.

The Application Group
200 Pine St # 200, San Francisco CA 94104-2702. 415/421-1627.

CG Computer Services
100 Spear St Ste 700, San Francisco CA 94105-1525. 415/777-1626.

Accounting Solution
685 Market St # 200, San Francisco CA 94105-4200. 415/546-0420.

Eico Inc.
1054 Yosemite Dr, Milpitas CA 95035-5410. 408/945-9898.

Disabled Programmers Inc.
151 Martinvale Ln, San Jose CA 95119-1319. 408/629-3700.

Certified Media Corp.
2050 Ringwood Ave, San Jose CA 95131-1728. 408/456-9090.

Tiburon Inc.
39350 Civic Center Dr, Fremont CA 94538-2331. 510/792-2108.

Aura Associates Inc.
2605 Winchester Blvd, Campbell CA 95008-5320. 408/364-6700.

Telos Consulting Services
3333 Bowers Ave Ste 151, Santa Clara CA 95054-2912. 408/438-6076.

Toner Corp.
601 University Ave Ste 225, Sacramento CA 95825-6706. 916/649-8330.

McCord Company
49 Stevenson St Ste 300, San Francisco CA 94105-2909. 415/978-5388.

Quickresponse Services Inc.
1400 Marina Way S, Richmond CA 94804-3747. 510/215-5000.

Jeppesen Dataplan Inc.
121 Albright Way, Los Gatos CA 95030-1801. 408/866-7611.

On Command Video
3301 Olcott St, Santa Clara CA 95054-3006. 408/496-1800.

COMPUTER RENTAL AND LEASING

Electro Rent Corporation
1905 Plymouth St, Mountain View CA 94043-1701. 415/964-5500.

Rent-A-Computer Inc.
4701 Patrick Henry Dr Ste 1501, Santa Clara CA 95054-1819. 408/727-7800.

Leasing Solutions Inc.
10 Almaden Blvd Ste 1500, San Jose CA 95113-2238. 408/995-6565.

CFR Computers For Rent Inc.
1300 Bayshore Hwy, Burlingame CA 94010-1803. 415/391-4801.

SWA Computers
1860 El Camino Real, Burlingame CA 94010-3127. 415/692-9210.

COMPUTER MAINTENANCE AND REPAIR

Ciber Network Services Inc.
74 New Montgomery St Ste 780, San Francisco CA 94105-3411. 415/974-7000.

Servcom
1155 Triton Dr Ste H, Foster City CA 94404-1213. 415/571-1344.

Tanthap Inc.
3445 Kifer Rd, Santa Clara CA 95051-0711. 408/746-3601.

Trilogy Magnetics
424 N Mill Creek Rd, Quincy CA 95971-9678. 916/283-3736.

React Computer Services
833 Mahler Rd, Burlingame CA 94010-1609. 415/692-1290.

Whole Earth Access
401 Bay Shore Blvd, San Francisco CA 94124-1508. 415/285-5244.

Entex Information Services
355 Lakeside Dr, Foster City CA 94404-1147. 415/525-4800.

Online Computers
2983 Jefferson Street, Napa CA 94558-4920. 707/253-8080.

The Computer Nurse
2101 Webster St Ste 150, Oakland CA 94612-3027. 510/645-1520.

On Line Computer Cleaning Service
1727 Telegraph Ave, Oakland CA 94612-2107. 510/832-3282.

Oakland Microcentre
1808 Franklin St, Oakland CA 94612. 510/836-0670.

Computer Choice
530 3rd St Ste B, San Rafael CA 94901-3384. 415/457-7636.

JRK Computer Service
37 Angela Ave, San Anselmo CA 94960-1316. 415/454-5340.

Trans Data Corp.
507 Valley Way, Milpitas CA 95035-4105. 408/956-5740.

The Fortel Group
4201 Burton Dr, Santa Clara CA 95054-1512. 408/980-6060.

Bell Atlantic Business Systems Service
4640 Northgate Blvd, Sacramento CA 95834-1126. 916/567-7800.

Copiers Plus
110 E Main St, Grass Valley CA 95945-6506. 916/273-5313.

COMPUTERS AND RELATED EQUIPMENT

Pro-Log Corporation
12 Upper Ragsdale Dr, Monterey CA 93940-5730. 408/372-4593.

Tangent Computer Inc.
197 Airport Blvd, Burlingame CA 94010-2006. 415/342-9388.

Domestic Automation Co.
125 Shoreway Rd, San Carlos CA 94070-2704. 415/592-6100.

Chaplet Systems USA Inc.
252 N Wolfe Rd, Sunnyvale CA 94086-4510. 408/732-7950.

Data Expert Corp.
1156 Sonora Ct, Sunnyvale CA 94086-5308. 408/737-8880.

Ampro Computers Inc.
990 Almanor Ave, Sunnyvale CA 94086-2902. 408/522-2100.

Netpower Inc.
545 Oakmead Pky, Sunnyvale CA 94086-4023. 408/522-9999.

Maspar Computer Corp.
749 N Mary Ave, Sunnyvale CA 94086-2909. 408/736-3300.

Arix Computer Corp.
1024 Morse Ave, Sunnyvale CA 94089-1602. 408/541-8700.

Graphics Microsystems Inc.
1284 Forgewood Ave, Sunnyvale CA 94089-2215. 408/745-7745.

Autographix Inc.
One Sansome St Ste 2100, San Francisco CA 94104-4432. 415/348-6946.

U Tron Inc.
47448 Fremont Blvd, Fremont CA 94538-6503. 510/656-3600.

Voysys Corp.
48634 Milmont Dr, Fremont CA 94538-7353. 510/252-1100.

Apaq Technology Inc.
45250 Northport Ct, Fremont CA 94538-6411. 510/226-7800.

First International Computer Inc.
5020 Brandin Ct, Fremont CA 94538-3140. 510/683-9200.

Elma Electronics Inc.
44350 S Grimmer Blvd, Fremont CA 94538-6385. 510/656-3400.

Amax Engineering Corp.
3288 Laurelview Ct, Fremont CA 94538-6535. 510/651-8886.

US Integrated Technologies
3023 Research Dr, Richmond CA 94806-5206. 510/223-1001.

Fuji Optical Systems Inc.
170 Knowles Dr, Los Gatos CA 95030-1833. 408/866-5466.

Zitel Corp.
630 Alder Dr, Milpitas CA 95035-7444. 408/321-9600.

Wedge Technology
1657 McCandless Dr, Milpitas CA 95035-8003. 408/263-9888.

Flytech Technology USA Inc.
3008 Scott Blvd, Santa Clara CA 95054-3323. 408/727-7373.

Cadam Inc.
One Almaden Blvd Ste 1200, San Jose CA 95113-2215. 408/534-4100.

Force Computers Inc.
2001 Logic Drive, San Jose CA 95124-3468. 408/371-5900.

Mitsuba Corporation
752 Charcot Ave, San Jose CA 95131-2223. 408/383-9356.

Ven-Tel Inc.
2121 Zanker Rd, San Jose CA 95131-2109. 408/436-7400.

Arix Corp.
871 Fox Ln, San Jose CA 95131-1601. 408/432-1200.

Sherpa Corp.
1511 Briartree Dr, San Jose CA 95131-2964. 408/433-0455.

Atalla Corp.
2304 Zanker Rd, San Jose CA 95131-1115. 408/435-8850.

Dyna Micro Inc.
30 W Montague Expy, San Jose CA 95134-2002. 408/943-0100.

Reply Corp.
4435 Fortran Dr, San Jose CA 95134-2300. 408/942-4804.

Oak Technology
139 Kifer Ct, Sunnyvale CA 94086-5120. 408/737-0888.

Smart Modular Technologies
4305 Cushing Pkwy, Fremont CA 94538-6408. 510/623-1231.

Sigma Designs Inc.
46501 Landing Pkwy, Fremont CA 94538-6421. 510/770-0100.

Avatar Systems Corp.
1455 McCarthy Blvd, Milpitas CA 95035-7433. 408/321-0110.

Cirexx Corp.
3391 Keller St, Santa Clara CA 95054-2617. 408/988-3980.

Areal Technology Inc.
2146 Bering Dr, San Jose CA 95131-2013. 408/436-6800.

Masstor Systems Corp.
1810-B Old Oakland Rd, San Jose CA 95131. 408/955-0160.

R-Byte Inc.
2299 Ringwood Ave Suite C4, San Jose CA 95131-1717. 408/452-8860.

Insite Peripherals Inc.
4433 Fortran Dr, San Jose CA 95134-2300. 408/946-8080.

Falco Data Products Inc.
1176 Aster Ave Ste H, Sunnyvale CA 94086-6803. 408/745-7123.

RJE Communications Inc.
765 N Mary Ave, Sunnyvale CA 94086-2909. 408/245-7532.

Jax International Inc.
5925 Redwood Dr, Rohnert Park CA 94928-2076. 707/584-7360.

ICT Inc.
2123 Ringwood Ave, San Jose CA 95131-1725. 408/434-0678.

Televideo Systems Inc.
PO Box 49048, San Jose CA 95161-9048. 408/954-8333.

Jameco Electronics
1355 Shoreway Rd, Belmont CA 94002-4100. 415/592-8097.

Proxim Inc.
295 Bernardo Ave, Mountain View CA 94043-5205. 415/960-1630.

Ampro Corporation
420-A N Bernardo Ave, Mountain View CA 94043. 510/962-8281.

EO Inc.
800 A E Middlefield Rd,

Mountain View CA 94043. 415/903-8100.

Digital Pathways Inc.
201 Ravendale Dr, Mountain View CA 94043-5216. 415/964-0707.

Cogent Electronics Inc.
210 Twin Dolphin Dr Suite A, Redwood City CA 94065-1402. 415/591-6617.

Torus Systems Inc.
240 Twin Dolphin Dr Ste C, Redwood City CA 94065-1403. 415/594-9336.

Crescendo Communications Inc.
930 E Arques Ave #3735, Sunnyvale CA 94086-4520. 408/732-5955.

Phoenix Service Inc.
525 Almanor Ave, Sunnyvale CA 94086-3512. 408/524-2300.

ASP Computer Products Inc.
285 N Wolfe Rd, Sunnyvale CA 94086. 408/746-2965.

American Advantech Corp.
750 E Arques Ave, Sunnyvale CA 94086-3830. 408/245-6678.

Gamma Link
1314 Chesapeake Ter, Sunnyvale CA 94089-1100. 408/744-1400.

Oce Graphics
1221 Innsbruck Dr, Sunnyvale CA 94089-1317. 415/966-9400.

Opcode Systems Inc.
3950 Fabian Way #100, Palo Alto CA 94303-4605. 415/856-3333.

Echelon Corporation
4015 Miranda Ave, Palo Alto CA 94304-1218. 415/855-7400.

Kensington Microware Ltd.
2855 Campus Dr, San Mateo CA 94403-2510. 415/572-2700.

Farallon Computing
2470 Mariner Square Loop, Alameda CA 94501-1010. 510/814-5100.

Kyocera Electronics Inc.
1321 Harbor Bay Pkwy, Alameda CA 94502-6541. 510/748-6680.

Tec America Electronics Inc.
2710 Lakeview Ct, Fremont CA 94538-6534. 510/651-5333.

Telco Systems Network Access Corp.
4305 Cushing Pkwy, Fremont CA 94538-6408. 510/490-3111.

TCL Inc.
41829 Albrae St, Fremont CA 94538-3120. 510/657-3800.

Compac Microelectronics Inc.
3797 Spinnaker Ct, Fremont CA 94538-6537. 510/656-3333.

MW Computer
41934 Christy St, Fremont CA 94538-3159. 510/659-8812.

Mouse Systems Corp.
47505 Seabridge Dr, Fremont CA 94538-6546. 510/656-1117.

Luxcom Inc.
3249 Laurelview Ct, Fremont CA 94538-6535. 510/770-3300.

Link Technology Inc.
46595 Landing Pkwy, Fremont CA 94538-6421. 510/651-8000.

ESS Technology Inc.
46107 Landing Pkwy, Fremont CA 94538-6407. 510/226-1088.

Elitegroup Computer Systems Inc.
45225 Northport Ct, Fremont CA 94538-6411. 510/226-7333.

Focus Information Systems Inc.
48860 Milmont Dr Ste 108C, Fremont CA 94538-7369. 510/657-2845.

Interlink Computer Sciences
47370 Fremont Blvd, Fremont CA 94538-6566. 510/657-9800.

In-Motion Inc.
46731 Fremont Blvd, Fremont CA 94538-6539. 510/651-2626.

Proxellent Inc.
41938 Christy St, Fremont CA 94538-3159. 510/785-4225.

Shuttle Technology Inc.
43116 Christy St, Fremont CA 94538-3167. 510/505-0567.

Puretek USA
44110 Old Warm Springs Blvd, Fremont CA 94538-6144. 510/656-8083.

Cache Computers Inc.
46600 Landing Pkwy, Fremont CA 94538-6420. 510/226-9922.

Umax Technologies Inc.
3353 Gateway Blvd, Fremont CA 94538-6526. 510/651-8883.

Ultima Electronics Corp.
3358 Gateway Blvd, Fremont CA 94538-6525. 510/659-1580.

PC Time Data
40555 Encyclopedia Cir, Fremont CA 94538-2469. 510/623-8862.

Deeco Products
31047 Genstar Rd, Hayward CA 94544. 510/471-4700.

Zypcom Inc.
2301 Industrial Pkwy W Ste 7, Hayward CA 94545-5029. 510/783-2501.

Appoint Inc.
6377 Clark Ave Ste 111, Dublin CA 94568-3034. 510/463-3003.

SBE Inc.
4550 Norris Canyon Rd, San Ramon CA 94583-1369. 510/355-2000.

Avi Systems Inc.
1830 Embarcadero, Oakland CA 94606-5226. 510/535-1020.

General Parametrics Corp.
1250 9th St, Berkeley CA 94710-1545. 510/524-3950.

Rhetorex Inc.
200 E Hacienda Ave, Campbell CA 95008-6617. 408/370-0881.

Personal Data Systems Inc.
100 W Rincon Ave Ste 103, Campbell CA 95008-2818. 408/866-1126.

Info Products
541 Division St, Campbell CA 95008-6905. 408/374-7290.

Advanced Computer Communications
10261 Bubb Rd, Cupertino CA 95014-4167. 408/864-0600.

Sage Instruments
240 Airport Blvd, Freedom CA 95019-2614. 408/761-1000.

Parity Systems Inc.
110 Knowles Dr, Los Gatos CA 95030. 408/378-1000.

Digicom Systems Inc.
188 Topaz St, Milpitas CA 95035-5429. 408/262-1277.

Dee One Systems
1558 Centre Pointe Dr, Milpitas CA 95035-8011. 408/956-8286.

Nexstor Inc.
631 S Milpitas Blvd, Milpitas CA 95035-5473. 408/262-1074.

Loral Fairchild Imaging
1801 McCarthy Blvd, Milpitas CA 95035-7407. 408/433-2500.

Jaton Corp.
556 S Milpitas Blvd, Milpitas CA 95035-5454. 408/942-9888.

Valuestor Inc.
105 Serra Way # 443, Milpitas CA 95035-5206. 408/945-1200.

Hi-Tech USA
1558 & 1562 Centre Pointe Dr , Milpitas CA 95035-8011. 408/262-8688.

Anritsu Wiltron Sales Co.
685 Jarvis Dr, Morgan Hill CA 95037-2813. 408/776-8300.

Imagen Corporation
2650 San Tomas Expressway, Santa Clara CA 95051-0953. 408/986-9400.

Canon USA Inc.
2051 Mission College Blvd, Santa Clara CA 95054-1519. 408/982-5200.

Basic Measuring Instruments Inc.
3250 Jay Street, Santa Clara CA 95054-3309. 408/970-3700.

Dtronix Inc.
3140 De La Cruz Blvd Ste 200 , Santa Clara CA 95054-2444. 408/982-9667.

Dextra Technology Corp.
5201 Great America Pkwy 320, Santa Clara CA 95054-1127. 408/562-5792.

Destiny Technology Corp
3255 Scott Blvd, Santa Clara CA 95054-3013. 408/262-9400.

Integrated Info Technology Inc.
2445 Mission College Blvd, Santa Clara CA 95054-1214. 408/727-1885.

Fujitsu Personal Systems Inc.
5200 Patrick Henry Dr, Santa Clara CA 95054-1152. 408/982-9500.

Peer Networks Inc.
3350 Scott Blvd Bldg 10, Santa Clara CA 95054-3116. 408/727-4111.

T3 Plus Networking Inc.
3393 Octavius Dr, Santa Clara CA 95054-3004. 408/986-4243.

Sundisk Corp.
3270 Jay St, Santa Clara CA 95054-3309. 408/562-0500.

Summit Memory Systems Inc.
360 El Pueblo Dr, Scotts Valley CA 95066-4212. 408/438-2660.

Datalogic
104 Whispering Pines Dr, Scotts Valley CA 95066-4734. 408/438-7000.

Syskonnect Inc
12930 Saratoga Ave, Saratoga CA 95070-4600. 408/725-4650.

Actrix Systems Inc.
6315 San Ignacio Ave, San

Jose CA 95119-1202. 408/281-4321.

Genoa Systems Corp.
6850 Santa Teresa Blvd, San Jose CA 95119-1205. 408/432-9090.

Bay Connection
2717 Buena View Ct, San Jose CA 95121-2911. 408/270-8070.

JDR Microdevices
2233 Samaritan Dr, San Jose CA 95124-4407. 408/559-1200.

Kansai Electric USA
2005 Hamilton Ave Ste 220, San Jose CA 95125-5917. 408/377-7062.

Alantec Corp.
2115 Onel Drive, San Jose CA 95131-2032. 408/955-9000.

Great Tek Inc.
2289 Ringwood Ave, San Jose CA 95131-1717. 408/943-1005.

Visionex Inc.
711 Charcot Ave, San Jose CA 95131. 408/954-0640.

CXR Telcom Corp.
2040 Fortune Dr #102, San Jose CA 95131-1860. 408/435-8520.

Tangram Technology Corp.
1528 Montague Expy, San Jose CA 95131-1408. 408/428-9165.

Seiko Instruments USA Inc.
1130 Ringwood Ct, San Jose CA 95131-1795. 408/922-5900.

Flexstar Inc.
2040 Fortune Dr, San Jose CA 95131-1823. 408/433-0770.

Quickcomm Inc.
2290 Ringwood Ave Ste K, San Jose CA 95131-1718. 408/956-9145.

Petronic International Inc.
2300 Zanker Rd Ste C, San Jose CA 95131-1114. 408/943-1717.

Pagine Corp.
2156 Zanker Rd, San Jose CA 95131-2113. 408/944-9200.

Indala Corp.
3041 Orchard Pky, San Jose CA 95134-2017. 408/434-7010.

Advanced Computer Link Inc.
2674 N 1st St, San Jose CA 95134-2003. 408/432-0270.

Cipher Data Products Inc.
3081 Zanker Rd Ms, San Jose CA 95134-2127. 415/967-9560.

Cygnet Systems Inc.
2560 Junction Ave, San Jose CA 95134-1902. 408/954-1800.

Grimes Company
1841 Enterprise Blvd, W Sacramento CA 95691-3423. 916/373-8888.

Removable Media Solutions
2700 Mercantile Dr Ste 100, Rncho Cordova CA 95742-6574. 916/933-0700.

Pasco Scientific
10101 Foothills Blvd, Roseville CA 95747-7100. 916/786-3800.

Jones Futurex Inc.
3715 Atherton Rd, Rocklin CA 95765-3701. 916/632-3456.

Hansen Information Tech
1745 Markston Rd, Sacramento CA 95825-4026. 916/921-0883.

FRS Inc.
1101 National Dr, Sacramento CA 95834-1901. 916/928-1107.

Immix
PO Box 2980, Grass Valley CA 95945-2980. 916/272-9800.

TDK Systems Development Center
136 New Mohawk Rd, Nevada City CA 95959-3262. 916/265-5395.

For more information on career opportunities in the computer industry:

<u>Associations</u>

ASSOCIATION FOR COMPUTING MACHINERY
1515 Broadway, 17th Floor, New York NY 10036. 212/869-7440.

INFORMATION TECHNOLOGY ASSOCIATION OF AMERICA
1616 North Fort Myer Drive, Suite 1300, Arlington VA 22209. 703/522-5055. World Wide Web address: http://www.itaa.org.

MULTIMEDIA DEVELOPMENT GROUP
2601 Mariposa Street, San Francisco CA 94110. 415/553-2300. Fax: 415/553-2403. E-Mail address: info@mdg.org. A nonprofit trade association dedicated to the business and market development of multimedia companies.

Magazines

COMPUTER-AIDED ENGINEERING
Penton Publishing, 1100 Superior Avenue, Cleveland OH 44114. 216/696-7000.

COMPUTERWORLD
IDG, 375 Cochituate Road, P.O. Box 9171, Framingham MA 01701-9171. 508/879-0700.

DATA COMMUNICATIONS
McGraw-Hill, 1221 Avenue of the Americas, New York NY 10020. 212/512-2000.

DATAMATION
Cahners Publishing, 275 Washington Street, Newton MA 02158. 617/964-3030.

IDC REPORT
International Data Corporation, 5 Speen Street, Framingham MA 01701. 508/872-8200.

EDUCATIONAL SERVICES

Job prospects for college and university faculty, elementary school teachers, counselors, and education administrators should show moderate improvement throughout the '90s, although most of the openings will result from retirements. Among kindergarten and elementary school teachers, the best opportunities await those with training in special education. The employment outlook is also good for teacher aides, as many assist special education teachers, as school reforms call for more individual attention to students, and as the number of students who speak English as a second language rises. Adult education and secondary school teachers, and sports and physical fitness instructors and coaches are other occupations expected to grow faster than average.

CALIFORNIA COLLEGE OF PODIATRIC MEDICINE
1210 Scott Street, San Francisco CA 94115. 415/563-8070. **Contact:** Sandra Piccini, Director of Human Resources. **Description:** A college/teaching hospital offering post-graduate programs in the field of podiatric medicine.

CALIFORNIA CULINARY ACADEMY, INC.
625 Polk Street, San Francisco CA 94102. 415/771-3536. **Contact:** Human Resources. **Description:** Founded in 1977, the California Culinary Academy is one of the largest accredited for-profit schools for professional chef training in the United States. The school has developed a highly-successful track record for the placement of graduates, low drop-out rates, and modest student loan default rates. The academy offers instruction in classical and modern methods of food preparation in its core degree program, specialized baking and pastry certificate programs, and a full range of evening and weekend classes for the cooking and wine enthusiast. The operations of the Academy include an A.O.S. Degree Program in Culinary Arts, a Certificate Program in Baking and Pastry Arts, weekend and short-course professional and vocational cooking classes, two public restaurants, three private dining rooms, and a small retail shop. **Corporate headquarters location:** This Location.

CALIFORNIA SCHOOL OF PROFESSIONAL PSYCHOLOGY
2749 Hyde Street, San Francisco CA 94109. 415/346-4500. **Contact:** Denise A. Hanson, Chief Human Resources Officer. **Description:** A nonprofit institution of higher learning which offers post-graduate programs leading to a doctorate in psychology. **Common positions include:** Accountant/Auditor; Administrative Services Manager; Administrative Worker/Clerk; Admissions Officer; Computer Programmer; Contract/Grant Administrator; Department Manager; Financial Aid Officer; Human Resources Specialist; Marketing Specialist; Public Relations Specialist; Systems Analyst. **Educational backgrounds include:** Accounting; Business Administration; Communications; Computer Science; Finance; Liberal Arts. **Benefits:** Cafeteria; Dental Insurance; Disability Coverage; Life Insurance; Medical Insurance; Pension Plan; Tuition Assistance. **Corporate headquarters location:** This Location. **Number of employees at this location:** 30. **Number of employees nationwide:** 1,100.

CALIFORNIA STATE UNIVERSITY/HAYWARD
258000 Carlos Bee Boulevard, Hayward CA 94542. 510/885-3634. **Contact:** Ms. Mardell Xavier, Associate Director/Human Resources. **Description:** A four-year

university. **Common positions include:** Accountant/Auditor; Administrator; Biological Scientist/Biochemist; Economist/Market Research Analyst; Human Resources Specialist; Marketing Specialist; Public Relations Specialist; Purchasing Agent and Manager. **Educational backgrounds include:** Accounting; Biology; Business Administration; Chemistry; Communications; Computer Science; Economics; Finance; Liberal Arts; Marketing; Mathematics; Physics. **Benefits:** Dental Insurance; Disability Coverage; Life Insurance; Medical Insurance; Pension Plan; Tuition Assistance. **Operations at this facility include:** Service.

CALIFORNIA STATE UNIVERSITY/TURLOCK
801 West Monte Vista, Turlock CA 95382. 209/667-3122. **Contact:** Human Resources. **Description:** A state university.

CHILDREN'S DISCOVERY CENTERS OF AMERICA, INC.
851 Irwin Street, Suite 200, San Rafael CA 94901. 415/257-4200. **Fax:** 415/459-1374. **Contact:** Human Resources. **Description:** Children's Discovery Centers of America is the fifth-largest chain of child care centers in the United States, operating 154 child care centers in 15 states with an aggregate licensed capacity of approximately 13,000 children. The company provides child care and preschool programs to children primarily between 2-1/2 and six years of age and, to a lesser extent, after school programs for older children and infant care. Children's Discovery operates 34 centers in conjunction with employer-sponsors, either on a management contract basis or with one or more types of employer subsidies, such as tuition subsidies, free or reduced rent, or provision of services. The company's proprietary computerized system monitors the staff-to-child ratio in all of its centers, enabling the company to staff efficiently in response to shifts in occupancy levels. **Corporate headquarters location:** This Location.

COLLEGE OF MARIN
935 College Avenue, Kentfield CA 94904. 415/457-8811. **Recorded Jobline:** 415/485-9693. **Contact:** Personnel. **Description:** A medium-sized, two-year community college.

CONTRA COSTA COMMUNITY COLLEGE DISTRICT
500 Court Street, Martinez CA 94553. 510/229-1000x207. **Fax:** 510/229-2490. **Contact:** Teresa Gula, District Human Resources Technician. **Description:** The community college district located just east of the San Francisco Bay area. Contra Costa Community College District offers two-year degrees, as well as vocational and transfer programs. The school has a culturally diverse student population. **Common positions include:** Education Administrator; Human Service Worker; Teacher. **Educational backgrounds include:** Master of Arts; Teaching. **Corporate headquarters location:** This Location.

FAR WEST LABORATORY FOR EDUCATIONAL RESEARCH & DEVELOPMENT
730 Harrison Street, San Francisco CA 94107. 415/565-3000. **Fax:** 415/565-3012. **Contact:** Joan Hukari, Personnel Manager. **Description:** A nonprofit educational agency created by Congress in 1966 engaged in improving the quality of education by helping policy makers and practitioners apply the best knowledge from research, development, and practice. The laboratory's professional staff combines state-of-the-art knowledge of educational research and development with a practical understanding of day-to-day school problems. AA/EOE. **Common positions include:** Computer Systems Analyst; Education Administrator; Mathematician; Secretary. **Educational backgrounds include:** Accounting; Computer Science; Education; Liberal Arts; Mathematics.

Benefits: Dental Insurance; Disability Coverage; Life Insurance; Medical Insurance; Pension Plan; Savings Plan. **Corporate headquarters location:** This Location. **Other U.S. locations:** Tucson AZ. **Operations at this facility include:** Research and Development. **Number of employees at this location:** 145. **Number of employees nationwide:** 165.

FOOTHILL & DE ANZA COMMUNITY COLLEGE
12345 El Monte Road, Los Altos Hills CA 94022-4599. 415/949-7777. **Contact:** Human Resources. **Description:** A two-year community college.

FREEMONT UNIFIED SCHOOL DISTRICT (FUSD)
P.O. Box 5008, Fremont CA 94537. 510/657-2350. **Contact:** Human Resources. **Description:** A school district. **Number of employees nationwide:** 1,250.

GOLDEN GATE UNIVERSITY
536 Mission Street, San Francisco CA 94105. 415/442-7000. **Contact:** Laverne Barnes, Personnel Coordinator. **Description:** An independent university specializing in business and pre-law undergraduate programs. Golden Gate University also offers graduate programs in law, business administration, public administration, and tax. **Educational backgrounds include:** Accounting; Business Administration; Computer Science; Economics; Finance; Liberal Arts; Marketing; Mathematics. **Benefits:** Dental Insurance; Employee Discounts; Life Insurance; Medical Insurance; Pension Plan; Tuition Assistance. **Number of employees at this location:** 325.

MILLS COLLEGE
5000 MacArthur Boulevard, Oakland CA 94613. 510/430-2282. **Recorded Jobline:** 510/430-2012. **Contact:** Personnel Department. **Description:** An independent liberal arts college for women. Founded in 1852, Mills College offers bachelor's and master's degrees.

OHLONE COLLEGE
P.O. Box 3909, Fremont CA 94539-0390. 510/659-6088. **TTY/TDD:** 510/659-6089. **Fax:** 510/659-6025. **Recorded Jobline:** 510/656-8295. **Contact:** Human Resources. **Description:** A college. **Number of employees at this location:** 550.

SAN FRANCISCO STATE UNIVERSITY
1600 Holloway Avenue, AD 252, San Francisco CA 94132. 415/338-1872. **Recorded Jobline:** 415/338-1871. **Contact:** Human Resources Department. **Description:** A state university. **NOTE:** Entry-level positions are available. **Common positions include:** Accountant/Auditor; Blue-Collar Worker Supervisor; Broadcast Technician; Budget Analyst; Buyer; Clerical Supervisor; Clinical Lab Technician; Computer Programmer; Computer Systems Analyst; Cost Estimator; Counselor; Draftsperson; Editor; Electrician; Financial Analyst; Hotel Manager/Assistant Manager; Human Resources Specialist; Internet Services Manager; Library Technician; Management Analyst/Consultant; Management Trainee; MIS Specialist; Pharmacist; Physician; Police/Law Enforcement Officer; Psychologist; Purchasing Agent and Manager; Radiologic Technologist; Registered Nurse; Teacher; Typist/Word Processor. **Educational backgrounds include:** Accounting; Business Administration; Communications; Computer Science; Education; Finance; Liberal Arts; MBA; Ph.D. **Benefits:** 401(k); Credit Union; Dental Insurance; Disability Coverage; Life Insurance; Mass Transit Available; Medical Insurance; Pension Plan; Profit Sharing; Tuition Assistance. **Special Programs:** Internships. **Corporate headquarters location:** Long

Beach CA. **Other U.S. locations:** CA. **Operations at this facility include:** Administration. **Number of employees at this location:** 3,000.

SANTA CLARA UNIVERSITY
500 El Camino Real, Santa Clara CA 95053. 408/554-4000. **Contact:** Director of Personnel. **Description:** A university offering undergraduate programs through its schools of Arts and Sciences, Business, Engineering, and Education. The university also offers graduate programs through its schools of Law, Engineering, Business, Agricultural Business, and Counseling Psychology.

SIERRA COMMUNITY COLLEGE
5000 Rocklin Road, Rocklin CA 95677. 916/781-0520. **Fax:** 916/781-0497. **Contact:** Peter Kolster, Director of Human Resources. **Description:** A community college offering degree and certificate programs and transfer curriculum. **Common positions include:** Accountant/Auditor; Administrative Services Manager; Advertising Clerk; Architect; Clerical Supervisor; Computer Programmer; Computer Systems Analyst; Counselor; Education Administrator; Human Resources Specialist. **Educational backgrounds include:** Accounting; Art/Design; Biology; Business Administration; Chemistry; Communications; Computer Science; Economics; Education; Engineering; Finance; Geology; Liberal Arts; Marketing; Mathematics; Physics. **Benefits:** 401(k); Dental Insurance; Disability Coverage; Life Insurance; Medical Insurance; Pension Plan. **Operations at this facility include:** Administration; Divisional Headquarters. **Number of employees at this location:** 450.

STANFORD UNIVERSITY
855 Serra Drive, Stanford CA 94305-6100. 415/723-0657. **Contact:** Kathy Davis, Manager/Human Resources. **Description:** A privately-endowed, non-sectarian institution of higher learning. Founded in 1885. The university offers undergraduate programs through its schools of Humanities and Sciences, Engineering, and Earth Sciences. Stanford University also offers graduate programs through its professional schools of Law, Medicine, Business, and Education.

UNIVERSITY OF CALIFORNIA/BERKELEY
2200 University Avenue, Room 7G, Berkeley CA 94720. 510/642-1011. **Contact:** Campus Personnel. **Description:** A university offering undergraduate and graduate programs in the liberal arts and professional fields. The university is a leader in teaching, research, and public service. Undergraduate divisions include the colleges of Chemistry, Engineering, Environmental Design, Letters and Science, and Natural Resources. Established in 1868, Berkeley is the oldest campus of the University of California system. **Common positions include:** Accountant/Auditor; Administrative Worker/Clerk; Administrator; Aerospace Engineer; Biological Scientist/Biochemist; Buyer; Chemist; Computer Programmer; Customer Service Representative; Department Manager; Editor; Financial Analyst; General Manager; Hotel Manager/Assistant Manager; Human Resources Specialist; Reporter; Student Services Specialist; Systems Analyst; Technical Writer/Editor; Transportation/Traffic Specialist. **Benefits:** Dental Insurance; Disability Coverage; Life Insurance; Medical Insurance; Pension Plan; Tuition Assistance. **Corporate headquarters location:** Oakland CA. **Operations at this facility include:** Administration; Research and Development.

UNIVERSITY OF CALIFORNIA/DAVIS
100 Administration Annex, Davis CA 95616. 916/752-0530. **Contact:** Personnel Department. **Description:** A location of the university.

UNIVERSITY OF CALIFORNIA/SANTA CRUZ
102 Communications Building, Santa Cruz CA 95064. 408/459-2011. **Contact:** Staff Personnel Office. **Description:** This campus of the University of California emphasizes undergraduate education in the arts and sciences. The predominant degrees offered are B.A. and B.S. degrees, but Master's and Doctoral degrees are also conferred.

UNIVERSITY OF SAN FRANCISCO
2130 Fulton Street, Campion C-7, San Francisco CA 94117-1080. 415/666-6707. **Fax:** 415/386-1074. **Recorded Jobline:** 415/666-5600. **Contact:** Nora Lee, Personnel Analyst. **Description:** Established as San Francisco's first institution of higher education in 1855, the University of San Francisco serves 8,000 students in the arts and sciences, business, education, nursing, and law. The university is a private, Jesuit institution and welcomes candidates who desire to work in such an environment. **Common positions include:** Accountant/Auditor; Budget Analyst; Computer Programmer; Computer Systems Analyst; Counselor; Financial Analyst; Human Resources Specialist; Librarian; Library Technician; Stationary Engineer; Typist/Word Processor. **Educational backgrounds include:** Business Administration; Communications; Liberal Arts. **Benefits:** Daycare Assistance; Dental Insurance; Disability Coverage; Life Insurance; Mass Transit Available; Medical Insurance; Pension Plan; Tuition Assistance. **Corporate headquarters location:** This Location. **Other U.S. locations:** San Ramon CA; Sacramento CA; Cupertino CA. **Operations at this facility include:** Administration. **Number of employees at this location:** 1,100.

UNIVERSITY OF THE PACIFIC
3601 Pacific Avenue, Administration Building, Stockton CA 95211. 209/946-2124. **Contact:** Human Resources. **Description:** A four-year university offering undergraduate and graduate programs.

Note: *Because addresses and telephone numbers of smaller companies can change rapidly, we recommend you call each company to verify the information below before inquiring about job opportunities. Mass mailings are not recommended.*

Additional small employers:

ELEMENTARY AND SECONDARY SCHOOLS

Saint Ignatius College Prep School
2001 37th Ave, San Francisco CA 94116-1165. 415/731-7500.

Head Royce School
4315 Lincoln Ave, Oakland CA 94602-2599. 510/531-1300.

Clovis Adult School
1452 David E Cook Way, Clovis CA 93611-0575. 209/292-3658.

Salinas Adult School
431 W Alisal St, Salinas CA 93901-1624. 408/758-0956.

Mountain View-Los Altos Adult School
333 Moffett Blvd, Mountain View CA 94043-4725. 415/940-1333.

San Lorenzo Adult Center
17250 Esteban St, Hayward CA 94541-1028. 510/481-4617.

Community Adult School
1505 E Main Ave, Morgan Hill CA 95037-3217. 408/779-5261.

Watsonville Aptos Adult School
550 Rodriguez St, Watsonville CA 95076-4210. 408/728-6330.

Lindbergh Adult School
311 E North St, Manteca CA 95336-4612. 209/825-3100.

James Rutter Middle School
7350 Palmer House Dr, Sacramento CA 95828-4027. 916/422-7590.

Clovis High School
1055 Fowler Ave, Clovis CA 93611-2099. 209/299-7211.

Clovis West High School
1070 E Teague Ave, Fresno CA 93720-1803. 209/431-6600.

Buchanan High School
1560 N Minnewawa Ave, Clovis CA 93611-7698. 209/298-3330.

Madera High School-South
26433 Avenue 13, Madera CA 93637-6190. 209/675-4450.

McLane High School
2727 N Cedar Ave, Fresno CA 93703-2097. 209/441-3500.

Fresno Senior High School
1839 N Echo Ave, Fresno CA 93704-6047. 209/441-3800.

Hoover Senior High School
5550 N 1st St, Fresno CA 93710-6201. 209/441-3888.

Galileo High School
1150 Francisco St, San Francisco CA 94109-1096. 415/749-3430.

Mission High School
3750 18th St, San Francisco CA 94114-2699. 415/241-6240.

Abraham Lincoln High School
2162-24th Avenue, San Francisco CA 94116. 415/759-2700.

George Washington High School
600 32nd Ave, San Francisco CA 94121-2794. 415/750-8400.

Lowell High School
1101 Eucalyptus Dr, San Francisco CA 94132-1499. 415/759-2730.

Antioch High School
700 W 18th St, Antioch CA 94509-1500. 510/706-5300.

Armijo High School
824 Washington St, Fairfield CA 94533-5586. 707/421-4230.

Fairfield High School
205 E Atlantic Ave, Fairfield CA 94533-1698. 707/422-4235.

Hayward High School
1633 East Ave, Hayward CA 94541-5399. 510/582-0102.

Napa High School
2475 Jefferson St, Napa CA 94558-4931. 707/253-3713.

Pittsburg High School
250 School St, Pittsburg CA 94565-3890. 510/473-4100.

James Logan High School
1800 H St, Union City CA 94587-3321. 510/471-2520.

Berkeley High School
2246 Milvia St, Berkeley CA 94704-1429. 510/644-6120.

Gilroy High School
750 W 10th St, Gilroy CA 95020-6399. 408/847-2424.

Live Oak High School
1505 E Main Ave, Morgan Hill CA 95037-3200. 408/779-5210.

Watsonville High School
250 E Beach St, Watsonville CA 95076-4831. 408/728-6386.

Yerba Buena High School
1855 Lucretia Ave, San Jose CA 95122-3799. 408/279-1500.

Overfelt High School
1835 Cunningham Ave, San Jose CA 95122-1799. 408/259-0540.

Oak Grove High School
285 Blossom Hill Rd, San Jose CA 95123-2099. 408/225-9332.

Santa Teresa High School
6150 Snell Ave, San Jose CA 95123-4796. 408/578-9100.

Mount Pleasant High School
1750 S White Rd, San Jose CA 95127-4799. 408/251-7820.

Independence High School
1776 Educational Park Dr, San Jose CA 95133-1703. 408/729-3911.

Edison Senior High School
1425 S Center St, Stockton CA 95206-2016. 209/953-4413.

Stagg Senior High School
1621 Brookside Rd, Stockton CA 95207-7804. 209/953-3053.

Lincoln High School
6844 Alexandria Pl, Stockton CA 95207-2498. 209/953-8921.

Franklin Senior High School
300 N Gertrude Ave, Stockton CA 95215-4820. 209/953-4363.

Tokay High School
1111 W Century Blvd, Lodi CA 95240-6699. 209/331-7990.

Lodi High School
3 S Pacific Ave, Lodi CA 95242-3023. 209/331-7815.

Atwater High School
PO Box 835, Atwater CA 95301-0835. 209/357-6013.

Merced High School
PO Box 2167, Merced CA 95344-0167. 209/385-6465.

Modesto High School
1st and H Streets, Modesto CA 95351. 209/576-4401.

Downey High School
1000 Coffee Rd, Modesto

CA 95355-4275. 209/576-4211.

Turlock High School
1600 E Canal Dr, Turlock CA 95380-4299. 209/667-4061.

Montgomery High School
1250 Hahman Dr, Santa Rosa CA 95405-6996. 707/528-5191.

Elk Grove High School
9800 Elk Grove Florin Rd, Elk Grove CA 95624-2599. 916/686-7741.

Oakmont High School
1710 Cirby Way, Roseville CA 95661-5599. 916/782-3781.

Roseville High School
601 Tahoe Ave, Roseville CA 95678-1799. 916/782-3753.

McClatchy High School
3066 Freeport Blvd, Sacramento CA 95818-4349. 916/264-4400.

Hiram Johnson High School
6879 14th Ave, Sacramento CA 95820-3499. 916/277-6300.

Valley High School
6300 Ehrhardt Ave, Sacramento CA 95823-5699. 916/689-6500.

Florin High School
7956 Cottonwood Ln, Sacramento CA 95828-5404. 916/689-8600.

Nevada Union High School
11761 Ridge Rd, Grass Valley CA 95945-5025. 916/273-4431.

Yuba City High School
850 B St, Yuba City CA 95991-4926. 916/741-5290.

Red Bluff High School
1260 Union St, Red Bluff CA 96080-3121. 916/529-8710.

Central Santa Clara School
760 Hillsdale Ave, San Jose CA 95136-1106. 408/723-6400.

SF Educational Services Inc.
1601 Lane St, San Francisco CA 94124-2732. 415/330-3100.

Jane Lathrop School
5325 Engle Rd, Carmichael CA 95608-3091. 916/481-7905.

San Mateo County Office Of Education
101 Twin Dolphin Dr, Redwood City CA 94065-1086. 415/802-5300.

Alameda Co. Supintendant Of Schools
313 W Winton Ave, Hayward CA 94544-1136. 510/887-0152.

Calaveras Co. Office Of Education
PO Box 760, Altaville CA 95221-0760. 209/736-4662.

Las Lomitas Elementary School District
1011 Altschul Ave, Menlo Park CA 94025-6706. 415/854-2880.

Pacific Grove Unified School District
555 Sinex Ave, Pacific Grove CA 93950-4320. 408/646-6520.

Belmont Elementary School District
2960 Hallmark Dr, Belmont CA 94002. 415/593-8203.

Hillsborough City School District
300 El Cerrito Ave, Burlingame CA 94010-6899. 415/342-5193.

Burlingame Elementary School District
2303 Trousdale Dr, Burlingame CA 94010-5704. 415/259-3814.

Whisman Elementary School District
750 San Pierre Way # A, Mountain View CA 94043-3133. 415/903-6900.

Moraga Elementary School District
PO Box 158, Moraga CA 94556-0158. 510/376-5943.

Mill Valley School District
411 Sycamore Ave, Mill Valley CA 94941-2231. 415/389-7700.

Scotts Valley Union School District
4444 Scotts Valley Dr Ste 5B , Scotts Valley CA 95066-4529. 408/438-1821.

Saratoga Union Elementary School District
20460 Forrest Hills Dr, Saratoga CA 95070-6020. 408/867-3424.

Healdsburg Union High School District
925 University St, Healdsburg CA 95448-3528. 707/431-3488.

Sebastopol Union Elementary School District
7905 Valentine Ave, Sebastopol CA 95472-3214. 707/829-4570.

Analy Union High School District
6980 Analy Ave, Sebastopol CA 95472-3493. 707/823-7623.

Black Oak Mine Unified School District
PO Box 349001,

Georgetown CA 95634-9001. 916/333-8300.

Winters Joint Unified School District
710 Railroad Ave, Winters CA 95694-1646. 916/795-6100.

Durham Unified School District
PO Box 300, Durham CA 95938-0300. 916/895-4675.

Los Altos Elementary School District
201 Covington Rd, Los Altos CA 94024-4030. 415/941-4010.

Mountain View Elementary School District
220 View St, Mountain View CA 94041-1344. 415/968-6565.

Laguna Salada Union School District
375 Reina Del Mar Ave, Pacifica CA 94044-3094. 415/359-1641.

Travis Unified School District
2751 De Ronde Dr, Fairfield CA 94533-9710. 707/437-4604.

Martinez Unified School District
921 Susana St, Martinez CA 94553-1848. 510/313-0480.

Tamalpais Union HS District
PO Box 605, Larkspur CA 94977-0605. 415/924-1801.

Mount Pleasant Elementary School District
14265 Story Rd, San Jose CA 95127-3823. 408/928-1200.

Stanislaus Union Elementary School District
3601 Carver Rd, Modesto CA 95356. 209/529-9546.

Rincon Valley Union Elementary School District
1000 Yulupa Ave, Santa Rosa CA 95405-7020. 707/542-7375.

Shasta Union High School District
1313 Yuba St, Redding CA 96001-1012. 916/241-3261.

Santa Cruz City School District
133 Mission St, Santa Cruz CA 95060-3747. 408/429-3800.

Merced Union High School District
PO Box 2147, Merced CA 95344-0147. 209/385-6400.

Eureka City School District
3200 Walford Ave, Eureka CA 95503-4828. 707/441-2400.

Washington Unified School District
930 W Acres Rd, W Sacramento CA 95691-3224. 916/371-9300.

New Haven Unified School District
34200 Alvarado Niles Rd, Union City CA 94587-4432. 510/471-1100.

Cupertino Union School District
10301 Vista Dr, Cupertino CA 95014-2091. 408/252-3000.

Oak Grove School District
6578 Santa Teresa Blvd, San Jose CA 95119-1297. 408/227-8300.

Vacaville Unified School District
751 School St, Vacaville CA 95688-3945. 707/453-6100.

Stockton Unified School District
701 N Madison St, Stockton CA 95202-1634. 209/953-4050.

COLLEGES, UNIVERSITIES, AND PROFESSIONAL SCHOOLS

Monterey Institute International Studies
425 Van Buren St, Monterey CA 93940-2691. 408/647-4100.

New College Of California
50 Fell St, San Francisco CA 94102-5206. 415/241-1300.

Dominican College San Rafael
50 Acacia Ave, San Rafael CA 94901-2298. 415/457-4440.

Santa Clara School Of Medical Technology
751 S Bascom Ave, San Jose CA 95128-2699. 408/299-5422.

Humphreys College
6650 Inglewood Ave, Stockton CA 95207-3896. 209/478-0800.

JUNIOR COLLEGES AND TECHNICAL INSTITUTES

Kings River Community College
995 N Reed Ave, Reedley CA 93654-2099. 209/638-3641.

John A O'Connell Community College
33 Gough St, San Francisco CA 94103-1214. 415/282-3100.

Vista Community College
2020 Milvia St Floor 3, Berkeley CA 94704-5102. 510/841-8431.

Indian Valley Colleges
1800 Ignacio Blvd, Novato

CA 94949-4912. 415/883-2211.

Columbia College
PO Box 1849, Columbia CA 95310-1849. 209/533-5100.

Mendocino College
PO Box 3000, Ukiah CA 95482-0300. 707/468-3100.

College Of The Siskiyous
800 College Ave, Weed CA 96094-2899. 916/938-4461.

Lassen College
PO Box 3000, Susanville CA 96130-3000. 916/257-6181.

Lake Tahoe Community College
1 College Dr, S Lake Tahoe CA 96150. 916/541-4660.

BUSINESS, SECRETARIAL, AND DATA PROCESSING SCHOOLS

Technology Education Center
PO Box 929, Fresno CA 93714-0929. 209/438-7547.

Compuquest For Kids
1332 Arleen Ave, Sunnyvale CA 94087. 408/732-7213.

La Lancha Computer Services
30048 Mission Blvd, Hayward CA 94544-7233.

Computer Systems Consulting
3290 La Canada Dr, Cameron Park CA 95682-7954. 916/672-2667.

VOCATIONAL SCHOOLS

Able Industries
1451 South O St, Dinuba CA 93618-2743. 209/591-2331.

Sierra Academy Of Aeronotics
PO Box 2429, Oakland CA 94614-0429. 510/568-6100.

ABC Technical & Trade School
41 W Yokuts Ave, Stockton CA 95207. 209/952-4164.

Timberline Construction Educational Center
8788 Greenback Ln, Orangevale CA 95662-4037. 916/989-5580.

American Schools
3517 Marconi Ave, Sacramento CA 95821-5328. 916/483-3800.

MISC. SCHOOLS AND EDUCATIONAL SERVICES

Berlitz Language Centers
1646 North California Boulevard, Walnut Creek CA 94596. 510/935-1386.

English Language Systems
4444 Geary Blvd, San Francisco CA 94118-3048. 415/387-2838.

Amigo Mio Spanish Connection
320 Judah St, San Francisco CA 94122. 415/566-4655.

Dawne Bernhardt Speech Communication
566 Vallejo St, San Francisco CA 94133-4064. 415/982-3314.

E&L School Of Travel
1952 Camden Ave, San Jose CA 95124. 408/879-9590.

Virtuoso
15 Mount Wittenberg Ct, San Rafael CA 94903-1057. 415/479-0703.

Wings Over California
2635 Cunningham Ave Ste G, San Jose CA 95148-1007. 408/251-6085.

Elk Grove Flying Service
9161 Locust St, Elk Grove CA 95624. 916/685-9780.

CFI
6151 Freeport Blvd, Sacramento CA 95822-3518. 916/427-7707.

Lamaze Childbirth Classes
4735 Lei St, Fair Oaks CA 95628-6018. 916/965-4911.

SF Theological Seminary
2 Kensington Rd, San Anselmo CA 94960-2905. 415/258-6500.

CHILD DAYCARE SERVICES

Kiddie Kollege
2765 E Olive Ave, Fresno CA 93701. 209/485-6271.

Childtime Children's Center
214 N Clark St, Fresno CA 93701-2109. 209/445-0216.

Nimitz School-Age Child Care
545 Cheyenne Dr, Sunnyvale CA 94087. 408/736-6176.

Tri-Cities Children Center
33905 Syracuse Ave, Union City CA 94587. 510/487-1689.

YMCA
6200 Encinal Dr, San Jose CA 95119. 408/226-3786.

YMCA
2720 Sonoma Pl, Santa Clara CA 95051. 408/243-6577.

YMCA
6990 Melvin Dr, San Jose CA 95129. 408/996-2308.

YMCA
200 Blossom Valley Dr, Los Gatos CA 95032-3809. 408/356-1866.

Cambrian Child Care
1975 Cambrianna Dr, San Jose CA 95124-2157. 408/559-6040.

Headsup Child Care
2841 Junction Ave Ste 100, San Jose CA 95134-1921. 415/424-1155.

Neighborhood Christian Pre-School
2575 Coit Dr, San Jose CA 95124-1609. 408/371-4222.

Dilworth Child Care
101 Strayer Drive, San Jose CA 95129. 408/446-5285.

Little Folks University
801 Sibley Street, Folsom CA 95630-3218. 916/985-7055.

Merryhill Country School
1370 Baseline Rd, Roseville CA 95747-9237. 916/782-2500.

La Petite Academy Inc.
1266 Stabler Ln, Yuba City CA 95993. 916/671-6771.

For more information on career opportunities in educational services:

Associations

AMERICAN ASSOCIATION OF SCHOOL ADMINISTRATORS
1801 North Moore Street, Arlington VA 22209-9988. 703/528-0700. Fax: 703/841-1543. An organization of school system leaders. Membership includes a national conference on education; programs and seminars; *The School Administrator,* a monthly magazine; *Leadership News,* a bi-monthly newspaper; *The AASA Professor,* a quarterly publication; and a catalog of other publications and audiovisuals.

AMERICAN FEDERATION OF TEACHERS
555 New Jersey Avenue NW, Washington DC 20001. 202/879-4400.

COLLEGE AND UNIVERSITY PERSONNEL ASSOCIATION
1233 20th Street NW, Suite 301, Washington DC 20036. 202/429-0311. World Wide Web address: http://www.jobweb.org/cohrma.mtml. Membership required.

NATIONAL ASSOCIATION OF BIOLOGY TEACHERS
11250 Roger Bacon Drive, Suite 19, Reston VA 22090-5202. 703/471-1134. Toll-free number: 800/406-0775. Fax: 703/435-5582. E-mail address: nabter@aol.com. World Wide Web address: http://www.nabt.org. A professional organization for biology and life science educators.

NATIONAL ASSOCIATION OF COLLEGE ADMISSION COUNSELORS
1631 Prince Street, Alexandria VA 22314. 703/836-2222. An education association of secondary school counselors, college and university admission officers, and related individuals who work with students as they make the transition from high school to post-secondary education.

NATIONAL ASSOCIATION OF COLLEGE AND UNIVERSITY BUSINESS OFFICERS
1 DuPont Circle, Suite 500, Washington DC 20036. 202/861-2500. Association for those involved in the financial administration and management of higher education. Membership required.

NATIONAL SCIENCE TEACHERS ASSOCIATION
1840 Wilson Boulevard, Arlington VA 22201-3000. 703/243-7100. World Wide Web address: http://www.nsta.org. Organization committed to the improvement of science education at all levels, preschool through college. Publishes five journals, a newspaper, and a number of special publications. Also conducts national and regional conventions.

Books

ACADEMIC LABOR MARKETS
Falmer Press, Taylor & Francis, Inc., 1900 Frost Road, Suite 101, Bristol PA 19007. 800/821-8312.

HOW TO GET A JOB IN EDUCATION
Adams Media Corporation, 260 Center Street, Holbrook MA 02343. 617/767-8100.

Directories

WASHINGTON HIGHER EDUCATION ASSOCIATION DIRECTORY
Council for Advancement and Support of Education, 11 DuPont Circle NW, Suite 400, Washington DC 20036 202/328-5900.

ELECTRONIC/INDUSTRIAL ELECTRICAL EQUIPMENT

Heading into 1996, industry analysts expect productivity in the fast-paced electronics industry to continue to spiral downward, even as the number of production workers in the industry levels off. Intense competition from overseas has companies cutting costs by sending labor-intensive operations to low-wage regions like the Far East and Mexico. On the other hand, the increased computerization of the industry is fueling the demand for highly trained, knowledgeable workers.

Semiconductor manufacturers, in particular, are growing steadily. At the start of 1995, the Semiconductor Industry Association forecasted a growth rate of about 15 percent. The year actually came in at 26 percent. Factors spawning a high demand for semiconductors: a surging PC market, new information highway markets, and stronger telecommunications and consumer electronics markets.

ADT SECURITY SYSTEMS WEST, INC.
3551 Arden Road, Hayward CA 94545. 510/785-2912. **Contact:** Antoinette Pace, Human Resources. **Description:** Designs, programs, markets, and installs protective systems to safeguard individuals and their property from hazards such as burglary, hold-up, and fire. The company operates through two major divisions: ADT Security Systems serves over 180,000 customers in the United States, Canada, and Western Europe; the ARI Group manufactures intrusion and smoke detection sensing and control equipment in the United States and Europe. **Corporate headquarters location:** Parsippany NJ.

ADVANCED MICRO DEVICES, INC.
One AMD Place, Sunnyvale CA 94088-3453. 408/732-2400. **Contact:** Human Resources. **World Wide Web address:** http://www.amd.com. **Description:** Designs, develops, manufactures and markets complex monolithic integrated circuits for use by manufacturers of a broad range of electronic equipment and systems, primarily for products for computation, communication, and instrument applications. The company operates worldwide. **Common positions include:** Computer Engineer; Electrical/Electronics Engineer; Materials Engineer. **Corporate headquarters location:** This Location. **Number of employees nationwide:** 11,550.

ALLEN-BRADLEY CO. INC.
5675 Gibraltar Drive, Pleasanton CA 94588. 510/227-0240. **Contact:** Human Resources. **Description:** Designs, manufactures, and markets high-quality electronic controls and control systems for industrial markets. The company's principal products are photoelectric controls, inductive proximity controls, sensing products, and mechanical limit switches for the automation of industrial processes.

AMPEX CORPORATION
401 Broadway, MS 3-20, Redwood City CA 94063-3199. 415/367-2011. **Contact:** Employment. **Description:** A manufacturer of equipment for professional television, mass data storage, and instrumentation including recorders, editors, switchers, special effects, robotic libraries, tapes, and interconnect equipment. **Common positions include:**

Accountant/Auditor; Budget Analyst; Buyer; Electrical/Electronics Engineer; Financial Analyst; Human Resources Specialist; Mechanical Engineer; Software Engineer. **Educational backgrounds include:** Accounting; Business Administration; Computer Science; Engineering; Finance; Marketing. **Benefits:** 401(k); Dental Insurance; Disability Coverage; Life Insurance; Medical Insurance; Savings Plan. **Corporate headquarters location:** This Location. **Operations at this facility include:** Administration; Divisional Headquarters; Research and Development; Sales; Service.

ANALOG DEVICES
2105 South Bascom Avenue, Suite 250, Campbell CA 95008-3277. 408/559-2037. **Contact:** Human Resources. **Description:** Designs, manufactures, and sells high-performance data-acquisition electronic components, subsystems, and systems. Analog Devices operates in two industry segments: Integrated Circuit Products, manufactured using semiconductor technology as either monolithic or hybrid circuits; and Assembled Products, manufactured from discrete components and subsystems made by the company and others. The company's products are used principally to acquire, amplify, condition, convert, and display analog electrical signals. Analog Devices offers more than 260 standard component products in two classifications: Data Acquisition Components (which process or convert analog electrical signals); and Instruments and Systems (temperature transducers, digital panel meters, data acquisition and control subsystems and systems, and linear component test systems). Markets served include defense and commercial aviation, industrial automation, health care, research and development, and energy management and development. Sales offices are located throughout the world.

ANDROS INC.
2332 Fourth Street, Berkeley CA 94710-2402. 510/849-5700. **Fax:** 510/849-5849. **Contact:** Human Resources. **Description:** Andros Inc. is a supplier of instrumentation and a leading worldwide designer and supplier to original equipment manufacturers of non-dispersive infrared gas analyzers. The largest current market for the company's products consists of manufacturers of automotive diagnostic equipment used in engine tune-ups and government-mandated emissions inspections. These devices measure concentrations of carbon dioxide, carbon monoxide, and hydrocarbons. Another market for Andros's products consists of manufacturers of medical respiratory monitoring equipment. Andros's medical products measure gases in human breath including carbon dioxide, halogenated hydrocarbon gases, and nitrous oxide. In December 1993, the company expanded its product line through the acquisition of Scitec Corporation, which designs, manufactures, and sells spectrum analysis instruments that analyze selected elements in material in its natural location and condition using X-ray fluorescence technology. These products are sold to end users, principally for the detection of lead in paint. **Corporate headquarters location:** This Location.

ANTHEM ELECTRONICS, INC.
1160 Ridder Park Drive, San Jose CA 95131. 408/453-1200. **Contact:** Human Resources. **Description:** Anthem Electronics, Inc. is an industrial distributor of electronic products. Products are distributed through 24 distribution centers and five sales offices throughout the United States. The company focuses on advanced technology, semiconductors, and disk drive products, and also provides materials and manufacturing management services to its customers. **Common positions include:** Accountant/Auditor; Blue-Collar Worker Supervisor; Buyer; Clerical Supervisor; Computer Systems Analyst; Credit Manager; Customer Service Representative; Electrical/Electronics Engineer; Human Resources Specialist; Operations/Production Manager; Quality Control Supervisor; Services Sales Representative; Technical

Writer/Editor. **Educational backgrounds include:** Business Administration; Computer Science; Engineering; Marketing. **Benefits:** 401(k); Dental Insurance; Life Insurance; Medical Insurance. **Corporate headquarters location:** This Location. **Operations at this facility include:** Administration; Sales; Service. **Listed on:** New York Stock Exchange. **Number of employees at this location:** 300. **Number of employees nationwide:** 700.

APPLIED MATERIALS, INC.
3050 Bowers Avenue, M/S 1826, Santa Clara CA 95054. 408/986-3400. **Fax:** 408/986-7940. **Contact:** Corporate Employment. **Description:** Applied Materials, Inc. is a leading producer of wafer fabrication systems for the worldwide semiconductor industry. The company also sells related spare parts and services. Applied Materials' products include dry etch systems for the creation of circuit paths in semiconductors and implementation products for silicon wafers. **Common positions include:** Electrical/Electronics Engineer; Financial Analyst; Human Resources Specialist; Marketing Specialist; Mechanical Engineer; Process Engineer; Sales Representative; Software Engineer. **Corporate headquarters location:** This Location. **Listed on:** NASDAQ. **Number of employees nationwide:** 5,000.

ATMEL CORPORATION
2325 Orchard Parkway, San Jose CA 95131. 408/441-0311. **Contact:** Human Resources. **Description:** Manufactures integrated microcircuits. **Common positions include:** Accountant/Auditor; Application Engineer; Design Engineer; Designer; Marketing Specialist; Product Engineer; Test Engineer.

AUTOMATIC SWITCH COMPANY
One Waters Park Drive, Suite 123, San Mateo CA 94403. 415/574-2726. **Contact:** Human Resources. **Description:** An international manufacturer of an extensive line of electronic control equipment used for the automation of machinery, equipment, and industrial processes, and the control of electric power. **NOTE:** Human Resources is located at the corporate headquarters. **Corporate headquarters location:** Florham Park NJ. **Parent company:** Emerson Electric.

AUTOMATIC SWITCH COMPANY
705 North Carlton Avenue, Stockton CA 95201. 209/941-4111. **Fax:** 209/948-1375. **Contact:** Zachary Styles, Human Resource Manager. **Description:** Manufactures and assembles electronic switchgear, housings, contactors, and motor controls. **Corporate headquarters location:** Florham Park NJ. **Parent company:** Emerson Electric.

BEI ELECTRONICS
One Post Street, Suite 2500, San Francisco CA 94104-5285. 415/956-4477. **Contact:** William Aber, Director of Human Resources. **Description:** BEI Electronics manufactures weapons systems, military avionics, and precision components. **NOTE:** Send resumes to: Corporate Personnel, 2700 Systron Drive, Concord CA 94518. **Common positions include:** Accountant/Auditor; Design Engineer; Electrical/Electronics Engineer; Mechanical Engineer.

C-CUBE MICROSYSTEMS INC.
1778 McCarthy Boulevard, Milpitas CA 95035. 408/944-6300. **Fax:** 408/944-6314. **Contact:** Human Resources. **Description:** Founded in 1988, C-Cube Microsystems Inc., a market leader in digital video compression, designs and markets integrated circuits that implement international standards for the compression of digital full-motion video and

still images for consumer electronics, communications and computer applications such as video CD players, direct broadcast of television programming by satellites, and multimedia computing. C-Cube's innovative encoder, decoder, and codec products allow high-quality full-motion video and still images to be cost-effectively provided by a broad range of end-user systems. **Corporate headquarters location:** This Location. **Number of employees at this location:** 130.

CALIFORNIA MICRO DEVICES CORPORATION
215 Topaz Street, Milpitas CA 95035. 408/263-3214. **Contact:** Human Resources. **Description:** California Micro Devices Corporation serves OEM and end-user electronic systems manufacturers who require higher performance, higher density, lower cost, and unique functionality by providing a line of specialty and precision electronic components. These components allow customers to build systems which provide superior value to their users by incorporating Integrated Passive Electronic Components. California Micro Devices has forged a leadership position with its proprietary materials and process technology which specializes in multiple thin passive electronic components and semiconductor devices. **Corporate headquarters location:** This Location.

CATALYST SEMICONDUCTOR, INC.
2231 Calle de Luna, Santa Clara CA 95054. 408/748-7700. **Fax:** 408/980-0318. **Contact:** Human Resources. **Description:** Founded in 1985, Catalyst Semiconductor is a supplier of nonvolatile semiconductors that provide design solutions for a broad range of applications including computers, wireless communications, networks, instrumentation, and automotive systems. Catalyst's family of nonvolatile devices includes FLASH, Serial and Parallel EEPROMs (electrical erasable read only memory), and NVRAMs. The company is dedicated to maintaining its position in EEPROM products while actively pursuing development of future generations of FLASH products. Catalyst's products are marketed through a direct sales force and a worldwide network of representatives and distributors. The company's employees work in technology development, engineering, marketing, and sales. Manufacturing and test locations include Japan, Singapore, Thailand, and the Philippines. **Corporate headquarters location:** This Location.

CENTRAL DYNAMICS
1983 Concourse Drive, San Jose CA 95131. 408/970-1600. **Contact:** Personnel. **Description:** Specializes in the design and manufacture of computer-controlled test, measurement, and development systems for a wide variety of customers in three high-technology markets: electronic equipment manufacturers, mechanical equipment manufacturers, and semiconductor manufacturers and users. **Corporate headquarters location:** Concord MA.

CHIPS AND TECHNOLOGIES, INC.
2950 Zanker Road, San Jose CA 95134. 408/434-0600. **Contact:** Human Resources. **Description:** Chips and Technologies supplies advanced semiconductor devices to the worldwide personal computer industry. The company pioneered the concept of implementing discrete system functions in highly-integrated chip sets. The company's products are found in a wide range of systems from compact portables to high-performance desktop computers. **Corporate headquarters location:** This Location.

CIRRUS LOGIC, INC.
3100 West Warren Avenue, Fremont CA 94538. 510/623-8300. **Contact:** Norman T. Brown, Employment Manager. **Description:** Cirrus Logic, Inc. develops innovative architectures for analog and digital systems functions and implements those architectures

in very large scale integrated (VLSI) circuits for applications that include mass storage, user interface (graphics, audio, and video), communications, and data acquisition. **Common positions include:** Accountant/Auditor; Buyer; Design Engineer; Electrical/Electronics Engineer; Software Engineer. **Educational backgrounds include:** Business Administration; Engineering; Finance. **Benefits:** 401(k); Dental Insurance; Disability Coverage; Life Insurance; Medical Insurance; Tuition Assistance. **Corporate headquarters location:** This Location. **Other U.S. locations:** San Diego CA; Broomfield CO; Raleigh NC; Austin TX; Dallas TX. **Operations at this facility include:** Administration; Divisional Headquarters; Manufacturing; Research and Development; Sales. **Listed on:** NASDAQ. **Annual sales/revenues:** More than $100 million. **Number of employees at this location:** 1,400. **Number of employees nationwide:** 2,850. **Number of employees worldwide:** 3,000.

COHERENT INC.
5100 Patrick Henry Drive, Santa Clara CA 95054. 408/764-4000. **Contact:** Human Resources. **Description:** A designer, manufacturer, and supplier of laser systems and medical instruments utilizing laser, precision optic, and microelectronic technologies for customers in science, industry, and medicine. **Common positions include:** Accountant/Auditor; Buyer; Computer Programmer; Customer Service Representative; Electrical/Electronics Engineer; Financial Analyst; General Manager; Manufacturing Engineer; Marketing Specialist; Operations/Production Manager; Physicist/Astronomer; Production Operator; Systems Analyst; Technical Representative; Technical Writer/Editor. **Educational backgrounds include:** Accounting; Business Administration; Chemistry; Computer Science; Engineering; Finance; Physics. **Benefits:** Dental Insurance; Disability Coverage; Employee Discounts; Life Insurance; Medical Insurance; Profit Sharing; Retirement Plan; Stock Option; Tuition Assistance. **Operations at this facility include:** Administration; Research and Development; Sales; Service.

COHERENT INC.
3270 West Bayshore Road, Palo Alto CA 94303. 415/858-2250. **Contact:** Human Resources. **Description:** A designer, manufacturer, and supplier of laser systems and medical instruments utilizing laser, precision optic, and microelectronic technologies for customers in science, industry, and medicine.

COHERENT INC.
AUBURN GROUP
2301 Lindbergh, Auburn CA 95602. 916/823-9550. **Contact:** Human Resources. **Description:** A designer, manufacturer, and supplier of laser systems and medical instruments using laser, precision optic, and microelectronic technologies for customers in science, industry, and medicine.

COMPUTER PRODUCTS
47173 Benecia Street, Fremont CA 94538. 510/657-6700. **Contact:** Human Resources. **Description:** Computer Products is a designer and producer of electronic products and subsystems. The company manufactures both standard and custom products used in an array of applications including powering communications networks, controlling the manufacture of fiber optics, enabling voice messaging, providing multimedia power for global Internet servers, and operating traffic signals with real-time embedded computers. The company consists of three business segments; Power Conversion, a supplier of power systems technology to the communications industry; RTP Corporation, an industrial automation business that delivers input/output products and intelligent

controllers; and Heurikon Corporation, a computer systems business that designs and provides real-time computers and subsystems tailored to the markets of voice messaging, graphics, video-on-demand, machine vision, and simulation.

CONDUCTUS, INC.
969 West Maude Avenue, Sunnyvale CA 94086. 408/523-9950. **Fax:** 408/523-9999. **Contact:** Human Resources. **Description:** Conductus develops, manufactures, and markets electronic systems and components based on superconductors. Since its founding in 1987, Conductus has pushed the development of high-temperature superconducting materials and devices to address the needs of large and growing markets. Conductus has successfully developed and currently markets magnetic sensors and laboratory instruments. The company is focused on developing additional products for applications in wireless communications, magnetic resonance instrumentation, and new applications of magnetic sensing. Research and development is largely funded by government contracts. **Corporate headquarters location:** This Location.

CREDENCE SYSTEMS CORPORATION
42808 Christy Street, Fremont CA 94538. 510/657-7400. **Fax:** 510/623-2560. **Contact:** Human Resources. **Description:** Credence Systems Corporation is a leader in the delivery of innovative, affordable solutions for high-volume production testing of digital and mixed-signal integrated circuits. Using its proprietary CMOS technologies, Credence manufactures automatic test equipment specifically designed to reduce the cost of testing without compromising performance, flexibility, or reliability. **Corporate headquarters location:** This Location.

CYPRESS SEMICONDUCTOR
3901 North 1st Street, San Jose CA 95134. 408/943-2600. **Contact:** Personnel. **Description:** Manufactures electronic parts and components.

EG&G/RETICON CORPORATION
345 Potrero Avenue, Sunnyvale CA 94086. 408/738-4266. **Contact:** Professional Employment Department. **Description:** Manufactures solid-state image sensors for electronics applications. Overall, EG&G provides a variety of specialized scientific products and services to governmental and industrial customers for technical applications. Business activities are conducted in five major market segments: instruments, which produces a wide range of mechanical, electronic, and electro-optical instruments used in industry and research; components, which produces mechanical, electronic, and electro-optical instruments for technologically-based industries; environmental & biomedical services, which provides specialized services in the environmental and health care fields including research in energy and biology; custom services & systems, which serves primarily government markets with technical and management services, energy-related research, and custom hardware and high-reliability electronic components for defense, space exploration, and environmental programs; and Department of Energy support, which provides support to DOE programs in nuclear and non-nuclear energy, and in weapons development and testing.

EATON CORPORATION
262 Santa Ana Court, Sunnyvale CA 94086. 408/730-6450. **Contact:** Human Resources. **Description:** A manufacturer of a wide variety of electronics equipment, including data processing systems and products and a line of communications equipment.

EMBEDDED PERFORMANCE INC.
1860 Barber Lane, Milpitas CA 95035. 408/434-2210. **Contact:** Employment Supervisor. **Description:** This location of Embedded Performance, Inc. produces electronic test equipment for commercial use. Embedded Performance is an integrated manufacturer and developer of electronic, electrical, battery, and industrial products. Electronic products include digital computer systems, torpedo systems for military applications, military and civilian communication systems, and servo motors and servo motor controllers for use in a wide variety of industries. Electrical products include industrial control equipment, light switches, circuit breakers, and a broad range of electrical products used in the construction industry. Battery products include a wide range of consumer and industrial batteries and casings. Industrial products include custom engineered parts, powder metal parts, and components used in hydraulic and other types of fluid systems. **Corporate headquarters location:** Rolling Meadows IL. **Listed on:** New York Stock Exchange.

EXAR CORPORATION
48720 Kato Road, Fremont CA 94538. 408/434-6400. **Contact:** Human Resources Department. **Description:** Exar Corporation is engaged in the design, manufacture, and marketing of analog and mixed-signal integrated circuits primarily for use in telecommunications, data communications, microperipherals, and consumer electronics products. **Common positions include:** Accountant/Auditor; Administrator; Buyer; Customer Service Representative; Department Manager; Electrical/Electronics Engineer; General Manager; Human Resources Specialist; Manufacturer's/Wholesaler's Sales Rep.; Marketing Specialist; Operations/Production Manager; Quality Control Supervisor. **Educational backgrounds include:** Accounting; Business Administration; Communications; Computer Science; Engineering; Marketing; Physics. **Benefits:** Dental Insurance; Disability Coverage; Employee Discounts; Life Insurance; Medical Insurance; Savings Plan; Stock Option; Tuition Assistance. **Corporate headquarters location:** This Location. **Operations at this facility include:** Administration; Manufacturing; Research and Development; Sales; Service. **Listed on:** NASDAQ. **Number of employees at this location:** 500.

FLEXTRONICS INTERNATIONAL
2241 Lundy Avenue, San Jose CA 95131. 408/428-1300. **Contact:** Human Resources Department. **Description:** Flextronics International is a manufacturer of a broad range of electron tubes.

GTE GOVERNMENT SYSTEMS CORPORATION
P.O. Box 7188, Mountain View CA 94039. 415/966-2995. **Fax:** 415/966-4621. **Contact:** Cecil Wright, Staffing. **Description:** GTE Government Systems Corporation is engaged in the advancement of information systems and command, control, communications, computer, and intelligence technology. GTE Government Systems Corporation designs and produces customized systems for defense, government, and industry. **Common positions include:** Electrical/Electronics Engineer; Software Engineer. **Benefits:** 401(k); Dental Insurance; Disability Coverage; Employee Discounts; Life Insurance; Medical Insurance; Pension Plan; Savings Plan; Tuition Assistance. **Corporate headquarters location:** Needham MA. **Parent company:** GTE Corporation. **Operations at this facility include:** Research and Development. **Number of employees at this location:** 1,200.

GENUS, INC.

1139 Karlstad Drive, Sunnyvale CA 94089. 408/747-7120. **Contact:** Human Resources. **Description:** Genus, Inc. designs, manufactures, markets, and services advanced thin film deposition, high-energy (MeV) ion implantation, and vapor phase wafer cleaning equipment used in the fabrication of complex ultra-large scale integration semiconductor devices. The company was the first to market chemical vapor deposition (CVD) tungsten silicide, CVD blanket tungsten, and MeV ion implantation systems -- three critical technologies for semiconductor manufacturing. Genus's products are used for several critical process steps required to produce integrated circuits for the computer, aerospace, communications, medical, military, aeronautical, automotive, and consumer electronics industries. The company's global customer base consists of semiconductor manufacturers in the United States, Europe, and countries in the Pacific Rim including Japan, Korea, and Taiwan. **Corporate headquarters location:** This Location.

HADCO CORPORATION

3080 Olcott Street, Suite 210-C, Santa Clara CA 95054. 408/986-8750. **Contact:** Human Resources. **Description:** A high-grade manufacturer of printed circuit boards and backpanel assemblies. Hadco produces multi-layer prototypes and volume orders.

HARRIS CORPORATION
DIGITAL TELEPHONE SYSTEMS

P.O. Box 1188, Novato CA 94948-1188. 415/382-5000. **Contact:** Joan VanderWerff, Human Resources Supervisor. **Description:** Harris Corporation is focused on four major businesses: advanced electronic systems, communications, semiconductors, and an office-equipment distribution network.

HARRIS SEMICONDUCTOR

3031 Tisch Way, One Plaza South, San Jose CA 95128. 408/985-7322. **Contact:** Human Resources. **Description:** Engaged in the research, design, application, and marketing of data acquisition semiconductors. **Common positions include:** Electrical/Electronics Engineer; Sales Engineer. **Educational backgrounds include:** Engineering. **Benefits:** 401(k); Dental Insurance; Disability Coverage; Life Insurance; Medical Insurance; Profit Sharing; Savings Plan; Tuition Assistance. **Corporate headquarters location:** Melbourne FL. **Parent company:** Harris Corporation. **Operations at this facility include:** Administration; Research and Development. **Number of employees at this location:** 80.

HEWLETT-PACKARD

3000 Hanover Street, MS 20APP, Palo Alto CA 94304-1181. 415/852-8473. **Fax:** 415/852-8138. **Contact:** Employment Response Center. **E-mail address:** hpresume@corp.hp.com. **World Wide Web address:** http://www.hp.com. **Description:** Nationally, the firm is engaged in the design, manufacture, marketing, and servicing of a broad array of precision electronics instruments and systems for measurement, analysis, and computation. **Educational backgrounds include:** Accounting; Business Administration; Chemistry; Engineering; Finance; Marketing; Mathematics; Physics. **Benefits:** Dental Insurance; Disability Coverage; Employee Discounts; Life Insurance; Medical Insurance; Pension Plan; Profit Sharing; Savings Plan; Tuition Assistance. **Special Programs:** Internships. **Operations at this facility include:** Administration; Manufacturing; Research and Development; Service. **Listed on:** New York Stock Exchange.

HEWLETT-PACKARD COMMUNICATIONS COMPONENTS
350-370 West Trimble Road, San Jose CA 95131. 408/435-7400. **Contact:** Personnel Department. **Description:** Hewlett-Packard is engaged in the design and manufacture of measurement and computation products and systems used in business, industry, engineering, science, health care, and education; principal products are integrated instrument and computer systems (including hardware and software), computer systems, and peripheral products; and medical electronic equipment and systems.

HEWLETT-PACKARD MICROWAVE INSTRUMENT DIVISION
1212 Valley House Drive, Rohnert Park CA 94928. 707/794-1212. **Contact:** Human Resources. **Description:** Produces radio-frequency, microwave, and millimeter wave spectrum analyzers and related signal analysis equipment. **Corporate headquarters location:** Palo Alto CA.

HEWLETT-PACKARD MICROWAVE TECHNOLOGY
1400 Fountain Grove Parkway, Santa Rosa CA 95403. 707/577-1400. **Contact:** Personnel. **Description:** Produces high-frequency transistors and diodes, SAW (surface-acoustic-wave) devices, YIG (yttrium-iron-garnet) spheres, integrated circuits, thick and thin film circuits, and microwave packages for all Hewlett-Packard divisions. As a whole, Hewlett-Packard is engaged in the design and manufacture of measurement and computation products and systems used in business, industry, engineering, science, health care, and education. Principal products are integrated instrument and computer systems (including hardware and software); computer systems and peripheral products; and medical electronic equipment and systems.

IMP, INC.
2830 North First Street, San Jose CA 95134. 408/432-9100. **Fax:** 408/434-0335. **Contact:** Human Resources. **Description:** IMP, Inc. develops and manufactures application-specific standard integrated circuits for mass storage applications. The company designs, develops, and manufactures certain custom memory integrated circuits. IMP also provides silicon foundry services to fabless semiconductor manufacturers and other companies. **Corporate headquarters location:** This Location.

IMPACT SYSTEMS, INC.
1075 East Brokaw Road, San Jose CA 95131. 408/453-3700. **Fax:** 408/453-4115. **Contact:** Human Resources. **Description:** Founded in 1980, Impact Systems, Inc. develops, manufactures, sells, and services a wide spectrum of computer-based measurement and control systems to the paper industry. Impact's cross-direction (CD) measurement and control systems reduce CD variations in key variables occurring in the production of virtually all grades of paper. Actuators and sensors primarily improve quality and reduce operating cost. The Spectrum drying products are mainly used to improve production. Control of these variables is critical to improving paper quality, increasing production capacity, and reducing rejects, energy consumption, and raw material costs. The company's products have been specifically designed for integration with existing paper machine measurement and control systems. Direct sales and service organizations located throughout the world. **Corporate headquarters location:** This location.

INFORMATION STORAGE DEVICES
2045 Hamilton Avenue, San Jose CA 95125. 408/369-2400. **Fax:** 408/369-2422. **Contact:** Human Resources. **Description:** Information Storage Devices (ISD) designs, develops and markets analog integrated circuit products for voice recording and playback using the company's proprietary ChipCorder high-density storage technology and mixed signal expertise. The company's products offer high-quality voice reproduction, ease of use, low-power consumption, and battery-less storage in a low-cost single-chip solution. These benefits have enabled the company's customers to develop diverse new applications. **Corporate headquarters location:** This Location.

INTEGRATED DEVICE TECHNOLOGY, INC.
2972 Stender Way, Santa Clara CA 95054. 408/727-6116. **Fax:** 408/944-2001. **Contact:** Staffing. **Description:** Integrated Device Technology, Inc. designs, manufactures, and markets high-speed CMOS VLSI integrated circuits with sub-half-micron feature sizes. The company's product lines are synergistic and are targeted at providing products that optimize the cost and performance of its customers' microprocessor-based systems. The company focuses its efforts on four product areas: SRAM cache, specialty memory products, logic, and RISC microprocessors that serve the desktop/server, data communications, and office automation markets. **Common positions include:** Chemical Engineer; Electrical/Electronics Engineer; Science Technologist; Statistician; Technical Writer/Editor. **Educational backgrounds include:** Chemistry; Engineering. **Benefits:** 401(k); Dental Insurance; Disability Coverage; Employee Discounts; Life Insurance; Medical Insurance; Profit Sharing; Savings Plan; Tuition Assistance. **Special Programs:** Internships. **Corporate headquarters location:** This Location. **Other U.S. locations:** San Jose CA. **Operations at this facility include:** Administration; Divisional Headquarters; Manufacturing; Research and Development; Sales. **Listed on:** NASDAQ. **Number of employees nationwide:** 2,800.

INTEGRATED SILICON SOLUTION, INC.
680 Almanor Avenue, Sunnyvale CA 94086. 408/733-4774. **Contact:** Human Resources. **Description:** Integrated Silicon Solution, Inc. (ISSI) designs, develops, and markets high-performance SRAM and nonvolatile memory integrated circuits used in personal computers, data communications, telecommunications, instrumentation, and consumer products. A substantial portion of the company's operations are located in Taiwan, where ISSI's facilities are used as a base for marketing and sales to Asian customers, manufacturing coordination, and product testing. Operations at this location include corporate headquarters, technology and product development, and some testing facilities. **Number of employees nationwide:** 230.

INTEL CORPORATION
Mail Stop FM4-145, P.O. Box 1141, Folsom CA 95763-1141. 408/987-8080. **Contact:** Staffing Department. **Description:** Intel is one of the largest semiconductor manufacturers in the world. Other operations include supercomputers; embedded control chips and flash memories; video technology software; multimedia hardware; personal computer enhancement products; and designing, making, and marketing microcomputer components, modules, and systems. Intel sells its products to original equipment manufacturers and other companies that incorporate them into their products. **Listed on:** NASDAQ.

INTEL CORPORATION
P.O. Box 58119, Santa Clara CA 95052-8119. 408/765-8080. **Contact:** Human Resources. **Description:** Intel is one of the largest semiconductor manufacturers in the

world. Other operations include supercomputers; embedded control chips and flash memories; video technology software; multimedia hardware; personal computer enhancement products; and designing, making, and marketing microcomputer components, modules, and systems. Intel sells its products to original equipment manufacturers and other companies that incorporate them into their products. **Corporate headquarters location:** This Location.

JOHNSON MATTHEY ELECTRICAL
677 River Oaks Parkway, San Jose CA 95134-1907. 408/943-1700. **Contact:** Human Resources. **Description:** A manufacturer of components for the electronics industry. Johnson Matthey Electrical also manufactures preforms and sputtering targets.

KLA INSTRUMENTS CORPORATION
P.O. Box 49055, San Jose CA 95161-9055. 408/456-6507. **Contact:** Human Resources. **Description:** KLA manufactures high-speed image-processing systems for the semiconductor industry. **Common positions include:** Accountant/Auditor; Buyer; Customer Service Representative; Draftsperson; Electrical/Electronics Engineer; Equipment Service Engineer; Financial Analyst; Human Resources Specialist; Manufacturer's/Wholesaler's Sales Rep.; Mechanical Engineer; Physicist/Astronomer; Purchasing Agent and Manager; Software Engineer; Systems Analyst; Technical Writer/Editor. **Educational backgrounds include:** Accounting; Business Administration; Computer Science; Engineering; Finance; Physics. **Benefits:** Daycare Assistance; Dental Insurance; Disability Coverage; Employee Discounts; Life Insurance; Medical Insurance; On-Site Gym; Pension Plan; Profit Sharing. **Special Programs:** Internships. **Corporate headquarters location:** This Location. **Operations at this facility include:** Administration; Divisional Headquarters; Manufacturing; Regional Headquarters; Research and Development; Sales; Service. **Listed on:** NASDAQ.

KENT ELECTRONICS CORPORATION
225 Charcot, San Jose CA 95731. 408/262-4300. **Contact:** Human Resources. **Description:** A multi-regional distributor of a wide variety of electronic products including wire and cable, connectors, and other passive and electromechanical products and interconnect assemblies used by customers in assembling and manufacturing electronic equipment. Kent Electronics Corporation also manufactures electronic interconnect assemblies that are built to customers' specifications.

KULICKE & SOFFA INDUSTRIES, INC.
U.S. WESTERN REGIONAL OFFICE
2210 Martin Avenue, Santa Clara CA 95050. 408/727-5040. **Fax:** 408/727-4929. **Contact:** Human Resources. **Description:** Kulicke & Soffa Industries, founded in 1951, is engaged in semiconductor assembly and services. The company designs, manufactures, markets, and supports equipment for IC and MCM/hybrid semiconductor manufacturers worldwide. Product lines include wafer and hard materials dicing, die bonding and wire bonding equipment, service and spare parts, and the Micro-Swiss line of bonding and dicing tools and production accessories.

LAM RESEARCH CORPORATION
4650 Cushing Parkway, Fremont CA 94538-6401. 510/659-0200. **Contact:** Human Resources. **Description:** LAM develops, manufactures, and markets single-water plasma etch systems that are used primarily in the fabrication of very large scale integrated (VLSI) circuits. The company's products are used to deposit specific film on a silicon wafer and selectively etch away portions of various films to create a circuit design.

Depositions and etch processes, which are repeated numerous times during the fabrication cycle, are required to manufacture virtually every semiconductor device produced today. The company currently sells a broad range of etch products to address specific applications including AutoEtch, Triode, Rainbow, and TCP product lines. **Common positions include:** Accountant/Auditor; Blue-Collar Worker Supervisor; Budget Analyst; Buyer; Chemical Engineer; Clerical Supervisor; Computer Programmer; Computer Systems Analyst; Credit Manager; Designer; Draftsperson; Electrical/Electronics Engineer; Financial Analyst; Human Resources Specialist; Industrial Engineer; Mechanical Engineer; Metallurgical Engineer; Software Developer; Technical Writer/Editor. **Educational backgrounds include:** Business Administration; Chemistry; Engineering; Finance. **Benefits:** 401(k); Dental Insurance; Disability Coverage; Employee Discounts; Life Insurance; Medical Insurance; Profit Sharing; Savings Plan; Tuition Assistance. **Corporate headquarters location:** This Location. **Other U.S. locations:** Nationwide. **Operations at this facility include:** Administration; Manufacturing; Sales; Service. **Number of employees at this location:** 1,600. **Number of employees nationwide:** 2,500.

LAMBDA ADVANCED ANALOG
2270 Martin Avenue, Santa Clara CA 95050. 408/727-0500. **Fax:** 408/988-2702. **Contact:** Sharon Allansmith, Human Resources Director. **Description:** Designs and manufactures hybrid, DC-DC converters, and VHF and HF communication systems for marine and land-based communications. **Common positions include:** Analog Circuit Design Engineer; Radio Frequency Engineer. **Educational backgrounds include:** Engineering. **Benefits:** 401(k); Bonus Award/Plan; Dental Insurance; Disability Coverage; Employee Discounts; Medical Insurance; Profit Sharing; Spending Account. **Corporate headquarters location:** New York. **Annual sales/revenues:** $21 - 50 million. **Number of employees at this location:** 170.

LINEAR TECHNOLOGY CORPORATION
1630 McCarthy Boulevard, Milpitas CA 95035-7487. 408/432-1900. **Contact:** Human Resources. **Description:** Designs and manufactures a broad line of standard high-performance linear integrated circuits. These circuits monitor, condition, amplify, or transform continuous analog signals. **Number of employees at this location:** 1,000.

LITTON APPLIED TECHNOLOGY
4747 Hellyer Avenue, P.O. Box 7012, San Jose CA 95150-7012. 408/365-4747. **Contact:** Professional Recruiting Department. **Description:** Designs and manufactures electronic defense systems used by Department of Defense, U.S. government agencies, and U.S. allies including radar warning receiving systems, cover and deception systems, and surveillance systems. **Common positions include:** Accountant/Auditor; Blue-Collar Worker Supervisor; Buyer; Computer Programmer; Electrical/Electronics Engineer; Financial Analyst; Industrial Engineer; Mechanical Engineer; Operations/Production Manager; Quality Control Supervisor; Systems Analyst; Technical Writer/Editor. **Educational backgrounds include:** Accounting; Business Administration; Engineering; Finance; Mathematics; Physics. **Benefits:** 401(k); Dental Insurance; Life Insurance; Medical Insurance; Pension Plan; Savings Plan; Stock Option; Tuition Assistance. **Corporate headquarters location:** Woodland Hills CA. **Parent company:** Litton Industries, Inc. **Operations at this facility include:** Administration; Divisional Headquarters; Manufacturing; Marketing; Research and Development; Sales; Service. **Listed on:** New York Stock Exchange.

LITTON ELECTRON DEVICES
960 Industrial Road, San Carlos CA 94070-4194. 415/591-8411. **Contact:** Adriana Lencarelli, Human Resources Recruiter. **Description:** A subsidiary of Litton, which serves worldwide markets with commercial, consumer, industrial, professional, and defense-related products. The major business area for the division is advanced microwave components and subsystems for military radar, communications, and electronic countermeasure markets. Product technologies are focused in high-power vacuum tubes, microwave semiconductors, amplifiers and oscillators, night vision and optical devices, and military switching power supplies. **Common positions include:** Accountant/Auditor; Administrator; Buyer; Computer Programmer; Department Manager; Draftsperson; Electrical/Electronics Engineer; Financial Analyst; Human Resources Specialist; Mechanical Engineer; Metallurgical Engineer; Operations/Production Manager; Systems Analyst. **Educational backgrounds include:** Accounting; Business Administration; Engineering; Physics. **Benefits:** Dental Insurance; Disability Coverage; Employee Discounts; Life Insurance; Medical Insurance; Pension Plan; Savings Plan; Tuition Assistance. **Corporate headquarters location:** Woodland Hills CA. **Parent company:** Litton Industries, Inc. **Operations at this facility include:** Administration; Divisional Headquarters; Manufacturing; Research and Development; Sales. **Listed on:** New York Stock Exchange.

LOCKHEED INFORMATION
3200 Zanker Road, P.O. Box 49041, San Jose CA 95134. 408/473-3000. **Contact:** Lisa Hoskins, Employment Representative. **Description:** Lockheed Information is a leading supplier of command, control, communications, and Intelligence (C3I) and training systems, with emphasis on large-scale systems integration, intelligence processing, exploration, and multilevel security and data storage technologies. The main complex at San Jose consists of a 23-acre parcel containing four multi-story buildings with more than 546,000 square feet of space. Facilities contain executive offices, engineering design groups, development labs, test installations, clean rooms, hybrid microelectronics laboratories, program offices, and administrative functions. **Common positions include:** Aerospace Engineer; Electrical/Electronics Engineer; Hardware Engineer; Software Engineer. **Educational backgrounds include:** Computer Science; Engineering; Finance; Mathematics; Physics. **Benefits:** Dental Insurance; Disability Coverage; Employee Discounts; Life Insurance; Medical Insurance; Pension Plan; Profit Sharing; Savings Plan; Tuition Assistance. **Parent company:** Lockheed Corporation. **Operations at this facility include:** Administration; Research and Development. **Number of employees at this location:** 800. **Number of employees nationwide:** 1,600.

LOCKHEED MARTIN FAIRCHILD SYSTEMS
1801 McCarthy Boulevard, Milpitas CA 95035. 408/433-2500. **Fax:** 408/433-2604. **Contact:** Human Resources. **Description:** Produces visible and infrared CCDs and cameras for use in military, space, and commercial applications. **Other area locations:** Newport Beach CA.

LOCKHEED MARTIN MICROWAVE NARDA WEST
11040 White Rock Road, Building 200, Rancho Cordova CA 95670. 916/638-5500. **Fax:** 916/638-8682. **Contact:** Human Resources. **Description:** Lockheed Martin Microwave is involved in the manufacture of filters/multiplexers, isolators, circulators, gain equalizers, oscillators (cavity and DRO), and integrated assemblies.

LOCKHEED MARTIN RANDTRON

130 Constitution Drive, Menlo Park CA 94025. 415/326-9500. **Contact:** Carinne Wickman, Human Resources Representative. **Description:** Designs and manufactures integrated microwave antenna subassemblies and low-radar cross-section antenna designs and measurements. **Common positions include:** Accountant/Auditor; Aerospace Engineer; Buyer; Computer Programmer; Cost Estimator; Department Manager; Human Resources Specialist; Mechanical Engineer; Microwave Engineer; Operations/Production Manager; Purchasing Agent and Manager; Quality Control Supervisor; Support Personnel; Systems Analyst. **Educational backgrounds include:** Accounting; Engineering; Finance. **Benefits:** Disability Coverage; Employee Discounts; Life Insurance; Savings Plan; Tuition Assistance. **Operations at this facility include:** Administration; Research and Development. **Number of employees at this location:** 240.

LOCKHEED MARTIN SPACE AND RANGE SYSTEMS

1260 Crossman Avenue, Sunnyvale CA 94089-1198. 408/734-6200. **Fax:** 408/734-6444. **Contact:** Human Resources. **Description:** Lockheed Martin Space and Range Systems is involved in automated command, control communications, instrumentation, telemetry, electronic warfare simulation, and expert systems (fixed and mobile applications) for space and range control facilities. The company also provides design, development, systems integration, operation, and maintenance support to space control systems and test, evaluation, and training ranges.

MEASUREX CORPORATION

One Results Way, Cupertino CA 95014-5991. 408/255-1500. **Fax:** 408/864-7570. **Contact:** Human Resources. **Description:** Measurex is a leading supplier of computer-integrated measurement, control, and information systems and services for continuous and batch manufacturing processes. The company believes its wide range of integrated products provides economic results for customers by improving product quality, increasing productivity, and reducing raw material usage. Industries served by the company include pulp and paper, plastics, nonwovens, aluminum, and rubber. Five business units are responsible for developing, marketing, and manufacturing Measurex product lines: Integrated Control Systems, located at the company's corporate headquarters in Cupertino, California, with another manufacturing plant in Waterford, Ireland, to serve European customers; Cross-Direction (CD) Profile Control Systems, produced by Measurex Devron Inc., in its plant in Vancouver, British Columbia, Canada; Web Inspection Products, manufactured by Measurex Roibox Oy in Kuopio, Finland; Millwide Production and Information Management Systems, produced by Measurex's management systems division in Cincinnati, Ohio; Industrial Systems Measurement, Control, and Information products, manufactured by Measurex's industrial systems division, located in Cupertino and in its Webart group offices in Cincinnati. Measurex customers are served by sales and service subsidiaries located in 44 offices in 30 countries around the world. **Corporate headquarters location:** This Location. **Number of employees worldwide:** 2,090.

MEGATEST CORPORATION

880 Fox Lane, San Jose CA 95131. 408/437-9700. **Contact:** Personnel. **Description:** An international manufacturer of automated test equipment for a wide range of original equipment manufacturers, particularly in semiconductor fabrication. **Common positions include:** Accountant/Auditor; Buyer; Computer Programmer; Electrical/Electronics

Engineer; Technical Writer/Editor. **Educational backgrounds include:** Computer Science; Engineering. **Benefits:** Disability Coverage; Life Insurance; Medical Insurance; Pension Plan; Tuition Assistance. **Corporate headquarters location:** This Location.

NEC ELECTRONICS, INC.
475 Ellis Street, Mountain View CA 94039. 415/960-6000. **Contact:** Human Resources Department. **Description:** NEC Electronics, Inc is one of the largest semiconductor manufacturers in the world, supplying a wide variety of micro-electronics components used in computers, telecommunications, data communications, instrumentation, automobiles, and consumer applications. **Common positions include:** Computer Programmer; Electrical/Electronics Engineer; Financial Analyst; Marketing Specialist; Technical Writer/Editor. **Educational backgrounds include:** Business Administration; Computer Science; Engineering; Marketing. **Benefits:** Dental Insurance; Disability Coverage; Life Insurance; Medical Insurance; Pension Plan; Tuition Assistance; Vision Insurance. **Corporate headquarters location:** This Location. **Other U.S. locations:** Roseville CA. **Parent company:** NEC Corporation. **Operations at this facility include:** Administration.

NATIONAL SEMICONDUCTOR CORPORATION
2900 Semiconductor Drive, MS 10-127, Santa Clara CA 95051. 408/721-5000. **Contact:** Kevin Wheeler, Human Resources. **Description:** National Semiconductor Corporation designs, develops, and manufactures microprocessors, consumer products, integrated circuits, memory systems, computer products, telecommunication systems, and high-speed bipolar circuits. National Semiconductor Corporation also operates seven plants in the U.S., the Pacific Rim, and Scotland. **Common positions include:** Computer Programmer; Department Manager; Electrical/Electronics Engineer; Financial Analyst; Human Resources Specialist; Industrial Engineer; Mechanical Engineer; Physicist/Astronomer; Technical Writer/Editor. **Educational backgrounds include:** Business Administration; Computer Science; Engineering; Finance; Marketing; Mathematics; Physics. **Benefits:** Dental Insurance; Disability Coverage; Employee Discounts; Life Insurance; Medical Insurance; Pension Plan; Profit Sharing; Savings Plan; Tuition Assistance. **Special Programs:** Internships. **Corporate headquarters location:** This Location. **Operations at this facility include:** Administration; Manufacturing; Research and Development; Sales; Service. **Listed on:** New York Stock Exchange.

NOVELLUS SYSTEMS INC.
3970 North First Street, San Jose CA 95134. 408/943-9700. **Fax:** 408/943-3422. **Contact:** Human Resources. **E-mail address:** novellushr@aol.com. **Description:** A manufacturer of advanced chemical vapor deposition systems used in the production of integrated circuits. **Common positions include:** Accountant/Auditor; Buyer; Chemical Engineer; Computer Programmer; Computer Systems Analyst; Designer; Draftsperson; Electrical/Electronics Engineer; Financial Analyst; Human Resources Specialist; Mechanical Engineer; Public Relations Specialist; Purchasing Agent and Manager; Software Engineer; Technical Writer/Editor. **Educational backgrounds include:** Accounting; Business Administration; Chemistry; Computer Science; Engineering; Marketing. **Benefits:** 401(k); Dental Insurance; Disability Coverage; Life Insurance; Medical Insurance; Profit Sharing; Stock Option; Tuition Assistance. **Corporate headquarters location:** This Location. **Other U.S. locations:** Nationwide. **Operations at this facility include:** Administration; Manufacturing; Research and Development; Sales; Service. **Listed on:** NASDAQ.

PHOTRONICS INC.
695 Vaqueros Avenue, Sunnyvale CA 94086-3540. 408/245-7342. **Contact:** Personnel Administrator. **Description:** Manufactures photo masks for the semiconductor industry. **Corporate headquarters location:** This Location.

PRESCOLITE, INC.
1251 Doolittle Drive, San Leandro CA 94577. 510/562-3500. **Contact:** Patt Lari, Human Resources Manager. **Description:** A manufacturer of incandescent and high-intensity discharge lighting fixtures.

RAYCHEM CORPORATION
300 Constitution Drive, Menlo Park CA 94025. 415/361-3333. **Contact:** College Relations Manager. **Description:** Raychem develops, manufactures, and markets a wide range of high-performance polymer and metal products and systems for the electronics, industrial, and telecommunications markets. Electronics products include insulation, wire, cable, fiber optics, circuit protection devices, and heating products. **Common positions include:** Electrical/Electronics Engineer; Financial Analyst; Manufacturer's/Wholesaler's Sales Rep.; Mechanical Engineer; Metallurgical Engineer. **Educational backgrounds include:** Chemistry; Engineering. **Benefits:** Dental Insurance; Employee Discounts; Life Insurance; Medical Insurance; Pension Plan; Profit Sharing; Savings Plan; Tuition Assistance. **Special Programs:** Internships. **Corporate headquarters location:** This Location. **Subsidiaries include:** Raynet designs, makes, and markets fiber-optic loop carrier systems for television and CATV systems. **Operations at this facility include:** Administration; Divisional Headquarters; Manufacturing; Regional Headquarters; Research and Development; Sales; Service. **Listed on:** New York Stock Exchange.

RAYTHEON SEMICONDUCTOR DIVISION
350 Ellis Street, Mountain View CA 94043. 415/968-9211. **Fax:** 415/966-7838. **Contact:** Staffing Manager. **Description:** Engaged in the manufacture, design, and development of semiconductor devices for commercial use. Products include standard linear and data conversion devices, Linear Arrays, LSI/VLSI gate arrays, high-density PROMS, and transistors. Raytheon is a diversified, international, multi-industry technology-based company ranked among the 100 largest U.S. industrial corporations. Raytheon has 110 facilities in 28 states, plus the District of Columbia. Overseas facilities and representative offices are located in 26 countries, principally in Europe, the Middle East, and the Pacific Rim. The company has four business segments: electronics; major appliances; aircraft products; and energy and environmental. **Common positions include:** Computer Systems Analyst; Designer; Electrical/Electronics Engineer; Manufacturer's/Wholesaler's Sales Rep. **Educational backgrounds include:** Engineering. **Benefits:** Dental Insurance; Disability Coverage; Employee Discounts; Life Insurance; Medical Insurance; Pension Plan; Savings Plan; Tuition Assistance; Vision Insurance. **Corporate headquarters location:** Lexington MA. **Parent company:** Raytheon. **Operations at this facility include:** Administration; Manufacturing; Research and Development; Sales; Service. **Listed on:** New York Stock Exchange. **Number of employees at this location:** 600.

REDMOND PRODUCTIONS INC. (RPI)
P.O. Box 14607, San Francisco CA 94114. **Contact:** Dave Mike, Human Resources Manager. **Description:** Engaged in the design of technical systems. **Common positions include:** Computer Programmer; Electrical/Electronics Engineer; Operations/Production Manager; Optical Engineer. **Educational backgrounds include:** Art/Design; Computer

Science; Engineering; Liberal Arts; Marketing; Physics. **Special Programs:** Internships. **Corporate headquarters location:** This Location. **Other U.S. locations:** Nationwide. **Operations at this facility include:** Administration; Manufacturing; Research and Development; Sales; Service. **Listed on:** Privately held.

RELIANCE ELECTRIC COMPANY
5675 Gibraltar Drive, Pleasanton CA 94588. 510/847-8883. **Contact:** Human Resources. **Description:** Manufactures electrical industrial products.

ROCKWELL INTERNATIONAL CORPORATION
3600 Pruneridge Avenue, Suite 100, Santa Clara CA 95051-5958. 408/249-9696. **Contact:** Human Resources. **Description:** Rockwell International Corporation provides products for the printing, military, automotive, and aerospace industries through its electronics, automotive, and graphics divisions. Products include military and commercial communication equipment, guidance systems, electronics, components for automobiles, and printing presses. A major client of Rockwell is the U.S. government. Rockwell provides the government with parts and services for bombers, as well as power systems for the space station, and is a major contractor for the Space Shuttle Orbiter program.

SAE ENGINEERING
282 Brokaw Road, Santa Clara CA 95050. 408/988-0700. **Contact:** Personnel. **Description:** An international manufacturer of interconnection hardware and systems for the original equipment market. The company is a minority manufacturer of a broad line of edgeboard connectors, flat ribbon cable interconnection systems, and wire wrapping services. **Corporate headquarters location:** Santa Clara CA. **Number of employees nationwide:** 1,200.

SCI SYSTEMS, INC.
2000 Ringwood Avenue, San Jose CA 95131. 408/943-6100. **Fax:** 408/943-6123. **Contact:** Glenn Burkhardt, Human Resources Generalist. **E-mail address:** glenn.burkhardt@scismail.sci.com. **Description:** Engaged in printed circuit board assembly (contract electronic manufacturing). **Common positions include:** Accountant/Auditor; Administrative Worker/Clerk; Buyer; Human Resources Specialist; MIS Specialist; Operations/Production Manager; Production Operator; Production/Material Planner; Quality Control Supervisor; Stock Clerk. **Educational backgrounds include:** Accounting; Business Administration; Communications; Computer Science; Engineering; Finance; Liberal Arts; Marketing. **Benefits:** 401(k); Dental Insurance; Disability Coverage; Employee Discounts; Life Insurance; Medical Insurance; Savings Plan; Tuition Assistance. **Corporate headquarters location:** Huntsville AL. **Operations at this facility include:** Administration; Manufacturing; Regional Headquarters; Sales; Service. **Annual sales/revenues:** More than $100 million. **Number of employees at this location:** 350. **Number of employees nationwide:** 8,000. **Number of employees worldwide:** 10,000.

ST MICROWAVE CORPORATION
955 Benecia Avenue, Sunnyvale CA 94086. 408/730-6300. **Contact:** Gloria L. Duran, Human Resources Manager. **Description:** Manufactures a wide variety of microwave and electronics components in four product areas: solid state devices, including test equipment and microwave assemblies and subsystems; microwave components, including isofilters and multiplexers; semiconductor products, including solid state RF switches and double balanced mixers; and YIG products, including harmonic generators

and tracking filter-oscillator sets. ST Microwave is a leader in components and subsystems for EW receiving systems and state-of-the-art thin-film technology. **Common positions include:** Department Manager; Draftsperson; Electrical/Electronics Engineer; Financial Analyst. **Educational backgrounds include:** Engineering; Marketing. **Benefits:** Dental Insurance; Disability Coverage; Employee Discounts; Life Insurance; Medical Insurance; Savings Plan; Tuition Assistance. **Corporate headquarters location:** This Location. **Parent company:** Signal Technology Corp. **Operations at this facility include:** Administration; Divisional Headquarters; Manufacturing; Research and Development; Sales; Service.

SANMINA CORPORATION
355 East Trimboe Road, San Jose CA 95131. 408/435-8444. **Fax:** 408/954-5560. **Contact:** Len Gilford, Director, Human Resources. **Description:** Specializes in using advanced manufacturing technologies and processes to manufacture custom-designed backpanel assemblies and subassemblies; multilayer, high-density printed circuit boards (PCBs); and surface mount technology (SMT) assemblies used in sophisticated electronics equipment. **Common positions include:** Accountant/Auditor; Budget Analyst; Buyer; Chemist; Customer Service Representative; Electrical/Electronics Engineer; Financial Analyst; Manufacturer's/Wholesaler's Sales Rep.; Manufacturing Engineer; Operations Research Analyst; Quality Control Supervisor. **Educational backgrounds include:** Accounting; Business Administration; Engineering; Finance; Marketing. **Benefits:** 401(k); Dental Insurance; Disability Coverage; Life Insurance; Medical Insurance; Tuition Assistance. **Corporate headquarters location:** This Location. **Operations at this facility include:** Administration; Manufacturing; Research and Development; Sales; Service. **Listed on:** NASDAQ. **Number of employees at this location:** 100. **Number of employees nationwide:** 750.

SIEMENS COMPONENTS, INC.
OPTOELECTRONICS DIVISION
19000 Homestead Road, Cupertino CA 95014. 408/257-7910. **Contact:** Personnel Manager. **Description:** Designs, manufactures, and sells optoelectronic component products for use in a variety of applications.

SIERRA SEMICONDUCTOR CORPORATION
2075 North Capitol Avenue, San Jose CA 95132. 408/263-9300. **Fax:** 408/263-1272. **Contact:** Professional Staffing. **Description:** Sierra Semiconductor designs, manufactures, and sells semiconductors for the communications market. **Common positions include:** Accountant/Auditor; Computer Systems Analyst; Electrical/Electronics Engineer; Financial Analyst; Food Scientist/Technologist; Science Technologist; Software Engineer. **Educational backgrounds include:** Computer Science; Engineering. **Benefits:** 401(k); Dental Insurance; Disability Coverage; Employee Discounts; Life Insurance; Medical Insurance; Stock Option; Vision Insurance. **Corporate headquarters location:** This Location. **Subsidiaries include:** PMC-Sierra and Prometheus. **Operations at this facility include:** Administration; Divisional Headquarters; Manufacturing; Research and Development; Sales. **Listed on:** NASDAQ. **Number of employees at this location:** 300.

SILICONIX INC.
A MEMBER OF THE TEMIC GROUP
2201 Laurelwood Road, Santa Clara CA 95056. 408/988-8000. **Fax:** 408/970-3929. **Contact:** Supervisor, Employee Relations/Communications. **Description:** Manufactures semiconductor products. **Common positions include:** Accountant/Auditor; Buyer;

Computer Programmer; Computer Systems Analyst; Electrical/Electronics Engineer; Financial Analyst; Human Resources Specialist; Industrial Engineer; Metallurgical Engineer. **Educational backgrounds include:** Accounting; Business Administration; Computer Science; Engineering; Marketing. **Benefits:** 401(k); Dental Insurance; Disability Coverage; Employee Discounts; Life Insurance; Medical Insurance; Pension Plan; Profit Sharing; Tuition Assistance. **Special Programs:** Internships. **Corporate headquarters location:** This Location. **Parent company:** AEG Capitol Corp. (Germany). **Operations at this facility include:** Administration; Manufacturing; Research and Development; Sales. **Listed on:** NASDAQ. **Number of employees at this location:** 800.

SIMCO ELECTRONICS
382 Martin Avenue, Santa Clara CA 95050. 408/727-3611. **Contact:** Jan Smith, Manager, Human Resources. **Description:** Engaged in the calibration and repair of electronic test and measuring equipment; electrical standards; physical, dimensional, mechanical gauges; and tools. Simco Electronics also performs inspection services. **Common positions include:** Quality Control Supervisor; Services Sales Representative; Technician. **Benefits:** 401(k); Credit Union; Dental Insurance; Disability Coverage; Life Insurance; Medical Insurance; Tuition Assistance. **Corporate headquarters location:** This Location. **Other U.S. locations:** Santa Fe Springs CA; Anaheim CA; Burbank CA; San Diego CA; Santa Clara CA; Austin TX; Dallas TX. **Operations at this facility include:** Administration; Sales; Service. **Listed on:** Privately held. **Annual sales/revenues:** $11 - $20 million. **Number of employees at this location:** 70. **Number of employees nationwide:** 230.

SOLECTRON CORPORATION
847 Gibraltar Drive, Milpitas CA 95035. 408/957-8500. **Contact:** Human Resources. **Description:** Manufactures complex printed circuitboards using surface mount technology (SMT) and pin-thought hole (PTH) interconnection technology. The company also provides for the testing and assembly of electronic subsystems for OEMs in the electronics industry. **Number of employees nationwide:** 3,000.

SPECTRA-MAT INC.
100 Westgate Drive, Watsonville CA 95076. 408/722-4116. **Contact:** Sandra Petznick, Personnel Manager. **Description:** Produces electronic components including electron emitters. **Common positions include:** Accountant/Auditor; Administrator; Blue-Collar Worker Supervisor; Buyer; Customer Service Representative; Draftsperson; Human Resources Specialist; Marketing Specialist; Operations/Production Manager. **Educational backgrounds include:** Accounting; Engineering. **Benefits:** Dental Insurance; Disability Coverage; Life Insurance; Medical Insurance; Stock Option; Tuition Assistance. **Corporate headquarters location:** This Location. **Operations at this facility include:** Administration; Manufacturing; Research and Development; Sales; Service.

SUPERTEX INC.
1235 Bordeaux Drive, Sunnyvale CA 94088. 408/744-0100. **Contact:** Melba L. Stathis, Personnel Manager. **Description:** Produces silicon integrated circuits and other microelectronic products for computer and electronics original equipment manufacturers. **Common positions include:** Accountant/Auditor; Buyer; Computer Programmer; Customer Service Representative; Electrical/Electronics Engineer; Systems Analyst. **Educational backgrounds include:** Accounting; Business Administration; Chemistry; Computer Science; Engineering; Marketing. **Benefits:** Dental Insurance; Disability

Coverage; Life Insurance; Medical Insurance; Profit Sharing; Savings Plan; Tuition Assistance. **Corporate headquarters location:** This Location. **Operations at this facility include:** Administration; Manufacturing; Research and Development; Sales; Service.

TEKTRONIX, INC.
3003 Bunker Hill Lane, Santa Clara CA 95052-8086. 408/496-0800. **Contact:** Human Resources. **Description:** Manufactures and markets electronic test and measurement equipment and a highly-specialized line of computer graphics terminals and peripherals for the engineering and scientific market.

TELEDYNE ELECTRONIC TECHNOLOGIES
P.O. Box 7127, Mountain View CA 94039-7126. 415/691-9800. **Fax:** 415/962-6982. **Contact:** Human Resources. **Description:** Engaged in the design and manufacture of passive and active devices, power supplies, and scientific instruments. Products include MMIC devices; amplifiers; integrated subsystems; voltage-controlled oscillators; microwave switches, filters, and ferrite devices; and mass spectrometry scientific instruments. **Common positions include:** Accountant/Auditor; Buyer; Chemical Engineer; Chemist; Designer; Draftsperson; Electrical/Electronics Engineer; Human Resources Specialist; Mechanical Engineer; Quality Control Supervisor; Software Engineer. **Educational backgrounds include:** Accounting; Business Administration; Chemistry; Engineering; Finance. **Benefits:** 401(k); Dental Insurance; Disability Coverage; Employee Discounts; Life Insurance; Medical Insurance; Pension Plan; Savings Plan; Tuition Assistance. **Corporate headquarters location:** Los Angeles CA. **Parent company:** Teledyne Inc. is a diversified producer of industrial and aviation machines, machine tools, aviation and electronics equipment, specialty metals, and consumer products. The company is close to completing a project which will eradicate operations that formerly accounted for nearly 15 percent of sales, in order to concentrate on technology-based lines while simultaneously consolidating the remaining units. Teledyne makes half the general aviation pistons in the U.S. Major products of industrial segments are internal combustion engines including air- and water-cooled, gasoline, and diesel fuel engines. **Operations at this facility include:** Administration; Divisional Headquarters; Research and Development; Sales. **Listed on:** New York Stock Exchange. **Number of employees at this location:** 250. **Number of employees nationwide:** 18,000.

TERADYNE, INC.
2625 Shadelands Drive, Walnut Creek CA 94598. 510/932-6900. **Contact:** Kyra Ritter, Personnel Administrator. **Description:** Teradyne internationally manufactures and sells in-circuit testers which analyze finished printed circuit board assemblies and confirm component specifications. The equipment then prints repair instructions if the assembly is faulty or defective. **Corporate headquarters location:** This Location.

TOSHIBA
1060 Rincon Circle, San Jose CA 95131. 408/456-8900. **Contact:** Personnel Department. **Description:** Produces integrated circuits for use in many electronics applications.

VLSI TECHNOLOGY INC.
1109 McKay Drive, San Jose CA 95131. 408/434-3000. **Contact:** Human Resources. **Description:** Designs and manufactures application-specific and application-standard integrated circuits for computer, telecommunication, consumer, and industrial uses.

Common positions include: Computer Systems Analyst; Electrical/Electronics Engineer; Financial Analyst; Software Engineer; Technician. **Educational backgrounds include:** Engineering. **Benefits:** 401(k); Dental Insurance; Disability Coverage; Life Insurance; Medical Insurance; Profit Sharing; Savings Plan; Tuition Assistance. **Special Programs:** Internships. **Corporate headquarters location:** This Location. **Other U.S. locations:** Tempe AZ; San Antonio TX. **Operations at this facility include:** Administration; Manufacturing; Research and Development; Sales. **Listed on:** NASDAQ. **Number of employees at this location:** 1,500. **Number of employees nationwide:** 3,000.

WATKINS-JOHNSON COMPANY
3333 Hillview Avenue, Palo Alto CA 94304-1204. 415/813-2210. **Fax:** 415/813-2452. **Contact:** Employment Office. **E-mail address:** staffing@wj.com. **Description:** Watkins-Johnson Company is a high-technology corporation specializing in semiconductor manufacturing equipment, subassemblies, and transceivers for wireless communications, and radio-frequency electronics for government applications. Watkins-Johnson produces chemical-vapor-deposition equipment for high-volume integrated circuit manufacturing. Components and equipment produced by Watkins-Johnson are used in base-station applications throughout the wireless communications industry. Watkins-Johnson's high-dynamic-range mixers are sold in high volume for cellular telephone base station functions. Radio-frequency products range from miniature, single-function components, through integrated subassemblies, to equipment for signal collection and analysis. **Common positions include:** Accountant/Auditor; Electrical/Electronics Engineer; Mechanical Engineer. **Educational backgrounds include:** Engineering. **Benefits:** 401(k); Disability Coverage; ESOP; Life Insurance; Mass Transit Available; Medical Insurance; Profit Sharing; Stock Option; Tuition Assistance. **Corporate headquarters location:** This Location. **Other U.S. locations:** Scotts Valley CA; San Jose CA; Gaithersburg MD. **Operations at this facility include:** Administration; Divisional Headquarters; Manufacturing; Research and Development; Sales. **Listed on:** New York Stock Exchange. **Annual sales/revenues:** More than $100 million. **Number of employees at this location:** 830. **Number of employees nationwide:** 2,200.

WATKINS-JOHNSON COMPANY
SEMICONDUCTOR EQUIPMENT GROUP
440 Kings Village Road, Scotts Valley CA 95066-4027. 408/438-2100. **Fax:** 408/439-4919. **Contact:** Rudy Fischer, Manager, Staffing and Employee Relations. **Description:** A diversified corporation comprised of the Defense Group (Palo Alto CA and Gaithersburg MD), specializing in defense electronics manufacturing; the Commercial Group (Scotts Valley CA and San Jose CA), producing CVD and HDPCVD furnaces and flat-panel manufacturing equipment; and the Electronics Group (San Jose CA and Gaithersburg MD), designing and manufacturing signal analysis equipment. Thsi location manufactures semiconductor equipment. **NOTE:** Entry-level positions are available at this location. **Common positions include:** Accountant/Auditor; Blue-Collar Worker Supervisor; Buyer; Chemical Engineer; Computer Systems Analyst; Design Engineer; Designer; Electrical/Electronics Engineer; Financial Analyst; Human Resources Specialist; Industrial Production Manager; Mechanical Engineer; MIS Specialist; Paralegal; Process Engineer; Purchasing Agent and Manager; Science Technologist; Software Engineer; Technical Writer/Editor. **Educational backgrounds include:** Engineering. **Benefits:** 401(k); Dental Insurance; Disability Coverage; Employee Discounts; Life Insurance; Medical Insurance; Profit Sharing; Savings Plan; Tuition Assistance. **Special Programs:** Internships. **Corporate headquarters location:**

Palo Alto CA. **Other U.S. locations:** San Jose CA; Gaithersburg MD. **Operations at this facility include:** Administration; Divisional Headquarters; Manufacturing; Research and Development; Sales; Service. **Listed on:** New York Stock Exchange. **Annual sales/revenues:** More than $100 million. **Number of employees at this location:** 2,100.

WESTINGHOUSE SECURITY ELECTRONICS

5452 Betsy Ross Drive, Santa Clara CA 95054-1184. 408/727-5170. **Fax:** 408/727-6707. **Contact:** Jo Ann Balesano, Human Resources Manager. **Description:** Manufactures access control systems. **Common positions include:** Customer Service Representative; Electrical/Electronics Engineer; Mechanical Engineer; Software Engineer; Technical Writer/Editor. **Educational backgrounds include:** Business Administration; Engineering. **Benefits:** 401(k); Dental Insurance; Disability Coverage; Employee Discounts; Life Insurance; Medical Insurance; Pension Plan; Vision Plan. **Corporate headquarters location:** This Location. **Parent company:** Westinghouse Electric Corporation is a diversified manufacturing company with interests in defense electronics, environmental services, broadcasting, mobile refrigeration units, office furniture, energy systems, and power generation. Subsidiaries of Westinghouse Electric include Thermo King, The Knoll Group, and Westinghouse Broadcasting. The company conducts operations through 791 locations in the U.S. and over 30 other countries. **Operations at this facility include:** Administration; Manufacturing; Research and Development. **Number of employees at this location:** 170. **Number of employees nationwide:** 195.

WYLE LABORATORIES
ELECTRONICS MARKETING GROUP

3000 Bowers Avenue, Santa Clara CA 95051. 408/727-2500. **Contact:** Personnel Department. **Description:** Engaged in the distribution of selected lines of electronic supplies and components primarily to the electronics and computer industries as well as military and aerospace oriented industries. Principal products include semiconductors, capacitors, resistors, and various computer products such as printers, video display terminals, and other products supplied by major computer manufacturing firms. This location is one of 13 nationwide operating divisions of Wyle Laboratories. **Common positions include:** Administrator; Buyer; Customer Service Representative; Electrical/Electronics Engineer; Human Resources Specialist; Marketing Specialist; Purchasing Agent and Manager; Services Sales Representative. **Educational backgrounds include:** Business Administration; Computer Science; Engineering; Liberal Arts; Marketing; Mathematics. **Benefits:** Dental Insurance; Disability Coverage; Employee Discounts; Life Insurance; Medical Insurance; Pension Plan; Savings Plan; Tuition Assistance. **Corporate headquarters location:** El Segundo CA. **Operations at this facility include:** Administration; Sales; Service. **Listed on:** New York Stock Exchange.

ZETA

2811 Orchard Parkway, San Jose CA 95134. 408/434-3580. **Contact:** Human Resources Department. **Description:** Manufactures and distributes microwave equipment and RF and DF systems. **Common positions include:** Accountant/Auditor; Assembly Worker; Buyer; Draftsperson; Electrical/Electronics Engineer; Mechanical Engineer; Microwave Technician; Radio Frequency Engineer; Radio Frequency Technician; Software Engineer. **Educational backgrounds include:** Engineering. **Benefits:** 401(k); Dental Insurance; Disability Coverage; Employee Discounts; Life Insurance; Medical Insurance;

Tuition Assistance. **Corporate headquarters location:** Buffalo NY. **Parent company:** Sierra Networks. **Operations at this facility include:** Administration. **Annual sales/revenues:** $11 million - $20 million. **Number of employees at this location:** 80.

ZILOG, INC.
210 East Hacienda Avenue, Campbell CA 95008-6600. 408/370-8000. **Fax:** 408/370-8056. **Contact:** Tony S. Perez, Principal Human Resources Representative. **Description:** Designs, develops, manufactures, and markets application-specific standard integrated circuits products (ASSPs) for the datacommunications, intelligent peripheral controller, consumer product controller, and memory markets. Zilog uses its proprietary superintegration design technology to combine cores and cells from its library of customer-familiar microprocessor, microcontroller, memory, and logic circuits to meet the design, cost, and time-to-market requirements of its customers. **Common positions include:** Chemical Engineer; Electrical/Electronics Engineer; Software Engineer. **Educational backgrounds include:** Engineering. **Benefits:** 401(k); Dental Insurance; Disability Coverage; Employee Discounts; Life Insurance; Medical Insurance; Profit Sharing; Savings Plan; Tuition Assistance. **Corporate headquarters location:** This Location. **Other U.S. locations:** Nampa ID. **Operations at this facility include:** Administration; Divisional Headquarters; Research and Development; Sales. **Listed on:** NASDAQ. **Number of employees at this location:** 250. **Number of employees nationwide:** 1,500.

ZYCON CORPORATION
445 El Camino Real, Santa Clara CA 95050. 408/241-9900. **Contact:** Brenda Mora, Human Resources Director. **Description:** Manufactures electron tubes.

Note: *Because addresses and telephone numbers of smaller companies can change rapidly, we recommend you call each company to verify the information below before inquiring about job opportunities. Mass mailings are not recommended.*

Additional small employers:

TRANSFORMERS

Kuhlman Transformer Salinas Pl
1056 Pellet Ave, Salinas CA 93901-4539. 408/758-1011.

Panamax Line Conditioning
150 Mitchell Blvd, San Rafael CA 94903-2046. 415/499-3900.

ELECTRICAL INDUSTRIAL APPARATUS

Scientific Technologies Inc.
6550 Dumbarton Cir, Fremont CA 94555-3611. 510/471-9717.

Tesco Controls Inc.
PO Box 239012, Sacramento CA 95823-9012. 916/395-8800.

ELECTRIC LIGHTING AND WIRING EQUIPMENT

Chicago Miniature Lamp Inc.
1021 S Wolfe Rd, Sunnyvale CA 94086-8806. 408/738-1617.

Circle AW Products Co.
1706 Lapham Dr, Modesto CA 95354-3812. 209/524-5281.

Pirelli Cable Corp.
1480 Will S Green Ave, Colusa CA 95932-3099. 916/458-5111.

B Lites Enterprises
2348 Auburn Blvd, Sacramento CA 95821-1756. 916/973-8196.

Wellmade Products
PO Box 6579, Oakland CA 94603-0579. 510/562-1878.

Peerless Lighting Corp.
PO Box 2556, Berkeley CA 94702-0556. 510/845-2760.

ELECTRONIC COMPONENTS AND ACCESSORIES

Altatron Inc.
47951 Westinghouse Dr,

Fremont CA 94539-7483. 510/440-0345.

Pycon Inc.
3501 Leonard Ct, Santa Clara CA 95054-2043. 408/727-1213.

Datacube Inc.
5201 Great America Pky Ste 320, Santa Clara CA 95054-1127. 408/562-6094.

Advanced Printed Circuit Technology
3495 De La Cruz Blvd, Santa Clara CA 95054-2165. 408/727-6442.

Comtronix Corp.
355 E Trimble Rd, San Jose CA 95131-1218. 408/954-5200.

Custom Arrays Corp.
525 Del Rey Ave Ste A, Sunnyvale CA 94086-3515. 408/749-1166.

Proto Engineering Corp.
183 Commercial St, Sunnyvale CA 94086-5202. 408/738-0693.

United Manufacturing Assembly Inc.
42680 Christy St, Fremont CA 94538-3135. 510/490-4680.

Trend Circuits
44358 Old Warm Springs Blvd, Fremont CA 94538-6189. 510/651-1150.

Dynamic Circuits
1831 Tarob Ct, Milpitas CA 95035-6825. 408/263-0940.

Paragon Inc.
2318 Calle De Luna, Santa Clara CA 95054-1003. 408/727-8824.

Isis Surface Mounting
1020 Rincon Cir, San Jose CA 95131-1325. 408/434-1841.

Lika
1443 Navy Dr, Stockton CA 95206-4103. 209/948-0944.

Static Ram Division
1566 Moffett St, Salinas CA 93905-3342. 408/424-7726.

Semialloys Inc.
5150 El Camino Real Suite B-11, Los Altos CA 94022-1527. 415/964-5400.

Ultra Clean Technology Systems
150 Independence Dr, Menlo Park CA 94025-1136. 415/323-4100.

Transition Technology International
75 Joaquin Rd, Portola Vally CA 94028-8114. 415/851-9225.

Unisil Purchasing Dept
614 National Ave, Mountain View CA 94043-2222. 415/962-0151.

Yieldup International
2672 Bayshore Pkwy, Mountain View CA 94043-1001. 415/964-0100.

Rudolph Research Co.
770 Lucerne Dr, Sunnyvale CA 94086-3844. 408/774-6250.

Ron Hauch Engineering
989 E California Ave, Sunnyvale CA 94086-4504. 408/720-1477.

Stec Instruments Inc.
1080 E Duane Ave Ste J, Sunnyvale CA 94086-2628. 408/730-8795.

Stanson Technology
491 Macara Ave, Sunnyvale CA 94086-2822. 408/720-9215.

Electrochemical Technology Corp.
764 San Aleso Ave, Sunnyvale CA 94086-1445. 408/744-0447.

Fusion Semicon Systems Corp.
770 Lucerne Dr, Sunnyvale CA 94086-3844. 408/774-6260.

Process Diagnostics Inc.
1050 Kifer Rd, Sunnyvale CA 94086-5301. 408/738-4315.

Oki Semiconductor Group
785 N Mary Ave, Sunnyvale CA 94086-2909. 408/720-1900.

Micro Dicing Service Inc.
1176 Aster Ave, Sunnyvale CA 94086-6803. 408/243-3326.

A&B International
1176 Aster Ave, Sunnyvale CA 94086-6803. 408/241-8174.

Axis
1290 Oakmead Pkwy, Sunnyvale CA 94086-4036. 408/522-9595.

Performance Semiconductor Corp.
630 E Weddell Dr, Sunnyvale CA 94089-1751. 408/734-8200.

Pacific Monolithics
1308 Moffett Park Dr, Sunnyvale CA 94089-1133. 408/732-8000.

Dynasty Technology Inc.
260 E Java Dr Suite G, Sunnyvale CA 94089-1303. 408/734-8388.

AG Processing Technologies Inc.
1325 Borregas Ave, Sunnyvale CA 94089-1003. 408/745-1790.

Catalyst Equipment Corporation
3784 Fabian Way, Palo Alto

CA 94303-4601. 415/856-1800.

KDH Sciences
3176 Stelling Dr, Palo Alto CA 94303-3962. 415/493-3147.

Vacua Techniques Co.
181 Easy St, Alamo CA 94507-1309. 510/939-0501.

Olin Hunt OCG Process Chemicals
148 Lawnview Cir, Danville CA 94526-5108. 510/831-9413.

WSI
47280 Kato Rd, Fremont CA 94538-7333. 510/656-5400.

Silicon Magic Corporation
20300 Stevens Creek Blvd, Cupertino CA 95014-2240. 408/366-0288.

Heraeus
19925 Stevens Creek Blvd, Cupertino CA 95014-2305. 408/379-6710.

Elantec Inc.
1996 Tarob Ct, Milpitas CA 95035-6841. 408/945-1323.

Semistar Inc.
265 Houret Dr, Milpitas CA 95035-6801. 408/956-9856.

Sensym Inc.
1804 McCarthy Blvd, Milpitas CA 95035-7410. 408/954-1100.

TDI Inc.
514 Valley Way, Milpitas CA 95035-4106. 408/956-8735.

Prime Solutions
461 Valley Way, Milpitas CA 95035-4105. 408/262-7224.

Insync Systems
1463 Centre Pointe Dr, Milpitas CA 95035-8010. 408/492-1363.

Opti Inc.
888 Tasman Dr, Milpitas CA 95035-7439. 408/980-8178.

LC Technology
2066 Walsh Ave, Santa Clara CA 95050-2527. 408/986-8456.

Intech Flash Analog Devices
2270 Martin Ave, Santa Clara CA 95050-2704. 408/727-0500.

Modular Process Technology Corp.
966 Shulman Ave, Santa Clara CA 95050-2822. 408/988-7808.

Micro Control Co.
2096 Walsh Ave, Santa Clara CA 95050-2543. 408/496-5778.

Semiconductor Automation
2094 Walsh Ave, Santa Clara CA 95050-2542. 408/986-0447.

Quality Semiconductor Inc.
851 Martin Ave, Santa Clara CA 95050-2952. 408/450-8000.

Synergy Semiconductor Corp.
3450 Central Expy, Santa Clara CA 95051-0703. 408/730-1313.

Synax USA
2352 Walsh Ave, Santa Clara CA 95051-1301. 408/496-5737.

Lark
3866 Shasta Dr, Santa Clara CA 95051. 408/243-9143.

Procon Technologies
1333 Lawrence Expy, Santa Clara CA 95051-3508. 408/246-4456.

Kawasaki Wafer Technology Inc.
2400 Walsh Ave, Santa Clara CA 95051-1303. 408/988-2600.

Alessi Inc.
3080 Olcott St, Santa Clara CA 95054-3209. 408/748-0209.

Brooks Instrument
3242 Scott Blvd, Santa Clara CA 95054-3011. 408/727-6054.

Celeritek Inc.
3236 Scott Blvd, Santa Clara CA 95054-3011. 408/986-5060.

Opal Inc.
2903 Bunker Hill Ln, Santa Clara CA 95054-1141. 408/727-6060.

Proto Logic
3375 Scott Blvd, Santa Clara CA 95054-3110. 408/980-9066.

Probus Technology
1900 Wyatt Dr, Santa Clara CA 95054-1529. 408/492-1200.

Shinkawa USA Inc.
2620 Augustine Dr, Santa Clara CA 95054-2903. 408/727-2601.

Tri Quint Semicon Inc. Computing
2300 Owen St, Santa Clara CA 95054-3210. 408/982-0900.

Trazar Co.
3250 Keller St, Santa Clara CA 95054-2613. 408/970-9501.

US Phicom A Inc.
4677 Old Ironsides Dr, Santa Clara CA 95054-1809. 408/748-6733.

Caltek Sales
3140 De La Cruz Blvd Ste 200, Santa Clara CA 95054-2444. 408/988-5153.

EPI Services
473 Sapena Ct Ste 13, Santa Clara CA 95054-2427. 408/748-1605.

Ecological Technologies Inc.
3281 Keller St, Santa Clara CA 95054-2646. 408/988-2050.

Genesis
3066 Scott Blvd, Santa Clara CA 95054-3325. 408/986-1636.

Equipment Resources Inc.
140 Sylvania Ave, Santa Cruz CA 95060-2134. 408/429-1300.

B&J Specialties
3004 Mission St, Santa Cruz CA 95060-5700. 408/454-0713.

DCT Technical Services
1592 Alum Rock Ave, San Jose CA 95116-2425. 408/254-3672.

Norsk Engineering
1961 Concourse Dr, San Jose CA 95131-1729. 408/943-0590.

Wafer Reclaim Service Inc.
2467 Autumnvale Dr, San Jose CA 95131-1802. 408/945-8112.

DuPont Photomasks
2235 Zanker Rd, San Jose CA 95131-1120. 408/435-8335.

Sputtering Materials
2029 Otoole Ave, San Jose CA 95131-1301. 408/954-1280.

Techlink Dry-Etch
1554 Montague Expy, San Jose CA 95131-1408. 408/435-1156.

Semi Supply
172 Component Dr, San Jose CA 95131-1119. 408/324-0700.

ITT Semiconductors
2540 N 1st St, San Jose CA 95131-1016. 408/526-2080.

SDL Inc.
80 Rose Orchard Way, San Jose CA 95134-1356. 408/943-9411.

IC Works Inc.
3725 N 1st St, San Jose CA 95134-1708. 408/922-0202.

Semiconductor Products Inc.
53 Bonaventura Dr, San Jose CA 95134-2105. 408/433-9576.

Winbic Semiconductor
90 Plumeria Dr, San Jose CA 95134-2134. 408/526-0888.

Paradigm Technology Inc.
71 Vista Montana, San Jose CA 95134-1507. 408/954-0500.

Ultrapointe Corp.
163 Baypointe Pkwy, San Jose CA 95134-1622. 408/894-7080.

JC & Company
PO Box 53572, San Jose CA 95153-0572. 408/226-2267.

Exel Microelectronics Inc.
PO Box 49038, San Jose CA 95161-9038. 408/432-0500.

Core Systems Inc.
7495 Doster Rd, Mountain Ranch CA 95246-9669. 209/754-0496.

CDS Electronic Payment Service
42 Woodward St, San Francisco CA 94103-2427. 415/252-1519.

McKenzie Technology
910 Page Ave, Fremont CA 94538-7340. 510/651-2700.

Cylink Corp
910 Hermosa Ct, Sunnyvale CA 94086-4103. 408/735-5800.

Contact International Corp.
1380 Bordeaux Dr, Sunnyvale CA 94089-1005. 408/734-0070.

Avex Electronics Inc.
760 Mission Ct, Fremont CA 94539-8204. 510/226-8133.

Leybold Materials Inc.
16035 Vineyard Blvd, Morgan Hill CA 95037-5480. 408/779-0636.

Paneltec Inc.
3307 Edward Ave, Santa Clara CA 95054-2332. 408/496-1174.

California Eastern Labs
4590 Patrick Henry Dr, Santa Clara CA 95054-1817. 408/988-3500.

Lucero Cables Inc.
1800 S 10th St, San Jose CA 95112-4108. 408/298-6001.

Topward Instruments
2031 Ringwood Ave, San Jose CA 95131-1703. 408/434-0888.

Pragmatech Inc.
101 Nicholson Ln, San Jose CA 95134-1359. 408/943-1151.

Hitachi Micro Systems Inc.
179 E Tasman Dr, San Jose CA 95134-1620. 408/433-1990.

Hybrinetics Inc.
PO Box 14399, Santa Rosa CA 95402-6399. 707/585-0333.

Microsource Inc.
1269 Corporate Center Pkwy, Santa Rosa CA 95407-5412. 707/527-7010.

ELECTRICAL EQUIPMENT, MACHINERY, AND SUPPLIES

Flash Electronics
48607 Warm Springs Blvd, Fremont CA 94539-7782. 510/440-2840.

LGE Electrical Sales Inc.
48531 Warm Springs Blvd, Fremont CA 94539-7793. 510/657-6732.

Challenger Electrical Equipment Corp.
151 N Sunrise Ave, Roseville CA 95661-2924. 916/773-3080.

Cyberoptics
48521 Warm Springs Blvd, Fremont CA 94539-7792. 510/770-0612.

Cambridge Lasers Inc.
853 Brown Rd, Fremont CA 94539-7090. 510/651-0110.

AEROSPACE AND/OR NAUTICAL SYSTEMS AND INSTRUMENTS

Ashtech Inc.
1170 Kifer Rd, Sunnyvale CA 94086-5303. 408/524-1400.

Continuum
3150 Central Expressway, Santa Clara CA 95051-0816. 408/727-3240.

Delfin Systems
3000 Patrick Henry Dr, Santa Clara CA 95054-1839. 408/748-1200.

ELECTRICAL EQUIPMENT WHOLESALE

Yokogawa Corp. of America
2001 Gateway Pl, San Jose CA 95110-1010. 408/441-8090.

California Software Systems Inc.
3454 Outlook Ct, San Jose CA 95132-2422. 408/251-4106.

CAD Services
3582 Springbrook Ave, San Jose CA 95148-3129. 408/223-8619.

All-Phase Electric Supply Co.
1359 E St, Fresno CA 93706-2001. 209/233-9981.

T&M Wholesale
856 Hillside Blvd, Daly City CA 94014-2309. 415/756-9297.

Phoenix Equipment
PO Box 13423, San Rafael CA 94913. 415/479-2080.

Hench Control
1101 S Winchester Blvd, San Jose CA 95128-3901. 408/296-4600.

Royal Wholesale Electric
816 E Church St, Stockton CA 95203-3629. 209/948-6410.

Endress & Hauser-Ondyne
2350 Endress Place, Greenwood CA 95635. 510/825-8282.

Yamas Controls Inc.
1041 Triangle Ct, West Sacramento CA 95691. 916/372-8800.

Consolidated Electrical Distributors
1787 E Main St Ste 14, Woodland CA 95776-6207. 916/666-5712.

Platt Electric Supply Inc.
460 N East St, Woodland CA 95776-6120. 916/661-0112.

Simplex Time Recorder Co.
3054 Gold Canal Dr, Rancho Cordova CA 95670-6116. 916/895-8664.

Baltech
7650 Newcastle Rd, Stockton CA 95215-9663. 209/546-7884.

Villares Corporation of America
255 Van Winkle Dr, San Anselmo CA 94960-1037. 415/485-0993.

Noah Industries
1360 East St, Tracy CA 95376-3621. 209/835-0886.

W.W. Grainger Inc.
1617 Industrial Pkwy W, Hayward CA 94544-7042. 510/670-1095.

ELECTRONIC PARTS AND EQUIPMENT WHOLESALE

Lodan West Inc.
1052 Commercial St, San Carlos CA 94070-4026. 415/592-4600.

Hamilton-Avnet Electronics
1175 Bordeaux Dr, Sunnyvale CA 94089-1299. 408/743-3300.

Bytex
1700 S Amphlett Blvd Ste 221, San Mateo CA 94402-2717. 415/286-3940.

Orchid Technology
221 E Warren Ave, Fremont CA 94539-7086. 510/683-0300.

Electronic Tele Communications
6689 Owens Dr Suite B, Pleasanton CA 94588-3335. 510/463-3393.

Western Micro Technology
254 E Hacienda Ave, Campbell CA 95008-6617. 408/725-1660.

AMP Inc.
19200 Stevens Creek Blvd 100, Cupertino CA 95014-2530. 408/255-3830.

Marshall Electronics Group
336 Los Coches St, Milpitas CA 95035-5427. 408/942-4600.

Applied Microsystems Corp.
3329 Kifer Rd, Santa Clara CA 95051-0719. 408/730-8694.

Micom Communications Corp.
5201 Great America Pky Ste 306, Santa Clara CA 95054-1127. 408/986-0890.

Beta Technology Inc.
105 Harvey West Blvd, Santa Cruz CA 95060-2126. 408/426-5890.

ACS Communications Inc.
250 Technology Cir, Scotts Valley CA 95066-3500. 408/438-3883.

Production Technologies
135 Aviation Way Ste 1, Watsonville CA 95076-2064. 408/724-6433.

Centon Electronics
1731 Technology Dr Ste 570, San Jose CA 95110-1326. 408/441-1200.

Arrow Schweber Electronics Inc.
1180 Murphy Ave, San Jose CA 95131-2418. 408/441-9700.

Baytech Sales Inc.
2700 Volley Cir, Meadow Vista CA 95722-9530. 916/878-7228.

Anthem Electronics
580 Menlo Dr Ste 8, Rocklin CA 95765-3706. 916/624-9744.

TIW Systems Inc.
2211 Lawson Ln, Santa Clara CA 95054-3311. 408/654-5600.

Motorola
10933 Trade Center Dr, Rancho Cordova CA 95670-6130. 916/635-2300.

International Paging Corp.
553 Pilgrim Dr, Foster City CA 94404-1211. 415/349-8866.

Lattice Semiconductor
1820 McCarthy Blvd, Milpitas CA 95035-7425. 408/433-8000.

Fleet Call Inc.
587 Kentucky Ave, Woodland CA 95695-2779. 916/662-1146.

For more information on career opportunities in the electronic/industrial electrical equipment industry:

Associations

AMERICAN CERAMIC SOCIETY
735 Ceramic Place, Westerville OH 43081. 614/890-4700. 800/837-1804. Provides ceramics futures information. Membership required.

ELECTROCHEMICAL SOCIETY
10 South Main Street, Pennington NJ 08534-2896. 609/737-1902. Fax: 609/737-2743. World Wide Web address: http://www.electrochem.org. An international society which holds bi-annual meetings internationally and periodic meetings through local sections. Publications include the monthly *Journal of the Electrochemical Society* and the quarterly *Interface*.

ELECTRONIC INDUSTRIES ASSOCIATION
2500 Wilson Boulevard, Arlington VA 22201-3834. 703/907-7500. World Wide Web address: http://www.eia.org.

ELECTRONICS TECHNICIANS ASSOCIATION
602 North Jackson Street, Greencastle IN 46135. 317/653-8262. Offers published job-hunting advice from the organization's officers and members. Also offers educational material and certification programs.

INSTITUTE OF ELECTRICAL AND ELECTRONICS ENGINEERS (IEEE)
345 East 47th Street, New York NY 10017. 212/705-7900. Toll-free number: 800/678-4333. World Wide Web address: http://www.ieee.org.

INSTITUTE OF ELECTRICAL AND ELECTRONICS ENGINEERS (IEEE)
1828 L Street NW, Suite 1202, Washington DC 20036-5104. Professional activities line: 202/785-0017. National information line: 202/785-2180.

INTERNATIONAL BROTHERHOOD OF ELECTRICAL WORKERS
1125 15th Street NW, Washington DC 20005. 202/833-7000.

INTERNATIONAL SOCIETY OF CERTIFIED ELECTRONICS TECHNICIANS
2708 West Berry Street, Ft. Worth TX 76109. 817/921-9101.

NATIONAL ELECTRONICS SALES AND SERVICES ASSOCIATION
2708 West Berry, Ft. Worth TX 76109. 817/921-9061. Provides newsletters and directories to members.

SOCIETY OF MANUFACTURING ENGINEERS (SME)
One SME Drive, P.O. Box 930, Dearborn MI 48121. 313/271-1500. Offers a resume database for members.

ENVIRONMENTAL AND WASTE MANAGEMENT SERVICES

According to the Environmental Protection Agency, the increase in environmental awareness over recent decades is more than just a trend. State and national legislation, such as the 1990 amendments to the Clean Air Act, have generated a new range of opportunities in skilled administrative, professional, and technical areas. However, the most critical positions needing to be filled are for scientists and engineers. These two groups develop new solutions to old problems, and therefore are instrumental in the research and development stages.

On the other hand, the current climate in the Congress is significantly cooler towards environmental regulation than in years past. Many members of Congress argue that American business is already overburdened by the Federal government, and some propose that the Environmental Protection Agency itself be disbanded.

ABATIX ENVIRONMENTAL CORPORATION
1664 Delta Court, Hayward CA 94544. 510/471-5997. **Contact:** Brian Mendelsohn, Branch Manager. **Description:** A full-line supplier of durable and nondurable supplies to the following industry segments: asbestos and lead abatement, hazardous material remediation, and construction. Supplies include industrial safety supplies, construction tools, general safety products such as protective clothing and eyewear, and clean-up equipment. Abatix Environmental Corporation has eight distribution centers serving customers throughout the Southwest, Midwest, and the Pacific Coast. The company plans to explore foreign business possibilities as developing countries are starting to realize the need for environmental clean-up. **Corporate headquarters location:** Dallas TX **Other U.S. locations:** Phoenix AZ; Denver CO; Seattle WA; and Corpus Christi TX. **Stock exchange symbol:** ABIX.

ACUREX ENVIRONMENTAL CORPORATION
555 Clyde Avenue, Mountain View CA 94043. 415/961-5700. **Fax:** 415/254-2498. **Contact:** Kay Sanford, Personnel. **Description:** Provides environmental engineering services. **Common positions include:** Accountant/Auditor; Chemical Engineer; Civil Engineer; Mechanical Engineer. **Educational backgrounds include:** Accounting; Engineering. **Benefits:** 401(k); Daycare Assistance; Dental Insurance; Disability Coverage; Employee Discounts; Life Insurance; Medical Insurance; Profit Sharing; Tuition Assistance. **Corporate headquarters location:** This Location. **Other U.S. locations:** Jefferson AR; Irvine CA; West Covina CA; Durham NC. **Parent company:** Geraghty and Miller, Inc. **Operations at this facility include:** Administration; Divisional Headquarters; Research and Development; Sales. **Listed on:** NASDAQ. **Number of employees at this location:** 65. **Number of employees nationwide:** 200.

BROWN & CALDWELL
P.O. Box 8045, Walnut Creek CA 94596-1220. 510/937-9010. **Toll-free phone:** 800/727-2224. **Contact:** Professional Staffing. **Description:** An employee-owned environmental engineering and consulting firm. Brown & Caldwell specializes in the

planning, engineering, and design of waste management systems. The company is also engaged in construction management and environmental analytical testing. Brown & Caldwell's laboratories are located in Northern and Southern California. **Common positions include:** Air Quality Scientist; Chemist; Environmental Engineer; Environmental Scientist; Hydrogeologist. **Educational backgrounds include:** Chemistry; Engineering; Environmental Science. **Benefits:** Daycare Assistance; Dental Insurance; Disability Coverage; Life Insurance; Medical Insurance; Pension Plan; Tuition Assistance. **Corporate headquarters location:** This Location.

CATALYTICA, INC.
430 Ferguson Drive, Building 3, Mountain View CA 94043. 415/960-3000. **Contact:** Human Resources. **Description:** Catalytica develops economical and environmentally advantageous catalytic technologies for the prevention of pollution in combustion systems, advanced process technologies, and fine chemical products manufacturing. The company is also developing an ultra low-emission combustion system for natural gas turbines. The company's subsidiary, Advanced Sensor Devices, is developing environmental monitoring devices including a continuous emissions monitor that is being introduced to the marketplace. Catalytica provides contract research, development, and consulting services to the petroleum refining and chemical industries. Additional programs include the development of a process for manufacturing gasoline alkylate to eliminate the use of liquid acid catalysts, the conversion of methane to transportation fuels, and the application of nanotechnology for new catalysts and materials. The company is also manufacturing fine chemical products and is developing more economical and environmentally compatible processes for the manufacture of fine chemicals for the pharmaceutical industry. **Corporate headquarters location:** This Location.

EMCON
400 South El Camino Real, Suite 1200, San Mateo CA 94402. 415/375-1522. **Fax:** 415/375-0763. **Contact:** Human Resources. **Description:** EMCON provides comprehensive environmental engineering and consulting services to a variety of public and private clients. EMCON is a leader in the design and remediation of solid and hazardous waste transfer, storage, and disposal facilities, having participated in the design and remediation of several hundred such facilities in the United States, Argentina, Canada, Hong Kong, Mexico, Peru, and Venezuela. EMCON's waste facility services include site selection and evaluation, facility design, development of preprocessing and operating plans, assistance in regulatory compliance and permitting, final closure, and end-use planning and design. The company's services also include the development of programs dealing with environmental assessments and remediation of contaminated sites, as well as services related to applied sciences such as fuel spill damage assessment, marine fate-and-effect studies, and natural resource damage assessment. The company also operates a full-service, integrated network of analytical laboratories in Alaska, Arizona, California, Florida, and Washington. **Corporate headquarters location:** This Location. **Number of employees nationwide:** 1,000.

HARDING LAWSON ASSOCIATES GROUP, INC.
7655 Redwood Boulevard, Novato CA 94945. 415/892-0821. **Contact:** Human Resources. **Description:** Harding Lawson Associates Group, Inc. offers clients a full spectrum of environmental services, with an emphasis on meeting the client's business needs. The company's engineering capabilities enable it to manage contaminated site restoration projects from investigation through design, construction management, and system operation. Harding Lawson Associates also provides a variety of complementary

services ranging from cost allocation analysis and strategic planning assistance to client representation before regulatory and other bodies. The company believes that the addition of enhanced capabilities in transportation and infrastructure design gives it new long-term growth opportunities at home and abroad. These capabilities include road, highway, and bridge design; traffic engineering; water and sewer system design; surface water management; facilities engineering; and wastewater collection and treatment. These complement existing services in waste disposal facility permitting, design, closure, resource recovery and recycling plans, and geotechnical engineering.

ICF KAISER INTERNATIONAL, INC.
1800 Harrison Street, Oakland CA 94612-3430. 510/419-6000. **Contact:** Personnel Department. **Description:** One of the nation's largest engineering, construction, and consulting services companies. ICF Kaiser provides fully integrated capabilities to clients worldwide in four related market areas: environment, infrastructure, industry, and energy. The majority of ICF Kaiser professionals study and resolve environmental problems. Projects address issues such as hazardous and radioactive waste cleanup, waste minimization and disposal, risk assessment, permitting, environmental compliance, global climate change and clean air, alternative fuels, groundwater contamination, and pollution of harbors and waterways. ICF Kaiser also has extensive experience in the infrastructure and industrial fields. Projects include the design, construction, and management of rapid transit systems, highways, hydroelectric plants, and mining and manufacturing facilities. **Corporate headquarters location:** Fairfax VA. **Other locations:** Perth; Taipei; Lisbon; London; Moscow; Paris; Mexico City. **Operations at this facility include:** Regional Headquarters. **Listed on:** New York Stock Exchange. **Number of employees worldwide:** 5,700.

QUANTERRA ENVIRONMENTAL SERVICES
880 Riverside Parkway, West Sacramento CA 95605. 916/373-5600. **Fax:** 916/371-8420. **Contact:** Human Resources. **Description:** In June 1994, Corning's Enseco division and IT Analytical Services, two of the largest commercial environmental analytical companies in the world, merged to become Quanterra, a completely new, independent company. Quanterra provides a complete range of environmental testing services to private industry, engineering consultants, and government agencies in support of major federal and state environmental regulations. The company also possesses a variety of special analytical capabilities including specializations in the following areas: air toxics; field analytical services, radiochemistry/mixed waste; and advanced technology. **Other U.S. locations:** CO; FL; MO; NC; OH; TN; TX; WA.

SIMMS LMC RECYCLERS
699 Seaport Boulevard, Redwood City CA 94063-2712. 415/369-4161. **Contact:** Human Resources. **Description:** A multi-faceted company involved in metals recycling and related ventures.

SIMMS LMC RECYCLERS
600 South 4th Street, Richmond CA 94804-3504. 510/236-0606. **Contact:** Human Resources. **Description:** A multi-faceted company involved in metals recycling and related ventures.

SIMMS LMC RECYCLERS
130 North 12th Street, Sacramento CA 95814. 916/444-3380. **Contact:** Human Resources. **Description:** A multi-faceted company involved in metals recycling and related ventures.

SMITH ENVIRONMENTAL TECHNOLOGY CORPORATION
1710 Main Street, Escalon CA 95320. 209/838-3507. **Contact:** Human Resources. **Description:** Formerly known as Canonie Environmental Services Corporation, Smith Environmental Technology performs comprehensive environmental consulting, engineering, and on-site remediation services throughout the United States for clients, including federal, state, and local government agencies, on properties contaminated with hazardous materials. Smith's services include assessment of environmental regulations, investigation of contaminated sites, and the design and engineering of methods to correct or prevent the contamination. The company also performs remedial actions including the construction and operation of required facilities, and emergency response actions in cases of spills and accidental releases of hazardous waste. The company uses a wide variety of technologies and construction processes and techniques to meet the needs of its clients in solving the problems caused by environmental pollutants. The company addresses hazardous and non-hazardous contaminants in municipal and industrial water supplies; wastewater and storm water from municipal, industrial, and military installations; groundwater, soils, and air space surrounding these types of complexes; and contaminants in the buildings and facilities themselves, such as asbestos, lead paint, and radioactive contamination.

SMITH ENVIRONMENTAL TECHNOLOGY CORPORATION
441 Whisman Road, Mountain View CA 94043. 415/960-1640. **Contact:** Human Resources. **Description:** Formerly known as Canonie Environmental Services Corporation, Smith Environmental Technology performs comprehensive environmental consulting, engineering, and on-site remediation services throughout the United States for clients, including federal, state, and local government agencies, on properties contaminated with hazardous materials. Smith's services include assessment of environmental regulations, investigation of contaminated sites, and the design and engineering of methods to correct or prevent the contamination. The company also performs remedial actions including the construction and operation of required facilities, and emergency response actions in cases of spills and accidental releases of hazardous waste. The company uses a wide variety of technologies and construction processes and techniques to meet the needs of its clients in solving the problems caused by environmental pollutants. The company addresses hazardous and non-hazardous contaminants in municipal and industrial water supplies; wastewater and storm water from municipal, industrial, and military installations; groundwater, soils, and air space surrounding these types of complexes; and contaminants in the buildings and facilities themselves, such as asbestos, lead paint, and radioactive contamination.

SMITH ENVIRONMENTAL TECHNOLOGY CORPORATION
7901 Stoneridge Drive, Suite 100, Pleasanton CA 94588. 510/463-9117. **Contact:** Human Resources. **Description:** Formerly known as Canonie Environmental Services Corporation, Smith Environmental Technology performs comprehensive environmental consulting, engineering, and on-site remediation services throughout the United States for clients, including federal, state, and local government agencies, on properties contaminated with hazardous materials. Smith's services include assessment of environmental regulations, investigation of contaminated sites, and the design and engineering of methods to correct or prevent the contamination. The company also performs remedial actions including the construction and operation of required facilities, and emergency response actions in cases of spills and accidental releases of hazardous waste. The company uses a wide variety of technologies and construction processes and techniques to meet the needs of its clients in solving the problems caused by environmental pollutants. The company addresses hazardous and non-hazardous

contaminants in municipal and industrial water supplies; wastewater and storm water from municipal, industrial, and military installations; groundwater, soils, and air space surrounding these types of complexes; and contaminants in the buildings and facilities themselves, such as asbestos, lead paint, and radioactive contamination.

SMITH ENVIRONMENTAL TECHNOLOGY CORPORATION
Gateway Center, 2900 Main Street, Building 140, Alameda CA 94501. 510/748-3800. **Contact:** Human Resources. **Description:** Formerly known as Canonie Environmental Services Corporation, Smith Environmental Technology performs comprehensive environmental consulting, engineering, and on-site remediation services throughout the United States for clients, including federal, state, and local government agencies, on properties contaminated with hazardous materials. Smith's services include assessment of environmental regulations, investigation of contaminated sites, and the design and engineering of methods to correct or prevent the contamination. The company also performs remedial actions including the construction and operation of required facilities, and emergency response actions in cases of spills and accidental releases of hazardous waste. The company uses a wide variety of technologies and construction processes and techniques to meet the needs of its clients in solving the problems caused by environmental pollutants. The company addresses hazardous and non-hazardous contaminants in municipal and industrial water supplies; wastewater and storm water from municipal, industrial, and military installations; groundwater, soils, and air space surrounding these types of complexes; and contaminants in the buildings and facilities themselves, such as asbestos, lead paint, and radioactive contamination.

THERMO ANALYTICAL
2030 Wright Avenue, Richmond CA 94804. 510/235-2633. **Fax:** 510/235-0438. **Contact:** Administrator. **Description:** Thermo Analytical is engaged in hazardous, radiological, and mixed-waste testing. The company's work is related to regulatory compliance, and all of their laboratories is extensively licensed and qualified to accept radioactive samples. The laboratories field support teams and the environmental science consultants throughout the U.S. are reputed for their technical qualifications and experience. Thermo Analytical's customers are diverse: industrial and commercial companies; engineering firms and architects; public and investor-owned utilities; and federal, state, and municipal agencies including the Environmental Protection Agency, the Department of Defense, and prime contractors for the Department of Energy. **Common positions include:** Administrative Services Manager; Biological Scientist/Biochemist; Buyer; Chemist; Computer Systems Analyst; Financial Analyst; General Manager; Human Resources Specialist; Laboratory Technician; Nuclear Engineer; Physicist/Astronomer; Purchasing Agent and Manager; Quality Control Supervisor; Technical Writer/Editor. **Educational backgrounds include:** Biology; Chemistry; Computer Science; Economics; Engineering; Physics. **Benefits:** 401(k); Bonus Award/Plan; Dental Insurance; Disability Coverage; Life Insurance; Medical Insurance; Pension Plan; Profit Sharing; Tuition Assistance. **Corporate headquarters location:** Waltham MA. **Other U.S. locations:** Nationwide. **Parent company:** Thermo Electron. **Operations at this facility include:** Administration; Divisional Headquarters; Research and Development; Sales; Service. **Listed on:** New York Stock Exchange. **Number of employees at this location:** 100. **Number of employees nationwide:** 1,500.

U.S. FILTER, INC.
960 Ames Avenue, Milpitas CA 95035. 408/946-1520. **Contact:** Human Resources. **Description:** Engaged in the manufacture and servicing of water purification and treatment equipment. Primary customers include the electronics industry, utilities,

pharmaceutical companies, and other entities that require highly-purified water. **Common positions include:** Accountant/Auditor; Financial Analyst. **Educational backgrounds include:** Business Administration; Engineering; Finance. **Benefits:** 401(k); Dental Insurance; Disability Coverage; Life Insurance; Medical Insurance; Profit Sharing; Tuition Assistance. **Corporate headquarters location:** This Location. **Operations at this facility include:** Administration; Marketing; Sales; Service.

WASTE MANAGEMENT/SANTA CLARA
715 Comstock, Santa Clara CA 95054-3403. 408/980-9900. **Contact:** Human Resources. **Description:** A subsidiary of WMX Technologies, an international provider of comprehensive waste management services, as well as engineering and construction, industrial, and related services, with operations in 19 countries.

Note: *Because addresses and telephone numbers of smaller companies can change rapidly, we recommend you call each company to verify the information below before inquiring about job opportunities. Mass mailings are not recommended.*

Additional small employers:

SANITARY SERVICES

Concord Disposal Service
4080 Mallard Dr, Concord CA 94520. 510/682-9113.

East Bay Disposal
4533 Mattos Dr, Fremont CA 94536-6736. 510/797-0440.

Richmond Sanitary Service Inc.
3260 Blume Dr, Richmond CA 94806-5203. 510/262-1600.

Marin Sanitary Service Inc.
1050 Andersen Dr, San Rafael CA 94901-5316. 415/456-2601.

Los Altos Garbage Co. Inc.
20863 Stevens Creek Blvd Ste 1, Cupertino CA 95014-2113. 408/993-9440.

Browning-Ferris Industries
1995 Oakland Rd, San Jose CA 95131-1688. 408/432-1234.

Burlington Environmental
PO Box 142, Folsom CA 95763-0142. 916/985-2370.

Western Waste Industries
4333 E Jefferson Ave, Fresno CA 93725-9707. 209/834-4070.

Valley Waste Management
1990 N California Blvd Ste 20 , Walnut Creek CA 94596-3711. 510/935-8900.

Yuba Sutter Disposal Inc.
3001 N Levee Rd, Marysville CA 95901-3600. 916/743-6933.

Grass Valley Disposal Inc.
640 E Main St, Grass Valley CA 95945-5806. 916/274-3090.

Joe's Trash & Appliance Hauling
424 Auzerais Ave, San Jose CA 95126-3608. 408/293-3582.

B&J Sanitary Landfill
6426 Hay Rd, Vacaville CA 95687-9433. 707/451-3276.

West Coast Recycling Co.
350 Rhode Island St, San Francisco CA 94103-5134. 415/621-6200.

Environmental Systems
PO Box 2483, Dublin CA 94568-0248. 510/828-6841.

A&B Sweeping & Marking
5033 Winkle Ave, Santa Cruz CA 95065-1147. 408/462-0400.

For more information on career opportunities in environmental and waste management services:

__Associations__

AIR & WASTE MANAGEMENT ASSOCIATION
One Gateway Center, Third Floor, Pittsburgh PA 15222. 412/232-3444. World Wide Web address: http://www.awma.org. A nonprofit, technical, and educational organization providing a neutral forum where all points of

view of an environmental management issue can be addressed.

ASSOCIATION OF STATE & INTERSTATE WATER POLLUTION CONTROL ADMINISTRATORS
750 First Street NE, Suite 910, Washington DC 20002. 202/898-0905. Fax: 202/898-0929. World Wide Web address: http://www.deq.state.la.us/asiwspca/welcome. A national, nonpartisan, professional organization comprised of government officials. Members implement surface and groundwater protection programs throughout the nation.

ENVIRONMENTAL INDUSTRY ASSOCIATION
4301 Connecticut Avenue NW, Suite 300, Washington DC 20008. 202/244-4700.

INSTITUTE OF CLEAN AIR COMPANIES
1707 L Street NW, Suite 570, Washington DC 20036. 202/457-0911-4201. A national association of companies involved in stationary source air pollution control.

WATER ENVIRONMENT FEDERATION
601 Wythe Street, Alexandria VA 22314. 703/684-2400. World Wide Web address: http://www.wef.org. Subscription to jobs newsletter required for career information.

Magazines

ENVIRONMENTAL CAREER OPPORTUNITIES
1776 I Street NW, Suite 710, Washington DC 20006. A publication that lists career opportunities in the environmental fields. $67 for 12 issues; $127 for 26 issues.

JOURNAL OF AIR AND WASTE MANAGEMENT ASSOCIATION
One Gateway Center, Third Floor, Pittsburgh PA 15222. 412/232-3444.

FABRICATED/PRIMARY METALS AND PRODUCTS

In 1995, the demand for steel dropped from 114 million to 110 million tons, and executives in the industry weren't expecting a turnaround in '96. While the price of structural beams rose, the price for flat-rolled steel -- used in automobiles, for example -- plummeted. Unfortunately, in early 1995, the industry was undergoing a boom in minimill construction. These new mills may add more capacity to an already glutted market.

AB&I
7825 San Leandro Street, Oakland CA 94621. 510/632-3467. **Contact:** Paul Quezada, Personnel Manager. **Description:** Manufactures cast iron soil pipe, fittings, and custom castings. **Common positions include:** Accountant/Auditor; Computer Programmer; Credit Manager; Customer Service Representative; Draftsperson; Human Resources Specialist; Manufacturer's/Wholesaler's Sales Rep.; Metallurgical Engineer; Quality Control Supervisor. **Educational backgrounds include:** Accounting; Business Administration; Engineering; Marketing. **Benefits:** Dental Insurance; Disability Coverage; Employee Discounts; Life Insurance; Medical Insurance; Pension Plan. **Corporate headquarters location:** This Location. **Operations at this facility include:** Manufacturing; Sales.

AMERICAN NATIONAL CAN CO.
2050 Williams Street, San Leandro CA 94577. 510/895-4700. **Contact:** Human Resources. **Description:** American National Can Co. manufactures a variety of container products. American National Can is 67-percent owned by Pechiney, a diversified international corporation that has operations in packaging, aluminum, turbine components, and related industrial sectors.

AMERICAN NATIONAL CAN CO.
567 South Riverside Drive, Modesto CA 95354-4008. 209/575-7100. **Contact:** Human Resources. **Description:** American National Can Co. manufactures a variety of container products. American National Can is 67-percent owned by Pechiney, a diversified international corporation that has operations in packaging, aluminum, turbine components, and related industrial sectors.

CBI SERVICES INC.
1390 Middlepath Road, Suite 550, Concord CA 94520. 510/688-1000. **Contact:** Personnel Manager. **Description:** Engaged primarily in the design, fabrication, and construction of large metal-plate structures and related systems. Customers include various original equipment manufacturers, utilities, and government bodies. Principal products include petroleum, petrochemical, and chemical storage tanks; cryogenic and low-temperature liquefaction and storage facilities; pressure vessels; and structures used in the exploration and production of offshore oil and gas. **Corporate headquarters location:** Oak Brook IL. **Listed on:** New York Stock Exchange.

CASTLE METALS
1625 Tillie Lewis Drive, Stockton CA 95206. 209/956-7900. **Contact:** Carol Smith, Administrative Supervisor. **Description:** Castle Metals is a large, independent metals service center.

GC INTERNATIONAL, INC.
156 Burns Avenue, Atherton CA 94027. 415/322-8449. **Contact:** Human Resources. **Description:** GC International, Inc. manufactures metal products primarily for inclusion in products sold by electronics, computer, and aerospace companies. GC's business units generally manufacture their own products from raw materials such as aluminum ingots, aluminum castings, aluminum discs, or semi-finished materials used by the A.L. Johnson division which are available from only one vendor. Raw materials and critical components are generally available from more than one source. **Subsidiaries include:** A.L. Johnson; ALJ Machining; and the Apollo Masters Division. **Number of employees nationwide:** 40.

THE HERRICK CORPORATION
P.O. Box 9125, Pleasanton CA 94566. 510/484-2900. **Contact:** Marie Davies, Personnel. **Description:** Engaged in steel fabrication and the providing of heavy industrial contracting services.

KAISER ALUMINUM CORPORATION
6177 Sunol Boulevard, Pleasanton CA 94566. 510/462-1122. **Contact:** Human Resources. **Description:** A manufacturer of aluminum plate, sheet, and coil products for a variety of end uses.

KAWNEER COMPANY INC.
7200 Doe Avenue, Visalia CA 93291. 209/651-4000. **Contact:** Personnel Manager. **Description:** Kawneer Company manufactures and markets fabricated products including non-residential architectural building products such as storefronts, building entrances, facings, window framing, and curtainwall systems. **Common positions include:** Accountant/Auditor; Blue-Collar Worker Supervisor; Buyer; Chemical Engineer; Civil Engineer; Computer Programmer; Credit Manager; Customer Service Representative; Department Manager; Draftsperson; Financial Analyst; General Manager; Human Resources Specialist; Industrial Engineer; Manufacturer's/Wholesaler's Sales Rep.; Purchasing Agent and Manager; Systems Analyst. **Educational backgrounds include:** Accounting; Business Administration; Chemistry; Engineering; Finance; Marketing. **Benefits:** Dental Insurance; Disability Coverage; Life Insurance; Medical Insurance; Pension Plan; Profit Sharing; Savings Plan; Stock Option; Tuition Assistance. **Corporate headquarters location:** Norcross GA. **Other U.S. locations:** AL; GA; IN; KY; PA. **Parent company:** Alumax is the third-largest aluminum producer in the United States and the fourth-largest in North America. The company operates more than 90 plants and facilities in the United States, Canada, and Western Europe. **Operations at this facility include:** Administration; Manufacturing; Sales; Service. **Listed on:** New York Stock Exchange. **Number of employees at this location:** 300. **Number of employees worldwide:** 14,000.

METALLURGICAL LABS INC.
1717 Solano Way, Suite 39, Concord CA 94520. 510/603-1080. **Contact:** Human Resources. **Description:** A metallurgical laboratory.

NOLL MANUFACTURING
P.O. Box 6010, San Pablo CA 94806-6010. 510/235-1014. **Contact:** Ed Rangel, Personnel. **Description:** Manufactures furnace pipe and fittings. **Common positions include:** Accountant/Auditor; Blue-Collar Worker Supervisor; Buyer; Purchasing Agent and Manager; Quality Control Supervisor. **Benefits:** Dental Insurance; Disability Coverage; Medical Insurance. **Corporate headquarters location:** This Location. **Operations at this facility include:** Administration; Divisional Headquarters; Manufacturing; Sales; Service.

PACIFIC STEEL CASTING COMPANY
1333 Second Street, Berkeley CA 94710. 510/525-9200. **Contact:** Ralph Hoover, Controller. **Description:** Produces steel castings and is engaged in the heat-treating of metals.

REYNOLDS METALS COMPANY/HAYWARD
P.O. Box 4157, Hayward CA 94540. 510/475-9324. **Contact:** Personnel Manager. **Description:** This facility primarily produces aluminum products. Founded in 1928, Reynolds Metals Company ia an international producer of primary aluminum and fabricated aluminum products. The company operates 50 plants in the United States. Operations include the mining and processing of bauxite, the refining of this ore into alumina, and the processing of the finished product. **Corporate headquarters location:** Richmond VA. **Listed on:** New York Stock Exchange.

C.E. TOLAND & SON
5300 Industrial Way, Benicia CA 94510. 707/747-1000. **Contact:** Jeannette Vaiana, Office Manager. **Description:** Engaged in metal and metal products fabrication. **Corporate headquarters location:** This Location.

USS-POSCO INDUSTRIES
P.O. Box 471, Pittsburg CA 94565. 510/439-6000. **Contact:** Human Resources. **Description:** A steel manufacturer.

WHITE CAP, INC.
P.O. Box 3337, Hayward CA 94545. 510/670-1600. **Contact:** Rudy Mondragon, Supervisor of Human Resources. **Description:** A manufacturer of vacuum metal closures (caps) for glass containers. **Parent company:** Continental Group.

***Note:** Because addresses and telephone numbers of smaller companies can change rapidly, we recommend you call each company to verify the information below before inquiring about job opportunities. Mass mailings are not recommended.*

Additional small employers:

WHOLESALE METALS SERVICE CENTERS AND OFFICES

Kearneys Manufacturing
PO Box 2926, Fresno CA 93745-2926. 209/233-2591.

Feralloy Reliance Co. LP
6850 Stevenson Blvd, Fremont CA 94538-2484. 510/651-7444.

Napa Pipe Corp.
1025 Kaiser Rd, Napa CA 94558-6257. 707/257-5000.

Joseph T. Ryerson & Son Inc.
PO Box 23070, Oakland CA 94623-2370. 510/653-2933.

JM Manufacturing
1051 Sperry Rd, Stockton CA 95206. 209/982-1500.

Mechano-Electro Works
8393 Capwell Dr Ste 210, Oakland CA 94621-2123. 510/638-7300.

Golden State Steel
104 Industrial Ct, Galt CA 95632-1562. 209/745-5200.

Aluserve Electrical Products
1937 Davis St, San Leandro CA 94577. 510/569-2012.

IRON AND STEEL FOUNDRIES

United States Pipe & Foundry
1295 Whipple Rd, Union City CA 94587-2025. 510/471-4711.

D&L Supply
3562 Shelter Creek Dr, Napa CA 94558. 707/224-2506.

NONFERROUS ROLLING AND DRAWING OF METALS

Ketema Inc. Pacific Extrusion
PO Box 1300, Watsonville CA 95077. 408/724-2244.

Columbia Pacific Aluminum Corp.
PO Box 576301, Modesto CA 95357. 209/521-6400.

FABRICATED STRUCTURAL METAL PRODUCTS

Salinas Reinforcing
355 S Vasco Rd, Livermore CA 94550-9256. 510/373-0733.

PSP Industries
300 Montague Expressway Suite 200, Milpitas CA 95035-6830. 408/942-1155.

Camblin Steel Company
PO Box 1400, Carmichael CA 95609. 916/922-6561.

Palm Iron & Bridge Works
8845 Elder Creek Rd, Sacramento CA 95828-1813. 916/386-1010.

International Window
PO Box 5025, Hayward CA 94540-5025. 510/487-1122.

Stiles Custom Metal Inc.
1885 Kinser Road, Ceres CA 95307-4606. 209/538-3667.

Milgard Manufacturing
PO Box 190, Rancho Cordova CA 95741-0190. 916/635-0700.

Devincenzi Metal Products
1655 Rollins Road, Burlingame CA 94010. 415/692-5800.

Critchfield Mechanical Inc.
4085 Campbell Ave, Menlo Park CA 94025-1006. 415/321-7801.

Forslund & Associates
PO Box 778, Madera CA 93639-0778. 209/673-8402.

Caltech Fence Co.
247 Quartz Circle, Livermore CA 94550. 510/449-7270.

Brian's Welding & Iron Works
197 Ryland Street, San Jose CA 95110-2241. 408/275-9834.

Iskon Imports
1655 Whipple Rd, Union City CA 94587. 510/429-1882.

Lodi Metal Technology Inc.
PO Box 967, Lodi CA 95241-0967. 209/334-2500.

SCREW MACHINE PRODUCTS

Rite Way Screw Products
6161 East Highway 12, Lodi CA 95240. 209/368-2640.

METAL STAMPINGS

California Metal Products Company
205 Apollo Way, Hollister CA 95023. 408/637-2250.

BP Chemicals Advanced Material Division
3525 Zephyr Street, Stockton CA 95206. 209/982-0160.

COATING, ENGRAVING, AND ALLIED SERVICES

Marwais Steel Co.
655 Montgomery St, San Francisco CA 94111-2635. 510/262-4838.

Courtaulds Aerospace
1608 4th Street, Berkeley CA 94710-1709. 510/526-1525.

For more information on career opportunities in the fabricated/primary metals and products industries:

Associations

ASM INTERNATIONAL: THE MATERIALS INFORMATION SOCIETY
Materials Park OH 44073. 800/336-5152. World Wide Web address: http://www.asm-intl.org. Gathers, processes, and disseminates technical information to foster the understanding and application of engineered materials.

AMERICAN FOUNDRYMEN'S SOCIETY
505 State Street, Des Plaines IL 60016. 847/824-0181.

AMERICAN WELDING SOCIETY
550 LeJeune Road NW, Miami FL 33126. 305/443-9353. World Wide Web address: http://www.amweld.org.

Directories

DIRECTORY OF STEEL FOUNDRIES IN THE UNITED STATES, CANADA, AND MEXICO
Steel Founder's Society of America, 455 State Street, Des Plaines IL 60016. 847/299-9160.

Magazines

AMERICAN METAL MARKET
25 7th Avenue, New York NY 10019. 212/887-8580.

IRON AGE NEW STEEL
191 South Gary, Carol Stream IL 60188. 708/462-2285.

IRON & STEEL ENGINEER
Association of Iron and Steel Engineers, Three Gateway Center, Suite 2350, Pittsburgh PA 15222. 412/281-6323.

MODERN METALS
625 North Michigan Avenue, Suite 2500, Chicago IL 60611. 312/654-2300.

FINANCIAL SERVICES

You can't get much better than 1995. The stock market soared throughout the year, boosting business at brokerage houses. And, although the market isn't expected to be as hot in '96, it appears likely that the Federal Reserve will lower interest rates, putting the pieces into place for another solid year.

Jobseekers who have experience with mergers and acquisitions should benefit. At the same time, expect more consolidation among brokerage houses themselves. Analysts believe that the largest houses will get larger and the small boutique firms will continue to prosper, but the firms in the middle may get crunched.

AMERICAN EXPRESS COMPANY
WESTERN REGIONAL OFFICE
525 Market Street, 38th floor, San Francisco CA 94105. 415/227-2827. **Contact:** Personnel Manager. **Description:** American Express Company, founded in 1850, is a diversified travel and financial services company operating in 160 countries around the world. American Express Travel Related Services offers consumers the Personal, Gold, and Platinum Cards, as well as revolving credit products such as Optima Cards, which allow customers to extend payments. Other products include the American Express Corporate Card which helps businesses manage their travel and entertainment expenditures; and the Corporate Purchasing Card, which helps business manage their expenditures on supplies, equipment, and services. Travel Related Services also offers American Express Travel Cheques and travel services, including trip planning, reservations, ticketing, and management information. American Express Financial Advisors provides a variety of financial products and services to help individuals, businesses, and institutions establish and achieve their financial goals. American Express Financial Advisors has a field of more than 8,000 financial advisors in the United States and offers financial planning, annuities, mutual funds, insurance, investment certificates, and institutional investment advisory trust, tax preparation, and retail securities brokerage services. American Express Bank seeks to meet the financial services needs of wealthy entrepreneurs and local financial service institutions through a global network of offices in 37 countries. **Corporate headquarters location:** New York NY.

BEAR, STEARNS & COMPANY, INC.
Citicorp Center, One Sansome Street, 41st Floor, San Francisco CA 94104. 415/772-2900. **Contact:** Human Resources. **Description:** Bear, Stearns & Company, Inc. is a leading worldwide investment banking, securities trading, and brokerage firm. With over $5.7 billion in total capital, Bear Stearns serves corporations, governments, institutions, and private investors worldwide. The firm's business includes corporate finance, mergers and acquisitions, public finance, institutional equities, fixed-income sales and trading, private client services, foreign exchange, future sales and trading, derivatives, and asset management. **Corporate headquarters location:** New York NY. **Other U.S. locations:** Los Angeles CA; Atlanta GA; Chicago IL; Boston MA; Dallas TX. **Parent company:** The Bear Stearns Companies Inc. also operates Bear Stearns Securities Corporation, providing professional and correspondent clearing services including securities lending; and Custodial Trust Company, providing master trust, custody, and government securities services.

CAPITAL ALLIANCE INVESTMENTS, INC.
50 California Street, Suite 2020, San Francisco CA 94111. 415/288-9575. **Contact:** Personnel Department. **Description:** Capital Alliance Investments is a securities firm offering a broad range of financial services.

CIGNA FINANCIAL ADVISORS
A DIVISION OF CIGNA CORPORATION
303 Second Street, Suite 660, San Francisco CA 94107. 415/546-9424. **Contact:** Lori Taylor, Director of Recruiting. **Description:** Markets financial services and products to high net worth individuals and business owners. **Common positions include:** Financial Services Sales Rep.; Securities Sales Representative. **Educational backgrounds include:** Accounting; Business Administration; Economics; Finance; Marketing. **Benefits:** 401(k); Dental Insurance; Disability Coverage; Life Insurance; Medical Insurance; Pension Plan. **Corporate headquarters location:** Bloomfield CT. **Parent company:** Cigna Corporation. **Operations at this facility include:** Administration; Sales; Service. **Listed on:** New York Stock Exchange. **Number of employees at this location:** 55.

DEAN WITTER REYNOLDS INC.
1400 Del Monte Center, Monterey CA 93940. 408/373-1861. **Contact:** Human Resources Department. **Description:** Dean Witter Reynolds offers diversified financial services including equities, fixed income securities, commodities, money market instruments, and investment banking services. The company operates in four groups: Dean Witter Reynolds, Inc.; Dean Witter Reynolds Capital Markets Group; Dean Witter Reynolds InterCapital Inc.; and Dean Witter Reynolds International Group. **Parent company:** Sears & Roebuck Financial Services Group. **Other area locations:** San Francisco CA.

DEAN WITTER REYNOLDS INC.
SAN FRANCISCO & LOS ANGELES
101 California Street, 7th Floor, San Francisco CA 94111. 415/693-6000. **Contact:** Brian Danbury, Manager of Personnel. **Description:** Dean Witter Reynolds offers diversified financial services including equities, fixed income securities, commodities, money market instruments, and investment banking services. The company operates in four groups: Dean Witter Reynolds, Inc.; Dean Witter Reynolds Capital Markets Group; Dean Witter Reynolds InterCapital Inc.; and Dean Witter Reynolds International Group. **Parent company:** Sears & Roebuck Financial Services Group. **Operations at this facility include:** Regional Headquarters.

FRANKLIN RESOURCES, INC.
777 Mariners Island Boulevard, San Mateo CA 94404. 415/312-2578. **Contact:** Human Resources. **Description:** A mutual fund and money market company. **Common positions include:** Accountant/Auditor; Administrative Worker/Clerk; Computer Programmer; Customer Service Representative; Systems Analyst; Technical Writer/Editor. **Educational backgrounds include:** Accounting; Business Administration; Computer Science; Liberal Arts; Marketing. **Benefits:** 401(k); Dental Insurance; Disability Coverage; Employee Discounts; Life Insurance; Medical Insurance; Profit Sharing; Tuition Assistance. **Corporate headquarters location:** This Location. **Listed on:** New York Stock Exchange.

GATX CAPITAL CORPORATION

4 Embarcadero Center, Suite 2200, San Francisco CA 94111. 415/955-3200. **Fax:** 415/403-3517. **Contact:** Marianne Matthews, Human Resources. **Description:** GATX Capital is a diversified, international financial services company providing asset-based financing for transportation and industrial equipment. The company arranges full payout financing leases, secured loans, operating leases, and other structured financing both as an investing principal and with institutional partners. The company's strategy is to invest in and to manage assets by combining asset knowledge, transaction structuring capabilities, and portfolio management expertise to control assets with significant upside potential. **Common positions include:** Accountant/Auditor; Attorney; Computer Programmer; Computer Systems Analyst; Credit Manager; Financial Analyst; Human Resources Specialist; Paralegal. **Educational backgrounds include:** Accounting; Business Administration; Computer Science; Finance; Liberal Arts; Marketing; Mathematics; MBA. **Benefits:** 401(k); Adoption Assistance; Dental Insurance; Disability Coverage; Life Insurance; Medical Insurance; Pension Plan; Tuition Assistance. **Corporate headquarters location:** This Location. **Subsidiaries include:** GATX Rail acquires, leases, and sells railcars and locomotives for GATX Capital's own portfolio and for managed portfolios. **Parent company:** GATX Corporation. **Operations at this facility include:** Administration; Divisional Headquarters. **Listed on:** New York Stock Exchange. **Number of employees at this location:** 190.

HOUSEHOLD FINANCE CORPORATION

388 Market Street, Suite 850, San Francisco CA 94111. 415/362-4542. **Fax:** 415/362-4548. **Contact:** Jerald Nielsen, Branch Manager. **Description:** Household Finance Corporation is a large, national, multi-industry corporation providing a wide range of financial services. **Common positions include:** Management Trainee. **Educational backgrounds include:** Business Administration; Economics; Finance. **Benefits:** 401(k); Daycare Assistance; Dental Insurance; Disability Coverage; Life Insurance; Medical Insurance; Pension Plan; Tuition Assistance. **Corporate headquarters location:** Chicago IL. **Parent company:** Household International. **Operations at this facility include:** Sales; Service. **Listed on:** New York Stock Exchange. **Number of employees nationwide:** 5,000.

IMPERIAL CREDIT INDUSTRIES, INC.

11151 Sun Center Drive, Rancho Cordova CA 95670. 916/638-7676. **Contact:** Human Resources. **Description:** Imperial Credit Industries is engaged primarily in the mortgage banking business, which consists of the origination or acquisition and subsequent sale of mortgage loans and the servicing of such loans. The company's mortgage banking operations relate principally to originating first lien mortgage loans secured by single (one to four members) family residences, the majority of which are located in California. The company, through its subsidiary Southern Pacific Thrift and Loan Association, accepts Federal Deposit Insurance Corporation insured deposits which are used to fund the company's mortgage banking business and to originate loans held for investment secured by residential and commercial properties. Additionally, in 1995, the company formed a new subsidiary, Imperial Credit Advisors, Inc., entering the company into the investment trust management business. **Corporate headquarters location:** Santa Ana CA.

IMPERIAL CREDIT INDUSTRIES, INC.

226 Airport Parkway, Suite 640, San Jose CA 95110. 408/453-8303. **Fax:** 408/453-8737. **Contact:** Human Resources. **Description:** Imperial Credit Industries is engaged

primarily in the mortgage banking business, which consists of the origination or acquisition and subsequent sale of mortgage loans and the servicing of such loans. The company's mortgage banking operations relate principally to originating first lien mortgage loans secured by single (one to four members) family residences, the majority of which are located in California. The company, through its subsidiary Southern Pacific Thrift and Loan Association, accepts Federal Deposit Insurance Corporation insured deposits which are used to fund the company's mortgage banking business and to originate loans held for investment secured by residential and commercial properties. Additionally, in 1995, the company formed a new subsidiary, Imperial Credit Advisors, Inc., entering the company into the investment trust management business. **Corporate headquarters location:** Santa Ana CA.

IMPERIAL CREDIT INDUSTRIES, INC.
1600 Riviera Avenue, Suite 375, Walnut Creek CA 94596. 510/930-7188. **Fax:** 510/930-8438. **Contact:** Human Resources. **Description:** Imperial Credit Industries is engaged primarily in the mortgage banking business, which consists of the origination or acquisition and subsequent sale of mortgage loans and the servicing of such loans. The company's mortgage banking operations relate principally to originating first lien mortgage loans secured by single (one to four members) family residences, the majority of which are located in California. The company, through its subsidiary Southern Pacific Thrift and Loan Association, accepts Federal Deposit Insurance Corporation insured deposits which are used to fund the company's mortgage banking business and to originate loans held for investment secured by residential and commercial properties. Additionally, in 1995, the company formed a new subsidiary, Imperial Credit Advisors, Inc., entering the company into the investment trust management business. **Corporate headquarters location:** Santa Ana CA.

ITOCHU INTERNATIONAL
One Maritime Plaza, Suite 920, San Francisco CA 94111. 415/399-3700. **Contact:** General Manager. **Description:** Itochu International is a multi-business trading and investment company. Itochu specializes in developing and sponsoring profitable opportunities in international and domestic commerce, industry, and finance, either as a principal or an agent. The company's services are designed to enhance virtually all aspects of business.

JEFFRIES & COMPANY, INC.
580 California Street, San Francisco CA 94104. 415/705-8444. **Contact:** Human Resources. **Description:** Jeffries & Company, founded in 1962, is engaged in equity, convertible debt and taxable fixed-income securities brokerage and trading, and corporate finance. Jeffries is one of the leading national firms engaged in the distribution and trading of blocks of equity securities and conducts such activities primarily in the third market, which refers to transactions in listed equity securities effected away from national securities exchanges. Jeffries's revenues are derived mostly from commission revenues and market-making or trading as principal in equity, taxable fixed-income and convertible securities with or on behalf of institutional investors, with the balance generated by corporate finance and other activities. **NOTE:** Send resumes to: Human Resources, 11100 Santa Monica Boulevard, Los Angeles CA 90025. **Corporate headquarters location:** Los Angeles CA. **Parent company:** Jeffries Group, Inc. is a holding company which, through Jeffries & Company and its three other primary subsidiaries (Investment Technology Group, Inc. Jeffries International Limited, and Jeffries Pacific Limited), is engaged in securities brokerage and trading, corporate finance, and other financial services.

MERRILL LYNCH
600 California Street, Eighth Floor, San Francisco CA 94108. 415/955-3700. **Contact:** Human Resources. **Description:** Merrill Lynch provides financial services in the following areas: securities, extensive insurance, and real estate and related services. One of the largest securities brokerage firms in the United States, it also brokers commodity futures and options, corporate and municipal securities, and is engaged in investment banking activities. The company operates three offices in San Francisco. **Common positions include:** Insurance Agent/Broker; Services Sales Representative. **Educational backgrounds include:** Accounting; Business Administration; Communications; Economics; Finance; Marketing. **Benefits:** Dental Insurance; Disability Coverage; Employee Discounts; Life Insurance; Medical Insurance; Pension Plan; Profit Sharing; Savings Plan; Tuition Assistance. **Corporate headquarters location:** New York NY. **Operations at this facility include:** Sales. **Listed on:** New York Stock Exchange.

MORGAN STANLEY & COMPANY, INC.
555 California Street, Suite 2200, San Francisco CA 94104. 415/576-2000. **Contact:** Ms. Pat Wong, Sales Assistant. **Description:** One of the largest investment banking firms in the world. **Common positions include:** Administrator; Branch Manager; Department Manager; Economist/Market Research Analyst; Financial Analyst; Management Trainee; Operations/Production Manager; Services Sales Representative; Underwriter/Assistant Underwriter. **Educational backgrounds include:** Accounting; Business Administration; Economics; Engineering; Mathematics. **Benefits:** Dental Insurance; Disability Coverage; Employee Discounts; Life Insurance; Medical Insurance; Pension Plan; Profit Sharing; Tuition Assistance. **Corporate headquarters location:** New York NY. **Operations at this facility include:** Regional Headquarters; Sales. **Listed on:** American Stock Exchange; New York Stock Exchange.

PACIFIC STOCK EXCHANGE
301 Pine Street, San Francisco CA 94104. 415/393-4000. **Contact:** Human Resources Department. **Description:** A regional stock exchange offering local stocks and securities as well as issues offered on such national exchanges as the New York and American Stock Exchanges. Pacific Stock Exchange has three trading floors: two are geographically separate equity floors (Los Angeles and San Francisco) and one is an options floor (San Francisco).

PAINE WEBBER
555 California Street, Suite 3200, San Francisco CA 94104. 415/398-6400. **Contact:** Stuart Spence, Branch Manager. **Description:** Paine Webber is a holding company that, together with operating subsidiaries, forms one of the world's largest investment services firms. Paine Webber assists corporations, governments, and individuals in meeting their long-term financial needs. Paine Webber also has operations in equity and fixed-income securities. **Corporate headquarters location:** New York NY.

PAINE WEBBER
100 California Street, Suite 400, San Francisco CA 94111. 415/954-6700. **Contact:** Connie Warner, Administrative Manager. **Description:** Paine Webber is a holding company that, together with operating subsidiaries, forms one of the world's largest investment services firms. Paine Webber assists corporations, governments, and individuals in meeting their long-term financial needs. Paine Webber also has operations in equity and fixed-income securities. **Corporate headquarters location:** New York NY.

PRUDENTIAL SECURITIES
Four Embarcadero Center, Suite 2400, San Francisco CA 94111. 415/981-0440. **Contact:** Personnel Department. **Description:** An international securities brokerage and investment firm (formerly operating as Bache Halsey Stuart Shields Inc.). The company offers clients more than 70 investment products including stocks, options, bonds, commodities, tax-favored investments, and insurance, as well as several specialized financial services. Prudential Securities operates more than 240 offices in 17 countries. **Corporate headquarters location:** New York NY. **Parent company:** Prudential Insurance Company.

CHARLES SCHWAB & COMPANY
101 Montgomery Street, San Francisco CA 94104. 415/627-7000. **Fax:** 415/627-7316. **Recorded Jobline:** 415/627-7227. **Contact:** Human Resources. **Description:** Charles Schwab & Company is one of the largest discount brokerage companies in the U.S. It has more than 200 branches and over 2.5 million active customer accounts. **Common positions include:** Accountant/Auditor; Administrative Services Manager; Advertising Clerk; Attorney; Branch Manager; Brokerage Clerk; Computer Programmer; Computer Systems Analyst; Customer Service Representative; Financial Analyst; Financial Services Sales Rep.; Human Resources Specialist; Management Analyst/Consultant; Management Trainee; Securities Sales Representative. **Educational backgrounds include:** Accounting; Business Administration; Communications; Computer Science; Economics; Finance; Liberal Arts; Marketing; Mathematics. **Benefits:** 401(k); Dental Insurance; Disability Coverage; Employee Discounts; Life Insurance; Medical Insurance; Pension Plan; Profit Sharing; Tuition Assistance. **Special Programs:** Internships. **Corporate headquarters location:** This Location. **Parent company:** Charles Schwab Corporation provides brokerages and investment services to 2.5 million investors with assets totaling $95.8 billion. The company services customers who primarily perform their own research and make their own decisions about investments but do not wish to pay for portfolio research and management. Schwab's services are fee-based, but securities are generally not sold to its investors. **Operations at this facility include:** Administration; Divisional Headquarters; Sales; Service. **Listed on:** American Stock Exchange; NASDAQ; New York Stock Exchange. **Number of employees at this location:** 2,200. **Number of employees nationwide:** 45,000.

SUTRO & COMPANY INC.
201 California Street, San Francisco CA 94111. 415/445-8201. **Fax:** 415/421-7632. **Contact:** Human Resources. **Description:** Established in 1858, Sutro & Company is a full-service, regional investment brokerage firm. **Common positions include:** Accountant/Auditor; Branch Manager; Brokerage Clerk; Budget Analyst; Computer Programmer; Computer Systems Analyst; Credit Manager; Editor; Financial Analyst; Human Resources Specialist; Insurance Agent/Broker; Operations/Production Manager; Purchasing Agent and Manager; Securities Sales Representative; Technical Writer/Editor. **Educational backgrounds include:** Accounting; Business Administration; Communications; Economics; Finance; Liberal Arts; Marketing. **Benefits:** 401(k); Dental Insurance; Disability Coverage; Health Club Discount; Life Insurance; Medical Insurance; Profit Sharing; Savings Plan; Tuition Assistance. **Corporate headquarters location:** This Location. **Parent company:** John Hancock Freedom Securities. **Operations at this facility include:** Administration; Divisional Headquarters; Regional Headquarters; Research and Development; Sales; Service. **Listed on:** Privately held. **Number of employees at this location:** 200. **Number of employees nationwide:** 650.

TRANSAMERICA CORPORATION
600 Montgomery Street, San Francisco CA 94111. 415/983-4177. **Contact:** Jackie Gentle, Manager of Human Resources. **Description:** The parent company for the diversified financial services and insurance companies of Transamerica. The company's personnel function is de-centralized and each company handles its own recruiting needs. **Common positions include:** Accountant/Auditor; Administrator; Financial Analyst; Human Resources Specialist; Secretary. **Educational backgrounds include:** Accounting; Business Administration; Economics; Finance. **Benefits:** 401(k); Dental Insurance; Disability Coverage; Life Insurance; Medical Insurance; Pension Plan; Tuition Assistance. **Corporate headquarters location:** This Location. **Operations at this facility include:** Administration. **Listed on:** New York Stock Exchange.

USL CAPITAL
733 Front Street, San Francisco CA 94111. 415/627-9000. **Fax:** 415/397-6543. **Contact:** Human Resources. **Description:** Provides general commercial financing and leasing. **NOTE:** USL Capital accepts written inquiries only. **Common positions include:** Accountant/Auditor; Administrator; Computer Programmer; Credit Manager; Customer Service Representative; General Manager; Marketing Specialist; Services Sales Representative; Systems Analyst. **Educational backgrounds include:** Accounting; Business Administration; Economics; Finance. **Benefits:** Dental Insurance; Disability Coverage; Life Insurance; Medical Insurance; Savings Plan; Tuition Assistance. **Corporate headquarters location:** This Location. **Parent company:** Ford Motor Company. **Operations at this facility include:** Administration; Sales; Service. **Number of employees nationwide:** 700.

Note: Because addresses and telephone numbers of smaller companies can change rapidly, we recommend you call each company to verify the information below before inquiring about job opportunities. Mass mailings are not recommended.

Additional small employers:

CREDIT AGENCIES AND INSTITUTIONS

Fresno Madera Farm Credit Service
426 S Madera Ave, Kerman CA 93630-1553. 209/846-5301.

First Mortgage Corporation
3616 Delta Fair Blvd, Antioch CA 94509-4006. 510/757-1707.

Ford Motor Credit Co.
4301 Hacienda Dr #400, Pleasanton CA 94588-2731. 510/463-9730.

Fireside Thrift Co.
475 14th St, Oakland CA 94612-1900. 510/444-1494.

The Money Store
2055 Gateway Pl Ste 400, San Jose CA 95110-1015. 408/436-7676.

Community Unity Lending
175 Bernal Rd, San Jose CA 95119-1343. 408/281-8383.

American Residential Lenders
5250 Claremont Ave, Stockton CA 95207-5700. 209/472-3411.

Equity Lending
9017 Thornton Rd, Stockton CA 95209-1847. 209/474-3700.

Federal Land Bank Association Yosemite
800 W Monte Vista Ave, Turlock CA 95382-7242. 209/667-2366.

Commerce Security Bank
1515 River Park Dr, Sacramento CA 95815-4610. 916/922-9501.

Transamerica Financial Service
1760 Creekside Oaks Dr, Sacramento CA 95833-3632. 916/641-5513.

Transamerica Financial Service
155 E Shaw Ave Ste 310, Fresno CA 93710-7619. 209/222-5256.

Heller Financial Inc.
1 Montgomery St, San

Francisco CA 94104-4505. 415/986-6933.

Cypress Financial Corp.
2300 Boynton Ave, Fairfield CA 94533-4354. 707/429-7074.

Machine Tool Finance Corp.
715 Southpoint Blvd, Petaluma CA 94954-6860. 707/765-0995.

Gold Key Credit
650 E Miner Ave, Stockton CA 95202-2608. 209/547-2922.

General Motors Acceptance Corp.
3255 W March Ln Ste 350, Stockton CA 95219-2304. 209/957-7901.

Westcorp Financial Services
1565 Exposition Blvd, Sacramento CA 95815-5147. 916/649-0100.

Westcorp Financial Services
39111 Paseo Padre Pkwy, Fremont CA 94538-1615. 510/797-1331.

County Financial Services
1111 Howe Ave, Sacramento CA 95825-8541. 916/646-0996.

First Federal Corp.
713 Del Paso Rd, Sacramento CA 95834-1106. 916/641-6527.

Silicon Valley Financial Service
2880 Lakeside Dr, Santa Clara CA 95054-2813. 408/980-6300.

MORTGAGE BANKERS

Community Lending
5619 Scotts Valley Dr Ste 120 , Scotts Valley CA 95066-3449. 408/438-5100.

First National Mortgage
350 S Winchester Blvd, San Jose CA 95128-2035. 408/241-5626.

GMAC Mortgage
2880 Sunrise Blvd Ste 218, Rancho Cordova CA 95742-6549. 916/638-7493.

Amerimac Mortgage Co.
1850 Warburton Ave, Santa Clara CA 95050-4111. 408/553-6000.

LOAN BROKERS

Royal Charter Mortgage
6442 N Maroa Ave, Fresno CA 93704-1247. 209/436-4020.

Service Mortgage Co.
1301 Shoreway Rd, Belmont CA 94002-4106. 415/594-1117.

Consulting Plus Inc.
664 W McKinley Ave, Sunnyvale CA 94086-6049. 408/735-7470.

Glendale Federal Bank
2 W 5th Ave, San Mateo CA 94402-2046. 415/579-6350.

Commerce Security Bank
995 Oliver Rd, Fairfield CA 94533-4300. 707/427-5180.

Wall Street Mortgage
39055 Hastings St Ste 210, Fremont CA 94538-1518. 510/745-8555.

Countrywide Funding Corp.
8080 Madison Ave Ste 100A, Fair Oaks CA 95628-3759. 916/965-1813.

Countrywide Funding Corp.
4309 Hacienda Dr Ste 390, Pleasanton CA 94588-2746. 510/460-9730.

Western Sunrise Mortgage
1981 N Broadway Ste 425, Walnut Creek CA 94596-3850. 510/933-1620.

Grant Mortgage Company
1450 Grant Ave, Novato CA 94945-3119. 415/892-6685.

Norwest Mortgage Banking Inc.
101 Larkspur Landing Cir, San Rafael CA 94901. 415/461-3938.

Norwest Mortgage Banking Inc.
1350 41st Ave, Capitola CA 95010-3906. 408/475-3607.

Aames Home Loan
3031 Tisch Way Ste 2, San Jose CA 95128-2530. 408/244-2600.

American General Finance Inc.
6015 Pacific Ave, Stockton CA 95207-3707. 209/478-5941.

American General Finance Inc.
811 E March Ln, Stockton CA 95207-5861. 209/951-7100.

American Savings Bank
1611 W March Ln, Stockton CA 95207-6401. 209/546-3035.

California West Mortgage
37 W Yokuts Ave, Stockton CA 95207-5721. 209/956-1190.

American General Finance
5808 Watt Ave, North Highlands CA 95660-4754. 916/331-0696.

American General Finance
1040 W Kettleman Ln Ste 6, Lodi CA 95240-6056. 209/369-5845.

American General Finance
11944 Masters Ct, Auburn CA 95603-2537. 916/888-6311.

The Cal Bay Mortgage Group
1211 N Dutton Ave, Santa Rosa CA 95401-4660. 707/795-8738.

Fair Oaks Mortgage
6939 Sunrise Blvd, Citrus Heights CA 95610-3153. 916/729-0364.

Stockmans Bank Of Commerce
9663 E Stockton Blvd, Elk Grove CA 95624-2565. 916/685-6546.

Sente Financial
1540 River Park Dr, Sacramento CA 95815-4611. 916/569-0700.

All Pacific Mortgage
1776 Tribute Rd Ste 205, Sacramento CA 95815-4410. 916/666-5626.

The Mortgage Network
3117 El Camino Ave, Sacramento CA 95821-6016. 916/972-1877.

Evans Mortgage Company
1350 Sutterville Rd, Sacramento CA 95822-1150. 916/731-4405.

Aspen Valley Mortgage
3040 Arden Way, Sacramento CA 95825-2049. 916/484-4475.

Directors Mortgage
2851 Park Marina Dr Ste 150, Redding CA 96001-2824. 916/224-2380.

SECURITY BROKERS AND DEALERS

Smith Barney Shearson Inc.
3000 Sand Hill Rd Ste 190, Menlo Park CA 94025-7116. 415/926-7600.

Smith Barney Shearson Inc.
350 California St, San Francisco CA 94104-1402. 415/955-1641.

Cowen & Co.
345 California St Ste 2600, San Francisco CA 94104-2624. 415/434-7800.

Coast Options Inc.
220 Montgomery St Ste 1019, San Francisco CA 94104-3402. 415/956-3498.

Goldman Sachs & Company
555 California St Ste 3120, San Francisco CA 94104-1607. 415/393-7500.

Emmett A. Larkin Company Inc.
100 Bush St Fl 100, San Francisco CA 94104-3904. 415/986-2332.

Salomon Brothers Inc.
555 California St Fl 39, San Francisco CA 94104-1502. 415/951-1777.

Sage Clearing Corp.
220 Bush St Ste 660, San Francisco CA 94104-3508. 415/781-7430.

Kidder, Peabody & Co. Inc.
555 California St Ste 3200, San Francisco CA 94104-1608. 415/398-6400.

Piper & Jaffray
345 California St Ste 2200, San Francisco CA 94104-2623. 415/421-1535.

Lehman Brothers
One Montgomery St, San Francisco CA 94104-4505. 415/955-9400.

Donaldson Lufkin & Jenrette
1 Montgomery St Ste 1210, San Francisco CA 94104-4572. 415/421-7600.

Babcock & Brown Inc.
2 Harrison St Fl 6, San Francisco CA 94105-1672. 415/512-1515.

Van Kasper & Co.
600 California St #1700, San Francisco CA 94108-2704. 415/391-5600.

Alex Brown & Sons Inc.
101 California St Fl 46, San Francisco CA 94111-5802. 415/544-2800.

O'Melveny & Myers
275 Battery St Ste 2600, San Francisco CA 94111-3338. 415/984-8700.

New York Life Insurance Co.
100 Pine St Ste 3000, San Francisco CA 94111-5216. 415/393-6060.

First Boston Corporation
101 California St Ste 4300, San Francisco CA 94111-5889. 415/765-7000.

Stone & Youngberg
50 California St Ste 3500, San Francisco CA 94111-4784. 415/981-1314.

Volpe Welty & Co.
1 Maritime Plz Ste 1100, San Francisco CA 94111-3414. 415/956-8120.

Kidder, Peabody & Co. Inc.
730 Welch Rd Ste 1, Palo Alto CA 94304-1506. 415/321-1500.

Glenborough Corp.
400 S El Camino Real Ste 1100, San Mateo CA 94402-1708. 415/343-9300.

AG Edwards & Sons Inc.
1099 D St, San Rafael CA 94901-2829. 415/454-9770.

Smith Barney Shearson Inc.
333 W San Carlos St Ste 900, San Jose CA 95110-2700. 408/947-2200.

Kidder, Peabody & Co. Inc.
50 W San Fernando St Ste 820, San Jose CA 95113-2413. 408/286-5500.

Cruttenden & Co.
3000 Sand Hill Rd, Menlo Park CA 94025-7116. 415/854-5516.

Robert W Baird & Co. Inc.
1 Sansome St, San Francisco CA 94104-4448. 415/956-6555.

Edward D Jones & Co.
39370 Fremont Blvd, Fremont CA 94538-1320. 510/790-1556.

Edward D Jones & Co.
410 Petaluma Blvd S, Petaluma CA 94952-4247. 707/763-1851.

Edward D Jones & Co.
9197 Greenback Ln, Orangevale CA 95662-4792. 916/989-0920.

Edward D Jones & Co.
312 Main St, Placerville CA 95667-5639. 916/626-8651.

Edward D Jones & Co.
2551 Park Marina Dr Ste C, Redding CA 96001-2842. 916/243-4707.

American Investors Company
21021 Corsair Blvd, Hayward CA 94545-1301. 510/732-9888.

Quick & Reilly Inc.
500 Ygnacio Valley Rd, Walnut Creek CA 94596-3840. 510/943-3112.

Mentor Capital
1901 S Bascom Ave, Campbell CA 95008-2215. 408/371-7144.

Wulff Hansen & Co.
1300 W Lodi Ave Ste A-10, Lodi CA 95242-3000. 209/368-2737.

Fortis Investors Inc.
1470 Enea Cir, Concord CA 94520-5217. 510/602-2733.

INVESTMENT ADVISORS

Smith Barney Shearson Inc.
1 Sansome St Fl 38, San Francisco CA 94104-4448. 415/984-6024.

Callan Associates
71 Stevenson St Ste 1300, San Francisco CA 94105-2938. 415/974-5060.

Physicians Planning Service
550 Sansome St Ste 300, San Francisco CA 94111-2928. 415/362-7308.

Bailard Biehl and Kaiser Inc.
2755 Campus Dr Fl 3, San Mateo CA 94403-2513. 415/571-5800.

Financial Network Investment Corp.
3478 Buskirk Ave Ste 300, Pleasant Hill CA 94523-4366. 510/944-9644.

Rosenberg Institutional Equity
4 Orinda Way, Orinda CA 94563-2515. 510/254-6464.

Lincoln Financial Insurance Service
3000 Executive Pkwy Ste 230, San Ramon CA 94583-4598. 510/275-0300.

IDS Financial Services Inc.
4000 Executive Pkwy Ste 250, San Ramon CA 94583-4206. 510/275-1944.

Northwest Asset Management Co.
100 Pringle Ave Ste 550, Walnut Creek CA 94596-3581. 510/945-1495.

SIA Financial
1590 The Alameda 200, San Jose CA 95126-2351. 408/280-0800.

Supermail International
2201 Park Towne Cir, Sacramento CA 95825-0401. 916/483-1131.

Swanee Group International
PO Box 306, San Jose CA 95103-0306. 408/446-2626.

Canaan Venture Partners
2884 Sand Hill Rd, Menlo Park CA 94025-7022. 415/854-8092.

Altamira Capital Corp.
883 Oak Grove Ave, Menlo Park CA 94025-4421. 415/322-3513.

Portola Co.
2400 Sand Hill Rd, Menlo Park CA 94025-6941. 415/854-1507.

Linsco Private Ledger Financial
3301 El Camino Real, Atherton CA 94027-3803. 415/306-0606.

Napoli & Associates Inc.
220 Montgomery St Ste 500, San Francisco CA 94104-3412. 415/398-1255.

McMorgan & Co.
1 Bush St Ste 800, San Francisco CA 94104-4441. 415/788-9300.

Boston Safe Deposit & Trust Co.
1 Embarcadero Ctr Ste 2200, San Francisco CA 94111-3711. 415/397-0600.

AMB Institutional Realty Advisors
505 Montgomery St, San

Francisco CA 94111-2561. 415/394-9000.

Technology Funding Inc.
2000 Alameda De Las Pulgas 011, San Mateo CA 94403-1269. 415/345-8899.

John Dugan & Associates
600 5th Ave, San Rafael CA 94901-3362. 415/454-2312.

Harrison Financial Associated Securities Corp.
10430 S De Anza Blvd, Cupertino CA 95014-3019. 408/725-2890.

George Devine Financial Plan
196 Dana Ave, San Jose CA 95126-2807. 408/293-1004.

American Express Financial Advisors
14570 Mono Way, Sonora CA 95370. 209/533-4457.

Spectrum Capital Management
1010 Racquet Club Dr, Auburn CA 95603-3060. 916/888-9000.

SJH Enterprises
8141 Walnut Villa Way, Fair Oaks CA 95628-2776. 916/961-4933.

MANAGEMENT INVESTMENT OFFICES

Dodge & Cox Income Fund
1 Sansome St Ste 3500, San Francisco CA 94104-4436. 415/981-1710.

REAL ESTATE INVESTMENT TRUSTS

Bay Apartment Communities Inc.
4340 Stevens Creek Blvd, San Jose CA 95129-1102.

For more information on career opportunities in financial services:

Associations

FINANCIAL EXECUTIVES INSTITUTE
P.O. Box 1938, Morristown NJ 07962-1938. 201/898-4600. Fee and membership required. Publishes biennial member directory. Provides member referral service.

INSTITUTE OF FINANCIAL EDUCATION
111 East Wacker Drive, Chicago IL 60601. 312/946-8800. World Wide Web address: http://www.theinstitute.com. Offers career development program.

NATIONAL ASSOCIATION OF BUSINESS ECONOMISTS
1233 20th Street NW, Suite 505, Washington DC 20036. 202/463-6223. Bulletin board number: 216/241-6254. Newsletter and electronic bulletin board list job openings. Members can upload resumes and listed positions desired to bulletin board.

NATIONAL ASSOCIATION OF CREDIT MANAGEMENT
8815 Centre Park Drive, Suite 200, Columbia MD 21045-2158. 410/740-5560. World Wide Web address: http://www.nacm.org. Contact: Delores Richman. Publishes a business credit magazine.

NATIONAL ASSOCIATION OF REAL ESTATE INVESTMENT TRUSTS
1129 20th Street NW, Suite 305, Washington DC 20036. 202/785-8717. Contact: Donna Smith, Membership.

PUBLIC SECURITIES ASSOCIATION
40 Broad Street, 12th Floor, New York NY 10004. 212/809-7000. Contact: Caroline Binn x427. Publishes an annual report and several newsletters.

SECURITIES INDUSTRY ASSOCIATION
120 Broadway, 35th Floor New York NY 10271. 212/608-1500. World Wide Web address: http://www.sia.com. Contact: Phil Williams/Membership. Publishes a security industry yearbook.

TREASURY MANAGEMENT ASSOCIATION
7315 Wisconsin Avenue, Suite 1250-W, Bethesda MD 20814. 301/907-2862. World Wide Web address: http://www.tma-net.org.

Directories

DIRECTORY OF AMERICAN FINANCIAL INSTITUTIONS
Thomson Business Publications, 6195 Crooked Creek Road, Norcross GA 30092. 770/448-1011. Sales 800/321-3373.

MOODY'S BANK AND FINANCE MANUAL
Moody's Investor Service, 99 Church Street, New York NY 10007. 212/553-0300.

Magazines

BARRON'S: NATIONAL BUSINESS AND FINANCIAL WEEKLY
Dow Jones & Co., 200 Liberty Street, New York NY 10281. 212/416-2700.

FINANCIAL PLANNING
40 West 57th Street, 11th Floor, New York NY 10019. 212/765-5311.

FINANCIAL WORLD
Financial World Partners, 1328 Broadway, 3rd Floor, New York NY 10001. 212/594-5030.

FUTURES: THE MAGAZINE OF COMMODITIES AND OPTIONS
250 South Wacker Drive, Suite 1150, Chicago IL 60606. 312/977-0999.

INSTITUTIONAL INVESTOR
488 Madison Avenue, 12th Floor, New York NY 10022. 212/303-3300.

FOOD AND BEVERAGES/AGRICULTURE

Employment in food processing is expected to fall slightly through 2005. Although the industry's output should grow, increasing automation and productivity will mean food can be produced with fewer workers. However, some food processing industries are likely to remain fairly labor intensive. For example, meat packing and poultry processing are difficult to fully automate because each animal processed is different. Professional specialty occupations, although small in number, are also expected to grow. The growth of these occupations -- including engineers, systems analysts, and food scientists -- reflects the industry's emphasis on scientific research to improve food products and production processes. Demand for food scientists will also grow in response to expanding government inspection and regulation of food production.

Several factors may slow the decline in food processing employment. As consumers increasingly seek "ready-to-heat" foods, the food processing industry has introduced many new products. Many of these new goods, which require more processing than the items they are replacing, will help maintain the demand for food processors in the future. In addition, the food processing industry is taking advantage of new technology to perform much of the processing formerly done by retailers. One other factor that may help stem employment decline is growing international trade in food products. Food processing firms expect growing trade to provide new markets for their products. The emerging field of biotechnology and other new food science technologies may also provide new jobs.

ALLIED SYSCO FOOD SERVICES
5900 Stewart Avenue, Fremont CA 94538. 510/226-3000. **Contact:** Human Resources. **Description:** A food services company. **Number of employees nationwide:** 600.

AMERICAN POULTRY, INC.
1925 Jerrold Avenue, San Francisco CA 94124. 415/648-9200. **Contact:** John McGirr, Controller. **Description:** Produces poultry and meat items.

BERINGER VINEYARDS
P.O. Box 111, St. Helena CA 94574. 707/963-7115. **Contact:** Karen Trenary, Personnel Coordinator. **Description:** Operates vineyards and makes wines. **Corporate headquarters location:** This Location.

BORDEN, INC.
NORTH AMERICAN FOODS DIVISION
2680 Bishop Drive, Suite 128, San Ramon CA 94583. 510/867-1950. **Contact:** Human Resources. **Description:** Major brands and businesses of Borden's North American Foods division include Pasta and Sauce (Creamette pasta, Catelli pasta and sauce, and regional U.S. and Canadian brands including Prince, R-F, Anthony's, Gioia and Ronco, Classico premium pasta sauce, and Aunt Millie's pasta sauce); Dairy (Borden, Meadow Gold, Viva, and Lite Line milk, ice cream, frozen desserts, and cultured products;

Borden process cheese; and Lite Line diet cheese products); and Nice Grocery (Cracker Jack popcorn and peanuts, Eagle brand sweetened condensed milk, ReaLemon juice, Wyler's bullion, and Cremora non-dairy creamer). Other divisions of Borden's include International Foods, European Bakery, International Dairy, European Grocery and Pasta; and Packaging and Industrial Products.

BUTTERBALL TURKEY COMPANY
P.O. Box 738, Turlock CA 95381-0738. 209/667-4664. **Contact:** Human Resources. **Description:** A fresh and frozen poultry processor. **Parent company:** ConAgra, Inc.

C.P.C. BAKERIES
264 South Spruce Avenue, South San Francisco CA 94080. 415/875-3100. **Contact:** Human Resources. **Description:** A bakery products firm, manufacturing and distributing a wide line of cakes, cookies, doughnuts, and similar baked products.

CAMPBELL SOUP COMPANY
6200 Franklin Boulevard, Sacramento CA 95824. 916/428-7890. **Contact:** Human Resources. **Description:** Campbell Soup is a major producer of commercial soups, juices, and pickles as well as frozen foods, canned beans and pasta products, spaghetti sauces, and baked goods. The company distributes its products worldwide. U.S. brands include Campbell's, Vlasic, V8, Chunky, Home Cookin', Prego, Pepperidge Farm, Inc., LeMenu, and Swanson. European foods are sold under brand names such as Pleybin, Biscuits Delacre, Freshbake, Groko, Godiva, and Betis. The company also owns Arnotts Biscuits of Australia.

CAMPBELL SOUP COMPANY
1836 Lapham Drive, Modesto CA 95354. 209/529-1100. **Contact:** Human Resources. **Description:** Campbell Soup is a major producer of commercial soups, juices, and pickles as well as frozen foods, canned beans and pasta products, spaghetti sauces, and baked goods. The company distributes its products worldwide. U.S. brands include Campbell's, Vlasic, V8, Chunky, Home Cookin', Prego, Pepperidge Farm, Inc., LeMenu, and Swanson. European foods are sold under brand names such as Pleybin, Biscuits Delacre, Freshbake, Groko, Godiva, and Betis. The company also owns Arnotts Biscuits of Australia.

CANANDAIGUA WINE CO.
P.O. Box 55, Woodbridge CA 95258-0055. 209/368-3113. **Contact:** Human Resources. **Description:** Canandaigua Wine Company is a leading producer and marketer of more than 125 national and regional beverage alcohol brands, distributed by more than 1,000 wholesalers as well as state alcoholic beverage control agencies, throughout the United States and in selected international markets. The company is the second-largest U.S. producer of wines in the categories of table wines, sparkling wines, and dessert wines. Products include Inglenook, Almaden Vineyards, and Paul Masson. The company is the fourth-largest importer of international beer brands, with three of the top 20 imported beer brands in the U.S. including Corona and St. Pauli Girl. The company is also the eighth-largest supplier of distilled spirits in the U.S. with products including bourbon, whiskey, gin, and vodka. **NOTE:** Send resumes to: Human Resources, P.O. Box 12667, Road 24, Madera CA 93639.

CARGILL SALT COMPANY
7220 Central Avenue, Newark CA 94560. 510/797-1820. **Contact:** Ilene Fox, Personnel Manager. **Description:** This location processes and distributes salt. The company, its

subsidiaries, and its affiliates are involved in nearly 50 individual lines of business. The company has 130 years of service and international expertise in commodity trading, handling, transporting, processing, and risk management. Cargill is a major trader of grains and oilseeds, as well as a marketer of many other agricultural and non-agricultural commodities. As a transporter, it uses a complex network of rail and road systems, inland waterways, and ocean-going routes combining its own fleet and transportation services purchased from outside sources to find the most efficient and economical modes of transport to move bulk commodities from point of origin to point of consumption. As an agricultural supplier, Cargill is a leader in developing high-quality, competitively-priced farm products and in supplying them to growers. Agricultural products include a wide variety of feed, seed, fertilizers, and other goods and services needed by producers worldwide. Cargill is also a leader in producing and marketing seed varieties and hybrids. Cargill Central Research, located at Cargill headquarters, is dedicated to developing new agricultural products to address the needs of customers around the world. The company also provides financial and technical services. Cargill's Financial Markets Division (FMD) supports Cargill and its subsidiaries with financial products and services that address the full spectrum of market conditions. These include financial instrument trading, emerging markets instrument trading, value investing, and money management. Cargill's worldwide food processing businesses supply products ranging from basic ingredients used in food production to recognized name brands. Cargill also operates a number of industrial businesses including the production of steel, industrial-grade starches, ethanol, and salt products. **Number of employees worldwide:** 70,000.

CHALONE WINE GROUP, LTD.
621 Airpark Road, Napa CA 94558-6272. 707/254-4200. **Fax:** 707/254-4201. **Contact:** Human Resources. **Description:** The Chalone Wine Group, Ltd. produces, markets, and sells premium white and red varietal table wines, primarily Chardonnay, Pinot Noir, Cabernet Sauvignon, and Sauvignon Blanc. The Chalone Wine Group, Ltd. operates five wineries, four located in different counties of California and the fifth located in eastern Washington state. The company's California wines are made principally from grapes grown at its Chalone Vineyard and Carmenet Vineyard facilities, at vineyards owned by the company's partner in the Edna Valley Vineyard joint venture, and, for the company's Acacia Winery facility, from grapes principally grown at neighboring independent vineyards, plus a small vineyard which is half owned and managed by the company. The Washington state wines are made from grapes grown at a nearby vineyard one-half owned by the company. **Corporate headquarters location:** This Location.

DNA PLANT TECHNOLOGY CORPORATION
6701 San Pablo Avenue, Oakland CA 94608. 510/547-2395. **Contact:** Human Resources. **Description:** DNA Plant Technology Corporation is a leading agribusiness biotechnology company focused on developing and marketing premium, fresh, and processed fruits and vegetables using advanced breeding, genetic engineering, and other biotechniques. FreshWorld Farms, a wholly-owned subsidiary of DNAP, markets a line of premium vegetables under the FreshWorld Farms brand including tomatoes, carrot bites, sweet red mini-peppers, and carrot sticks. DNAP's two-track strategy uses advanced breeding to develop and market improved products today, and genetic engineering to further improve products for tomorrow. **Corporate headquarters location:** This Location.

DEL MONTE CORPORATION
P.O. Box 69, San Jose CA 95103. 408/291-2420. **Contact:** Human Resources

Department. **Description:** A producer of canned fruits and vegetables, tomato sauces, condiments, and dessert products for the consumer, institutional, and military markets. The company operates over 60 plants worldwide at which it processes food and makes, labels, and packs its own cans. Brand names include Del Monte, Morton Munchwich, Snack Cups, Bonanza, Ortega, Sunkist Plus, and Summer Crisp.

DOLE DRIED FRUIT & NUT CO.
P.O. Box 2565, Fresno CA 93745-2565. 209/499-6600. **Contact:** Human Resources. **Description:** This location packages dried fruits and nuts. Overall, Dole Food is a worldwide producer, packager, packer, and marketer of fresh produce including pineapples, bananas, grapes, and apples, as well as nearly 30 varieties of fresh vegetables. Using either the Dole label or others, Dole Food also deals in packaged foods such as canned fruits, juices, and dried fruits and nuts. The company also operates residential, commercial, and industrial real estate in Hawaii, California, and Arizona under the Castle & Cooke name.

DREYER'S GRAND ICE CREAM, INC.
5929 College Avenue, Oakland CA 94618. 510/652-8187. **Contact:** Human Resources. **Description:** Dreyer's Grand Ice Cream manufactures and distributes premium-quality ice cream and other dairy dessert products. Its ice cream is one of the leading premium packaged ice cream products in most areas of the western U.S. In addition, the company's products are sold in various midwestern, mid-Atlantic, and southeastern markets, as well as in the New York metropolitan area, under the name Edy's Grand Ice Cream. **Number of employees nationwide:** 1,150.

THE EARTHGRAINS COMPANY
P.O. Box 2093, Oakland CA 94604. 510/436-5350. **Contact:** Personnel. **Description:** Produces and distributes a wide range of baked goods.

FRITO-LAY INC.
600 Garner Road, Modesta CA 95357. 209/544-5400. **Contact:** Personnel. **Description:** A worldwide manufacturer and wholesaler of snack products including Fritos Corn Chips, Lays Potato Chips, Doritos Tortilla Chips, and a wide range of other snack foods. The parent company operates on a worldwide basis within three industry segments: beverages, snack foods, and restaurants. The beverage segment primarily markets its brands worldwide and manufactures concentrates for its brands for sale to franchised bottlers worldwide. The segment also operates bottling plants and distribution facilities of its own located in the U.S. and key international markets, and distributes ready-to-drink Lipton tea products under a joint-venture agreement. In addition, under separate distribution and joint-venture agreements, the segment distributes certain previously existing, as well as jointly-developed Ocean Spray juice products. The international snack food business includes major operations in Mexico, the United Kingdom, and Canada. The restaurant segment consists primarily of the operations of the worldwide Pizza Hut, Taco Bell, and KFC chains. PFS, PepsiCo's restaurant distribution operation, supplies company-owned and company-franchised restaurants principally in the U.S. **Common positions include:** Blue-Collar Worker Supervisor; Electrical/Electronics Engineer; Industrial Engineer; Mechanical Engineer. **Educational backgrounds include:** Engineering; Food Science. **Benefits:** Dental Insurance; Disability Coverage; Employee Discounts; Life Insurance; Medical Insurance; Pension Plan; Savings Plan; Tuition Assistance. **Corporate headquarters location:** Plano TX. **Parent company:** PepsiCo. **Operations at this facility include:** Manufacturing. **Listed on:** New York Stock Exchange.

GALLO SALAME
2411 Baumann Avenue, San Lorenzo CA 94580. 510/276-1300. **Contact:** Personnel. **Description:** Manufactures and distributes sausage and sausage products. **Corporate headquarters location:** This Location.

GALLO SALES COMPANY
440 Forbes Boulevard, South San Francisco CA 94080. 415/794-6000. **Contact:** Director of Training and Recruitment. **Description:** Produces and markets premium wines and brandy.

GENERAL MILLS, INC.
7041 Koll Center Parkway, Pleasanton CA 94566-3128. 510/426-8005. **Contact:** Human Resources. **Description:** Produces and markets consumer foods. Food products include Cheerios, Wheaties, and Total cereals; Betty Crocker desserts, frostings, and mixes; Pop Secret microwave popcorn; Gorton's frozen seafood; Yoplait yogurt; Bisquick pancake mix; and Gold Medal flour. General Mills is also engaged in the full-service dinnerhouse restaurant business, operating over 1,000 company-owned Red Lobster and Olive Garden restaurants in North America. Founded in 1928. **NOTE:** Send resumes to: Human Resources, 500 North State College Boulevard, Orange CA 92668.

GILROY FOODS INC.
P.O. Box 1088, Gilroy CA 95021-1088. 408/847-1414. **Contact:** Personnel. **Description:** A dehydrator of vegetable products. **Common positions include:** Accountant/Auditor; Agricultural Scientist; Biological Scientist/Biochemist; Buyer; Chemical Engineer; Chemist; Computer Programmer; Department Manager; Draftsperson; Electrical/Electronics Engineer; Food Scientist/Technologist; Human Resources Specialist; Industrial Engineer; Management Trainee; Manufacturer's/Wholesaler's Sales Rep.; Marketing Specialist; Mechanical Engineer; Operations/Production Manager; Quality Control Supervisor. **Educational backgrounds include:** Accounting; Biology; Business Administration; Chemistry; Computer Science; Engineering; Food Science; Manufacturing Management; Operations. **Benefits:** 401(k); Dental Insurance; Disability Coverage; Employee Discounts; Life Insurance; Medical Insurance; Pension Plan; Profit Sharing; Stock Option; Tuition Assistance. **Corporate headquarters location:** Hunt Valley MD. **Parent company:** McCormick & Company, Inc. (Baltimore MD). **Operations at this facility include:** Divisional Headquarters.

GOLDEN GRAIN
4576 Willow Road, Pleasanton CA 94588-2708. 510/734-8800. **Contact:** Human Resources. **Description:** Producers of Rice-a-Roni as well as all types of macaroni products.

GRANNY GOOSE FOODS INC.
930 98th Avenue, Oakland CA 94603. 510/635-5400. **Contact:** Personnel. **Description:** Manufactures and distributes potato chips and other snack specialty foods.

H.J. HEINZ COMPANY
P.O. Box 57, Stockton CA 95201-3057. 209/948-2782. **Contact:** Human Resources. **Description:** H.J. Heinz Company is a worldwide producer of food products including ketchup, sauces, condiments, baby food, seafood, pet food, frozen potato products, frozen meats, beverages, and a wide selection of other processed consumables. These foods are marketed under brand names including Heinz, Steak-Umm, and Ore-Ida. The

company also operates and sells franchise licenses for Weight Watchers International weight control classes and related programs.

H.J. HEINZ COMPANY
P.O. Box 57, Tracy CA 95378. 209/832-4241. **Contact:** Human Resources. **Description:** H.J. Heinz Company is a worldwide producer of food products including ketchup, sauces, condiments, baby food, seafood, pet food, frozen potato products, frozen meats, beverages, and a wide selection of other processed consumables. These foods are marketed under brand names including Heinz, Steak-Umm, and Ore-Ida. The company also operates and sells franchise licenses for Weight Watchers International weight control classes and related programs.

H.J. HEINZ COMPANY
P.O. Box 5150, San Ramon CA 94583. 510/830-0577. **Contact:** Human Resources. **Description:** H.J. Heinz is a worldwide producer of food products including ketchup, sauces, condiments, baby food, seafood, pet food, frozen potato products, frozen meats, beverages, and a wide selection of other processed consumables. These foods are marketed under brand names including Heinz, Steak-Umm, and Ore-Ida. The company also operates and sells franchise licenses for Weight Watchers International weight control classes and related programs.

HUNT-WESSON INC.
1111 East Covell Boulevard, Davis CA 95616-1209. 916/753-4071. **Contact:** Human Resources. **Description:** Hunt-Wesson is an integrated food, vegetable, and convenience food manufacturer, and is one of the nation's largest producers of tomato-based products. **Corporate headquarters location:** Fullerton CA. **Parent company:** ConAgra, Inc.

KELLOGG COMPANY
P.O. Box 5191, San Jose CA 95150. 408/295-8656. **Contact:** Human Resources. **Description:** Founded in 1906. Kellogg, a diversified international company, specializes in the manufacturing and marketing of ready-to-eat cereals, as well as frozen waffles, toaster pastries, cereal bars, frozen pies, and other convenience foods. Kellogg products are manufactured in 18 countries in North America, Europe, Asia-Pacific, and Latin America, and are distributed in more than 150 countries. This location is also the headquarters of the Kellogg USA Convenience Foods Division, formed in 1993. This division's production facilities in California, Georgia, New Jersey, Pennsylvania, and Tennessee manufacture products such as Kellogg's Pop-Tarts toaster pastries, Eggo waffles, Kellogg's Nutri-Grain bars, Kellogg's Low Fat Granola bars, Kellogg's Croutettes stuffing mix, and Kellogg's Corn Flake Crumbs. **Corporate headquarters location:** Battle Creek MI. **Other U.S. locations:** Ontario, Canada; San Leandro CA; Atlanta GA; Omaha NE; Blue Anchor NJ; Lancaster PA; Muncy PA; Pottstown PA; Memphis TN; Rossville TN. **Listed on:** New York Stock Exchange.

KRAFT GENERAL FOODS CORPORATION
P.O. Box 5500, San Leandro CA 94577. 510/639-5000. **Contact:** Dick Sewell, Human Resources Manager. **Description:** Engaged in the production of such goods as coffee, Jell-O, Log Cabin Syrup, and Tang. The company also produces packaged grocery products nationally.

McCORMICK & COMPANY
P.O. Box 81311, Salinas CA 93912-1311. 408/758-2411. **Contact:** David Miller, Manager of Human Relations. **Description:** A diversified specialty food company

engaged in the manufacturing and marketing of seasonings and flavoring products to the food industry. Products are sold in 84 countries and processed at more than 40 facilities throughout the world. Principal products include spices, herbs, seeds, vegetable products, seasoning blends, food seasoning mixes, and specialty frozen foods. **Common positions include:** Accountant/Auditor; Agricultural Engineer; Industrial Engineer. **Educational backgrounds include:** Business Administration; Engineering. **Benefits:** Dental Insurance; Disability Coverage; Employee Discounts; Life Insurance; Medical Insurance; Pension Plan; Profit Sharing; Savings Plan; Tuition Assistance. **Corporate headquarters location:** Hunt Valley MD. **Operations at this facility include:** Manufacturing. **Listed on:** NASDAQ.

MOTHER'S COOKIES
810 81st Avenue, Oakland CA 94621. 510/569-2323. **Contact:** Barbara Granat, Human Resources Manager. **Description:** Develops, manufactures, imports, and markets cookies in the western United States. Primary customers are wholesale food distributors and retail food markets. **Common positions include:** Accountant/Auditor; Blue-Collar Worker Supervisor; Branch Manager; Buyer; Computer Programmer; Credit Manager; Customer Service Representative; Department Manager; Draftsperson; Food Scientist/ Technologist; Human Resources Specialist; Manufacturer's/Wholesaler's Sales Rep.; Marketing Specialist; Mechanical Engineer; Operations/Production Manager; Quality Control Supervisor; Systems Analyst. **Educational backgrounds include:** Accounting; Business Administration; Computer Science; Engineering; Marketing. **Benefits:** 401(k); Dental Insurance; Disability Coverage; Employee Discounts; Life Insurance; Medical Insurance; Pension Plan; Savings Plan; Tuition Assistance. **Corporate headquarters location:** This Location.

NESTLE BEVERAGE COMPANY
P.O. Box 7449, San Francisco CA 94120. 415/546-4600. **Fax:** 415/543-6864. **Contact:** Recruiter, Employee Relations. **Description:** An international manufacturer of beverage products. Formerly Hills Bros., the Nestle Company was founded in 1878. **Common positions include:** Accountant/Auditor; Administrative Services Manager; Budget Analyst; Buyer; Chemical Engineer; Claim Representative; Clerical Supervisor; Computer Programmer; Computer Systems Analyst; Credit Manager; Customer Service Representative; Designer; Food Scientist/Technologist; General Manager; Management Analyst/Consultant; Management Trainee; Manufacturer's/Wholesaler's Sales Rep.; Operations/Production Manager; Public Relations Specialist; Purchasing Agent and Manager; Quality Control Supervisor; Services Sales Representative; Transportation/Traffic Specialist; Wholesale and Retail Buyer. **Benefits:** 401(k); Daycare Assistance; Dental Insurance; Disability Coverage; Employee Discounts; Life Insurance; Medical Insurance; Pension Plan; Savings Plan; Tuition Assistance. **Parent company:** Nestle U.S.A.; Nestle S.A. **Listed on:** European Bourse. **Number of employees at this location:** 550.

PEPSI-COLA BOTTLING COMPANY
7550 Reese Road, Sacramento CA 95828. 916/423-1000. **Contact:** Human Resources. **Description:** A bottling facility for the international soft drink company. PepsiCo, Inc. operates on a worldwide basis within three industry segments: beverages, snack foods, and restaurants. The beverage segment primarily markets its brands worldwide and manufactures concentrates for its brands for sale to franchised bottlers worldwide. The segment also operates bottling plants and distribution facilities of its own located in the U.S. and key international markets and distributes ready-to-drink Lipton tea products under a joint venture agreement. In addition, under separate distribution and joint-

venture agreements, the segment distributes certain previously existing, as well as jointly-developed, Ocean Spray juice products.

THE QUAKER OATS COMPANY
P.O. Box 2205, Oakland CA 94621. 510/261-5800. **Contact:** Cassandra Nevins, Personnel. **Description:** A manufacturing facility producing beverages and consumer food products. **NOTE:** Entry-level positions are available. **Common positions include:** Production Manager. **Educational backgrounds include:** Food Science; Liberal Arts. **Benefits:** 401(k); Daycare Assistance; Dental Insurance; Disability Coverage; Life Insurance; Mass Transit Available; Medical Insurance; Pension Plan; Profit Sharing; Savings Plan; Tuition Assistance. **Special Programs:** Internships. **Corporate headquarters location:** Chicago IL. **Other U.S. locations:** Nationwide. **Operations at this facility include:** Manufacturing. **Number of employees at this location:** 200.

RED WING COMPANY, INC.
NATIONAL PRESERVE COMPANY
P.O. Box 49009, San Jose CA 95161-9009. 408/254-5226. **Contact:** Helen Wesson, Human Resources Manager. **Description:** Manufactures jams, jellies, preserves, tomato products, and peanut butter products.

RUIZ FOOD PRODUCTS, INC.
P.O. Box 37, Dinuba CA 93618. 209/591-5510. **Contact:** Juana Lacy, Human Resources Manager. **Description:** Produces Mexican frozen foods that are distributed throughout the U.S., Mexico, and Canada. **Common positions include:** Accountant/Auditor; Blue-Collar Worker Supervisor; Budget Analyst; Buyer; Claim Representative; Clerical Supervisor; Computer Programmer; Computer Systems Analyst; Education Administrator; Financial Analyst; Food Scientist/Technologist; Human Resources Specialist; Industrial Engineer; Industrial Production Manager; Public Relations Specialist; Purchasing Agent and Manager; Quality Control Supervisor; Teacher; Transportation/Traffic Specialist. **Educational backgrounds include:** Accounting; Business Administration; Computer Science; Finance; Marketing. **Benefits:** Dental Insurance; Life Insurance; Medical Insurance; Pension Plan. **Corporate headquarters location:** This Location. **Operations at this facility include:** Administration; Divisional Headquarters; Manufacturing; Regional Headquarters; Research and Development; Sales; Service. **Listed on:** Privately held. **Number of employees at this location:** 1,000.

SEE'S CANDY SHOPS INC.
210 El Camino Real, South San Francisco CA 94080. 415/583-7307. **Contact:** Human Resources. **Description:** Corporate offices of the candy manufacturer.

SHAKLEE CORPORATION
444 Market Street, San Francisco CA 94111. 415/954-3000. **Contact:** Emily Williams, Personnel Manager. **Description:** Engaged in the manufacture and marketing of a number of proprietary nutritional products, including vitamins, minerals, protein powders, and other nutritional food products. The company also markets a wide variety of household products. **Common positions include:** Accountant/Auditor; Buyer; Chemical Engineer; Chemist; Customer Service Representative. **Educational backgrounds include:** Chemistry; Finance; Marketing. **Benefits:** 401(k); Dental Insurance; Disability Coverage; Employee Discounts; Life Insurance; Medical Insurance; Pension Plan; Profit Sharing; Tuition Assistance. **Corporate headquarters location:** This Location. **Parent company:** Yamanuchi. **Listed on:** Privately held.

SHASTA BEVERAGES INC.
BEVPAK MANUFACTURING
P.O. Box 4617, Hayward CA 94540. 510/783-3200. **Contact:** Human Resources Director. **Description:** A producer of a variety of regular and diet soft drinks. **Common positions include:** Accountant/Auditor; Blue-Collar Worker Supervisor; Computer Programmer; Customer Service Representative; Financial Analyst; Manufacturer's/Wholesaler's Sales Rep.; Secretary; Systems Analyst. **Educational backgrounds include:** Business Administration; Finance. **Special Programs:** Internships. **Corporate headquarters location:** This Location. **Parent company:** National Beverage.

SPRECKELS SUGAR COMPANY
4256 Hacienda Drive, P.O. Box 8025, Pleasanton CA 94588-8625. 510/463-3400. **Contact:** Mel Voos, Personnel Supervisor. **Description:** A sugar processing firm. **Corporate headquarters location:** This Location.

SPRECKELS SUGAR COMPANY
P.O. Box 1287, Manteca CA 95336. 209/823-3121. **Contact:** Human Resources. **Description:** A sugar processing firm. **Corporate headquarters location:** Pleasanton CA.

SUN GARDEN PACKING COMPANY
P.O. Box 6180, San Jose CA 95150-6180. 408/283-8200. **Contact:** Human Resources. **Description:** A food products company.

SUN SEEDS, LTD., L.P.
P.O. Box 2078, Morgan Hill CA 95038. 408/776-1111. **Contact:** Human Resources. **Description:** A producer of seeds and related products for the agricultural industry. **Number of employees at this location:** 125.

SUN-DIAMOND GROWERS OF CALIFORNIA
P.O. Box 9024, Pleasanton CA 94566. 510/463-8200. **Contact:** Human Resources. **Description:** Produces and packages nationally-distributed food products such as walnuts, prunes, dried fruit, and other fruit and nut products.

SUN-MAID GROWERS OF CALIFORNIA
13525 South Bethel Avenue, Kingsburg CA 93631. 209/896-8000. **Contact:** Personnel Department. **Description:** Processes and distributes raisins, apricots, prunes, figs, and related by-products.

SUPERIOR COFFEE AND FOODS
20389 Corsair Boulevard, Hayward CA 94545. 510/785-8600. **Contact:** Jim Frisby, General Manager. **Description:** Since 1908, Superior Coffee and Foods has been a roaster of coffee for foodservice, specialty coffee, espresso, vending, convenience store, and office coffees. The company is a manufacturer of salad dressings and sauces, and a distributor of spices, tea, specialty tea, syrups, hot chocolate, cappuccino, and vending products. Superior Coffee and Foods also offers full equipment-service programs. **NOTE:** Entry-level positions are available. **Common positions include:** Accountant/Auditor; Administrative Services Manager; Branch Manager; Buyer; Clerical Supervisor; Credit Manager; Customer Service Representative; Financial Analyst; Food Scientist/Technologist; General Manager; Human Resources Specialist; Management Trainee; Manufacturer's/Wholesaler's Sales Rep.; Public Relations Specialist; Purchasing Agent and Manager; Quality Control Supervisor; Services Sales Representative;

Telecommunications Manager; Typist/Word Processor. **Educational backgrounds include:** Accounting; Business Administration; Communications; Liberal Arts; Marketing. **Benefits:** 401(k); Dental Insurance; Disability Coverage; Employee Discounts; Life Insurance; Medical Insurance; Pension Plan; Savings Plan; Tuition Assistance. **Special Programs:** Internships. **Corporate headquarters location:** Bensenville IL. **Other U.S. locations:** Nationwide. **Parent company:** Sara Lee. **Operations at this facility include:** Administration; Divisional Headquarters; Manufacturing; Research and Development; Sales; Service. **Listed on:** New York Stock Exchange. **Number of employees at this location:** 140. **Number of employees worldwide:** 1,300.

TRI-VALLEY GROWERS
P.O. Box 7114, San Francisco CA 94120-7114. 415/837-4000. **Contact:** Manager of Employee Relations. **Description:** Administrative offices for a large fruit processor and cannery. **Common positions include:** Accountant/Auditor; Blue-Collar Worker Supervisor; Computer Programmer; Credit Manager; Customer Service Representative; Department Manager; Electrical/Electronics Engineer; Financial Analyst; Food Scientist/Technologist; General Manager; Human Resources Specialist; Industrial Engineer; Management Trainee; Marketing Specialist; Mechanical Engineer; Operations/Production Manager; Purchasing Agent and Manager; Quality Control Supervisor; Systems Analyst. **Educational backgrounds include:** Accounting; Agricultural Science; Business Administration; Computer Science; Engineering; Finance; Food Science; Liberal Arts. **Benefits:** Dental Insurance; Disability Coverage; Employee Discounts; Life Insurance; Medical Insurance; Pension Plan; Profit Sharing; Savings Plan; Tuition Assistance. **Corporate headquarters location:** Modesto CA.

TRI-VALLEY GROWERS
3200 East Eight Mile Road, Stockton CA 95212-9414. 209/931-8000. **Contact:** Human Resources. **Description:** A large fruit processing and canning company.

WM. WRIGLEY JR. COMPANY
2801 Mission Street, Santa Cruz CA 95060. 408/423-8800. **Contact:** Joe Torres, Personnel Manager. **Description:** Manufactures and markets chewing gums under several name brands including Wrigley's Spearmint and Hubba Bubba.

***Note:** Because addresses and telephone numbers of smaller companies can change rapidly, we recommend you call each company to verify the information below before inquiring about job opportunities. Mass mailings are not recommended.*

Additional small employers:

VEGETABLES AND MELONS

Lindemann Produce Inc.
825 G St, Los Banos CA 93635-3734. 702/323-2442.

Fowler Packing Co. Inc.
8570 S Cedar Ave, Fresno CA 93725-9747. 209/834-5911.

Merrill Farms Inc.
PO Box 659, Salinas CA 93902-0659. 408/424-7365.

Sea Mist Farms
118 Molera Rd, Castroville CA 95012. 408/633-3211.

CA Artichoke & Vegetable Growers Corp.
PO Box 1247, Castroville CA 95012-1247. 408/633-2144.

Blue Anchor Inc.
Walnt Grove-Thornton Rd, Walnut Grove CA 95690. 916/776-1708.

Naumes Inc.
7216 Dantoni Rd, Marysville CA 95901. 916/743-2052.

PR Farms Inc.
2917 East Shepherd Avenue, Clovis CA 93611-9152. 209/299-7270.

FLORICULTURE AND NURSERY PRODUCTS

Ferry-Morse Seed Company
PO Box 4938, Modesto CA 95352-4938. 209/579-7333.

Harris Moran Seed Company Inc.
100 Breen Rd, San Juan Batista CA 95045-9522. 408/623-4323.

CROP FARMS

Ruann Dairy
7285 W Davis Ave, Riverdale CA 93656-9735. 209/867-4457.

Cecchini & Cecchini Incorporated
Highway 4, Byron CA 94514. 510/634-4400.

John Kautz Farms
5920 East Live Oak Road, Lodi CA 95240. 209/931-0782.

Bouldin Farming Company
20101 State Highway 12, Isleton CA 95641-9602. 916/777-6091.

Alkop Farms
PO Box 1560, Chico CA 95927-1560. 916/891-6881.

BEEF

Wolfsen Inc.
PO Box 311, Los Banos CA 93635-0311. 209/827-7700.

GENERAL FARMS

Yosuba Farms Incorporated
Everglade Road, Robbins CA 95676. 916/738-4462.

CROP SERVICES

Fresh World
1188 Padre Drive, Salinas CA 93901-2253. 408/755-1721.

Youngstown Grape Distributing Inc.
1750 16th St, Reedley CA 93654-3439. 209/638-2271.

Frazier Nut Farms Inc.
10830 Yosemite Blvd, Waterford CA 95386-9637. 209/522-1406.

Mount Konocti Growers
PO Box 365, Kelseyville CA 95451-0365. 707/279-4213.

ANIMAL SPECIALTY SERVICES

Golden Genes Inc.
3899 W Davis Ave, Riverdale CA 93656-9417. 209/867-3545.

American Breeders Service
9311 Trenary Court, Elk Grove CA 95624. 916/686-1777.

FARM MANAGEMENT AND LABOR SERVICES

Fresh West Harvesting
29701 River Road, Gonzales CA 93926. 408/675-0202.

Terranova Ranch Incorporated
27450 Road 19, Chowchilla CA 93610. 209/665-2441.

De Benedetto Agriculture
26393 Road 22 1/2, Chowchilla CA 93610. 209/665-1712.

Met West Agribusiness
PO Box 509, Del Rey CA 93616-0509. 209/445-1574.

Braden Farms
PO Box 1022, Hughson CA 95326-1022. 209/883-4061.

MEAT AND POULTRY PROCESSING

Beef Packers Inc.
PO Box 12503, Fresno CA 93778-2503. 209/268-5586.

Alpine Packing Co.
9900 Lower Sacramento Rd, Stockton CA 95210-3912. 209/477-2691.

Superior Packing
PO Box 940, Dixon CA 95620-0940. 916/678-3091.

Gainers
5777 Madison Ave, Sacramento CA 95841-3315. 916/348-1633.

Columbus Salame
465 Cabot Rd, South San Francisco CA 94080-4819. 415/583-9333.

DAIRY PRODUCTS

Danish Creamery Assoc.
755 F St, Fresno CA 93706-3416. 209/233-5154.

Sorrento Cheese Co.
1451 Sunny Court, San Jose CA 95116. 408/288-5151.

Hilmar Cheese Co. Inc.
9001 N Lander St, Hilmar CA 95324. 209/667-6076.

Suprema Specialties West
14253 S Airport Way, Manteca CA 95336-8641.

San Joaquin Valley Dairymens
PO Box 2198, Los Banos CA 93635-2198. 209/826-4901.

Challenge Dairy Products
11875 Dublin Blvd Ste B 200, Dublin CA 94568-2842. 510/828-6160.

Safeway Inc.
2000 Adams Ave, San Leandro CA 94577-1008. 510/613-2900.

Berkeley Farms Inc.
PO Box 8465, Emeryville CA 94662-0465. 510/420-5600.

California Cooperative
PO Box 871, Petaluma CA 94953-0871. 707/763-1931.

Foster Farms Dairy
1707 McHenry Ave, Modesto CA 95350-4371. 209/576-3400.

PRESERVED FRUITS AND VEGETABLES

Fruitful Valley Sun
2063 E El Monte Way, Dinuba CA 93618-9352. 209/591-7044.

Beech-Nut Nutrition Corp.
1661 Senter Rd, San Jose CA 95112-2522. 408/293-8330.

Pacific Coast Producers
929 S Stockton St, Lodi CA 95240-4850. 209/367-7239.

Pacific Coast Producers
101 Woodland Ave, Woodland CA 95695-2761. 916/666-0056.

Ehmann Olive Company
1800 Idora St, Oroville CA 95966-6767. 916/533-3303.

The JM Smucker Co.
PO Box 81447, Salinas CA 93912-1447. 408/424-2761.

Odwalla Inc.
120 Stone Pine Road, Half Moon Bay CA 94019. 415/726-1888.

Vandenbergh Foods Co.
1400 Waterloo Rd, Stockton CA 95205-3743. 209/466-9580.

Quality Assured Packing Inc.
PO Box 55308, Stockton CA 95205-8808. 209/931-6700.

Atwater Canning Co. Inc.
901 Packers St, Atwater CA 95301-4614. 209/358-5616.

Escalon Packers Inc.
1905 McHenry Ave, Escalon CA 95320-9601. 209/838-7341.

Manzana Products Co. Inc.
9141 Green Valley Rd, Sebastopol CA 95472-2245. 707/823-5313.

Helnke's Inc.
PO Box 369, Chico CA 95927-0369. 916/891-1517.

Champion Raisin International
PO Box 219, Fowler CA 93625-0219. 209/834-5981.

San-Francisco Quality Products Co.
535 Railroad Ave, South San Francisco CA 94080-3450. 415/871-2446.

Horn Of Plenty
3851 Charter Park Dr Ste H, San Jose CA 95136-1384. 408/274-7443.

Rogers Foods
151 S Walnut Rd, Turlock CA 95380-5127. 209/667-2777.

Pacific Choice Brands Inc.
4667 E Date Ave, Fresno CA 93725-2101. 209/237-5583.

Hollar Pepper Company Inc.
PO Box 487, Stockton CA 95201-0487. 209/465-0842.

Escalon Frozen Foods
19901 McHenry Ave, Escalon CA 95320-9614. 209/838-3564.

Eckert Cold Storage
757 Moffat Blvd, Manteca CA 95336-5819. 209/823-3181.

Wawona Frozen Foods
100 W Alluvial Ave, Clovis CA 93611-9176. 209/299-2901.

Rich Products Corporation
320 O St, Fresno CA 93721-3086. 209/486-7380.

Nancy's Specialty Foods
6500 Overlake Pl, Newark CA 94560-1084. 510/494-1100.

GRAIN MILL PRODUCTS

Pacific International Rice Mills Inc.
PO Box 652, Woodland CA 95776-0652. 916/666-1691.

Pacific Rice Products Inc.
PO Box 2060, Woodland CA 95776-2060. 916/662-5056.

Comet Rice Maxwell
PO Box 398, Maxwell CA 95955-0398. 916/438-2265.

PREPARED FEEDS AND INGREDIENTS FOR ANIMALS

Nutrena Feed Division
PO Box 369, Stockton CA 95201-3069. 209/982-4632.

Nulaid Foods Inc.
200 W 5th St, Ripon CA 95366-2766. 209/599-2121.

BAKERY PRODUCTS

Rainbo Bakeries Of San Joaquin
PO Box 832, Fresno CA 93712-0832. 209/233-5191.

Flowers Baking Company
PO Box 11458, Fresno CA 93773-1458. 209/485-0671.

Rolling Pin Manufacturing
1511 Grandview Dr, South San Francisco CA 94080-4911. 415/952-7323.

Andre-Boudin Bakeries Inc.
132 Hawthorne St, San Francisco CA 94107-1308. 415/882-1849.

Parisian Bakeries
1995 Evans Ave, San Francisco CA 94124-1105. 415/641-1000.

SUGAR AND CONFECTIONERY PRODUCTS

Liquid Sugars Inc.
PO Box 96, Oakland CA 94604-0096. 510/420-7100.

Holly Sugar Corporation
PO Box 60, Tracy CA 95378-0060. 209/835-3210.

Delta Sugar Corporation
35265 Willow Ave, Clarksburg CA 95612. 916/665-1840.

Herman Goelitz Candy Co. Inc.
2400 N Watney Way, Fairfield CA 94533-6722. 707/428-2800.

Guittard Chocolate Company
10 Guittard Rd, Burlingame CA 94010-2203. 415/697-4427.

Blommer Chocolates
1515 Pacific St, Union City CA 94587. 510/471-4300.

BEVERAGES

Golden State Brewing Co.
333 California Dr, Burlingame CA 94010-4114. 415/344-6050.

Sterling Vineyards
1111 Dunaweal Ln, Calistoga CA 94515-9799. 707/942-3300.

Wente Bros
5565 Tesla Rd, Livermore CA 94550-9149. 510/447-3603.

Domaine Chandon
1 California Drive, Yountville CA 94599. 707/944-8844.

HSE Daniels Inc. Golden Gate
12 Harbor Drive, Novato CA 94945-3507. 415/892-6949.

Mirassou Vineyards
3000 Aborn Road, San Jose CA 95135-1799. 408/274-4000.

Robert Mondavi Winery
PO Box 1260, Woodbridge CA 95258-1260. 209/369-5861.

Bronco Wine
6342 Bystrum Road, Ceres CA 95307-9513. 209/538-3131.

Heublein Wine Inc.
21801 State Highway 120, Escalon CA 95320-9771. 209/838-3575.

Heublein Inc.
151 Commonwealth Dr, Menlo Park CA 94025-1105. 415/324-2751.

Sebastiani Vineyards Inc.
PO Box A, Deer Park CA 94576-0501. 707/938-5532.

Vine Cliff Winery
7400 Silverado Trail, Napa CA 94558-9425. 707/944-1364.

Opus One
PO Box 6, Oakville CA 94562-0006. 707/944-9442.

E&J Gallo Winery
PO Box 1081, Fresno CA 93714-1081. 209/453-2400.

E&J Gallo Winery
18000 River Rd, Livingston CA 95334. 209/394-6219.

E&J Gallo Winery
5953 Weir Ave, Livingston CA 95334-9509. 209/394-6271.

E&J Gallo Winery
5511 Griffith Ave, Livingston CA 95334-9513. 209/394-6281.

Kendall Jackson Distribution Center
981 Airway Ct, Santa Rosa CA 95403-2049. 707/579-3040.

The Wine Alliance
PO Box 948, Healdsburg CA 95448-0948. 707/433-8268.

Black Mountain Spring Water
PO Box 3010, San Carlos CA 94070-1310. 415/595-3800.

7-Up Bottling Company
1590 Yosemite Ave, San Francisco CA 94124-3239. 415/822-4700.

Coca Cola Bottling Co.
14655 Wicks Blvd, San Leandro CA 94577-6715. 510/667-6300.

COFFEE

Premium Food Imports Inc.
44777 S Grimmer Blvd Ste G, Fremont CA 94538-7604. 510/490-3485.

CHIPS AND SNACKS

Cornnuts Inc.
1320 Harbor Bay Parkway Suite 250 , Alameda CA 94502-6556. 510/523-3949.

PASTA

Hershey Pasta Group
PO Box 12146, Fresno CA 93776-2146. 209/485-8110.

Diana's Noodle Corporation
PO Box 7555, San Mateo CA 94403-7555. 415/378-5165.

FOOD PREPARATIONS

Folgers Coffee Co.
PO Box 2048, San Francisco CA 94126-2048. 415/875-1500.

Integrated Ingredients
1420 Harbor Bay Parkway Suite 210, Alameda CA 94502-7083. 510/748-6300.

FOOD WHOLESALE

Durkee Foods
2855 S East Avenue, Fresno CA 93725-1908. 209/486-1337.

Malt-O-Meal Co.
1143 Crane St # 203, Menlo Park CA 94025-4313. 415/322-7764.

Van Den Bergh Foods Co.
1484 Kifer Rd, Sunnyvale CA 94086-5306. 408/739-8800.

West Coast Distributing
23363 Thurston Ct, Hayward CA 94541-4569. 510/537-9940.

Raybern Quality Foods
311 West A Street, Hayward CA 94541-4838. 510/786-3900.

Food Service Cash & Carry
19367 Mission Blvd, Hayward CA 94541-1242. 510/481-1515.

Gourmet Specialties
21001 Cabot Blvd, Hayward CA 94545-1109. 510/887-7322.

Bromar
4256 Hacienda Drive, Pleasanton CA 94588-2719. 510/463-3450.

Fleming Co. Inc. Western Region
4457 Willow Rd, Pleasanton CA 94588-8554. 510/847-1940.

Cook Harms Le Baron Co.
5064 Franklin Dr, Pleasanton CA 94588-3354. 510/463-5600.

Yosemite Wholesale Inc.
2674 Vassar Ave, Merced CA 95340-9005. 209/384-1600.

Villa Mexican Food Distributors
903 Kansas Ave, Modesto CA 95351-1552. 209/521-8768.

Quality Products & Services
903 Kansas Ave, Modesto CA 95351-1552. 209/522-6681.

Market Wholesale Grocery
536 S Mariposa Rd, Modesto CA 95354-4124. 408/526-8511.

Superb Farms
PO Box 610, Turlock CA 95381-0610. 209/664-2222.

JFC International Inc.
545 Jefferson Blvd, Broderick CA 95605-2351. 916/373-9151.

La Provence
1735 Arden Way, Sacramento CA 95815-5001. 916/641-8709.

Bay Pacific Marketing
20955 Foothill Blvd, Hayward CA 94541-1511. 510/727-0600.

Pacific Sun Industries Inc.
710 Sandoval Way, Hayward CA 94544-7111. 510/489-7405.

Kelley-Clarke Inc.
6300 Dumbarton Cir, Fremont CA 94555-3644. 510/790-6300.

Select Foods Inc.
22885 Amador St, Hayward CA 94541-6207. 510/785-1000.

Mountain Peoples Warehouse
12745 Earhart Ave, Auburn CA 95602-9027. 916/889-9531.

Foster Farms
415 Kansas Ave, Modesto CA 95351-1515. 209/576-3470.

Foster Farms Dairy & Food Products
3380 W Ashlan Ave, Fresno CA 93722-4448. 209/224-3900.

Berkeley Farms
2065 Oakdale Ave, San Francisco CA 94124-2040. 415/821-5900.

Mid-Valley Dairy Inc.
PO Box 2898, Fairfield CA 94533-0289. 707/864-0502.

Two Count Holding Co.
37590 Sycamore Street, Newark CA 94560. 510/795-4100.

F&A Dairy California
691 Inyo, Newman CA 95360. 209/862-1732.

Gonzales Distributing
1104 Bristol Avenue, Stockton CA 95204. 209/465-8771.

Avoset Food Corporation
299 5th Ave, Gustine CA 95322-1202. 209/854-6461.

California Cooperative Creamery
2331 Tully Rd, Hughson CA 95326. 209/883-4461.

Race Street Fish and Poultry
PO Box 28385, San Jose CA 95159-8385. 408/294-6161.

Setton Pistachio Co. Inc.
2901 Falcon Dr, Madera CA 93637-9287. 209/673-4949.

Poppy Creek Farms
2910 Falcon Dr, Madera CA 93637-9287. 209/661-6176.

M-T Trading Co. Inc.
24431 Avenue 14, Madera CA 93637-9276. 209/661-1556.

Villa DiNoce Company
2701 N Alpine Rd, Stockton CA 95215-9581. 209/931-2755.

Del Mar Seafoods
PO Box 5969, Salinas CA 93915-5969. 408/753-5100.

California Shellfish Co.
2601 5th St, Sacramento CA 95818-2802. 916/446-0251.

Fresno Meat Co.
3115 S Fig Ave, Fresno CA 93706-5647. 209/265-4380.

Facciola Meat Company
941 E Charleston Rd, Palo Alto CA 94303-4998. 415/494-7200.

Weber Quality Meats
990 Carden St, San Leandro CA 94577-1164. 510/635-9892.

Young's Meat & Provisions
2981 Mead Ave, Santa Clara CA 95051-0818. 408/987-2788.

Durham Meat Company
160 Sunol St, San Jose CA 95126-3064. 408/291-3600.

Food Service of America Inc.
2155 E Muscat Ave, Fresno CA 93725-2326. 209/497-7000.

Super Value Stores Inc.
4930 E Yale Avenue, Fresno CA 93727-1517. 209/255-1886.

Bob's Produce
2095 Jerrold Ave, San Francisco CA 94124-1628. 415/695-1155.

Bill's Finest Produce Co.
1969 Jerrold Ave, San Francisco CA 94124-1602. 415/647-5500.

Cooks Co.
1942 Jerrold Ave, San Francisco CA 94124-1603. 415/824-2800.

Cal-Bay Produce
1908 Innes Ave, San Francisco CA 94124-1623. 415/824-3735.

City Fruit & Produce Co.
1985 Jerrold Ave, San Francisco CA 94124-1602. 415/647-1213.

RP Roberti & Co.
1600 Weaverly Dr, Petaluma CA 94954-3730. 707/778-2347.

Royal Foods Co. Inc.
1885 Las Plumas Ave, San Jose CA 95133-1706. 408/729-4200.

Kings Crown Packing
11611 Clifton Court Rd, Stockton CA 95206-9664. 209/466-9146.

Maui Pineapple
5440 E Harney Lane, Lodi CA 95240-6903. 209/367-1780.

DiMare Bros.
Fresno & N St, Newman CA 95360. 209/862-2872.

JC Produce Inc.
PO Box 1027, W Sacramento CA 95691-1027. 916/372-4050.

General Produce
1330 North B St, Sacramento CA 95814-0605. 916/441-6431.

Just Desserts Inc.
1970 Carroll Ave, San Francisco CA 94124-2511. 415/330-3600.

Linda's Tortillas
5542 Monterey Hwy #306, San Jose CA 95138-1529. 408/286-8585.

Pacific Tomato Growers
425 Sperry Ave, Patterson CA 95363. 209/892-2551.

Pasta Fresh
PO Box 2301, Benicia CA 94510-5301. 707/747-1800.

Pacific International Rice Mills Inc.
845 Kentucky Ave, Woodland CA 95695-2744. 916/666-1691.

Odwalla Juices
1900 E Davis Drive, Dinuba CA 93618-9372. 209/591-4089.

Odwalla Juices
182 Beacon St, South San Francisco CA 94080-6913. 415/952-1562.

Marin Organic Juice Company
6 Bank St #A, San Anselmo CA 94960-2505. 415/459-1339.

Martinelli's & Co.
230 Center St, Watsonville CA 95076-4707. 408/761-4570.

Joule Beverage Inc.
360 Industrial Way, Benicia CA 94510. 707/747-1090.

Champion Nutrition Inc.
2615 Stanwell Dr, Concord CA 94520-4814. 510/689-1790.

Country Farm Food Co.
1900 Railroad Dr, Sacramento CA 95815-3514. 916/564-6020.

Kilpatrick's Bakeries Inc.
629 Lindaro St, San Rafael CA 94901-3935. 415/454-7576.

Kilpatrick's Bakeries Inc.
1801 Somersville Rd, Antioch CA 94509-1354. 510/754-2535.

Colombo Baking Co.
42000 Boyce Rd, Fremont CA 94538-3111. 510/651-1992.

Alvarado Street Bakery & Nutritional Foods
500 Martin Ave, Rohnert Park CA 94928-2047. 707/585-3293.

Entenmann's
2475 Fruitridge Rd, Sacramento CA 95822-2243. 916/731-7138.

First Colony Coffee & Tea
8788 Elk Grove Blvd, Elk Grove CA 95624-1766. 916/686-8140.

Boyd Coffee Co.
4592 E 2nd St, Benicia CA 94510-1000. 707/747-6459.

Cargill Coffee
1640 School St, Moraga CA 94556-1123. 510/631-1000.

Hillside Coffee Co.
11480 Commercial Pkwy, Castroville CA 95012-3202. 408/633-6300.

Barbour Vineyard Enterprises
500 Tokay Lane, Saint Helena CA 94574. 707/963-0540.

Continental Grain Co.
1805 Harbor Ave, Stockton CA 95203. 209/466-4261.

ALCOHOL WHOLESALE

Markstein Distributing Co.
60 Main Avenue, Sacramento CA 95838. 916/920-9070.

Markstein Distributing Co.
101 Park Place, San Ramon CA 94583-1759. 510/831-1919.

Showermans Distributing
2265 Junction Ave, San Jose CA 95131. 408/432-9393.

Horizon Beverage Co.
1700 20th St, Oakland CA 94607-1639. 510/465-2212.

Heublein Inc.
815 Atlantic Ave # 100, Alameda CA 94501-2274. 510/521-1116.

Fetzer Vineyards Inc.
5801 Christie Ave, Emeryville CA 94608-1923. 510/653-7400.

Couch Distributing Co.
PO Box 50004, Watsonville CA 95077. 408/724-0649.

Glen Ellen Winery
1883 London Ranch Rd, Glen Ellen CA 95442-9728. 707/935-3000.

FARM SUPPLIES WHOLESALE

Harris Moran Seed Co.
4511 Willow Rd, Pleasanton CA 94588-2709. 510/416-8400.

Valent USA Corp.
PO Box 8025, Walnut Creek CA 94596-8025. 510/256-2700.

Simplot Co.
16777 Howland Rd, Lathrop CA 95330-9777. 209/858-2511.

Sun Valley Floral Farms
3100 Upper Bay Rd, Arcata CA 95521-9690. 707/826-8700.

Peto Seed Co. Inc.
37437 State Highway 16, Woodland CA 95695-9353. 916/666-0931.

TOBACCO AND TOBACCO PRODUCTS WHOLESALE

Core-Mark Distributors
31300 Medallion Dr, Hayward CA 94544-7902. 510/487-3000.

Core-Mark Distributors
3970 Pell Circle, Sacramento CA 95838. 916/927-0795.

For more information on career opportunities in the food, beverage, and agriculture industries:

Associations

AMERICAN ASSOCIATION OF CEREAL CHEMISTS (AACC)
3340 Pilot Knob Road, St. Paul MN 55121. 612/454-7250. World Wide Web address: http://www.scisoc.org/aacc. Contact: Marla Meyers. Dedicated to the dissemination of technical information and continuing education in cereal science.

AMERICAN FROZEN FOOD INSTITUTE
1764 Old Meadow Lane, Suite 350. McLean VA 22102. 703/821-0770. A national trade association representing the interests of the frozen food industry.

AMERICAN SOCIETY OF AGRICULTURAL ENGINEERS
2950 Niles Road, St. Joseph MI 49085. 616/429-0300. Contact: Julie Swim.

AMERICAN SOCIETY OF BREWING CHEMISTS ASSOCIATION
3340 Pilot Knob Road, St. Paul MN 55121. 612/454-7250. World Wide Web address: http://www.scisoc.org/asbc. Founded in 1934 to improve and bring uniformity to the brewing industry on a technical level.

CIES - THE FOOD BUSINESS FORUM
3800 Moore Plaza, Alexandria VA 22305. 703/549-4525. A global food business network. Membership is on a company basis. Members learn how to manage their businesses more effectively and gain access to information and contacts.

DAIRY AND FOOD INDUSTRIES SUPPLY ASSOCIATION (DFISA)
1451 Dolly Madison Boulevard, McLean VA 22101-3850. 703/761-2600. Contact: Dorothy Brady. A trade association whose members are suppliers to the food, dairy, liquid processing, and related industries.

MASTER BREWERS ASSOCIATION OF THE AMERICAS (MBAA)
2421 North Mayfair Road, Suite 310, Wauwatosa, WI 53226. 414/774-8558. Promotes, advances, improves, and protects the professional interests of brew and malt house production and technical personnel. Disseminates technical and practical information.

NATIONAL AGRICULTURAL CHEMICALS ASSOCIATION
1156 15th Street NW, Suite 900, Washington DC 20005. 202/296-1585. World Wide Web address: http://www.acpa.org.

NATIONAL BEER WHOLESALERS' ASSOCIATION
1100 South Washington Street, Alexandria VA 22314-4494. 703/683-4300. Fax: 703/683-8965. Contact: Karen Craig.

NATIONAL FOOD PROCESSORS ASSOCIATION
1401 New York Avenue NW, Suite 400, Washington DC 20005. 202/639-5900. Contact: Ned Endler.

NATIONAL SOFT DRINK ASSOCIATION
1101 16th Street NW, Washington DC 20036. 202/463-6732.

UNITED DAIRY INDUSTRY ASSOCIATION (UDIA)
10255 West Higgins Road, Suite 900, Rosemont IL 60018. 847/803-2000. A federation of state and regional dairy promotion organizations that develop and execute effective programs to increase consumer demand for U.S.-produced milk and dairy products.

Directories

FOOD ENGINEERING'S DIRECTORY OF U.S. FOOD PLANTS
Chilton Book Company, Chilton Way, Radnor PA 19089. 800/695-1214.

THOMAS FOOD INDUSTRY REGISTER
Thomas Publishing Company, Five Penn Plaza, New York NY 10001. 212/695-0500.

Magazines

BEVERAGE WORLD
Keller International Publishing Corporation. 150 Great Neck Road, Great Neck NY 11021. 516/829-9210.

FOOD PROCESSING
301 East Erie Street, Chicago IL 60611. 312/644-2020.

FROZEN FOOD AGE
Maclean Hunter Media, #4 Stamford Forum, Stamford CT 06901. 203/325-3500.

PREPARED FOODS
Gorman Publishing Company, 8750 West Bryn Mawr, Chicago IL 60631. 312/693-3200.

GOVERNMENT

While the federal government is still the nation's largest employer, the number of federal jobs is rapidly on the decline. Adding to this instability was the federal government's shutdown on more than one occasion while the President and Congress were in budgetary deadlock. The decrease in Department of Defense employment that started with the collapse of the Soviet Union has only increased due to federal deficits. The Defense Department is expected to reduce its workforce through attrition over the next decade.

Employment in other executive agencies is also expected to fall. Many workers are being offered buyouts, early retirement, and other incentives to leave the federal government. Demand remains strong, however, for nurses and engineers.

The outlook for state and local government workers is somewhat better. While opportunities vary from one state to the next, the Bureau of Labor Statistics forecasts a 16 percent job rise through 2005. Adding to the demand is the rising need for services. Since the early '80s, the government has decentralized and states have assumed more responsibility for providing services. Many policy decisions have been shifted to individual state governments, which are increasingly dealing with transportation problems, health care issues, energy policies, and poverty.

Even so, future job growth may be slowed by budgetary constraints. Local governments are struggling to meet the demand for services because tax revenues and federal aid are declining. Many states have cut their workforces to reduce spending and keep budgets balanced.

ANTIOCH, CITY OF
P.O. Box 5007, Antioch CA 94531-5007. 510/779-7020. **Contact:** Janet Sanchez, Personnel Technician. **Description:** Administrative offices for the city of Antioch. **Common positions include:** Accountant/Auditor; Attorney; Automotive Mechanic/Body Repairer; Blue-Collar Worker Supervisor; Civil Engineer; Clerical Supervisor; Computer Programmer; Construction and Building Inspector; Human Resources Specialist; Purchasing Agent and Manager. **Educational backgrounds include:** Accounting; Engineering; Finance. **Benefits:** Dental Insurance; Disability Coverage; Life Insurance; Medical Insurance; Tuition Assistance. **Corporate headquarters location:** This Location. **Operations at this facility include:** Administration. **Number of employees at this location:** 300.

CALIFORNIA HIGHWAY PATROL
1551 Benecia Road, Vallejo CA 94951. 707/648-4180. **Contact:** Officer Linda Sanders, Recruitment Unit. **Description:** A law enforcement agency. **Common positions include:** Computer Programmer. **Educational backgrounds include:** Liberal Arts. **Benefits:** 401(k); Dental Insurance; Disability Coverage; Life Insurance; Medical Insurance; Pension Plan. **Corporate headquarters location:** Sacramento CA. **Number of employees:** 6,000.

CLOVIS, CITY OF
1033 5th Street, Clovis CA 93612. 209/297-2320. **Contact:** Mark Rau, Personnel. **Description:** Administrative offices of the city of Clovis. **NOTE:** Please send resumes only for advertised positions. **Common positions include:** Accountant/Auditor; Automotive Mechanic/Body Repairer; Blue-Collar Worker Supervisor; Budget Analyst; Buyer; Civil Engineer; Clerical Supervisor; Computer Programmer; Computer Systems Analyst; Construction and Building Inspector; Customer Service Representative; Draftsperson; Electrician; Emergency Medical Technician; Financial Analyst; Geographer; Human Resources Specialist; Management Analyst/Consultant; Surveyor; Urban/Regional Planner; Water Transportation Specialist. **Educational backgrounds include:** Accounting; Business Administration; Engineering; Finance. **Benefits:** Dental Insurance; Disability Coverage; Employee Discounts; Life Insurance; Medical Insurance; Pension Plan; Tuition Assistance. **Special Programs:** Internships. **Corporate headquarters location:** This Location. **Operations at this facility include:** Administration. **Number of employees at this location:** 320.

CONTRA COSTA COUNTY GOVERNMENT
651 Pine Street, 3rd Floor, Martinez CA 94553. 510/646-4054. **Contact:** Personnel Department. **Description:** Offices of Contra Costa County. Services offered include health services, social services, law and justice, public works, building inspection, agricultural inspection, animal control, and fire protection. **Common positions include:** Accountant/Auditor; Administrator; Attorney; Blue-Collar Worker Supervisor; Buyer; Civil Engineer; Computer Programmer; Dietician/Nutritionist; Draftsperson; Human Resources Specialist; Management Trainee; Mental Health Worker; Police/Law Enforcement Officer; Purchasing Agent and Manager; Registered Nurse; Systems Analyst. **Educational backgrounds include:** Accounting; Business Administration; Computer Science; Engineering; Liberal Arts; Psychology; Social Work. **Benefits:** Credit Union; Dental Insurance; Disability Coverage; Life Insurance; Medical Insurance; Pension Plan; Tuition Assistance. **Corporate headquarters location:** This Location. **Operations at this facility include:** Administration; Service.

FRESNO COUNTY
2220 Tulare Street, 14th Floor, Fresno CA 93721. 209/488-3364. **Fax:** 209/262-4800. **Recorded Jobline:** 209/488-3017. **Contact:** Janet L. Coleman, Deputy Personnel Director. **Description:** Government offices of Fresno County. **Common positions include:** Accountant/Auditor; Adjuster; Administrative Services Manager; Agricultural Scientist; Architect; Attorney; Automotive Mechanic/Body Repairer; Blue-Collar Worker Supervisor; Budget Analyst; Buyer; Chemist; Civil Engineer; Clerical Supervisor; Clinical Lab Technician; Computer Programmer; Computer Systems Analyst; Construction and Building Inspector; Counselor; Dental Assistant/Dental Hygienist; Dentist; Dietician/Nutritionist; Draftsperson; EEG Technologist; EKG Technician; Electrician; Emergency Medical Technician; Financial Analyst; Health Services Manager; Human Resources Specialist; Human Service Worker; Librarian; Library Technician; Licensed Practical Nurse; Management Analyst/Consultant; Medical Records Technician; Nuclear Medicine Technologist; Occupational Therapist; Paralegal; Pharmacist; Physical Therapist; Physician; Property and Real Estate Manager; Psychologist; Purchasing Agent and Manager; Quality Control Supervisor; Radiologic Technologist; Recreational Therapist; Registered Nurse; Respiratory Therapist; Restaurant/Food Service Manager; Social Worker; Stationary Engineer; Structural Engineer; Surveyor; Urban/Regional Planner. **Educational backgrounds include:** Accounting; Business Administration; Communications; Computer Science; Economics; Engineering; Finance; Liberal Arts. **Benefits:** Credit Union; Deferred Compensation;

Dental Insurance; Disability Coverage; Life Insurance; Medical Insurance; Pension Plan. **Corporate headquarters location:** This Location. **Operations at this facility include:** Administration; Service. **Number of employees at this location:** 7,000.

HAYWARD, CITY OF
25151 Clawiter Road, Hayward CA 94545. 510/293-8669. **Contact:** Human Resources. **Description:** Government offices for the city of Hayward. **Common positions include:** Accountant/Auditor; Attorney; Budget Analyst; Buyer; Civil Engineer; Clerical Supervisor; Computer Programmer; Construction and Building Inspector; Counselor; Electrical/Electronics Engineer; Electrician; Human Resources Specialist; Librarian; Mechanical Engineer; Surveyor. **Educational backgrounds include:** Business Administration; Engineering; Liberal Arts. **Benefits:** 401(k); Dental Insurance; Disability Coverage; Life Insurance; Medical Insurance; Pension Plan; Tuition Assistance. **Special Programs:** Internships. **Corporate headquarters location:** This Location. **Operations at this facility include:** Administration. **Number of employees at this location:** 700.

PUBLIC UTILITIES COMMISSION
1155 Market Street, 8th Floor, San Francisco CA 94103. 415/554-1600. **Contact:** Personnel Department. **Description:** The Public Utilities Commission (PUC) has three separate divisions under its direction: Municipal Railway, Water Department, and Hetch Hetchy Power. The PUC employs people in all areas, including administrative, professional, technical, skilled craft, and clerical. **Common positions include:** Accountant/Auditor; Architect; Civil Engineer; Claim Representative; Electrical/Electronics Engineer; General Manager; Human Resources Specialist; Industrial Engineer; Mechanical Engineer; Statistician; Systems Analyst; Transportation/Traffic Specialist. **Educational backgrounds include:** Accounting; Business Administration; Computer Science; Economics; Engineering; Finance; Liberal Arts. **Benefits:** Dental Insurance; Medical Insurance; Savings Plan; Tuition Assistance. **Special Programs:** Internships. **Corporate headquarters location:** San Francisco CA. **Operations at this facility include:** Administration. **Number of employees nationwide:** 5,000.

SAN FRANCISCO MEDICAL EXAMINER'S OFFICE
850 Bryant Street, San Francisco CA 94103. 415/553-1694. **Contact:** Human Resources. **Description:** The medical examiner's office for the city of San Francisco.

SAN FRANCISCO PORT COMMISSION
Ferry Building, Suite 3100, San Francisco CA 94111. 415/274-0400. **Contact:** Nancy Woo, Personnel Director. **Description:** Operates city and county port facilities as an agency of both the city and county of San Francisco. The agency's professional work force is small and stable.

SANTA CLARA COUNTY TRANSPORTATION AGENCY
3331 North First Street, San Jose CA 95134. 408/321-5575. **Contact:** Personnel Director. **Description:** Provides transportation services to the San Jose area. **Common positions include:** Driver.

U.S. ENVIRONMENTAL PROTECTION AGENCY
75 Hawthorne Street, San Francisco CA 94105. 415/744-1500. **Contact:** Human Resources. **Description:** The Environmental Protection Agency was created in 1970 through an executive reorganization plan designed to consolidate the environmental activities of the federal government into a single agency. The EPA is dedicated to

improving and preserving the quality of the environment, both national and global, and protecting human health and the productivity of natural resources. The agency is committed to ensuring that federal environmental laws are implemented and enforced effectively; U.S. policy, both foreign and domestic, fosters the integration of economic development and environmental protection so that economic growth can be sustained over the long term; and public and private decisions affecting energy, transportation, agriculture, industry, international trade, and natural resources fully integrate considerations of environmental quality. As part of Region 9, this location of the EPA covers Arizona, California, Hawaii, Nevada, American Samoa, Guam, and Trust Territories of the Pacific. **Benefits:** Daycare Assistance; Fitness Program; Flextime Plan; Incentive Plan; Leave Time; Retirement Plan. **Special Programs:** Internships. **Corporate headquarters location:** Washington DC. **Other U.S. locations:** Denver CO; Atlanta GA; Chicago IL; Kansas City KS; Boston MA; New York NY; Philadelphia PA; Dallas TX; Seattle WA. **Number of employees nationwide:** 19,000.

For more information about career opportunities in the government:

Directories

ACCESS...FCO ON-LINE
Federal Research Service, Inc., P.O. Box 1059, 243 Church Street, Vienna VA 22183-1059. 703/281-0200. This is the online service of the *Federal Career Opportunities* publication. To join online, the cost is $25 for the set-up and $45 for one hour, payable by credit card over the phone.

HEALTH CARE: SERVICES, EQUIPMENT, AND PRODUCTS

With no time to worry about the failure of government-proposed health care reforms, the health care industry is surging ahead with its own solutions, pressured by a competitive marketplace to cut costs. HMOs and insurance providers are looking to nursing homes and home care companies as an alternative to long-term hospital stays, and shifting from inpatient to less expensive outpatient care. Hospitals are streamlining operations and consolidating, with cutback efforts targeting staff, as well as unnecessary tests and laboratory fees. Hospital cost-cutting has also hurt medical equipment suppliers, as many hospitals form networks to share expensive equipment.

Even so, from 1990 to 1995, the number of health care workers in the United States grew from 8.86 million to 10.5 million. Despite pressure to cut back, the health care industry remains a growth area. As the elderly population continues to grow faster than the population as a whole and the survival rate of the severely ill continues to improve, the need for new workers will continue to increase, and the large employment base will create replacement needs.

ABBOTT LABORATORIES
DIAGNOSTIC DIVISION
39300 Civic Center Drive, Suite 280, Fremont CA 94538-2324. 510/745-8613. **Contact:** Human Resources. **Description:** This location is a sales office. Abbott Laboratories manufactures a wide range of health care products, including pharmaceuticals, hospital products, diagnostic products, chemical products, and nutritional products. Abbott Laboratories has international facilities.

ABBOTT LABORATORIES
HOSPITAL PRODUCTS DIVISION
1212 Terra Bella Avenue, Mountain View CA 94043. 415/961-4380. **Fax:** 415/961-4380. **Contact:** Patrick Eagan, Director of Human Resources. **Description:** Designs, develops, and manufactures automated laboratory instruments, primarily used in the fields of clinical chemistry, microbiology, and therapeutic drug monitoring. This location of Abbott Laboratories is the business unit headquarters location. **Common positions include:** Accountant/Auditor; Administrator; Biomedical Engineer; Blue-Collar Worker Supervisor; Buyer; Chemist; Computer Programmer; Computer Systems Analyst; Customer Service Representative; Department Manager; Draftsperson; Electrical/Electronics Engineer; Financial Analyst; Human Resources Specialist; Industrial Engineer; Marketing Specialist; Mechanical Engineer; Operations/Production Manager; Purchasing Agent and Manager; Quality Control Supervisor; Software Engineer; Technical Writer/Editor. **Educational backgrounds include:** Accounting; Business Administration; Computer Science; Engineering; Finance; Liberal Arts; Marketing; Mathematics; Physics. **Benefits:** 401(k); Credit Union; Dental Insurance; Disability Coverage; Employee Discounts; Life Insurance; Medical Insurance; Pension Plan; Profit Sharing; Spending Account; Tuition Assistance. **Corporate headquarters**

location: Abbott Park IL. **Operations at this facility include:** Administration; Divisional Headquarters; Manufacturing; Research and Development; Sales; Service. **Listed on:** New York Stock Exchange. **Number of employees at this location:** 800.

ACCESS HEALTH MARKETING, INC.
11020 White Rock Road, Rancho Cordova CA 95670. 916/851-4000. **Fax:** 916/852-3890. **Contact:** Human Resources. **Description:** Access Health Marketing is committed to delivering a comprehensive approach to consumer health care information resulting in better health care decisions, lower medical costs, and improved patient health and satisfaction. Access Health's personal management products incorporate the following capabilities: assisting members in evaluating their health symptoms, enabling members to understand and manage serious health care episodes, providing assistance in administering at-home health remedies, offering educational information on a variety of topics, including disease prevention and helping members to find the right physician to meet their specific needs. Through personal health management services, members are actively involved in managing their own health, and empowered to make better-informed health care decisions. **Corporate headquarters location:** This Location.

ACUSON
P.O. Box 7393, Mountain View CA 94039. 415/969-9112. **Contact:** Employee Relations, G-10. **Description:** Acuson manufactures ultrasound medical instruments. **Common positions include:** Accountant/Auditor; Financial Analyst; Hardware Engineer; Manager of Information Systems; Marketing Specialist; Mechanical Engineer; Sales Representative; Software Engineer. **Number of employees at this location:** 1,700.

ADAC LABORATORIES
NUCLEAR MEDICINE DIVISION
540 Alder Drive, Milpitas CA 95035. 408/321-9100. **Contact:** Bob Starr, Director of Personnel. **Description:** Produces medical diagnostic computer systems and components including state-of-the-art digital radiography image processing, nuclear medicine image processing, and radiation therapy planning systems. **Common positions include:** Accountant/Auditor; Design Engineer; Electrical/Electronics Engineer; Financial Analyst; Manufacturing Engineer; Marketing Specialist; Mechanical Engineer; Software Engineer. **Corporate headquarters location:** This Location.

ALAMEDA COUNTY MEDICAL CENTER
1411 East 31st Street, Oakland CA 94602. 510/437-4800. **Contact:** Aracelia G. Esparza, Medical Center Recruiter. **Description:** A 300-bed, adult acute care facility. Alameda County Medical Center distinguishes itself as a teaching hospital. Up-to-date clinical knowledge helps to create an environment conducive to performing quality nursing care. **Common positions include:** Licensed Practical Nurse; Registered Nurse; Surgical Technician. **Benefits:** 401(k); Dental Insurance; Disability Coverage; Life Insurance; Medical Insurance; Pension Plan; Tuition Assistance. **Corporate headquarters location:** Oakland CA. **Operations at this facility include:** Service.

ALLIED HEALTHCARE PRODUCTS, INC.
ARCHITECTURAL PRODUCTS DIVISION
5301 Adeline Street, Oakland CA 94608. 510/652-7771. **Contact:** Human Resources. **Description:** Allied Healthcare Products, Inc. is a leading manufacturer of respiratory products used in the health care industry in a wide range of hospital and alternate site settings, including post-acute care facilities, home health care and trauma care. The company's product lines include respiratory therapy equipment, medical gas equipment,

and emergency medical products. The company believes that it is one of the largest U.S. manufacturers of respiratory therapy products with leading market shares in many of its principal product lines. As a result of six acquisitions completed within the last two years, the company has diversified its product lines and expanded its distribution channels. While maintaining its position as a leading manufacturer in its traditional product lines, the company has broadened its focus to emphasize more technologically-advanced respiratory therapy products for which it anticipates significant growth. Allied offers a broad spectrum of respiratory therapy products for use in the trauma, hospital, home, and post-acute care settings. The company's products are marketed under well-recognized and respected brand names to hospitals, hospital equipment dealers, hospital construction contractors, home health care dealers, emergency medical products dealers and others. Allied's product lines include respiratory therapy equipment (respiratory care/anesthesia products and home respiratory care products); emergency medical products (respiratory/resuscitation products); and medical gas equipment (medical gas system construction products, medical gas system regulation devices, disposable oxygen and specialty gas cylinders, and portable suction equipment). **Parent company:** Harbour Group.

AMERICAN SHARED HOSPITAL SERVICES
1400 Lone Palm Avenue, Modesto CA 95351. 415/788-5300. **Contact:** Human Resources. **Description:** American Shared Hospital Services provides shared diagnostic imaging services and respiratory therapy contract management to approximately 178 hospitals, medical centers, and medical offices located in 20 states and one hospital in the United Kingdom. The company's strategy is to provide shared diagnostic imaging, therapeutic services, and hospital department contract management on a national scale on a fee-per-procedure basis that is less expensive and more cost-efficient than that which the client health care provider could offer itself. The four diagnostic imaging services provided by the company are Magnetic Resonance Imaging (MRI), Computed Axial Tomography Scanning (CT), Ultrasound, and Nuclear Medicine. The company also provides respiratory therapy and diagnostic imaging department management. In addition, the company provides a Gamma Knife to a major university medical center and has an option to acquire a second Gamma Knife located in another major university medical center. **Corporate headquarters location:** This Location.

BAYER INC.
P.O. Box 1986, Berkeley CA 94701. 510/705-5000. **Contact:** Personnel. **Description:** Engaged in the development, manufacture, and distribution of health care products, including pharmaceuticals and a wide range of hospital equipment. This is the group headquarters location.

BIGGS-GRIDLEY MEMORIAL HOSPITAL
240 Spruce Street, Gridley CA 95948. 916/846-5671. **Fax:** 916/846-6406. **Contact:** Human Resources. **Description:** A hospital. **Common positions include:** Accountant/Auditor; Biological Scientist/Biochemist; Blue-Collar Worker Supervisor; Clinical Lab Technician; Credit Manager; Customer Service Representative; EEG Technologist; EKG Technician; Environmental Engineer; Human Resources Specialist; Licensed Practical Nurse; Medical Records Technician; Occupational Therapist; Purchasing Agent and Manager; Radiologic Technologist; Registered Nurse; Respiratory Therapist; Restaurant/Food Service Manager; Social Worker; Speech-Language Pathologist. **Educational backgrounds include:** Accounting; Biology; Business Administration; Health Care. **Benefits:** Disability Coverage; Employee Discounts; Life Insurance; Medical Insurance; Pension Plan; Savings Plan. **Corporate headquarters**

location: This Location. **Operations at this facility include:** Administration. **Listed on:** Privately held.

BROOKSIDE HOSPITAL
2023 Vale Road, Suite 102, San Pablo CA 94806. 510/235-7006x2875. **Recorded Jobline:** 510/235-7006x2020. **Contact:** Personnel. **Description:** An acute care hospital. **Common positions include:** Biomedical Engineer; Clinical Lab Technician; Computer Systems Analyst; Dietician/Nutritionist; EKG Technician; Financial Analyst; Health Services Manager; Human Resources Specialist; Licensed Practical Nurse; Medical Records Technician; Nuclear Medicine Technologist; Occupational Therapist; Pharmacist; Physical Therapist; Purchasing Agent and Manager; Radiologic Technologist; Recreational Therapist; Registered Nurse; Respiratory Therapist; Social Worker; Stationary Engineer; Surgical Technician. **Educational backgrounds include:** Health Care. **Benefits:** 401(k); Dental Insurance; Disability Coverage; Life Insurance; Medical Insurance; Pension Plan. **Corporate headquarters location:** This Location. **Number of employees at this location:** 900.

CALIFORNIA DENTAL ASSOCIATION
P.O. Box 13749, Sacramento CA 95853. 916/443-0505. **Fax:** 916/498-6105. **Recorded Jobline:** 916/443-4526x3814. **Contact:** Lynn Rossi, Human Resources Director. **Description:** California Dental Association is a nonprofit dental association providing membership programs and services for California dentists. **Common positions include:** Accountant/Auditor; Adjuster; Administrative Services Manager; Attorney; Claim Representative; Clerical Supervisor; Computer Programmer; Computer Systems Analyst; Customer Service Representative; Dental Assistant/Dental Hygienist; Dentist; Editor; Financial Analyst; Human Resources Specialist; Insurance Agent/Broker; Public Relations Specialist; Reporter; Stationary Engineer; Technical Writer/Editor; Travel Agent; Underwriter/Assistant Underwriter. **Educational backgrounds include:** Accounting; Business Administration; Communications; Finance; Marketing. **Benefits:** Dental Insurance; Disability Coverage; Employee Discounts; Life Insurance; Medical Insurance; Pension Plan; Tuition Assistance. **Corporate headquarters location:** This Location. **Operations at this facility include:** Administration; Divisional Headquarters; Sales; Service. **Listed on:** Privately held. **Number of employees at this location:** 175.

CHEMTRAK INC.
929 East Arques Avenue, Sunnyvale CA 94086. 408/773-8156. **Toll-free phone:** 800/927-7776. **Fax:** 408/773-1651. **Contact:** Human Resources. **Description:** ChemTrak was founded in 1985 to bring health care closer to the patient by changing the way many in vitro diagnostic tests are performed. The company develops, manufactures, and markets quantitative and qualitative easy-to-use, disposable diagnostic tests for the worldwide point-of-care markets, including the consumer retail and physician office markets. The company's strategy is to develop tests for high-volume markets to meet the diagnostic needs of an aging, health- and cost-conscious population. **Corporate headquarters location:** This Location.

COMMUNITY HOSPITALS OF CENTRAL CALIFORNIA
P.O. Box 1232, Human Resources, Fresno CA 93715. 209/442-6000. **Toll-free phone:** 800/442-3944. **Contact:** Employment. **Description:** A comprehensive medical system with three acute care hospitals, three long-term care facilities, and home care services. Specialties include cancer, cardiology, emergency services, rehabilitation, and family birthing centers. **Common positions include:** Accountant/Auditor; Assistant Manager; Budget Analyst; Cashier; Chef/Cook/Kitchen Worker; Clerical Supervisor; Clinical Lab

Technician; Computer Operator; Computer Programmer; Computer Systems Analyst; Construction Trade Worker; Department Manager; Dietician/Nutritionist; EEG Technologist; EKG Technician; Electrician; Employment Interviewer; Financial Manager; Health Services Manager; Human Resources Specialist; Interviewing Clerk; Librarian; Licensed Practical Nurse; Medical Records Technician; Nuclear Medicine Technologist; Occupational Therapist; Payroll Clerk; Pharmacist; Physical Therapist; Physician; Psychologist; Radiologic Technologist; Receptionist; Recreation Worker; Recreational Therapist; Registered Nurse; Respiratory Therapist; Secretary; Social Worker; Sociologist; Speech-Language Pathologist; Stock Clerk; Surgical Technician; Systems Analyst; Typist/Word Processor. **Educational backgrounds include:** Accounting; Business Administration. **Benefits:** 403(b); Daycare Assistance; Dental Insurance; Disability Coverage; Employee Discounts; Life Insurance; Medical Insurance; Pension Plan; Tuition Assistance. **Corporate headquarters location:** This Location. **Number of employees at this location:** 4,200.

EP TECHNOLOGIES, INC.
350 Potrero Avenue, Sunnyvale CA 94086. 408/481-3800. **Fax:** 408/481-3801. **Contact:** Human Resources. **Description:** EP Technologies, Inc. designs, develops, manufactures, and markets electrophysiology catheters and systems for use in minimally-invasive procedures to diagnose and treat cardiac tachyarrhythmias. The company has received approval from the Food and Drug Administration of its Premarket Approval application for use of its RF Cardiac Ablation System to treat certain types of tachyarrhythmias. This system incorporates temperature monitoring which assists the clinician in verifying that the catheter is in contact with and is ablating (destroying) the cardiac tissue. The RF Cardiac Ablation System, consisting of a control module and steerable ablation catheters, has been used successfully in clinical trials to ablate supra-ventricular tachycardias inducing tissue in 1,400 patients. In the United States, the company has established a direct sales force to market diagnostic and ablation catheter products. Internationally, the company's products are marketed in Canada and 35 countries in Europe and Asia. EP Technologies provides clinical education and training for physicians and supports research programs directed at expanding the range of tachyarrhythmias treatable by ablation. **Corporate headquarters location:** This Location.

ENDOSONICS CORPORATION
6616 Owens Drive, Pleasanton CA 94588. 510/734-0464. **Fax:** 510/734-0465. **Contact:** Human Resources. **Description:** Endosonics Corporation addresses the treatment of atherosclerosis with new technologies. The company develops, manufactures, and markets interventional catheter products, such as balloon angioplasty catheters, ultrasound imaging, and site-specific drug delivery catheters, in combination or on a stand-alone basis. These products target applications such as coronary angioplasty, peripheral vascular, neurointerventional, and drug delivery procedures. The company's core technology foundation, intravascular ultrasound (IVUS), enhances the effectiveness of the diagnosis and treatment of coronary and other vascular diseases by aiding the interventional cardiologist, radiologist, and vascular surgeon in identifying lesion-specific characteristics, selecting an optimum course of treatment, positioning a therapeutic device, treating disease sites, and assessing results of treatment immediately. Endosonics' angioplasty imaging catheters combine an angioplasty balloon and intravascular ultrasound imaging in a single catheter. The company's subsidiary, CardioVascular Dynamics, Inc. has developed products that include site-specific drug delivery technology to allow the accurate delivery of therapeutic solutions and drugs to

remote anatomical locations within the body such as the coronaries, as well as in peripheral vascular and neurovascular applications. **Corporate headquarters location:** This Location.

FRESENIUS U.S.A., INC.
2637 Shadelands Drive, Walnut Creek CA 94598. 510/295-0200. **Contact:** Dominic Capurro, Human Resources Manager. **Description:** Fresenius U.S.A., Inc. primarily manufactures, sells, and distributes systems and supplies for hemodialysis and peritoneal dialysis. The products include machines, dialysizers, equipment solutions in bio-compatible flexible plastic bags, and associated disposable tubing assemblies, serving the entire range of end-stage renal disease patients. **NOTE:** Entry-level positions are available. **Common positions include:** Biomedical Engineer; Computer Programmer; Customer Service Representative; Design Engineer; Draftsperson; Electrical/Electronics Engineer; MIS Specialist; Operations/Production Manager; Quality Control Supervisor. **Benefits:** 401(k); Dental Insurance; Disability Coverage; Life Insurance; Medical Insurance; Savings Plan. **Special programs:** Training programs. **Corporate headquarters location:** This Location. **Other U.S. locations:** Nationwide. **Parent company:** Fresenius AG (Germany). **Operations at this facility include:** Administration; Divisional Headquarters; Manufacturing; Sales; Service. **Listed on:** American Stock Exchange. **Annual sales/revenues:** $51 million - $100 million. **Number of employees at this location:** 375.

HELIAN HEALTH GROUP, INC.
26415 Carmel Rancho Boulevard, Carmel CA 93921. 408/646-9000. **Contact:** Human Resources. **Description:** Helian Health Group, Inc. is a progressive medical services company that concentrates on specialty surgical centers and occupational health care. Helian is dedicated to finding ways to lower the high cost of medical care. Its occupational health and surgical operations provide high quality medical services at affordable prices.

IMATRON INC.
389 Oyster Point Boulevard, South San Francisco CA 94080. 415/583-9964. **Fax:** 415/871-0418. **Contact:** Vicky Kallas, Human Resources Manager. **Description:** Manufactures high-speed CT scanners and other medical imaging devices. **Common positions include:** Designer; Draftsperson; Electrical/Electronics Engineer; Field Service Engineer; Mechanical Engineer; Physicist/Astronomer; Purchasing Agent and Manager; Quality Control Supervisor; Radiologic Technologist; Software Engineer. **Educational backgrounds include:** Business Administration; Computer Science; Engineering; Mathematics; Physics. **Benefits:** 401(k); Bonus Award/Plan; Dental Insurance; Disability Coverage; EAP; Employee Discounts; Life Insurance; Medical Insurance; Pension Plan; Savings Plan; Stock Option; Tuition Assistance. **Corporate headquarters location:** This Location. **Operations at this facility include:** Administration; Divisional Headquarters; Manufacturing; Regional Headquarters; Research and Development; Sales; Service. **Listed on:** NASDAQ. **Number of employees at this location:** 130. **Number of employees nationwide:** 160.

KAISER PERMANENTE
2025 Morse Avenue, Sacramento CA 95825. 916/973-6848. **Contact:** Personnel. **Description:** A nonprofit public benefit and charitable health care corporation that enrolls members and arranges for their medical, hospital, and related services nationwide. **Common positions include:** Accountant/Auditor; Chiropractor; Claim Representative; Computer Programmer; Customer Service Representative; Dietician/Nutritionist;

Education Administrator; EEG Technologist; EKG Technician; Electrical/Electronics Engineer; Human Resources Specialist; Human Service Worker; Librarian; Licensed Practical Nurse; Mechanical Engineer; Medical Records Technician; Nuclear Medicine Technologist; Occupational Therapist; Operations/Production Manager; Pharmacist; Physician; Physician Assistant; Psychologist; Purchasing Agent and Manager; Quality Control Supervisor; Radiologic Technologist; Registered Nurse; Respiratory Therapist; Social Worker; Speech-Language Pathologist; Stationary Engineer; Surgical Technician. **Educational backgrounds include:** Business Administration; Engineering; Health Care. **Other U.S. locations:** Nationwide; Oakland CA. **Number of employees at this location:** 3,200.

LASERCOPE SURGICAL SYSTEMS
3052 Orchard Drive, San Jose CA 95134. 408/943-0636. **Fax:** 408/944-9401. **Contact:** Human Resources. **Description:** Lasercope, a leading provider of minimally-invasive surgical systems, designs and markets an advanced line of medical laser systems, surgical delivery devices, reusables, and disposables. It markets its products to hospitals, outpatient surgical centers, and physician offices in the U.S., the U.K., and France through its own direct sales force and through exclusive distributor arrangements in Europe, Asia, the Middle East, and Pacific Rim. **Common positions include:** Accountant/Auditor; Design Engineer; Mechanical Engineer; MIS Specialist; Operations/Production Manager; Software Engineer. **Educational backgrounds include:** Engineering. **Benefits:** 401(k); Dental Insurance; Disability Coverage; Domestic Partner Benefits; Employee Discounts; Job Sharing; Life Insurance; Medical Insurance; Profit Sharing; Tuition Assistance. **Operations at this facility include:** Administration; Divisional Headquarters; Manufacturing; Research and Development; Sales; Service. **Listed on:** NASDAQ. **Annual sales/revenues:** $21 - 50 million. **Number of employees at this location:** 170. **Number of employees nationwide:** 220.

LODI MEMORIAL HOSPITAL
975 South Fairmont Avenue, Lodi CA 95241. 209/334-3411. **Fax:** 209/339-8587. **Recorded Jobline:** 209/339-7562. **Contact:** Hugh Sadler, Human Resources Manager. **Description:** A nonprofit 186-bed acute care hospital. Services include acute physical rehabilitation, subacute care, long-term care, home health, and adult daycare. **Common positions include:** Accountant/Auditor; Computer Programmer; Computer Systems Analyst; Dietician/Nutritionist; Financial Analyst; Human Resources Specialist; Licensed Practical Nurse; Medical Records Technician; Nuclear Medicine Technologist; Occupational Therapist; Pharmacist; Physical Therapist; Physician; Public Relations Specialist; Radiologic Technologist; Recreational Therapist; Registered Nurse; Respiratory Therapist; Social Worker; Speech-Language Pathologist; Stationary Engineer; Surgical Technician. **Benefits:** 401(k); 403(b); Dental Insurance; Disability Coverage; EAP; Employee Discounts; Life Insurance; Medical Insurance; Section 125 Plan. **Number of employees at this location:** 800.

MAXXIM MEDICAL
14300 Winchester Boulevard, Los Gatos CA 95030. 408/379-0350. **Contact:** Human Resources. **Description:** Principally engaged in the manufacture and sale of a broad line of health care products used by hospitals, laboratories, pharmaceutical companies, medical schools, dentists, and the general public. This facility primarily manufactures disposable medical gloves for use in hospitals and laboratories. **Common positions include:** Accountant/Auditor; Administrator; Buyer; Chemist; Mechanical Engineer; Purchasing Agent and Manager; Quality Control Supervisor. **Educational backgrounds include:** Accounting; Chemistry; Computer Science; Engineering. **Benefits:** Dental

Insurance; Disability Coverage; Life Insurance; Medical Insurance; Pension Plan; Savings Plan; Tuition Assistance. **Corporate headquarters location:** Franklin Lakes NJ. **Operations at this facility include:** Manufacturing. **Listed on:** New York Stock Exchange.

McKESSON CORPORATION
One Post Street, San Francisco CA 94104. 415/983-9087. **Fax:** 415/983-7114. **Contact:** Employment and Staffing. **Description:** McKesson Corporation is a *Fortune* 500 managed health care and pharmaceuticals distribution company. The corporation's business segments include Drug and Health Care; Car Care Products; Water and Beverages; Third Party Prescription Billing and Administration. **Common positions include:** Accountant/Auditor; Attorney; Computer Programmer; Computer Systems Analyst; Human Resources Specialist; Operations/Production Manager; Paralegal; Pharmacist; Wholesale and Retail Buyer. **Educational backgrounds include:** Accounting; Computer Science; Finance; Liberal Arts; Marketing; Mathematics. **Benefits:** 401(k); Dental Insurance; Disability Coverage; Life Insurance; Medical Insurance; Pension Plan; Profit Sharing; Savings Plan; Tuition Assistance. **Corporate headquarters location:** This Location. **Other U.S. locations:** Nationwide. **Subsidiaries include:** McKesson Water; Service Merchandising; Armor All. **Operations at this facility include:** Administration; Divisional Headquarters. **Listed on:** New York Stock Exchange. **Number of employees at this location:** 700. **Number of employees nationwide:** 14,000.

MERCED COMMUNITY MEDICAL CENTER
301 East 13th Street, Merced CA 95304. 209/385-7114. **Fax:** 209/385-7062. **Contact:** Jeff Braga, Director of Human Resources. **Description:** A community medical center. **Common positions include:** Clinical Lab Technician; Computer Systems Analyst; EEG Technologist; Financial Analyst; Licensed Practical Nurse; Medical Records Technician; Nuclear Medicine Technologist; Pharmacist; Physical Therapist; Physician; Radiologic Technologist; Registered Nurse; Respiratory Therapist; Social Worker; Surgical Technician. **Educational backgrounds include:** Accounting; Business Administration; Chemistry; Computer Science; Finance; Health Care; Marketing. **Benefits:** Dental Insurance; Disability Coverage; Life Insurance; Medical Insurance; Tuition Assistance. **Operations at this facility include:** Administration; Service. **Number of employees at this location:** 800.

MERCY HEALTHCARE NORTH
2175 Roseline Avenue, Redding CA 96001. 916/225-6132. **Fax:** 916/225-7297. **Recorded Jobline:** 916/223-2324. **Contact:** Alan H. Gugin, Director of Human Resources. **Description:** A medical center. **Common positions include:** Computer Programmer; Computer Systems Analyst; Credit Manager; Dietician/Nutritionist; EEG Technologist; EKG Technician; Electrician; Emergency Medical Technician; Environmental Engineer; Human Resources Specialist; Librarian; Library Technician; Licensed Practical Nurse; Medical Records Technician; Nuclear Medicine Technologist; Occupational Therapist; Paralegal; Pharmacist; Physical Therapist; Purchasing Agent and Manager; Radiologic Technologist; Registered Nurse; Respiratory Therapist; Restaurant/Food Service Manager; Social Worker; Speech-Language Pathologist; Stationary Engineer; Surgical Technician. **Educational backgrounds include:** Accounting; Business Administration; Communications; Computer Science; Health Care. **Benefits:** 403(b); Dental Insurance; Disability Coverage; Employee Discounts; Life Insurance; Medical Insurance; Pension Plan; TSAs; Tuition Assistance. **Corporate**

headquarters location: San Francisco CA. **Parent company:** Catholic Healthcare West. **Operations at this facility include:** Administration; Regional Headquarters; Service. **Number of employees at this location:** 1,500.

MERIT BEHAVIORAL CARE
400 Oyster Point Boulevard, Suite 306, South San Francisco CA 94080. 415/742-0980. **Contact:** Personnel. **Description:** Provides comprehensive managed mental health and substance abuse treatment programs for insurance companies, employers, health maintenance organizations, and other providers of mental health benefits in Arizona, Illinois, Hawaii, Indiana, Ohio, Texas, Florida, and Michigan.

NELLCOR, INC.
4280 Hacienda Drive, Pleasanton CA 94588. 510/463-4000. **Fax:** 510/463-4718. **Contact:** Professional Employment. **Description:** Founded in 1981, the company designs, manufactures, and markets high-performance monitoring equipment, sensors, and accessories for patient safety and management throughout the hospital, in emergency care, and in the home. Nellcor is the leading producer of pulse oximeters used in hospitals for the continuous measurement of patient oxygen status. Nellcor's line of oximetry sensors is the broadest in the medical equipment industry and includes both adhesive and reusable sensors as well as a sensor recycling program. **Common positions include:** Accountant/Auditor; Biomedical Engineer; Clinical Lab Technician; Computer Operator; Computer Programmer; Computer Systems Analyst; Customer Service Representative; Electrical/Electronics Engineer; Financial Analyst; Human Resources Specialist; Mechanical Engineer; Paralegal; Purchasing Agent and Manager; Registered Nurse; Respiratory Therapist; Software Engineer; Technical Writer/Editor. **Educational backgrounds include:** Business Administration; Computer Science; Engineering; Marketing; Physics. **Benefits:** Dental Insurance; Disability Coverage; Life Insurance; Medical Insurance; Profit Sharing; Savings Plan; Tuition Assistance. **Corporate headquarters location:** This Location. **Other locations:** Tijuana, Mexico. **Other U.S. locations:** Chula Vista CA; Lenexa KS; Eden Prairie MN. **Subsidiaries include:** EdenTec. **Operations at this facility include:** Administration; Research and Development; Sales; Service. **Listed on:** NASDAQ. **Number of employees at this location:** 400. **Number of employees nationwide:** 800.

PILKINGTON, BARNES, HIND, INC.
810 Kifer Road, Sunnyvale CA 94086. 408/736-5462. **Fax:** 408/524-5104. **Contact:** John Reasner, Vice President of Human Resources. **Description:** A manufacturer of vision care products including lenses and solutions. **Common positions include:** Accountant/Auditor; Biological Scientist/Biochemist; Buyer; Chemical Engineer; Chemist; Clinical Lab Technician; Computer Programmer; Computer Systems Analyst; Economist/Market Research Analyst; Financial Analyst; Human Resources Specialist; Industrial Engineer; Librarian; Marketing Specialist; Mechanical Engineer; Operations/Production Manager; Quality Control Supervisor; Systems Analyst. **Educational backgrounds include:** Accounting; Business Administration; Chemistry; Engineering; Finance; Marketing. **Benefits:** 401(k); Dental Insurance; Disability Coverage; Life Insurance; Medical Insurance; Pension Plan; Savings Plan; Tuition Assistance. **Corporate headquarters location:** This Location. **Other U.S. locations:** Phoenix AZ; San Diego CA. **Operations at this facility include:** Divisional Headquarters; Manufacturing; Research and Development; Sales. **Number of employees at this location:** 130.

SIEMENS MEDICAL LABORATORIES INC.
4040 Nelson Avenue, Concord CA 94520. 510/246-8200. **Contact:** Employment Representative. **Description:** Engaged in the design and manufacturing of medical linear accelerators for use in radiation therapy. **Common positions include:** Electrical/Electronics Engineer; Mechanical Engineer; Physicist/Astronomer; Software Engineer; Technical Writer/Editor. **Educational backgrounds include:** Computer Science; Engineering; Physics. **Corporate headquarters location:** This Location. **Parent company:** Siemens AG (Germany). **Operations at this facility include:** Administration; Manufacturing; Research and Development; Sales; Service.

SUNRISE MEDICAL
QUICKIE DESIGNS
2842 Business Park Avenue, Fresno CA 93727. 209/292-2171. **Fax:** 209/292-7412. **Contact:** Human Resources. **Description:** Designs, manufactures, and markets internationally a broad line of medical products used in institutional and home care settings which address the recovery, rehabilitation, and respiratory needs of the patient. Its products are designed to address the elderly, the disabled, recovering patients, and health-conscious consumers.

SUTTER ROSEVILLE MEDICAL CENTER
333 Sunrise Avenue, Roseville CA 95661. 916/781-1527. **Fax:** 916/781-2588. **Recorded Jobline:** 916/781-1090. **Contact:** Employment Coordinator. **Description:** Sutter Roseville Medical Center is a 205-bed, acute care hospital that serves the health care needs of the Roseville community and its surrounding areas. **Common positions include:** Emergency Medical Technician; Medical Records Technician; Pharmacist; Physical Therapist; Radiologic Technologist; Registered Nurse; Respiratory Therapist; Social Worker; Speech-Language Pathologist; Surgical Technician. **Benefits:** Dental Insurance; Disability Coverage; Life Insurance; Medical Insurance; Pension Plan. **Corporate headquarters location:** Sacramento CA. **Other U.S. locations:** Honolulu HI. **Operations at this facility include:** Health Care; Service. **Number of employees at this location:** 1,250. **Number of employees nationwide:** 34,500.

THERMO-SEPARATION PRODUCTS
P.O. Box 49031, San Jose CA 95161-9031. 408/526-1100. **Contact:** Human Resources. **Description:** This company manufactures laboratory instruments and supplies for the health care industry. **Number of employees at this location:** 300.

WASHINGTON HOSPITAL
2000 Mowry Avenue, Fremont CA 94538. 510/791-3428. **Contact:** Human Resources. **Description:** A hospital. **Number of employees nationwide:** 1,300.

***Note:** Because addresses and telephone numbers of smaller companies can change rapidly, we recommend you call each company to verify the information below before inquiring about job opportunities. Mass mailings are not recommended.*

Additional small employers:

MEDICAL EQUIPMENT

Origin Medsystems Inc.
135 Constitution Dr, Menlo Park CA 94025-1118. 415/617-5000.

Menlo Care Inc.
1350 Willow Rd Ste 101, Menlo Park CA 94025-1516. 415/325-2500.

Biotrak Inc.
1058 Huff Ave, Mountain

View CA 94043-1226. 415/965-7400.

Cardiac Pathways Corporation
995 Benicia Ave, Sunnyvale CA 94086-2805. 408/737-0505.

Cavro Scientific Instruments Inc.
242 Humboldt Ct, Sunnyvale CA 94089-1315. 408/745-7400.

Surgical Dynamics Inc.
2575 Stanwell Dr, Concord CA 94520-4812. 510/687-2192.

Boehringer Mannheim Advanced
48431 Milmont Dr, Fremont CA 94538-7327. 510/252-9216.

The Furon Company
322 E Warren Ave, Fremont CA 94539-7966. 510/651-2022.

Sparta Surgical Corp.
7068 Koll Center Pkwy, Pleasanton CA 94566-3100. 510/417-8812.

Target Therapeautics Inc.
99 W Tasman Dr, San Jose CA 95134-1712. 408/435-7700.

Applied Vascular Engineering
5355 Skylane Blvd, Santa Rosa CA 95403-1046. 707/525-0111.

Baxter Diagnostics Microscan
2040 Enterprise Blvd, W Sacramento CA 95691-3427. 916/374-3075.

Baxter Healthcare Corp.
1584 Enterprise Blvd, W Sacramento CA 95691-3422. 916/372-1900.

Saf-T-Cab Inc.
PO Box 2587, Fresno CA 93745-2587. 209/268-5541.

Resound Corp.
220 Saginaw Dr, Redwood City CA 94063-4725. 415/480-7800.

Robbins Scientific Corp.
814 San Aleso Ave, Sunnyvale CA 94086-1411. 408/734-8500.

Hosmer Dorrance Corp.
PO Box 37, Campbell CA 95009-0037. 408/379-5151.

AD Craig Co. Inc.
937 Coffee Rd Ste 1, Modesto CA 95355-4240. 209/529-7221.

Loredan Biomedical Inc.
3650 Industrial Blvd, W Sacramento CA 95691-6501. 916/374-8009.

Faro USA Corporation
1320 Marsten Rd, Burlingame CA 94010-2406. 415/348-3763.

Lares Research
295 Lockheed Ave, Chico CA 95973-9026. 916/345-1767.

Advanced Research & Applications Corp.
425 Lakeside Dr, Sunnyvale CA 94086-4704. 408/733-7780.

Eigen
PO Box 848, Nevada City CA 95959-0848. 916/265-2020.

Lightwave Electronics Corp.
1161 San Antonio Rd, Mountain View CA 94043-1002. 415/962-0755.

S-Tron
303 Ravendale Dr, Mountain View CA 94043-5233. 415/903-4949.

Hoetron Inc.
776 Palomar Ave, Sunnyvale CA 94086-2914. 408/720-1800.

Medasonics Inc.
47233 Fremont Blvd, Fremont CA 94538-6502. 510/623-0626.

Myrenne Instruments Inc.
PO Box 1383, Fremont CA 94538-0138. 510/490-4385.

Lexel Laser Inc.
48503 Milmont Dr, Fremont CA 94538-7336. 510/770-0800.

Hospital Systems Inc.
5301 Adeline St, Oakland CA 94608-3107. 510/652-7771.

Heraeus Laser Sonics Inc.
575 Cottonwood Dr, Milpitas CA 95035-7434. 408/954-4040.

Quantronix Western
2368 Walsh Ave # C, Santa Clara CA 95051-1301. 408/727-9984.

Visx Inc.
3400 Central Expressway, Santa Clara CA 95051-0703. 408/733-2020.

UTI Instruments Co.
2030 Fortune Dr Ste C, San Jose CA 95131-1823. 408/428-9400.

Cardiorhythm
130 Rio Robles, San Jose CA 95134-1813. 408/943-6510.

Ocular Sciences
601 Gateway Blvd, South San Francisco CA 94080-7013. 415/583-1400.

Con-Cise Lens Co.
14520 Doolittle Dr, San Leandro CA 94577-6615. 510/483-9400.

Franklin Optical Co
428 Santander Dr, San Ramon CA 94583-2143. 510/803-0100.

VETERINARY SERVICES

Pet Prevent A Care Vaccination
4122 S Moorland Ave, Santa Rosa CA 95407-8141. 707/584-8222.

Animal Den Annex
4060 Power Inn Rd, Sacramento CA 95826-4345. 916/456-4723.

Bradshaw Veterinary Clinic Inc.
9609 Bradshaw Rd, Elk Grove CA 95624-9406. 916/685-4673.

Rancho Cordova Animal Medical Center
3342 Mather Field Rd, Rancho Cordova CA 95670-5966. 916/362-1863.

Sacramento Animal Medical Group Inc.
1550 Jefferson Blvd, W Sacramento CA 95691-3950. 916/371-8900.

MEDICAL EQUIPMENT AND SUPPLIES WHOLESALE

Aesculap Inc.
1000 Gateway Blvd, South San Francisco CA 94080-7030. 415/876-7000.

Philips Medical Systems
7020 Koll Center Pkwy Bldg 110, Pleasanton CA 94566-3107. 510/463-1700.

Biodental Technologies Corp.
11277 Sunrise Park Dr, Rncho Cordova CA 95742-6528. 916/638-8147.

Arthrotek Medical Systems
771 Twin View Blvd, Redding CA 96003-2008. 916/225-8835.

Solano Ambulance Co. Inc.
1027 Alabama St, Vallejo CA 94590-4597. 707/552-6212.

Visionex
PO Box 2744, Sunnyvale CA 94087-0744. 408/730-1924.

Professional Hospital Supply
2373 N Watney Way, Fairfield CA 94533-6746. 707/429-2884.

MHS & Associates
1142 Rivergate Dr, Lodi CA 95240-0553. 209/333-3758.

Life Medical Industries Inc.
2607 Wigwam Dr, Stockton CA 95205-2434. 209/462-4294.

Troy Mao
3039 Baronscourt Way, San Jose CA 95132-1708. 408/929-1915.

Generic-Pentron
3805 Pasadena Ave, Sacramento CA 95821-2815. 916/489-6047.

United Rubber Group
3423 Investment Blvd, Hayward CA 94545-3802. 510/732-9010.

Stuart Medical Inc.
6150 Las Positas Rd, Livermore CA 94550-7809. 510/606-1133.

Kid's Korner Medical Supply
97 Willow Street, San Jose CA 95110-3141. 408/971-1034.

Kinetic Concepts Therapeutic
1040 Commercial Street, San Jose CA 95112. 408/437-1649.

KCI
4630 Northgate Blvd, Sacramento CA 95834-1125. 916/923-4470.

DOCTORS' OFFICES AND CLINICS

West Oakland Health Center
700 Adeline St, Oakland CA 94607-2608. 510/835-9610.

Redwood Medical Group Inc.
805 Veterans Blvd, Redwood City CA 94063-1700. 415/261-2300.

Contra Costa Industial Medical Clinic
2339 Buchanan Rd, Antioch CA 94509-4402. 510/777-9194.

John C. Fremont Medical Clinic
5186 Hospital Rd, Mariposa CA 95338. 209/966-0850.

Pacific Northwest Physical Therapy
540 H St, Crescent City CA 95531-3744. 707/464-9511.

Novacare Outpatient
3947 Lennane Dr Ste 150, Sacramento CA 95834-1957. 916/929-0237.

Warrack Hospital
2449 Summerfield Rd, Santa Rosa CA 95405-7880. 707/542-9030.

Qualmed Plans For Health
155 Grand Ave, Oakland CA 94612-3724. 510/465-9600.

Lifeguard
1851 McCarthy Blvd, Milpitas CA 95035-7452. 408/943-9400.

Health Net
8880 Cal Center Dr Ste 360, Sacramento CA 95826-3266. 916/255-0100.

Bay Valley Medical Group
27212 Calaroga Ave, Hayward CA 94545-4349. 510/785-5000.

Dos Palos Health Center
1405 California Ave, Dos Palos CA 93620-2300. 209/392-2111.

Hill Physicians Medical Group Inc.
2401 Crow Canyon Rd, San Ramon CA 94583-1545. 510/820-8300.

DENTISTS' OFFICES AND CLINICS

Daniel D. Barry III DDS
450 Sutter, San Francisco CA 94108. 415/421-2723.

Dental Health Center
2180 Tully Rd, San Jose CA 95122-1345. 408/238-1806.

Evergreen Dental Group
2451 S King Rd, San Jose CA 95122. 408/274-9600.

Napa Solano Dental Society
1023 Empire St, Fairfield CA 94533-5706. 707/428-3894.

San Joaquin Dental Society
7849 N Pershing Ave, Stockton CA 95207-1749. 209/951-1311.

OFFICES AND CLINICS OF HEALTH PRACTITIONERS

Jette Chiropractic Center
200 4th St, Petaluma CA 94952-4261. 707/765-1928.

Bourque Chiropractic Clinic
10 W 5th St, Watsonville CA 95076-4202. 408/728-4266.

Chiropractic Referral Resource
6693 Folsom Auburn Rd Ste F, Folsom CA 95630-2130. 916/989-6689.

Visioncare Of California
777 Grand Ave, San Rafael CA 94901-3500. 415/457-0766.

Veterans Workshop Inc.
795 Willow Rd, Menlo Park CA 94025-2539. 415/325-9555.

Back To Form
2160 Appian Way, Pinole CA 94564-2524. 510/724-7133.

Kentfield Rehabilitation Hospital
1125 Sir Francis Drake Blvd, Kentfield CA 94904-1455. 415/485-3541.

Davis Physical Therapy
635 Anderson Rd Ste 11, Davis CA 95616-3505. 916/756-1010.

Cordova Physical Therapy Caremark
11000 Olson Dr, Rancho Cordova CA 95670-5653. 916/635-1443.

Alta Therapies
7041 Koll Center Pkwy, Pleasanton CA 94566-3128. 510/484-9610.

Visiting Nurse & Hospice
600 Nut Tree Rd, Vacaville CA 95687-4669. 707/453-8225.

NURSING AND PERSONAL CARE FACILITIES

University Convalescent Hospital
2122 Santa Cruz Ave, Menlo Park CA 94025-6308. 415/854-4020.

San Bruno Skilled Nursing Hospital
890 El Camino Real, San Bruno CA 94066-3137. 415/583-7768.

Hayward Convalescent Hospital
1832 B St, Hayward CA 94541-3198. 510/538-3866.

Barrett Skilled Nursing Hospital
1625 Denton Ave, Hayward CA 94545-1943. 510/782-2133.

Bancroft Convalescent Hospital
1475 Bancroft Ave, San Leandro CA 94577-5178. 510/483-1680.

Chowchilla Convalescent Hospital
1010 Ventura Ave, Chowchilla CA 93610-2368. 209/665-4826.

Los Banos Convalescent Hospital
931 Idaho Ave, Los Banos CA 93635-3405. 209/826-0790.

Oakhurst Community Living Center
40131 Highway 49, Oakhurst CA 93644-9560. 209/683-2244.

Sierra View Homes Inc.
1155 E Springfield Ave, Reedley CA 93654-3225. 209/638-9226.

Selma Convalescent Home
2108 Stillman St, Selma CA 93662-3097. 209/896-4990.

Fresno Care & Guidance Center
1715 S Cedar Ave, Fresno CA 93702-4398. 209/237-8377.

Golden Cross Health Care Fresno
1233 A St, Fresno CA 93706-3202. 209/268-6317.

Community Alzheimers Living Center
668 E Bullard Ave, Fresno

CA 93710-5401. 209/439-4461.

Hillcrest Convalescent Hospital
3672 N 1st St, Fresno CA 93726-6810. 209/227-5383.

Valley Convalescent Center
4840 E Tulare Ave, Fresno CA 93727-3099. 209/251-7161.

Salinas Care Center
637 E Romie Ln, Salinas CA 93901-4205. 408/424-0687.

Katherine Convalescent Hospital
315 Alameda Ave, Salinas CA 93901-4198. 408/424-1878.

Skyline Skilled Nursing Facility
348 Iris Dr, Salinas CA 93906-3514. 408/449-5496.

Crestwood Skilled Nursing Facility
350 Iris Dr, Salinas CA 93906-3514. 408/449-1515.

Beverly Healthcare Center
23795 Holman Hwy, Monterey CA 93940-5903. 408/624-1875.

Pacific Grove Convalescent Hospital
200 Lighthouse Ave, Pacific Grove CA 93950-3022. 408/375-2695.

Eden Valley Care Center
612 Main St, Soledad CA 93960-2533. 408/678-2462.

Carlmont Convalescent Hospital
2140 Carlmont Dr, Belmont CA 94002-3417. 415/591-9601.

Hillhaven Convalescent Hospital
1609 Trousdale Dr, Burlingame CA 94010-4520. 415/697-1865.

Villa Convalescent Center & Residential Facility
130 Vale St, Daly City CA 94014-2516. 415/755-0411.

Pilgrim Haven Retirement Community
373 Pine Ln, Los Altos CA 94022-1696. 415/948-8291.

The Nursing Inn Of Menlo Park
16 Coleman Pl, Menlo Park CA 94025-2406. 415/326-0802.

Sharon Heights Convalescent Hospital
1185 Monte Rosa Dr, Menlo Park CA 94025-6763. 415/854-3300.

Linda Mar Health Care & Rehabilitation
751 San Pedro Terrace Rd, Pacifica CA 94044-4101. 415/359-4800.

Sunnyvale Convalescent Hospital
1291 S Bernardo Ave, Sunnyvale CA 94087-2075. 408/245-8070.

Hy-Lond Convalescent Hospital
797 E Fremont Ave, Sunnyvale CA 94087-2805. 408/738-4880.

Mission Bay Convalescent Hospital
331 Pennsylvania Ave, San Francisco CA 94107-2950. 415/647-3587.

Mission Villa Convalescent Hospital
1420 Hampshire St, San Francisco CA 94110-4818. 415/285-7660.

Sheffield Convalescent Hospital
1133 S Van Ness Ave, San Francisco CA 94110-3214. 415/647-3117.

Convalescent Center
5767 Mission St, San Francisco CA 94112-4208. 415/584-3294.

Central Gardens Convalescent Hospital
1355 Ellis St, San Francisco CA 94115. 415/567-2967.

PARC Pacific Convalescent Hospital
1421 Broderick St, San Francisco CA 94115-3304. 415/922-3244.

Hayes Convalescent Hospital
1250 Hayes St, San Francisco CA 94117-1597. 415/931-8806.

Little Sisters Of The Poor
300 Lake St, San Francisco CA 94118. 415/751-6510.

Palo Alto Nursing Center
911 Bryant St, Palo Alto CA 94301-2798. 415/327-0511.

San Mateo Convalescent Hospital
453 N San Mateo Dr, San Mateo CA 94401-2453. 415/342-6255.

South Shore Convalescent Hospital
625 Willow St, Alameda CA 94501-5711. 510/523-3772.

Geriatric Crestwood Treatment Center
295 Pine Breeze Dr, Angwin CA 94508-9620. 707/965-2461.

Baywood Care Center
550 Patterson Blvd, Pleasant Hill CA 94523-4155. 510/939-5400.

Rosewood Care Center
1911 Oak Park Blvd, Pleasant Hill CA 94523-4601. 510/935-6630.

Shields Nursing Center
3230 Carlson Blvd, El

Cerrito CA 94530-3907. 510/525-3212.

Sierra Solano Care Center
1260 Travis Blvd, Fairfield CA 94533-4802. 707/425-0669.

La Mariposa Nursing & Rehabilitation Center
1244 Travis Blvd, Fairfield CA 94533-4802. 707/422-7750.

Fairfield Nursing & Rehabilitation Center
1255 Travis Blvd, Fairfield CA 94533-4801. 707/425-0623.

Carewest Park Central Nursing Center
2100 Parkside Dr, Fremont CA 94536-5326. 510/797-5300.

Carewest Petaluma Nursing
1115 B St, Petaluma CA 94952-4028. 707/765-3030.

Carewest Manzanita Nursing
300 Cherry Creek Rd, Cloverdale CA 95425-3811. 707/894-5201.

Carewest Gateway Nursing Center
26660 Patrick Ave, Hayward CA 94544-3808. 510/782-1845.

Hayward Hills Convalescent Hospital
1768 B St, Hayward CA 94541-3102. 510/538-4424.

Glen Ellen Intermediate Care
21568 Banyan St, Hayward CA 94541-2429. 510/538-2348.

Saint Anthony Care Center Inc.
553 Smalley Ave, Hayward CA 94541-4919. 510/733-3877.

Saint Christopher Convalescent Hospital Inc.
22822 Myrtle St, Hayward CA 94541-6321. 510/537-4844.

Saint Francis Extended Care
718 Bartlett Ave, Hayward CA 94541-3614. 510/785-5737.

Saint Michael Convalescent Hospital Inc.
25919 Gading Rd, Hayward CA 94544-2725. 510/782-8424.

Saint Joseph Convalescent Hospital Inc.
18949 Redwood Rd, Castro Valley CA 94546-3153. 510/886-1101.

Saint Luke's Sub-Acute Care Hospital
1652 Mono Ave, San Leandro CA 94578-2020. 510/357-5351.

Saint John Kronstadt Convalescent Center
4432 James Ave, Castro Valley CA 94546-3533. 510/889-7000.

Saint Theresa Convalescent Hospital
21863 Vallejo St, Hayward CA 94541-2599. 510/538-3811.

Driftwood Manor
19700 Hesperian Blvd, Hayward CA 94541-4704. 510/785-2880.

Eden West Rehabilitation & Convalescent Care Center
1805 West St, Hayward CA 94545-1932. 510/783-4811.

Stanton Hill Convalescent Hospital
20090 Stanton Ave, Castro Valley CA 94546-5299. 510/538-8464.

Redwood Convalescent Hospital
22103 Redwood Rd, Castro Valley CA 94546-7173. 510/537-8848.

Castro Valley Care Center
20259 Lake Chabot Rd, Castro Valley CA 94546-5307. 510/351-3700.

Woodland Nursing Inn
3721 Mount Diablo Blvd, Lafayette CA 94549-3538. 510/284-5544.

Lafayette Convalescent Hospital
1010 1st St, Lafayette CA 94549-3875. 510/284-1420.

Community Convalescent Center
1790 Muir Rd, Martinez CA 94553-4718. 510/228-8383.

Martinez Convalescent Hospital
4110 Alhambra Way, Martinez CA 94553-3924. 510/228-4260.

Alhambra Convalescent Hospital
331 Ilene Street, Martinez CA 94553-2631. 510/228-2020.

Rheem Valley Convalescent Hospital
348 Rheem Blvd, Moraga CA 94556-1516. 510/376-5995.

Roberts Nursing Home
3415 Browns Valley Rd, Napa CA 94558-5497. 707/257-3515.

Orinda Rehabilitation & Convalescent Hospital
11 Altarinda Road, Orinda CA 94563-2602. 510/254-6500.

Marlinda Convalescent Hospital
830 Pratt Ave, Saint Helena CA 94574-1035. 707/963-2791.

Vallejo Convalescent Hospital
900 Sereno Dr, Vallejo CA 94589-2400. 707/643-8453.

Manor Care Nursing & Rehabilitation Center
1226 Rossmoor Pkwy, Walnut Creek CA 94595-2538. 510/975-5000.

Guardian Of Rossmoor
1224 Rossmoor Pkwy, Walnut Creek CA 94595-2501. 510/937-7450.

Guardian Foundation
2580 Samaritan Dr, San Jose CA 95124-4101. 408/356-8181.

Guardian Ignacio
1449 Ygnacio Valley Rd, Walnut Creek CA 94598-2932. 510/939-5820.

Immaculate Care Center
3003 Fruitvale Ave, Oakland CA 94602-2110. 510/534-3219.

Lakeshore Convalescent Hospital
1901 3rd Ave, Oakland CA 94606-1853. 510/834-9880.

MacArthur Nursing Center
309 MacArthur Blvd, Oakland CA 94610-3233. 510/836-3777.

Rounseville Rehabilitation Center
210 40th Street Way, Piedmont CA 94611-5612. 510/658-2041.

High Street Nursing Center
3145 High Street, Oakland CA 94619-1839. 510/533-9970.

Willow Tree Convalescent Hospital
2124 57th Ave, Oakland CA 94621-4399. 510/261-2628.

Chaparral House Inter Care
1309 Allston Way, Berkeley CA 94702-1998. 510/848-8774.

Kyakameena Skilled Nursing
2131 Carleton St, Berkeley CA 94704-3213. 510/843-2131.

Live Oak Living Center Greenridge
2150 Pyramid Dr, El Sobrante CA 94803-3220. 510/222-1242.

Claritas Inter Care Hospital
955 23rd St, Richmond CA 94804-1250. 510/237-5182.

Creekside Care Center
1900 Church Ln, San Pablo CA 94806. 510/235-5514.

Hillside Care Center
81 Professional Center Pkwy, San Rafael CA 94903-2702. 415/479-5161.

Northgate Convalescent Hospital
40 Professional Center Pkwy, San Rafael CA 94903-2703. 415/479-1230.

Pine Ridge Care Center
45 Professional Center Pkwy, San Rafael CA 94903-2702. 415/479-3610.

The Oaks
450 Hayes Ln, Petaluma CA 94952-4010. 707/778-8686.

Beverly Manor Of Petaluma
101 Monroe St, Petaluma CA 94954-2393. 707/795-9641.

Camden Convalescent Hospital
1331 Camden Ave, Campbell CA 95008-6799. 408/377-4030.

Golden Age Convalescent Hospital
523 Burlingame Ave, Capitola CA 95010-3307. 408/475-0722.

Forum At Rancho San Antonio
23600 Via Esplendor, Cupertino CA 95014-6513. 415/969-0300.

Pleasant Care Convalescent Gilroy
8170 Murray Ave, Gilroy CA 95020-4605. 408/842-9311.

Hazel Hawkins Convalescent Hospital
3110 Southside Rd, Hollister CA 95023-9631. 408/637-5353.

Terreno Gardens Skilled Care
14966 Terreno De Flores Ln, Los Gatos CA 95032-2000. 408/356-8136.

Oak Meadows Convalescent Hospital
350 De Soto Dr, Los Gatos CA 95032. 408/356-9151.

Pacific Hills Manor
370 Noble Ct, Morgan Hill CA 95037-4134. 408/779-7346.

Winchester Convalescent Hospital
1250 N Winchester Blvd, Santa Clara CA 95050-6324. 408/241-3844.

Brommer Manor
2000 Brommer St, Santa Cruz CA 95062-3049. 408/476-4415.

Batterson Convalescent Hospital
2555 Mattison Ln, Santa Cruz CA 95062-1924. 408/475-4065.

Odd Fellows Health Center
14500 Fruitvale Ave, Saratoga CA 95070-6129. 408/867-3891.

Valley Convalescent Hospital
919 Freedom Blvd, Watsonville CA 95076-3804. 408/722-3581.

Watsonville Care Center West
525 Auto Center Dr, Watsonville CA 95076-3727. 408/724-7505.

Homewood Convalescent Hospital
75 N 13th St, San Jose CA 95112-3493. 408/295-2665.

Mount Pleasant Convalescent Hospital
1355 Clayton Rd, San Jose CA 95127-4307. 408/251-3070.

Bellerose Convalescent Hospital
100 Bellerose Dr, San Jose CA 95128-1701. 408/286-4161.

Plymouth Square
1319 N Madison, Stockton CA 95202. 209/466-4341.

Beverly Manor Of Stockton
2740 N California St, Stockton CA 95204-5529. 209/466-3522.

Pleasant Care Stockton
9289 Branstetter Pl, Stockton CA 95209-1700. 209/477-5252.

Heritage Of Stockton
9107 Davis Rd, Stockton CA 95209-1807. 209/478-6488.

Gross Convalescent Hospital
321 W Turner Road, Lodi CA 95240-0517. 209/334-3760.

Crescent Court Nursing Home
610 S Fairmont Ave, Lodi CA 95240-3835. 209/367-7400.

San Andreas Convalescent Hospital
556 Toyon Dr, San Andreas CA 95249. 209/754-4213.

Mark Twain Convalescent Hospital
900 Mountain Ranch Rd, San Andreas CA 95249-9713. 209/754-3823.

Hale Aloha Convalescent Hospital
1711 Richland Ave, Ceres CA 95307-4599. 209/537-4581.

La Sierra Care Center
2424 M St, Merced CA 95340-2808. 209/723-4224.

Casa De Modesto Retirement Center
1745 Eldena Way, Modesto CA 95350-3568. 209/529-4950.

Orangeburg Convalescent Hospital
823 E Orangeburg Ave, Modesto CA 95350-4619. 209/524-4641.

Colony Park Care Center
159 E Orangeburg Ave, Modesto CA 95350-5334. 209/526-2811.

Modesto Convalescent Hospital
515 E Orangeburg Ave, Modesto CA 95350-5599. 209/529-0516.

Reno Avenue Convalescent Hospital
1028 Reno Ave, Modesto CA 95351-1127. 209/524-1146.

Scenic Circle Care Center
1611 Scenic Dr, Modesto CA 95355-4907. 209/523-5667.

Vintage Faire Convalescent Hospital
3620 Dale Rd, Modesto CA 95356-0500. 209/521-2094.

Oak Valley Care Center
275 S Oak Ave, Oakdale CA 95361-3517. 209/847-0367.

Bethany Home
930 W Main St, Ripon CA 95366-2325. 209/599-4221.

Valley View Care Center
2649 Topeka St, Riverbank CA 95367-2248. 209/869-2568.

New Hope Care Center
2586 Buthmann Ave, Tracy CA 95376-2165. 209/832-2273.

Tracy Convalescent Hospital
545 W Beverly Place, Tracy CA 95376-3099. 209/835-6034.

Bel Air Lodge Convalescent Hospital
180 Starr Ave, Turlock CA 95380-3323. 209/632-1075.

Montgomery Convalescent Hospital
3751 Montgomery Dr, Santa Rosa CA 95405-5271. 707/525-1250.

Santa Rosa Convalescent Hospital
446 Arrowood Dr, Santa Rosa CA 95407-7591. 707/528-2100.

Meadowood Nursing Center
3805 Dexter Ln, Clearlake CA 95422-8850. 707/994-7738.

Sherwood Oaks Health Center
130 Dana St, Fort Bragg CA 95437-4506. 707/964-6333.

Lakeport Skilled Nursing Center Inc.
625 16th St, Lakeport CA 95453-3500. 707/263-6101.

Apple Valley Convalescent Hospital
1035 Gravenstein Ave, Sebastopol CA 95472-4537. 707/823-7675.

Fircrest Convalescent Hospital Inc.
7025 Corline Ct, Sebastopol CA 95472-4520. 707/823-7444.

Ukiah Convalescent Hospital
1349 S Dora St, Ukiah CA 95482-6512. 707/462-8864.

Sunset Convalescent Hospital
2353 23rd St, Eureka CA 95501-3201. 707/445-3261.

Pacific Convalescent Hospital
2211 Harrison Ave, Eureka CA 95501-3275. 707/443-9767.

Granada Convalescent Hospital
2885 Harris St, Eureka CA 95503-4808. 707/443-1627.

Sea View Convalescent Hospital
8400 Purdue Dr, Eureka CA 95503-7049. 707/443-5668.

Crescent City Convalescent Hospital
1280 Marshall St, Crescent City CA 95531-2298. 707/464-6151.

Foothill Oaks Care Center
3400 Bell Rd, Auburn CA 95603-9241. 916/888-6257.

Brittany Healthcare Center
3900 Garfield Ave, Carmichael CA 95608-6647. 916/481-6455.

Carmichael Convalescent Hospital
8336 Fair Oaks Blvd, Carmichael CA 95608-1906. 916/944-3100.

Rosewood Terrace
6041 Fair Oaks Blvd, Carmichael CA 95608-4816. 916/483-8103.

Whitney Walnut Convalescent Hospital
3529 Walnut Ave, Carmichael CA 95608-3049. 916/488-8601.

Mountain Manor Inter Care
6101 Fair Oaks Blvd, Carmichael CA 95608-4895. 916/488-7211.

Hillhaven Convalescent Hospital
600 Sunrise Ave, Roseville CA 95661-4110. 916/782-3131.

Sierra Hills Care Center
1139 Cirby Way, Roseville CA 95661. 916/782-7007.

Placerville Pines Convalescent Hospital
1040 Marshall Way, Placerville CA 95667-5706. 916/622-3400.

El Dorado Convalescent Hospital
3280 Washington St, Placerville CA 95667-5838. 916/622-6842.

Winsor House Convalescent Hospital
101 S Orchard Ave, Vacaville CA 95688-3693. 707/448-6458.

Sommerset Nursing Center
2215 Oakmont Way, W Sacramento CA 95691-3022. 916/371-1890.

Stollwood Convalescent Hospital
135 Woodland Ave, Woodland CA 95695-2759. 916/662-9674.

Woodland Skilled Nursing Facility
678 3rd St, Woodland CA 95695-4034. 916/662-9643.

Pioneer House-Retirement Residence
415 P St, Sacramento CA 95814-5339. 916/442-4906.

Sacramento Convalescent Hospital
3700 H St, Sacramento CA 95816-4611. 916/452-3592.

Trinity House Retirement Residence
2701 Capitol Ave, Sacramento CA 95816-6036. 916/446-4806.

Saint Claire's Nursing Center
6248 66th Ave, Sacramento CA 95823-2733. 916/392-4440.

Briarwood Health Care
5901 Lemon Hill Ave, Sacramento CA 95824-3231. 916/383-2741.

Sutter Oaks Nursing Centers
3400 Alta Arden Expressway, Sacramento CA 95825-2103. 916/481-5500.

Asian Community Nursing Home
7801 Rush River Dr, Sacramento CA 95831-4602. 916/393-9020.

Sutter Oaks Alzheimer's Center
500 Jessie Ave, Sacramento CA 95838-2698. 916/922-7177.

Parkview Care Center
1617 Ramirez St, Marysville CA 95901-4334. 916/742-7311.

Oak Park Nursing Center Inc.
10716 Cedar Ave, Grass Valley CA 95945-6007. 916/273-2470.

Meadow View Manor
396 Dorsey Dr, Grass Valley CA 95945-5368. 916/272-2273.

Valley Oaks Health Care Center
246 Spruce St, Gridley CA 95948-2216. 916/846-6266.

Live Oak Care Center
9000 Larkin Rd, Live Oak CA 95953-9599. 916/695-8020.

Paradise Health Care Center
7419 Skyway, Paradise CA 95969-3230. 916/877-7676.

The Fountains
1260 Williams Way, Yuba City CA 95991-2400. 916/751-4888.

Terrace Care Center
1220 Plumas St, Yuba City CA 95991-3411. 916/671-0550.

Brentwood Skilled Nursing Rehabilitation
1795 Walnut St, Red Bluff CA 96080-3645. 916/527-2046.

Modoc Medical Center
228 McDowell St, Alturas CA 96101. 916/233-3416.

Clovis Community Hospital
88 N Dewitt Ave, Clovis CA 93612-0311. 209/299-8200.

Fowler Convalescent Hospital
1306 E Sumner Ave, Fowler CA 93625-2627. 209/834-2542.

Alice Manor
8448 E Adams Ave, Fowler CA 93625-9773. 209/834-2519.

Raintree Convalescent Hospital
5265 E Huntington Ave, Fresno CA 93727-4099. 209/251-8244.

Carmel Valley Manor
8545 Carmel Valley Rd, Carmel CA 93923-9557. 408/624-1281.

Mount Zion Medical Center
1600 Divisadero St, San Francisco CA 94115-3066. 415/885-7555.

California Pacific Medical Center
3698 California St, San Francisco CA 94118-1702. 415/750-6460.

Marina Convalescent Center
3201 Fernside Blvd, Alameda CA 94501-1709. 510/523-2363.

Mount Diablo Medical Pavilion
2740 Grant Street, Concord CA 94520-2265. 510/674-4107.

Bethesda Home
22427 Montgomery St, Hayward CA 94541-3945. 510/538-8300.

Wisteria Care Center
20524 Wisteria St, Castro Valley CA 94546-5523. 510/727-9169.

Dowling Convalescent Hospital
451 28th Street, Oakland CA 94609-3602. 510/893-4066.

Lake Park Retirement Residence
1850 Alice St, Oakland CA 94612-4195. 510/835-5511.

Herrick Campus
2001 Dwight Way, Berkeley CA 94704-2608. 510/204-4409.

Nazareth House
245 Nova Albion Way, San Rafael CA 94903-3596. 415/479-8282.

Green Hills Manor
238 Virginia Ave, Campbell CA 95008-3908. 408/379-8114.

Sunny View Lutheran Home
22445 Cupertino Rd, Cupertino CA 95014-1043. 408/253-4300.

Los Gatos Meadows Geriatric Hospital
110 Wood Rd, Los Gatos CA 95030. 408/354-0211.

Milpitas Convalescent Hospital
120 Corning Ave, Milpitas CA 95035-5225. 408/262-0217.

Healdsburg Convalescent Hospital
14745 Grove St, Healdsburg CA 95448. 707/433-4813.

Sebastopol Convalescent Hospital
477 Petaluma Ave, Sebastopol CA 95472-4250. 707/823-7855.

Ukiah Valley Medical Center
1120 S Dora St, Ukiah CA 95482-6340. 707/462-3111.

Eskaton Village Care Center
3847 Walnut Ave, Carmichael CA 95608-2148. 916/974-2060.

Clovis Convalescent Hospital
111 Barstow Ave, Clovis CA 93612-2225. 209/299-2591.

Reedley Convalescent Hospital
1090 E Dinuba Ave, Reedley CA 93654. 209/638-3577.

Sanger Convalescent Hospital
2550 9th St, Sanger CA 93657-2716. 209/875-6501.

Bethel Lutheran Home
2280 Dockery Ave, Selma CA 93662-3898. 209/896-4900.

Valley Care Guidance Center
9919 S Elm Ave, Fresno CA 93706-9220. 209/834-5351.

Country View Alzheimer's Center
925 N Cornelia Ave, Fresno CA 93706-1096. 209/275-4785.

Manning Gardens Convalescent Hospital
2113 E Manning Ave, Fresno CA 93725-9681. 209/834-2586.

Twilight Haven Convalescent Hospital
1717 S Winery Ave, Fresno CA 93727-5011. 209/251-8417.

Carmel Convalescent Hospital
Hwy 1 & Valley Way, Carmel CA 93921. 408/624-8296.

Greenery Rehabilitation Center
385 Esplanade, Pacifica CA 94044-1882. 415/993-5576.

Hillhaven Victorian
2121 Pine St, San Francisco CA 94115-2829. 415/922-5085.

Hillhaven Lawton Convalescent Hospital
1575 7th Ave, San Francisco CA 94122-3704. 415/566-1200.

Hillsdale Manor Convalescent Hospital
2883 S Norfolk St, San Mateo CA 94403-1698. 415/378-3191.

Majestic Pines Care Center
1628 B St, Hayward CA 94541-3081. 510/582-4636.

Home For Jewish Parents
2780 26th Ave, Oakland CA 94601-1998. 510/536-4604.

Garfield Mental Health Center
1451 28th Ave, Oakland CA 94601-1632. 510/261-9191.

Oakridge Care Center
2919 Fruitvale Ave, Oakland CA 94602-2108. 510/261-8564.

Clinton Village Convalescent Hospital
1833 10th Ave, Oakland CA 94606-3023. 510/536-6512.

Excell Care Center
3025 High St, Oakland CA 94619-1807. 510/261-5200.

Shields Richmond Nursing Center
1919 Cutting Blvd, Richmond CA 94804-2662. 510/233-8513.

Fifth Avenue Convalescent Hospital
1601 5th Ave, San Rafael CA 94901-1808. 415/456-7171.

Guardian Of Greenbrae
1220 S Eliseo Dr, Greenbrae CA 94904-2006. 415/461-9700.

Canyon Manor
655 Canyon Road, Novato CA 94947-4399. 415/892-1628.

Terraces Of Los Gatos
800 Blossom Hill Rd, Los Gatos CA 95032. 408/356-1006.

Watsonville Care Center East
421 Auto Center Dr, Watsonville CA 95076-3725. 408/724-0671.

East Valley Pavillion
645 S Bascom Ave, San Jose CA 95128-2602. 408/299-8364.

Good Samaritan Rehabilitation & Care Center
1630 N Edison St, Stockton CA 95204-5633. 209/948-8762.

Chateau Convalescent Hospital
1221 Rosemarie Ln, Stockton CA 95207-6798. 209/477-2664.

Fairmont Rehabilitation Hospital
950 S Fairmont Ave, Lodi CA 95240-5131. 209/368-0693.

Delta Convalescent Hospital
1334 South Ham Lane, Lodi CA 95242-3903. 209/334-3825.

St. Dominic's Hospital
1777 W Yosemite Ave, Manteca CA 95337-5187. 209/825-3500.

Franciscan Convalescent Hospital
3169 M St, Merced CA 95348-2497. 209/722-6231.

Sonora Community Hospital
538 Ponderosa Dr, Sonora CA 95370-4805. 209/532-3161.

London House Convalescent Hospital
4650 Hoen Ave, Santa Rosa CA 95405. 707/546-0471.

London House Care Home
678 2nd St W, Sonoma CA 95476-6901. 707/938-1096.

Spring Lake Village
5555 Montgomery Dr, Santa Rosa CA 95409-8844. 707/538-8400.

Valley View Skilled Nursing Center
1162 S Dora St, Ukiah CA 95482-6340. 707/462-1436.

Willits Nursing & Rehabilitation Center
64 Northbrook Way, Willits CA 95490. 707/459-5592.

Crestwood Manor
2370 Buhne St, Eureka CA 95501-3205. 707/442-5721.

Eskaton Manzanita Manor
5318 Manzanita Ave, Carmichael CA 95608-0512. 916/331-8513.

Royal Oaks Convalescent Hospital
114 F St, Galt CA 95632-1833. 209/745-1537.

Gold Country Health Center
4301 Golden Center Dr, Placerville CA 95667-6260. 916/621-1100.

Garden Skilled Nursing Facility
2291 Fair Oaks Blvd, Sacramento CA 95825-5501. 916/927-1802.

Beverly Manor Convalescent Hospital
188 Cohasset Lane, Chico CA 95926-2271. 916/343-6084.

Crestwood Treatment Center
3062 Churn Creek Rd, Redding CA 96002-2124. 916/221-0976.

Tehama County Health Center
1850 Walnut St, Red Bluff CA 96080-3611. 916/527-0350.

Regency Hills Convalescent Hospital
2351 Loveridge Rd, Pittsburg CA 94565-5117. 510/427-4444.

Emmanuel Convalescent Hospital
180 N Jackson Ave, San Jose CA 95116-1907. 408/259-8700.

Colusa Community Hospital
PO Box 331, Colusa CA 95932-0331. 916/458-5821.

Morton Bakar Center
494 Blossom Way, Hayward CA 94541. 510/582-7676.

HOSPITALS AND MEDICAL CENTERS

Los Banos Community Hospital
520 West I St, Los Banos CA 93635-3419. 209/826-0591.

George L. Mee Memorial Hospital
300 Canal Street, King City CA 93930-3431. 408/385-6000.

Kaiser Foundation Hospital
1330 Cutting Blvd, Richmond CA 94804-2555. 510/596-6000.

Vitel International Inc.
100 Shoreline Hwy # 190, Mill Valley CA 94941-3645. 415/332-5134.

St. Josephs Behavioral Health Center
2510 N California St, Stockton CA 95204-5502. 209/948-2100.

Healdsburg General Hospital
1375 University St, Healdsburg CA 95448-3363. 707/431-6500.

Palm Drive Hospital
501 Petaluma Ave, Sebastopol CA 95472-4215. 707/823-8511.

Sonoma Valley Hospital District
347 Andrieux St, Sonoma CA 95476-6811. 707/935-5000.

Sutter Davis Hospital
PO Box 1617, Davis CA 95617-1617. 916/756-6440.

Vencor Hospital
223 Fargo Way, Folsom CA 95630-2961. 916/351-9151.

US Air Force Hospital
10535 Hospital Way, Mather CA 95655-4200. 916/643-7166.

Siskiyou General Hospital
818 South Main Street, Yreka CA 96097-3395. 916/842-4121.

Crestwood Geriatric Treatment Center
2171 Mowry Ave, Fremont CA 94538-1717. 510/793-8383.

Oak Creek Mental Health Recovery Service
455 Silicon Valley Blvd, San Jose CA 95138-1858. 408/224-2020.

Neurocare Inc.
1001 Galaxy Way, Concord CA 94520-5725. 510/686-5500.

Shriners Hospital For The Crippled
1701 19th St, Sacramento CA 95814-6711. 916/457-1800.

HOME HEALTH CARE SERVICES

Reedley Home Health Service A Division
1592 11th St, Reedley CA 93654-2938. 209/638-8994.

Curaflex Infusion Services
21020 Alexander Ct, Hayward CA 94545-1234. 510/782-9553.

Option Home Care IV & Nutrition
2165 Francisco Blvd E, San Rafael CA 94901-5522. 415/721-2273.

Olsten Kimberly Qualitycare
5405 N Pershing Ave Ste C3, Stockton CA 95207-5451. 209/474-7881.

Carepoint Nursing Services
604 W Cross St, Woodland CA 95695-3602. 916/753-2122.

Sutter Visiting Nursing Association
1455 Response Rd Ste 200, Sacramento CA 95815-4849. 916/927-3481.

Casha Resource Home Health Service Inc.
4600 Northgate Blvd, Sacramento CA 95834-1103. 916/565-0270.

Trinity Home Health Services
PO Box 1229, Weaverville CA 96093-1229. 916/623-5541.

SPECIALTY OUTPATIENT FACILITIES

Salvation Army Adult Rehabilitation Center
1500 Valencia St, San Francisco CA 94110-4406. 415/695-8000.

Renaissance Adolescent Center
2025 E Dakota Ave, Fresno CA 93726-4804. 209/435-7669.

Parkside Recovery Home Los Gatos
1101 S Winchester Blvd, San Jose CA 95128-3901. 408/358-2553.

Capital Counseling Services
650 Howe Ave, Sacramento CA 95825-4732. 916/646-1647.

CHANGE Alcoholism Counseling
2701 Cottage Way, Sacramento CA 95825-1223. 916/489-3552.

Beat It Program Inc.
PO Box 20896, San Jose CA 95160-0896. 408/241-3644.

Chemical Dependency Center
1507 21st St Ste 100, Sacramento CA 95814-5220. 916/448-2951.

American Lung Association
PO Box 23817, San Jose CA 95153-3817. 408/298-4277.

Tobacco Reduction Amador County
1001 Broadway Ste 106, Jackson CA 95642-2649. 209/223-6638.

Mental Health Association
199 Greenfield Ave, San Rafael CA 94901-2622. 415/456-7693.

Mill Valley House
60 Rancho Dr, Mill Valley CA 94941-1612. 415/381-4443.

Harbor Hills
1171 7th Ave, Santa Cruz CA 95062. 408/476-1700.

Litteral House
96 S 14th St, San Jose CA 95112-2015. 408/998-3293.

Recovery Inc.
PO Box 214344, Sacramento CA 95821. 916/483-5616.

HEALTH AND ALLIED SERVICES

Peninsula Blood Bank
1791 El Camino Real, Burlingame CA 94010-3284. 415/697-4034.

Stanford Medical School Blood Center
800 Welch Rd, Palo Alto CA 94304-1603. 415/723-7994.

Novacare Outpatient Rehabilitation
920 Yount St, Napa CA 94559-1800. 707/255-0711.

J&J Moroschok Enterprises
1480 Mallard Ln, Oakley CA 94561-2013. 510/625-2345.

Occupational Health Service Inc.
125 E Sir Francis Drake Blvd Larkspur CA 94939-1860. 415/461-8100.

San Joaquin Valley Health Center
425 N California St, Stockton CA 95202-2130. 209/463-4125.

Sierra Foothills Blood Center
11960 Heritage Oak Pl, Auburn CA 95603-2401. 916/823-0655.

Adventist Health System West
PO Box 619002, Roseville CA 95661-9002. 916/781-2000.

Center Point Programs
1050 B St, San Rafael CA 94901-2923. 415/454-7777.

RESIDENTIAL CARE

Loyd's Liberty Homes
2519 W Shaw Ave, Fresno CA 93711-3311. 209/226-5611.

Easton Creek Villa
1268 Balboa Ave, Burlingame CA 94010-4835. 415/344-7066.

Colony Residential Care Home
1991 Colony St, Mountain View CA 94043-1728. 415/968-4699.

Navarrete's Rest Home
693 7th Ave, San Bruno CA 94066-4523. 415/583-6003.

Joy's Aloha Lodge
969 Henderson Ave, Sunnyvale CA 94086-9061. 408/732-2499.

GM Residential Care
4924 Omar St, Fremont CA 94538-3248. 510/226-0102.

Saint Regis Retirement Center
23950 Mission Blvd, Hayward CA 94544-1091. 510/881-7888.

King's Rock Manor
2525 Oak Rd, Walnut Creek CA 94596-3131. 510/947-1550.

Sleepy Hollow Serenity Home
17 Fawn Ct, San Anselmo CA 94960-1125. 415/456-1854.

National Homecare Systems
831 Bay St, Santa Cruz CA 95060-4701. 408/464-1055.

Golden-Ager's Homes
1905 Kinross Way, San Jose CA 95122-2943. 408/947-8587.

Westgate Villa
5425 Mayme Ave, San Jose CA 95129-4899. 408/366-6510.

Brobergs Residential Care Homes
1733 Oldtree Ct, San Jose CA 95131-1931. 408/729-9019.

Sunrise Community
7501 Sunrise Boulevard, Citrus Heights CA 95610. 916/726-3315.

Eucalyptus Tree Lodge
1532 Rosalind St, Sacramento CA 95838-4535. 916/925-9655.

Families First
2025 Gateway Pl, San Jose CA 95110-1014. 408/452-0490.

Park Towers
700 Laurel Ave, San Mateo CA 94401-4144. 415/342-2051.

Byron Park Retirement Residence
1700 Tice Valley Blvd, Walnut Creek CA 94595-1634. 510/937-1700.

Piedmont Gardens
110 41st St, Piedmont CA 94611-5250. 510/654-7172.

Forum At Rancho San Antonio
23500 Cristo Rey Dr, Cupertino CA 95014. 415/969-0600.

Villa Dolce Vita
627 N Grant St, Stockton CA 95202-2232. 209/931-1800.

Plymouth Place
1320 N Monroe, Stockton CA 95203. 209/466-4345.

Casa Manana Inn
3700 North Sutter St, Stockton CA 95204. 209/466-4046.

Park Place Apartments
13th & North Street, Sacramento CA 95814. 916/444-8400.

Pioneer Tower
515 P St, Sacramento CA 95814-6349. 916/443-6548.

For more information on career opportunities in the health care industry:

Associations

ACCREDITING COMMISSION ON EDUCATION FOR HEALTH SERVICES ADMINISTRATION
1911 North Fort Myer Drive, Suite 503, Arlington VA 22209. 703/524-0511.

AMERICAN ACADEMY OF FAMILY PHYSICIANS
8880 Ward Parkway, Kansas City MO 64114. 816/333-9700. Promotes continuing education for family physicians.

AMERICAN ACADEMY OF PHYSICIAN ASSISTANTS
950 North Washington Street, Alexandria VA 22314. 703/836-2272. Promotes the use of physician assistants.

AMERICAN ASSOCIATION FOR CLINICAL CHEMISTRY
2101 Lovely Street NW, Suite 202, Washington, DC 20037-1526. 202/857-0717. A nonprofit association for clinical, chemical, medical, and technical doctors.

AMERICAN ASSOCIATION FOR RESPIRATORY CARE
11030 Ables Lane, Dallas TX 75229-4593. 214/243-2272. World Wide Web address: http://www.aarc.org. Promotes the art and science of respiratory care, while focusing on the needs of the patients.

AMERICAN ASSOCIATION OF COLLEGES OF OSTEOPATHIC MEDICINE
6110 Executive Boulevard, Suite 405, Rockville MD 20852. 301/468-2037. World Wide Web address: http://www.aacom.org. Provides applications processing services for colleges of osteopathic medicine.

AMERICAN ASSOCIATION OF COLLEGES OF PODIATRIC MEDICINE
1350 Piccard Drive, Suite 322, Rockville MD 20850. 301/990-7400. World Wide Web address: http://www.podiatry.org/podiatry.html. Provides applications processing services for colleges of podiatric medicine.

AMERICAN ASSOCIATION OF DENTAL SCHOOLS
1625 Massachusetts Avenue NW, Washington DC 20036-2212. 202/667-9433. Fax: 202/667-0642. E-mail address: aads@aads.jhu.edu. Represents all 54 of the dental schools in the U.S. as well as individual members. Goals of the organization include the expansion of postdoctoral training and increasing the number of women and minorities in the dental field.

AMERICAN ASSOCIATION OF HEALTHCARE CONSULTANTS
11208 Waples Mill Road, Suite 109, Fairfax VA 22030. 703/691-2242. World Wide Web address: http://www.mcninet.com/aahc.

AMERICAN ASSOCIATION OF HOMES AND SERVICES FOR THE AGING
901 E Street NW, Suite 500, Washington DC 20004-2037. 202/783-2242.

AMERICAN ASSOCIATION OF MEDICAL ASSISTANTS
20 North Wacker Drive, Suite 1575, Chicago IL 60606. 312/899-1500.

AMERICAN ASSOCIATION OF NURSE ANESTHETISTS
222 South Prospect Avenue, Park Ridge IL 60068-4001. 847/692-7050.

AMERICAN CHIROPRACTIC ASSOCIATION
1701 Clarendon Boulevard, Arlington VA 22209. 703/276-8800. World Wide Web address: http://www.amerchiro.org/aca. A national, nonprofit professional membership organization. Provides educational services (through films, booklets, texts, and kits), regional seminars and workshops, and major health and education activities to provide information on public health, safety, physical fitness, and disease prevention.

AMERICAN COLLEGE OF HEALTHCARE ADMINISTRATORS
325 South Patrick Street, Alexandria VA 22314. 703/549-5822. A professional membership society for individual long-term care professionals. Sponsors educational programs, supports research, and produces a number of publications, including the *Journal of Long-Term Care Administration* and *The Long-Term Care Administrator.*

AMERICAN COLLEGE OF HEALTHCARE EXECUTIVES
One North Franklin, Suite 1700, Chicago IL 60606-3491. 312/424-2800. Offers credentialing and educational programs. Publishes *Hospital & Health Services Administration* (a journal), and *Healthcare Executive* (a magazine).

AMERICAN COLLEGE OF MEDICAL PRACTICE EXECUTIVES
104 Inverness Terrace, East Englewood CO 80112-5306. 303/397-7869.

AMERICAN COLLEGE OF PHYSICIAN EXECUTIVES
4890 West Kennedy Boulevard, Suite 200, Tampa FL 33609-2575. 813/287-2000. World Wide Web address: http://www.acpe.org.

AMERICAN DENTAL ASSOCIATION
211 East Chicago Avenue, Chicago IL 60611. 312/440-2500.

AMERICAN DENTAL HYGIENISTS ASSOCIATION
Division of Professional Development, 444 North Michigan Avenue, Suite 3400, Chicago IL 60611. 312/440-8900. World Wide Web address: http://www.adha.org.

AMERICAN DIETETIC ASSOCIATION
216 West Jackson Boulevard, Chicago IL 60606-6995. 312/899-0040 or 800/877-1600.

Promotes optimal nutrition to improve public health and well-being.

AMERICAN HEALTH INFORMATION MANAGEMENT ASSOCIATION
919 North Michigan Avenue, Suite 1400, Chicago IL 60611. 312/787-2672. World Wide Web address: http://www.ahima.org.

AMERICAN HOSPITAL ASSOCIATION
One North Franklin Street, Suite 2700, Chicago IL 60606. 312/422-3000.

AMERICAN MEDICAL ASSOCIATION
515 North State Street, Chicago IL 60610. 312/464-5000. An organization for medical doctors.

AMERICAN MEDICAL TECHNOLOGISTS
710 Higgins Road, Park Ridge IL 60068. 847/823-5169.

AMERICAN NURSES ASSOCIATION
600 Maryland Avenue SW, Suite 100W, Washington DC 20024-2571. 202/554-4444.

AMERICAN OCCUPATIONAL THERAPY ASSOCIATION
4720 Montgomery Lane, Bethesda MD 20824-1220. 301/652-2682. 800/377-8555. Fax: 301/652-7711.

AMERICAN OPTOMETRIC ASSOCIATION
243 North Lindbergh Boulevard, St. Louis MO 63141. 314/991-4100. Offers publications, discounts, and insurance programs for members.

AMERICAN ORGANIZATION OF NURSE EXECUTIVES
One North Franklin Street, Suite 3400, Chicago IL 60606. 312/422-2800.

AMERICAN PHYSICAL THERAPY ASSOCIATION
1111 North Fairfax Street, Alexandria VA 22314. 703/684-2782. World Wide Web address: http://www.apta.org. Small fee required for information.

AMERICAN PUBLIC HEALTH ASSOCIATION
1015 15th Street NW, Suite 300, Washington DC 20005. 202/789-5600. World Wide Web address: http://www.apha.org.

AMERICAN VETERINARY MEDICAL ASSOCIATION
1931 North Meacham Road, Suite 100, Schaumburg IL 60173-4360. 847/925-8070. World Wide Web address: http://www.avma.org. Provides a forum for the discussion of issues of importance to the veterinary profession.

ASSOCIATION OF MENTAL HEALTH ADMINISTRATORS
60 Revere Drive, Suite 500, Northbrook IL 60062. 847/480-9626.

ASSOCIATION OF UNIVERSITY PROGRAMS IN HEALTH ADMINISTRATION
1911 North Fort Myer Drive, Suite 503, Arlington VA 22209. 703/524-5500.

GROUP HEALTH ASSOCIATION OF AMERICA, INC.
1129 20th Street NW, Suite 600, Washington DC 20036. 202/778-3200.

HEALTHCARE FINANCIAL MANAGEMENT ASSOCIATION
Two Westbrook Corporate Center, Suite 700, Westchester IL 60154. 708/531-9600. World Wide Web address: http://www.hfma.org.

NATIONAL MEDICAL ASSOCIATION
1012 Tenth Street NW, Washington DC 20001. 202/347-1895.

Magazines

AMERICAN JOURNAL OF NURSING
555 West 57th Street, New York NY 10019. Publishes five editions: *Hospital*, *Critical Care*, *Continuing Care*, *Regular*, and *Nurse Practitioner*. Accredited as a provider of continuing education in nursing by the American Nurses Credentialing Center.

AMERICAN MEDICAL NEWS
American Medical Association, 515 North State Street, Chicago IL 60605. 312/464-5000.

CHANGING MEDICAL MARKETS
Theta Corporation, Theta Building, Middlefield CT 06455. 860/349-1054.

HEALTH CARE EXECUTIVE
American College of Health Care Executives, One North Franklin, Suite 1700, Chicago IL 60606. 312/424-2800.

NURSEFAX
Springhouse Corporation, 1111 Bethlehem Pike, P.O. Box 908, Springhouse PA 19477. 215/646-8700. This is a jobline service designed to be used in conjunction with *Nursing* magazine. Please call to obtain a copy of a magazine or the *Nursing* directory.

MODERN HEALTHCARE
Crain Communications, 740 North Rush Street, Chicago IL 60611. 312/649-5374.

HOTELS AND RESTAURANTS

Job opportunities in the restaurant industry are plentiful. A number of trends will boost job growth, including population growth, rising incomes, and more dual-income families. Some demand will be met through labor saving innovations like salad bars, untended meal stations, automated beverage stations, and central kitchens that serve a number of establishments in the same restaurant chain. In the fast-food sector, use of labor-saving technology is essential to remain competitive. Since the most time-consuming transaction at drive-in windows is making change, some restaurants are experimenting with debit and credit cards to reduce transaction time. However, despite labor-saving innovations, the increased demand for services will increase the need for workers.

Jobs in hotels, motels, and other lodging places will be plentiful throughout the next decade. Driving the growth will be many of the same trends affecting the restaurant industry, as well as low-cost airfares and foreign tourism in the U.S. Another hot trend: legalized gambling. The hotel and motel industry invests heavily in the gaming industry, and that has further fueled job growth. This growth will continue as hotels increasingly attract families by offering relatively inexpensive casino vacation packages.

The greatest growth is in all-suite properties and budget motels. Since they don't have restaurants, dining rooms, lounges, or kitchens, these properties offer few jobs for food and beverage workers, but jobs should be available for managers and assistant managers. The trend toward chain-affiliated lodging places should provide managers with opportunities for advancement into general manager positions and corporate administrative jobs.

DAVRE'S INC.
555 California Street, Carnelium Room, 52nd Floor, San Francisco CA 94104. 415/433-7505. **Contact:** Conrad Sunga, Personnel. **Description:** Owns and operates a chain of popularly-priced restaurants. **Parent company:** Aramark.

DUNFEY SAN MATEO HOTEL
1770 South Amphlett Boulevard, San Mateo CA 94402. 415/573-7661. **Contact:** Personnel. **Description:** Operates a full-service hotel with a variety of facilities.

EL TORITO RESTAURANTS INC.
379 Gellert Boulevard, Daly City CA 94015. 415/994-3210. **Contact:** General Manager. **Description:** Operates a chain of Mexican-style and continental dinnerhouses. **Corporate headquarters location:** This Location.

FAIRMONT HOTEL
950 Mason Street, San Francisco CA 94108. 415/772-5129. **Fax:** 415/772-5049. **Contact:** Ms. Jamie Franks, Employment Manager. **Description:** Operates numerous hotels. **Common positions include:** Accountant/Auditor; Employment Interviewer; Food and Beverage Service Worker; Hotel Manager/Assistant Manager; Hotel/Motel

Clerk; Human Resources Specialist; Human Service Worker; Payroll Clerk; Secretary; Stationary Engineer.

FRESH CHOICE, INC.
2901 Tasman Drive, Suite 109, Santa Clara CA 95054. 408/986-8661. **Fax:** 408/450-0198. **Contact:** Recruiter. **Description:** Operates 58 casual, upscale restaurants in northern California, Washington, Texas, and Washington DC under the Fresh Choice name. The restaurants feature an extensive selection of high-quality, freshly made specialty and traditional salads, hot pasta dishes, soups, bakery goods, and desserts, offered in a self-service distinctive dining experience that combines the selection, quality, and ambiance of full-service casual restaurants, and the convenience and low-price appeal of traditional buffet restaurants. **Common positions include:** Restaurant/Food Service Manager. **Benefits:** Dental Insurance; ESOP; Life Insurance; Medical Insurance. **Special Programs:** Internships. **Corporate headquarters location:** This Location. **Other U.S. locations:** Washington DC; TX; WA. **Listed on:** NASDAQ. **Number of employees at this location:** 60. **Number of employees nationwide:** 3,000.

HOLIDAY INN CIVIC CENTER
50 Eighth Street, San Francisco CA 94103. 415/626-6103. **Contact:** Director of Personnel. **Description:** Operates a full-service hotel as part of the international Holiday Inn chain, whose operations include the management of more than 1,750 company-owned and franchised hotels, gaming operations, restaurants, and a sea transportation subsidiary. **Corporate headquarters location:** Memphis TN. **Listed on:** New York Stock Exchange.

HYATT REGENCY AT SAN FRANCISCO AIRPORT
1333 Old Bayshore Highway, Burlingame CA 94010. 415/347-1234. **Contact:** Human Resources. **Description:** Operates a full-service hotel complex which includes restaurants, banquet rooms, and recreational and convention facilities. Hyatt hotels are located throughout the world. **Common positions include:** Accountant/Auditor; Food and Beverage Service Worker; Hotel Manager/Assistant Manager; Services Sales Representative. **Educational backgrounds include:** Accounting; Business Administration; Hospitality/Restaurant. **Benefits:** Dental Insurance; Employee Discounts; Free Meals; Life Insurance; Medical Insurance; Pension Plan; Tuition Assistance. **Corporate headquarters location:** Chicago IL. **Parent company:** Hyatt Corporation. **Operations at this facility include:** Service.

HYATT REGENCY MONTEREY HOTEL CONFERENCE CENTER
One Old Golf Course Road, Monterey CA 93940. 408/372-1234. **Fax:** 408/647-2075. **Contact:** Alex Ortiz, Employment Coordinator. **Description:** Part of the Hyatt chain of hotels, this location is one of over 100 worldwide. **Common positions include:** Accountant/Auditor; Bank Officer/Manager; Blue-Collar Worker Supervisor; Clerical Supervisor; Credit Manager; Customer Service Representative; General Manager; Hotel Manager/Assistant Manager; Human Resources Specialist; Management Trainee; Restaurant/Food Service Manager; Services Sales Representative. **Educational backgrounds include:** Accounting; Business Administration; Communications; Finance. **Benefits:** 401(k); Dental Insurance; Disability Coverage; Employee Discounts; Life Insurance; Medical Insurance; Pension Plan; Tuition Assistance. **Corporate headquarters location:** Chicago IL. **Operations at this facility include:** Administration; Sales; Service. **Number of employees at this location:** 430. **Number of employees nationwide:** 40,000.

HYATT REGENCY SAN FRANCISCO
Five Embarcadero Center, San Francisco CA 94111. 415/788-1234. **Fax:** 415/398-2567. **Contact:** Human Resources Manager. **Description:** Operates a hotel with a complete range of services as part of the Hyatt chain of hotels, which operates hotel and recreational facilities throughout the world. **Corporate headquarters location:** Chicago IL.

LE BARON HOTEL
1350 North First Street, San Jose CA 95112. 408/453-6200. **Contact:** Personnel Assistant. **Description:** Operates a full-service hotel with a wide range of facilities, including convention facilities, meeting rooms, suites, three lounges, two restaurants, and an exercise room. **Common positions include:** Accountant/Auditor; Hotel Manager/Assistant Manager; Human Resources Specialist; Marketing Specialist; Services Sales Representative. **Educational backgrounds include:** Marketing. **Benefits:** Dental Insurance; Disability Coverage; Life Insurance; Medical Insurance. **Corporate headquarters location:** This Location. **Operations at this facility include:** Administration; Sales; Service.

LYON'S RESTAURANTS INC.
1165 Triton Drive, Foster City CA 94404. 415/349-5966. **Contact:** Personnel Department. **Description:** Operates a chain of restaurants. **Common positions include:** Management Trainee. **Educational backgrounds include:** Business Administration; Liberal Arts. **Benefits:** Credit Union; Dental Insurance; Disability Coverage; Life Insurance; Medical Insurance; Pension Plan; Tuition Assistance.

MARRIOTT SANTA CLARA
2700 Mission College Boulevard, Santa Clara CA 95054. 408/988-1500. **Contact:** Ms. Reine Garcia, Recruiter. **Description:** Operates a hotel with complete dining and recreational facilities.

MONTEREY PASTA COMPANY
353 Sacramento, Suite 500, San Francisco CA 94111. 415/397-7782. **Contact:** Human Resources. **Description:** Monterey Pasta Company manufactures and markets a premium line of fresh gourmet pasta and pasta sauces, emphasizing natural ingredients, and owns and operates 20 quick-service pasta restaurants. In addition to offering its products in its quick-service restaurants, the company markets and sells its products primarily in California, Colorado, Washington, and Arizona through approximately 945 leading grocery and club stores, such as Safeway, Ralphs, Vons, QFC, King Soopers, and Price/Costco. Monterey Pasta seeks to build brand recognition and customer loyalty by developing complementary channels of distribution and multiple points of sale for the company's products. A key component of the company's strategy is to cross market between grocery stores and its restaurants. Monterey Pasta currently offers 29 gourmet pasta products that are prepared using the company's proprietary recipes, including cut pasta, ravioli, pasta sauces, and pasta soups. To distinguish itself from more traditional Italian-style competitors, the company focuses on gourmet, premium pasta products in line with contemporary California cuisine. The company emphasizes the fresh, healthful, all-natural, and preservative-free quality of its products. The company's pasta and pasta sauces include Snow Crab Ravioli, Smoked Salmon Ravioli, Gorgonzola Roasted Walnut Ravioli, Sweet Red Pepper Fettucini, Santa Fe Linguine, Sun Dried Tomato Pesto Sauce, and Monterey Clam and Mushroom Sauce. The company is committed to

diversifying its product line by introducing innovative new pasta products on a regular basis.

OAKLAND MARRIOTT CITY CENTER
1001 Broadway, Oakland CA 94607. 510/451-4000. **Fax:** 510/832-1730. **Recorded Jobline:** 510/466-6440. **Contact:** Suzy Martinez DeSousa, Director of Human Resources. **Description:** A full-service luxury hotel and restaurant with 488 rooms. Oakland Marriott City Center also has conference rooms and meeting space available, connected directly to the hotel. **NOTE:** Entry-level positions are available. **Common positions include:** Accountant/Auditor; Customer Service Representative; General Manager; Hotel Manager/Assistant Manager; Human Resources Specialist; Restaurant/Food Service Manager; Typist/Word Processor. **Educational backgrounds include:** Accounting; Business Administration. **Benefits:** 401(k); Dental Insurance; Disability Coverage; Employee Discounts; Life Insurance; Mass Transit Available; Medical Insurance; Tuition Assistance. **Special programs**: Internships; Training programs. **Corporate headquarters location:** San Francisco CA. **Parent company:** Park Lane Hotels International. **Operations at this facility include:** Administration; Sales; Service. **Listed on:** Privately held. **Number of employees at this location:** 270.

RAMADA HOTEL/SAN FRANCISCO
1231 Market Street, San Francisco CA 94103. 415/626-8000. **Contact:** Gina Marzouk, Personnel Manager. **Description:** Operates a hotel with a variety of facilities. **Common positions include:** Accountant/Auditor; Credit Manager; Hotel Manager/Assistant Manager; Human Resources Specialist; Management Trainee; Operations/Production Manager; Purchasing Agent and Manager; Restaurant/Food Service Manager; Services Sales Representative. **Benefits:** Credit Union; Daycare Assistance; Disability Coverage; Employee Discounts; Life Insurance; Medical Insurance; Pension Plan; Tuition Assistance. **Operations at this facility include:** Administration; Regional Headquarters; Sales; Service.

RAMADA PLAZA HOTEL/FISHERMAN'S WHARF
590 Bay Street, San Francisco CA 94133. 415/885-4700. **Contact:** Personnel Department. **Description:** Operates a hotel with complete facilities as a part of Ramada Inns, Inc., which operates in two industry segments: Hotel and Gaming/Hotel. The company owns or licenses more than 600 hotels, including some overseas. **Listed on:** New York Stock Exchange.

SAN FRANCISCO AIRPORT HILTON
San Francisco International Airport, San Francisco CA 94128. 415/875-3060. **Contact:** Employment Manager. **Description:** Operates a hotel as part of the Hilton Hotels chain. Nationally, Hilton Hotels Corporation owns, leases, and operates more than 40 hotels under the Hilton name, and operates 150 Hilton hotels on a franchise basis. **Common positions include:** Cashier; Chef/Cook/Kitchen Worker; Department Manager; Food and Beverage Service Worker; Hotel/Motel Clerk; Restaurant/Food Service Manager; Stationary Engineer. **Educational backgrounds include:** Business Administration; Hospitality/Restaurant; Marketing. **Benefits:** Dental Insurance; Disability Coverage; Employee Discounts; Life Insurance; Medical Insurance; Pension Plan; Savings Plan. **Corporate headquarters location:** Beverly Hills CA. **Parent company:** Hilton Hotels Corporation. **Operations at this facility include:** Administration; Sales; Service. **Listed on:** New York Stock Exchange.

SAN FRANCISCO HILTON AND TOWERS
333 O'Farrell Street, San Francisco CA 94102. 415/771-1400. **Contact:** Human Resources. **Description:** A 1,900-room convention hotel with 110,000 square feet of meeting space. **Common positions include:** Customer Service Representative; Hotel Manager/Assistant Manager. **Educational backgrounds include:** Business Administration; Communications; Hospitality/Restaurant; Hotel Administration; Restaurant Management. **Benefits:** 401(k); Dental Insurance; Employee Discounts; Life Insurance; Medical Insurance; Pension Plan; Tuition Assistance. **Special Programs:** Internships. **Corporate headquarters location:** Beverly Hills CA. **Other U.S. locations:** Nationwide. **Listed on:** New York Stock Exchange. **Number of employees at this location:** 1,200.

SHERATON AT FISHERMAN'S WHARF
2500 Mason Street, San Francisco CA 94133. 415/362-5500. **Fax:** 415/627-6529. **Recorded Jobline:** 415/627-6567. **Contact:** Karen Crouch, Director of Human Resources. **Description:** Operates as part of the Sheraton Corporation, which has hotels and other interests in most major United States cities. **Common positions include:** Accountant/Auditor; Computer Programmer; Credit Manager; Customer Service Representative; Financial Analyst; Hotel Manager/Assistant Manager; Human Resources Specialist; Restaurant/Food Service Manager; Services Sales Representative; Systems Analyst. **Educational backgrounds include:** Communications; Hospitality/Restaurant; Liberal Arts. **Benefits:** Dental Insurance; Employee Discounts; Life Insurance; Medical Insurance; Pension Plan; Tuition Assistance. **Corporate headquarters location:** Boston MA.

***Note:** Because addresses and telephone numbers of smaller companies can change rapidly, we recommend you call each company to verify the information below before inquiring about job opportunities. Mass mailings are not recommended.*

Additional small employers:

EATING PLACES

Pizza Hut
4793 East Olive Avenue, Fresno CA 93702. 209/453-1111.

Pizza Hut
4134 North West Avenue, Fresno CA 93705. 209/222-2491.

Pizza Hut
2111 North Blackstone Avenue, Fresno CA 93703-2109. 209/224-6770.

Pizza Hut
1140 Waterloo Road, Stockton CA 95205. 209/467-1111.

Pizza Hut
27548 Tampa Ave, Hayward CA 94544. 510/782-2828.

Pizza Hut
720 West 11th Street, Tracy CA 95376-3715. 209/832-5100.

Pizza Hut
21 West Lodi Avenue, Lodi CA 95240-3515. 209/369-1961.

Pizza Hut
1773 Decoto Road, Union City CA 94587. 510/489-3600.

Pizza Hut
4607 Cherry Ave, San Jose CA 95118-3708. 408/978-5151.

Pizza Hut
560 Raleys Towne Ctr, Rohnert Park CA 94928-2444. 707/584-4600.

Applebee's Neighborhood Bar & Grill
Fig Garden Village Shopping Center, Fresno CA 93704. 209/244-6904.

Kentucky Fried Chicken
3218 E Jensen Ave, Fresno CA 93706-5114. 209/268-6311.

Ole Frijole Restaurant
5279 N Blackstone Ave, Fresno CA 93710-6703. 209/435-6570.

Sizzler Restaurant
1962 W El Camino Real,

Mountain View CA 94040-2002. 415/967-5574.

Sizzler Restaurant
1035 S Winchester Blvd, San Jose CA 95128-3702. 408/248-8189.

Sizzler Restaurant
7006 N Cedar Ave, Fresno CA 93720-3300. 209/323-9701.

Sizzler Restaurant
3725 Redwood Hwy, San Rafael CA 94903-3900. 415/472-1621.

Paradise Cafe
909 Van Ness Ave, Fresno CA 93721-2009. 209/266-3324.

Wendy's
1377 E Monte Vista Ave, Vacaville CA 95688-3082. 707/446-8669.

Wendy's
499 El Camino Real, San Bruno CA 94066-4246. 415/873-3810.

Wendy's
2326 Tulare Street, Fresno CA 93721-2206. 209/497-8085.

Sky Chefs Inc.
810 Malcolm Rd, Burlingame CA 94010-1407. 415/692-3941.

Charley Brown's
1550 Old Bayshore Hwy, Burlingame CA 94010. 415/697-6907.

Joe's Of Westlake
11 Glenwood Ave, Daly City CA 94015-3030. 415/755-7400.

Bartels & Blaine
180 Constitution Dr, Menlo Park CA 94025-1117. 415/324-1882.

Treasure Pot Seafood Restaurant
2650 W El Camino Real, Mountain View CA 94040-1117. 415/948-8999.

Tony & Alba's Pizza & Pasta
619 Escuela Ave, Mountain View CA 94040-2008. 415/968-5089.

Hong Kong Cafe
455 Oceana Blvd, Pacifica CA 94044-1901. 415/359-6088.

Bangkok Bay Thai Cuisine
825 El Camino Real, Redwood City CA 94063-1538. 415/365-5369.

Los Molcajetes Restaurant
175 5th Ave, Redwood City CA 94063-3603. 415/364-9685.

Tacos El Tulense
2391 Spring St, Redwood City CA 94063-3025. 415/367-1944.

Barney's Bar & Grill
590 Veterans Blvd, Redwood City CA 94063-1122. 415/365-8145.

Wang's House
586 San Mateo Ave, San Bruno CA 94066-4325. 415/871-6190.

Great Steak & Fry
2448 Town Center Ln, Sunnyvale CA 94086-6103. 408/739-3188.

Postrio Restaurant
545 Post St, San Francisco CA 94102-1228. 415/776-7825.

Silks At Mandarin Oriental Hotel
222 Sansome St, San Francisco CA 94104-2703. 415/986-2020.

Boulevard Restaurant
One Mission St, San Francisco CA 94105-1209. 415/543-6084.

Palomino European San Francisco Bistro
345 Spear St, San Francisco CA 94105-1673. 415/512-7400.

Lulu Cafe
816 Folsom St, San Francisco CA 94107-1123. 415/495-5775.

Cathay House
718 California St, San Francisco CA 94108-2404. 415/982-3388.

Village Pizzeria
1243 Van Ness Ave, San Francisco CA 94109-5534. 415/673-7771.

McCormick & Kuleto's Seafood
900 N Point St, San Francisco CA 94109-1154. 415/929-1730.

Thai Stick Restaurant
698 Post St, San Francisco CA 94109. 415/928-7730.

TGI Friday's
10343 N Wolfe Rd, Cupertino CA 95014-2507. 408/257-9600.

TGI Friday's
3101 S El Camino Real, San Mateo CA 94403-3429. 415/570-4684.

TGI Friday's
685 Beach St, San Francisco CA 94109. 415/775-8443.

Hard Rock Cafe
1699 Van Ness Ave, San Francisco CA 94109-3608. 415/885-1699.

Coconut Grove Supper Club
1415 Van Ness Ave, San

Francisco CA 94109-4607. 415/776-1616.

The Wok Shop Cafe
1307 Sutter St, San Francisco CA 94109-5415. 415/771-2142.

Salmagundi
425 Battery St, San Francisco CA 94111-3210. 415/398-4801.

Scott's Seafood Grill & Bar
2400 Lombard St, San Francisco CA 94123-2604. 415/563-8988.

Cafe General
1165 Revere Ave, San Francisco CA 94124-3422. 415/822-4123.

Olive Garden Italian Restaurant
2515 El Camino Real, Palo Alto CA 94306-1704. 415/326-5673.

Olive Garden Italian Restaurant
3251 20th Ave, San Francisco CA 94132-1900. 415/661-6770.

Olive Garden Italian Restaurant
1780 Challenge Way, Sacramento CA 95815-5006. 916/649-8305.

Scoma's Fisherman's Wharf
Foot Of Jones & Jefferson Pier 4, San Francisco CA 94133. 415/771-4383.

Expo Family Restaurant
160 Jefferson St, San Francisco CA 94133-1202. 415/673-9400.

Piatti Ristorante
2 Stanford Shopping Ctr, Palo Alto CA 94304-1401. 415/324-9733.

Fish Market Restaurants
3150 El Camino Real, Palo Alto CA 94306-2298. 415/493-9188.

Old Bayshore Grill
330 N Bayshore Blvd, San Mateo CA 94401-1235. 415/343-4110.

Carl's Jr.
1530 Kirker Pass Rd, Clayton CA 94517-1072. 510/672-9324.

Carl's Jr.
875 E Stanley Blvd, Livermore CA 94550-4008. 510/443-1565.

Carl's Jr.
4595 Century Blvd, Pittsburg CA 94565-7103. 510/754-5423.

Mai Food To Go
1303 W Texas St, Fairfield CA 94533-5918. 707/429-0194.

Los Gallos Taqueria
936 W Texas St, Fairfield CA 94533-5742. 707/429-2155.

London Fish & Chips
108 Sunset Center, Fairfield CA 94533. 707/421-0635.

Market Broiler
39195 Farwell Dr, Fremont CA 94538-1051. 510/791-8675.

Grand Taipei
40460 Albrae St, Fremont CA 94538-2483. 510/490-3337.

Joey D's Tamarack Inn
32681 Mission Blvd, Hayward CA 94544-8261. 510/471-8411.

Las Casuelas Grill
28257 Mission Blvd, Hayward CA 94544-4853. 510/581-1883.

Ski's Hot Dogs
31103 Mission Blvd, Hayward CA 94544-7603. 510/489-7030.

Bakers Square Restaurant & Pie Shop
1304 First Street, Livermore CA 94550-4202. 510/443-0241.

Canton Village
1100 E Stanley Blvd, Livermore CA 94550-4156. 510/373-3900.

Phoenix Garden
34123 Fremont Blvd, Fremont CA 94555-2230. 510/795-6611.

Mustards Grill
7399 Saint Helena Hwy, Napa CA 94558-9726. 707/944-2424.

Sunset Cactus Cafe
5416 Milani Ave, Newark CA 94560-3211. 510/657-4440.

Coco's Bakery Restaurant
7944 Dublin Blvd, Dublin CA 94568-2925. 510/829-4779.

Trilogy
1234 Main Street, Saint Helena CA 94574. 707/963-5507.

Horatio's Restaurant
60 San Leandro Marina, San Leandro CA 94577-4001. 510/351-5556.

Kings Wok Chinese Restaurant
34316 Alvarado Niles Rd, Union City CA 94587-4454. 510/475-1118.

The New Yorker Pizza
34391 Alvarado Niles Rd, Union City CA 94587-4455. 510/471-3400.

Vie De France
29320 Union City Blvd, Union City CA 94587-1219. 510/429-0500.

Round Table Pizza
1744 Decoto Rd, Union City CA 94587-3524. 510/489-3131.

Taos Grill
1345 Treat Blvd, Walnut Creek CA 94596-2173. 510/934-3850.

Creative Croissants
24 Broadway Ln, Walnut Creek CA 94596-5104. 510/930-9609.

The Fisherman
6534 Washington St, Yountville CA 94599-1397. 707/944-0170.

Cafe Kinyon
Vintage 1870, Yountville CA 94599. 707/944-2788.

Gum Kuo Restaurant
388 9th St Ste 182, Oakland CA 94607-4292. 510/268-1288.

Hambrick's Giant Burgers
4203 MacArthur Blvd, Oakland CA 94619-1907. 510/482-5656.

Chez Panisse
1517 Shattuck Ave, Berkeley CA 94709. 510/548-5072.

Golden Gate Catering
1100 Eastshore Hwy, Berkeley CA 94710-1002. 510/559-7400.

California Bakery and Restaurant
41 Simms St, San Rafael CA 94901-5415. 415/453-3513.

Red Boy Pizza
1115 4th St, San Rafael CA 94901-3006. 415/454-3131.

Pinkys Pizza Parlor San Rafael
345 3rd St, San Rafael CA 94901-3547. 415/453-3582.

Rosalind Catering
1545 4th Street, San Rafael CA 94901-2744. 415/454-3858.

Gonzales Hacienda San Rafael
809 B St, San Rafael CA 94901-3002. 415/459-9863.

Zims Restaurants
Northgate Shopping Center, San Rafael CA 94903. 415/479-9384.

Hof Brau-Roast Haus
276 Northgate One, San Rafael CA 94903-3416. 415/472-2233.

International House Of Pancakes
6480 Redwood Dr, Rohnert Park CA 94928-2326. 707/586-3698.

High Tech Burrito
118 Strawberry Village, Mill Valley CA 94941-2329. 415/388-7002.

Jennie Low's Chinese Cuisine
38 Miller Ave, Mill Valley CA 94941-1927. 415/388-8868.

Holey Bagel
308 Strawberry Village, Mill Valley CA 94941-2331. 415/381-2600.

Dipsea Cafe
200 Shoreline Hwy, Mill Valley CA 94941-3605. 415/381-0298.

Denny's Restaurant
7330 Redwood Blvd, Novato CA 94945-3212. 415/897-6086.

Buona Sera Cucina Italiana
148 Kentucky St, Petaluma CA 94952-2995. 707/763-3333.

Ferrais Restaurant & Coffee Shop
5101 Old Redwood Hwy, Petaluma CA 94954. 707/792-1710.

Burger King
5304 Old Redwood Hwy, Petaluma CA 94954. 707/664-9385.

Burger King
4960 Auburn Blvd, McClellan Afb CA 95652. 916/344-6421.

Taqueria La Quinta
150 A, Point Reyes Station CA 94956. 415/663-8868.

Hot Wok Chinese Food
898 Sir Francis Drake Blvd, San Anselmo CA 94960-1914. 415/454-0877.

King's Table Buffet
1955 41st Ave, Capitola CA 95010-2514. 408/475-4043.

Golden West Pancake House
11 Green Valley Rd, Freedom CA 95019-3108. 408/722-2424.

Brandons
1800 Barber Ln, Milpitas CA 95035-7422. 408/432-6311.

Fresh Choice Restaurant
5353 Almaden Expy, San Jose CA 95118-3601. 408/723-7991.

Fresh Choice Restaurant
3041 Stevens Creek Blvd, Santa Clara CA 95050-6704. 408/243-7402.

Fish Market Restaurant
3775 El Camino Real, Santa Clara CA 95051-2612. 408/246-3474.

Erik's Deli Cafe Inc.
365 Coral St, Santa Cruz CA 95060-2106. 408/458-1818.

Chaminade At Santa Cruz
1 Chaminade Ln, Santa Cruz CA 95065-1524. 408/475-5600.

The City Bar & Grill
300 Almaden Blvd, San Jose CA 95110-2703. 408/947-4444.

Bac Ha Restaurant
3120 Senter Rd, San Jose CA 95111-1257. 408/972-2736.

Angelo's Pepper Steak House
344 Tully Rd, San Jose CA 95111-1913. 408/288-7622.

Florentine Italian Foods Inc.
1070 Commercial St Ste 107, San Jose CA 95112-1420. 408/452-0170.

George's Arena Grill
525 W Santa Clara St, San Jose CA 95113-1520. 408/999-6800.

Les Saisons Restaurant & Bar
170 S Market St, San Jose CA 95113-2307. 408/998-3950.

Bakers Square Restaurant & Bake Shop
5055 Almaden Expy, San Jose CA 95118-2051. 408/267-6760.

El Grullo Restaurant
1210 Story Rd, San Jose CA 95122-2606. 408/993-1220.

Hoi Kee
1818 Tully Rd, San Jose CA 95122-1883. 408/238-3011.

Goveas Restaurant
1996 Tully Road, San Jose CA 95122-1889. 408/270-0973.

Ling's Chinese Food
362 Eastridge Mall, San Jose CA 95122-1402. 408/274-5221.

La Ostioneria
2155 Story Rd, San Jose CA 95122-1671. 408/923-7492.

Xinh Xinh Cafe
1075 Tully Rd, San Jose CA 95122-4237. 408/286-6611.

Wong Kee Barbeque Chinese Food
1818 Tully Rd, San Jose CA 95122-1883. 408/238-8230.

McTamal
2001 Story Rd, San Jose CA 95122-1617. 408/923-3660.

Robin Red Grill & Spirits Emporium
398 Eastridge Mall, San Jose CA 95122-1402. 408/223-1000.

Teriyaki Express
356 Eastridge Mall, San Jose CA 95122-1402. 408/274-7382.

Tay Ho Restaurant
1818 Tully Rd, San Jose CA 95122-1883. 408/238-9397.

Marie Callenders Restaurant & Bakeries
2628 W March Ln, Stockton CA 95207-6523. 209/952-0054.

Marie Callenders Restaurant & Bakeries
620 Blossom Hill Rd, San Jose CA 95123-3003. 408/578-0643.

Marie Callenders Restaurant & Bakeries
18599 Sutter Blvd, Morgan Hill CA 95037-2817. 408/778-7373.

Union Chinese Restaurant
2615 Union Ave, San Jose CA 95124-1349. 408/559-1688.

Togo's Eatery
173 W Santa Clara St, San Jose CA 95113-1707. 408/286-9394.

Togo's Eatery
900 North First Street, San Jose CA 95112-4918. 408/287-4570.

Togo's Eatery
40714 Grimmer Blvd, Fremont CA 94538-2845. 510/651-9053.

Togo's Eatery
14944 Camden Ave, San Jose CA 95124-2801. 408/371-3352.

Togo's Eatery
39308 Argonaut Way, Fremont CA 94538-1308. 510/790-8907.

Cozy Family Restaurants
2089 The Alameda, San Jose CA 95126-1136. 408/244-9085.

Chili's Grill & Bar
2980 Stevens Creek Blvd, San Jose CA 95128-2023. 408/241-8833.

Chili's Grill & Bar
5303 Sunrise Blvd, Fair Oaks CA 95628-3539. 916/962-0404.

Chili's Grill & Bar
5756 Pacific Ave, Stockton CA 95207-5160. 209/474-9004.

Taco Bell
840 S Bascom Ave, San Jose CA 95128-2605. 408/280-1728.

Armadillo Willy's BBQ
995 Saratoga Ave, San Jose CA 95129-2335. 408/255-7427.

Kitahama Japanese Restaurant
974 S Saratoga-Sunnyvale Rd, San Jose CA 95129. 408/257-6449.

Shang Yun Chinese Restaurant
1231 Kentwood Ave Ste A, San Jose CA 95129-3600. 408/996-0818.

Goldilocks Bakeshop & Restaurant
1698 Hostetter Rd # M, San Jose CA 95131-3333. 408/453-2537.

Fortune Chinese Restaurant
2530 Berryessa Rd # 913, San Jose CA 95132-2903. 408/723-8954.

Dong Thanh Restaurant
2095 N Capitol Ave, San Jose CA 95132-1009. 408/263-4730.

Trine's Cafe
2825 S White Rd, San Jose CA 95148-2933. 408/223-1563.

Bing's Cafe
701 E Main St, Stockton CA 95202-3132. 209/943-6974.

Dairy Queen Restaurant
9299 Thornton Rd, Stockton CA 95209-1858. 209/473-1929.

Mandarin House
9238 Thornton Rd, Stockton CA 95209-1833. 209/951-2034.

Paprika Hungarian Restaurant
9263 Fitzpatrick Cir, Stockton CA 95210-1446. 209/368-2925.

Jack In The Box
4989 Kingsley Rd, Stockton CA 95215-8320. 209/943-2157.

Brooks Ranch
4300 E Waterloo Rd, Stockton CA 95215-2334. 209/931-5611.

Denny's
5033 S US Highway 99, Stockton CA 95215-8248. 209/937-0665.

Mario's Pizza Place
322 Rose Garden Ct, Manteca CA 95336-3221. 209/869-0582.

McDonald's
2350 W Kettleman Ln, Lodi CA 95242. 209/368-1467.

McDonald's
7850 Lichen Dr, Citrus Heights CA 95621-1000. 916/721-7773.

McDonald's
2444 Notre Dame Blvd, Chico CA 95928-7136. 916/899-1285.

McDonald's
200 Richards Blvd, Sacramento CA 95814-0236. 916/444-2395.

McDonald's
901 N Carpenter Rd, Modesto CA 95351-1191. 209/544-2350.

Plascencia's Restaurant
128 W 10th St, Tracy CA 95376-3904. 209/835-9331.

Stony Point Grill
130 Stony Point Rd, Santa Rosa CA 95401-4120. 707/578-1953.

Coco's Family Restaurant
1501 Farmers Ln, Santa Rosa CA 95405-7525. 707/545-2626.

Mary's Pizza Shack
535 Summerfield Rd, Santa Rosa CA 95405-5202. 707/538-1888.

Mary's Pizza Shack
18636 Sonoma Hwy, Sonoma CA 95476-4418. 707/938-3600.

Pizza Express
2705 Bell Rd, Auburn CA 95603-2538. 916/823-9700.

David's Thai Cuisine
13338 Lincoln Way, Auburn CA 95603-3226. 916/888-6444.

Esperanca's Restaurant
1501 Grass Valley Hwy, Auburn CA 95603-2806. 916/885-1367.

Courtland Docks
11740 State Highway 160, Courtland CA 95615-9732. 916/775-1172.

Steve's Place Pizza
314 F St, Davis CA 95616-4118. 916/758-2800.

Pizza-Take & Bake
670 Pleasant Valley Rd, Diamond Springs CA 95619-9241. 916/626-0550.

Poor Red's Bar-B-Q
6221 Pleasant Valley Rd, El Dorado CA 95623-4232. 916/622-2901.

Old Mill Restaurant
9380 Elk Grove Florin Rd, Elk Grove CA 95624-1635. 916/685-7494.

Pizza Mill
16902 Yolo Ave, Esparto CA 95627. 916/787-4658.

Cafe Bergeron
919 Yolo Av, Esparto CA 95627. 916/787-3812.

Cliff House Of Folsom
9900 Greenback Ln, Folsom CA 95630-2117. 916/989-9243.

Spices Grill & Bar
419 Main St Ste 300, Placerville CA 95667-5600. 916/966-7555.

Mandarin Chinese Restaurant
4570 Pleasant Valley Rd, Placerville CA 95667-8404. 916/647-8111.

Round Table Pizza
2875 Ray Lawyer Dr, Placerville CA 95667-3914. 916/621-0682.

Las Primas Mexican Restaurant
3181 Cameron Park Dr, Cameron Park CA 95682-7980. 916/677-9791.

Coffee Tree
100 Nut Tree Pkwy, Vacaville CA 95687-3251. 707/448-8435.

Wah Shine Restaurant
145 Peabody Rd, Vacaville CA 95687-4708. 707/448-0785.

Uncle Reds American Grill
321 Nut Tree Rd, Vacaville CA 95687-3242. 707/452-8322.

El Caracol
201 Dobbins St, Vacaville CA 95688. 707/449-3798.

Nyack Coffee Shop
41800 Nyack Rd, Emigrant Gap CA 95715. 916/389-2611.

Cattlemens Restaurant
12409 Folsom Blvd, Rncho Cordova CA 95742-6413. 916/985-3030.

Hannibals Restaurant & Catering
535 L St, Sacramento CA 95814-3310. 916/443-5767.

Monterey Bay Canners Restaurant
400 Bercut Dr, Sacramento CA 95814. 916/441-3474.

Penny's Coffee Shop
1901 L St, Sacramento CA 95814-4108. 916/448-6059.

Cafe Europa
1689 Arden Way, Sacramento CA 95815-4030. 916/929-4140.

Chowders Arden Fair
1689 Arden Way, Sacramento CA 95815-4030. 916/927-7687.

California Pizza Kitchen Inc.
1735 Arden Way Ste 220, Sacramento CA 95815-5009. 916/568-0932.

El Gordo Carnitas
1022 Del Paso Blvd, Sacramento CA 95815-3605. 916/922-8188.

Ogden Entertainment Services
1600 Exposition Blvd, Sacramento CA 95815-5104. 916/924-1953.

Old Land Park Inland Boat Club
1704 Broadway, Sacramento CA 95818-2320. 916/447-9227.

Gallagher's Bar & Grill
5100 Folsom Blvd, Sacramento CA 95819-4535. 916/451-3444.

Chargin's Bar & Grill
4900 J Street, Sacramento CA 95819-3829. 916/454-1524.

Walt's Restaurant
2721 El Camino Ave, Sacramento CA 95821-5903. 916/488-5440.

Woody's Grill & Bar
2751 Fulton Ave, Sacramento CA 95821-5101. 916/485-4886.

Futami Restaurant
5609 Freeport Blvd, Sacramento CA 95822-3501. 916/428-0975.

Eat Your Vegetables
1841 Howe Ave, Sacramento CA 95825-1025. 916/922-8413.

Chili's Restaurant
2100 Arden Way Ste 185, Sacramento CA 95825-2217. 916/929-5838.

Flamingo Chinese Restaurant
9170 Kiefer Blvd, Sacramento CA 95826-5106. 916/362-8282.

Bradshaw's Restaurant
9647 Micron Ave, Sacramento CA 95827-2605. 916/362-3274.

Jasper's Giant Hamburgers
2946 Bradshaw Rd, Sacramento CA 95827-1602. 916/363-2112.

Fortune House Seafood Restaurant
7438 Windbridge Dr, Sacramento CA 95831-4707. 916/443-3128.

Carl Karcher Enterprises
3841 N Freeway Blvd Ste 185, Sacramento CA 95834-1948. 916/922-2029.

Java City Inc.
717 Del Paso Rd, Sacramento CA 95834-1106. 916/641-1330.

Eppie's Restaurants
4600 Madison Ave, Sacramento CA 95841-2515. 916/332-6277.

Hometown Buffet
2021 Whitman Ave Ste A, Chico CA 95928-6791. 916/899-1507.

Bettys Authentic Mexican Restaurant
10180 Live Oak Blvd, Live Oak CA 95953-2014. 916/695-3535.

Cornucopia Restaurants
515 Montgomery St, Oroville CA 95965-4510. 916/534-9025.

Long John Silver's Seafood Restaurant
1780 Oro Dam Blvd E, Oroville CA 95966-5909. 916/533-1541.

Jerry's Restaurants
590 Colusa Ave, Yuba City CA 95991-4009. 916/673-7254.

Strings Italian Cafe
1185 Colusa Ave, Yuba City CA 95991-3665. 916/673-7881.

Paul Kennedy's Steakhouse
4114 Lake Tahoe Blvd, S Lake Tahoe CA 96150-6965. 916/541-5077.

Zoo Frozen Yogurt
246 Jackson St, San Jose CA 95112-3201. 408/288-7858.

More Than Yogurt
3436 W Hammer Ln, Stockton CA 95219-4599. 209/957-9696.

Double Rainbow Gourmet Ice Cream
2532 Watt Ave, Sacramento CA 95821-6312. 916/973-1678.

Haagen-Dazs Co. Inc.
1045 National Dr Ste 11, Sacramento CA 95834-1930. 916/928-8493.

M&M Chicken
109 Appian Way, Union City CA 94587-3703. 510/487-6525.

Pagliacci Pizza
42 Greenfield Ave, San Anselmo CA 94960-2415. 415/459-4744.

Taste Of China
1659 Branham Ln # 1, San Jose CA 95118-2291. 408/448-3748.

Daddio's Deli & Cafe
1329 Columbus Ave, San Francisco CA 94133-1303. 415/771-8761.

Bolo's Pizza
PO Box 8014, Fremont CA 94537-8014. 510/460-8400.

J Bud's Grill
2025 W El Camino Real, Mountain View CA 94040-2217. 415/969-8209.

Cable Car Corner
1099 Powell St, San Francisco CA 94108-1513. 415/362-5925.

Cosmos Sandwich Shop
22 Peace Plz Ste 170, San Francisco CA 94115-3611. 415/931-7888.

New Thanh Huong
1156 Story Road, San Jose CA 95122-2635. 408/288-8851.

Submarine 21 Sandwich & Salads
1290 S Bascom Ave, San Jose CA 95128-3513. 408/286-2121.

Me-N-Ed's Pizza Parlors
7080 N Cedar Ave, Fresno CA 93720-3300. 209/298-7824.

Round Table Pizza
2401 Waterman Blvd, Fairfield CA 94533-1869. 707/425-3127.

Little Caesar's Pizza
100 E Tabor Ave, Fairfield CA 94533-3908. 707/422-3100.

Little Caesar's Pizza
2566 Grass Valley Hwy, Auburn CA 95603-2532. 916/885-9999.

Domino's Pizza
8743 Elk Grove Blvd, Elk Grove CA 95624-1742. 916/685-3030.

Mountain Mike's Pizza
2011 Naglee Ave, San Jose CA 95128-4801. 408/280-5070.

Churchill's Pizza & Pub
219 Taylor Rd, Newcastle CA 95658-9601. 916/663-2380.

Godfather's Pizza
6716 Madison Ave Ste 5, Fair Oaks CA 95628-3151. 916/965-1318.

Godfather's Pizza
1913 Douglas Blvd, Roseville CA 95661-3832. 916/773-2000.

Murphy's Take & Bake Pizza
Anderson Square Shopping Center, Anderson CA 96007. 916/378-2375.

Lunardis Market
1085 Alameda De Las Pulgas, Belmont CA 94002. 415/591-5768.

De La Cruz Deli
908 W Maude Ave, Sunnyvale CA 94086-2801. 408/245-3354.

Creative Gourmets
1375 Geneva Dr, Sunnyvale CA 94089-1121. 408/745-8700.

Court Cafe
1 Lombard St, San Francisco CA 94111-1132. 415/433-5502.

Vintage Catering
6034 Stewart Ave, Fremont CA 94538-3152. 510/657-1149.

Linda Thomas Catering
6528 Washington St, Yountville CA 94599-1397. 707/944-8096.

Country Delights Deli
27000 Highway 1, Tomales CA 94971. 707/878-2732.

Zanotto's Custom Catering
14 Victor Sq, Scotts Valley CA 95066-3564. 408/438-0982.

Genes Fine Foods Deli
18850 Cox Ave, Saratoga CA 95070-4196. 408/374-5198.

DRINKING PLACES

Hollywood Bar & Grill
5399 Farwell Pl, Fremont CA 94536-7222. 510/790-7007.

Foggs An International Tavern
303 Bryant Ave, Mountain View CA 94040-4520. 415/390-9696.

Reno Club
2348 W Capitol Ave, W Sacramento CA 95691-2426. 916/371-3333.

HOTELS AND MOTELS

The Highlands Inn
PO Box 1700, Carmel CA 93921-1700. 408/624-3801.

Quail Lodge Resort & Golf Club
8205 Valley Greens Dr, Carmel CA 93923-9513. 408/624-1581.

Doubletree Hotel At San Francisco
835 Airport Blvd, Burlingame CA 94010-1922. 415/344-5500.

Crown Sterling Suites
150 Anza Blvd, Burlingame CA 94010-1924. 415/342-4600.

California Innkeepers
1350 Bayshore Hwy, Burlingame CA 94010-1823. 415/348-7400.

Sheraton Inn San Francisco Airport
1177 Airport Blvd, Burlingame CA 94010-1909. 415/342-9200.

Stanford Park Hotel
100 El Camino Real, Menlo Park CA 94025-5292. 415/322-1234.

Clarion Hotel
401 E Millbrae Ave, Millbrae CA 94030-3189. 415/692-6363.

Crown Sterling Suites Hotel
250 Gateway Blvd, S San Fran CA 94080-7018. 415/589-3400.

Hotel Group Of America
693 Sutter St Floor 2, San Francisco CA 94102-1023. 415/202-8700.

Handlery Union Square Hotel
351 Geary St, San Francisco CA 94102-1801. 415/781-0269.

Best Western Americana
121 7th St, San Francisco CA 94103-2835. 415/863-2529.

El Drisco Hotel
2901 Pacific Ave, San Francisco CA 94115-1097. 415/346-2880.

Islander Motels
2428 Central Ave, Alameda CA 94501-4566. 510/523-7927.

Inn At Napa Valley
1075 California Blvd, Napa CA 94559-1061. 707/253-9540.

Days Inn
4200 Great America Pkwy, Santa Clara CA 95054-1210. 408/980-1525.

Red Lion Hotel Modesto
1150 9th St, Modesto CA 95354-0839. 209/526-6000.

Best Western Heritage Inn
11269 Point East Dr, Rncho Cordova CA 95742-6239. 916/635-4040.

Best Western John Jay Inn
301 W Pacheco Blvd, Los Banos CA 93635-4046. 209/827-0954.

Motel Six
1240 Camden Ave, Campbell CA 95008-6702. 408/371-8870.

E-Z 8 Motels Inc.
3550 El Camino Real, Santa Clara CA 95051-2136. 408/246-3119.

Motel Orleans
3951 Budweiser Ct, Stockton CA 95215-2301. 209/931-9341.

Lake Alpine Lodge
Alpine Lake, Bear Valley CA 95223. 209/753-6358.

Chateau By Piccadilly Inns
5113 E McKinley Ave, Fresno CA 93727-2033. 209/456-1418.

Holiday Inn Crowne Plaza
600 Airport Blvd, Burlingame CA 94010-1920. 415/340-8500.

Sir Francis Drake Hotel
450 Powell St, San Francisco CA 94102-1591. 415/392-7755.

Holiday Inn Financial District
750 Kearny St, San Francisco CA 94108-1809. 415/433-6600.

Parc Oakland Hotel
1001 Broadway, Oakland CA 94607. 510/451-4000.

Red Lion Hotel-Sonoma County
One Red Lion Drive, Rohnert Park CA 94928. 707/584-5466.

Holiday Inn
1355 Flora Ave, San Jose CA 95130. 408/453-5340.

Calaveras Lodging
1211 S Main St, Angels Camp CA 95222-9000. 209/736-0049.

Powderbears Log Cabin
Toll Gate Rd, Bear Valley CA 95223. 209/753-2136.

Trend West Resorts Inc.
1792 Tribute Rd Ste 270, Sacramento CA 95815-4305. 916/921-2022.

For more information on career opportunities in hotels and restaurants:

Associations

AMERICAN HOTEL AND MOTEL ASSOCIATION
1201 New York Avenue NW, Suite 600, Washington DC 20005-3931. 202/289-3100. World Wide Web address: http://www.ahma.com. Provides lobbying services and educational programs, maintains and disseminates industry data, and produces a variety of publications.

THE EDUCATIONAL FOUNDATION OF THE NATIONAL RESTAURANT ASSOCIATION
250 South Wacker Drive, 14th Floor, Chicago IL 60606. 312/715-1010. Offers educational products, including textbooks, manuals, instruction guides, manager and employee training programs, videos, and certification programs.

NATIONAL RESTAURANT ASSOCIATION
1200 17th Street NW, Washington DC 20036. 202/331-5900. World Wide Web address: http://www.restaurant.org. Provides a number of services, including government lobbying, communications, research, and information, and operates the Educational Foundation (see separate address).

Directories

DIRECTORY OF CHAIN RESTAURANT OPERATORS
Business Guides, Inc., Lebhar-Friedman, Inc., 3922 Coconut Palm Drive, Tampa FL 33619-8321. 813/664-6700.

DIRECTORY OF HIGH-VOLUME INDEPENDENT RESTAURANTS
Lebhar-Friedman, Inc., 3922 Coconut Palm Drive, Tampa FL 33619-8321. 813/664-6700.

Magazines

CORNELL HOTEL AND RESTAURANT ADMINISTRATION QUARTERLY
Cornell University School of Hotel Administration, Statler Hall, Ithaca NY 14853-6902. 607/255-9393.

HOTEL AND MOTEL MANAGEMENT
120 West 2nd Street, Duluth MN 55802.

INNKEEPING WORLD
Box 84108, Seattle WA 98124. 206/362-7125.

NATION'S RESTAURANT NEWS
Lebhar-Friedman, Inc., 3922 Coconut Palm Drive, Tampa, FL 33619. 813/664-6700.

INSURANCE

What's the job outlook in insurance? That depends on which industry segment you're looking at. Health insurers, who have avoided any Washington-based reforms, are reaping record profits, while property-casualty and life insurers are still struggling. The industry has been consolidating with major mergers, and that's likely to continue in 1996. Under pressure from low returns, and a growing number of environmental claims, the property-casualty industry needs to cut overhead. In many cases, that also means jobs.

The picture in health insurance is much brighter. Many of the biggest players in the insurance industry have moved into managed care, benefiting from the economies of scale.

ALEXANDER & ALEXANDER
333 Bush Street, Suite 600, San Francisco CA 94104. 415/391-2600. **Contact:** Mary Fenton, Office Manager. **Description:** Operates an insurance brokerage firm. **Common positions include:** Accountant/Auditor; Claim Representative; Financial Analyst; Insurance Agent/Broker; Underwriter/Assistant Underwriter. **Educational backgrounds include:** Accounting; Business Administration. **Benefits:** Dental Insurance; Disability Coverage; Life Insurance; Medical Insurance; Pension Plan; Savings Plan; Tuition Assistance. **Corporate headquarters location:** This Location.

AMERICAN INTERNATIONAL INC.
3 Embarcadero Center, Suite 302, San Francisco CA 94111. 415/445-2700. **Contact:** Liz Skorupa, Human Resources Manager. **Description:** An international insurance firm providing primarily property and casualty coverages in 50 states and 130 jurisdictions throughout the world. **Common positions include:** Services Sales Representative; Underwriter/Assistant Underwriter. **Benefits:** Life Insurance; Medical Insurance; Pension Plan; Stock Option; Tuition Assistance. **Corporate headquarters location:** New York NY. **Other U.S. locations:** Phoenix AZ; Los Angeles CA; Chicago IL; Dallas TX; Seattle WA. **Operations at this facility include:** Administration; Sales; Service. **Listed on:** New York Stock Exchange.

ARGONAUT INSURANCE COMPANY
250 Middlefield Road, Menlo Park CA 94025. 415/326-0900. **Contact:** Karen Borden, Manager of Human Resources. **Description:** A commercial lines property casualty insurer specializing in workers' compensation insurance. **Common positions include:** Accountant/Auditor; Actuary; Branch Manager; Claim Representative; Computer Programmer; Financial Analyst; Systems Analyst; Underwriter/Assistant Underwriter. **Educational backgrounds include:** Accounting; Business Administration; Computer Science. **Benefits:** 401(k); Dental Insurance; Disability Coverage; Life Insurance; Medical Insurance; Pension Plan; Stock Option; Stock Purchase. **Corporate headquarters location:** This Location. **Operations at this facility include:** Administration.

BLUE SHIELD OF CALIFORNIA/SAN FRANCISCO
P.O. Box 7168, San Francisco CA 94120. 415/445-5000. **Contact:** Human Resources. **Description:** A health care financing plan organization which provides a variety of

group and individual health plan coverages and professional medical services from doctors, dentists, psychiatrists, and other medical professionals. **Common positions include:** Accountant/Auditor; Actuary; Administrator; Department Manager; Financial Analyst; General Manager; Human Resources Specialist; Marketing Specialist; Mathematician; Public Relations Specialist; Services Sales Representative; Systems Analyst; Technical Writer/Editor; Underwriter/Assistant Underwriter. **Educational backgrounds include:** Accounting; Business Administration; Communications; Economics; Liberal Arts; Marketing; Mathematics; Nursing. **Benefits:** Dental Insurance; Disability Coverage; Life Insurance; Medical Insurance; Pension Plan; Savings Plan. **Corporate headquarters location:** This Location.

CII FINANCIAL, INC.
P.O. Box 9025, Pleasanton CA 94566-9025. 510/416-8700. **Fax:** 510/416-0771. **Contact:** Human Resources. **Description:** CII Financial is a holding company primarily engaged in writing workers' compensation insurance through its wholly-owned subsidiaries, California Indemnity Insurance Company and Commercial Casualty Insurance Company. CII Financial is also engaged in the electronic door lock manufacturing business through its 80 percent-owned subsidiary, InteLock Technologies, and in the insurance premium finance business through its wholly-owned subsidiary, CII Premium Finance Company. In addition, CII Financial has two operating insurance agencies and a managing general agent for a small start-up operation to write property-casualty insurance. **Corporate headquarters location:** This Location.

CSE INSURANCE GROUP
P.O. Box 7764, San Francisco CA 94120. 415/495-6800. **Contact:** Personnel Director. **Description:** A fire, casualty, and life insurance company.

CALIFORNIA CASUALTY MANAGEMENT COMPANY
P.O. Box M, San Mateo CA 94402. 415/574-4000. **Contact:** Employment. **Description:** An insurance firm offering business insurance and personal insurance. **Common positions include:** Accountant/Auditor; Actuary; Administrator; Attorney; Claim Representative; Commercial Artist; Computer Programmer; Customer Service Representative; Financial Analyst; Human Resources Specialist; Insurance Agent/Broker; Marketing Specialist; Statistician; Systems Analyst; Underwriter/Assistant Underwriter. **Educational backgrounds include:** Accounting; Business Administration; Computer Science; Finance; Mathematics. **Benefits:** Credit Union; Dental Insurance; Disability Coverage; Employee Discounts; Life Insurance; Medical Insurance; Pension Plan; Savings Plan; Tuition Assistance. **Corporate headquarters location:** This Location. **Operations at this facility include:** Administration; Sales; Service.

CALIFORNIA STATE AUTO ASSOCIATION
150 Van Ness Avenue, 5th Floor, San Francisco CA 94102. 415/565-4185. **Fax:** 415/565-4582. **Recorded Jobline:** 415/565-2194. **Contact:** Employment. **Description:** California State Auto Association provides automobile and homeowners insurance in California, Nevada, and Utah. The association also provides road services and travel services. **Common positions include:** Accountant/Auditor; Actuary; Attorney; Claim Representative; Commercial Artist; Computer Programmer; Customer Service Representative; Draftsperson; Financial Analyst; Human Resources Specialist; Public Relations Specialist; Services Sales Representative; Systems Analyst; Technical Writer/Editor; Transportation/Traffic Specialist; Underwriter/Assistant Underwriter. **Educational backgrounds include:** Accounting; Art/Design; Business Administration; Communications; Computer Science; Economics; Finance. **Benefits:** 401(k); Dental

Insurance; Disability Coverage; Employee Discounts; Life Insurance; Medical Insurance; Pension Plan; Tuition Assistance. **Corporate headquarters location:** This Location. **Parent company:** AAA National. **Operations at this facility include:** Administration; Sales; Service. **Number of employees at this location:** 1,700. **Number of employees nationwide:** 6,200.

CHUBB GROUP OF INSURANCE COMPANIES
Two Embarcadero Center, #1500, San Francisco CA 94111. 415/989-3000. **Contact:** Russell Kaltschmidt, Human Resources Manager. **Description:** A multiple-line property and casualty insurance group serving the public through independent agents and brokers. **Common positions include:** Claim Representative; Loss Prevention Specialist; Management Trainee; Operations/Production Manager; Underwriter/Assistant Underwriter. **Educational backgrounds include:** Business Administration; Liberal Arts. **Benefits:** Daycare Assistance; Dental Insurance; Disability Coverage; Life Insurance; Medical Insurance; Pension Plan; Profit Sharing; Savings Plan; Stock Option; Tuition Assistance. **Corporate headquarters location:** Warren NJ. **Operations at this facility include:** Administration; Sales; Service. **Listed on:** New York Stock Exchange.

CITATION INSURANCE GROUP
P.O. Box 28586, San Jose CA 95159. 408/292-0222. **Contact:** Carol Dickerson, Manager of Human Resources. **Description:** Founded in 1981, Citation Insurance Group is a holding company principally engaged in writing workers' compensation and commercial property and casualty insurance through its wholly-owned subsidiaries, Citation Insurance Company and Citation National Insurance Company. In its workers' compensation business, Citation Insurance Company (CIC) has historically specialized in providing coverage for California businesses but has recently begun to provide such coverage in Arizona, Colorado, and Utah. CIC focuses on insuring smaller accounts in those classifications it believes to be more historically profitable. CIC believes that by maintaining its focus on a limited number of employment classifications it can provide claim management and loss control services to the smaller accounts at a level appropriate to the size and type of business of the policyholder. Historically, CIC competed with other workers' compensation insurers principally on the basis of it loss control expertise, claim management services and policy holder dividends. Citation Insurance Company and Citation National Insurance Company specialize in insuring accounts in commercial property-oriented business classifications including investment properties, retail operations, restaurants, wholesale distribution operations, and other service-related businesses. **Common positions include:** Accountant/Auditor; Claim Representative; Clerical Supervisor; Computer Programmer; Computer Systems Analyst; Typist/Word Processor; Underwriter/Assistant Underwriter. **Educational backgrounds include:** Insurance. **Benefits:** 401(k); Dental Insurance; Disability Coverage; Life Insurance; Mass Transit Available; Medical Insurance; Profit Sharing; Tuition Assistance. **Corporate headquarters location:** This Location. **Other U.S. locations:** AZ; CO. **Operations at this facility include:** Administration. **Listed on:** NASDAQ. **Stock exchange symbol:** CITN. **Annual sales/revenues:** $51 - $100 million. **Number of employees at this location:** 100. **Number of employees nationwide:** 175.

DELTA DENTAL PLAN OF CALIFORNIA
Delta Tower, 100 First Street, 8th Floor, San Francisco CA 94105. 415/972-8300. **Contact:** Recruitment and Selection. **Description:** A prepaid dental insurance firm. **NOTE:** Entry-level positions are available. **Common positions include:** Accountant/Auditor; Actuary; Customer Service Representative; Dental Assistant/Dental Hygienist; Financial Analyst; Underwriter/Assistant Underwriter. **Educational**

backgrounds include: Accounting; Business Administration; Economics; Finance. **Benefits:** Dental Insurance; Disability Coverage; EAP; Employee Discounts; Life Insurance; Medical Insurance; Pension Plan; Prescription Drugs; Tuition Assistance. **Corporate headquarters location:** This Location. **Other U.S. locations:** Sacramento CA; Cerritos CA; Atlanta GA. **Subsidiaries include:** Private Medical Care, Inc. (PMI); Delta Dental Insurance Company (DDIC). **Operations at this facility include:** Administration; Sales; Service. **Annual sales/revenues:** More than $100 million. **Number of employees at this location:** 1,000. **Number of employees nationwide:** 1,500.

FIDELITY NATIONAL TITLE INSURANCE COMPANY
98 Battery Street, 4th Floor, San Francisco CA 94111. 415/421-1919. **Fax:** 415/788-0101. **Contact:** Human Resources. **Description:** Administrative offices for the title insurance company.

FIREMAN'S FUND INSURANCE CORPORATION
777 San Marin Drive, Novato CA 94998. 415/899-2000. **Contact:** Personnel. **Description:** An insurance company offering a wide range of coverage and policies.

GAB ROBINS
201 Mission Street, Suite 280, San Francisco CA 94105. 415/979-0909. **Contact:** David Flitton, Branch Manager. **Description:** Provides adjustment, inspection, appraisal, and claims management services to 15,000 insurance industry customers through over 550 branch offices. Specific services include the settlement of claims following major disasters; and the appraisal, investigation, and adjustment of auto insurance, casualty, fire, marine, life, accident, health, and disability claims. **Common positions include:** Accountant/Auditor; Claims Investigator; Computer Operator; Human Resources Specialist. **Educational backgrounds include:** Accounting; Business Administration; Liberal Arts. **Corporate headquarters location:** Parsippany NJ. **Parent company:** SGS North America. **Number of employees nationwide:** 3,400.

INDUSTRIAL INDEMNITY COMPANY
P.O. Box 7468, 255 California Street, San Francisco CA 94120. 415/627-5000. **Contact:** Personnel Director. **Description:** A state underwriter of casualty, property, and life insurance. **Corporate headquarters location:** This Location.

JOHNSON & HIGGINS
345 California Street, Suite 1700, San Francisco CA 94104. 415/981-6700. **Contact:** Linda Crawford, Human Resources. **Description:** An insurance brokerage firm specializing in employee benefits, property, casualty, mass coverage, and marine/aviation insurance lines. Johnson & Higgins has more than 140 offices worldwide.

KEMPER INSURANCE
P.O. Box 7993, San Francisco CA 94120. 415/421-2400. **Contact:** Dianne Whaley, Personnel Director. **Description:** A national/international insurance corporation. Engaged in a wide range of insurance, financial, and related activities. The company provides property, casualty, life insurance, reinsurance, and a wide range of diversified financial services operations. **Corporate headquarters location:** Long Grove IL.

LIBERTY MUTUAL INSURANCE COMPANY
P.O. Box 9117, Pleasanton CA 94566-9117. 510/734-9200. **Contact:** Personnel Department. **Description:** A full-line insurance firm offering life, medical, and business

insurance, as well as investment and retirement plans. **Corporate headquarters location:** Boston MA.

MARSH & McLENNAN/SAN FRANCISCO
P.O. Box 193880, San Francisco CA 94119. 415/393-5000. **Contact:** Human Resources. **Description:** A professional firm which provides advice and services worldwide through an insurance brokerage and risk management firm, reinsurance intermediary facilities, and a consulting and financial services group to clients concerned with the management of assets and risks. Specific services include Insurance and Risk Management Services, Reinsurance, Consulting and Financial Services, Consulting, Merchandising, and Investment Management. The company has subsidiaries and affiliates in 57 countries, and correspondents in 20 more. **Corporate headquarters location:** New York NY. **Listed on:** New York Stock Exchange.

METRAHEALTH, INC.
WESTERN REGION
425 Market Street, 13th Floor, San Francisco CA 94105. 415/546-3355. **Contact:** Human Resources Director. **Description:** Regional headquarters for MetraHealth's group managed care division. **Corporate headquarters location:** Hartford CT.

MUTUAL OF AMERICA
4000 Executive Parkway, Suite 512, San Ramon CA 94583. 510/244-0500. **Contact:** Todd Moriarty, Vice President. **Description:** An insurance company.

NATIONAL INSURANCE GROUP
395 Oyster Point Boulevard, Suite 500, South San Francisco CA 94080-1928. 415/872-6772. **Contact:** Human Resources. **Description:** An insurance company.

NORCAL MUTUAL INSURANCE COMPANY
50 Fremont Street, 17th Floor, San Francisco CA 94105. 415/777-4200. **Fax:** 415/512-1868. **Contact:** Felicia Field-Watson, Human Resources Representative. **Description:** Provides physicians with professional liability insurance. **Common positions include:** Attorney; Budget Analyst; Buyer; Claim Representative; Computer Programmer; Economist/Market Research Analyst; Editor; Financial Analyst; Human Resources Specialist; Paralegal; Services Sales Representative; Systems Analyst; Technical Writer/Editor; Underwriter/Assistant Underwriter. **Educational backgrounds include:** Business Administration; Communications; Finance; Liberal Arts. **Benefits:** Dental Insurance; Disability Coverage; Life Insurance; Medical Insurance; Pension Plan; Profit Sharing; Savings Plan; Tuition Assistance; Vision Insurance. **Special Programs:** Internships. **Corporate headquarters location:** This Location. **Other U.S. locations:** Anchorage AK; Pasadena CA. **Operations at this facility include:** Administration; Sales. **Listed on:** Privately held. **Number of employees at this location:** 170.

PRUDENTIAL PREFERRED INSURANCE COMPANY
651 Gateway Boulevard, Suite 700, South San Francisco CA 94080. 415/952-1111. **Contact:** Stan Chin, General Manager. **Description:** The largest multi-line financial services organization in the world with offices located throughout the United States and Canada. Prudential Preferred Insurance provides a wide range of financial services for individuals and groups, including individual insurance; personal investments; group insurance; reinsurance; institutional investments; group pension; and health care programs. Canadian operations are based in Toronto, Ontario. **Common positions**

include: Insurance Agent/Broker; Management Trainee; Marketing Specialist; Services Sales Representative. **Educational backgrounds include:** Finance; Marketing. **Benefits:** Dental Insurance; Life Insurance; Medical Insurance. **Corporate headquarters location:** Newark NJ. **Other U.S. locations:** Westlake CA; Jacksonville FL; Chicago IL; Boston MA; Minneapolis MN; South Plainfield NJ; Philadelphia PA; Houston TX. **Operations at this facility include:** Sales; Service. **Listed on:** New York Stock Exchange. **Number of employees at this location:** 65.

ROLLINS HUDIG HALL
One Market Plaza, Spear Street Tower, Suite 2100, San Francisco CA 94105. 415/543-9360. **Contact:** Mary Ericson, Human Resources Manager. **Description:** The San Francisco Profit Center of a large international insurance brokerage. Rollins Hudig Hall is primarily involved with property and casualty, marine, and public entities specialties. **Common positions include:** Accountant/Auditor; Administrator; Customer Service Representative; Industrial Agent/Broker; Marketing Specialist. **Benefits:** Dental Insurance; Disability Coverage; Life Insurance; Medical Insurance; Pension Plan; Savings Plan; Tuition Assistance. **Corporate headquarters location:** Briarcliff Manor NY. **Operations at this facility include:** Administration; Sales; Service. **Listed on:** New York Stock Exchange.

SAFECO INSURANCE COMPANY OF AMERICA
SAFECO CORPORATION
3000 Executive Parkway, Suite 300, San Ramon CA 94583. 510/277-8600. **Toll-free phone:** 800/816-6594. **Contact:** Greg Smith, Personnel Manager. **Description:** Safeco's primary business is in property and casualty insurance with strong subsidiaries in life insurance, surety, property development, credit, and investments/asset management. Safeco emphasizes employee development, innovation, professionalism, and a conservative approach to business. Regional and branch offices are located across the United States. **Common positions include:** Attorney; Claim Representative; Marketing Specialist; Underwriter/Assistant Underwriter. **Educational backgrounds include:** Accounting; Business Administration; Communications; Finance; Liberal Arts; Marketing; Psychology. **Benefits:** Bonus Award/Plan; Life Insurance; Medical Insurance; Profit Sharing; Savings Plan; Tuition Assistance. **Corporate headquarters location:** Seattle WA. **Operations at this facility include:** Administration; Marketing.

SCOR REINSURANCE
One Market, Steuart Street Tower, Suite 1275, San Francisco CA 94105-1008. 415/247-6565. **Fax:** 415/247-6569. **Contact:** Human Resources. **Description:** A property and casualty insurance and reinsurance company. **Corporate headquarters location:** New York NY. **Other U.S. locations:** Hartford CT; Chicago IL; Dallas TX. **Parent company:** SCOR U.S. Corporation.

SEDGEWICK OF CALIFORNIA
600 Montgomery Street, San Francisco CA 94111. 415/983-5600. **Contact:** Director, Human Resources. **Description:** Offers a full range of insurance brokerage and consulting services. **Common positions include:** Account Executive; Underwriter/Assistant Underwriter. **Educational backgrounds include:** Business Administration; Marketing. **Benefits:** Dental Insurance; Disability Coverage; Employee Discounts; Life Insurance; Medical Insurance; Pension Plan; Profit Sharing; Savings Plan; Tuition Assistance. **Corporate headquarters location:** New York NY. **Operations at this facility include:** Administration; Divisional Headquarters; Sales; Service.

STATE COMPENSATION INSURANCE FUND
1275 Market Street, San Francisco CA 94103. 415/565-1169. **Contact:** Personnel. **Description:** One of California's largest writers of workers' compensation insurance through 21 district offices.

TAKECARE, INC.
2300 Clayton Road, Suite 1000, Concord CA 94520-2100. 510/246-1300. **Contact:** Human Resources. **Description:** A managed health care company that provides complete health care services through HMOs operating in California, Colorado, Illinois, and Ohio. TakeCare's HMOs operate under the network and IPA models. The company provides services through roughly 742,000 members. **Number of employees nationwide:** 1,070.

THE TRAVELERS INSURANCE COMPANY
WALNUT CREEK
P.O. Box 8112, Walnut Creek CA 94596. 510/945-4000. **Contact:** Department of Interest. **Description:** One of the largest investor-owned insurance and financial service institutions in the world. The Travelers writes every principal form of life, accident, health, and casualty/property insurance. The company offers a broad range of pension and other investment management services. The Travelers operates more than 375 field offices through the country, and has assets of over $20 billion and more than $100 billion of life insurance in force. **Corporate headquarters location:** Hartford CT. **Listed on:** New York Stock Exchange.

VISION SERVICE PLAN
3333 Quality Drive, Rancho Cordova CA 95670. 916/851-5000. **Fax:** 916/851-4858. **Recorded Jobline:** 916/851-4700. **Contact:** Corporate Recruiter. **Description:** Vision Service Plan sells and administers a pre-paid vision care plan as an employee benefit purchased by employers for their employees. **Common positions include:** Accountant/Auditor; Computer Programmer; Computer Systems Analyst; Customer Service Representative; Economist/Market Research Analyst; Financial Analyst; Human Resources Specialist; Public Relations Specialist; Purchasing Agent and Manager; Technical Writer/Editor. **Educational backgrounds include:** Accounting; Business Administration; Computer Science; Finance; Health Care; Marketing. **Benefits:** Dental Insurance; Disability Coverage; Employee Discounts; Life Insurance; Medical Insurance; Tuition Assistance. **Special Programs:** Internships. **Corporate headquarters location:** This Location. **Other U.S. locations:** Nationwide. **Subsidiaries include:** Altair Eyewear. **Operations at this facility include:** Administration; Research and Development; Sales; Service. **Listed on:** Privately held. **Number of employees at this location:** 1,000. **Number of employees nationwide:** 1,300.

WEST COAST LIFE INSURANCE COMPANY
343 Sansome Street, 16th Floor, San Francisco CA 94104. 415/433-6200. **Fax:** 415/433-9423. **Contact:** Tracy Barker, Manager/Human Resources. **Description:** West Coast Life Insurance Company offers a complete range of life insurance services. **Common positions include:** Accountant/Auditor; Actuary; Customer Service Representative; Department Manager; Human Resources Specialist; Insurance Agent/Broker; Management Trainee; Marketing Specialist; Operations/Production Manager; Statistician; Systems Analyst; Underwriter/Assistant Underwriter. **Educational backgrounds include:** Accounting; Business Administration; Communications; Economics; Finance; Leasing; Liberal Arts; Marketing; Mathematics. **Benefits:** 401(k);

Credit Union; Dental Insurance; Disability Coverage; Employee Discounts; Life Insurance; Medical Insurance; Pension Plan; Tuition Assistance. **Corporate headquarters location:** This Location. **Parent company:** Nationwide Insurance. **Operations at this facility include:** Administration; Sales; Service. **Number of employees at this location:** 125.

Note: *Because addresses and telephone numbers of smaller companies can change rapidly, we recommend you call each company to verify the information below before inquiring about job opportunities. Mass mailings are not recommended.*

Additional small employers:

INSURANCE COMPANIES

California Capital Insurance Company
2300 Garden Rd, Monterey CA 93940-5326. 408/649-1155.

Leland A. Wolf & Associates
100 Foster City Blvd, Foster City CA 94404-1148. 415/573-8041.

New York Life Insurance Co.
70 Washington St Ste 200, Oakland CA 94607-3738. 510/268-3300.

US Behavioral Health
2000 Powell St Ste 1180, Emeryville CA 94608-1832. 510/601-2200.

Zurich American Insurance Group
44 Montgomery St Fl 27, San Francisco CA 94104-4602. 415/986-4900.

RLI Northern CA Regional Office
425 California St Ste 2101, San Francisco CA 94104-2206. 415/397-9937.

Wausau Insurance Co.
425 Market St Ste 800, San Francisco CA 94105-2423. 415/541-0144.

Zenith Insurance Co.
353 Sacramento St # 1001, San Francisco CA 94111-3620. 510/460-0600.

Fremont Compensation
100 California St Ste 700, San Francisco CA 94111-4512. 415/362-3333.

Republic Indemnity Co. America
100 Pine St Ste 1400, San Francisco CA 94111-5102. 415/981-3200.

Home Insurance Co.
1 Embarcadero Ctr Ste 1400, San Francisco CA 94111-3703. 415/544-3000.

Ohio Casualty Group
1390 Willow Pass Rd Ste 440, Concord CA 94520-5250. 510/825-4141.

Associated Claims Management Inc.
390 N Wiget Ln # 300, Walnut Creek CA 94598-2406. 510/930-9883.

California Compensation Insurance Co.
504 Redwood Blvd, Novato CA 94947-6921. 415/883-2503.

Jaffee Bonds
809 2nd Street, Santa Rosa CA 95404-4619. 707/546-4910.

INSURANCE AGENTS, BROKERS, AND SERVICES

Alburger Basso De Grosz Insurance
301 Island Pkwy, Belmont CA 94002-4109. 415/598-0900.

CNA Insurance
999 Bayhill Dr, San Bruno CA 94066-3000. 415/872-5300.

Benefit Consultants Inc.
1125 Industrial Rd, San Carlos CA 94070-4133. 510/595-8500.

Workers Compensation Insurance Rating Bureau
1 Market Plz, San Francisco CA 94105-1019. 415/777-0777.

Heffernan & Gallagher
160 Spear St, San Francisco CA 94105. 415/375-8855.

William M. Mercer Inc.
3 Embarcadero Ctr Ste 1250, San Francisco CA 94111-4015. 415/393-5200.

Equifax Services
2010 Crow Canyon Pl Ste 230, San Ramon CA 94583-1344. 510/830-0844.

Blue Shield Of California
6436 Oakdale Rd, Riverbank CA 95367-9648. 209/572-7500.

Allied Group
2301 Circadian Way, Santa Rosa CA 95407-5416. 707/542-2502.

Hoyt-Petersen & Co.
PO Box 3042, Sacramento CA 95812. 916/631-1200.

Aetna
6795 N Palm Ave, Fresno CA 93704-1056. 209/436-3100.

Rathbone King & Seeley Insurance Service
2547 W Shaw Ave Ste 113, Fresno CA 93711-3321. 209/248-8085.

Farmers Insurance Group
1201 Howard Ave Ste 302, Burlingame CA 94010-4224. 415/342-3960.

State Farm Insurance
1950 Kearny St, San Francisco CA 94133-2130. 415/693-4100.

Classic Insurance Service
1470 Enea Circle, Concord CA 94520-5217. 510/602-0850.

Reliance Insurance Co.
10989 Trade Center Dr, Rancho Cordova CA 95670-6152. 916/638-8300.

For more information on career opportunities in insurance:

Associations

ALLIANCE OF AMERICAN INSURERS
1501 Woodfield Road, Suite 400 West, Schaumburg IL 60173-4980. 847/330-8500.

HEALTH INSURANCE ASSOCIATION OF AMERICA
555 13th Street North, Suite 600E, Washington DC 20004. 202/824-1600.

INSURANCE INFORMATION INSTITUTE
110 William Street, 24th Floor, New York NY 10038. 212/669-9200. World Wide Web address: http://www.iii.org. Provides informational products on property/casualty insurance.

SOCIETY OF ACTUARIES
475 North Martingale Road, Suite 800, Schaumburg IL 60173-2226. 847/706-3500.

Directories

INSURANCE ALMANAC
Underwriter Printing and Publishing Company, 50 East Palisade Avenue, Englewood NJ 07631. 201/569-8808. Hardcover annual, 639 pages, $115. Available at libraries.

INSURANCE MARKET PLACE
Rough Notes Company, Inc., P.O. Box 564, Indianapolis IN 46206. 317/634-1541.

INSURANCE PHONE BOOK AND DIRECTORY
Reed Reference Publishing, 121 Chanlon Road, New Providence NJ 07974. Toll-free phone: 800/521-8110. $89.95, new editions available every other year. Also available at libraries.

NATIONAL DIRECTORY OF HEALTH MAINTENANCE ORGANIZATIONS
Group Health Association of America, 1129 20th Street NW, Suite 600, Washington DC 20036. 202/778-3200.

Magazines

BEST'S REVIEW
A.M. Best Company, A.M. Best Road, Oldwick NJ 08858-9988. 908/439-2200. Monthly.

INSURANCE JOURNAL
Wells Publishing, 9191 Towne Centre Drive, Suite 550, San Diego, CA 92122-1231 619/455-7717. A biweekly magazine covering the insurance industry. Subscription: $78 per year, $3 for a single issue.

INSURANCE TIMES
M & S Communications, 20 Park Plaza, Suite 1101, Boston MA 02116. 617/292-7117. A regional biweekly insurance newspaper for insurance professionals.

LEGAL SERVICES

The number of people working in the legal services field has exploded since the early '70s. According to a 1969 survey by the Bureau of Labor Statistics (BLS), there were 387,000 workers in legal services. Today, that number is well over 1 million. The glut of lawyers has led to tremendous competition in the legal profession. Law firms are laying off associates and firing unproductive partners. Graduates of prestigious law schools face tough competition for jobs, but for the top graduates, the offers will be there. According to Jon Sargent, an economist for the Office of Economic Growth at the BLS, some jobseekers looking to break into this industry may need to look outside the mainstream legal services industry: nonprofit companies, government positions, or law firms in smaller communities.

Paralegals have carved out a niche for themselves and continue to be the fastest-growing profession in legal services. "Paralegals have become a cost-effective way to provide legal services in many cases," says Sargent, referring to the realization by many employers that paralegals can do many of the same jobs as associates, at a much lower cost.

COBLENTZ CAHEN McCABE & BREYER
222 Kearney Street, 7th Floor, San Francisco CA 94108. 415/391-4800. **Contact:** Human Resources Department. **Description:** Coblentz Cahen McCabe & Breyer is a law firm.

KORNBLUM & FERRY LAW OFFICES
550 Montgomery Street, 8th Floor, San Francisco CA 94111. 415/392-7800. **Contact:** Human Resources. **Description:** The law offices of Kornblum & Ferry provide a wide range of legal services.

LAW OFFICES OF RONALD E. HOTHEM
369 Broadway Street, San Francisco CA 94133. 415/421-8222. **Contact:** Human Resources. **Description:** A law firm.

LEMPRES & WULFSBERG PRO CORP.
300 Lakeside Drive, 24th Floor, Oakland CA 94612-3524. 510/835-9100. **Contact:** Human Resources. **Description:** A law firm.

MORRISON & FOERSTER LLP
345 California Street, San Francisco CA 94104-2675. 415/677-7000. **Contact:** Human Resources. **Description:** A legal services firm. **Corporate headquarters location:** This Location.

SACK & ASSOCIATES
1433 Webster Street, Suite 200, Oakland CA 94612-3205. 510/444-6453. **Contact:** Human Resources Department. **Description:** A law firm.

Note: *Because addresses and telephone numbers of smaller companies can change rapidly, we recommend you call each company to verify the information below before inquiring about job opportunities. Mass mailings are not recommended.*

Additional small employers:

LEGAL SERVICES

Jackson Hargrove Emerich
7108 N Fresno St Ste 400, Fresno CA 93720-2938. 209/261-0200.

Berry and Berry
1300 Clay St Floor 9, Oakland CA 94612-1425. 510/835-8330.

Low Ball & Lynch
255 Shoreline Dr Floor 4, Redwood City CA 94065-1404. 415/591-8822.

Gibson Dunn & Crutcher
1 Montgomery St Ste 2600, San Francisco CA 94104-5526. 415/393-8200.

McGee Lafayette Willis & Green
71 Stevenson St #19F, San Francisco CA 94105-2934. 415/956-4747.

Preuss Walker and Shanagher
595 Market St Floor 16, San Francisco CA 94105-2802. 415/978-2600.

Sedgwick Detert Moran & Arnold
1 Embarcadero Ctr Floor 16, San Francisco CA 94111-3607. 415/781-7900.

Limbach and Limbach
2001 Ferry Bldg, San Francisco CA 94111-4207. 415/433-4150.

Lillick and Charles
2 Embarcadero Ctr, San Francisco CA 94111-3823. 415/984-8200.

Brown and Bain
600 Hansen Way Ste 100, Palo Alto CA 94304-1090. 415/856-9411.

Larson and Burnham
PO Box 119, Oakland CA 94604-0119. 510/444-6800.

Skjerven Morrill MacPherson
601 California St Ste 800, San Francisco CA 94108-2813. 415/986-8383.

Skjerven Morrill MacPherson
25 Metro Dr Ste 700, San Jose CA 95110-1339. 408/283-1222.

Hopkins & Carley
150 Almaden Blvd Floor 15, San Jose CA 95113-2009. 408/286-9800.

McCutchen Doyle Brown & Enersen
55 S Market St Ste 1500, San Jose CA 95113-2327. 408/947-8400.

Robinson and Wood Inc.
227 N 1st St Ste 300, San Jose CA 95113-1016. 408/298-7120.

Diepenbrock Wulff Plant & Hann
PO Box 3034, Sacramento CA 95812-3034. 916/444-3910.

Kronick Moskovitz Tiedemann
400 Capitol Mall Floor 27, Sacramento CA 95814-4417. 916/321-4500.

Greve Clifford Diepenbrock
980 9th St Ste 1700, Sacramento CA 95814-2737. 916/443-2011.

Orrick Herrington & Sutcliffe
400 Capitol Mall # 3000, Sacramento CA 95814-4407. 916/447-9200.

Littler Mendelson Fastiff
400 Capitol Mall, Sacramento CA 95814-4407. 916/448-7164.

Mastagni Holstedt & Chiurazzi
1912 I St, Sacramento CA 95814-3112. 916/446-4692.

Fliesler Dubb Meyer & Lovejoy
4 Embarcadero Ctr, San Francisco CA 94111-4106. 415/362-3800.

Fliesler Dubb Meyer & Lovejoy
1281 Oakmead Pkwy, Sunnyvale CA 94086-4040. 408/773-9100.

Blakely Sokoloff Taylor
1279 Oakmead Pkwy, Sunnyvale CA 94086-4040. 408/720-8598.

Oblon Spivak McClelland Maier
224 Airport Pkwy Ste 300, San Jose CA 95110-1022. 408/436-2070.

Rosenblum Parish & Isaacs
160 W Santa Clara St Ste 1500, San Jose CA 95113-1700. 408/977-0120.

Attorneys Diversified Services
577 2nd St, San Francisco CA 94107-1410. 415/882-1700.

Mullen & Filippi
50 Fremont St Floor 19, San

Francisco CA 94105-2230. 415/979-1900.

Thomas Snell Jamison Russell
2445 Capitol St, Fresno CA 93721-2224. 209/442-0600.

Shartsis Friese & Ginsburg
1 Maritime Plz, San Francisco CA 94111-3404. 415/421-6500.

Goldstein & Phillips PC
1 Embarcadero Ctr Floor 8, San Francisco CA 94111-3607. 415/981-8855.

Williams Romanski Et Al PC
1775 Woodside Rd, Redwood City CA 94061-3436. 415/364-9110.

Williams Romanski Et Al PC
152 N 3rd St Ste 600, San Jose CA 95112-5581. 408/275-8262.

Keesal Young & Logan PC
4 Embarcadero Ctr Ste 1500, San Francisco CA 94111-4122. 415/398-6000.

Ropers Majeski Kohn & Bentley
670 Howard St, San Francisco CA 94105-3916. 415/543-4800.

Ropers Majeski Kohn & Bentley
80 N 1st St, San Jose CA 95113-1298. 408/287-6262.

Ropers Majeski Kohn & Bentley
3558 Round Barn Blvd Ste 300 , Santa Rosa CA 95403-0992. 707/524-4200.

McCormick Barstow Et Al
5 River Park Pl E, Fresno CA 93720-1501. 209/433-1300.

Tobin & Tobin PC
1 Montgomery St Floor 15, San Francisco CA 94104-4505. 415/433-1400.

Leland Parachini Et Al
333 Market St, San Francisco CA 94105-2102. 415/957-1800.

Landels Ripley & Diamond
350 Steuart Street, San Francisco CA 94105. 415/788-5000.

Pettit & Martin PC
101 California St, San Francisco CA 94111-5802. 415/434-4000.

Law Office Of Robert Savage
433 Airport Blvd, Burlingame CA 94010-2017. 415/344-5875.

Murphy Weir & Butler PC
101 California St Floor 39, San Francisco CA 94111-5802. 415/398-4700.

Howard Rice Nemerovski Et Al
7th Floor, 3 Embarcadero Ctr, San Francisco CA 94111. 415/434-1600.

Hardy Erich Brown & Wilson PC
1000 G St, Sacramento CA 95814-0840. 916/449-3800.

Fenton & Keller
2801 Salinas Hwy, Monterey CA 93940-6401. 408/373-1241.

Wright Robinson McCammon
44 Montgomery St, San Francisco CA 94104-4602. 415/391-7111.

Tarkington O'Connor & O'Neill
Spear St Floor 41, San Francisco CA 94105-1504. 415/777-5501.

Murphy Pearson Bradley
86 Kearny St Floor 11, San Francisco CA 94108-5502. 415/788-1900.

Thornton Taylor Downs Et Al PC
505 Sansome St Floor 16, San Francisco CA 94111-3106. 415/421-8890.

Cartwright Slobodin Et Al
101 California St Ste 2600, San Francisco CA 94111-5853. 415/433-0440.

Laughlin Falbo Levy & Moresi
2 Embarcadero Ctr Ste 5, San Francisco CA 94111-3823. 415/781-6676.

Lynch Loofbourrow Et Al PC
50 Francisco St Ste 400, San Francisco CA 94133-2114. 415/397-2800.

Hothem & Isele
369 Broadway, San Francisco CA 94133-4512. 415/421-8222.

Gray Cary Ware & Freidenrich
400 Hamilton Ave, Palo Alto CA 94301-1809. 415/328-6561.

Hallgrimson McNichols Et Al
5000 Hopyard Rd Ste 400, Pleasanton CA 94588-3352. 510/460-3700.

McNamara Houston Dodge
1211 Newell Ave Floor 2, Walnut Creek CA 94596-5331. 510/939-5330.

Saperstein Goldstein Et Al PC
1300 Clay St Floor 11, Oakland CA 94612-1425. 510/763-9800.

Stark Wells Rahl Et Al
1999 Harrison St Ste 1300, Oakland CA 94612-3517. 510/834-2200.

Haworth Bradshaw & Chaney Inc.
PO Box 147, San Jose CA 95103-0147. 408/293-9393.

Pillsbury Madison & Sutro
10 Almaden Blvd Ste 800, San Jose CA 95113-2237. 408/947-4000.

Mayall Hurley Knutsen Et Al PC
2453 Grand Canal Blvd Ste 2, Stockton CA 95207-8259. 209/477-3833.

Kroloff Belcher Smart Et Al
PO Box 692050, Stockton CA 95269-2050. 209/478-2000.

Diehl Steinheimer Riggio Et Al
400 E Main St Ste 600, Stockton CA 95290-0299. 209/464-8732.

Curtis & Arata
PO Box 3030, Modesto CA 95353-3030. 209/521-1800.

Bolling Walter & Gawthrop PC
PO Box 255200, Sacramento CA 95865-5200. 916/369-0777.

Wild Carter Tipton & Oliver PC
246 W Shaw Ave, Fresno CA 93704-2663. 209/224-2131.

Dowling Magarian Aaron Et Al
6051 N Fresno St Ste 200, Fresno CA 93710-5280. 209/432-4500.

Venture Law Group
2800 Sand Hill Rd, Menlo Park CA 94025-7022. 415/854-4488.

Rogers Joseph O'Donnell Et Al
311 California St, San Francisco CA 94104-2602. 415/956-2828.

Carroll Burdick & McDonough
44 Montgomery St Ste 400, San Francisco CA 94104-4706. 415/989-5900.

American Arbitration Association
417 Montgomery St, San Francisco CA 94104-1129. 415/981-3901.

Marron Reid & Sheehy PC
610 California St Ste 1200, San Francisco CA 94108-2701. 415/434-0800.

Rosenblum Parish & Isaacs PC
555 Montgomery St Ste 1500, San Francisco CA 94111-2545. 415/421-8232.

Epstein Becker & Green
2 Embarcadero Ctr Ste 1650, San Francisco CA 94111-3994. 415/398-3500.

Cooper White & Cooper PC
201 California St Floor 15, San Francisco CA 94111-5002. 415/433-1900.

Keker & Van Nest PC
710 Sansome St, San Francisco CA 94111-1704. 415/391-5400.

Brobeck Phleger & Harrison PC
2200 Geng Rd, Palo Alto CA 94303-3317. 415/424-0160.

Wilson Sonsini Goodrich Et Al
650 Page Mill Rd, Palo Alto CA 94304-1050. 415/493-9300.

Cooley Godward Castro Huddleso
5 Palo Alto Sq Ste 400, Palo Alto CA 94306-2122. 415/843-5000.

Cooley Godward Castro Huddleso
1 Maritime Plz Floor 20, San Francisco CA 94111-3404. 415/693-2000.

Berding & Weil
3240 Stone Valley Rd W Ste 102, Alamo CA 94507-1563. 510/838-2090.

Dickenson Peatman & Fogarty
809 Coombs St, Napa CA 94559-2937. 707/252-7122.

Wendel Rosen Black & Dean
1111 Broadway, Oakland CA 94607-4036. 510/834-6600.

Donahue Gallagher Woods & Wood
300 Lakeside Dr Ste 1900, Oakland CA 94612-3538. 510/451-0544.

Ricksen Knox
1999 Harrison St Ste 1700, Oakland CA 94612-3517. 510/893-1000.

Downey Brand Seymour & Rohwer
555 Capitol Mall Ste 1050, Sacramento CA 95814-4601. 916/441-0131.

Weintraub Genshlea & Sproul PC
400 Capitol Mall Floor 11, Sacramento CA 95814-4407. 916/558-6000.

Hefner Stark & Marois
2710 Gateway Oaks Dr, Sacramento CA 95833-3505. 916/925-6620.

Gagen McCoy McMahon
279 Front St, Danville CA 94526-3401. 510/837-0585.

Baker & McKenzie
2 Embarcadero Ctr Ste 24, San Francisco CA 94111-3823. 415/576-3000.

Nossaman Guthner Knox Et Al
50 California St, San Francisco CA 94111-4624. 415/398-3600.

Neumiller & Beardslee Pc
509 W Weber Ave, Stockton CA 95203-3167. 209/948-8200.

John J. Mullane Jr. Inc.
601 California St 21st Floor, San Francisco CA 94108. 415/981-6630.

Fitzgerald Abbott & Beardsley
1221 Broadway Floor 21, Oakland CA 94612-1837. 510/451-3300.

Nielsen Merksamer Et Al PC
650 California St Ste 2650, San Francisco CA 94108-2607. 415/389-6800.

Dryden Margoles Et Al
1 California St Ste 2600, San Francisco CA 94111-5427. 415/362-6715.

Kincaid Gianunzio Caudle
500 Ygnacio Valley Rd Ste 400, Walnut Creek CA 94596-3847. 510/930-9111.

Sellar Hazard Snyder Et Al PC
PO Box 3510, Walnut Creek CA 94598-0510. 510/938-1430.

Hoge Fenton Jones & Appel Inc.
60 South Market Street, San Jose CA 95113. 408/287-9501.

Stanton Kay & Watson
180 Sutter St, San Francisco CA 94104-4001. 415/788-3496.

Breon O'Donnell Miller Et Al
71 Stevenson St Ste 1900, San Francisco CA 94105-2939. 415/543-4111.

Van Bourg Weinberg Roger
180 Grand Ave # 1400, Oakland CA 94612-3741. 510/839-6600.

Archer McComas & Lageson PC
2033 N Main St Ste 800, Walnut Creek CA 94596-3728. 510/930-6600.

Gassett Perry & Frank
210 N 4th St Ste 400, San Jose CA 95112-5500. 408/295-7034.

Porter Scott Weiberg Et Al PC
350 University Ave Ste 200, Sacramento CA 95825-6517. 916/929-1481.

Motschiedler Michaelides Et Al
1690 W Shaw Ave Ste 200, Fresno CA 93711-3516. 209/439-4000.

Stammer McKnight Barnum Et Al
2540 W Shaw Ln Ste 110, Fresno CA 93711-2700. 209/449-0571.

Arnberger Kim Baxbaum & Choy
44 Montgomery St Ste 500, San Francisco CA 94104-4607. 415/955-0553.

O'Connor Cohn Dillon & Barr PC
101 Howard St Floor 5, San Francisco CA 94105-1629. 415/281-8888.

Long & Levit PC
101 California St Ste 2300, San Francisco CA 94111-5895. 415/397-2222.

Bartko Zankel Tarrant & Miller
900 Front St Floor 3, San Francisco CA 94111-1427. 415/956-1900.

Berliner Cohen PC
Ten Almaden Blvd 11th Floor, San Jose CA 95113. 408/286-5800.

Matheny Poidmore & Sears
PO Box 13711, Sacramento CA 95853-4711. 916/929-9271.

Keck Mahin & Cate PC
Golden Gateway Ctr 23rd Floor, San Francisco CA 94111. 415/392-7077.

Miller Starr & Regalia PC
16th Floor One Kaiser Plaza, Oakland CA 94612. 510/465-3800.

Berg Ziegler Anderson & Parker
4 Embarcadero Ctr Ste 1400, San Francisco CA 94111-4164. 415/397-6000.

Clapp Moroney Bellagamba Et Al
4400 Bohannon Dr Ste 100, Menlo Park CA 94025-1041. 415/327-1300.

Branson Fitzgerald & Howard
643 Bair Island Rd Ste 400, Redwood City CA 94063-2758. 415/365-7710.

Preston Steffen Katzen
100 Van Ness Ave, San Francisco CA 94102-5209. 415/565-2811.

Brown & Wood
555 California St, San Francisco CA 94104-1502. 415/772-1200.

Sonnenschein Nath & Rosenthal
685 Market St # 1000, San Francisco CA 94105-4200. 415/882-5000.

Hanson Bridgett Marcus
333 Market St Floor 23, San Francisco CA 94105-2102. 415/777-3200.

Zelle & Larson
Steuart St 15th Floor, San Francisco CA 94105. 415/978-9788.

Latham & Watkins
505 Montgomery St Ste 1900, San Francisco CA 94111. 415/391-0600.

Heller Ehrman White
525 University Ave Ste 1100, Palo Alto CA 94301-1900. 415/324-7000.

Townsend & Townsend Khourie
379 Lytton Ave, Palo Alto CA 94301. 415/326-2400.

Morgan Miller & Blair
1676 N California Blvd Ste 200, Walnut Creek CA 94596-4137. 510/937-3600.

Corbett & Kane
2000 Powell St Ste 1450, Emeryville CA 94608-1859. 510/547-2434.

Jackson Tufts Cole & Black PC
650 California St, San Francisco CA 94108-2702. 415/433-1950.

Hessinger & Associates
950 S Bascom Ave Ste 1113, San Jose CA 95128-3537. 408/494-0345.

Cinnamon Casterton & Hagedorn
1515 River Park Dr, Sacramento CA 95815-4610. 916/929-6800.

For more information on career opportunities in legal services:

Associations

AMERICAN BAR ASSOCIATION
750 North Lake Shore Drive, Chicago IL 60611. 312/988-5000. World Wide Web address: http://www.abanet.org.

FEDERAL BAR ASSOCIATION
1815 H Street NW, Suite 408, Washington DC 20006-3697. 202/638-0252. World Wide Web address: http://www.access.digex.net/fedbar.

NATIONAL ASSOCIATION OF LEGAL ASSISTANTS
1516 South Boston, Suite 200, Tulsa OK 74119-4013. 918/587-6828. World Wide Web address: http://www.nala.org. An educational association. Offers the National Voluntary Association Exam. Memberships are available.

NATIONAL FEDERATION OF PARALEGAL ASSOCIATIONS
P.O. Box 33108, Kansas City MO 64114-0108. 816/941-4000. World Wide Web address: http://www.paralegals.org. Offers magazines, seminars, and Internet job listings.

NATIONAL PARALEGAL ASSOCIATION
P.O. Box 629, 6186 Honey Hollow Road, Doylestown PA 18901. 215/297-8333.

MANUFACTURING: MISCELLANEOUS CONSUMER

The consumer goods manufacturing industry is more than just one industry. To generally forecast about the entire range of companies that make products for consumers is risky, since so much can differ from one segment to the next. In fact, many consumer manufacturers are listed under more specific categories in this book.

With that said, some general statements can be made about the outlook for this gigantic field. Over the long term, many analysts are optimistic. An improved economy, as well as an aging baby boom generation with growing disposable income, should provide stimulus for increases in personal durables. Continued growth in international trade should also point to a favorable long-term outlook for household consumer durables.

U.S. exports of household durables should also expand as trade barriers drop. The North American Free Trade Agreement (NAFTA), passed in early 1994, will give U.S. manufacturers even greater access to what is already the second-largest export market for U.S. household durables. Other trade agreements may follow with several Latin American countries. Potential markets in Eastern Europe and independent states of the former Soviet Union may also open.

ALADDIN MECHANICAL SERVICES
1111 Aladdin Avenue, San Leandro CA 94577. 510/357-6711. **Contact:** Betty Foott, Accounting Manager. **Description:** Manufactures furnaces and other heating products.

ATARI CORPORATION
455 South Matilda Avenue, Sunnyvale CA 94086. 408/328-0900. **Contact:** Gayle McKim, Personnel Director. **Description:** Administrative and sales office for the video systems company. Atari manufactures and distributes video gaming systems.

BLACK & DECKER CORPORATION
15401 Hesperian Boulevard, San Leandro CA 94578. 510/276-1610. **Contact:** Human Resources. **Description:** With products and services marketed in more than 100 countries, Black & Decker is a global marketer and manufacturer of products used in and around the home and for commercial applications. It is also a major supplier of information technology and services to governmental and commercial clients worldwide. The company is the world's largest producer of power tools, power tool accessories, security hardware, and electric lawn and garden tools, and they are the largest global supplier of engineered fastening systems to the markets they serve.

CENTRAL GARDEN & PET COMPANY
P.O. Box 899, Lafayette CA 94549. 510/283-4573. **Contact:** Human Resources. **Description:** Central Garden & Pet Company is the nation's largest supplier and merchandiser of lawn and garden and pet products and a major distributor of pool

supplies. Through a network of 32 distribution centers and unparalleled service to more than 10,000 retail stores each week, Central is maximizing sales and profitability for both manufacturers and retailers. The company's strategy is to rapidly consolidate the lawn and garden and pet supplies industries through internal growth and acquisition. **Corporate headquarters location:** This Location. **Number of employees nationwide:** 1,450.

THE CLOROX COMPANY
P.O. Box 24305, Oakland CA 94623. 510/271-7615. **Contact:** Corporate Staffing. **Description:** A diversified *Fortune* 500 international manufacturer and marketer of consumer products. **Common positions include:** Accountant/Auditor; Buyer; Chemical Engineer; Chemist; Civil Engineer; Computer Programmer; Financial Analyst; Food Scientist/Technologist; Human Resources Specialist; Industrial Engineer; Manufacturer's/Wholesaler's Sales Rep.; Marketing Specialist; Mechanical Engineer; Operations/Production Manager; Systems Analyst; Technical Writer/Editor; Transportation/Traffic Specialist. **Educational backgrounds include:** Accounting; Business Administration; Chemistry; Computer Science; Engineering; Finance; Liberal Arts; Marketing. **Benefits:** Dental Insurance; Disability Coverage; Life Insurance; Medical Insurance; Pension Plan; Profit Sharing; Savings Plan; Tuition Assistance. **Corporate headquarters location:** This Location. **Listed on:** New York Stock Exchange.

THE CLOROX TECHNICAL CENTER
P.O. Box 493, Pleasanton CA 94566. 510/847-6100. **Contact:** Human Resources. **Description:** Conducts research and development for the Clorox Company, which manufactures and markets a variety of consumer products. **Parent company:** The Clorox Company.

EBSCO INDUSTRIES INC.
920 41st Avenue, Santa Cruz CA 95062. 408/475-5020. **Contact:** Office Manager. **Description:** Ebsco is an office products dealer. The company also provides administrative functions for a national sales force selling to the federal government. **Common positions include:** Accountant/Auditor; Administrative Services Manager; Blue-Collar Worker Supervisor; Buyer; Computer Programmer; Customer Service Representative; Department Manager; Marketing Specialist; Purchasing Agent and Manager; Services Sales Representative; Systems Analyst. **Educational backgrounds include:** Business Administration; Marketing. **Benefits:** Disability Coverage; Employee Discounts; Life Insurance; Medical Insurance; Pension Plan; Profit Sharing; Savings Plan; Tuition Assistance. **Corporate headquarters location:** Birmingham AL. **Operations at this facility include:** Divisional Headquarters; Sales; Service.

LEWIS GALOOB TOYS, INC.
500 Forbes Boulevard, South San Francisco CA 94080. 415/952-1678. **Contact:** Human Resources. **Description:** Lewis Galoob Toys, Inc. designs, develops, markets, and sells high-quality toys worldwide and has been in business since 1957. The company's strategies in selecting and developing lines are to focus primarily on low to medium-priced product lines that are brandable, to capitalize on current trends in the toy industry and popular culture and to expand and diversify its product categories. The company's products are generally sold worldwide, with a substantial portion of its revenues derived from sales in the United States and Europe. The company sells its products principally to retailers in the United States and to toy distributors outside of the United States. U.S. retail outlets for the products include specialty toy retailers, discount and chain stores,

catalog and mail order companies, department stores, and variety stores. The company's products are generally manufactured overseas, primarily in the People's Republic of China.

MEDIA ARTS GROUP, INC.
10 Almaden Boulevard, 9th Floor, San Jose CA 95113. 408/947-4680. **Contact:** Human Resources. **Description:** Media Arts designs, manufactures, markets, and distributes fine-quality collectible, gift, and art products. Since its inception, the company has developed a marketing and distribution program designed to maximize sales and profitability. The company has assembled a team of managers that it feels has extensive experience in the areas of product design, development, marketing, and sales to implement this marketing and distribution program. In December 1993, Media Arts acquired a 51 percent interest and an option to acquire an additional 46 percent interest in John Hine Limited, a United Kingdom company that manufactures, markets, and distributes hand-painted miniature cottages and other miniature buildings and figurines to customers primarily in the United States and the United Kingdom. **Number of employees nationwide:** 580.

MEMTEK PRODUCTS INC.
1600 Memorex Drive, Santa Clara CA 95050. 408/982-5084. **Fax:** 408/982-5045. **Contact:** Angie Gehman, Human Resources Manager. **Description:** A distributor of Memorex audio, video, and computer supplies, as well as Dysan disks. **Common positions include:** Accountant/Auditor; Adjuster; Computer Programmer; Computer Systems Analyst; Credit Manager; Customer Service Representative; Financial Analyst; Human Resources Specialist; Manufacturer's/Wholesaler's Sales Rep.; Purchasing Agent and Manager; Software Engineer; Wholesale and Retail Buyer. **Educational backgrounds include:** Accounting; Art/Design; Business Administration; Computer Science; Finance; Marketing. **Benefits:** 401(k); Dental Insurance; Disability Coverage; Life Insurance; Medical Insurance. **Parent company:** Hanny America. **Operations at this facility include:** Administration; Divisional Headquarters; Sales. **Listed on:** NASDAQ. **Number of employees nationwide:** 200.

MONROE SYSTEMS FOR BUSINESS INC.
20988 Corsair Boulevard, Hayward CA 94545. 510/293-9900. **Contact:** Mike McCormick, District Manager. **Description:** Manufactures and markets a wide range of large- and small-scale electronic calculators, programmable calculators, electronic accounting machines, facsimile, shredders, and copy machines. Products are used in a wide range of business, governmental, medical, and educational applications. International operations reach 70 countries, with facilities in Venezuela, Puerto Rico, Hong Kong, and Zurich. Products are sold through more than 250 company-owned branches in the United States and Canada. **Common positions include:** Branch Manager; Services Sales Representative. **Educational backgrounds include:** Marketing. **Benefits:** Dental Insurance; Disability Coverage; Employee Discounts; Life Insurance; Medical Insurance; Pension Plan; Savings Plan; Tuition Assistance. **Corporate headquarters location:** Morris Plains NJ. **Operations at this facility include:** Administration; Sales; Service. **Number of employees nationwide:** 2,000.

THE NORTH FACE
2013 Sarallon Drive, San Leandro CA 94577. 510/618-3500. **Contact:** Human Resources. **Description:** A manufacturer, wholesaler, and retailer of outdoor equipment and apparel including tents, backpacks, sleeping bags, outerwear, skiwear, and sportswear. **Common positions include:** Accountant/Auditor; Blue-Collar Worker

Supervisor; Computer Programmer; Credit Manager; Customer Service Representative; Human Resources Specialist; Industrial Engineer; Manufacturer's/Wholesaler's Sales Rep.; Marketing Specialist; Operations/Production Manager; Purchasing Agent and Manager; Quality Control Supervisor. **Educational backgrounds include:** Accounting; Business Administration; Computer Science; Finance; Marketing. **Benefits:** Dental Insurance; Disability Coverage; Employee Discounts; Life Insurance; Medical Insurance; Pension Plan; Savings Plan; Tuition Assistance. **Corporate headquarters location:** This Location. **Operations at this facility include:** Administration; Divisional Headquarters; Manufacturing; Regional Headquarters; Research and Development; Sales; Service.

PROCTER & GAMBLE
P.O. Box 4368, Modesto CA 95352-4368. 209/538-5000. **Contact:** Human Resources. **Description:** This location manufactures Pampers diapers for the consumer market. Procter & Gamble operates manufacturing facilities worldwide.

TAB PRODUCTS COMPANY
1400 Page Mill Road, Palo Alto CA 94304. 415/852-2567. **Fax:** 415/852-2524. **Contact:** Staffing Manager. **E-mail address:** Bannier@aol.com. **Description:** Provides efficient record-keeping management products. Products include lateral color-coding files, a file tracker bar code system, unit space finders, and high-density mobile filing systems. **Common positions include:** Accountant/Auditor; Adjuster; Budget Analyst; Buyer; Computer Programmer; Computer Systems Analyst; Credit Manager; Customer Service Representative; Economist/Market Research Analyst; Financial Analyst; Services Sales Representative; Software Engineer; Technical Writer/Editor. **Educational backgrounds include:** Accounting; Business Administration; Communications; Computer Science; Engineering; Finance; Marketing; Mathematics. **Benefits:** 401(k); Dental Insurance; Disability Coverage; Employee Discounts; Life Insurance; Medical Insurance; Pension Plan; Savings Plan; Tuition Assistance. **Corporate headquarters location:** This Location. **Other U.S. locations:** Nationwide. **Operations at this facility include:** Administration; Divisional Headquarters; Regional Headquarters; Research and Development; Sales; Service. **Number of employees at this location:** 120. **Number of employees nationwide:** 1,000.

THOMAS INDUSTRIES
ARCHITECTURAL OUTDOOR DIVISION
2661 Alvarado Street, San Leandro CA 94577. **Contact:** Byron Geils, Human Resources Manager. **Description:** Thomas Industries has been providing lighting and compressor/vacuum pump products since 1953. The Architectural Outdoor Products Division provides outdoor area and flood lighting applications. **Common positions include:** Accountant/Auditor; Budget Analyst; Buyer; Computer Programmer; Computer Systems Analyst; Customer Service Representative; Draftsperson; Electrical/Electronics Engineer; Financial Analyst; General Manager; Industrial Engineer; Production Manager. **Educational backgrounds include:** Engineering; Finance; Marketing. **Benefits:** 401(k); Dental Insurance; Disability Coverage; Employee Discounts; Life Insurance; Medical Insurance; Pension Plan; Profit Sharing; Savings Plan; Tuition Assistance. **Special Programs:** Internships. **Corporate headquarters location:** Louisville KY. **Other U.S. locations:** Nationwide. **Operations at this facility include:** Administration; Divisional Headquarters; Sales. **Listed on:** New York Stock Exchange. **Number of employees at this location:** 200. **Number of employees nationwide:** 3,000.

Note: *Because addresses and telephone numbers of smaller companies can change rapidly, we recommend you call each company to verify the information below before inquiring about job opportunities. Mass mailings are not recommended.*

Additional small employers:

HOUSEHOLD FURNITURE

Stuart's Fine Furniture
3419 Railroad Ave, Ceres CA 95307. 209/537-4751.

Metropolitan Furniture Corp.
1635 Rollins Rd, Burlingame CA 94010. 415/697-7900.

SCALES/BALANCES

Paxall Parsons Machinery
31800 Hayman St, Hayward CA 94544. 510/489-3900.

Eagle Packaging Group
2107 Livingston St, Oakland CA 94606. 510/533-3000.

HOUSEHOLD AUDIO AND VIDEO EQUIPMENT

AKG Acoustics Company
1525 Alvarado St, San Leandro CA 94577-2640. 510/351-3500.

BATTERIES

Portable Energy Products
170 Technology Cir, Scotts Valley CA 95066-3520. 408/439-5100.

TOYS AND SPORTING GOODS

Discovery Toys
2530 Arnold Dr Ste 400, Martinez CA 94553-4359. 510/370-3400.

Oceanic
2002 Davis St, San Leandro CA 94577. 510/352-5001.

Giro Sport Design Inc.
380 Encinal St, Santa Cruz CA 95060. 408/479-8020.

For more information on career opportunities in consumer manufacturing:

Associations

ASSOCIATION FOR MANUFACTURING TECHNOLOGY
7901 Westpark Drive, McLean VA 22102. 703/893-2900. World Wide Web address: http://www.mfgtech.org. Offers research services.

ASSOCIATION OF HOME APPLIANCE MANUFACTURERS
20 North Wacker Drive, Chicago IL 60606. 312/984-5800.

NATIONAL ASSOCIATION OF MANUFACTURERS
1331 Pennsylvania Avenue NW, Suite 1500, Washington DC 20004. 202/637-3000. World Wide Web address: http://www.nam.org. A lobbying association for manufacturers.

NATIONAL HOUSEWARES MANUFACTURERS ASSOCIATION
6400 Schafer Court, Suite 650, Rosemont IL 60018. 847/292-4200. World Wide Web address: http://www.housewares.org. Offers shipping discounts and other services.

SOCIETY OF MANUFACTURING ENGINEERS
P.O. Box 930, One SME Drive, Dearborn MI 48121. 313/271-1500. World Wide Web address: http://www.sme.org. Offers educational events and educational materials on manufacturing.

Directories

APPLIANCE MANUFACTURER ANNUAL DIRECTORY
Appliance Manufacturer, 5900 Harper Road, Suite 105, Solon OH 44139. 216/349-3060. $25.00.

HOUSEHOLD AND PERSONAL PRODUCTS INDUSTRY BUYERS GUIDE
Rodman Publishing Group, 17 South Franklin Turnpike, Ramsey NJ 07446. 201/825-2552. $12.00.

Magazines

APPLIANCE
1110 Jorie Boulevard, Oak Brook IL 60522-9019. 708/990-3484. Monthly. $70.00 for a one-year subscription.

COSMETICS INSIDERS REPORT
Advanstar Communications, 131 West 1st Street, Duluth MN 55802. Toll-free phone: 800/346-0085. $189.00 for a one year subscription; 24 issues annually. Features timely articles on cosmetics marketing and research.

MANUFACTURING: MISCELLANEOUS INDUSTRIAL

New investments by American businesses have generated much of the U.S. economy's expansion in recent years. That's good news for machinery manufacturers, who have been very busy. Through October 1995, the manufacturing of machinery and equipment was up about 12 percent over the previous year.

AMERICAN METER COMPANY
1350 Bayshore Highway, Suite 750, Burlingame CA 94010. 415/340-1414. **Contact:** Human Resources. **Description:** Manufactures vapor gas measurement products.

AMERICAN STANDARD INC.
799 Main Street, Suite E, Half Moon Bay CA 94019. 415/712-8401. **Contact:** Personnel. **Description:** A worldwide manufacturer operating in four diversified areas: Transportation Products, Building Products, Security and Graphic Products, and Construction and Mining Equipment. American Standard conducts manufacturing operations in more than 20 countries. **NOTE:** Send resumes to: P.O. Box 6820, One Centennial Plaza, Piscataway NJ 08855-6820. **Corporate headquarters location:** Piscataway NJ. **Listed on:** New York Stock Exchange.

AMERON INTERNATIONAL
CONCRETE AND STEEL PIPE GROUP
10100 Linne Road, Tracy CA 95376. 209/836-5050. **Contact:** Joan Medlin, Personnel Manager. **Description:** Manufactures concrete and steel pipe as part of Ameron's Concrete and Steel Pipe Group. Overall, the Concrete and Steel Pipe Group supplies products and services used in the construction of pipeline facilities for various utilities. Eight plants manufacture concrete cylinder pipe, prestressed concrete cylinder pipe, steel pipe, and reinforced concrete pipe for water transmission, storm and industrial wastewater, and sewage collection. Overall, Ameron International manufactures and supplies goods and services to the industrial, utility, marine, and construction markets. The business of the company is divided into four groups: the Concrete and Steel Pipe Group, the Protective Coatings Group, the Fiberglass Pipe Group, and the Construction and Allied Products Group. The Protective Coatings Group develops, manufactures, and markets high-performance coatings and surfacer systems on a worldwide basis. These products are utilized for the preservation of major structures, such as metallic and concrete facilities and equipment, to prevent their degradation by corrosion, abrasion, marine fouling, and other forms of chemical and physical attack. The Fiberglass Pipe Group develops, manufactures, and markets filament-wound and molded fiberglass pipe fittings. The Construction & Allied Products Group includes the HC&D Division, which supplies ready-mix concrete, crushed and sized basaltic aggregates, dune sand, concrete pipe, and box culverts, primarily to the construction industry in Hawaii. **Corporate headquarters location:** Monterey Park CA. **Listed on:** New York Stock Exchange.

B&H MANUFACTURING COMPANY
P.O. Box 247, Ceres CA 95307. 209/537-5785. **Contact:** Dolores Brooks, Personnel Manager. **Description:** A manufacturer of labeling machines.

BOC COATING TECHNOLOGY
P.O. Box 2529, Fairfield CA 94533. 707/423-2100. **Contact:** Wendy Clappis, Human Resources Manager. **Description:** Produces high vacuum systems and equipment for industrial applications. **Common positions include:** Designer; Manufacturing Engineer; Science Technologist. **Educational backgrounds include:** Engineering; Optics; Physics. **Benefits:** 401(k); Dental Insurance; Disability Coverage; Life Insurance; Medical Insurance; Pension Plan; Tuition Assistance. **Corporate headquarters location:** Murray Hill NJ. **Other U.S. locations:** Concord CA. **Parent company:** The BOC Group, Inc. **Operations at this facility include:** Administration; Divisional Headquarters; Manufacturing; Sales. **Listed on:** London Stock Exchange. **Number of employees at this location:** 170. **Number of employees nationwide:** 250.

BW/IP INTERNATIONAL, INC.
6077 Egret Court, Benicia CA 94510. 707/745-3773. **Contact:** Human Resources. **Description:** Manufactures fluid control systems.

BW/IP INTERNATIONAL, INC.
1132 North Seventh Street, San Jose CA 95112-4427. 408/298-0123. **Contact:** Kerry Kirkpatrick, Human Resources Manager. **Description:** Manufactures fluid control systems.

BECKMAN INSTRUMENTS, INC.
1050 Page Mill Road, Palo Alto CA 94304. 415/857-1150. **Contact:** Human Resources. **Description:** Designs, develops, manufactures, markets, and services laboratory analytical instruments and related consumable chemical products, industrial instruments, control systems, and precision electronic components. Primarily serves three markets: health care, biomedical research, and scientific products. The company also has research, development, and engineering offices. **Corporate headquarters location:** Fullerton CA. **Listed on:** New York Stock Exchange.

BEMIS COMPANY INC.
P.O. Box 396, Union City CA 94587-0396. 510/471-2811. **Contact:** Human Resources. **Description:** Bemis is a diversified producer of consumer and industrial packaging materials, film products, and business products. Packaging products include tapes, paper bags, and packaging for pharmaceuticals, candy, toilet paper, and detergents. The company also produces sheetprint stock, roll labels, laminates, and adhesive products.

CPI
3200 Patrick Henry Drive, Santa Clara CA 95054-1814. 408/496-6273. **Contact:** Human Resources. **Description:** Engaged in the research, development, manufacture, and marketing of various products and services in the fields of communications, industrial equipment, medicine, and scientific research.

CAL-AIR CONDITIONING
1355 South 7th Street, San Jose CA 95112. 408/947-0155. **Fax:** 408/293-9511. **Contact:** Claude Dubreuil, Administration Manager. **Description:** A mechanical contractor (HVAC and piping). Cal-Air Conditioning installs and services air conditioning and heating systems, and is also engaged in energy management and sheet

metal fabrication. **Common positions include:** Cost Estimator; Draftsperson; Mechanical Engineer; Purchasing Agent and Manager. **Educational backgrounds include:** Accounting; Engineering. **Benefits:** Dental Insurance; Disability Coverage; Employee Discounts; Life Insurance; Medical Insurance; Profit Sharing; Savings Plan; Tuition Assistance. **Corporate headquarters location:** Whittier CA. **Other U.S. locations:** Glendale CA; Sacramento CA. **Parent company:** Cal-Air, Inc. **Operations at this facility include:** Administration; Divisional Headquarters; Sales; Service. **Number of employees at this location:** 150. **Number of employees nationwide:** 400.

THE COAST DISTRIBUTION SYSTEM
P.O. Box 26888, San Jose CA 95159. 408/436-8611. **Contact:** Human Resources. **Description:** The Coast Distribution System is one of North America's largest distributors of parts and accessories to the recreational vehicle and boating industries. Coast supplies a broad line of products to parts and accessory supply stores, recreational vehicle and marine dealerships, chain stores, and mass merchandisers. These products include awnings, electrical and plumbing items, towing equipment and hitches, appliances, marine electronics and safety equipment, and various accessories and consumables. The company distributes its products to an active customer base of over 15,000 retailers through 19 distribution centers located throughout the United States and Canada. **Corporate headquarters location:** This Location.

DSP TECHNOLOGY INC.
48500 Kato Road, Fremont CA 94538. 510/657-7555. **Fax:** 510/657-7576. **Contact:** Human Resources. **Description:** DSP Technology Inc. is an industry leader in the design and manufacture of state-of-the-art, computer-automated measurement and control systems. Major vehicle manufacturers, aerospace companies, and government-funded agencies employ these systems to gather data, analyze information, and monitor the results of research and development projects. This advanced technology is helping companies solve real-world problems in areas such as vehicle powertrain performance, automotive passenger safety, general research, and environmental pollution. The company's products are used by engineers and scientists to gather and measure analog signals generated by transducers and/or detectors which measure physical properties such as temperature, pressure, acceleration and radiation. These products have been used in applications as diverse as automotive combustion research, vehicle impact testing, powertrain dynamometer control, ultrasonics, chemical kinetics, plasma diagnostics, spectroscopy, fusion research, explosives testing, liquid chromatography, vibration analysis, and analysis of the Earth's ozone layer. **Corporate headquarters location:** This Location.

DIONEX CORPORATION
501 Mercury Drive, Sunnyvale CA 94088. 408/481-4125. **Fax:** 408/739-8015. **Contact:** Jana Usher, Human Resources Representative. **Description:** Dionex Corporation develops, manufactures, sells, and services systems and related products that isolate and identify the components of chemical mixtures. The company's products are used extensively in environmental analysis and by the pharmaceutical, life science, biotechnology, chemical, petrochemical, power generation, and electronics industries. Its customers include industrial companies worldwide, government agencies, research institutions, and universities. Working with customers, the research and development teams explore new technologies to enhance the performance of ion technology, high-performance liquid chromatography, capillary electrophoresis, and supercritical fluid extraction and chromatography technologies. The companies has subsidiaries in Italy, Japan, Switzerland, and Germany. **Common positions include:** Accountant/Auditor;

Biological Scientist/Biochemist; Chemist; Computer Programmer; Customer Service Representative; Services Sales Representative; Software Engineer. **Educational backgrounds include:** Chemistry; Engineering; Marketing. **Benefits:** 401(k); Dental Insurance; Disability Coverage; Employee Discounts; Life Insurance; Medical Insurance; Profit Sharing; Tuition Assistance. **Special Programs:** Internships. **Corporate headquarters location:** This Location. **Other U.S. locations:** Atlanta GA; OH; Salt Lake City UT. **Operations at this facility include:** Administration; Manufacturing; Regional Headquarters; Research and Development; Sales; Service. **Listed on:** NASDAQ. **Number of employees nationwide:** 570.

DOVER ELEVATOR COMPANY
590 Laurelwood Road, Santa Clara CA 95054. 408/980-5150. **Contact:** Human Resources. **Description:** Services and sells equipment for elevator maintenance.

ELECTROGLAS, INC.
2901 Coronado Drive, Santa Clara CA 95054. 408/727-6500. **Contact:** Human Resources. **Description:** Electroglas, Inc. is a leader in the development, manufacture, marketing, and servicing of automatic wafer probing equipment for use in the fabrication of semiconductor devices. The company's wafer probers position individual semiconductor devices still in wafer form under contact test probes to facilitate testing of the devices and manage information collected during the testing process. The company's primary products are its 2000 Series wafer probers and its Horizon 4000 Series wafer probers. All of Electroglas' wafer probers feature the company's linear motor technology and offer advanced vision processing, sophisticated system software, and high throughput. **Corporate headquarters location:** This Location.

FAFCO INC.
2690 Middlefield Road, Redwood City CA 94063-3455. 415/363-2690. **Contact:** Vice President of Finance. **Description:** Manufactures and distributes solar heat exchangers and related equipment.

FISHER SCIENTIFIC
2170 Martin Avenue, Santa Clara CA 95050-2780. 408/727-0660. **Contact:** Human Resources. **Description:** Manufactures, distributes, and sells a wide range of products used in laboratories. Fisher Scientific is a supplier to industrial labs and to medical labs. Products include analytical and measuring instruments, apparatus, and appliances; reagent chemicals and diagnostics; glassware and plasticware; and laboratory furniture. Customers are primarily industrial laboratories, medical and hospital laboratories serving the health care industry, and educational and research laboratories. Manufacturing operations are carried out by six operating divisions in 11 United States locations.

FOR BETTER LIVING, INC.
13620 Lincoln Way, Suite 380, Auburn CA 95603. 916/823-9600. **Fax:** 916/823-9650. **Contact:** Human Resources. **Description:** For Better Living, Inc. manufactures and distributes precast concrete and plastic products, and publishes specialty magazines. Associated Concrete Products, Inc., Dalworth Concrete Products, Inc., and Associated Plastics, Inc. comprise the concrete and plastic products segment. The concrete segment designs, manufactures, and distributes underground precast concrete structures. This group has developed a patented line of precast concrete sectional boxes to house underground transformers, distribution systems, and splicing manholes. The plastics segment produces plastics products using a fiber reinforced plastic process and a structural foam process developed for injection molding. Surfer Publications

(Communications Group) constitutes the specialty magazine publications segment, publishing *Surfer*, *Powder*, *Snowboarder*, and *Bike Magazine*. The Communications Group also produces cable television and home video programs. **Corporate headquarters location:** This Location.

GASONICS INTERNATIONAL CORPORATION
2730 Junction Avenue, San Jose CA 95134. 408/944-0212. **Contact:** Human Resources. **Description:** GaSonics International is a leading supplier of process systems used in the fabrication of advanced integrated circuits. The company is the world's largest supplier of equipment for dry removal of photoresist and other mask layer materials applied to semiconductor wafers during fabrication. GaSonics International also offers leading-edge systems for related phases of semiconductor manufacture, including thermal growth of oxide layers and selective cleaning applications. GaSonics International products feature proprietary technologies that help semiconductor manufacturers increase fabrication throughput and reduce wafer damage, which in turn raise production yields. GaSonics sells and services its products in the U.S., Europe, and the Pacific Rim. **Corporate headquarters location:** This Location.

HEXCEL CORPORATION
5794 West Las Positas Boulevard, Pleasanton CA 94588. 510/847-9500. **Contact:** Corporate Staffing. **Description:** A manufacturing firm engaged in two primary business segments: structural materials (aerospace products, non-aerospace honeycomb, resin-impregnated industrial fabrics, non-impregnated fabrics) and specialty chemicals (including bulk pharmaceuticals, custom and special-purpose chemicals, specialty resins, and industrial maintenance chemicals). **Common positions include:** Ceramics Engineer; Chemical Engineer; Computer Programmer; Computer Systems Analyst; Materials Engineer. **Educational backgrounds include:** Accounting; Chemistry; Computer Science; Engineering; Finance. **Benefits:** 401(k); Dental Insurance; Disability Coverage; Employee Discounts; Life Insurance; Medical Insurance; Tuition Assistance. **Corporate headquarters location:** This Location. **Other U.S. locations:** Nationwide. **Operations at this facility include:** Research and Development. **Listed on:** New York Stock Exchange. **Number of employees at this location:** 250. **Number of employees nationwide:** 1,800.

HOSOKAWA MANUFACTURING
P.O. Box 880, Santa Rosa CA 95402. 707/585-2373. **Contact:** Personnel. **Description:** Produces food and chemical processing machinery. **Common positions include:** Accountant/Auditor; Department Manager; Draftsperson; General Manager; Manufacturer's/Wholesaler's Sales Rep.; Mechanical Engineer; Operations/Production Manager; Purchasing Agent and Manager. **Educational backgrounds include:** Accounting; Business Administration; Engineering; Marketing. **Benefits:** 401(k); Dental Insurance; Disability Coverage; Life Insurance; Medical Insurance; Pension Plan; Tuition Assistance. **Corporate headquarters location:** This Location. **Parent company:** Berwind Corp. **Operations at this facility include:** Administration; Divisional Headquarters; Service.

HUSSMANN CORPORATION
P.O. Box 649005, San Jose CA 95164-9005. 510/354-2040. **Contact:** Human Resources. **Description:** Hussmann Corporation produces merchandising and refrigeration systems for the world's food industry. It is a market share leader in every

country in which it has a manufacturing presence, including Canada, Mexico, the United Kingdom, and the United States. Products include refrigerated display cases, refrigeration systems, beverage coolers, walk-in coolers, and industrial refrigeration equipment. Markets include supermarkets, convenience and specialty stores, and industrial refrigeration applications in the United States, Canada, Mexico, and the United Kingdom. Hussmann's principal strategies for growth include the following: to develop and introduce new and innovative products; to invest and improve productivity and profit margins and to continue to expand in markets outside the U.S.

HUSSMANN CORPORATION
4244 South Market Court, Suite C, Sacramento CA 95834. 916/920-4993. **Contact:** Human Resources. **Description:** Hussmann Corporation produces merchandising and refrigeration systems for the world's food industry. It is a market share leader in every country in which it has a manufacturing presence, including Canada, Mexico, the United Kingdom, and the United States. Products include refrigerated display cases, refrigeration systems, beverage coolers, walk-in coolers, and industrial refrigeration equipment. Markets include supermarkets, convenience and specialty stores, and industrial refrigeration applications in the United States, Canada, Mexico, and the United Kingdom. Hussmann's principal strategies for growth include the following: to develop and introduce new and innovative products; to invest and improve productivity and profit margins and to continue to expand in markets outside the U.S. In addition to Hussmann, Whitman's other operating subsidiaries include Pepsi-Cola General Bottlers, headquartered in Rolling Meadows IL; and Midas International Corporation, headquartered in Chicago.

ILC TECHNOLOGY INC.
399 Java Drive, Sunnyvale CA 94089. 408/745-7900. **Contact:** Ms. Pat Sanborn, Human Resources Director. **Description:** ILC is a manufacturer of specialty lamps and equipment for laser pump, medical, industrial, and aerospace applications. The company grew with the laser industry as a premier designer and supplier of arc lamps for optical pumping of solid waste, other lasers, and specialty equipment. **Common positions include:** Accountant/Auditor; Chemical Engineer; Customer Service Representative; Draftsperson; Electrical/Electronics Engineer; Mechanical Engineer; Metallurgical Engineer; Operations/Production Manager; Purchasing Agent and Manager. **Educational backgrounds include:** Business Administration; Engineering; Finance; Marketing. **Benefits:** Dental Insurance; Disability Coverage; Employee Discounts; Life Insurance; Medical Insurance; Pension Plan; Profit Sharing; Savings Plan; Tuition Assistance. **Operations at this facility include:** Administration; Manufacturing; Research and Development; Sales; Service. **Listed on:** American Stock Exchange. **Number of employees at this location:** 360.

INGERSOLL-RAND EQUIPMENT SALES
1944 Marina Boulevard, San Leandro CA 94577-3207. 510/357-9131. **Contact:** Human Resources. **Description:** Manufactures compressors, pumps, and other non-electrical industrial equipment and machinery. Products include air compression systems, antifriction systems, construction equipment, air tools, bearings, locks, tools, and pumps. The company operates 93 production facilities throughout the world.

INTERLAKE INC.
1029 South Sacramento Street, Lodi CA 95240-4799. 209/333-3500. **Contact:** Personnel Director. **Description:** Manufactures and distributes materials handling equipment and other industrial and agricultural products.

LANDIS & GYR SYSTEMS, INC.
1730 Technology Drive, San Jose CA 95110. 408/453-5222. **Contact:** Human Resources Manager. **Description:** Manufactures supervisory control and energy management equipment for the power and utility industries. **Corporate headquarters location:** This Location.

LIBBEY-OWENS-FORD COMPANY
P.O. Box 128, Lathrop CA 95330. 209/858-5151. **Contact:** Jim Woehrle, Personnel Director. **Description:** A diversified industrial manufacturer whose operating divisions produce glass, laminated and molded plastic products, fluid power and fluid systems components, and valves, gaskets, and fittings, among other products. This facility primarily produces automobile window and windshield glass, and other glass products. **Corporate headquarters location:** Toledo OH. **Listed on:** New York Stock Exchange.

MATERIALS RESEARCH CORPORATION
2350 Mission College Boulevard, Suite 1140, Santa Clara CA 95054. 408/748-0902. **Contact:** Human Resources. **Description:** Designs and manufactures thin-film coating and etching systems which are utilized in the manufacturing of integrated circuits for sale principally to the semiconductor, computer, and telecommunications industries. Materials Research Corporation also processes and fabricates ultra-high purity metals and metal alloys, principally for thin film purposes. Materials Research Corporation's thin-film technology products are also used in nonelectronic applications such as protective coatings for corrosion and wear-resistance in razor blades and various automotive products. The company operates in three segments: Sputtering Equipment, Associated Target Materials, and Other High Purity Materials. The company operates five sales offices in the United States. Sales and manufacturing facilities are located throughout the world.

MILLAR ELEVATOR SERVICE CO.
500 Carlton Court, South San Francisco CA 94080. 415/873-8222. **Contact:** Human Resources. **Description:** A firm specializing in the repair, servicing, and renovation of office and apartment building elevators.

MOTION INDUSTRIES, INC.
4165 Commercial Drive, Tracy CA 95376. 209/836-3830. **Contact:** Personnel Director. **Description:** Distributes bearings, power transmission components, and fluid power components.

OPTICAL COATING LABORATORY, INC.
2789 North Point Parkway, Santa Rosa CA 95407. 707/525-7555. **Contact:** Judy Matteucci, Employment Manager. **Description:** Engaged in the design, development, manufacturing, and marketing of vacuum-deposited thin film coatings and optics used in photographic products, office equipment, and computers. **Common positions include:** Electrical/Electronics Engineer; Industrial Engineer; Materials Engineer; Mechanical Engineer. **Educational backgrounds include:** Engineering. **Benefits:** 401(k); Dental Insurance; Disability Coverage; Life Insurance; Medical Insurance; Profit Sharing; Tuition Assistance. **Corporate headquarters location:** This Location. **Operations at this facility include:** Manufacturing. **Listed on:** NASDAQ. **Number of employees at this location:** 900.

OTIS ELEVATOR COMPANY
2303 Camino Ramon, Suite 180, San Ramon CA 94583. 510/824-4780. **Contact:** Personnel Director. **Description:** An area sales office for the producer of elevators and escalators.

PACIFIC ROLLER DIE COMPANY INC.
P.O. Box 3398, Hayward CA 94540. 510/782-7242. **Contact:** Human Resources. **Description:** Manufactures machine tools.

PETERSON TRACTOR COMPANY
955 Marina Boulevard, P.O. Box 5258, San Leandro CA 94577. 510/357-6200. **Contact:** Personnel Director. **Description:** A dealer of Caterpillar heavy construction equipment and diesel engines. **Common positions include:** Mechanic; Services Sales Representative. **Benefits:** Dental Insurance; Life Insurance; Medical Insurance; Pension Plan; Profit Sharing. **Corporate headquarters location:** This Location. **Operations at this facility include:** Administration; Regional Headquarters; Sales; Service.

PITNEY BOWES INC.
MAILING DIVISION
5000 Executive Parkway 140, San Ramon CA 94583. 510/830-0799. **Fax:** 510/830-0985. **Contact:** Patricia Brown, Western Division Personnel Director. **Description:** Pitney Bowes Inc. is a *Fortune* 150 company. The mailing division manufactures and markets postage meters, mail processing and shipping systems, addressing systems, manifesting systems, folding and inserting systems, and mailing software throughout the United States and internationally. **Common positions include:** Customer Service Representative; Manufacturer's/ Wholesaler's Sales Rep.; Services Sales Representative. **Educational backgrounds include:** Business Administration; Liberal Arts; Marketing. **Benefits:** 401(k); Daycare Assistance; Dental Insurance; Disability Coverage; Employee Discounts; Life Insurance; Medical Insurance; Pension Plan; Savings Plan; Tuition Assistance. **Special Programs:** Internships. **Corporate headquarters location:** Stamford CT. **Other U.S. locations:** Nationwide. **Operations at this facility include:** Divisional Headquarters. **Listed on:** New York Stock Exchange. **Number of employees nationwide:** 10,000.

QUADREP
2635 North First Street, Suite 116, San Jose CA 95134. 408/432-3300. **Contact:** Personnel. **Description:** A manufacturer's representative specializing in the sale of connectors, cable assemblies, and other products produced by Amphenol.

RAY BURNER COMPANY
401 Parr Boulevard, Richmond CA 94801. 415/333-5800. **Contact:** Russ Westover, Office Manager. **Description:** Manufactures and distributes boilers and gas burners.

SCHLAGE LOCK COMPANY
2401 Bayshore Boulevard, San Francisco CA 94134. 415/467-1100. **Fax:** 415/330-5620. **Recorded Jobline:** 415/330-5664. **Contact:** Human Resources Department. **Description:** Schlage Lock Company is a manufacturer of door hardware and security systems. **Common positions include:** Accountant/Auditor; Administrator; Blue-Collar Worker Supervisor; Buyer; Commercial Artist; Computer Programmer; Computer Systems Analyst; Credit Manager; Customer Service Representative; Department Manager; Designer; Draftsperson; Editor; Electrical/Electronics Engineer; Financial Analyst; General Manager; Human Resources Specialist; Industrial Engineer;

Management Analyst/Consultant; Management Trainee; Manufacturer's/Wholesaler's Sales Rep.; Marketing Specialist; Mechanical Engineer; Operations/Production Manager; Public Relations Specialist; Purchasing Agent and Manager; Quality Control Supervisor; Reporter; Statistician; Systems Analyst; Technical Writer/Editor; Transportation/Traffic Specialist. **Educational backgrounds include:** Accounting; Art/Design; Business Administration; Communications; Computer Science; Economics; Engineering; Finance; Marketing; Mathematics. **Benefits:** 401(k); Daycare Assistance; Dental Insurance; Disability Coverage; Employee Discounts; Life Insurance; Medical Insurance; Pension Plan; Savings Plan; Tuition Assistance. **Special Programs:** Internships. **Corporate headquarters location:** Woodcliff Lake NJ. **Other U.S. locations:** Security CO; Lenexa KS. **Parent company:** Ingersoll-Rand. **Operations at this facility include:** Administration; Divisional Headquarters; Manufacturing; Research and Development; Sales; Service. **Number of employees at this location:** 600. **Number of employees nationwide:** 3,000.

SOUTHWEST DO-ALL COMPANY
3201 Diablo Avenue, Hayward CA 94545. 415/697-7620. **Contact:** Personnel. **Description:** A distributor of machine tools and other industrial supplies. Southwest Do-All Company operates 50 branches throughout the United States. **Corporate headquarters location:** Des Plaines IL.

ULTRATECH STEPPER
3050 Zanker Road, San Jose CA 95134. 408/727-4930. **Fax:** 408/577-3378. **Contact:** Human Resources. **Description:** Ultratech Stepper develops, manufactures, and markets photo lithography equipment designed to reduce the cost of ownership for manufacturers of integrated circuits (IC) and thin-film head magnetic recording devices.

VARIAN ASSOCIATES
3100 Hansen Way, M/S E-140, Palo Alto CA 94304. 415/493-4000. **Fax:** 415/424-6343. **Contact:** Human Resources. **Description:** Varian is a diversified, international manufacturing company with sales in excess of $1 billion annually. Varian operates manufacturing facilities in seven nations and sales and service offices worldwide. The company is organized around the following core businesses: Health Care Systems; Instruments; Electronic Devices; and Semiconductor Equipment. Each day, more than 80,000 people receive cancer treatments from over 2,300 Varian medical linear accelerators, treatment stimulators, and information management systems in service at hospitals and clinics worldwide. The company is also a leading supplier of X-ray tubes for imaging systems of all types. Leading semiconductor chip manufacturers worldwide rely on Varian's leading edge manufacturing systems to give them performance down to the sub-micron level and the flexibility necessary to compete in rapidly changing global markets. The company believes that unsurpassed reliability and precision make Varian analytical instruments key tools in environmental control, providing accurate testing and analysis of air, water, and soil. The company's instruments also aid physicians and researchers in the fight against diseases such as AIDS. Varian instruments can be found in laboratories regulating the quality of products ranging from petroleum and pharmaceuticals to ice cream and champagne. Its vacuum pumps and leak detectors are essential to the number of highly sophisticated processes that require a vacuum environment. Varian's electron tubes help to bring nations and cultures together through modern communications links. Varian is a worldwide leader in the manufacture of devices that power the information age by generating, amplifying, and defining signals for radio and television broadcasting and satellite communications. They are also essential elements in air traffic control, navigation, radar, fusion energy, and other

scientific research applications. **Common positions include:** Accountant/Auditor; Biomedical Engineer; Buyer; Ceramics Engineer; Chemical Engineer; Computer Programmer; Computer Systems Analyst; Customer Service Representative; Designer; Electrical/Electronics Engineer; Financial Analyst; Human Resources Specialist; Materials Engineer; Mechanical Engineer; Metallurgical Engineer; Nuclear Engineer; Operations/Production Manager; Paralegal; Services Sales Representative; Software Engineer; Technical Writer/Editor. **Educational backgrounds include:** Accounting; Business Administration; Chemistry; Computer Science; Engineering; Finance; Marketing; Physics. **Benefits:** 401(k); Daycare Assistance; Dental Insurance; EAP; Employee Discounts; Life Insurance; Medical Insurance; Profit Sharing; Tuition Assistance. **Special Programs:** Internships. **Corporate headquarters location:** This Location. **Other U.S. locations:** AZ; MA; UT. **Operations at this facility include:** Administration; Manufacturing; Research and Development; Sales; Service. **Listed on:** New York Stock Exchange. **Number of employees at this location:** 3,000. **Number of employees nationwide:** 6,500.

**VARIAN ASSOCIATES
CHROMATOGRAPHY SYSTEMS**
2700 Mitchell Drive, Walnut Creek CA 94598-1602. 510/939-2400. **Contact:** Human Resources. **Description:** Varian is a diversified, international manufacturing company with sales in excess of $1 billion annually. Varian operates manufacturing facilities in seven nations and sales and service offices worldwide. The company is organized around the following core businesses: Health Care Systems; Instruments; Electronic Devices; Semiconductor Equipment. Each day, more than 80,000 people receive cancer treatments from over 2,300 Varian medical linear accelerators, treatment stimulators, and information management systems in service at hospitals and clinics worldwide. The company is also a leading supplier of X-ray tubes for imaging systems of all types. Leading semiconductor chip manufacturers worldwide rely on Varian's leading edge manufacturing systems to give them performance down to the sub-micron level and the flexibility necessary to compete in rapidly changing global markets. The company believes that unsurpassed reliability and precision make Varian analytical instruments key tools in environmental control, providing accurate testing and analysis of air, water, and soil. The company's instruments also aid physicians and researchers in the fight against diseases such as AIDS. Varian instruments can be found in laboratories regulating the quality of products ranging from petroleum and pharmaceuticals to ice cream and champagne. Its vacuum pumps and leak detectors are essential to the number of highly sophisticated processes that require a vacuum environment. Varian's electron tubes help to bring nations and cultures together through modern communications links. Varian is a worldwide leader in the manufacture of devices that power the information age by generating, amplifying, and defining signals for radio and television broadcasting and satellite communications. They are also essential elements in air traffic control, navigation, radar, fusion energy, and other scientific research applications.

W.P.W. CRANE SERVICES
3077 Tea Garden Street, San Leandro CA 94577. 510/483-2102. **Contact:** Human Resources. **Description:** A producer of equipment such as cranes, wire rope, and chain hoists.

WATERMAN INDUSTRIES INC.
P.O. Box 458, Exeter CA 93221. 209/592-3174. **Contact:** Personnel Department. **Description:** Produces water and flow control valves and irrigation equipment.

WEIGH-TRONIX, INC.
2320 Airport Boulevard, Santa Rosa CA 95403. 707/527-5555. **Fax:** 707/579-1655. **Contact:** Terry Cheney, Human Resources Assistant. **Description:** Manufactures electronic weighing systems, thermal and impact printers, POS scales, mailing systems, and related products. **Common positions include:** Accountant/Auditor; Blue-Collar Worker Supervisor; Buyer; Draftsperson; Electrical/Electronics Engineer; Financial Analyst; General Manager; Human Resources Specialist; Operations/Production Manager; Purchasing Agent and Manager; Quality Control Supervisor; Software Engineer. **Educational backgrounds include:** Accounting; Business Administration; Engineering; Finance. **Benefits:** 401(k); Daycare Assistance; Dental Insurance; Disability Coverage; Employee Discounts; Life Insurance; Medical Insurance; Pension Plan; Profit Sharing; Tuition Assistance. **Corporate headquarters location:** Norwalk CT. **Other U.S. locations:** Nationwide. **Parent company:** Staveley. **Operations at this facility include:** Administration; Divisional Headquarters; Manufacturing; Research and Development; Sales; Service. **Listed on:** Privately held. **Number of employees at this location:** 85. **Number of employees nationwide:** 1,000.

WESGO
477 Harbor Boulevard, Belmont CA 94002. 415/592-9440. **Contact:** Pam Salloum, Human Resources Manager. **Description:** Manufactures technical ceramics and brazing alloys. **Common positions include:** Accountant/Auditor; Blue-Collar Worker Supervisor; Buyer; Computer Programmer; Customer Service Representative; Department Manager; Draftsperson; Financial Analyst; Human Resources Specialist; Mechanical Engineer; Metallurgical Engineer; Operations/Production Manager; Purchasing Agent and Manager; Quality Control Supervisor; Services Sales Representative. **Educational backgrounds include:** Accounting; Business Administration; Computer Science; Engineering; Marketing. **Benefits:** Dental Insurance; Disability Coverage; Life Insurance; Medical Insurance; Pension Plan; Savings Plan; Tuition Assistance. **Operations at this facility include:** Administration; Manufacturing; Research and Development; Sales.

WESTBURNE SUPPLY INC.
2901 Spring Street, Redwood City CA 94063. 415/306-1350. **Contact:** Personnel Manager. **Description:** Manufactures plumbing, heating, and industrial supplies.

WIEGMANN & ROSE
P.O. Box 4187, Oakland CA 94614. 510/529-2121. **Contact:** John Gasparini, Vice President of Personnel. **Description:** Manufactures fabricated heat exchangers.

YORK INTERNATIONAL CORPORATION
7060 Koll Center Parkway, Suite 312, Pleasanton CA 94566-3118. 510/426-1144. **Contact:** Human Resources. **Description:** York International manufacturers a full line of residential, commercial, and industrial air-conditioning and refrigeration equipment and systems, heating systems, and food systems. The company recruits internationally. York employs 2,300 technicians throughout the world who provide service and repairs. The company markets its products in over 110 countries through 42 exclusive distribution facilities, 10 co-owned centers, and over 200 other wholesalers.

***Note:** Because addresses and telephone numbers of smaller companies can change rapidly, we recommend you call each company to verify the information below before inquiring about job opportunities. Mass mailings are not recommended.*

Additional small employers:

COMMERCIAL FURNITURE AND FIXTURES

Metropolitan Furniture Corp.
245 E Harris Ave, South San Francisco CA 94080-6807. 415/871-6222.

The McGuire Furniture
1201 Bryant St, San Francisco CA 94103-4306. 415/626-1414.

Harbor Universal Inc.
1900 Marina Blvd, San Leandro CA 94577-3207. 510/352-2100.

METAL HARDWARE

EJ Brooks Co.
PO Box 2939, San Rafael CA 94912. 415/456-3453.

Schlage Lock Company
540 Dado St, San Jose CA 95131-1229. 408/435-8435.

ORDNANCE AND ACCESSORIES

RCBS Operations
605 Oro Dam Blvd, Oroville CA 95965. 916/533-5191.

Autocam California
2545 Barrington Ct, Hayward CA 94545-1134. 510/782-4545.

MacCal Co. Inc.
1737 Junction Ave, San Jose CA 95112. 408/441-1435.

METAL CUTTING OR FORMING TOOLS

Branson International Plasma Corp.
31172 Huntwood Ave, Hayward CA 94544-7817. 510/489-3030.

MISC. INDUSTRIAL MACHINE TOOLS

Idylwid Corporation
2620 Augustine Dr Ste 120, Santa Clara CA 95054-2908. 408/727-9300.

INDUSTRIAL WELDING AND SOLDERING EQUIPMENT

Metcal Inc.
1530 Obrien Dr, Menlo Park CA 94025-1434. 415/325-3291.

WOODWORKING MACHINERY

Voorwood Co.
2350 Barney Rd, Anderson CA 96007-4395. 916/365-3311.

SPECIAL INDUSTRIAL MACHINERY

Nikon Precision Inc.
1399 Shoreway Rd, Belmont CA 94002-4105. 415/508-4674.

Pacific Western Systems Inc.
505 E Evelyn Ave, Mountain View CA 94041-1613. 415/961-8855.

Micro Mask Inc.
695 Vaqueros Ave, Sunnyvale CA 94086-3524. 408/245-7342.

Therma Wave Inc.
1250 Reliance Way, Fremont CA 94539-6100. 510/490-3663.

Semiconductor Systems
47003 Mission Falls Ct, Fremont CA 94539-7819. 510/683-8858.

Tegal Corp.
2201 S McDowell Blvd, Petaluma CA 94954-5661. 707/763-5600.

ET Systems Inc.
3350 Scott Blvd Bldg 8, Santa Clara CA 95054-3108. 408/727-5501.

PUMPS AND PUMPING EQUIPMENT

Weir Floway Inc.
2494 S Railroad Ave, Fresno CA 93706. 209/442-4000.

PACKAGING MACHINERY

Salwasser Manufacturing Co. Inc.
1949 E Manning Ave # 548, Reedley CA 93654-9462. 209/638-8484.

INDUSTRIAL PROCESS FURNACES AND OVENS

Retech Inc.
PO Box 997, Ukiah CA 95482-0997. 707/462-6522.

MISC. INDUSTRIAL MACHINERY AND EQUIPMENT

Kubota Pacific Computer
2880 Lakeside Dr Ste 131, Santa Clara CA 95054-2814. 408/727-8100.

INDUSTRIAL AND COMMERCIAL MACHINERY AND EQUIPMENT

George Martin
1250 67th St, Emeryville CA 94608-1184. 510/652-2200.

Triple A Machine Shop
2801 Giant Rd, Richmond CA 94806-2246. 510/233-0444.

Ra-Tek
PO Box 550, Morgan Hill

CA 95038-0550. 408/778-0888.

Connor Formed Metal Products
PO Box 151, San Jose CA 95103-0151. 408/436-8585.

Nelms Donham Machining Inc.
6341 San Ignacio Ave, San Jose CA 95119-1202. 408/297-9724.

GL Precision Machining
1465 Ellerd Dr, Turlock CA 95380-5749. 209/667-0890.

True Spex Precision Machining
2286 Mora Dr, Mountain View CA 94040-1549. 415/967-0120.

JLK Engineering
926 W Evelyn Ave, Sunnyvale CA 94086-5957. 408/481-0769.

H&J Machine Shop
643 E Arques Ave, Sunnyvale CA 94086-3832. 408/245-8168.

True-Tech
4050 Technology Pl, Fremont CA 94538-6362. 510/353-1000.

Moss Precision Inc.
24619 Oneil Ave, Hayward CA 94544-1627. 510/886-1440.

Turner Tooling
29870 Larrabee St, Hayward CA 94544-6806. 510/581-2641.

Arthur Langlie Services
782 Park Avenue, San Jose CA 95126-4800. 408/297-2396.

Norcal Pump & Machine
896 Stokes Ave, Stockton CA 95215. 209/465-4544.

Central Valley Machine Works
3516 Atwater Blvd, Atwater CA 95301-9501. 209/358-5694.

MOTORS AND GENERATORS

Arcadian Power Corp.
PO Box 1149, Tracy CA 95378-1149. 510/416-0600.

MEASURING AND CONTROLLING EQUIPMENT

Tri-Continent Scientific
12555 Loma Rica Dr, Grass Valley CA 95945-9090. 916/273-8888.

Nanometrics Inc.
310 Deguigne Dr, Sunnyvale CA 94086-3906. 408/746-1600.

IA Corp.
PO Box 4004, Alameda CA 94501-0404. 510/769-5400.

Ixys Corp.
3540 Bassett St, Santa Clara CA 95054-2704. 408/982-0700.

Prometrix Corp.
2500 Augustine Dr, Santa Clara CA 95054-3001. 408/970-9500.

Raytek Inc.
PO Box 1820, Santa Cruz CA 95061. 408/458-1110.

Sierra Instruments Inc.
5 Harris Ct Bldg L, Monterey CA 93940-5752. 408/373-0200.

Aehr Test Systems
1667 Plymouth St, Mountain View CA 94043-1231. 415/691-9400.

Giga-Tronics Inc.
4650 Norris Canyon Rd, San Ramon CA 94583-1320. 510/328-4650.

DCM Industries Inc.
2930 Faber St, Union City CA 94587-1214. 510/429-9500.

Telecommunications Technology
195 S Milpitas Blvd, Milpitas CA 95035-5425. 408/945-1700.

Probe Technology Corporation
2424 Walsh Ave, Santa Clara CA 95051-1303. 408/980-1740.

Everett Charles Technologies
138 Charcot Ave, San Jose CA 95131. 408/922-0120.

Verilink Corp.
145 Baytech Drive, San Jose CA 95134. 408/945-1199.

Pacific Western Systems
8794 Airport Rd, Redding CA 96002. 916/221-8855.

Fisons Instruments Manufacturing Inc.
355 Shoreway Rd, San Carlos CA 94070-2708. 415/591-3600.

Molecular Devices
1311 Orleans Dr, Sunnyvale CA 94089. 408/747-1700.

JRH Biosciences
One Harter Avenue, Woodland CA 95776-5901. 916/666-9835.

Lucas Novasensor
1055 Mission Court, Fremont CA 94539. 510/490-9100.

Gas Tech Inc.
8407 Central Ave, Newark CA 94560-3431. 510/794-6200.

For more information on career opportunities in industrial manufacturing:

Associations

ASSOCIATION FOR MANUFACTURING TECHNOLOGY
7901 Westpark Drive, McLean VA 22102. 703/893-2900. A trade association.

INSTITUTE OF INDUSTRIAL ENGINEERS
25 Technology Park, Norcross GA 30092. 770/449-0460. A nonprofit organization with 27,000 members. Conducts seminars and offers reduced rates on its books and publications.

NATIONAL ASSOCIATION OF MANUFACTURERS
1331 Pennsylvania Avenue NW, Suite 1500, Washington DC 20004. 202/637-3000. A lobbying association.

NATIONAL SCREW MACHINE PRODUCTS ASSOCIATION
6700 West Snowville Road, Brecksville OH 44141. 216/526-0300. World Wide Web address: http://www.pmpa.org. Provides resource information.

NATIONAL TOOLING AND MACHINING ASSOCIATION
9300 Livingston Road, Fort Washington MD 20744. 301/248-1250. Reports on wages and operating expenses. Produces monthly newsletters. Offers legal advice.

SOCIETY OF MANUFACTURING ENGINEERS
P.O. Box 930, One SME Drive, Dearborn MI 48121. 313/271-1500. Offers educational events and educational materials on manufacturing.

Special Programs

BUREAU OF APPRENTICESHIP AND TRAINING
U.S. Department of Labor, 200 Constitution Avenue NW, Washington, DC 20210. 202/219-6540.

MINING/GAS/PETROLEUM/ENERGY RELATED

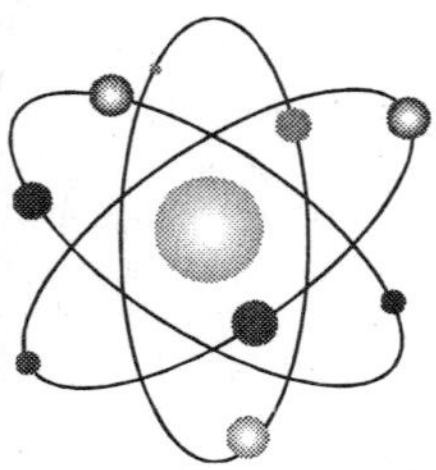

The energy industry just isn't what it used to be. In recent years, energy companies have been restructuring their operations in order to insure solid cash flows even in an era of low prices. Smaller, independent companies are now able to finance new production and land purchases with cash generated from stock sales.

Even so, jobseekers can't expect increased production to lead to much employment growth. Layoffs are expected to continue, but advanced technologies used by the energy industry continue to crop up, and jobseekers with engineering backgrounds should watch for energy-related, high-tech jobs.

In mining, earnings are much higher than average, but technological innovations, international competition, and environmental regulation will reduce employment. Best bets in the mining industry are for scientific technicians, professional specialty workers (such as geologists), and truck drivers.

AIR LIQUIDE AMERICA CORPORATION
2121 North California Boulevard, Walnut Creek CA 94596-7390. 510/977-6500. **Contact:** Human Resources. **Description:** A diversified manufacturer engaged primarily in the recovery and sale of atmospheric industrial gases, the manufacture and sale of oil field equipment and supplies, and the distribution of welding and industrial equipment and supplies. Air Liquide America operates in the following business segments: the Gas Group produces and sells oxygen, nitrogen, and argon in liquid and gaseous forms in approximately 20 locations in Texas, Louisiana, Florida, California, and Hawaii, operating more than 1,000 miles of pipeline. The Energy Group operates under two names (Bowen Tools and Dia-Log Companies), and manufactures and sells equipment to petroleum and natural gas companies. The Welding Group distributes electric arc welding equipment and supplies in Texas, Louisiana, California, and Hawaii for Lincoln Electric Company. **NOTE:** All hiring is done through the Houston office. Applicants should send resumes to: Deborah Alfred, Human Resources, P.O. Box 460229, Houston TX 77056.

AIR LIQUIDE AMERICA CORPORATION
700 Decoto Road, Union City CA 94597-3513. 510/429-4200. **Contact:** Human Resources. **Description:** A diversified manufacturer engaged primarily in the recovery and sale of atmospheric industrial gases, the manufacture and sale of oil field equipment and supplies, and the distribution of welding and industrial equipment and supplies. Operates in the following business segments: the Gas Group produces and sells oxygen, nitrogen, and argon in liquid and gaseous forms in approximately 20 locations in Texas, Louisiana, Florida, California, and Hawaii, operating more than 1,000 miles of pipeline. The Energy Group operates under two names (Bowen Tools, or Dia-Log Companies), and manufactures and sells equipment to petroleum and natural gas companies. The Welding Group distributes electric arc welding equipment and supplies in Texas, Louisiana, California, and Hawaii for Lincoln Electric Company. **NOTE:** Please send resumes to: Deborah Alfred, Human Resources, P.O. Box 460229, Houston TX 77056.

ARCO PETROLEUM PRODUCTS
2000 Alameda, Suite 218, De Las Pulgas CA 94403. 415/571-2402. **Contact:** Judy Martinez, Personnel Representative. **Description:** A prime resource recovery company, specializing in exploration and production of crude oil and natural gas, as well as petroleum products and petrochemical feed stocks. Overall, Arco is primarily an energy company involved in all phases of the petroleum energy business. The company also manufactures and markets petrochemicals; has interests in coal, copper, molybdenum, and other minerals; and produces a wide range of metal products and solar energy devices.

BHP MINERALS INC.
550 California Street, San Francisco CA 94104. 415/981-1515. **Contact:** Janice Davis, Personnel Supervisor. **Description:** Mines coal and other minerals.

CALPINE CORPORATION
50 West San Fernando Street, San Jose CA 95113. 408/995-5115. **Contact:** Human Resources. **Description:** Calpine is a power company. Calpine sells its products -- steam and electricity -- to electric utilities, industrial companies, and government institutions. The company develops, owns, and operates independent power projects, including three geothermal and two natural gas-fired plants. In addition, the company owns 363 megawatts of geothermal fields that supply 15 utility power plants. The company is the second-largest producer of geothermal energy in the United States. **Corporate headquarters location:** This Location.

CHEVRON CORPORATION
575 Market Street, San Francisco CA 94105. 415/894-7700. **Contact:** Human Resources. **Description:** An international oil firm with operations in more than 90 countries. Chevron Corporation is engaged in worldwide integrated petroleum operations, including the exploration and production of crude oil and natural gas reserves; the transportation of crude oil, natural gas, and petroleum products by pipeline, tanker, and motor equipment; the operation of oil-refining complexes; and the wholesale and retail marketing of hundreds of petroleum products. **NOTE:** Entry-level positions are available. **Common positions include:** Accountant/Auditor; Chemical Engineer; Chemist; Computer Programmer; Computer Systems Analyst; Geologist/Geophysicist; Mechanical Engineer; Petroleum Engineer. **Educational backgrounds include:** Accounting; Business Administration; Engineering; Finance; Geology; Marketing. **Benefits:** 401(k); Dental Insurance; Disability Coverage; Employee Discounts; Job Sharing; Life Insurance; Medical Insurance; Pension Plan; Profit Sharing; Savings Plan. **Special Programs:** Internships. **Corporate headquarters location:** This Location. **Other U.S. locations:** San Ramon CA; Southern CA; New Orleans LA; Houston TX. **Operations at this facility include:** Administration. **Listed on:** New York Stock Exchange. **Annual sales/revenues:** More than $100 million. **Number of employees at this location:** 3,000. **Number of employees nationwide:** 28,000. **Number of employees worldwide:** 40,000.

CHEVRON RESEARCH & TECHNOLOGY
A SUBSIDIARY OF CHEVRON CORPORATION
100 Chevron Way, Richmond CA 94801. 510/242-3000. **Contact:** Human Resources. **Description:** Engaged in research and development, design, and technical services for petroleum and petrochemical processes and products. Chevron is an international oil firm with operations in more than 90 countries engaged in worldwide integrated petroleum operations, including the exploration and production of crude oil and natural gas

reserves; the transportation of crude oil, natural gas, and petroleum products by pipeline, tanker, and motor equipment; the operation of oil-refining complexes; and the wholesale and retail marketing of hundreds of petroleum products. **NOTE:** Please apply only when openings occur. **Number of employees nationwide:** 2,000.

HOMESTAKE MINING COMPANY
650 California Street, 11th Floor, San Francisco CA 94108. 415/981-8150. **Contact:** Mary T. Schuba, Manager of Human Resources. **Description:** One of the largest gold mining companies in the world, Homestake Mining has production facilities in the United States, Canada, and Australia, with minor interests in Chile, Mexico, and Venezuela. **Common positions include:** Accountant/Auditor; Computer Systems Analyst; Financial Analyst; Mining Engineer. **Educational backgrounds include:** Accounting; Business Administration; Computer Science; Engineering; Finance; Geology. **Benefits:** 401(k); Commuter Bonus Plan; Dental Insurance; Disability Coverage; EAP; Life Insurance; Medical Insurance; Pension Plan; Tuition Assistance. **Corporate headquarters location:** This Location. **Other U.S. locations:** SD. **Operations at this facility include:** Administration. **Listed on:** New York Stock Exchange. **Number of employees at this location:** 70. **Number of employees nationwide:** 2,100.

INSPECTORATE AMERICA CORPORATION
3773 Pacheco Boulevard, Martinez CA 94553-2130. 510/372-0958. **Contact:** Human Resources. **Description:** An oil and gas field services company.

KENETECH CORPORATION
500 Sansome Street, San Francisco CA 94111. 415/398-3825. **Contact:** Human Resources. **Description:** Kenetech Corporation is a leading provider of products and services to the electric power industry. Through its subsidiaries, the company designs, develops, builds, finances, and maintains power plants that use environmentally-preferred technologies -- principally wind, biomass, and natural gas. **NOTE:** Send resumes to: Human Resources, 6952 Preston Avenue, Livermore CA 94550. **Common positions include:** Accountant/Auditor; Attorney; Electrical/Electronics Engineer; Financial Analyst; Human Resources Specialist; Industrial Production Manager; Mechanical Engineer; Metallurgical Engineer; Meteorologist; Paralegal; Software Engineer. **Educational backgrounds include:** Accounting; Business Administration; Engineering; Finance. **Benefits:** 401(k); Dental Insurance; Disability Coverage; ESOP; Medical Insurance; Tuition Assistance. **Corporate headquarters location:** This Location. **Other U.S. locations:** Livermore CA. **Operations at this facility include:** Administration. **Number of employees at this location:** 200. **Number of employees nationwide:** 900.

OLYMPIAN
260 Michele Court, South San Francisco CA 94080. 415/873-8200. **Contact:** Barbara Kittelman, Personnel Director. **Description:** Distributes a wide variety of petroleum products. **Common positions include:** Computer Programmer; Credit Manager; Customer Service Representative; Department Manager; Environmental Engineer; General Manager; Hazardous Materials Driver; Human Resources Specialist; Marketing Specialist; Warehouse Manager. **Benefits:** 401(k); Dental Insurance; Life Insurance; Medical Insurance. **Corporate headquarters location:** This Location.

PLANT MAINTENANCE INC.
P.O. Box 48, Martinez CA 94553. 510/228-3285. **Contact:** Human Resources. **Description:** An oil field services company.

SHELL OIL COMPANY/MARTINEZ
P.O. Box 711, Martinez CA 94553. 510/228-6161. **Contact:** Employee Relations Manager. **Description:** Engaged in the exploration, development, production, purchase, transportation, and marketing of crude oil, natural gas, and related chemical products. The Oil Products segment is engaged primarily in the marketing and sale of its oil products in the United States. The Chemical Products segment is engaged principally in the production of detergent alcohols, agricultural herbicides and insecticides, and other petrochemicals. **Corporate headquarters location:** Houston TX. **Listed on:** New York Stock Exchange.

TOSCO CORPORATION
2300 Clayton Road, Suite 1100, Concord CA 94520-2148. 510/602-4000. **Contact:** Human Resources. **Description:** Tosco Corporation is a refiner of crude oil and marketer of wholesale petroleum products. The company has interests in over 23,000 acres of oil shale property in Colorado and over 20,000 acres in Vermont. Tosco refines the crude oil of some five domestic and two foreign companies, and then distributes the oil and related products through its subsidiary, Tosco Refining Corporation. The company has acquired Bayway, a refining company in New Jersey; and Pacific Northwest, which operates retail marketing and distribution facilities in Washington and Oregon.

TOSCO REFINING CORPORATION
Waterfront Road and Solano Way, Martinez CA 94553. 510/228-1220. **Contact:** Human Resources. **Description:** Tosco Refining Corporation distributes oil and related products that are refined by Tosco Corporation. **Parent company:** Tosco Corporation is a refiner of crude oil and marketer of wholesale petroleum products. The company has interests in over 23,000 acres of oil shale property in Colorado and over 20,000 acres in Vermont. Tosco refines the crude oil of some five domestic and two foreign companies. The company has acquired Bayway, a refining company in New Jersey; and Pacific Northwest, which operates retail marketing and distribution facilities in Washington and Oregon.

Note: *Because addresses and telephone numbers of smaller companies can change rapidly, we recommend you call each company to verify the information below before inquiring about job opportunities. Mass mailings are not recommended.*

Additional small employers:

LUBRICATING OILS AND GREASES

Wickland Oil Terminals
90 San Pablo Avenue, Crockett CA 94525. 510/787-1076.

PETROLEUM REFINING

Coast Gas Inc.
432 Westridge Dr, Watsonville CA 95076. 408/724-1921.

PETROLEUM AND PETROLEUM PRODUCTS WHOLESALE

Pacific Refining Co.
4901 San Pablo Ave, Hercules CA 94547-2100. 510/799-8000.

Proflame Inc.
400 Bel Marin Keys Boulevard Floor 3 , Novato CA 94949-5650. 415/883-8717.

Amerigas
210 Canyon View Rd, Colfax CA 95713-9707. 916/346-2241.

Petro Speed
324 N 16th St, Sacramento CA 95814. 916/446-0771.

Pennzoil Products Company
Distribution Center, San Jose CA 95112. 408/298-7373.

Wickland Oil Martinez
2801 Waterfront Rd, Martinez CA 94553-1454. 510/228-3227.

For more information on career opportunities in the mining, gas, petroleum, and energy industries:

Associations

AMERICAN ASSOCIATION OF PETROLEUM GEOLOGISTS
P.O. Box 979, Tulsa OK 7410-0979. 918/584-2555. World Wide Web address: http://www.geobyte.com. International headquarters for petroleum geologists.

AMERICAN GEOLOGICAL INSTITUTE
4220 King Street, Alexandria VA 22302-1507. 703/379-2480. World Wide Web address: http://www.agi.umd.edu/agi/agi.html. Scholarships available. Publishes monthly *Geotimes*. Offers job listings.

AMERICAN NUCLEAR SOCIETY
555 North Kensington Avenue, La Grange Park IL 60525. 708/352-6611. World Wide Web address: http://www.ans.org. Offers educational services.

AMERICAN PETROLEUM INSTITUTE
1220 L Street NW, Suite 900, Washington DC 20005. 202/682-8000. World Wide Web address: http://www.api.org. A trade association.

GEOLOGICAL SOCIETY OF AMERICA
3300 Penrose Place, P.O. Box 9140, Boulder CO 80301. 303/447-2020. Membership of over 17,000. Offers sales items and publications. Also conducts society meetings.

SOCIETY OF EXPLORATION GEOPHYSICISTS
P.O. Box 702740, Tulsa OK 74170-2740. 918/493-3516. A membership association. Offers publications.

Directories

BROWN'S DIRECTORY OF NORTH AMERICAN AND INTERNATIONAL GAS COMPANIES
Advanstar Communications, 7500 Old Oak Boulevard, Cleveland OH 44130. Toll-free phone: 800/225-4569.

NATIONAL PETROLEUM NEWS FACT BOOK
Adams/Hunter Publishing Company, 2101 South Arlington Heights Road, Suite 150, Arlington Heights IL 60005-4142. 847/427-9512.

OIL AND GAS DIRECTORY
Geophysical Directory, Inc., P.O. Box 130508, Houston TX 77219. 713/529-8789.

Magazines

AMERICAN GAS MONTHLY
1515 Wilson Boulevard, Arlington VA 22209. 703/841-8686.

GAS INDUSTRIES
Gas Industries News, Inc., 6300 North River Road, Suite 505, Rosemont IL 60018. 312/693-3682.

NATIONAL PETROLEUM NEWS
Adams/Hunter Publishing Company, 2101 South Arlington Heights Road, Suite 150, Arlington Heights IL 60005. 847/427-9512.

OIL AND GAS JOURNAL
PennWell Publishing Company, 1421 South Sheridan Road, P.O. Box 1260. Tulsa OK 74101. 918/835-3161.

PAPER AND WOOD PRODUCTS

The year 1995 was a dramatic one for the paper industry. Prices jumped higher and faster than they had at any time since World War II. According to Dean Witter, profits were up an astounding 180 percent during the year at the nation's 19 largest paper and paperboard companies.

By mid-1995, however, customers had begun to hoard paper, forcing prices back down. Luckily, even as profits soared in the early part of the year, the industry played its hand conservatively by resisting the impulse to expand capacity. Analysts expect prices to continue to stay down during 1996. That means that jobseekers shouldn't anticipate a major increase in industry hiring.

One hot trend, however, may provide opportunity. Environmental concerns should give the paper packaging segment an advantage over plastics, as companies move to become "green." The industry hopes to recycle at least half of the paper it produces by the turn of the century. Minimills, which convert cardboard into pulp, are springing up nationwide. Among the industry's recycling leaders: Weyerhaeuser and Boise Cascade.

AMERICAN ENVELOPE
900 David Road, Burlingame CA 94010. 415/348-4891. **Contact:** Linda Blackwell, Office Manager. **Description:** A manufacturer and distributor of plain and printed envelopes. **Common positions include:** Manufacturer's/Wholesaler's Sales Rep. **Benefits:** Dental Insurance; Disability Coverage; Life Insurance; Medical Insurance; Pension Plan; Savings Plan; Tuition Assistance. **Operations at this facility include:** Manufacturing. **Listed on:** New York Stock Exchange.

BEMISS-JASON CORPORATION
37600 Central Court, Newark CA 94560. 510/713-6400. **Contact:** Lesley Williams, Human Resources Manager. **Description:** Produces a myriad of paper products for educational, art and crafts, retail, display, and medical purposes. **Common positions include:** Accountant/Auditor; Administrator; Advertising Clerk; Bank Officer/Manager; Blue-Collar Worker Supervisor; Buyer; Commercial Artist; Computer Programmer; Credit Manager; Customer Service Representative; Department Manager; Financial Analyst; General Manager; Industrial Engineer; Manufacturer's/Wholesaler's Sales Rep.; Mechanical Engineer; Systems Analyst. **Educational backgrounds include:** Accounting; Art/Design; Business Administration; Communications; Computer Science; Economics; Engineering; Finance; Liberal Arts; Marketing; Mathematics. **Benefits:** Dental Insurance; Disability Coverage; Life Insurance; Medical Insurance; Profit Sharing; Savings Plan; Tuition Assistance. **Corporate headquarters location:** This Location. **Operations at this facility include:** Administration; Manufacturing; Research and Development; Sales; Service.

CALPINE CONTAINERS INC.
140 Gregory Lane, Suite 180, Pleasant Hill CA 94523-3357. 510/798-3010. **Fax:** 510/686-0152. **Contact:** Jan Tibbetts, Personnel Director. **Description:** Produces wooden and corrugated paper boxes. **Common positions include:** Administrator; Branch Manager; Computer Programmer; Department Manager; Management Trainee;

Manufacturer's/Wholesaler's Sales Rep. **Educational backgrounds include:** Accounting; Business Administration. **Benefits:** Dental Insurance; Disability Coverage; Life Insurance; Medical Insurance; Pension Plan; Profit Sharing; Vision Insurance. **Corporate headquarters location:** This Location. **Operations at this facility include:** Regional Headquarters. **Number of employees at this location:** 20. **Number of employees nationwide:** 300.

CELEBRATE PAPER COMPANY
245 South Spruce Avenue, South San Francisco CA 94080. 415/266-7211. **Fax:** 415/266-7239. **Contact:** Felicia Washington, Human Resources Department. **Description:** The distribution division of the Mead Corporation. Product line includes paper and paper products; office supplies and equipment; packaging supplies and equipment; and consumables. **Common positions include:** Accountant/Auditor; Administrator; Budget Analyst; Buyer; Claim Representative; Clerical Supervisor; Credit Manager; Customer Service Representative; Dental Lab Technician; EKG Technician; Financial Analyst; General Manager; Human Resources Specialist; Marketing Specialist; Mechanical Engineer; Operations/Production Manager; Public Relations Specialist; Purchasing Agent and Manager; Services Sales Representative; Statistician; Systems Analyst; Teacher. **Educational backgrounds include:** Accounting; Business Administration; Communications; Computer Science; Finance; Liberal Arts; Marketing. **Benefits:** 401(k); Dental Insurance; Disability Coverage; Life Insurance; Medical Insurance; Pension Plan; Savings Plan; Tuition Assistance. **Parent company:** Mead Corporation (Dayton OH). **Operations at this facility include:** Administration; Regional Headquarters; Sales; Service. **Number of employees at this location:** 160. **Number of employees nationwide:** 2,000.

FIBREBOARD CORPORATION
California Plaza, 2121 North California Boulevard, Suite 560, Walnut Creek CA 94596. 510/274-0700. **Contact:** Human Resources. **Description:** Fibreboard is a leader in the building products industry, manufacturing wood, vinyl, and industrial insulation products. Registered trade names include Norandex and Pabco. In addition to owning approximately 80,000 acres of timberland in the central Sierra Nevada Mountains of California, the company also owns and operates two California resorts: Northstar-at-Tahoe, an all-season ski and golf resort and conference center, and Sierra-at-Tahoe, a day ski facility. The company's building products operations are made up of the Wood Products Group, Norandex, and Pabco. Wood products include lumber, molding, millwork, and hardwood plywood panels. Norandex is a manufacturer and distributor of vinyl siding and residential building products. Pabco produces calcium silicate molded industrial insulation, Super Firetemp panel fireproofing board, metal jacketing, and elbows.

GEORGIA-PACIFIC CORPORATION
PACKAGING DIVISION
249 East Grand Avenue, South San Francisco CA 94080. 415/873-7800. **Contact:** Jim McGee, Human Resources Manager. **Description:** This location produces corrugated containers. **Common positions include:** Blue-Collar Worker Supervisor; Customer Service Representative; Electrician; Human Resources Specialist; Manufacturer's/ Wholesaler's Sales Rep.; Payroll Clerk; Printing Press Operator; Production Manager; Production Operator; Quality Control Supervisor; Receptionist; Secretary; Services Sales Representative; Transportation/Traffic Specialist; Welder. **Educational backgrounds include:** Accounting; Business Administration; Finance; Liberal Arts. **Benefits:** Dental Insurance; Disability Coverage; Life Insurance; Medical Insurance; Pension Plan;

Savings Plan; Tuition Assistance. **Corporate headquarters location:** Atlanta GA. **Operations at this facility include:** Administration; Manufacturing; Research and Development; Sales. **Listed on:** New York Stock Exchange. **Number of employees at this location:** 220. **Number of employees nationwide:** 52,000.

HUDSON ICS
P.O. Box 2338, San Leandro CA 94577. 510/351-5872. **Contact:** Charlie Novotny, Personnel Director. **Description:** Operates a sawmill and lumber yard.

INLAND CONTAINER CORPORATION
P.O. Box 565, Newark CA 94560-0565. 510/797-2020. **Contact:** Human Resources. **Description:** A manufacturer of corrugated shipping containers and boxes.

INTERNATIONAL PAPER COMPANY
2826 Teepee Drive, Stockton CA 95205-2462. 209/463-4736. **Contact:** Human Resources. **Description:** One of the world's largest forest products companies, with 72,500 employees in over 300 locations worldwide. International Paper is a manufacturer of pulp and paper, packaging, and wood products as well as a range of specialty products. Millions of acres of timberland are controlled by International Paper, making it the largest private landowner in the United States. The company is organized into five business segments: Printing Papers, in which principal products include uncoated papers, coated papers, bristles, and pulp; Packaging, which includes industrial packaging, consumer packaging, and kraft and specialty papers; Distribution, which includes sales of printing papers, graphic arts equipment and supplies, packaging materials, industrial supplies, and office products; Specialty Products, which include imaging products, specialty panels, nonwovens, chemicals, and minerals; and Forest Products, including logs and wood products.

INTERNATIONAL PAPER COMPANY
1900 South Norfolk Street, Suite 323, San Mateo CA 94403-1151. 415/572-1373. **Contact:** Human Resources. **Description:** One of the world's largest forest products companies, with 72,500 employees in over 300 locations worldwide. International Paper is a manufacturer of pulp and paper, packaging, and wood products as well as a range of specialty products. Millions of acres of timberland are controlled by International Paper, making it the largest private landowner in the United States. The company is organized into five business segments: Printing Papers, in which principal products include uncoated papers, coated papers, bristles, and pulp; Packaging, which includes industrial packaging, consumer packaging, and kraft and specialty papers; Distribution, which includes sales of printing papers, graphic arts equipment and supplies, packaging materials, industrial supplies, and office products; Specialty Products, which include imaging products, specialty panels, nonwovens, chemicals, and minerals; and Forest Products, including logs and wood products.

JEFFERSON SMURFIT
201 South Hillview Drive, Milpitas CA 95035. 408/946-3600. **Contact:** Human Resources. **Description:** A large producer of paperboard packaging. Manufacturing facilities are located throughout the world. Some products include shipping containers, folding cartons, composite cans, plastic drums, and many others.

JEFFERSON SMURFIT
2600 De La Cruz Boulevard, Santa Clara CA 95050. 408/496-5118. **Contact:** Human Resources. **Description:** A large producer of paperboard packaging. Manufacturing

facilities are located throughout the United States and in foreign locations. Some products include shipping containers, folding cartons, composite cans, plastic drums, and many others.

LASERCRAFT
P.O. Box 696, Santa Rosa CA 95402. 707/528-1060. **Contact:** Controller. **Description:** A manufacturer of laser-engraved wood and paper giftware including stationery and special occasion note cards. **Common positions include:** Accountant/Auditor; Blue-Collar Worker Supervisor; Buyer; Commercial Artist; Customer Service Representative; Draftsperson; Operations/Production Manager. **Educational backgrounds include:** Accounting; Art/Design; Business Administration; Marketing. **Benefits:** Dental Insurance; Disability Coverage; Employee Discounts; Life Insurance; Medical Insurance; Pension Plan; Savings Plan; Tuition Assistance. **Corporate headquarters location:** This Location. **Other U.S. locations:** Healdsburg CA. **Operations at this facility include:** Administration; Manufacturing; Research and Development; Sales.

LONGVIEW FIBRE COMPANY
120 Montgomery Street, Suite 2200, San Francisco CA 94104-4325. 415/362-8670. **Contact:** Human Resources. **Description:** Longview Fibre Company owns and operates 530,000 acres of tree farms in Oregon and Washington and is a major pulp, wood, and paper products manufacturer. The company has 14 converting plants in 10 states which produce shipping containers and merchandise and grocery bags.

LOUISIANA-PACIFIC CORPORATION
WESTERN DIVISION
P.O. Box 158, Samoa CA 95564. 707/443-7511. **Fax:** 707/443-0522. **Contact:** Human Resources. **Description:** A forest products firm which harvests timber and converts it into a wide range of wood products including lumber, panel products, doors, and other goods. Operates more than 100 manufacturing facilities and 20 distribution centers in the United States and Canada.

THE MARLEY COOLING TOWER COMPANY
150 North Sinclair Avenue, Stockton CA 95215. 209/465-3451. **Contact:** Personnel. **Description:** Manufactures wooden cooling towers that are used in various industry applications. **Corporate headquarters location:** This Location.

NATIONWIDE PAPERS, INC.
P.O. Box 7895, San Francisco CA 94120. 415/586-9160. **Contact:** Carol Curbischley, Operations Manager. **Description:** A distributor of paper products.

PACIFIC LUMBER COMPANY
P.O. Box 37, Scotia CA 95565. 707/764-2222. **Contact:** Personnel Department. **Description:** A lumber company.

POTLATCH CORPORATION
P.O. Box 193591, San Francisco CA 94119-3591. 510/947-5500. **Contact:** Lois Seguin, Employee Relations Administrator. **Description:** Potlatch is a fully-integrated manufacturer of forest products including lumber, plywood, paper, bleached paperboard, and consumer products. Wood products are produced at plants in Arkansas, Idaho, and Minnesota and are marketed through company sales representatives to wholesalers for distribution nationwide. Coated papers for magazines, catalogs, and direct-mail

advertising are produced in Minnesota and sold mostly to merchants. **Listed on:** New York Stock Exchange.

SIMPSON PAPER COMPANY
989 Hillsdale Boulevard, Suite 370, Foster City CA 94404. 415/358-9970. **Contact:** Human Resources. **Description:** Produces a wide range of paper products at mills throughout the United States.

SIMPSON PAPER COMPANY
942 South Stockton Avenue, Ripon CA 95366. 209/599-4241. **Contact:** Human Resources. **Description:** Produces a wide range of paper products at mills throughout the United States.

SIMPSON PAPER COMPANY
P.O. Box 637, Anderson CA 96007-0637. 916/365-2711. **Contact:** Human Resources. **Description:** Produces a wide range of paper products at mills throughout the United States.

SIMPSON PAPER COMPANY
1900 Vendissen, Samoa CA 95564. 707/443-9771. **Contact:** Human Resources. **Description:** Produces a wide range of paper products at mills throughout the United States.

WEYERHAEUSER PAPER COMPANY
1801 Hibbard Street, Alameda CA 94501. 510/523-6121. **Contact:** Human Resources. **Description:** Weyerhaeuser's principal businesses are the growing and harvesting of timber; the manufacture, distribution, and sale of forest products including logs, wood chips, and building products; real estate development and construction; and financial services. Weyerhaeuser is one of the world's largest private owners of merchantable softwood timber and also on of the largest producers of softwood lumber and pulp. The company is also one of North America's largest producers of forest products and recyclers of office wastepaper, newspaper, and corrugated boxes. Weyerhaeuser also sells electricity to utility companies generated from its 15 trash-to-energy plants and six small cogeneration or recycling plants. The Water Division manufactures and operates facilities and systems for water purification, water treatment, and managed by-products. The Air Division designs, manufactures, and integrates air-pollution emission control and measurement systems and related equipment. **Common positions include:** Accountant/Auditor; Blue-Collar Worker Supervisor; Customer Service Representative; Department Manager; General Manager; Human Resources Specialist; Manufacturer's/Wholesaler's Sales Rep.; Operations/Production Manager. **Educational backgrounds include:** Accounting; Engineering. **Benefits:** Dental Insurance; Disability Coverage; Employee Discounts; Life Insurance; Medical Insurance; Pension Plan; Profit Sharing; Savings Plan; Tuition Assistance. **Corporate headquarters location:** Tacoma WA. **Listed on:** New York Stock Exchange. **Number of employees nationwide:** 37,000.

WEYERHAEUSER PAPER COMPANY
1345 Harkins Road, Salinas CA 93901. 408/757-5381. **Contact:** Kathy Clark, Human Resources Director. **Description:** This location produces pine lumber and plywood. Weyerhaeuser is a manufacturer of forest products. The company's principal businesses are the growing and harvesting of timber; the manufacture, distribution, and sales of forest products including logs, wood chips, building products, pulp, paper, and

packaging products; real estate development and construction; and financial services. The company is the world's largest private owner of merchantable softwood timber and a large producer of softwood lumber and market pulp. It is also one of the largest North American producers of forest products and recyclers of office wastepaper, newspaper, and corrugated boxes. Weyerhaeuser emphasizes minimum-impact (on the environment) manufacturing; a safe, well-managed, team-oriented workplace; and good community relations.

WEYERHAEUSER PAPER COMPANY
P.O. Box 5143, San Ramon CA 94583-5143. 510/830-1240. **Contact:** Human Resources. **Description:** This location produces pine lumber and plywood. Weyerhaeuser is a manufacturer of forest products. The company's principal businesses are the growing and harvesting of timber; the manufacture, distribution, and sales of forest products including logs, wood chips, building products, pulp, paper, and packaging products; real estate development and construction; and financial services. The company is the world's largest private owner of merchantable softwood timber and a large producer of softwood lumber and market pulp. It is also one of the largest North American producers of forest products and recyclers of office wastepaper, newspaper, and corrugated boxes. Weyerhaeuser emphasizes minimum-impact (on the environment) manufacturing; a safe, well-managed, team-oriented workplace; and good community relations.

WILLAMETTE INDUSTRIES
P.O. Box 1878, 2800 Alvarado Street, San Leandro CA 94577. 510/357-5400. **Fax:** 510/352-5518. **Contact:** Jack Sullivan, Personnel and Safety Director. **Description:** This location manufactures corrugated shipping cartons. **Benefits:** Dental Insurance; Disability Coverage; Life Insurance; Medical Insurance; Pension Plan; Profit Sharing; Tuition Assistance. **Corporate headquarters location:** Portland OR. **Operations at this facility include:** Manufacturing; Sales.

***Note:** Because addresses and telephone numbers of smaller companies can change rapidly, we recommend you call each company to verify the information below before inquiring about job opportunities. Mass mailings are not recommended.*

Additional small employers:

LUMBER AND WOOD WHOLESALE

Collins Pine Co.
PO Box 796, Chester CA 96020. 916/258-2111.

United Pacific Forest Products
101 H St, Petaluma CA 94952. 707/762-9060.

Schmidbauer Lumber
1046 Koster Road, Eureka CA 95501. 707/443-7024.

Wisconsin CA First Product Inc.
PO Box 2125, Redding CA 96099. 916/241-8310.

Roof Structures Inc.
4433 Enterprise St, Fremont CA 94538. 510/226-7171.

Redwood Empire Sawmills
31401 McCray Rd, Cloverdale CA 95425-9503. 707/894-4241.

INDUSTRIAL PAPER AND RELATED PRODUCTS WHOLESALE

Kirk Paper & Graphics
1059 Vine St, Sacramento CA 95814-0339. 916/441-5793.

National Self Storage
4950 Watt Ave, N Highlands CA 95660-5195. 916/338-1609.

National Self Storage
7245 55th St, Sacramento

CA 95823. 916/422-6043.

CONVERTED PAPER AND PAPERBOARD PRODUCTS

Down River Int'l
PO Box 15290 C, Sacramento CA 95851. 916/920-0290.

DIE-CUT PAPER AND PAPER PRODUCTS

Atapco Office Products
PO Box 12266, Fresno CA 93777. 209/441-0180.

Bindco
1089 Mills Way, Redwood City CA 94063. 415/363-2200.

PAPER BAGS

Kent H. Landsberg Co.
31067 San Clemente St, Hayward CA 94544-7894. 510/489-8200.

COATED AND LAMINATED PAPER

Bay Area Labels
1980 Lundy Ave, San Jose CA 95131. 408/432-1980.

PAPERBOARD CONTAINERS AND BOXES

San Joaquin Packaging
PO Box 720, Stockton CA 95201. 209/464-7000.

Gaylord Container
1779 Wilbur Avenue, Antioch CA 94509. 510/779-3200.

Gaylord Container
6400 Jamieson Way, Gilroy CA 95020. 408/847-6400.

Tharco
2222 Grant Ave, San Lorenzo CA 94580-1892. 510/276-8600.

Mercury Container
33463 Western Ave, Union City CA 94587-3201. 510/487-1211.

Keyes Fibre Company
6341 Folsom Blvd, Sacramento CA 95819-4618. 916/689-2020.

Sonoco Industrial Container
701 Willow Pass Rd, Pittsburg CA 94565-1803. 510/439-3786.

Pacific Coast Packaging
1401 S Madera Ave, Kerman CA 93630. 209/846-6644.

Valley View Packing
PO Box 5699, San Jose CA 95150-5699. 408/269-1275.

PAPER MILLS

Ledger Paper Company
5601 Cedars Rd, Redding CA 96001. 916/243-8076.

Newark Sierra Paperboard
800 W Church Street, Stockton CA 95203. 209/466-5251.

WOOD PRESERVING

California Casc Woodland
1492 Churchill Downs Ave, Woodland CA 95776. 916/666-1261.

WOOD CONTAINERS

Wood Fiber Products
12686 Locke Road, Lockeford CA 95237. 209/727-3731.

WOOD PALLETS AND SKIDS

Sonoma Pacific Co. Inc.
2100 Embarcadero Ste 105, Oakland CA 94606-5309. 510/261-1843.

Lodi Fab Industries Inc.
1029 South Sacramento St, Lodi CA 95240-4712. 209/333-3500.

WOOD PRODUCTS

Sierra Pine Ltd.
4300 Dominguez Rd, Rocklin CA 95677-2103. 916/624-2473.

Custodis-Ecodyne Inc.
PO Box 1267, Santa Rosa CA 95402. 707/544-5833.

Wetsel-Oviatt Lumber
PO Box 910, Folsom CA 95763. 916/939-8700.

P&M Cedar Products
PO Box 7349, Stockton CA 95267. 209/957-2802.

The Dorris Lumber & Moulding Co.
2601 Redding Ave, Sacramento CA 95820-2155. 916/452-7531.

Sacramento A-1 Door
PO Box 214446, Sacramento CA 95821. 916/481-5030.

Thunderbird Moulding
8180 Industrial Pkwy, Sacramento CA 95824-2340. 916/381-4200.

Morrison Building Materials
PO Box 7120, Chico CA 95927. 916/345-3999.

Miller Redwood Co.
PO Box 247, Crescent City CA 95531. 707/464-3144.

Standard Structures
PO Box K, Santa Rosa CA 95402. 707/544-2982.

Hi-Ridge Lumber Co.
PO Box 458, Yreka CA 96097. 916/842-4451.

LOGGING

Eel River Sawmills Inc.
S Hwy 101, Redcrest CA 95569. 707/764-5636.

Capital Lumber Co.
13480 Old Redwood Hwy, Healdsburg CA 95448. 707/433-7070.

Harwood Products Inc.
PO Box 224, Branscomb CA 95417. 707/984-6181.

WOOD MILLS

P&M Cedar Products
6199 State Highway 273, Anderson CA 96007-9418.

Big Valley Lumber
PO Box 617, Bieber CA 96009. 916/294-5221.

Sierra Lumber Manufacturers
PO Box 6216, Stockton CA 95206-0216. 209/943-7777.

For more information on career opportunities in the paper and wood products industries:

Associations

AMERICAN FOREST AND PAPER ASSOCIATION
1111 19th Street NW, Suite 700, Washington DC 20036. 202/463-2700. A lobbying group that conducts informational gatherings.

AMERICAN FOREST AND PAPER ASSOCIATION
260 Madison Avenue, New York NY 10016. 212/340-0600. Headquartered in Washington DC. A lobbying group that conducts informational gatherings.

FOREST PRODUCTS SOCIETY
2801 Marshall Court, Madison WI 53705-2295. 608/231-1361. An international, nonprofit, educational association that provides an information network for all segments of the forest products industry. Offers employment referral service.

NATIONAL PAPER TRADE ASSOCIATION
111 Great Neck Road, Great Neck NY 11021. 516/829-3070. World Wide Web address: http://www.papertrade.com. Offers management services to wholesalers.

PAPERBOARD PACKAGING COUNCIL
888 17th Street NW, Suite 900, Washington DC 20006. 202/289-4100. Offers statistical and lobbying services.

TECHNICAL ASSOCIATION OF THE PULP AND PAPER INDUSTRY
P.O. Box 105113, Atlanta GA 30348. 404/446-1400. World Wide Web address: http://www.tappi.org. Nonprofit. Offers conferences and education.

Directories

DIRECTORY OF THE FOREST PRODUCTS INDUSTRY
Miller Freeman Publications, Inc., 600 Harrison Street, San Francisco CA 94107. 415/905-2200.

LOCKWOOD-POST'S DIRECTORY OF THE PAPER AND ALLIED TRADES
Miller Freeman Publications, Inc., 600 Harrison Street, San Francisco CA 94107. 415/905-2200.

POST'S PULP AND PAPER DIRECTORY
Miller Freeman Publications, Inc., 600 Harrison Street, San Francisco CA 94107. 415/905-2200.

Magazines

PAPERBOARD PACKAGING
Advanstar Communications, 131 West First Street, Duluth MN 55802. 218/723-9200.

PULP AND PAPER WEEK
Miller Freeman Publications, Inc., 600 Harrison Street, San Francisco CA 94107. 415/905-2200.

WOOD TECHNOLOGIES
Miller Freeman Publications, Inc., 600 Harrison Street, San Francisco CA 94107. 415/905-2200.

PRINTING AND PUBLISHING

The big news in publishing in 1995 was the paper shortage. Paper costs account for 30 to 40 percent of the manufacturing costs of a book. Many companies compensated for the rising costs by stockpiling paper, designing books more tightly, lowering paper grades, and increasing book prices. The paper pinch also affected the magazine and newspaper industries. Newsprint prices rose more than 30 percent from early 1994 to early 1995. Magazines became noticeably shorter. One good sign for newspapers and magazines: As the economy improves, companies will increase their print advertising budgets. And, with a presidential election and a Summer Olympics on the calendar in '96, spending for advertising will increase.

Another way some publishers are balancing their books against the paper crunch is by looking to electronic media, a competitive and rapidly expanding medium. Many book publishers are offering CD-ROM versions of popular books, especially educational, reference, and children's books. Also, books-on-tape are growing in popularity. Magazines and newspapers also are joining the electronic bandwagon -- many periodicals and newspapers are now available online.

Book printing and distribution are also evolving. Traditionally, long print runs were necessary to keep costs down. But thanks to new digital presses that don't use plates, books can now be printed and distributed in small batches according to demand. Instead of printing and then distributing, publishers can now distribute and then print. Publishers will be able to use many small presses across the country, instead of one or two strategically placed large presses. The result: increased demand for computer-savvy printing professionals and dramatic cuts in shipping and warehousing.

ADDISON-WESLEY PUBLISHING COMPANY
2725 Sand Hill Road, Menlo Park CA 94025. 415/854-0300. **Fax:** 415/853-2530. **Contact:** Human Resources Department. **Description:** Publishes and distributes educational materials for use in elementary and high schools, universities, and industry, covering essentially all the major disciplines. Addison-Wesley also publishes professional, reference, and nonfiction trade books. The company operates in three industry segments: Higher Education, School, and General Books. Sales are made internationally. This facility is primarily involved in the school and higher education segments. **Corporate headquarters location:** Reading MA.

ALAMEDA NEWSPAPER GROUP
P.O. Box 5050, Hayward CA 94540. 510/783-6111. **Contact:** Human Resources. **Description:** The Alameda Newspaper Group publishes five daily newspapers with a combined daily circulation of about 232,000. **Common positions include:** Administrative Worker/Clerk; Customer Service Representative; Editor; Reporter; Services Sales Representative. **Benefits:** 401(k); Dental Insurance; Life Insurance; Medical Insurance; Vision Insurance. **Parent company:** Garden State Newspapers.

Operations at this facility include: Administration; Manufacturing; Regional Headquarters; Sales; Service. **Number of employees nationwide:** 1,000.

AMERICAN BANK NOTE COMPANY
55 New Montgomery Street, Suite 206, San Francisco CA 94105. 415/543-8585. **Fax:** 413/543-6565. **Contact:** Human Resources. **Description:** A national sales office for the 200-year-old American Bank Note Company. The company is a printer of counterfeit-resistant documents and one of the largest security printers in the world. American Bank Note creates secure documents of value for governments and corporations worldwide. Products include currencies; passports; stock and bond certificates; and bank, corporate, government, and travelers cheques, as well as food coupons, gift vouchers and certificates, driver's licenses, product authentication labels, and vital documents. **Corporate headquarters location:** New York NY. **Other U.S. locations:** Burbank CA; Long Beach CA; Washington DC; Atlanta GA; Bedford Park IL; Needham MA; St. Louis MO; Horsham PA; Huntington Valley PA; Philadelphia PA; Pittsburgh PA; Dallas TX. **Parent company:** United States Banknote Corporation operates two other subsidiaries: American Bank Note Holographics, Inc., one of the world's largest producers of the laser-generated, three-dimensional images that appear on credit cards and products requiring proof of authenticity; and American Bank Note Company Brazil, one of Brazil's largest private security printers and a provider of personalized checks, financial transaction cards, and pre-paid telephone cards. **Listed on:** New York Stock Exchange.

BANCROFT-WHITNEY COMPANY, LAW PUBLISHERS
P.O. Box 7005, San Francisco CA 94111-7005. 415/732-8500. **Fax:** 415/732-8874. **Contact:** Maria Sutter, Human Resources Manager. **E-mail address:** Msutter@Bancroft.com. **Description:** Publishes legal research information in CD-ROM and book formats for law practitioners and the judiciary. **Common positions include:** Attorney; Computer Programmer; Computer Systems Analyst; Customer Service Representative; Paralegal. **Educational backgrounds include:** Computer Science; Juris Doctorate; Marketing. **Benefits:** 401(k); Dental Insurance; Disability Coverage; Life Insurance; Medical Insurance; Pension Plan; Tuition Assistance. **Corporate headquarters location:** Toronto, Ontario. **Other U.S. locations:** Stamford CT. **Parent company:** Thomson Professional Publishing/The Thomson Corp. **Operations at this facility include:** Administration; Research and Development; Sales; Service. **Number of employees at this location:** 200.

BOWNE OF SAN FRANCISCO, INC.
343 Samsone Street, 15th Floor, San Francisco CA 94104. 415/362-2300. **Contact:** Human Resources. **Description:** Provides financial and corporate printing. **Parent company:** Bowne & Company, Inc.

THE CALIFORNIAN
P.O. Box 81091, Salinas CA 93912. 408/424-2221. **Contact:** Ms. Jenine Paul, Personnel Director. **Description:** Publishes a daily newspaper. **Common positions include:** Advertising Clerk; Customer Service Representative; District Manager; Editor; Graphic Artist; Reporter; Services Sales Representative. **Educational backgrounds include:** Accounting; Art/Design; Business Administration; Communications; Finance; Journalism; Marketing. **Benefits:** 401(k); Daycare Assistance; Dental Insurance; Disability Coverage; Employee Discounts; Life Insurance; Medical Insurance; Pension Plan; Savings Plan; Tuition Assistance. **Parent company:** Gannett Company, Inc.

Operations at this facility include: Administration; Sales; Service. **Number of employees at this location:** 180.

CONTRA COSTA TIMES
P.O. Box 5088, Walnut Creek CA 94596. 510/935-2525. **Contact:** Laurie Fox, Human Resources Manager. **Description:** Publishes multiple daily newspapers with a circulation of over 200,000. **Common positions include:** Accountant/Auditor; Advertising Clerk; Cashier; Clerical Supervisor; Computer Operator; Computer Programmer; Credit Clerk and Authorizer; Credit Manager; Customer Service Representative; Editor; Financial Manager; Human Resources Specialist; Library Technician; Machinist; Market Research Analyst; Marketing/Advertising/PR Manager; Payroll Clerk; Printing Press Operator; Receptionist; Reporter; Secretary; Services Sales Representative; Truck Driver; Typist/Word Processor. **Educational backgrounds include:** Accounting; Art/Design; Business Administration; Communications; Computer Science; Finance; Liberal Arts; Marketing. **Benefits:** Dental Insurance; Disability Coverage; Life Insurance; Medical Insurance; Pension Plan; Savings Plan. **Corporate headquarters location:** This Location. **Operations at this facility include:** Administration; Manufacturing. **Number of employees at this location:** 1,700.

DELUXE CHECK PRINTERS INC.
1551 Dell Avenue, Campbell CA 95008. 408/370-8801. **Contact:** Mimi Adame, Personnel Director. **Description:** Deluxe Check Printers is engaged in printing and selling a variety of checks, deposit tickets, and related forms to banks and other financial institutions. The company also manufactures documents imprinted on magnetic ink. Printing operations are carried out at more than 50 plants throughout the United States. **Benefits:** Dental Insurance; Disability Coverage; Employee Discounts; Life Insurance; Medical Insurance; Pension Plan; Profit Sharing; Savings Plan; Tuition Assistance. **Corporate headquarters location:** Shoreview MN. **Parent company:** Deluxe Corporation, was founded in 1915 and provides check printing, electronic funds transfer processing services, and related services to the financial industry; check authorization and collection services to retailers; and electronic benefit transfer services to state governments. Deluxe also produces forms, specialty papers, and other products for small businesses, professional practices, and medical/dental offices; and provides tax forms and electronic tax filing services to tax preparers. Through the direct mail channel, Deluxe sells greeting cards, gift wrap, and related products to households. The company entered the lithographic ink market in 1994 as a result of developing a breakthrough water-washable ink. Deluxe is a *Fortune* 500 company with facilities located in the United States, Canada, and the United Kingdom.

DEVON PUBLISHING GROUP
770 Tamalpais Drive, Corte Madera CA 94925. 415/924-5652. **Contact:** Human Resources. **Description:** Devon Publishing Group is one of the largest publishers of original artwork, posters, prints, cards, calendars, and related products. Its principal company, Portal Publications, Ltd. (Corte Madera, California; England), markets its products to a broad spectrum of more than 10,000 retail stores, identifying marketplace trends and computerizing the ordering process. Divisions of Devon Publishing Group include The Winn Devon Art Group, Ltd. (Seattle); Regency House Pictures and Frames, Inc. (Decatur, Georgia); and Aird Imports Pty. Ltd. (South Australia). **Benefits:** Pension Plan; Profit Sharing; Stock Option. **Corporate headquarters location:** Stamford CT. **Parent company:** Devon Group, Inc. **Listed on:** NASDAQ.

DIMAT DIRECT

4142 Point Eden Way, Hayward CA 94545. 510/786-5500. **Contact:** Personnel Assistant. **Description:** Provides web offset printing services, with advertising circulars as the company's primary product. Dimat Direct also provides mailing and marketing services. **Corporate headquarters location:** This Location.

FOR BETTER LIVING, INC.

13620 Lincoln Way, Suite 380, Auburn CA 95603. 916/823-9600. **Fax:** 916/823-9650. **Contact:** Human Resources. **Description:** For Better Living, Inc. manufactures and distributes precast concrete and plastic products, and publishes specialty magazines. Associated Concrete Products, Inc., Dalworth Concrete Products, Inc., and Associated Plastics, Inc. comprise the concrete and plastic products segment. The concrete segment designs, manufactures, and distributes underground precast concrete structures. This group has developed a patented line of precast concrete sectional boxes to house underground transformers, distribution systems, and splicing manholes. The plastics segment produces plastics products using a fiber reinforced plastic process and a structural foam process developed for injection molding. Surfer Publications (Communications Group) constitutes the specialty magazine publications segment, publishing *Surfer*, *Powder*, *Snowboarder*, and *Bike Magazine*. The Communications Group also produces cable television and home video programs. **Corporate headquarters location:** This Location.

GEORGE LITHOGRAPH COMPANY

460 Valley Drive, Brisbane CA 94005. 415/397-2400. **Contact:** Debbi Barnes, Director of Human Resources. **Description:** George Lithograph Company is a typesetting and printing firm.

HARPERCOLLINS SAN FRANCISCO

1160 Battery Street, San Francisco CA 94111. 415/477-4400. **Fax:** 415/477-4589. **Contact:** Human Resources Director/Manager. **Description:** HarperCollins is an English-language book publisher. The San Francisco division specializes in the publishing of religious, academic, and psychology titles, as well as visual books (cookbooks and giftbooks). **Common positions include:** Accountant/Auditor; Customer Service Representative; Designer; Editor; Financial Analyst; Human Resources Specialist; Operations/Production Manager. **Educational backgrounds include:** Accounting; Art/Design; Computer Science; Finance; Liberal Arts; Marketing. **Benefits:** 401(k); Dental Insurance; Disability Coverage; Employee Discounts; Life Insurance; Medical Insurance; Tuition Assistance. **Special Programs:** Internships. **Corporate headquarters location:** New York NY. **Other U.S. locations:** Glenview IL; Scranton PA. **Subsidiaries include:** Scott Foresman & Company; Zondervan. **Parent company:** HarperCollins Publishers. **Operations at this facility include:** Administration; Divisional Headquarters; Sales. **Listed on:** Privately held. **Number of employees at this location:** 135. **Number of employees nationwide:** 3,000.

HOUGHTON MIFFLIN COMPANY

925 East Meadow Drive, Palo Alto CA 94303. 415/857-0211. **Contact:** Laura Folkner, Human Resources Administrator. **Description:** This location of the worldwide publishing company is a sales office for the elementary school division in the Western region. **Common positions include:** Sales Representative. **Educational backgrounds include:** Education. **Corporate headquarters location:** Boston MA. **Other U.S. locations:** New York NY. **Operations at this facility include:** Sales. **Number of employees at this location:** 40.

K.P. CORPORATION
2350 Zanker Road, San Jose CA 95131. 408/736-5810. **Contact:** Human Resources. **Description:** A commercial lithographic printer.

LAWSON MARDON LABEL
1990 North California Boulevard, Suite 710, Walnut Creek CA 94596. 510/975-0777. **Contact:** Personnel Director. **Description:** Executive offices for a lithography and printing services firm.

MAYFIELD PUBLISHING COMPANY
1280 Villa Street, Mountain View CA 94041. 415/960-3222. **Contact:** Pamela Trainer, Personnel Director. **Description:** Publishes college textbooks. **Common positions include:** Acquisition Editor; Administrator; Art Director; Book Production Worker; Credit Manager; Customer Service Representative; Editor; Human Resources Specialist; Marketing Specialist; Operations/Production Manager; Order Clerk; Purchasing Agent and Manager. **Educational backgrounds include:** Communications; Liberal Arts. **Benefits:** Bonus Award/Plan; Dental Insurance; Disability Coverage; Employee Discounts; Life Insurance; Medical Insurance; Pension Plan; Tuition Assistance. **Corporate headquarters location:** This Location. **Operations at this facility include:** Administration; Divisional Headquarters; Sales; Service.

McCLATCHEY NEWSPAPERS, INC.
2100 Q Street, Sacramento CA 95816. 916/321-1846. **Contact:** Human Resources. **Description:** McClatchey Newspapers publishes 12 daily and eight community newspapers in California, Washington, Alaska, and South Carolina. Their combined average circulation is 825,800 daily and 977,200 Sunday. In 1857, James McClatchey became the founding editor of *The Sacramento Bee* in California's Central Valley. In the 1920s, the *Fresno Bee* and *Modesto Bee* were added; subsequently, the company acquired four other dailies, the *Anchorage Daily News*, *The* (Tacoma) *News Tribune* and the *Pasco Tri-City Herald* in Washington; and *The* (Rock Hill) *Herald* in South Carolina. The company's seven largest dailies are located in growing markets in which they are the primary news sources.

MILLER FREEMAN PUBLICATIONS, INC.
600 Harrison Street, San Francisco CA 94107. 415/905-2200. **Contact:** Norma Kanamori, Human Resources. **Description:** Publishes magazines and books, as well as maps, directories, and other publications. **Parent company:** United Newspapers.

THE MODESTO BEE
P.O. Box 3928, Modesto CA 95352. 209/578-2093. **Fax:** 209/578-2095. **Recorded Jobline:** 209/578-2004. **Contact:** Human Resources. **Description:** A newspaper. **Common positions include:** Advertising Clerk; Blue-Collar Worker Supervisor; Clerical Supervisor; Computer Programmer; Computer Systems Analyst; Credit Manager; Customer Service Representative; Editor; Electrician; General Manager; Human Resources Specialist; Librarian; Library Technician; Reporter; Technical Writer/Editor. **Educational backgrounds include:** Accounting; Business Administration; Communications; Computer Science; Finance; Marketing. **Benefits:** 401(k); Dental Insurance; Disability Coverage; Employee Discounts; Life Insurance; Medical Insurance; Pension Plan; Savings Plan; Tuition Assistance. **Special Programs:** Internships. **Corporate headquarters location:** Sacramento CA. **Parent company:** McClatchey Newspapers, Inc. **Operations at this facility include:** Manufacturing; Sales. **Number of employees at this location:** 600.

MOORE BUSINESS FORMS & SYSTEMS
5000 Executive Parkway, Suite 200, San Ramon CA 94583. 510/901-5200. **Contact:** Personnel. **Description:** This location is the Western Operations Office. A manufacturer of business systems, forms, and equipment. Moore Business Forms & Systems has branches in 39 countries and maintains 280 sales offices worldwide.

MOORE BUSINESS FORMS & SYSTEMS
1400 Fashion Island Boulevard, Suite 701, San Mateo CA 94404. 415/578-8900. **Contact:** Human Resources. **Description:** A manufacturer of business systems, forms, and equipment, with more than 280 sales offices and branches in 39 countries.

MOORE BUSINESS FORMS & SYSTEMS
2354 Lapham Drive, Modesto CA 95350. 209/524-4311. **Contact:** Human Resources. **Description:** A manufacturer of business systems, forms, and equipment, with more than 280 sales offices and branches in 39 countries.

MOORE BUSINESS FORMS & SYSTEMS
P.O. Box 5005, Visalia CA 93278-5005. 209/651-2153. **Contact:** Human Resources. **Description:** A manufacturer of business systems, forms, and equipment, with more than 280 sales offices and branches in 39 countries.

MOORE BUSINESS FORMS & SYSTEMS
1300 East Shaw Avenue, Suite 135, Fresno CA 93710-7903. 209/227-0786. **Contact:** Human Resources. **Description:** A manufacturer of business systems, forms, and equipment, with more than 280 sales offices and branches in 39 countries.

MOTHER JONES MAGAZINE
731 Market Street, Sixth Floor, San Francisco CA 94103. 415/357-0509. **Contact:** Human Resources. **Description:** A magazine that specializes in investigative reporting and political and cultural analysis. Established in 1976.

OAKLAND TRIBUNE, INC.
P.O. Box 28884, Oakland CA 94604. 510/208-6300. **Contact:** Human Resources. **Description:** Publishes a daily metropolitan newspaper with a circulation of approximately 155,000. **Common positions include:** Accountant/Auditor; Advertising Clerk; Computer Programmer; Credit Manager; Customer Service Representative; Department Manager; Human Resources Specialist; Manufacturer's/Wholesaler's Sales Rep.; Marketing Specialist; Operations/Production Manager; Purchasing Agent and Manager; Reporter; Systems Analyst; Technical Writer/Editor; Transportation/Traffic Specialist. **Educational backgrounds include:** Accounting; Advertising; Business Administration; Communications; Computer Science; Journalism; Marketing. **Benefits:** Daycare Assistance; Disability Coverage; Employee Discounts; Life Insurance; Medical Insurance; Pension Plan; Tuition Assistance.

THE RECORD
P.O. Box 900, Stockton CA 95201. 209/943-6397. **Contact:** Personnel Department. **Description:** Publishes a daily newspaper with a circulation of more than 55,000 as part of the Gannett Newspapers Group.

REDDING RECORD SEARCHLIGHT
P.O. Box 492397, Redding CA 96049-2397. 916/243-2424. **Contact:** Bonnie Pask, Human Resources Director. **Description:** Publishes a daily newspaper in northern California with a circulation of more than 39,000 as part of the John P. Scripps Newspapers Group. **Common positions include:** Advertising Clerk; Clerical Supervisor; Customer Service Representative; Editor; Reporter; Services Sales Representative. **Benefits:** 401(k); Dental Insurance; Disability Coverage; Employee Discounts; Life Insurance; Medical Insurance; Pension Plan; Savings Plan; Tuition Assistance. **Special Programs:** Internships. **Corporate headquarters location:** Cincinnati OH. **Other U.S. locations:** Nationwide. **Parent company:** Scripps Howard (E.W. Scripps). **Operations at this facility include:** Administration; Sales; Service. **Listed on:** NASDAQ. **Number of employees at this location:** 180. **Number of employees nationwide:** 10,000.

MIKE ROBERTS COLOR PRODUCTIONS/SCENIC ART
P.O. Box 24122, Oakland CA 94623. 510/652-1500. **Contact:** Personnel Department. **Description:** Provides processing and printing services for film.

SKC AMERICA
307 North Pastoria, Sunnyvale CA 94086. 408/739-4170. **Contact:** Linda Allmendinger, Human Resources Manager. **Description:** Develops, manufactures, and markets microfilm and microfilm-related products and services. The two operating divisions produce diazo and vesicular films used in computer output microfilm duplication, microprinting, and aperture and engineering applications. The two divisions also provide related microfilm products and services, including microprinting, supplies and equipment distribution, and the production of coated films. **Common positions include:** Accountant/Auditor; Administrator; Chemist; Computer Programmer; Customer Service Representative; Electrical/Electronics Engineer; Financial Analyst; Human Resources Specialist; Industrial Engineer; Manufacturer's/Wholesaler's Sales Rep.; Marketing Specialist; Mechanical Engineer; Operations/Production Manager; Quality Control Supervisor; Systems Analyst. **Educational backgrounds include:** Accounting; Business Administration; Chemistry; Communications; Computer Science; Engineering; Finance; Marketing; Physics. **Benefits:** Dental Insurance; Disability Coverage; Employee Discounts; Life Insurance; Medical Insurance; Pension Plan; Profit Sharing; Savings Plan; Stock Option; Tuition Assistance. **Operations at this facility include:** Manufacturing. **Listed on:** New York Stock Exchange.

SAN FRANCISCO EXAMINER
110 5th Street, San Francisco CA 94103. 415/777-2424. **Contact:** Metro Editor. **Description:** Operates a daily afternoon newspaper with a circulation of more than 155,000. As part of the Hearst Corporation, the company jointly publishes a Sunday edition with competitor *San Francisco Chronicle*. **Common positions include:** Editor; Reporter.

SAN FRANCISCO NEWSPAPER AGENCY
925 Mission Street, San Francisco CA 94103. 415/777-7642. **Contact:** Betty Cutter, Personnel Director. **Description:** Provides business services to San Francisco's two major newspapers (*Chronicle* and *Examiner*).

SAN JOSE MERCURY NEWS WEST
1875 South Bascom Avenue #2450, Campbell CA 95008-2336. 408/559-5804. **Contact:** Human Resources. **Description:** An office of the San Jose Mercury News, Inc., which

publishes an daily newspaper with a circulation of 320,000. **NOTE:** Interested applicants should send resumes to: 750 Riddle Park Drive, San Jose CA 95190.

SAN JOSE MERCURY NEWS, INC.
750 Ridder Park Drive, San Jose CA 95190. 408/920-5000. **Contact:** Employment Manager. **Description:** Publishes an daily newspaper with a circulation of 320,000. **Common positions include:** Accountant/Auditor; Commercial Artist; Computer Programmer; Photographer/Camera Operator; Reporter; Services Sales Representative. **Educational backgrounds include:** Accounting; Business Administration; Journalism. **Benefits:** 401(k); Dental Insurance; Disability Coverage; Life Insurance; Medical Insurance; Pension Plan; Stock Option; Tuition Assistance. **Parent company:** Knight-Ridder, Inc. (Miami FL). **Operations at this facility include:** Manufacturing; Sales; Service. **Listed on:** New York Stock Exchange.

SEQUOIA PACIFIC SYSTEMS CORPORATION
1030 North Anderson Road, Exeter CA 93221. 209/592-2191. **Contact:** Sharon Burd, Director/Industrial Relations. **Description:** A graphic arts specialty firm engaged in the printing of labels, business forms, and elections materials. This location is the division's major manufacturing facility and corporate office.

SEQUOIA PACIFIC SYSTEMS CORPORATION
480 2nd Avenue, Suite 203, San Francisco CA 94107-1426. 415/442-0500. **Contact:** Human Resources. **Description:** A graphic arts specialty firm engaged in the printing of labels, business forms, and election materials.

TIMES-HERALD, INC.
P.O. Box 3188, Vallejo CA 94590. 707/644-1141. **Contact:** Joan Rondoni, Personnel Secretary. **Description:** Operates a daily newspaper with a circulation of more than 25,000. Times-Herald, Inc. is part of the Donrey Media Group.

TRU-COLOR PHOTO
27105 Industrial Boulevard, Hayward CA 94545. 510/783-7000. **Contact:** Personnel Department. **Description:** Provides wholesale photo-finishing services and related sales and service activities. **Common positions include:** Photographer/Camera Operator; Photographic Process Worker; Printing Press Operator; Production Operator; Quality Control Supervisor. **Corporate headquarters location:** This Location.

Note: *Because addresses and telephone numbers of smaller companies can change rapidly, we recommend you call each company to verify the information below before inquiring about job opportunities. Mass mailings are not recommended.*

Additional small employers:

COMMERCIAL ART AND GRAPHIC DESIGN

SBG Partners
1725 Montgomery St, San Francisco CA 94111-1030. 415/391-9070.

Capitol Color
2250 Walsh Ave, Santa Clara CA 95050-2514. 408/727-7560.

Fong & Fong Printers
3009 65th St, Sacramento CA 95820-2021. 916/739-1313.

Graphics Unlimited
807 E Street, San Rafael CA 94901-2818. 415/485-1082.

Expressions In Concept & Design
23785 Cabot Blvd, Hayward CA 94545-1660. 510/784-0733.

California Concepts
2450 Washington Avenue Suite 26, San Leandro CA 94577-5943. 510/357-0935.

MJ Design
98 Trinidad Drive, Tiburon CA 94920-1036. 415/435-4669.

ASI Sign Systems
1111 Joellis Way, Sacramento CA 95815-3914. 916/924-1939.

Ellis & Ellis Signs-Displays
1111 Joellis Way, Sacramento CA 95815-3914. 916/924-1936.

Communication Associates
5630 Kiva Dr, Sacramento CA 95841-4328. 916/487-3000.

Allgood Industries
3466 Enterprise Ave, Hayward CA 94545-3219. 510/785-0220.

Custom Paper Products
2360 Teagarden St, San Leandro CA 94577-4341. 510/352-6880.

Chartmasters
201 Filbert St, San Francisco CA 94133-3203. 415/421-6591.

COMMERCIAL PHOTOGRAPHY

Richard Stacks Creative Photo
490 Talbot Avenue, Pacifica CA 94044-2600. 415/738-2070.

Gregory Blore Photography
164 Team Track Road, Auburn CA 95603. 916/888-8661.

Flashback Photographics
PO Box 701, Lotus CA 95651-0701. 916/626-7855.

BOOKS, PERIODICALS, AND NEWSPAPERS WHOLESALE

Publishers Group West
4065 Hollis St, Emeryville CA 94608-3547. 510/658-3453.

ARAMARK Services Inc.
6211 Power Inn Rd, Sacramento CA 95824-2323. 916/381-3810.

PRINTING TRADE SERVICES

Walker Graphics
333 Fremont St, San Francisco CA 94105-2384. 415/433-7900.

BUSINESS FORMS

Stocktab
1236 San Luis Obispo Street, Hayward CA 94544-7916. 510/487-1060.

Vanier Business Forms & Service
5775 Brisa Street, Livermore CA 94550-9273. 510/449-3700.

GKM Corp.
986 South Canyon Way, Colfax CA 95713. 916/823-7070.

COMMERCIAL PRINTING

Certified Ad Services
PO Box 12025, Fresno CA 93776-2025. 209/233-1891.

Anderson Lithograph Company
533 Airport Boulevard Suite 400, Burlingame CA 94010-2013. 415/348-0446.

Color Copy Printing Inc.
2798 Bay Road, Redwood City CA 94063. 415/369-4440.

Warren's Waller Press
339 Harbor Way, South San Francisco CA 94080-6919. 415/589-6262.

Louis Roesch Co.
1886 Mission St, San Francisco CA 94103-3585. 415/621-4700.

Graphic Arts Center
832 Sansome St, San Francisco CA 94111-1508. 415/981-2742.

Ford Graphics Co.
PO Box 192224, San Francisco CA 94119-2224. 415/777-9346.

America Computer Graphics Inc.
2200 Jerrold Ave, San Francisco CA 94124-1012. 415/824-8695.

Advance Reproductions
2248 Jerrold Ave, San Francisco CA 94124-1012. 415/648-9118.

Watt-Peterson Inc.
1900 Embarcadero Rd, Palo Alto CA 94303-3327. 415/493-6979.

American Lithographers
21062 Forbes Ave, Hayward CA 94545-1169. 510/732-1650.

RJ Print Service
2222 2nd St Ste 4, Livermore CA 94550-4555. 510/373-1006.

Sullivan Graphics
1221 California Ave, Pittsburg CA 94565-4112. 510/439-3700.

Bawden Printing Inc.
1933 Davis St, San Leandro CA 94577-1260. 510/729-6355.

First Western Graphics
1345 Doolittle Dr, San

Leandro CA 94577-2223. 510/632-5595.

Gilmore Envelope Corporation
510 North First Street, San Jose CA 95112-5321. 408/294-2524.

CANN Copy-Print
150 East Santa Clara Street, San Jose CA 95113-1901. 408/298-8841.

Academy Press
3929 Woodford Dr, San Jose CA 95124-3738. 408/266-6642.

Graphic Center
953 South Bascom Avenue, San Jose CA 95128. 408/293-0882.

Mustang Press
1442 South Winchester Boulevard, San Jose CA 95128-4330. 408/378-1945.

Quebecor Printing San Jose Inc.
PO Box 6363, San Jose CA 95150-6363. 408/435-2300.

Calcentral Press Inc.
2629 5th Street, Sacramento CA 95818-2802. 916/441-5392.

Graphic Center
3925 Power Inn Rd, Sacramento CA 95826-4334. 916/453-1332.

Griffin Printing & Lithograph
4141 North Freeway Boulevard, Sacramento CA 95834-1209. 916/448-3511.

Personalized Software
665 Clyde Ave, Mountain View CA 94043-2235. 415/968-4121.

Pacific Imprints
1706 3rd Ave, Walnut Creek CA 94596. 510/934-8553.

Green Valley Products
1200 Glenmore Way, El Dorado Hls CA 95762-5612. 916/933-6659.

MISC. PUBLISHING

Aircraft Technical Publishers
101 S Hill Drive, Brisbane CA 94005-1203. 415/468-1705.

Krames Communications
1100 Grundy Ln, San Bruno CA 94066-3030. 415/742-0400.

Color 2000
1269 Howard St, San Francisco CA 94103-2711. 415/861-5151.

Solzer & Hail
515 Folsom St, San Francisco CA 94105-3132. 415/495-8440.

Rapid
633 Battery St, San Francisco CA 94111-1809. 415/982-6071.

Thomas Bros. Maps
550 Jackson St, San Francisco CA 94133-5188. 415/981-7520.

Copy Rite
1301 Fourth Street, San Rafael CA 94901-2809. 415/456-1144.

Landmark General Corp.
51 Digital Drive, Novato CA 94949-5754. 415/883-1600.

Designs For Success
PO Box 932, Ross CA 94957-0932. 415/721-0104.

Infocorp
2880 Lakeside Drive Suite 300, Santa Clara CA 95054-2826. 408/980-4300.

Hispanic Yellow Pages
2025 Gateway Place Suite 340, San Jose CA 95110-1006.

Penny Saver
11370 Sunrise Park Dr, Rancho Cordova CA 95742-6542. 916/636-2200.

Type Faces
504 Southgate Rd, Sacramento CA 95815-3715. 916/641-2352.

Quadra Color Inc.
7917 Fruitridge Rd, Sacramento CA 95820-6746. 916/386-1204.

AGI Publishing Inc.
1850 North Gateway Boulevard Suite 132, Fresno CA 93727-1626. 209/251-8888.

Mass Micro Systems Inc.
1582 Centre Pointe Dr, Milpitas CA 95035-8011. 408/956-5999.

BOOKS: PUBLISHING AND/OR PRINTING

Victory Press
543 Lighthouse Ave, Monterey CA 93940-1460. 408/883-1725.

Evan-Moor Publishers
18 Lower Ragsdale Dr, Monterey CA 93940-5728. 408/649-5901.

Brooks/Cole Publishing Co.
511 Forest Lodge Rd, Pacific Grove CA 93950-5040. 408/373-0728.

Fearon-Janus Book Publishers
500 Harbor Blvd, Belmont CA 94002-4075. 415/592-7810.

Dale Seymour Publications
PO Box 10888, Palo Alto CA 94303-0879. 415/324-2800.

Creative Publications
1300 Villa St, Mountain View CA 94041-1197. 415/988-1000.

Benjamin Cummings Publishing
390 Bridge Pkwy, Redwood City CA 94065-1522. 415/594-4400.

Jossey-Bass Inc. Publishers
350 Sansome Street Floor 5, San Francisco CA 94104-1304. 415/433-1740.

McGraw-Hill Inc.
55 Francisco St Ste 700, San Francisco CA 94133-2117. 415/433-2821.

Osborne McGraw-Hill
2600 10th Street, Berkeley CA 94710-2586. 510/548-2805.

Journal Lithographic Co.
PO Box 5226, San Mateo CA 94402-0226. 415/573-8877.

Sybex Inc.
2021 Challenger Drive, Alameda CA 94501-1038. 510/523-8233.

Matthew Bender & Co. Inc.
PO Box 2077, Oakland CA 94604-2077. 510/446-7100.

Ziff-Davis Press
5903 Christie Ave, Emeryville CA 94608-1925. 510/601-2000.

ETR Associates
PO Box 1830, Santa Cruz CA 95061. 408/438-4060.

O'Reilly and Associates
103 Morris Street SuiteA, Sebastopol CA 95472-3873. 707/829-0515.

Siempre Adelante Publishing
1190 Alta Mesa Rd, Monterey CA 93940-4603. 408/646-0553.

Monterey Publishing
479 Pacific St Ste 4, Monterey CA 93940-2716. 408/648-1547.

Monterey Press
467 Alvarado Street, Monterey CA 93940. 408/657-9542.

General Education Publications
99 S Van Ness Ave, San Francisco CA 94103-1226. 415/554-1000.

Chronicle Books
275 Fifth Street, Sacramento CA 94203. 415/777-7240.

Tien Wah Press
2236B Sixth Street, Berkeley CA 94710-2219. 510/845-9532.

Consolidated Printers Inc.
2630 Eighth Street, Berkeley CA 94710-2588. 510/843-8524.

The Compleat Works
1021 Cedar Street, Berkeley CA 94710-1522. 510/528-4403.

PERIODICALS: PUBLISHING AND/OR PRINTING

Casey Printing Inc.
398 San Antonio Dr, King City CA 93930-3821. 408/385-3222.

Sunset Publishing Corp.
80 Willow Rd, Menlo Park CA 94025. 415/321-3600.

Track & Field News Inc.
2570 West El Camino Real Suite 606, Mountain View CA 94040-1300. 415/948-8188.

Barclays Law Publishers
PO Box 3066, South San Francisco CA 94083-3066. 415/589-8200.

Sunset Publishing
33 New Montgomery St Ste 2050, San Francisco CA 94105-4506. 415/543-8100.

Parenting Magazine
301 Howard St Floor 17, San Francisco CA 94105-2252. 415/546-7575.

PC World Communications
501 2nd St Ste 600, San Francisco CA 94107-1431. 415/546-7722.

Research Holdings Ltd.
2201 3rd St, San Francisco CA 94107-3125. 415/621-0220.

Infoworld Publishing Corp.
155 Bovet Rd Ste 800, San Mateo CA 94402-3115. 415/572-7341.

GPI Publications
411 Borel Ave, San Mateo CA 94402-3522. 415/358-9500.

CMP Publications Inc.
2800 Campus Dr, San Mateo CA 94403-2530. 415/525-4300.

Medior Inc.
2800 Campus Dr, San Mateo CA 94403-2530. 415/525-4000.

Mac User
110 Marsh Dr Ste 250, Foster City CA 94404-1173. 415/570-5110.

Bam Publications
3740 Buskirk Ave, Pleasant Hill CA 94523. 510/934-3700.

Touchdown Publications
2815 Mitchell Dr Ste 202, Walnut Creek CA 94598-1626. 510/933-0230.

Computer Currents Publishing
5720 Hollis Street,

Emeryville CA 94608. 510/547-6800.

Infotainment World
951 Mariners Island Boulevard, San Mateo CA 94404-1558. 415/349-4300.

BNA California
770 L Street, Sacramento CA 95814-3325. 916/552-6500.

NEWSPAPERS: PUBLISHING AND/OR PRINTING

Greenfield News
845 Oak Avenue, Greenfield CA 93927-5663. 408/674-5907.

Monterey County Herald
PO Box 271, Monterey CA 93942-0271. 408/372-3311.

Cross Communications
PO Box 51542, Pacific Grove CA 93950-6542. 408/375-9377.

Voice Of Mountain-Advertising
PO Box 405, Mountain View CA 94042-0405. 415/964-8222.

Sacramento Bee Legal News
760 Market Street, San Francisco CA 94102-2401. 415/433-0510.

The Recorder
625 Polk Street Suite 500, San Francisco CA 94102-3368. 415/749-5400.

Neue Presse German Lang Newspaper
655 Sutter Street Suite 405, San Francisco CA 94102-1032. 415/567-5050.

The Clarion Call
988 Market Street Suite 311, San Francisco CA 94102-4004. 415/922-7401.

American Music Press
325 10th Street, San Francisco CA 94103. 415/864-4512.

Howard Quinn Co.
298 Alabama Street, San Francisco CA 94103-4218. 415/621-3750.

Korea Central Daily News
1245 Howard Street, San Francisco CA 94103-2711. 510/522-5100.

World Journal Inc.
824 Stockton Street, San Francisco CA 94108-2121. 415/397-8473.

Oversea Distributors
546 Kearny Street, San Francisco CA 94108-2503. 415/421-5729.

International Daily News
632 Kearny Street, San Francisco CA 94108-1830. 415/956-5338.

Herald
708 Sacramento Street, San Francisco CA 94108-2505. 415/781-6338.

San Francisco Bay Guardian
520 Hampshire Street, San Francisco CA 94110-1417. 415/255-3100.

Outside Magazine
353 Sacramento Street Suite 600, San Francisco CA 94111-3604. 415/398-2627.

Hokubei Mainichi
PO Box 193321, San Francisco CA 94119-3321. 415/567-7323.

San Francisco Independent
1201 Evans Avenue, San Francisco CA 94124-1717. 415/826-1100.

Palo Alto Weekly
703 High Street, Palo Alto CA 94301-2486. 415/326-8216.

Dow Jones & Co. Inc.
1701 Page Mill Rd, Palo Alto CA 94304-1210. 415/493-2800.

San Mateo Times & Daily News Ledger
1080 South Amphlett Boulevard, San Mateo CA 94402-1802. 415/348-4321.

Coverstory
1080 South Amphlett Boulevard, San Mateo CA 94402-1802. 415/348-4444.

Lesher Communications
PO Box 2299, Antioch CA 94531-2299. 510/757-2525.

The Argus
PO Box 5100, Fremont CA 94537-5100. 510/794-0111.

Napa Valley Register
1615 Second Street, Napa CA 94559-2818. 707/226-3711.

West County Times
PO Box 100, Pinole CA 94564-0100. 510/758-8400.

Daily Ledger Post-Dispatch
515 Railroad Ave, Pittsburg CA 94565-2304. 510/432-7336.

Valley Times
127 Spring St, Pleasanton CA 94566-6680. 510/462-4160.

St. Helena Star
1328 Main St, Saint Helena CA 94574-1905. 707/963-2731.

Diablo Dealer Inc.
2610 Crow Canyon Road

Suite 100, San Ramon CA 94583-1547. 510/820-0664.

Vallejo Times Herald
440 Curtola Pkwy, Vallejo CA 94590-6923. 707/644-1141.

Solano Times
2640 Shadelands Dr, Walnut Creek CA 94598-2513. 707/747-1192.

The Montclarion Publications
5707 Redwood Rd, Oakland CA 94619-2400. 510/339-4030.

The Daily Californian
2150 Dwight Way, Berkeley CA 94704-2000. 510/849-2482.

Court Reporter
124 Paul Drive, San Rafael CA 94903-2024. 415/479-4311.

Petaluma Weekly News
135 Keller Street, Petaluma CA 94952-2943. 707/769-9958.

Argus-Courier
PO Box 1091, Petaluma CA 94953-1091. 707/762-4541.

North Monterey County Fortnighter
PO Box 1104, Castroville CA 95012-1104. 408/663-3939.

Santa Cruz Sentinel Publishing Co.
207 Church St, Santa Cruz CA 95060-3809. 408/423-4242.

Register Pajaronian
PO Box 50055, Watsonville CA 95077-5055. 408/761-7300.

Metro Publishing Inc.
550 South First Street, San Jose CA 95113-2806. 408/298-8000.

Nichi Bei Times San Jose
1423 Vinci Park Way, San Jose CA 95131-2777. 408/923-2727.

Sing Tao Newspaper Limited
1628 Hostetter Rd Ste E, San Jose CA 95131-3309. 408/453-9080.

Bay Area Chinese News
1630 Oakland Rd Ste A20, San Jose CA 95131-2449. 408/453-1605.

Bizspo News
PO Box 8688, San Jose CA 95155-8688. 408/265-9717.

The Portuguese Tribune
PO Box 3477, San Jose CA 95156-3477. 408/729-6197.

Lodi News-Sentinel
PO Box 1360, Lodi CA 95241-1360. 209/369-2761.

Manteca Bulletin
531 E Yosemite Ave, Manteca CA 95336-5806. 209/239-3531.

Lesher Newspapers Inc.
3033 G Street, Merced CA 95340-2108. 209/722-1511.

Union Democrat Corp.
84 S Washington St, Sonora CA 95370-4711. 209/532-7151.

Tracy Press Inc.
PO Box 419, Tracy CA 95378-0419. 209/835-3030.

Mid-Valley Publishers
202 West Main Street, Turlock CA 95380-4813. 209/632-0677.

Turlock Journal
PO Box 800, Turlock CA 95381-0800. 209/634-9141.

The Waterford News
216 E St, Waterford CA 95386. 209/874-1927.

Lake County Publishing Inc.
PO Box 849, Lakeport CA 95453-0849. 707/994-0106.

Sonoma Index-Tribune Inc.
117 West Napa Street, Sonoma CA 95476-6639. 707/938-2111.

Ukiah Daily Journal
590 South School Street, Ukiah CA 95482-5438. 707/468-0123.

VP Publishing Inc.
527 D St, Eureka CA 95501-0308. 707/443-8703.

Humboldt Newspapers Inc.
PO Box 3580, Eureka CA 95502-3580. 707/442-1711.

Auburn Journal Inc.
PO Box 5910, Auburn CA 95604-5910. 916/885-5656.

The Davis Enterprise
PO Box 1470, Davis CA 95617-1470. 916/756-0800.

Herburger Publications
604 North Lincoln Way, Galt CA 95632-8601. 916/685-5533.

Delta Publishing
16074 Harbor Drive, Isleton CA 95641-9724. 916/777-2233.

Amador Ledger-Dispatch
10776 Argonaut Ln, Jackson CA 95642-9465. 209/223-1767.

Neighbors
3628 Madison Ave Ste 3, N Highlands CA 95660-5096. 916/348-2700.

The Press Tribune Inc.
188 Cirby Way, Roseville CA 95678-6420. 916/786-6500.

John Rico Publishing Co.
916 Cotting Ln, Vacaville CA 95688. 707/448-6401.

The Wheatland Review
501 Third Street, Wheatland CA 95692. 916/633-4742.

Spectrum Newspapers
PO Box 1030, Rancho Cordova CA 95741-1030. 916/852-6222.

The Daily Democrat
PO Box 730, Woodland CA 95776-0730. 916/662-5421.

The Los Angeles Daily News
925 L Street, Sacramento CA 95814-3702. 916/446-6723.

Lesher Capitol Bureau
925 L Street, Sacramento CA 95814-3702. 916/441-2101.

The Business Journal
1401 21st St Ste 200, Sacramento CA 95814-5221. 916/447-7661.

The Chico Enterprise-Record
PO Box 9, Chico CA 95927-0009. 916/891-1234.

Territorial Dispatch
412 4th Street, Marysville CA 95901-5910. 916/743-6643.

The Chico News and Review
PO Box 7847, Chico CA 95927-7847. 916/894-2300.

Feather Publishing Company Inc.
PO Box B, Quincy CA 95971. 916/283-0800.

The Union
11464 Sutton Way, Grass Valley CA 95945-5304. 916/273-9561.

The Oroville Mercury Register
2081 Second Street, Oroville CA 95965-3400. 916/533-3131.

PHOTOGRAPHIC EQUIPMENT AND SUPPLIES

Konica Quality Photo Systems
1725 Comstock St, Santa Clara CA 95054-3409. 408/727-8581.

NEWS SYNDICATES

Bay City News Service
70 W Hedding St, San Jose CA 95110-1705. 408/287-3639.

For more information on career opportunities in printing and publishing:

<u>Associations</u>

AMERICAN BOOKSELLERS ASSOCIATION
828 South Broadway, Tarrytown NY 10591. 914/591-2665. World Wide Web address: http://www.bookweb.org.

AMERICAN INSTITUTE OF GRAPHIC ARTS
919 3rd Avenue, 22nd Floor, New York NY 10003-3004. 212/807-1990. A 36-chapter, nationwide organization sponsoring programs and events for graphic designers and related professionals.

AMERICAN SOCIETY OF NEWSPAPER EDITORS
P.O. Box 4090, Reston VA 22090-1700. 703/648-1144. World Wide Web address: http://www.nc.net/asne.

ASSOCIATION OF GRAPHIC ARTS
330 7th Avenue, 9th Floor, New York NY 10001-5010. 212/279-2100. World Wide Web address: http://www.agcomm.org. Offers educational classes and seminars.

BINDING INDUSTRIES OF AMERICA
70 East Lake Street, Suite 300, Chicago IL 60601. 312/372-7606. Offers credit collection, government affairs, and educational services.

THE DOW JONES NEWSPAPER FUND
P.O. Box 300, Princeton NJ 08543-0300. 609/520-4000. World Wide Web address: http://www.dowjones.com.

GRAPHIC ARTISTS GUILD
11 West 20th Street, 8th Floor, New York NY 10011. 212/463-7730. World Wide Web address: http://www.gag.org. A union for artists.

INTERNATIONAL GRAPHIC ARTS EDUCATION ASSOCIATION
4615 Forbes Avenue, Pittsburgh PA 15213. 412/682-5170.

MAGAZINE PUBLISHERS ASSOCIATION
919 Third Avenue, 22nd Floor, New York NY 10022. 212/752-0055. World Wide Web address: http://www.magazine.org. A membership association.

NATIONAL ASSOCIATION OF PRINTERS AND LITHOGRAPHERS
780 Pallisade Avenue, Teaneck NJ 07666. 201/342-0700. World Wide Web address: http://www.napl.org. Membership required. Offers consulting services and a publication.

NATIONAL NEWSPAPER ASSOCIATION
1525 Wilson Boulevard, Arlington VA 22209. 703/907-7900. World Wide Web address: http://www.oweb.com/nna.

NATIONAL PRESS CLUB
529 14th St. NW, 13th Floor, Washington DC 20045. 202/662-7500. Offers professional seminars, career services, and conference facilities, as well as members-only restaurants and a health club.

NEWSPAPER ASSOCIATION OF AMERICA
Newspaper Center, 11600 Sunrise Valley Drive, Reston VA 22091. 703/648-1000. World Wide Web address: http://www.naa.org. The technology department publishes marketing research.

THE NEWSPAPER GUILD
Research and Information Department, 8611 2nd Avenue, Silver Spring MD 20910. 301/585-2990. A trade union.

PRINTING INDUSTRIES OF AMERICA
100 Dangerfield Road, Alexandria VA 22314. 703/519-8100. World Wide Web address: http://www.printing.org. Members are offered publications, insurance, and political action.

TECHNICAL ASSOCIATION OF THE GRAPHIC ARTS
68 Lomb Memorial Drive, Rochester NY 14623. 716/475-7470. Conducts an annual conference and offers newsletters.

WRITERS GUILD OF AMERICA WEST
8955 Beverly Boulevard, West Hollywood CA 90048. 310/550-1000. World Wide Web address: http://www.wga.org. A membership association which registers scripts.

Directories

EDITOR & PUBLISHER INTERNATIONAL YEARBOOK
Editor & Publisher Company Inc., 11 West 19th Street, New York NY 10011. 212/675-4380. $100.00. Offers newspapers to editors in both the United States and foreign countries throughout the world.

GRAPHIC ARTS BLUE BOOK
A.F. Lewis & Company, 245 Fifth Avenue, New York NY 10016. 212/679-0770. $80.00. Manufacturers and dealers.

JOURNALISM CAREER AND SCHOLARSHIP GUIDE
The Dow Jones Newspaper Fund, P.O. Box 300, Princeton NJ 08543-0300. 609/520-4000.

Magazines

AIGA JOURNAL
American Institute of Graphic Arts, 164 Third Avenue, New York NY 10010. 212/807-1990. $21.50. A 56-page quarterly magazine dealing with contemporary issues.

EDITOR & PUBLISHER
Editor & Publisher Company Inc., 11 West 19th Street, New York NY 10011. 212/675-4380.

GRAPHIC ARTS MONTHLY
249 West 49th Street, New York NY 10011. 212/463-6836.

GRAPHIS
141 Lexington Avenue, New York NY 10016. 212/532-9387. $89.00. Magazine covers portfolios, articles, designers, advertising, and photos.

PRINT
104 Fifth Avenue, 19th Floor New York NY 10011. 212/463-0600. Offers a graphic design magazine. $55.00 for subscription.

PUBLISHER'S WEEKLY
249 West 17th Street, New York NY 10011. Weekly publication for book publishers and sellers.

Special Book and Magazine Programs

THE NEW YORK UNIVERSITY SUMMER PUBLISHING PROGRAM
48 Cooper Square, Room 108, New York NY 10003. 212/998-7219. A seven week, intensive program for individuals interested in the field of publishing as a career.

THE RADCLIFFE PUBLISHING COURSE
77 Brattle Street, Cambridge MA 02138. 617/495-8678.

RICE UNIVERSITY PUBLISHING PROGRAM
Office of Continuing Studies, P.O. Box 1892, Houston TX 77251-1892. 713/520-6022.

UNIVERSITY OF DENVER PUBLISHING INSTITUTE
2075 South University Boulevard, #D-114, Denver CO 80208. 303/871-4868.

REAL ESTATE

Rising interest rates in early 1995 caused housing starts to drop and sales of existing single-family homes to moderately decline. However, by mid-summer, rates began falling once more. Solid opportunities for jobseekers are available for those looking to enter the real estate field. Occupancy will go up in the office sector, as few new office properties are being built. Apartment construction, on the other hand, is on the rise. Commercial property sales will help maintain employment opportunities for real estate agents, brokers, and appraisers. The number of job openings in these occupations is expected to match the number of openings for most other careers nationwide. The majority of these openings, however, will be replacement positions, as agents return or leave the field, rather than new positions.

Property and real estate managers will have even greater opportunities to find employment, as more openings appear for these positions than for other occupations. The people with the most qualified backgrounds for these jobs will be those with college degrees in business administration and other related studies.

BRE PROPERTIES, INC.
One Montgomery Street, Suite 2500, San Francisco CA 94104. 415/445-6550. **Contact:** James Bailey, Office Manager. **Description:** A real estate investment firm.

CATELLUS DEVELOPMENT CORPORATION
201 Mission Street, San Francisco CA 94105. 415/974-4500. **Contact:** Human Resources. **Description:** Catellus Development Corporation is an owner, developer, and manager of industrial, retail, and office projects. These properties and the company's other land holdings and joint venture interests are located in major markets in California and 11 other states. The company develops and manages its operating properties which consist primarily of industrial facilities and a limited number of office and retail buildings. **Corporate headquarters location:** This Location.

COLDWELL BANKER
2633 Ocean Avenue, San Francisco CA 94111. 415/334-1880. **Contact:** Human Resources. **Description:** Coldwell Banker is one of the largest residential real estate companies in the United States and Canada in terms of total home sales transactions. In the late 1970s, Coldwell Banker purchased a 51 percent interest in Executrans, Inc., a corporate relocation management company, from Allstate. That company became Coldwell Banker Relocation Services. Coldwell Banker was acquired by Sears, Roebuck & Co. in late 1981. At the same time, the company launched Coldwell Banker Residential Affiliates, Inc., aimed at franchising select brokers who served small- to medium-sized markets. In October 1993, The Fremont Group, together with Coldwell Banker senior management, purchased the company from Sears, Roebuck & Co.

DIGIORGIO CORPORATION
One Samsone, Suite 2100, San Francisco CA 94104. 415/984-3161. **Contact:** Human Resources. **Description:** Operates nonresidential buildings.

GRUBB & ELLIS COMPANY
One Montgomery Street, Telesis Tower, 9th Floor, San Francisco CA 94104. 415/956-1990. **Contact:** Personnel Administrator. **Description:** A commercial and residential real estate brokerage firm. **Common positions include:** Accountant/Auditor; Administrator; Financial Analyst; Systems Analyst. **Educational backgrounds include:** Accounting; Business Administration; Computer Science; Finance; Liberal Arts. **Benefits:** 401(k); Dental Insurance; Life Insurance; Medical Insurance; Tuition Assistance. **Corporate headquarters location:** This Location.

MERIDIAN INDUSTRIAL TRUST
455 Market Street, 17th Floor, San Francisco CA 94105. 415/956-3031. **Contact:** Human Resources. **Description:** A real estate firm. **Common positions include:** Accountant/Auditor; Customer Service Representative; Financial Analyst; General Manager; Systems Analyst. **Educational backgrounds include:** Accounting; Business Administration; Finance; Real Estate. **Benefits:** 401(k); Dental Insurance; Life Insurance; Medical Insurance. **Corporate headquarters location:** This Location. **Operations at this facility include:** Administration; Service.

Note: *Because addresses and telephone numbers of smaller companies can change rapidly, we recommend you call each company to verify the information below before inquiring about job opportunities. Mass mailings are not recommended.*

Additional small employers:

LAND SUBDIVIDERS AND DEVELOPERS

White Land Co.
2882 Sand Hill Rd, Menlo Park CA 94025-7022. 415/854-9035.

Access Land Development Service
550 Hamilton Ave, Menlo Park CA 94025-1302. 415/325-0735.

Harrington Development
2400 W El Camino Real, Mountain View CA 94040-1421. 415/961-6495.

Wilfred T. Ussery & Associates
690 Market St, San Francisco CA 94104-5101. 415/788-6580.

Oak Hill Capital Corp.
601 Montgomery St Ste 1010, San Francisco CA 94111-2613. 415/986-7398.

Anthony Hay & Associates
3 Embarcadero Ctr, San Francisco CA 94111-4003. 415/956-2579.

Kintetsu Enterprises Co.
1790 Post St, San Francisco CA 94115-3606. 415/922-9300.

Savoy Corp.
170 Columbus Ave # 450, San Francisco CA 94133-5160. 415/421-5521.

Columbia Sales Information
22 Moore Ct, Alameda CA 94502-7745. 510/865-7253.

John H. Dyer Constructon Co. Inc.
44380 S Grimmer Blvd, Fremont CA 94538-6385. 510/651-9129.

Autumn Valley New Home Development
4593 Maureen Cir, Livermore CA 94550-8002. 510/373-2544.

Friedrich Company Inc.
633 Main St, Saint Helena CA 94574-2004. 707/963-1401.

Hodge Companies Inc.
250 Camino Alto, Mill Valley CA 94941-1400. 415/383-9221.

Kings Mill
410 Nottingham Ct, Petaluma CA 94954-8507. 707/763-9547.

Brusa Corp.
333 W San Carlos St, San Jose CA 95110-2711. 408/288-7790.

Vineland Sales Office
5602 Bellagio Dr, San Jose CA 95118-3900. 408/448-2327.

Lion Development Co.
2296 Quimby Rd, San Jose

CA 95122-1356. 408/238-4896.

Glen Hidden Evergreen Sales Office
2511 Glen Dundee Way, San Jose CA 95148-4135. 408/270-1697.

Avery Land Co. Inc.
571 Stanislaus Ave, Angels Camp CA 95222. 209/736-4774.

Professional Apartment Management Inc.
2020 W Kettleman Ln, Lodi CA 95242-4317. 209/334-6565.

Liberty Development Co.
3109 Santa Fe St, Riverbank CA 95367-2312. 209/869-3667.

Ram Development Group Inc.
8539 Via Gwynn Way, Fair Oaks CA 95628-3847. 916/863-7826.

Lake Canyon Estates Sales Office
884 Lake Canyon Ave, Galt CA 95632-8129. 209/745-5009.

Sacher Properties
PO Box 179, Newcastle CA 95658-0179. 916/663-1923.

Community Land Development
6225 Trajan Dr, Orangevale CA 95662-3834. 916/989-1303.

Heritage Funding Corp.
9152 Greenback Ln, Orangevale CA 95662-4740. 916/989-9755.

Windsor Meadows Development Co.
3103 Canvasback Way, W Sacramento CA 95691-4425. 916/371-3700.

HCF Inc.
11335 Folsom Blvd, Rancho Cordova CA 95742-6224. 916/638-0640.

Andrews & Associates
2966 Richardson Cir, El Dorado Hills CA 95762-4207. 916/933-1214.

Spieker Partners
8880 Cal Center Dr Ste 160, Sacramento CA 95826-3266. 916/369-8880.

Spieker Properties
2150 River Plaza Dr Ste 160, Sacramento CA 95833-3882. 916/922-5600.

Robbins Land Co.
3426 American River Dr, Sacramento CA 95864-5715. 916/971-1088.

RL Holderbein Construction Inc.
11256 Banner Mine Way, Nevada City CA 95959-3453. 916/477-8020.

REAL ESTATE AGENTS AND MANAGERS

All-Star International
505 W Olive Ave, Sunnyvale CA 94086. 408/736-8888.

Bank Of America Corporate Real Estate
560 Davis St Ste 2, San Francisco CA 94111-1999. 415/953-0500.

Norris Beggs and Simpson
535 Pacific Ave, San Francisco CA 94133-4635. 415/362-5660.

Lincoln Property Co.
101 Lincoln Centre Dr Fl 4, Foster City CA 94404-1130. 415/571-2200.

Barcelon Associates Management
3685 Mount Diablo Blvd Ste 201, Lafayette CA 94549-3736. 510/284-7101.

John M. Grubb Relocation
1301 Ygnacio Valley Rd, Walnut Creek CA 94598-2817. 510/947-0511.

Wells & Bennett Realtors
1451 Leimert Blvd, Oakland CA 94602. 510/531-7000.

Kaiser Center Inc.
300 Lakeside Dr Ste 130, Oakland CA 94612-3534. 510/271-6146.

Frank Howard Allen Realtors
383 Miller Ave, Mill Valley CA 94941. 415/381-3000.

Frank Howard Allen Realtors
1013 2nd St, Novato CA 94945-2405. 415/897-4444.

KCS Properties Inc.
7919 Folsom Blvd Ste 300, Sacramento CA 95826-2617. 916/381-1225.

Pacific Union Co.
417 Montgomery St Ste 1000, San Francisco CA 94104-1123. 415/834-3488.

Remax East Bay Group Inc.
1333 Willow Pass Rd, Concord CA 94520-5225. 510/602-4747.

Remax In Motion
519 Estudillo Ave, San Leandro CA 94577-4600. 510/357-3700.

Fox & Carskadon Better Homes
36 Tiburon Blvd, Mill Valley CA 94941-5103. 415/388-5060.

Fox & Carskadon Better Homes
901 Reichert Ave, Novato CA 94945-7023. 707/792-0686.

Prudential California Realty
333 S McDowell Blvd, Petaluma CA 94954-3507. 707/795-1023.

Contempo Realty Inc.
215 W Hamilton Ave, Campbell CA 95008-0558. 408/370-6611.

Century 21 Golden Bay Regional Office
3170 De La Cruz Blvd, Santa Clara CA 95054-2411. 408/727-7345.

BT Commercial
2425 Porter St, Soquel CA 95073-2444. 408/476-8000.

Lyon & Associates Realtors
1919 Grass Valley Hwy, Auburn CA 95603-2852. 916/888-1928.

Lyon & Associates Realtors
6815 Madison Ave, Fair Oaks CA 95628-3126. 916/962-0111.

Kyle Realty
820 Wales Dr Ste 2, Folsom CA 95630-5546. 916/983-5100.

Cochlan Associates Management Co.
120 I St Ste 300, Sacramento CA 95814-2213. 916/443-6637.

Sierra Hills Properties
11172 Golden Way, Nevada City CA 95959-3461. 916/273-6102.

CB Commercial
1776 W March Ln, Stockton CA 95207-6450. 209/473-7800.

Royal Management Group
5080 N Fruit Ave, Fresno CA 93711-3062. 209/221-9475.

Woodmont Managements
1050 Ralston Ave, Belmont CA 94002-2243. 415/592-3960.

Brighton Pacific Management Co.
25 Ecker Pl, San Francisco CA 94105-2753. 415/543-3680.

Pacific Property Services
4 Embarcadero Ctr Ste 2600, San Francisco CA 94111-5994. 415/772-0500.

Bluth Realty and Investments
39600 Fremont Blvd, Fremont CA 94538-2112. 510/438-9816.

Sammis PCA Partners
2815 Whipple Rd, Union City CA 94587-1233. 510/429-1180.

Aspen Property Management
2700 Ygnacio Valley Rd, Walnut Creek CA 94598-3455. 510/943-1889.

Rubicon Property Services
2000 Embarcadero Ste 201, Oakland CA 94606-5300. 510/534-4700.

Metro Plaza
25 Metro Dr, San Jose CA 95110-1316. 408/453-3434.

Porta Management Group
4300 Stevens Creek Blvd Ste 13, San Jose CA 95129. 408/296-4990.

21st Century Investments
11335 Folsom Blvd, Rncho Cordova CA 95742-6224. 916/638-3837.

The John Stewart Company
906 G St, Sacramento CA 95814-1800. 916/448-1172.

Timberlake Rental Office
1005 Fulton Ave, Sacramento CA 95825-4240. 916/488-3777.

Harbor Oaks
2227 River Plaza Dr, Sacramento CA 95833-3800. 916/641-7999.

Newport Pacific Funding
6060 Sunrise Vista Dr, Citrus Hts CA 95610-7053. 916/725-3403.

Brown Chudleigh Schuler
101 S Ellsworth Ave, San Mateo CA 94401-3911. 415/579-0772.

REAL ESTATE OPERATORS

Bill Graham Civic Auditorium
747 Howard St, San Francisco CA 94103-3118. 415/974-4060.

Wells Fargo Center Property Management
400 Capitol Mall, Sacramento CA 95814-4407. 916/448-0400.

Marina Square Outlet Shopping Center
I-880 At Marina B1, San Leandro CA 94577. 510/351-5600.

Gerson Bakar & Associates
333 Park Plaza Dr, Daly City CA 94015-1538. 415/755-1313.

Drever Partners Inc.
4 Embarcadero Ctr Ste 1810, San Francisco CA 94111-4190. 415/433-1773.

The Peninsula Regent
1 Baldwin Ave, San Mateo CA 94401-3846. 415/579-5500.

Floral Garden Apartments
2375 Floral Ave, Selma CA 93662-2720. 209/896-0971.

Arbor Apartments
5669 N Fresno St, Fresno CA 93710-8301. 209/435-2475.

Millbrook Garden Apartments
3302 N Millbrook Ave, Fresno CA 93726-5810. 209/229-4689.

Camelot Lakes Apartments
937 N Peach Ave, Fresno CA 93727-2485. 209/251-4554.

Central Park Apartments
90 Sierra Vista Ave, Mountain View CA 94043. 415/964-5600.

El Mirador Apartments
165 Bernardo Ave, Mountain View CA 94043-5203. 415/964-4884.

Thomas Jefferson Apartments
107 South Mary Avenue, Sunnyvale CA 94086. 408/773-8448.

Villa Deste Apartments
112 N Bayshore Blvd, San Mateo CA 94401-2071. 415/344-1914.

Del Norte Place
11720 San Pablo Ave, El Cerrito CA 94530-1750. 510/237-8300.

Countrywood
4555 Thornton Ave, Fremont CA 94536-5667. 510/797-9628.

Roberts Lane Townhouses
41240 Roberts Avenue, Fremont CA 94538. 510/656-4021.

Pebble Creek Apartments
40777 High St, Fremont CA 94538-3733. 510/651-9080.

Lund Avenue Garden Apartments
90 Lund Ave, Hayward CA 94544-2800. 510/886-4769.

Riverside Apartments
211 Riverside Dr, Napa CA 94559-3905. 707/255-5925.

East Bluff Apartments
1813 Marlesta Ct, Pinole CA 94564-2016. 510/724-8480.

Valley Plaza Villages II Apartments
4411 Valley Ave, Pleasanton CA 94566-5580. 510/426-0377.

Ashland Village Apartments
1300 Kentwood Ln, San Leandro CA 94578-2372. 510/481-2565.

Lakeside Village Apartments
4170 Springlake Dr, San Leandro CA 94578-4599. 510/352-5900.

Parkside Apartments
1501 Decoto Rd, Union City CA 94587-3529. 510/487-2733.

Franciscan Apartments
1975 Sereno Dr, Vallejo CA 94589-2872. 707/552-4000.

Camelot Apartments
61 Novato Street, San Rafael CA 94901-4606. 415/457-5522.

Pilgrim Park Apartments
96 Pilgrim Way, San Rafael CA 94903-4006. 415/479-4091.

Brander Mill Apartments
440 Dixon Landing Rd, Milpitas CA 95035. 408/946-2955.

Villa Monterey
2898 Villa Monterey, San Jose CA 95111-2173. 408/365-9200.

Saratoga Gardens
1240 San Tomas Aquino Rd, San Jose CA 95117. 408/243-7103.

Hillsdale House
1640 Hillsdale Ave, San Jose CA 95124-3231. 408/448-2131.

Meridian Heights Apartments
1035 Meridian Ave, San Jose CA 95125-4351. 408/723-4959.

Glen Fairway Apartments
448 Toyon Ave, San Jose CA 95127. 408/926-3100.

Kelley Drive Condominium
7667 Kelley Dr, Stockton CA 95207-1153. 209/957-4316.

Laguna Park Apartments
3639 W Benjamin Holt Dr, Stockton CA 95219-3323. 209/477-8366.

San Andreas Apartments
441 E Saint Charles St, San Andreas CA 95249-9659. 209/754-1453.

Sierra Village Apartments
250 Greenley Rd, Sonora CA 95370-5928. 209/532-0817.

Driftwood Apartments
800 W Grant Line Rd, Tracy CA 95376-2429. 209/835-3187.

Las Palmas Apartments
1545 N Palm St, Turlock CA 95380-3225. 209/632-5958.

Brentwood Apartments
303 Wayside Dr, Turlock CA 95380-3249. 209/668-8001.

Vineyard Manor
19 Clark Ave, Cloverdale CA 95425-3957. 707/894-5426.

The CBM Group Inc.
1010 Racquet Club Dr Ste 108, Auburn CA 95603-3060. 916/823-5206.

Sutter Court Apartments
5930 Sutter Ave, Carmichael CA 95608. 916/489-5014.

Sunrise Commons
8123 Sunrise Blvd, Citrus Heights CA 95610. 916/723-7900.

Sojourner Truth Apartments
1205 Fifth Street, Davis CA 95616-3956. 916/756-9495.

Summer Hills
5900 Sperry Dr, Citrus Heights CA 95621. 916/962-3679.

Fair Oaks Towers
8065 Sacramento St, Fair Oaks CA 95628-7561. 916/966-4864.

Park Folsom Retirement Apartments
255 Wales Dr, Folsom CA 95630-2953. 916/985-7580.

Lakeridge Rental Condominiums
2400 Natoma Station Dr, Folsom CA 95630-8150. 916/985-8500.

Jackson Hills Apartments
300 New York Ranch Rd, Jackson CA 95642-9425. 209/223-0128.

Deer Valley Apartments
1801 Eureka Rd, Roseville CA 95661-7710. 916/782-3338.

The Meadows
10108 Malaga Way, Rancho Cordova CA 95670-3385. 916/363-6005.

La Loma Apartments
2088 West La Loma Drive, Rancho Cordova CA 95670-3208. 916/366-5796.

Zinfandel Ranch Apartments
10833 Folsom Blvd, Rancho Cordova CA 95670. 916/638-1644.

The Apollo Gardens
10401 Rockingham Dr, Rancho Cordova CA 95670-5857. 916/362-7363.

Woodstream Townhomes
6115 Brookside Circle Rocklin CA 95677. 916/783-0555.

Heritage Apartments
200 Leisure Way, Vacaville CA 95687-3408. 707/448-7978.

Shasta Terrace Apartments
293 Shasta Drive, Vacaville CA 95687. 707/447-3651.

Sycamore Apartments
901 Sara Court, Vacaville CA 95687. 707/446-3219.

Aegean Apartments
199 Aegean Way, Vacaville CA 95687. 707/448-7056.

Touch Stone Duplexes
2604 Duet Dr, West Sacramento CA 95691-4522. 916/372-7168.

Capitol City Apartments
1608 Madrone Ave, W Sacramento CA 95691-2610. 916/371-6376.

Glen Cherry Apartments
762 W Lincoln Ave, Woodland CA 95695-3656. 916/666-0152.

Camelot South
1222 E St, Sacramento CA 95814-1449. 916/443-2847.

River Park Vista
5975 Newman Ct, Sacramento CA 95819-2624. 916/457-2503.

Greystone Place
3545 41st Avenue, Sacramento CA 95824. 916/395-3252.

Warren House Apartments
610 Howe Avenue, Sacramento CA 95825. 916/927-4185.

Arden-Towne Apartments
2400 Arden Way, Sacramento CA 95825-2432. 916/925-3609.

Fox Ridge Apartments
3715 Tallyho Dr, Sacramento CA 95826. 916/364-7770.

Casa De Angelo Apartments
3151 Notre Dame Dr, Sacramento CA 95826-3539. 916/381-1962.

Kohler Gardens Apartments
5454 Kohler Ave, Sacramento CA 95841-2780. 916/332-1420.

Summertime Apartments
6830 Walerga Rd, Sacramento CA 95842. 916/348-0400.

Antelope Vista Apartments
3600 Elverta Road, Sacramento CA 95843. 916/338-0722.

Parkfair Garden Apartments
431 Parkfair Drive, Sacramento CA 95864. 916/487-5424.

Henson Gardens Apartments
1225 Morse Ave, Sacramento CA 95864-3899. 916/487-1393.

Colusa Gardens
Highway 20 & Wescott Road, Colusa CA 95932. 916/458-7811.

Orland Manor Apartments
817 Newport Avenue, Orland CA 95963-1660. 916/865-9634.

Silverwood Estates
One Ilahee Lane, Chico CA 95973-7247. 916/343-0291.

4 Seasons Mobile Home Commmunity
3138 West Dakota Avenue, Fresno CA 93722-4900. 209/224-4034.

Town & Country Mobile Village
1060 San Miguel Rd, Concord CA 94518-2044. 510/689-5551.

For more information on career opportunities in real estate:

Associations

INSTITUTE OF REAL ESTATE MANAGEMENT
430 North Michigan Avenue, P.O. Box 109025, Chicago IL 60610-9025. 312/661-1930. Dedicated to educating and identifying real estate managers who are committed to meeting the needs of real estate owners and investors.

INTERNATIONAL ASSOCIATION OF CORPORATE REAL ESTATE EXECUTIVES
440 Columbia Drive, Suite 100, West Palm Beach FL 33409. 407/683-8111. World Wide Web address: http://www.nacare.org. An international association of real estate brokers.

Magazines

JOURNAL OF PROPERTY MANAGEMENT
Institute of Real Estate Management, 430 North Michigan Avenue, Chicago IL 60610. 312/661-1930.

NATIONAL REAL ESTATE INVESTOR
6151 Powers Ferry Road, Atlanta GA 30339. 404/955-2500.

RETAIL

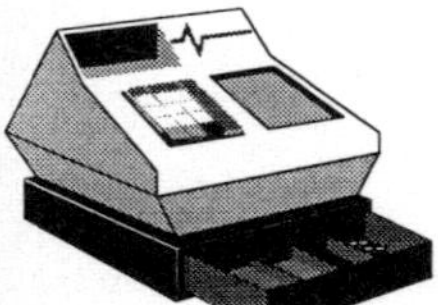

The '90s have been turbulent times for the retail industry. During the early years of the decade, the industry struggled as the national economy remained mired in recession. Now that the recession has technically been over for several years, one would think that shoppers would be flocking back to stores. Think again.

During 1995, sales rose by only 4.5 percent, and analysts expected about the same for '96. During 1995 alone, 15,000 retailers filed for Chapter 11 bankruptcy. Many of them, according to Business Week, *were regional chains with outdated stores and merchandise.*

The problem is simple: Consumers just aren't spending like they used to, and when customers insist on cut-rate bargains, only the giants, like Wal-Mart and Target, can survive. And not even all of them are safe from the threat of red ink. Kmart, the nation's third-largest chain, is closing 70 stores; while Bradlees and Ames are both having financial problems of their own.

ANDRONICO'S PARK AND SHOP
1109 Washington Avenue, Albany CA 94706. 510/524-2696. **Contact:** M. Paige Ellis, Director of Personnel. **Description:** Operates a chain of upscale retail grocery stores. **Common positions include:** Butcher; Grocery Clerk. **Educational backgrounds include:** Accounting; High School Diploma. **Benefits:** Dental Insurance; Disability Coverage; Life Insurance; Medical Insurance; Pension Plan. **Corporate headquarters location:** This Location. **Operations at this facility include:** Administration.

BIOBOTTOMS
P.O. Box 6009, Petaluma CA 94953. 707/778-1948. **Contact:** Human Resources. **Description:** A mail-order retailer of infants' and children's apparel and accessories.

BROOKS BROTHERS
201 Post Street, San Francisco CA 94108. 415/397-4500. **Contact:** Human Resources. **Description:** Operates a specialty retailing chain with 46 stores in the United States, and 14 in Japan. **NOTE:** Send resumes to Judy Flaa, West Coast Group Manager, 10250 Santa Monica Boulevard, Los Angeles CA 90067. **Corporate headquarters location:** New York NY. **Parent company:** Allied Stores Corporation.

BROOKS CAMERA
125 Kearney Street, San Francisco CA 94108. 415/362-4708. **Contact:** Don Boyle, Manager. **Description:** A retailer of photography equipment. **Common positions include:** Accountant/Auditor; Buyer; Civil Engineer; Photographic Process Worker; Quality Control Supervisor; Retail Sales Worker. **Benefits:** Employee Discounts; Medical Insurance; Pension Plan. **Corporate headquarters location:** This Location. **Parent company:** Inventory Supply Company, Inc. **Operations at this facility include:** Administration; Regional Headquarters; Sales.

GAP INC.
900 Cherry Avenue, San Bruno CA 94066. 415/952-4400. **Contact:** Personnel. **Description:** A nationwide retailer of moderately-priced casual apparel for men, women,

and children. The company operates over 1,500 stores in a number of metropolitan areas under the names Gap, GapKids, babyGap, Banana Republic, and Old Navy Clothing Company. Gap and GapKids stores can also be found in the United Kingdom, France, and Canada. **Corporate headquarters location:** This location. **Listed on:** New York Stock Exchange.

GOOD GUYS INC.
7000 Marina Boulevard, Brisbane CA 94005. 415/615-5000. **Contact:** Human Resources. **Description:** Owns a chain of retail consumer electronic products stores specializing in televisions, videos, home audio systems, telephones, home office systems, car phones, cellular phones, photographic equipment, and other related electronic products. **Corporate headquarters location:** This Location.

GOTTSCHALKS
P.O. Box 28920, Fresno CA 93729. 209/434-4711. **Contact:** Renee Jones, Director of Recruitment. **Description:** A large, full-line fashion department store with locations in California, Washington, Oregon, and Nevada.

GRAND AUTO, INC.
7200 Edgewater Drive, Oakland CA 94621. 510/577-2500. **Contact:** Human Resources. **Description:** A retailer and distributor of automotive aftermarket products. As a multimillion-dollar power retailer, Grand Auto operates nearly 100 locations. **Common positions include:** Assistant Manager; Store Manager. **Benefits:** Dental Insurance; Disability Coverage; Employee Discounts; Life Insurance; Medical Insurance; Savings Plan. **Operations at this facility include:** Sales; Service.

GUMP'S
135 Post Street, San Francisco CA 94108. 415/984-9218. **Fax:** 415/984-9200. **Contact:** Diana Holland-Cramer, Director of Human Resources. **Description:** Operates retail department stores. **Common positions include:** Accountant/Auditor; Buyer; Customer Service Representative; General Manager. **Educational backgrounds include:** Accounting; Business Administration; Marketing. **Benefits:** 401(k); Dental Insurance; Disability Coverage; Employee Discounts; Life Insurance; Medical Insurance; Profit Sharing. **Corporate headquarters location:** Weehawken NJ. **Parent company:** Hanover Direct. **Operations at this facility include:** Administration; Sales. **Listed on:** New York Stock Exchange. **Number of employees at this location:** 140.

GYMBOREE
700 Airport Boulevard, Suite 200, Burlingame CA 94010. 415/579-0600. **Fax:** 415/696-7400. **Contact:** Human Resources. **Description:** Operates a chain of retail stores selling apparel and accessories for children's activewear. **Common positions include:** Accountant/Auditor; Computer Systems Analyst; Designer; Operations/Production Manager; Paralegal; Transportation/Traffic Specialist. **Educational backgrounds include:** Accounting; Art/Design; Business Administration; Computer Science; Finance. **Benefits:** 401(k); Dental Insurance; Disability Coverage; Employee Discounts; Life Insurance; Medical Insurance; Tuition Assistance. **Operations at this facility include:** Administration; Research and Development. **Listed on:** NASDAQ. **Number of employees at this location:** 100. **Number of employees nationwide:** 3,700.

HIT OR MISS, INC.
685 Market Street, San Francisco CA 94105. 415/243-8465. **Fax:** 415/243-0641. **Contact:** Human Resources. **Description:** The nation's leading chain of off-price

women's fashion stores with over 500 stores in 35 states. **Common positions include:** Assistant Manager; Management Trainee; Store Manager. **Benefits:** 401(k); Dental Insurance; Disability Coverage; Employee Discounts; Life Insurance; Medical Insurance; Tuition Assistance. **Corporate headquarters location:** Stoughton MA. **Parent company:** TJX Companies, Inc. **Operations at this facility include:** Sales. **Listed on:** New York Stock Exchange.

LONGS DRUG STORES
141 North Civic Drive, P.O. Box 5222, Walnut Creek CA 94596. 510/937-1170. **Contact:** Employment. **Description:** Corporate office for a company that owns and operates retail drug stores, offering a broad range of pharmaceuticals and personal care products. The company operates over 130 locations nationwide. **Corporate headquarters location:** This Location.

LUCKY STORES INC.
NORTHERN DIVISION
P.O. Box 5008, San Leandro CA 94577. 510/678-4200. **Contact:** Human Resources. **Description:** A high-volume retailer operating over 400 supermarkets in California and Nevada. In addition to retail stores, the company also operates warehouses, distribution facilities, and manufacturing plants to supply the stores. **Parent company:** American Stores. **Operations at this facility include:** Administration; Divisional Headquarters. **Listed on:** New York Stock Exchange.

MACY'S STONESTOWN
One Stonestown Mall, San Francisco CA 94132. 415/753-4000. **Contact:** Human Resources. **Description:** A full-line department store chain with alternative career paths in store management, central merchandising, and planning. Both programs are designed to prepare talented individuals for careers in retail. A vast majority of executive positions are filled from within the company.

MACY'S UNION SQUARE
170 O'Farrell Street, San Francisco CA 94102. 415/397-3333. **Contact:** Human Resources. **Description:** One of three divisions of R.H. Macy Company (New York NY). Macy's Union Square operates 50 stores regionally as part of the full-line department store chain. **Common positions include:** Administrator; Buyer; Customer Service Representative; Department Manager; Management Trainee. **Educational backgrounds include:** Business Administration; Communications; Economics; Liberal Arts; Marketing. **Benefits:** Dental Insurance; Disability Coverage; Employee Discounts; Life Insurance; Medical Insurance; Pension Plan; Savings Plan. **Corporate headquarters location:** New York NY. **Operations at this facility include:** Divisional Headquarters.

MARSHALL'S OF SAN FRANCISCO
901 Market Street, San Francisco CA 94103-1729. 415/974-5368. **Contact:** Human Resources. **Description:** An off-price retail organization providing wide assortments of men's, women's, and children's apparel, footwear, accessories, and selected home furnishings in over 500 locations nationwide.

NATURAL WONDERS INC.
4209 Technology Drive, Fremont CA 94538. 510/252-9600. **Contact:** Human Resources. **Description:** Operates mall-based specialty retail stores which offer an

assortment of nature- and science-related products including telescopes, maps, globes, and bird feeders. **Number of employees nationwide:** 1,300.

NORDSTROM
285 Winston Drive, San Francisco CA 94132. 415/753-1344. **Contact:** Human Resources. **Description:** A specialty retailer which sells apparel, shoes, and accessories for the family. Nordstrom operates 74 stores including 18 clearance stores. The company recently entered the direct sales market with a mail-order catalog division and is testing interactive TV shopping. Most sales are derived from California operations. The company also leases shoe departments from 11 stores in Hawaii and operates a men's boutique.

NORDSTROM
865 Market Street, San Francisco CA 94103. 415/243-8500. **Contact:** Human Resources. **Description:** A specialty retailer which sells apparel, shoes, and accessories for the family. Nordstrom operates 74 stores including 18 clearance stores. The company recently entered the direct sales market with a mail-order catalog division and is testing interactive TV shopping. Most sales are derived from California operations. The company also leases shoe departments from 11 stores in Hawaii and operates a men's boutique.

ORCHARD SUPPLY HARDWARE STORES CORPORATION
6450 Via Del Oro, San Jose CA 95119. 408/365-2699. **Fax:** 408/365-2690. **Recorded Jobline:** 800/529-5229. **Contact:** Richard Dawson, Human Resources Recruitment Coordinator. **World Wide Web address:** http://www.osh.com. **Description:** Orchard Supply Hardware is an operator of hardware superstores in Northern and Southern California. Founded in 1931, the company currently operates 62 stores. Orchard primarily targets the fix-it homeowner focused on repair and maintenance projects and is positioned in an unique niche between the small, high-priced independent hardware retailers and the large warehouse home center chains. **NOTE:** The jobline can be accessed only by local callers. **Common positions include:** Accountant/Auditor; Advertising Clerk; Budget Analyst; Buyer; Cashier; Claim Representative; Clerical Supervisor; Computer Programmer; Computer Systems Analyst; Construction Contractor and Manager; Credit Manager; Customer Service Representative; Department Manager; Draftsperson; Editor; Financial Analyst; Gardener; General Manager; Human Resources Specialist; Management Trainee; Operations/Production Manager; Property and Real Estate Manager; Quality Control Supervisor; Sales Associate; Transportation/Traffic Specialist; Travel Agent; Wholesale and Retail Buyer. **Educational backgrounds include:** Accounting; Business Administration; Computer Science; Finance; Marketing. **Benefits:** 401(k); Dental Insurance; Disability Coverage; Employee Discounts; Life Insurance; Medical Insurance; Pension Plan; Profit Sharing; Savings Plan; Tuition Assistance. **Corporate headquarters location:** This Location. **Listed on:** NASDAQ; New York Stock Exchange. **Number of employees at this location:** 300. **Number of employees nationwide:** 5,000.

RALEY'S INC.
P.O. Box 15618, Sacramento CA 95852. 916/373-3333. **Contact:** Personnel. **Description:** Raley's is Sacramento's largest supermarket chain with more than 50 locations in Northern California and Nevada.

RUSS BERRIE & COMPANY WEST INC.
2249 South McDowell Boulevard Extension, Petaluma CA 94954-6901. 707/763-7877. **Fax:** 707/765-9572. **Contact:** Mike Hope, Vice President/General Manager. **Description:** An international retail company engaged in the giftware and toys industries including impulse, plush, souvenir, and licensed products. Russ Berrie has an extensive line of over 8,000 items. The company has locations in all 50 states. **Common positions include:** Manufacturer's/Wholesaler's Sales Rep. **Educational backgrounds include:** Business Administration; Communications; Marketing; Sales. **Benefits:** 401(k); Dental Insurance; Disability Coverage; Life Insurance; Medical Insurance; Pension Plan; Tuition Assistance. **Corporate headquarters location:** Oakland NJ. **Other U.S. locations:** Columbus OH. **Parent company:** Russ Berrie & Company Inc. **Operations at this facility include:** Administration; Divisional Headquarters; Regional Headquarters; Sales; Service. **Listed on:** New York Stock Exchange. **Number of employees at this location:** 140. **Number of employees nationwide:** 2,000.

SAFEWAY STORES, INC.
201 4th Street, Oakland CA 94660. 510/891-3000. **Fax:** 510/891-3603. **Contact:** Peter Chen, Director of Human Resources and Planning. **Description:** Safeway Stores, Inc. is one of the world's largest food retailers. The company operates approximately 1,080 stores in the Western, Rocky Mountain, Southwestern, and Mid-Atlantic regions of the United States and in western Canada. In support of its stores, the company has an extensive network of distribution, manufacturing, and food processing facilities. Safeway also holds a 35 percent interest in The Vons Companies, Inc., the largest supermarket chain in Southern California, and a 49 percent interest in Casa Ley, S.A. de C.V., which operates food/variety, clothing, and wholesale outlet stores in western Mexico.

SAKS FIFTH AVENUE
384 Post Street, San Francisco CA 94108. 415/986-4300. **Contact:** Ms. Bobi Eisenberg, Personnel Director. **Description:** A fashion forward specialty store designed to provide a high degree in fashion and quality for women, men, and children. Saks Fifth Avenue also offers a gift department. **Corporate headquarters location:** New York NY. **Other U.S. locations:** Palo Alto CA; New York NY.

SAVE MART SUPERMARKETS
P.O. Box 4278, Modesto CA 95352. 209/577-1600. **Contact:** Kit Serpa, Employment Supervisor. **Description:** A grocery retailer.

SHARPER IMAGE CORPORATION
650 Davis Street, San Francisco CA 94111. 415/445-6000. **Contact:** Mary Mackenzie, Vice President of Human Resources. **Description:** A retailer and catalog marketing firm.

THE SHERWIN-WILLIAMS COMPANY INC.
320 4th Street, San Francisco CA 94107-1207. 415/495-5720. **Contact:** Human Resources. **Description:** A retail paint and wall covering store. Brands sold include Sherwin-Williams, Dutch Boy, Martin Senour, Baltimore, and Kem paints, as well as related packaging.

THE SHERWIN-WILLIAMS COMPANY INC.
696 Broadway, Redwood City CA 94063-3103. 415/366-5786. **Contact:** Human Resources. **Description:** A retail paint and wall covering store. Brands sold include Sherwin-Williams, Dutch Boy, Martin Senour, Baltimore, and Kem paints, as well as related packaging.

THE SHERWIN-WILLIAMS COMPANY INC.
1525 Rollins Road, Burlingame CA 94010-2305. 415/697-2595. **Contact:** Human Resources. **Description:** A retail paint and wall covering store. Brands sold include Sherwin-Williams, Dutch Boy, Martin Seymour, Baltimore, and Kem paints, as well as such related packaging products as paint cans, sprays, and labels. The Sherwin-Williams labeled architectural and industrial coatings are sold through approximately 2,000 co-owned specialty paint and wall covering stores located in 48 states. Coatings are produced for original equipment manufacturers in various industries, as well as for the automobile aftermarket, the industrial maintenance market, and the traffic paint market. **Corporate headquarters location:** Cleveland OH. **Listed on:** New York Stock Exchange.

THE SHERWIN-WILLIAMS COMPANY INC.
3301 McHenry Avenue, Modesto CA 95350-1443. 209/521-1577. **Contact:** Human Resources. **Description:** A retail paint and wall covering store. Brands sold include Sherwin-Williams, Dutch Boy, Martin Senour, Baltimore, and Kem paints, as well as related packaging.

THE SHERWIN-WILLIAMS COMPANY INC.
WEST AREA OFFICE
2125 Oak Grove Road, #324, Walnut Creek CA 94598. 510/932-3363. **Fax:** 510/930-7118. **Contact:** Jim Pfohl, Area Personnel Director. **Description:** Markets paint, coatings, and related products through a network of company owned sales branches throughout California and the western United States. **Common positions include:** Management Trainee; Manufacturer's/Wholesaler's Sales Rep.; Store Manager. **Educational backgrounds include:** Business Administration; Management/Planning; Marketing. **Benefits:** 401(k); Dental Insurance; Disability Coverage; Employee Discounts; Life Insurance; Medical Insurance; Pension Plan; Profit Sharing; Savings Plan; Tuition Assistance. **Special Programs:** Internships. **Corporate headquarters location:** Cleveland OH. **Other U.S. locations:** Nationwide. **Operations at this facility include:** Administration; Regional Headquarters. **Listed on:** New York Stock Exchange. **Number of employees at this location:** 20. **Number of employees nationwide:** 20,000.

WILLIAMS-SONOMA, INC.
100 North Point Street, San Francisco CA 94133. 415/421-7900. **Contact:** Human Resources. **Description:** A retailer of cookware, serving equipment, and other specialty items. Products are sold both through retail stores and mail-order catalogs with the following brand names: Williams-Sonoma, Hold Everything, Gardener's Eden, Pottery Barn, and Chambers.

Note: *Because addresses and telephone numbers of smaller companies can change rapidly, we recommend you call each company to verify the information below before inquiring about job opportunities. Mass mailings are not recommended.*

Additional small employers:

DEPARTMENT STORES

K-Mart
1075 Shaw Ave, Clovis CA 93612-3933. 209/298-9772.

K-Mart
4987 E Kings Canyon Rd, Fresno CA 93727-3812. 209/456-1116.

K-Mart
270 Mount Hermon Rd, Scotts Valley CA 95066-4024. 408/438-0545.

K-Mart
2344 Sunrise Blvd, Rancho Cordova CA 95670-4343. 916/635-3400.

K-Mart
5615 Pacific Street, Rocklin CA 95677-3174. 916/624-7003.

K-Mart
2323 McKee Rd, San Jose CA 95116-1609. 408/272-0110.

K-Mart
13220 San Pablo Ave, San Pablo CA 94806-3986. 510/232-1822.

K-Mart
1200 El Camino Real, Colma CA 94014-3237. 415/756-7440.

JCPenney Co. Inc.
484 Sun Valley Mall, Concord CA 94520-5814. 510/687-6000.

JCPenney Co. Inc.
70 Westlake Mall, Daly City CA 94015-1407. 415/756-3000.

Macy's
2210 Tully Road, San Jose CA 95122-1347. 408/238-3333.

Macy's
5411 Thornwood Dr, San Jose CA 95123-1215. 408/224-3333.

Macy's
1400 Hilltop Mall Rd, Richmond CA 94806-1913. 510/222-3333.

Macy's
15555 E 14th St, San Leandro CA 94578-1947. 510/797-3333.

Macy's
115 Hillsdale Mall, San Mateo CA 94403-3408. 415/341-3333.

Macy's
1400 Redwood Hwy, Corte Madera CA 94925-1201. 415/927-3333.

Macy's
One Serramonte Ctr, Daly City CA 94015-2345. 415/994-3333.

Mervyn's Department Store
9175 E Stockton Blvd, Elk Grove CA 95624-9505. 916/686-6700.

Mervyn's Department Store
2855 Story Road, San Jose CA 95127-3924. 408/259-8800.

Mervyn's Department Store
545 Southland Mall, Hayward CA 94545-2149. 510/276-8800.

Mervyn's Department Store
63 Serramonte Ctr, Daly City CA 94015-2345. 415/756-9022.

Mervyn's Department Store
855 Broadway, Millbrae CA 94030-1911. 415/692-4490.

Sears Roebuck & Co.
3400 S El Camino Real, San Mateo CA 94403-3400. 415/572-6400.

Sears Roebuck & Co.
455 San Antonio Rd, Mountain View CA 94040-1215. 415/948-8511.

Sears Roebuck & Co.
2600 Somersville Rd, Antioch CA 94509-4428. 510/706-6600.

Sears Roebuck & Co.
1178 El Camino Real, San Bruno CA 94066-2406. 415/244-5000.

Neiman-Marcus
150 Stockton St, San Francisco CA 94108-4680. 415/362-3900.

Emporium
3251 20th Ave, San Francisco CA 94132-1900. 415/753-4000.

Emporium
40 Hillsdale Mall, San Mateo CA 94403-3407. 415/572-5555.

Emporium
410 Sun Valley Mall, Concord CA 94520-5815. 510/671-8400.

Emporium
400 Newpark Mall, Newark CA 94560-5200. 510/791-3600.

Emporium
2500 Hilltop Mall Rd, Richmond CA 94806-1917. 510/222-1111.

Emporium
701 E El Camino Real, Mountain View CA 94040-2889. 415/969-1111.

Emporium
5353 Almaden Expy, San Jose CA 95118-3601. 408/265-1111.

Weinstock's
3401 Dale Rd Ste 200, Modesto CA 95356-0502. 209/527-8888.

Ross Stores Inc.
9135 E Stockton Blvd, Elk Grove CA 95624-9506. 916/685-3327.

Target Stores
555 Showers Dr, Mountain View CA 94040-1432. 415/965-7764.

Target Stores
4301 Century Boulevard, Pittsburg CA 94565. 510/778-8950.

Target Stores
7200 Amador Plaza Rd, Dublin CA 94568-2320. 510/829-8900.

Target Stores
1871 N Main St, Walnut Creek CA 94596-4106. 510/947-0650.

Target Stores
20745 Stevens Creek Blvd, Cupertino CA 95014-2123. 408/725-2651.

Target Stores
3155 Silver Creek Rd, San Jose CA 95121-1730. 408/238-7800.

Target Stores
1925 Douglas Blvd, Roseville CA 95661-3834. 916/786-8787.

Target Stores
10881 Olson Dr, Rancho Cordova CA 95670-5646. 916/638-4971.

Target Stores
6051 Mack Road, Sacramento CA 95823-4668. 916/395-9454.

Target Stores
5001 Madison Ave, Sacramento CA 95841-2604. 916/348-3701.

Van Heusen Factory Store
1937 State Highway 273, Anderson CA 96007-4264. 916/378-2607.

Smith & Hawken Outlet
1330 10th Street, Berkeley CA 94710-1510. 510/525-2944.

Corning-Revere Factory Store
2200 Petaluma Blvd N, Petaluma CA 94952-1968. 707/766-8405.

Price Club
2200 Middlefield Rd, Redwood City CA 94063-2882. 415/369-3321.

Ross Dress For Less
140 Cochrane Plz, Morgan Hill CA 95037-2812. 408/779-4212.

Family Bargain Center
48 N American St, Stockton CA 95202-3019. 209/469-2080.

Costco Wholesale
1900 Santa Rosa Ave, Santa Rosa CA 95407-7621. 707/578-0428.

Beno's Inc.
2070 State Highway 88, Jackson CA 95642. 209/223-1791.

Troutman 's
1922 East 20th Street, Chico CA 95928. 916/345-2551.

MISC. GENERAL MERCHANDISE STORES

98 Cent Clearance Centers
1682 E Hammer Ln, Stockton CA 95210-4119. 209/478-0233.

GROCERY AND CONVENIENCE STORES

Vons Grocery Store
3850 N Cedar Ave, Fresno CA 93726-5263. 209/229-9755.

Monte Mart-Grocery Warehouse
Food Centers, Monterey CA 93940. 408/394-6575.

Cala Foods Inc.
Stanyan & Haight, San Francisco CA 94117. 415/752-3940.

Cala Foods Inc.
250 Skyline Plz, Daly City CA 94015-3825. 415/992-3355.

Grant & Green Market
1401 Grant Ave, San Francisco CA 94133-3303. 415/986-1801.

Centromart Stores
7820 Brentwood Blvd, Brentwood CA 94513-1039. 510/634-4435.

Quik Stop Market Inc.
PO Box 5745, Fremont CA 94537-5745. 510/657-8500.

Cost Less Foods
26905 Mission Blvd, Hayward CA 94544-4131. 510/733-6041.

OFC Market
426 W Harder Rd, Hayward CA 94544-2130. 510/732-6562.

Petrini's
4015 Castro Valley, Castro Valley CA 94546. 510/889-7575.

Albertson's Food Centers
919 E Stanley Blvd, Livermore CA 94550-4009. 510/443-9500.

Fast & Easy Mart
34759 Ardenwood Blvd, Fremont CA 94555-3654. 510/795-1213.

C Mini Mart
6000 Dougherty Rd, Dublin CA 94568-2634. 510/828-0696.

E Street Market
33503 Mission Blvd, Union City CA 94587-1427. 510/487-7658.

Food 4 Less
941 Alamo Drive, Vacaville CA 95687-5601. 707/446-8831.

Food 4 Less
605 Rohnert Park Expy W, Rohnert Park CA 94928-2021. 707/584-1200.

Food 4 Less
5184 Sonoma Blvd, Vallejo CA 94589-1661. 707/552-0956.

E-Z Market
3305 San Felipe Rd, San Jose CA 95135-2000. 408/270-5304.

Pak'N Save Foods
375 N Capitol Ave, San Jose CA 95133-1906. 408/258-1195.

Pak'N Save Foods
762 Sunnyvale Saratoga Rd, Sunnyvale CA 94087-1462. 408/720-0244.

Pak'N Save Foods
4950 Almaden Expy, San Jose CA 95118-2007. 408/267-1200.

Pak'N Save Foods
555 Floresta Blvd, San Leandro CA 94578-4125. 510/483-2681.

Pak'N Save Foods
640 Hegenberger Rd, Oakland CA 94621-1914. 510/636-7970.

Whole Foods Market
3000 Telegraph Ave, Berkeley CA 94705-2014. 510/649-1333.

Whole Foods Market
414 Miller Ave, Mill Valley CA 94941-2904. 415/381-1200.

Canned Foods Inc.
2000 5th St, Berkeley CA 94710-1918. 510/845-1999.

Oliver's Market
546 East Cotati Avenue, Cotati CA 94931-4090. 707/795-9501.

Nob Hill Foods
809 Bay Avenue, Capitola CA 95010-2146. 408/476-5600.

Nob Hill Foods
451 Vineyard Town Ctr, Morgan Hill CA 95037-5631. 408/779-8485.

24 Markets
1846 Story Rd, San Jose CA 95122-1923. 408/251-3480.

Charlee's Jiffy Market
2905 S Bascom Ave, San Jose CA 95124. 408/371-6790.

Norooz Bazaar
1390 S Bascom Ave, San Jose CA 95128-4502. 408/295-2323.

Trader Joe's
5269 Prospect Rd, San Jose CA 95129-5031. 408/446-5055.

Trader Joe's
5311 Sunrise Blvd, Fair Oaks CA 95628-3539. 916/863-1744.

Yaohan USA
675 Saratoga Ave, San Jose CA 95129-2052. 408/255-6690.

Alamar Store
147 N Aurora St, Stockton CA 95202-2614. 209/946-4357.

Centro-Mart Inc.
310 W Charter Way, Stockton CA 95206-1763. 209/465-2706.

Circle K Store
8606 Thornton Rd, Stockton CA 95209-1815. 209/478-8959.

United States Market
705 S Carroll Ave, Stockton CA 95215-6801. 209/942-4012.

Super Store Industries
2800 W March Ln Ste 210, Stockton CA 95219-8218. 209/473-8100.

Estrella's Market
1804 Minnie St, Patterson CA 95363. 209/895-5244.

Garcia's Market
6450 3rd St, Riverbank CA 95367-2418. 209/869-2940.

Circle T Market
5925 Terminal Ave, Riverbank CA 95367-2921. 209/869-4985.

G&G Super Market
1211 W College Ave, Santa Rosa CA 95401-5044. 707/546-6877.

Capay Grocery
7544 Cutting Av, Capay CA 95607. 916/865-2058.

Albertson's Food Centers
6335 Commerce Blvd, Rohnert Park CA 94928-2403. 707/585-1101.

Albertson's Food Centers
550 E Perkins St, Ukiah CA 95482-4509. 707/462-3843.

Albertson's Food Centers
5025 Marconi Ave, Carmichael CA 95608-4205. 916/481-6530.

Albertson's Food Centers
5330 Stockton Blvd, Sacramento CA 95820-5412. 916/451-0806.

Albertson's Food Centers
1050 Oro Dam Blvd E, Oroville CA 95965-5834. 916/533-6523.

Schwan Sales
9919 Kent St, Elk Grove CA 95624-1401. 916/686-8662.

Clark's Market
Road 99W & Road 17, Yolo CA 95697. 916/662-1371.

Sacramento Natural Foods Co-Op
1900 Alhambra Blvd, Sacramento CA 95816-7013. 916/455-2667.

Holiday Quality Foods
1947 East Main Street, Quincy CA 95971-9657. 916/283-2370.

Tropic-Cal Ice Cream
1716 Ocala Ave, San Jose CA 95122-2078. 408/272-7775.

Parkside Deli & Cafe
4200 N Freeway Blvd Ste 5, Sacramento CA 95834-1235. 916/924-7009.

Bell Avenue Deli
2150 Bell Ave, Sacramento CA 95838-3000. 916/923-2098.

MISC. FOOD STORES

R Fish & Co.
2539 Esplanade, Chico CA 95973-1163. 916/895-3474.

Honeybaked Ham Co.
4959 Mowry Ave, Fremont CA 94538-1159. 510/796-0336.

DPM Family Pack Meat Store
905 B St, Marysville CA 95901-5311. 916/743-4707.

Perry Farms
34600 Ardenwood Blvd, Fremont CA 94555-3645. 510/791-0340.

Poindexter Nut
5414 E Floral Ave, Selma CA 93662-9505. 209/834-1555.

Imperial Nut Inc.
592 N 5th St, San Jose CA 95112-3232. 408/294-0336.

Conagra Dried Fruit and Nut Co.
1403 S Fresno Ave, Stockton CA 95206-1175. 209/465-9181.

Yumi Yogurt
805 E El Camino Real, Mountain View CA 94040-2807. 415/960-1919.

Yogurt Park
80 Broadway Ln, Walnut Creek CA 94596-5104. 510/944-4748.

Yogurt Delite
897 E El Camino Real, Sunnyvale CA 94087-2937. 408/720-1819.

Yogurt Delite
4750 Almaden Expy, San Jose CA 95118-2052. 408/266-8783.

Yogurt Delite
1080 Saratoga Ave, San Jose CA 95129-3431. 408/243-7349.

Parkwood's Yogurt Shoppe
1756 W Hammer Ln, Stockton CA 95209-2922. 209/473-8969.

Bread Of Life Alternative Food
1690 S Bascom Ave, Campbell CA 95008-0606. 408/371-5000.

General Nutrition Center
5435 Clayton Rd, Clayton CA 94517-1075. 510/672-6854.

General Nutrition Center
1855 41st Ave, Capitola CA 5010. 408/462-0244.

General Nutrition Center
1689 Arden Way Ste 2108, Sacramento CA 95815-4039. 916/646-9855.

Rhapsody Herbal Supply
1307 4th St, San Rafael CA 94901-2809. 415/454-9696.

Melaleuca Independent Distributor Mark
8501 Hans Engel Way, Fair Oaks CA 95628-6245. 916/965-6352.

Herb World Company
5075 Pasadena Ave, Sacramento CA 95841-4149. 916/487-6767.

Starbucks Coffee
195 E El Camino Real, Sunnyvale CA 94087-1937. 408/749-8158.

Cupps Fine Coffee Tea & Cocoa
880 Market St, San Francisco CA 94102-3001. 415/989-8745.

Java City
1800 Capitol Ave, Sacramento CA 95814-4105. 916/444-5282.

Weatherstone Coffee & Trade Co.
812 21st St, Sacramento CA 95814-3106. 916/443-6340.

The Perrier Group
39159 Paseo Padre Pkwy, Fremont CA 94538-1600. 510/797-0616.

Two Virgins Gourmet Foods & Wine
900 N Point St, San Francisco CA 94109-1154. 415/775-7589.

Wing Hanh Co.
654 Pacific Ave, San Francisco CA 94133-4410. 415/956-4339.

RETAIL BAKERIES

La Petite Boulangerie Inc.
851 Cherry Ave, San Bruno CA 94066-2949. 415/871-7177.

Rolling Pin Donuts
429 San Bruno Ave W, San Bruno CA 94066-3527. 415/589-9687.

Boogie Woogie Bagel Boy
1227 Park St, Alameda CA 94501-5211. 510/523-8979.

Wonder Hostess
40667 Fremont Blvd, Fremont CA 94538-4336. 510/490-5326.

Model Bakery
1357 Main St, Saint Helena CA 94574-1904. 707/963-8192.

San Rafael French Bakery
1512 4th St, San Rafael CA 94901-2713. 415/453-2957.

Old Country Bakery
55 Lovell Ave, San Rafael CA 94901-3920. 415/485-1934.

Sweet Cheeses Cheesecakes
625 San Anselmo Ave, San Anselmo CA 94960-2615. 415/457-2733.

Magic Muffins
Redhill Shopping Center, San Anselmo CA 94960. 415/454-0615.

The Hickory Pit Original
980 E Campbell Ave, Campbell CA 95008-2303. 408/371-2400.

Il Fornaio Panetteria Bakery
302 S Market St, San Jose CA 95113-2817. 408/271-3399.

PW Supermarkets
6938 Almaden Expy, San Jose CA 95120-3201. 408/997-2202.

Hong Kong Bakery Inc.
1818 Tully Rd Ste 198, San Jose CA 95122-1883. 408/238-8866.

Clover Cake Shop
4342 Moorpark Ave, San Jose CA 95129-2030. 408/257-3412.

La Bou
8109 Fruitridge Rd, Sacramento CA 95820-6750. 916/386-1515.

Mrs Fields' Chocolate Chippery
32 347 Gallert Blvd, Daly City CA 94015. 415/992-7077.

Great American Cookie
Weberstown Mall, Stockton CA 95207. 209/474-2447.

A-1 Donut Plus
4662 Meridian Ave, San Jose CA 95118-2326. 408/265-1440.

Yum Yum Donut Shop
544 E Charter Way, Stockton CA 95206-1534. 209/946-9024.

Donut Appetit
707 E March Ln Ste 14, Stockton CA 95207-5864. 209/957-3553.

The Donut Queen
8651 Elk Grove Blvd, Elk Grove CA 95624-1790. 916/686-8144.

Donut Spot
8853 Greenback Ln, Orangevale CA 95662-4058. 916/989-1269.

Spudnut Donuts
1495 East St, Woodland CA 95776-6334. 916/661-9514.

CK's Doughnuts
8333 Folsom Blvd, Sacramento CA 95826-3538. 916/381-3818.

Mazeria's Pie
683 Manor Drive, Pacifica CA 94044-2117. 415/355-9791.

AUTO DEALERS

Monti's Chevrolet
222 San Bruno Ave E, San Bruno CA 94066-3626. 415/589-8850.

Melody Toyota Inc.
750 El Camino Real, San Bruno CA 94066-3427. 415/588-2313.

Regal Dodge
1095 W El Camino Real, Sunnyvale CA 94087-1030. 408/738-0400.

Larry Hopkins Honda
1048 W El Camino Real, Sunnyvale CA 94087-1024. 408/720-1999.

Royal Motor Sales
1525 Howard St, San Francisco CA 94103-2524. 415/241-8100.

Walnut Creek Ford
1800 N Main St, Walnut Creek CA 94596-4107. 510/932-2900.

St. Claire Cadillac
4343 Stevens Creek Blvd, Santa Clara CA 95051-6998. 408/244-1000.

Smythe Buick Inc.
4201 Stevens Creek Blvd, Santa Clara CA 95051-6937. 408/983-5300.

Stevens Creek Toyota
4425 Stevens Creek Blvd, Santa Clara CA 95051-6855. 408/984-1234.

John L. Sullivan Chevrolet-Geo
700 Automall Dr, Roseville CA 95661-3024. 916/782-1243.

Winter Volvo & Lincoln Mercury
3805 Florin Rd, Sacramento CA 95823-1884. 916/421-3400.

Wes Lasher Inc.
5830 Florin Rd, Sacramento CA 95823-2301. 916/392-1400.

Niello Co.
2701 Arden Way, Sacramento CA 95825-1366. 916/482-5790.

Barber Dealer Group
850 Redwood St, Vallejo CA 94590-2942. 707/648-8170.

Elk Grove Chrysler Plymouth
Hwy 99, Elk Grove CA 95624. 916/685-1750.

Big Valley Ford Inc.
Stockton Auto Center, Stockton CA 95212. 209/956-6711.

Stevens Creek Honda
4590 Stevens Creek Blvd, San Jose CA 95129-1197. 408/247-2550.

Honda Of Santa Rosa
2750 Corby Ave, Santa Rosa CA 95407-5745. 707/542-5377.

Hayward Hyundai
25601 Mission Blvd, Hayward CA 94544-2526. 510/582-8000.

Wilmshurst Forty Niner Subaru
Main, Angels Camp CA 95222. 209/736-2515.

European Motors Ltd.
1480 Folsom St, San Francisco CA 94103-3702. 415/673-2000.

Fremont Nissan
5633 John Muir Dr, Newark CA 94560-5363. 510/651-5800.

Stevens Creek Nissan
4855 Stevens Creek Blvd, Santa Clara CA 95051-6660. 408/983-5900.

Key Auto Sales
845 Vallejo Ave, Novato CA 94945-2430. 415/892-6122.

Geweke Used Cars & Used Trucks
40 S Cherokee Ln, Lodi CA 95240-3019. 209/462-6451.

CONSUMER SUPPLY STORES

Tire Service By Wheel Works
2107 N 1st St Ste 580, San Jose CA 95131-2026. 408/436-7644.

Fitzgerald Enterprises
PO Box 1754, Pacifica CA 94044-6754. 415/355-7669.

American Racing Equipment Inc.
1832 G St, Fresno CA 93706-1617. 209/233-8571.

Wire Wheels
1636 H St, Fresno CA 93721-1629. 209/268-8270.

America's Tire Company
32 W El Camino Real, Mountain View CA 94040-2602. 415/988-9611.

Auto Parts Club
1220 Diamond Way, Concord CA 94520-5210. 510/603-7676.

Kragen Auto Works
41085 Fremont Blvd, Fremont CA 94538-4866. 510/490-9986.

Kragen Auto Parts
501 S State Highway 49, Jackson CA 95642-2534. 209/223-3256.

Performance Plus
6052 Dougherty Rd, Dublin CA 94568-2634. 510/833-9870.

Shops Automotive Performance Centers
4401 Stevens Creek Blvd, Santa Clara CA 95051-6855. 408/247-3564.

Sparks Racing Enterprises
10 Boston Ave, San Jose CA 95128-1901. 408/275-1356.

Von Housen Auto Parts
703 E Bidwell St, Folsom CA 95630-3341. 916/983-6100.

Von Housen Auto Parts
1722 Mangrove Ave, Chico CA 95926-2300. 916/343-8272.

America's Tire Co.
8881 Greenback Ln, Orangevale CA 95662-4060. 916/989-2882.

NAPA Auto Parts
200 Palm Ave, Auburn CA 95603-3906. 916/885-5134.

Wheatland Auto Parts Mapco
424 Front St, Wheatland CA 95692-9442. 916/633-4581.

Grand Auto Supply
73 W Court St, Woodland CA 95695-3011. 916/662-3982.

BMW Parts & Service
5001 Florin Perkins Rd, Sacramento CA 95826-4811. 916/383-4586.

Auto Parts Headquarters
9971 Horn Rd, Sacramento CA 95827-1946. 916/361-2886.

Riebe's Auto Parts
4914 Auburn Blvd, Sacramento CA 95841-2619. 916/332-1564.

Riebe's Auto Parts
129 Idaho Maryland Rd, Grass Valley CA 95945-5813. 916/273-4000.

Bay Area Performance
2560 Wyandotte St, Mountain View CA 94043-2315. 415/969-0372.

Alouis Auto Radiator Inc.
650 Divisadero St, San Francisco CA 94117-1502. 415/923-1446.

Wings Corporate USA
48511 Warm Springs Blvd

Ste 21, Fremont CA 94539-7765. 510/490-7078.

Bowers Performance
3557 1st St, Livermore CA 94550-2201. 510/294-8241.

ARE Racing Engine Systems
8848 Steven Ave, Orangevale CA 95662-2113. 916/987-7629.

Goodyear Tire Centers
6000 Dougherty Rd, Dublin CA 94568-2634. 510/833-9700.

H&J Tire-Goodyear
7426 Redwood Blvd, Novato CA 94945-2457. 415/897-1185.

Goodyear Auto Service Center
3146 Stevens Creek Blvd, San Jose CA 95117-1140. 408/296-7435.

Goodyear Commercial Tire & Service Center
3801 Wilcox Rd, Stockton CA 95215. 209/931-4442.

Goodyear Tire Center
2621 El Camino Ave, Sacramento CA 95821-5901. 916/972-9033.

Jensen's Tire Service
2410 Pratt Avenue, Hayward CA 94544-7828. 510/487-1266.

Tire Service By Wheel Works
1205 Parkside Dr, Walnut Creek CA 94596-3693. 510/945-1900.

Tire Service By Wheel Works
802 S 1st St, San Jose CA 95110-3122. 408/297-5700.

Tire Service By Wheel Works
2955 S King Rd, San Jose CA 95122-1500. 408/270-8400.

Winston Tire Company
1845 Hillsdale Ave, San Jose CA 95124-3027. 408/267-1012.

Winston Tire Company
923 South Cherokee Lane, Lodi CA 95240-4304. 209/369-1025.

Winston Tire Company
363 N Blackstone Ave, Fresno CA 93701-1916. 209/443-5223.

Winston Tire Company
504 San Bruno Ave W, San Bruno CA 94066-3113. 415/589-5273.

Stones Country Tire & Automotive
26 Commerce Pl, Vacaville CA 95687-4102. 707/447-4312.

Dooley Commercial Tire Service Inc.
1348 Terminal St, W Sacramento CA 95691-3515. 916/373-0600.

FUEL DEALERS

Campora Propane Service
2850 Willow Pass Rd, Pittsburg CA 94565-3237. 510/458-2120.

Campora Propane Service
6151 Pony Express Trail, Pollock Pines CA 95726-9649. 916/644-4932.

C&J Propane Service
1390 Norman Ave, Santa Clara CA 95054-2056. 408/727-2117.

Arrow Propane Inc.
5787 Pleasant Valley Rd, Placerville CA 95667. 916/642-0140.

Amerigas
5060 Pony Express Trail, Camino CA 95709-9620. 916/644-7646.

Nero's Designer Firewood
998 Rush Creek Pl, Novato CA 94945-2427. 415/892-1480.

California Hot Wood
6001 S 5th Ave, Oroville CA 95965. 916/533-3122.

CATALOG AND MAIL-ORDER HOUSES

Red Rose Collection Inc.
PO Box 280140, San Francisco CA 94128-0140. 415/692-4500.

Sierra Catalog Sales
140 French Bar Rd, Jackson CA 95642-2515. 209/223-5417.

CAMERA AND PHOTOGRAPHIC SUPPLY STORES

Zytron
1156 Aster Ave, Sunnyvale CA 94086-6810. 408/243-3838.

HOBBY, TOY, AND GAME SHOPS

SS Retail Stores Corp.
30587 Huntwood Ave, Hayward CA 94544-7019. 510/429-1515.

The Ribbon Outlet
330 Nut Tree Rd, Vacaville CA 95687-3200. 707/449-4888.

Evans Ceramics
355 Healdsburg Ave, Healdsburg CA 95448-4137. 707/433-2502.

Imaginarium
1145 Broadway Plz, Walnut Creek CA 94596-5130. 510/932-2040.

Toy Liquidators
1949 State Highway 273, Anderson CA 96007-4265. 916/378-0527.

STATIONERY AND OFFICE SUPPLY STORES

Office Depot Inc.
121 E El Camino Real, Sunnyvale CA 94087-1937. 408/746-2040.

Eastman Inc.
7711 Murray Dr, Stockton CA 95210-5316. 209/473-4281.

Eastman Inc.
737 Del Paso Rd, Sacramento CA 95834-1106. 916/927-0171.

Schwabacher Frey
1123 West North Market Boulevard, Sacramento CA 95838. 916/646-2022.

BOOKSTORES

Turk Street News
66 Turk St, San Francisco CA 94102-2808. 415/885-2040.

Franciscan Shops
1650 Holloway Ave, San Francisco CA 94132-1722. 415/338-2023.

Crown Books
3923 Piedmont Ave, Piedmont CA 94611-5351. 510/654-8424.

Super Crown
858 Blossom Hill Rd, San Jose CA 95123-2725. 408/629-1033.

Book Warehouse Of California
312 Nut Tree Rd, Vacaville CA 95687-3200. 707/446-6688.

SPORTING GOODS STORES

REI-Recreational Equipment Inc.
1975 Diamond Blvd, Concord CA 94520-5716. 510/825-9400.

Burt Copel Co.
1345 Industrial Ave, Petaluma CA 94952-6500. 707/765-4512.

Big 5 Sporting Goods
105 N McDowell Blvd, Petaluma CA 94954-2304. 707/765-6811.

Nevada Bob's Golf & Tennis
Camden & Union Ave, San Jose CA 95124. 408/371-8544.

Exercise Equipment Company
610 Francisco Boulevard West, San Rafael CA 94901-3926. 415/453-8396.

Santa Cruz Billiards Supply
4300 Capitola Road, Capitola CA 95010. 408/462-2025.

Copeland's Sports
1689 Arden Way, Sacramento CA 95815-4030. 916/648-0551.

DRUG STORES

Drug Barn Inc.
4921 Junipero Serra Blvd, Daly City CA 94014-3216. 415/997-4861.

Drug Emporium
4946 Almaden Expy, San Jose CA 95118-2007. 408/266-2633.

Costco Wholesale
380 W Ashlan Ave, Clovis CA 93612-5611. 209/291-1084.

Costco Wholesale
3150 Fostoria Way, Danville CA 94526-5553. 510/277-1800.

Diabetes Care
450 Sutter, San Francisco CA 94108. 415/956-6743.

Sub-Co Generic Drugs
2101 Forest Ave, San Jose CA 95128-1424. 408/298-6664.

Bel Air Markets
8787 Elk Grove Blvd, Elk Grove CA 95624-1742. 916/685-2225.

Bel Air Markets
4008 Foothills Blvd, Roseville CA 95747-7233. 916/783-1173.

Bel Air Markets
2341 Sunset Blvd, Rocklin CA 95765-4337. 916/632-0184.

Bel Air Markets
7901 Walerga Rd, Sacramento CA 95843-5722. 916/725-0333.

Bel Air Markets
1286 Stabler Ln, Yuba City CA 95993-2620. 916/755-3991.

RECORD AND PRERECORDED TAPE STORES

Camelot Music
900 Dana Dr Ste 52A, Redding CA 96003-4825. 916/221-3295.

Camelot Music
347 Gellert Blvd, Daly City CA 94015. 415/755-9870.

G&G World Of Nintendo
1264 E Gibson Rd Ste F607, Woodland CA 95776-6319. 916/661-0511.

Collector's Record Shop
844 B St, San Rafael CA 94901-3003. 415/459-2870.

Blockbuster Music
5353 Almaden Expy, San

Jose CA 95118-3601. 408/723-4130.

Minnie Photo Album
4573 Fellows Street, Union City CA 94587. 510/429-8122.

COMPUTER AND SOFTWARE STORES

Tesseract Corp.
475 Sansome St Floor 21, San Francisco CA 94111-3103. 415/981-1800.

Optic Computer Communication
386 2nd Avenue, San Francisco CA 94118. 415/386-1638.

Lighting Development
2800 W Bayshore Rd, Palo Alto CA 94303-3843. 415/496-1000.

Computerland
1590 Solano Way, Concord CA 94520. 510/687-4400.

Whole Earth Access Computers
2990 7th St, Berkeley CA 94710. 510/843-1700.

Compucom Systems
10860 Gold Center Dr, Rncho Cordova CA 95670-6034. 916/631-9835.

Ameridata Inc.
1812 Tribute Rd, Sacramento CA 95815-4311. 916/569-5200.

Seneca Laser Systems-Facs Line
1340 Tully Rd Ste 315, San Jose CA 95122-3055. 408/292-2369.

Richard Young Products
11344 Coloma Rd Ste 890, Gold River CA 95670-4465. 916/852-1117.

Softnet Solutions
1870 Embarcadero Rd, Palo Alto CA 94303-3308. 415/321-3000.

Power Up Software
2929 Campus Drive, San Mateo CA 94403. 415/345-5900.

Uniface Corp.
1320 Harbor Bay Parkway Suite 240, Alameda CA 94502-6556. 510/748-6145.

Synon Corporation
1100 Larkspur Landing Cir, Larkspur CA 94939-1827. 415/461-5000.

CONSUMER ELECTRONICS STORES

Satellite Cable Center
PO Box 5498, Redwood City CA 94063. 415/599-9800.

Coit Com
1111 Story Road, San Jose CA 95122-2633. 408/286-0597.

Video Only
6920 Amador Plaza Rd, Dublin CA 94568-2314. 510/829-2900.

Circuit City
5795 Christie Ave, Emeryville CA 94608-2412. 510/655-2200.

Cambridge Soundworks
1050 Contra Costa Blvd, Concord CA 94523-1943. 510/685-8000.

Audio Designs
4046 Ashbrook Cir, San Jose CA 95124-3332. 408/377-3580.

R-J Electronics
5277 Larchwood Dr, San Jose CA 95118-3039. 408/264-5513.

Owl TV
1440 Crespi Drive, Pacifica CA 94044-3606. 415/359-7672.

Astro Television Service
1501 Adrian Way, San Jose CA 95122. 408/261-1105.

Rentronics
3245 South White Road, San Jose CA 95148. 408/270-5522.

MOTORCYCLE DEALERS

Your Scooter Shop
1700 El Camino Real, Menlo Park CA 94027-4127. 415/327-3010.

Western Cycles
649 Escuela Ave, Mountain View CA 94040-2008. 415/968-8558.

Motorcycle Performance Center
8303 Sierra College Blvd Suite 126, Roseville CA 95661-9485. 916/791-2000.

RV DEALERS

Vactach Co.
14305 Holden Court, San Jose CA 95124. 408/377-2022.

Foothill RV
167 Taylor Avenue, Newcastle CA 95658. 916/663-9402.

BOAT DEALERS

West Marine
295 Harbor Drive, Sausalito CA 94965-1424. 415/332-0202.

West Marine
2450 17th Avenue, Santa Cruz CA 95062. 408/476-1800.

For more information on career opportunities in retail:

Associations

INTERNATIONAL ASSOCIATION OF CHAIN STORES
3800 Moor Place, Alexandria VA 22305. 703/549-4525.

NATIONAL AUTOMOTIVE DEALERS ASSOCIATION
8400 Westpark Drive, McLean VA 22102. 703/821-7000.

NATIONAL INDEPENDENT AUTOMOTIVE DEALERS ASSOCIATION
2521 Brown Boulevard, Suite 100, Arlington TX 76006. 817/640-3838. World Wide Web address: http://www.niada.com.

NATIONAL RETAIL FEDERATION
325 7th Street NW, Suite 1000, Washington DC 20004. 202/783-7971. World Wide Web address: http://www.nrf.com. Provides information services, industry outlooks, and a variety of educational opportunities and publications.

Directories

AUTOMOTIVE NEWS MARKET DATA BOOK
Automotive News, Crain Communication, 1400 Woodbridge Avenue, Detroit MI 48207-3187. 313/446-6000.

STONE, CLAY, GLASS, AND CONCRETE PRODUCTS

Growth in stone, clay, glass, concrete, and related materials is closely tied to the success of the construction industry. On the one hand, analysts believe that the fortunes of the construction industry should remain solid in the short term, despite the added pressure of an economy that has cooled from its torrid pace of growth in 1994 and early 1995. On the other hand, the longer-term forecast is for much slower growth, since infrastructure construction is dependent on declining local government budgets. In general, the stone, clay, glass, and concrete industry should see revenue growth of about 1 to 2 percent annually over the next few years.

AMERICAN OLEAN TILE CO.
350 Littlefield, South San Francisco CA 94080-6103. 415/589-2013. **Contact:** Human Resources. **Description:** A ceramic tile manufacturer and distributor.

HYDRO CONDUIT CORPORATION
4150 North Brawley Avenue, Fresno CA 93722-3914. 209/275-2241. **Contact:** Human Resources. **Description:** Manufactures and sells water transmission products (including pipe and tubing), concrete pipe, and reinforced concrete pipe. Hydro Conduit Corporation is an international company.

NATIONAL REFRACTORIES & MINERALS CORPORATION
1852 Rutan Drive, Livermore CA 94550-7635. 510/449-5010. **Fax:** 510/455-8362. **Contact:** Director of Human Resources. **Description:** A manufacturer of refractory products and minerals. **Common positions include:** Accountant/Auditor; Administrative Services Manager; Attorney; Biological Scientist/Biochemist; Budget Analyst; Buyer; Chemical Engineer; Chemist; Financial Analyst; Geologist/Geophysicist; Human Resources Specialist; Industrial Production Manager; Management Analyst/Consultant; Metallurgical Engineer; Mining Engineer; Operations/Production Manager; Paralegal; Physicist/Astronomer; Purchasing Agent and Manager; Quality Control Supervisor; Science Technologist. **Educational backgrounds include:** Accounting; Chemistry; Engineering; Physics. **Benefits:** 401(k); Dental Insurance; Disability Coverage; ESOP; Life Insurance; Medical Insurance. **Corporate headquarters location:** This Location. **Other U.S. locations:** Moss Landing CA; Salinas CA; Mexico MO; Columbiana OH. **Operations at this facility include:** Administration; Research and Development. **Number of employees at this location:** 100. **Number of employees nationwide:** 900.

OWENS-BROCKWAY GLASS CONTAINER PLANT
P.O. Box 1019, 3600 Alameda Avenue, Oakland CA 94604. 510/436-2000. **Contact:** Personnel Director. **Description:** A diversified manufacturer of packaging products including glass containers.

SYAR INDUSTRIES INC.
P.O. Box 2540, Napa CA 94558. 707/252-8711. **Contact:** Human Resources. **Description:** Manufactures concrete products.

WALKER'S CONCRETE INC.
457 Queens Lane, San Jose CA 95112. 408/436-8100. **Contact:** Human Resources. **Description:** A producer of ready-mixed concrete and concrete products. **Corporate headquarters location:** This Location. **Other area locations:** 2400 Peralta Street, Oakland CA 94607, 510/452-1663; 1844 West Winton Avenue, Hayward CA 94545, 510/782-2323.

Note: *Because addresses and telephone numbers of smaller companies can change rapidly, we recommend you call each company to verify the information below before inquiring about job opportunities. Mass mailings are not recommended.*

Additional small employers:

DIMENSION STONE

Hogan Quarry
Hogan Dam Rd & Silver Rapids Rd, Valley Springs CA 95252. 209/772-2775.

CRUSHED AND BROKEN STONE

Gallagher & Burk Inc.
344 High St, Oakland CA 94601-3902. 510/251-0466.

GLASS AND GLASS PRODUCTS

Guardian Industries Corp.
11535 E Mountain View Ave, Kingsburg CA 93631-9211. 209/896-6400.

PPG Industries Inc.
PO Box 2748, Fresno CA 93745-2748. 209/485-4660.

O'Keeffe's Inc.
75 Williams Ave, San Francisco CA 94124-2693.

Anchor Glass Co.
22302 Hathaway Ave, Hayward CA 94541-4861.

CEMENT

Calaveras Cement Co.
2033 N Main St Ste 500, Walnut Creek CA 94596-3734. 510/256-8837.

Kaiser Cement Corp.
PO Box 8019, Walnut Creek CA 94596. 510/256-3050.

Kaiser Cement Corp.
24001 Stevens Creek Blvd, Cupertino CA 95014-5660. 408/996-4203.

MINERAL PRODUCTS

Parex Inc.
11290 Vallejo Ct, French Camp CA 95231-9771. 209/983-8002.

For more information on career opportunities in stone, clay, glass, and concrete products:

<u>Associations</u>

THE AMERICAN CERAMIC SOCIETY
735 Ceramic Place, Westerville OH 43081. 614/890-4700. Offers a variety of publications, meetings, information, and educational services. Also operates Ceramic Futures, an employment service with a resume database.

NATIONAL GLASS ASSOCIATION
8200 Greensboro Drive, Suite 802, McLean VA 22102. 703/442-4890.

<u>Magazines</u>

GLASS MAGAZINE
National Glass Association, 8200 Greensboro Drive, McLean VA 22102. 703/442-4890.

ROCK PRODUCTS
MacLean Hunter Publishing Company, 29 North Wacker Drive, Chicago IL 60606. 312/726-2805.

TRANSPORTATION

According to Labor Department estimates the number of jobs in the air transportation industry will increase faster than average. Passenger and cargo traffic should increase in response to a rise in population, incomes, and business activity. Employment in other air transport activities will also increase as more aircraft are purchased for business, agriculture, and recreation. Despite this expected growth, jobseekers should expect strong competition as the number of applicants for airline jobs exceeds the number of jobs available. Not only are airline jobs highly sought after, but the industry has been going through a period of consolidation, and today more and more of the business is concentrated with a handful of the major carriers, such as American, Delta, United, and USAir.

In the trucking and warehousing industry, the number of jobs created is very closely related to the health of the national economy. Competition in the industry is intense, both among truckers and with the railroads. Trucking companies compete by slashing rates or offering more customized service. Motor carriers must quote rates high enough to cover costs but low enough to remain competitive. Still, job opportunities for truckers are expected to be good. In some areas, companies have had trouble recruiting well-trained drivers. Although some routes have switched to intermodal transportation and recent downturns in the economy have eased some driver shortages, turnover is relatively high. That should ensure a steady supply of jobs.

On the railroads, the use of both freight and passenger rail will climb. And according to the U.S. Commerce Department, increased trade and stronger freight rates should help the performance of U.S. flag liner companies operating in the Asian markets. Domestic use of water transportation should also increase, especially between Alaska and the lower 48 states.

A SWEEP IN THE DEEP
1815 Clement Avenue, Alameda CA 94501-1376. 510/523-5541. **Contact:** Human Resources. **Description:** A boat upkeep and maintenance company specializing in underwater services.

AVIATION METHODS INC.
San Francisco International Airport, San Francisco CA 94128. 415/875-1700. **Contact:** Human Resources. **Description:** Aviation Methods Inc. is a charter airplane management company.

BART (BAY AREA RAPID TRANSIT)
P.O. Box 12688, Oakland CA 94604-2688. 510/464-6200. **Recorded Jobline:** 415/464-OPEN. **Contact:** Employment Office. **Description:** The public transportation department for the Bay Area. **NOTE:** Please call the jobline for current openings; unsolicited resumes will not be accepted.

CHIPMAN UNITED
1521 Bueno Vista, Alameda CA 94501. 510/748-8700. **Contact:** Department of Interest. **Description:** Engaged in providing moving and storage services. **Corporate headquarters location:** This Location.

CONSOLIDATED FREIGHTWAYS CORPORATION
3240 Hillview Avenue, Palo Alto CA 94304. 415/494-2900. **Contact:** Personnel. **Description:** A motor freight carrier and air freight forwarder operating in all 50 states. Operations include export/import brokerage, overseas forwarding, and warehousing and distribution services. **Corporate headquarters location:** This Location. **Listed on:** New York Stock Exchange.

CROWLEY MARITIME CORPORATION
155 Grand Avenue, Oakland CA 94612. 510/251-7500. **Contact:** Personnel Department. **Description:** Provides marine transportation and construction services.

DHL WORLDWIDE EXPRESS
333 Twin Dolphin Drive, Redwood City CA 94065. 415/593-7474. **Contact:** Human Resources. **Description:** An air express services company. The DHL Worldwide Network is an air express network that services national and foreign markets reaching over 190 countries. The company is made up of two separate, independently-owned organizations: DHL International Ltd. and DHL Airways Inc., the U.S.-based company.

DI SALVO TRUCKING COMPANY
P.O. Box 193765, San Francisco CA 94119. 415/495-1800. **Contact:** Janet Mayer, Personnel Director. **Description:** Operates an area trucking and trucking terminal services firm. **Corporate headquarters location:** This Location.

DOLLAR RENT-A-CAR SYSTEMS
1815 Old Bayshore Highway, Burlingame CA 94010. 415/692-1204. **Contact:** Human Resources. **Description:** A nationwide car rental system with hundreds of outlets throughout the United States. **Corporate headquarters location:** This Location.

FEDERAL EXPRESS CORPORATION
950 Tower Lane, 10th Floor, Metro Center Boulevard, Foster City CA 94404. 415/578-5144. **Contact:** Personnel Department. **Description:** Specializes in the overnight, door-to-door transportation of packages and documents (more than 180,000 shipments daily) through an operating fleet of more than 60 aircrafts. Nationwide, the company operates a network of 207 full-service stations throughout the United States, providing daily service to 281 major markets and 17,000 smaller communities. Federal Express owns and operates its own fleet of aircraft, and more than 4,500 radio-equipped vans which pick up and deliver shipments. **NOTE:** This firm does not accept unsolicited resumes. Please only respond to advertised openings. **Corporate headquarters location:** Memphis TN. **Listed on:** New York Stock Exchange.

FRITZ COMPANIES, INC.
706 Mission Street, San Francisco CA 94103. 415/904-8360. **Contact:** Human Resources. **Description:** Founded in 1933, Fritz Companies, Inc. is a leader in global integrated transportation logistics and related information services for importers and exporters worldwide. The company's principal services include international airfreight and ocean freight forwarding, warehousing and distribution, customs brokerage, and

other value-added services for the international movement of goods. **Corporate headquarters location:** This Location.

GENERAL STEAMSHIP AGENCIES, INC.
P.O. Box 193450, San Francisco CA 94119-3450. 415/772-9200. **Contact:** Janis Mahoney, Vice President of Human Resources. **Description:** Operates a shipping agency.

HARPER GROUP CIRCLE INTERNATIONAL
260 Townsend Street, San Francisco CA 94107. 415/978-0600. **Contact:** Kathy McFarland, Manager of Human Resources. **Description:** Provides international air and ocean freight forwarding services.

HELLENIC MEDITERRANEAN LINES
One Hallidie Plaza, San Francisco CA 94102. 415/989-7434. **Fax:** 415/986-4037. **Contact:** Human Resources. **Description:** A steamship transportation company operating in the Mediterranean.

LANDSTAR ITCO, INC.
6250 Village Parkway, Dublin CA 94568. 510/829-4300. **Contact:** Human Resources. **Description:** A subsidiary of one of the largest multi-modal transportation service companies in North America, ITCO is an intermodal marketing company. **Corporate headquarters location:** Shelton CT. **Parent company:** Landstar System, Inc. is divided into specialized freight transportation segments. Its business is a mix of regular accounts and spot hauls, with the top 100 clients generating more than one-third of the revenue. Landstar is the only publicly-traded trucking company relying on independent owner-operators rather than salaried company drivers, with the company owning just 10 percent of the trucks in its fleet. Landstar buys many trucking supplies co-op, so its drivers receive large discounts on trucks, tires, gas, and lodging, in addition to getting 75 percent of the gross revenue from a load. Other subsidiaries of Landstar System include Landstar Expedited, Inc., Landstar Express America, Inc., Landstar Gemini, Inc., Landstar Inway, Inc., Landstar Ligon, Inc., Landstar Poole, Inc., Landstar Ranger, Inc., Landstar T.L.C., Inc., Landstar Transportation Service, Inc.

LYKES BROTHERS STEAMSHIP CORPORATION
180 Howard Street, Suite 450, San Francisco CA 94105. 415/227-2000. **Contact:** Personnel Department. **Description:** Operates an American flag steamship company with a fleet of 46 ships serving virtually every major marketplace in the world. **Corporate headquarters location:** New Orleans LA. **Parent company:** LTV Corporation.

OOCL (USA) INC.
(ORIENT OVERSEAS CONTAINER LINE)
4141 Hacienda Drive, Pleasanton CA 94588. 510/460-4800. **Contact:** Human Resources. **Description:** During the early days of containerization in the late 1960s, OOCL was the first Asian shipping line to introduce fully-containerized transport services. By the end of the next decade, services were expanded worldwide from the Far East to North America, Europe, and Australia. The 1980s saw further expansion to the Transatlantic, as well as the development of OOCL's intermodal capabilities to meet customers' demands of a door-to-door service that included total road and rail transportation. Today, OOCL, with interests in various terminals and land-side transportation networks, is a company that offers shippers around the world a comprehensive, containerized cargo distribution system.

PORT OF OAKLAND
P.O. Box 2064, Oakland CA 94604. 510/272-1515. **Fax:** 510/272-1172. **Contact:** Manager of Personnel and Employee Services. **Description:** Operates Oakland International Airport, maritime facilities, and commercial real estate. **Common positions include:** Accountant/Auditor; Attorney; Buyer; Civil Engineer; Claim Representative; Clerical Supervisor; Computer Programmer; Computer Systems Analyst; Construction and Building Inspector; Construction Trade Worker; Department Manager; Draftsperson; Electrical/Electronics Engineer; Employment Interviewer; Financial Manager; Heating/AC/Refrigeration Technician; Human Resources Specialist; Human Service Worker; Payroll Clerk; Property and Real Estate Manager; Public Relations Specialist; Purchasing Agent and Manager; Receptionist; Secretary; Typist/Word Processor. **Educational backgrounds include:** Accounting; Business Administration; Computer Science; Finance; Marketing. **Benefits:** Dental Insurance; Disability Coverage; Employee Discounts; Life Insurance; Medical Insurance; Pension Plan; Savings Plan; Tuition Assistance. **Special Programs:** Internships. **Corporate headquarters location:** This Location. **Operations at this facility include:** Administration; Service. **Number of employees at this location:** 600.

ROYAL CRUISE LINE
One Maritime Plaza, Suite 1400, San Francisco CA 94111. 415/956-7200. **Contact:** Human Resources. **Description:** An ocean cruise line.

SFO AIRPORTER INC.
325 5th Street, San Francisco CA 94107. 415/495-8404. **Contact:** Jeff Leonoudakis, President. **Description:** Operates a bus line service.

SAN JOSE, CITY OF
SAN JOSE INTERNATIONAL AIRPORT
801 North First Street, Room 207, San Jose CA 95110. 408/277-4205. **Contact:** Personnel. **Description:** Operates and manages the city's airport facilities. The airport is a city-funded department and all airport staff are city of San Jose employees. **NOTE:** Employment applications must be obtained from the city of San Jose's Human Resources Department. Applications and resumes are accepted only for current openings. **Common positions include:** Accountant/Auditor; Administrator; Advertising Clerk; Airport Staff Worker; Airport Superintendent; Blue-Collar Worker Supervisor; Civil Engineer; Draftsperson; Marketing Specialist; Planner; Public Relations Specialist; Real Estate Agent. **Educational backgrounds include:** Accounting; Business Administration; Communications; Computer Science; Economics; Engineering; Finance; Liberal Arts; Marketing; Mathematics.

SOUTHERN PACIFIC TRANSPORTATION COMPANY
One Market Plaza, Room 860, San Francisco CA 94105. 415/541-1973. **Contact:** Ellen O'Donnell, Manager of Employment. **Description:** Southern Pacific Transportation Company is a national common carrier trucking and railroad firm, with facilities throughout the country. The company has more than five area locations, including Sacramento. **Corporate headquarters location:** This Location. **Parent company:** Southern Pacific Corporation. **Listed on:** New York Stock Exchange.

STOCKTON PORT DISTRICT
P.O. Box 2089, Stockton CA 95201. 209/946-0246. **Contact:** Administrative Service. **Description:** Provides berthing and warehousing facilities for inbound and outbound marine shipping. The port also provides domestic office and warehouse space, and has

land available for industrial development. **Common positions include:** Accountant/Auditor; Blue-Collar Worker Supervisor; Computer Programmer; Department Manager; General Manager; Human Resources Specialist; Management Trainee; Operations/Production Manager; Police/Law Enforcement Officer; Purchasing Agent and Manager; Systems Analyst; Transportation/Traffic Specialist. **Educational backgrounds include:** Accounting; Business Administration; Computer Science; Marketing; Transportation/Logistics. **Benefits:** Dental Insurance; Disability Coverage; Life Insurance; Medical Insurance; Pension Plan; Tuition Assistance. **Corporate headquarters location:** This Location. **Operations at this facility include:** Administration.

TRANSCISCO INDUSTRIES INC.
TRANSCISCO RAIL
601 California Street, Suite 1301, San Francisco CA 94108. 415/397-1010. **Contact:** Patricia Pierce, Director of Human Resources. **Description:** Manufactures and provides maintenance on railcars.

WALLACE TRANSPORT INC.
P.O. Box 67, Planada CA 95365. 209/382-0239. **Contact:** Dixie Fox, Director of Personnel & Safety. **Description:** A common carrier trucking firm. **Common positions include:** Services Sales Representative; Transportation/Traffic Specialist; Truck Driver.

WORLD EXPLORER CRUISES
555 Montgomery Street, Suite 1400, San Francisco CA 94111. 415/393-1565. **Contact:** Human Resources. **Description:** An ocean cruise line ship.

Note: *Because addresses and telephone numbers of smaller companies can change rapidly, we recommend you call each company to verify the information below before inquiring about job opportunities. Mass mailings are not recommended.*

Additional small employers:

WHOLESALE OF TRANSPORTATION EQUIPMENT AND SUPPLIES

Jarlin Aviation Services
301 County Airport Rd, Vacaville CA 95688-3101. 707/448-2041.

Formula Power
2956 Treat Boulevard, Concord CA 94518. 510/685-1689.

M&W Tool Co.
97 Juniper Drive, Atherton CA 94027-2121. 415/327-3500.

MARINE CARGO HANDLING

Hall-Buck Marine Inc.
Benicia Industrial Park, Benicia CA 94510. 707/745-1101.

Crawley Marine Services
2900 Main St, Alameda CA 94501-7522. 415/546-2600.

PASSENGER TRANSPORTATION ARRANGEMENT SERVICES

Casto Travel Inc.
1154 Sonora Ct, Sunnyvale CA 94086. 408/737-7000.

Corporate Travel Services
550 California St Floor 3, San Francisco CA 94104-1006. 415/433-4700.

Rosenbluth International
49 Stevenson St Ste 1100, San Francisco CA 94105-2909. 415/512-4500.

China Travel Service
1523 Ofarrell St, San Francisco CA 94115-3758. 415/921-3533.

Apex Travel-Page Mill Travel
3000 El Camino Real, Palo Alto CA 94306-2120. 415/494-6011.

Travel Logistics Group
3190 Clearview Way, San Mateo CA 94402-3751. 415/358-8800.

Q-Travel
3190 Stevens Creek Blvd, San Jose CA 95117-1142. 408/244-4424.

Suntrips Inc.
2350 Paragon Dr, San Jose CA 95131-1308. 408/432-0700.

Funfare Travel
5275 Sunny Orchard Ln, San Jose CA 95135-1237. 408/270-8644.

Cali Travel
2670 S White Rd, San Jose CA 95148-2071. 408/223-2120.

Patterson Travel Agency
1107 21st St, Sacramento CA 95814-4267. 916/441-1526.

Tiem'Po Travel
2015 21st St, Sacramento CA 95818-1752. 916/453-0329.

Carlson Travel Network
3099 Fair Oaks Blvd, Sacramento CA 95864-5613. 916/489-2323.

Runaway Tours Inc.
120 Montgomery St Ste 800, San Francisco CA 94104-4311. 415/788-0224.

Cost Less Travel Bargain Center Inc.
674 Broadway, San Francisco CA 94133-4406. 415/397-6868.

Giselle's Travel Bureau
508 2nd St, Davis CA 95616-4619. 916/756-7770.

Giselle's Travel Bureau
5667 Freeport Blvd, Sacramento CA 95822-3525. 916/421-6616.

Betty Fong Travel
5874 S Land Park Dr, Sacramento CA 95822-3311. 916/424-0414.

Council Travel
394 University Dr, Menlo Park CA 94025-5224. 415/325-3888.

Transmarine Navigation Corp.
2321 W Washington St Ste K, Stockton CA 95203-2948. 209/465-9599.

AIR TRANSPORTATION AND SERVICES

Delta Air Lines Inc.
710 McDonell Dr, S San Fran CA 94080-1121. 415/872-4233.

Japan Air Lines Co. Ltd.
275 Ofarrell St, San Francisco CA 94102-2121. 415/765-8548.

Japan Air Lines Co. Ltd.
PO Box 280025, San Francisco CA 94128-0025. 415/877-3214.

Philippine Airlines Inc.
447 Sutter St, San Francisco CA 94108-4601. 415/391-0270.

TWA Inc.
PO Box 280008, San Francisco CA 94128-0008. 415/877-4112.

Faucett Airlines
24 E 3rd Ave, San Mateo CA 94401-4011. 415/348-1767.

Aircargo Handling Services Inc.
270 Lawrence Ave, S San Fran CA 94080-6817. 415/583-1968.

Ameriflight
9171 Earhart Rd # 2, Oakland CA 94621-4514. 510/569-6000.

Westair Cargo
5175 E Clinton Way, Fresno CA 93727-2046. 209/251-8444.

NSI Technology Services
155 Moffett Park Dr # 220-A, Sunnyvale CA 94089-1323. 415/968-2797.

Dynair Corp.
San Francisco International Airport, San Francisco CA 94128. 415/877-0358.

Plumas District Hospital Airport
1065 Bucks Lake Rd, Quincy CA 95971-9507. 916/283-2121.

MISC. WATER TRANSPORTATION SERVICES

Det Norske Veritas Class
1350 Treat Blvd Ste 110, Walnut Creek CA 94596-2134. 510/939-1045.

Bureau Veritas
1777 N California Blvd, Walnut Creek CA 94596-4150. 510/934-7434.

WATER TRANSPORTATION OF PASSENGERS

Red & White Fleet
41 Pier, San Francisco CA 94133. 415/546-2800.

WATER TRANSPORTATION OF FREIGHT

Orient Overseas Container Line
4141 Hacienda Dr, Pleasanton CA 94588-8549. 510/460-4800.

Matson Navigation Co.
3050 7th St, Oakland CA 94607-1047. 510/271-9754.

OSK Mitsui Lines Inc.
600 California St Ste 1450,

San Francisco CA 94108-2704. 415/982-8360.

P&O Containers Ltd.
450 Sansome St Ste 410, San Francisco CA 94111-3312. 415/956-4358.

WAREHOUSING AND STORAGE

Larson Cooling Company
706 W Market St, Salinas CA 93901-1426. 408/424-4137.

TPE Services Inc.
7041 Las Positas Rd, Livermore CA 94550-0212. 510/447-2400.

J&R Distribution Service Inc.
1867 Whipple Rd, Hayward CA 94544-7834. 510/489-3230.

Public Storage
1870 Arnold Industrial Pl, Concord CA 94520-5324. 510/680-1902.

Public Storage
601 Sunset Dr, Antioch CA 94509-2827. 510/754-7134.

Public Storage
1455 Concord Ave, Concord CA 94520-4909. 510/671-9276.

Public Storage
2325 Soquel Dr, Santa Cruz CA 95065-1935. 408/462-0990.

Servex Inc.
30870 San Clemente St, Hayward CA 94544-7135. 510/429-2929.

Peppertree Warehouse & Distributing Co.
30527 San Antonio St, Hayward CA 94544-7101. 510/487-1119.

New Breed
2055 Burroughs Ave, San Leandro CA 94577-5611. 510/352-2552.

Tab Warehouse & Distribution
2444 Station Dr, Stockton CA 95215-7958. 209/943-4777.

A Low Cost Self Storage
3860 Benatar Way, Chico CA 95928-7113. 916/891-1259.

Westlam Foods-Sutter Division
1493 Acacia Ave, Sutter CA 95982-9310. 916/755-0033.

Safe Place Storage
6880 Santa Teresa Blvd, San Jose CA 95119-1205. 408/281-0400.

Valley 99 Mini Storals
4100 S US Highway 99, Stockton CA 95215-8238. 209/463-8419.

Mid-Valley Portable Storage
1333 E Turner Rd, Lodi CA 95240-0730. 209/368-0629.

AAA Security Mini Storage
4325 Marconi Ave, Sacramento CA 95821-4309. 916/481-9930.

Golden State Services
2055 S 7th St, San Jose CA 95112-6011. 408/288-3030.

Arden & 80 RV Storage
1200 Arden Way, Sacramento CA 95815-3302. 916/927-9802.

The File Keeper
640 E Main St, Grass Valley CA 95945-5806. 916/274-3547.

COURIER SERVICES

United States Courier
365 Brannan St, San Francisco CA 94107-1810. 415/495-3003.

California Couriers
30914 San Antonio St, Hayward CA 94544-7110. 510/471-7100.

Express-It Courier Service Inc.
1855 Norman Ave, Santa Clara CA 95054-2029. 408/734-1999.

United Couriers Inc.
2153 Otoole Ave Ste E, San Jose CA 95131-1331. 408/441-0141.

TRUCKING

CH Robinson Company
2491 W Shaw Ave, Fresno CA 93711-3306. 209/244-0411.

Northwest Transport Service Inc.
4014 E California Ave, Fresno CA 93725-1004. 209/233-7792.

TLC Lines Inc.
4887 E Annadale Ave, Fresno CA 93725-2209. 209/485-0692.

Roy Miller Freight Lines Inc.
3053 S Golden State Blvd, Fresno CA 93725-2321. 209/486-2957.

Truck A Way
325 Airport Rd, King City CA 93930-2505. 408/385-5451.

Adams Air Cargo
468 Littlefield Ave, South San Francisco CA 94080-6105. 415/871-9851.

RWL Investments Inc.
859 Harrison St, San Francisco CA 94107-1124. 415/495-1800.

TWI Domestic Transportaion Systems
3190 Clearview Way, San

Mateo CA 94402-3751. 415/573-6900.

PSB Trucking
43978 Fremont Blvd, Fremont CA 94538-6057. 510/659-9706.

Yellow Freight System Inc.
25555 Clawiter Rd, Hayward CA 94545-2740. 510/783-7010.

Overnite Transportation
2348 Industrial Parkway West, Hayward CA 94545. 510/785-6432.

Old Dominion Freight Line Inc.
2340 Industrial Pkwy W, Hayward CA 94545-5006. 510/785-9155.

MGM Transport
2976 Alvarado St, San Leandro CA 94577-5706. 510/483-7440.

Clipper Hill Transportation Co.
2900 Volpey Way, Union City CA 94587-1206. 510/487-8620.

Logistics Express Inc.
700 Decoto Rd, Union City CA 94587. 510/487-7443.

JT Trucking Company
1849 Sunnyvale Ave, Walnut Creek CA 94596-1811. 510/763-9413.

Condor Enterprises Inc.
4919 Tidewater Ave, Oakland CA 94601-4914. 510/534-7200.

Pacific Motor Trucking Co.
650 Hammond Way, Milpitas CA 95035-5328. 408/945-0589.

Ego Line Moving & Storage
1596 S 7th St, San Jose CA 95112-5929. 408/275-8964.

TNT Canada Truck Line
3018 Loomis Rd, Stockton CA 95205-8051. 209/941-8032.

Williams Tank Lines Inc.
1477 Tillie Lewis Dr, Stockton CA 95206-1130. 209/944-5613.

Independent Trucking
1145 W Charter Way, Stockton CA 95206-1106. 209/462-6009.

California Bulk Inc.
3939 Producers Dr, Stockton CA 95206-4204. 209/983-1069.

American Transfer
2701 S US Highway 99, Stockton CA 95215-7838. 209/466-0111.

T&T Trucking Inc.
11396 N US Highway 99, Lodi CA 95240-7349. 209/931-6000.

Frank C. Alegre Trucking Inc.
802 N Cluff Avenue, Lodi CA 95240-0707. 209/334-2112.

Donohue Trucking
PO Box 39, Carmichael CA 95609-0039. 916/485-4546.

Brashers Sacramento Auto Auction
6233 Blacktop Rd, Rio Linda CA 95673-3000. 916/991-5555.

Superior California Trucking Co.
604 Galveston St, W Sacramento CA 95691-2212. 916/371-7520.

Western Transportation Service
840 S River Rd, W Sacramento CA 95691-2826. 916/372-5395.

Pre-Fab Transit Co.
Road 101 & Beamer, Woodland CA 95695. 916/666-7100.

Pioneer Fleet Service Inc.
6225 Turner Rd, Sacramento CA 95829-9324. 916/381-4228.

Vecta Transportation Systems Inc.
1621 Main Ave, Sacramento CA 95838-2427. 916/921-6696.

Western Parcel Express
1015 North Market Blvd, Sacramento CA 95838. 916/928-9430.

Matheson Fast Freight Inc.
2391 Court St, Redding CA 96001-2527. 916/243-6292.

Hospenthal Livestock Transportation
10554 Bruceville Rd, Elk Grove CA 95758-9539. 916/684-2600.

Peninsula Moving & Storage
1500 Whipple Rd, Union City CA 94587-2046. 510/549-1971.

A&A Freight Lines
2520 Hilton St, Union City CA 94587-4309. 510/489-9401.

North Coast Messenger
10966 Bigge St, San Leandro CA 94577-1121. 510/351-3339.

Tricor California
1679 Enterprise Blvd, W Sacramento CA 95691-3447. 916/371-1704.

Frank J. Warn Inc.
2480 Whipple Rd, Hayward CA 94544. 510/471-8900.

Conway Western Express
2200 Claremont Ct, Hayward

CA 94545-5002. 510/785-6920.

Bigge Crane & Rigging Co.
PO Box 1657, San Leandro CA 94577. 510/638-8100.

Tri State Motor Transit
3841 Bithell Ln, Suisun City CA 94585. 707/427-5530.

Falcon Charter Service Inc.
350 8th St, San Francisco CA 94103. 415/558-7300.

Norris Trailer Transport
9th & Pierce, College City CA 95931. 916/476-3228.

Keep On Trucking Company Inc.
370 8th Ave, Oakland CA 94606-5104. 510/893-6011.

Valley South Bay North American
660 N King Rd, San Jose CA 95133-1715. 510/490-2994.

LOCAL AND INTERURBAN PASSENGER TRANSIT

Laidlaw Transit Inc.
801 Wilbur Ave, Antioch CA 94509. 510/754-4878.

Laidlaw Transit Inc.
1001 Galaxy Way, Concord CA 94520. 510/685-3204.

Fairfield Suisun Transit Systems
1705 Enterprise Dr, Fairfield CA 94533. 707/429-1296.

Dave Transportation Service Inc.
1705 Enterprise Dr, Fairfield CA 94533-5801. 707/422-6378.

Golden Gate Industries
2829 California St, San Francisco CA 94115-2515. 415/922-9400.

Star Limousine
PO Box 2762, South San Francisco CA 94083-2762. 415/761-2434.

A Perfect Experience Limo Service
1679 Novato Blvd, Novato CA 94947-3251. 707/585-1320.

Central Valley Ridesharing
2100 Tulare Street, Suite 619, Fresno CA 93721-2111. 209/441-7433.

Baystar Medical Services
9828 Business Park Dr, Sacramento CA 95827-1704. 916/856-1650.

Foothill Ambulance Service
PO Box 15145, Sacramento CA 95851. 916/348-4412.

Indian Valley Hospital
174 Hot Springs Rd, Greenville CA 95947-9746. 916/284-7828.

Oroville Express
1825 Montgomery St, Oroville CA 95965-4822. 916/534-9999.

Mayflower Contract Service Inc.
100 Howe Rd, Martinez CA 94553-2067. 510/228-9200.

Gold Rush Charters
PO Box 5278, Stockton CA 95205-0278. 209/462-9879.

Amador Tours
1331 C St, Sacramento CA 95814-0913. 916/444-7880.

Servicar Of Santa Clara County
1506 White Oaks Rd, Campbell CA 95008-6724. 408/377-6655.

RAILROAD TRANSPORTATION

Union Pacific Fruit Express
833 E 8th St, Stockton CA 95206-2203. 209/948-0428.

Stockton Terminal & Eastern RR
1282 Shaw Rd, Stockton CA 95215-4016. 209/464-8730.

SHIP/BOAT BUILDING AND REPAIRING

Malibu Boats West Inc.
1861 Grogan Ave, Merced CA 95340. 209/383-7469.

TRANSPORTATION EQUIPMENT

Zieman Manufacturing Co.
1805 E Beamer St, Woodland CA 95776-6220. 916/666-0383.

For more information on career opportunities in transportation:

Associations

AIR TRANSPORT ASSOCIATION OF AMERICA
1301 Pennsylvania Avenue NW, Suite 1100, Washington DC 20004. 202/626-4000. World Wide Web address: http://www.air-transport.org.

AMERICAN BUREAU OF SHIPPING
2 World Trade Center, 106th Floor, New York NY 10048. 212/839-5000.

AMERICAN MARITIME ASSOCIATION
380 Madison Avenue, 17th Floor, New York NY 10017. 212/557-9520. A trade association which offers collection and bargaining services.

AMERICAN SOCIETY OF TRAVEL AGENTS
1101 King Street, Suite 200, Alexandria VA 22314. 703/739-2782. World Wide Web address: http://www.astanet.com. For information about the American Society of Travel Agents, send a SASE with $.75 postage to the attention of the Fulfillment Department.

AMERICAN TRUCKING ASSOCIATION
2200 Mill Road, Alexandria VA 22314-4677. 703/838-1700. World Wide Web address: http://www.cais.com/ata.

ASSOCIATION OF AMERICAN RAILROADS
50 F Street NW, Washington DC 20001. 202/639-2100.

FUTURE AVIATION PROFESSIONALS OF AMERICA
4959 Massachusetts Boulevard, Atlanta GA 30337. 404/997-8097. Future Aviation Professionals of America publishes a monthly newsletter which monitors the job market for flying jobs; a pilot employment guide, outlining what is required to become a pilot; and a directory of aviation employers.

INSTITUTE OF TRANSPORTATION ENGINEERS
525 School Street SW, Suite 410, Washington DC 20024-2797. 202/554-8050. World Wide Web address: http://www.ite.org. The Institute of Transportation Engineers is a scientific and educational association, providing for professional development of members and others.

MARINE TECHNOLOGY SOCIETY
1828 L Street NW, Suite 906, Washington DC 20036. 202/775-5966.

NATIONAL MARINE MANUFACTURERS ASSOCIATION
401 North Michigan Avenue, Suite 1150, Chicago IL 60611. 312/836-4747. The National Marine Manufacturers Association is a partnership of three manufacturer groups: The National Association of Boat Manufacturers; The Association of Marine Engine Manufacturers; and The National Association of Marine Products & Services. Subscription to job listing publication is available for a fee.

NATIONAL MOTOR FREIGHT TRAFFIC ASSOCIATION
2200 Mill Road, Alexandria VA 22314-4654. 703/838-1810. World Wide Web address: http://www.erols.com/nmfta. The National Motor Freight Travel Association works towards the improvement and advancement of the interests and welfare of motor common carriers.

NATIONAL TANK TRUCK CARRIERS
2200 Mill Road, Alexandria VA 22314. 703/838-1700. The National Tank Truck Carriers is a trade association representing and promoting the interests of the highway bulk transportation community.

Directories

MOODY'S TRANSPORTATION MANUAL
Moody's Investors Service, Inc., 99 Church Street, New York NY 10007. 212/553-0300. $12.95 per year with weekly updates.

NATIONAL TANK TRUCK CARRIER DIRECTORY
2200 Mill Road, Alexandria VA 22314. 703/838-1700.

OFFICIAL MOTOR FREIGHT GUIDE
1700 West Courtland Street, Chicago IL 60622. 312/278-2454.

Magazines

AMERICAN SHIPPER
P.O. Box 4728, Jacksonville FL 32201. 904/355-2601. Monthly.

FLEET OWNER
707 Westchester Avenue, White Plains NY 10604-3102. 914/949-8500.

HEAVY DUTY TRUCKING
Newport Communications, P.O. Box W, Newport Beach CA 92658. 714/261-1636.

ITE JOURNAL
Institute of Transportation Engineers, 525 School Street SW, Suite 410, Washington DC 20024-2797. 202/554-8050. One year subscription (12 issues): $50.

MARINE DIGEST AND TRANSPORTATION NEWS
P.O. Box 3905, Seattle WA 98124. 206/682-3607.

SHIPPING DIGEST
51 Madison Avenue, New York NY 10010. 212/689-4411.

TRAFFIC WORLD MAGAZINE
741 National Press Building, Washington DC 20045. 202/383-6140.

TRANSPORT TOPICS
2200 Mill Road, Alexandria VA 22314. 703/838-1772.

UTILITIES: ELECTRIC/GAS/WATER

With deregulation looming closer and closer, utilities are adjusting by cutting costs and providing better service. This is a good sign for the industry but a bad sign for jobseekers, as employment should remain just about flat. Job prospects in the utilities industry are probably best with large electric utilities, water supply facilities, and sanitary services right now. The most common positions with public utilities are precision production workers and operators, fabricators, and laborers.

CALIFORNIA WATER SERVICE COMPANY
P.O. Box 1150, San Jose CA 95108-1150. 408/451-8200. **Contact:** Human Resources. **Description:** California Water Service Company is a public utility supplying water service through 20 separate water systems to 365,000 customers living in 38 California communities. The company's rates and operations are regulated by the California Public Utilities Commission with the rates for each district determined separately. **Corporate headquarters location:** This Location.

CITIZENS TELECOM
P.O. Box 496035, Redding CA 96049. **Toll-free phone:** 800/726-3539. **Contact:** Personnel. **Description:** Provides one or more of five basic utility services -- telephone, electric, gas, water, and wastewater -- to hundreds of communities in several states.

CITIZENS TELECOM
9701 Elk Grove Florin Road, Elk Grove CA 95624. 916/686-3000. **Contact:** Personnel. **Description:** Provides one or more of five basic utility services -- telephone, electric, gas, water, and wastewater -- to hundreds of communities in several states.

PACIFIC GAS & ELECTRIC COMPANY
Mail Code N2F, P.O. Box 770000, San Francisco CA 94177. 415/973-7000. **Fax:** 415/973-4572. **Contact:** Human Resources. **Description:** An operating investor-owned utility engaged in supplying electric and natural gas service throughout most of northern and central California, with more than 4 million customers. **Common positions include:** Accountant/Auditor; Attorney; Budget Analyst; Chemist; Civil Engineer; Computer Systems Analyst; Customer Service Representative; Draftsperson; Economist/Market Research Analyst; Electrical/Electronics Engineer; Financial Analyst; Human Resources Specialist; Industrial Engineer; Mechanical Engineer; Nuclear Engineer; Software Engineer; Systems Analyst; Technical Writer/Editor. **Educational backgrounds include:** Accounting; Business Administration; Computer Science; Economics; Engineering; Finance; Human Resources; Information Systems. **Benefits:** Credit Union; Daycare Assistance; Disability Coverage; Employee Discounts; Life Insurance; Medical Insurance; Pension Plan; Profit Sharing; Savings Plan; Tuition Assistance. **Corporate headquarters location:** This Location. **Operations at this facility include:** Administration. **Listed on:** New York Stock Exchange. **Number of employees nationwide:** 23,000.

Note: *Because addresses and telephone numbers of smaller companies can change rapidly, we recommend you call each company to verify the information below before inquiring about job opportunities. Mass mailings are not recommended.*

Additional small employers:

ELECTRIC SERVICES

Bureau of Electricity
2000 Grand St, Alameda CA 94501-1228. 510/748-3901.

Soquel Electric Co.
24 Pepperwood Way, Soquel CA 95073. 408/464-6836.

GAS AND/OR WATER SUPPLY

Westland Water District
Fresno-Coalinga Rd, Five Points CA 93624.

Nevada Irrigation District
10836 Rough & Ready Hwy, Grass Valley CA 95945-8522. 916/273-6185.

San Francisco Water Department
1000 El Camino Real, Millbrae CA 94030-2048. 415/872-5900.

For more information on career opportunities in the utilities industry:

Associations

AMERICAN PUBLIC GAS ASSOCIATION
Lee Highway, Suite 102, Fairfax VA 22030. 703/352-3890. Publishes a weekly newsletter.

AMERICAN PUBLIC POWER ASSOCIATION (APPA)
2301 M Street NW, Washington DC 20037. 202/467-2970. Represents publicly-owned utilities. Provides many services including: government relations, educational programs, and industry-related information publications.

AMERICAN WATER WORKS ASSOCIATION
6666 West Quincy Drive, Denver CO 80235. 303/794-7711.

NATIONAL RURAL ELECTRIC COOPERATIVE ASSOCIATION
1800 Massachusetts Avenue NW, Washington DC 20036. 202/857-9500. World Wide Web address: http://www.nreca.org.

Directories

MOODY'S PUBLIC UTILITY MANUAL
Moody's Investors Service, Inc., 99 Church Street, New York NY 10007. 212/553-0300. Annually available at libraries.

Magazines

PUBLIC POWER
2301 M Street NW, Washington DC 20037. 202/467-2900.

MISCELLANEOUS WHOLESALING

Employment in the wholesale trade sector is closely tied to the growth of the economy. However, industry trends will change a good portion of the composition and nature of wholesale trade employment. Consolidation of the industry into fewer firms and the spread of new technology should slow growth in some occupations, but many new jobs will be created in others as firms provide a growing array of support services. In addition, these trends will change the role of many other workers.

Heightened competition and pressure to lower operating costs should continue to force distributors to merge with or acquire other firms. The resulting consolidation of wholesale trade among fewer, larger firms will reduce the demands for some workers as merged companies eliminate duplicated staff. Consolidation and greater competition among wholesale trade firms, however, will lead more firms to expand customer service, increasing the demand for these types of workers. Clerks or sales workers will advance to many of these new customer service or marketing jobs, and new workers may be needed for financial, logistical, technical, or advertising positions.

BUTLER-JOHNSON CORPORATION
5031 24th Street, Sacramento CA 95822-2297. 916/454-3512. **Contact:** Human Resources. **Description:** A wholesaler of a wide range of building and flooring products.

W.W. GRAINGER
1617 Industrial Place West, Hayward CA 94544. 510/471-6374. **Contact:** Human Resources. **Description:** A wholesaler of HVAC, electrical, and various other industrial supplies and equipment.

HARRINGTON INDUSTRIAL PLASTICS
1100 Industrial Road, Unit 15, San Carlos CA 94070. 415/637-9910. **Contact:** Human Resources. **Description:** A wholesaler of plastic piping, fittings, and other related products.

J&S WHOLESALE COMPANY
P.O. Box 638, Jackson CA 95642. 209/223-3091. **Contact:** Human Resources. **Description:** A wholesaler of firearms, ammunition, and reloading components.

PEAK PRODUCTS
2501 Mercantile Drive, Unit E, Rancho Cordova CA 95741. 916/852-5111. **Contact:** Human Resources. **Description:** A wholesaler of abrasives.

WILBUR-ELLIS COMPANY
CONNELL BROS. COMPANY
320 California Street, Suite 2, San Francisco CA 94104. 415/772-4000. **Contact:** Ofelia Lee, Personnel Manager. **Description:** International merchants and distributors involved in importing and exporting goods. Wilbur-Ellis trades agricultural feed and chemical products. **Common positions include:** Accountant/Auditor; Buyer; Chemical Engineer; Manufacturer's/Wholesaler's Sales Rep.; Transportation/Traffic Specialist. **Educational**

backgrounds include: Accounting; Business Administration; Marketing. **Benefits:** 401(k); Dental Insurance; Disability Coverage; Life Insurance; Medical Insurance; Pension Plan; Tuition Assistance. **Corporate headquarters location:** This Location. **Operations at this facility include:** Administration.

Note: *Because addresses and telephone numbers of smaller companies can change rapidly, we recommend you call each company to verify the information below before inquiring about job opportunities. Mass mailings are not recommended.*

Additional small employers:

WHOLESALE FURNITURE AND HOME FURNISHINGS

Eastman
2900 Faber St, Union City CA 94587. 510/475-1500.

Kielty & Dayton Inc.
23125 Bernhardt St, Hayward CA 94545-1622. 510/732-9200.

Coast To Coast Mattresses
168 Williams Rd, Salinas CA 93905-2838. 408/753-9445.

Peninsula Floors Inc.
PO Box 71, Livermore CA 94551-0071. 510/449-6000.

Bacar Inc.
1855 Dobbin Dr, San Jose CA 95133. 408/926-1110.

A&R Drapery
3060 Cyrus Ave, San Jose CA 95124. 408/374-4410.

Delta Pi Design Inc.
510 Dana Ave, San Jose CA 95126-2001. 408/286-0776.

Window Fashions
6424 10th Ave, Lucerne CA 95458. 707/274-2620.

OFFICE EQUIPMENT WHOLESALE

Solano Cash Register
810 Davis St, Vacaville CA 95687-5421. 707/448-3114.

Gestetner Corp.
6715 N Palm Ave Ste 103, Fresno CA 93704-1073. 209/436-6730.

Buresh Co.
595 Taylor Rd, Newcastle CA 95658-9780. 916/663-3301.

Taylor Made Office Systems
1326 Northmarket Blvd, Sacramento CA 95834. 916/928-2900.

COMMERCIAL EQUIPMENT WHOLESALE

Global Steel Products Corp.
1331 T St, Sacramento CA 95814-7107. 916/443-4433.

Capitol Interiors Inc.
1334 Bynum Way, Oakley CA 94561-3113. 510/625-4272.

National Bandsaw Service
4450 Desin Dr, San Jose CA 95118-2032. 408/978-3532.

LPC Packaging Inc.
1195 N Gertrude Ave, Stockton CA 95215-4034. 209/948-8112.

Casa Herrera Inc.
4560 Sherbourne Dr, San Jose CA 95124-4842. 408/723-0627.

Esselte Meto
2672 Bayshore Pkwy, Mountain View CA 94043-1001. 415/966-1661.

HARDWARE WHOLESALE

Santa Rosa Wholesale
4055 Santa Rosa Ave, Santa Rosa CA 95407-8222. 707/584-7822.

Cooper Machinery & Supply
135 Crest Rd, Novato CA 94945-2729. 415/892-4355.

Empire Equipment Co. Ltd.
2850 El Centro Rd, Sacramento CA 95833-9703. 916/922-7181.

Windmaster
Byron Hot Springs Rd, Byron CA 94514. 510/634-0777.

Superior Engineered Products
20187 Mack St, Hayward CA 94545-1202. 510/487-2442.

E&E Enterprises
PO Box 956, Newark CA 94560-0956. 510/796-1790.

Sym-Tex Systems Inc.
2255 Martin Ave Ste G, Santa Clara CA 95050-2709. 408/748-7611.

Specialty Rubber & Gasket
187 Arthur Road, Martinez CA 94553-2205. 510/370-7733.

Olander Fasteners Inc.
4708 Roseville Road Suite 105, North Highlands CA 95660-5172. 916/344-8747.

SPORTING AND RECREATIONAL GOODS AND SUPPLIES WHOLESALE

Fitart Sports Inc.
30616 San Antonio Street, Hayward CA 94544-7104. 510/475-7800.

All Logo Sports
16860 Joleen Way, Morgan Hill CA 95037-4607. 408/779-0777.

Orcal Pool Supplies Inc.
2325 Paragon Drive, San Jose CA 95131-1309. 408/943-9030.

Redi Golf
PO Box 70813, Sunnyvale CA 94086. 408/241-3868.

Court Works Equipment
1755 E Bayshore Rd, Redwood City CA 94063-4142. 415/306-0114.

SCRAP AND WASTE MATERIALS WHOLESALE

LMC Recyclers
699 Seaport Blvd, Redwood City CA 94063-2712. 415/369-4161.

LMC Recyclers
130 N 12th St, Sacramento CA 95814-0615. 916/444-3380.

Markovits & Fox
1633 Oakland Rd, San Jose CA 95131. 408/453-7888.

Hillman Metals
1273 Industrial Pkwy West, Hayward CA 94544-7025. 510/889-8222.

PAPER AND OFFICE SUPPLIES WHOLESALE

BT Redwood Inc.
1195 Hamilton Ct, Menlo Park CA 94025-1424. 415/321-0870.

Schwabacher Frey Hanson
30773 Wiegman Rd, Hayward CA 94544-7045. 510/475-7700.

Rubberstampede
PO Box 246, Berkeley CA 94701-0246. 510/420-6800.

Classico San Francisco Inc.
15 Koch Rd Ste B, Corte Madera CA 94925-1231. 415/459-3830.

Duplex Products Inc.
851 Traeger Ave, San Bruno CA 94066-3037. 415/574-3322.

Allante Business Systems & Forms
PO Box 1851, Orangevale CA 95662. 916/989-5128.

For more information on career opportunities in the wholesaling industry:

Associations

APPLIANCE PARTS DISTRIBUTORS ASSOCIATION
228 East Baltimore Street, Detroit MI 48202. 313/875-8455. An association for wholesale distributors of appliance parts.

EMPLOYMENT SERVICES

NOTE: *While every effort is made to keep the addresses and phone numbers of these companies up-to-date, employment services often move or change hands and are therefore more difficult to track. Please notify the publisher if you find any discrepancies.*

TEMPORARY EMPLOYMENT AGENCIES

CDI
44 Montgomery Street, Suite 2120, San Francisco CA 94104. 415/434-1846. **Contact:** Debra Jaron, Branch Manager. **Description:** A temporary agency. Company pays fee. **Specializes in the areas of:** Secretarial; Word Processing. **Number of placements per year:** 500 - 999.

EDP/TEMPS AND CONTRACT SERVICES
685 Market Street, Suite 470, San Francisco CA 94105. 415/952-5010. **Contact:** Office Manager. **Description:** A temporary agency. Company pays fee. **Specializes in the areas of:** Accounting/Auditing; Banking; Computer Hardware/Software; Engineering; Finance; Insurance; Manufacturing; MIS/EDP; Nonprofit; Personnel/Labor Relations; Printing/Publishing; Technical and Scientific. **Positions commonly filled include:** Computer Operator; Computer Programmer; EDP Specialist; MIS Specialist; Systems Analyst; Technical Writer/Editor. **Number of placements per year:** 1000+.

EDP/TEMPS AND CONTRACT SERVICES
3180 Crow Canyon Place, Suite 100, San Ramon CA 94583. 510/866-1030. **Contact:** Office Manager. **Description:** A temporary agency. Company pays fee. **Specializes in the areas of:** Accounting/Auditing; Banking; Computer Hardware/Software; Engineering; Finance; Insurance; Manufacturing; MIS/EDP; Nonprofit; Personnel/Labor Relations; Printing/Publishing; Technical and Scientific. **Positions commonly filled include:** Computer Programmer; EDP Specialist; MIS Specialist; Systems Analyst; Technical Writer/Editor. **Number of placements per year:** 1000+.

INTERIM PERSONNEL
24301 Southland Drive, Suite 207, Hayward CA 94545. 510/785-5300. **Contact:** Office Manager. **Description:** A temporary agency. Company pays fee. **Specializes in the areas of:** Non-Specialized. **Positions commonly filled include:** Bookkeeper; Clerk; Computer Operator; Customer Service Representative; Data Entry Clerk; Draftsperson; Electronics Technician; Factory Worker; Legal Assistant; Light Industrial Worker; Medical Secretary; Receptionist; Secretary; Stenographer; Systems Analyst; Technician; Typist/Word Processor. **Number of placements per year:** 1000+.

INTERIM PERSONNEL
966 Fulton Avenue, Suite 297, Sacramento CA 95825. 916/929-0600. **Contact:** Office Manager. **Description:** A temporary agency. Company pays fee. **Specializes in the areas of:** Non-Specialized. **Positions commonly filled include:** Bookkeeper; Clerk; Computer Operator; Customer Service Representative; Data Entry Clerk; Draftsperson; Factory Worker; Legal Secretary; Light Industrial Worker; Medical Secretary; Receptionist; Secretary; Stenographer; Technician; Typist/Word Processor. **Number of placements per year:** 1000+.

KELLY SERVICES

1111 Civic Drive, Suite 240, Walnut Creek CA 94596. 510/746-1460. **Contact:** Mrs. Jo Tieslau, Customer Service/Operations Manager. **Description:** A temporary agency. Company pays fee. **Specializes in the areas of:** Accounting/Auditing; Advertising; Architecture/Construction/Real Estate; Banking; Clerical; Computer Hardware/Software; Engineering; Finance; Food Industry; Health/Medical; Legal; Manufacturing; MIS/EDP; Printing/Publishing; Sales and Marketing; Secretarial; Technical and Scientific. **Positions commonly filled include:** Accountant/Auditor; Administrative Assistant; Aerospace Engineer; Agricultural Engineer; Architect; Biological Scientist/Biochemist; Biomedical Engineer; Bookkeeper; Ceramics Engineer; Civil Engineer; Clerk; Commercial Artist; Computer Programmer; Customer Service Representative; Data Entry Clerk; Dietician/Nutritionist; Draftsperson; Economist/Market Research Analyst; Editor; Electrical/Electronics Engineer; Factory Worker; Financial Analyst; Industrial Designer; Industrial Engineer; Legal Secretary; Light Industrial Worker; Marketing Specialist; Mechanical Engineer; Medical Secretary; Metallurgical Engineer; Petroleum Engineer; Purchasing Agent and Manager; Receptionist; Sales Representative; Secretary; Statistician; Stenographer; Systems Analyst; Technical Writer/Editor; Technician; Typist/Word Processor; Underwriter/Assistant Underwriter. **Number of placements per year:** 1000+.

MANPOWER TEMPORARY SERVICES

124 University Avenue, Palo Alto CA 94301. 415/323-2200. **Contact:** Mandy Santos, Manager. **Description:** A temporary agency. Company pays fee. **Positions commonly filled include:** Accountant/Auditor; Administrative Assistant; Advertising Clerk; Biological Scientist/Biochemist; Bookkeeper; Buyer; Ceramics Engineer; Chemical Engineer; Clerk; Computer Operator; Computer Programmer; Construction Trade Worker; Customer Service Representative; Data Entry Clerk; Draftsperson; Driver; EDP Specialist; Electrical/Electronics Engineer; Factory Worker; Industrial Engineer; Legal Secretary; Light Industrial Worker; Mechanical Engineer; Medical Secretary; Nurse; Operations/Production Manager; Public Relations Specialist; Purchasing Agent and Manager; Quality Control Supervisor; Receptionist; Secretary; Stenographer; Systems Analyst; Technical Writer/Editor; Technician; Typist/Word Processor.

MANPOWER TEMPORARY SERVICES OF CALIFORNIA

480 South Ellsworth, San Mateo CA 94401. 415/342-2700. **Contact:** Vernon Hill, Manager. **Description:** A temporary agency. Company pays fee. **Specializes in the areas of:** Non-Specialized. **Positions commonly filled include:** Accountant/Auditor; Administrative Assistant; Advertising Clerk; Biological Scientist/Biochemist; Bookkeeper; Buyer; Ceramics Engineer; Chemical Engineer; Clerk; Computer Operator; Computer Programmer; Construction Trade Worker; Customer Service Representative; Data Entry Clerk; Draftsperson; Driver; EDP Specialist; Electrical/Electronics Engineer; Factory Worker; Industrial Engineer; Legal Secretary; Light Industrial Worker; Mechanical Engineer; Medical Secretary; Nurse; Operations/Production Manager; Public Relations Specialist; Purchasing Agent and Manager; Quality Control Supervisor; Receptionist; Secretary; Stenographer; Systems Analyst; Technical Writer/Editor; Technician; Typist/Word Processor.

OLSTEN STAFFING

1000 Broadway, Suite 248, Oakland CA 94607. 510/987-7555. **Contact:** Peggy Poole, Branch Manager. **Description:** A temporary agency. **Specializes in the areas of:** Accounting/Auditing; Clerical; Legal; Secretarial. **Positions commonly filled include:** Administrative Assistant; Bookkeeper; Claim Representative; Clerk; Customer Service

Representative; Data Entry Clerk; Driver; Legal Secretary; Light Industrial Worker; Medical Secretary; Receptionist; Secretary; Typist/Word Processor. **Number of placements per year:** 1000+.

PERSONNEL POOL OF SACRAMENTO
2862 Arden Way, Suite 225, Sacramento CA 95825. 916/484-1450. **Contact:** Mark Binneboese, General Manager. **Description:** A temporary agency. Company pays fee. **Specializes in the areas of:** Clerical; Construction; Food Industry; Health/Medical; Industrial; Insurance; Legal; Manufacturing; MIS/EDP; Sales and Marketing. **Positions commonly filled include:** Administrative Assistant; Bookkeeper; Clerk; Computer Programmer; Construction Trade Worker; Customer Service Representative; Data Entry Clerk; Draftsperson; Driver; Editor; EDP Specialist; Factory Worker; Food Production Worker; Legal Secretary; Light Industrial Worker; Medical Secretary; Receptionist; Sales Representative; Secretary; Statistician; Stenographer; Transcriptionist; Typist/ Word Processor. **Number of placements per year:** 1000+.

SIERRA TECHNOLOGY CORPORATION
4150 Manzanita Avenue, Suite 100, Carmichael CA 95608. 916/488-4960. **Contact:** General Manager. **Description:** A temporary agency. Company pays fee. **Specializes in the areas of:** Architecture/Construction/Real Estate; Computer Hardware/Software; Engineering; Manufacturing; Technical and Scientific. **Positions commonly filled include:** Aerospace Engineer; Agricultural Engineer; Architect; Biological Scientist/ Biochemist; Biomedical Engineer; Ceramics Engineer; Chemical Engineer; Chemist; Civil Engineer; Computer Operator; Computer Programmer; Data Entry Clerk; Draftsperson; EDP Specialist; Electrical/Electronics Engineer; Financial Analyst; Industrial Designer; Industrial Engineer; Mechanical Engineer; Metallurgical Engineer; Mining Engineer; Operations/Production Manager; Petroleum Engineer; Purchasing Agent and Manager; Quality Control Supervisor; Systems Analyst; Technical Writer/ Editor; Technician. **Number of placements per year:** 200 - 499.

STAFF BUILDERS INC. OF CALIFORNIA
1010 Hurley Way, Suite 185, Sacramento CA 95825. 916/923-3600. **Contact:** Office Manager. **Description:** A temporary agency. Company pays fee. **Specializes in the areas of:** Non-Specialized. **Positions commonly filled include:** Accountant/Auditor; Administrative Assistant; Bookkeeper; Clerk; Computer Operator; Computer Programmer; Customer Service Representative; Data Entry Clerk; Draftsperson; Driver; EDP Specialist; Factory Worker; Health Services Worker; Legal Secretary; Light Industrial Worker; Medical Secretary; Nurse; Public Relations Specialist; Receptionist; Sales Representative; Secretary; Stenographer; Technician; Typist/Word Processor. **Number of placements per year:** 1000+.

TECH/AID OF CALIFORNIA
1291 East Hillsdale Boulevard, Suite 140, Foster City CA 94404. 415/574-7645. **Contact:** Office Manager. **Description:** A temporary agency. Company pays fee. **Specializes in the areas of:** Computer Hardware/Software; Design; Engineering; Manufacturing. **Positions commonly filled include:** Aerospace Engineer; Architect; Biological Scientist/Biochemist; Chemist; Civil Engineer; Commercial Artist; Designer; Draftsperson; Electrical/Electronics Engineer; Industrial Designer; Industrial Engineer; Light Industrial Worker; Mechanical Engineer; Physicist/Astronomer; Quality Control Supervisor; Technical Writer/Editor; Technician. **Number of placements per year:** 1000+.

TECH/AID OF CALIFORNIA
7700 Edgewater, Suite 543, Oakland CA 94621. 510/577-6700. **Contact:** Office Manager. **Description:** A temporary agency. Company pays fee. **Specializes in the areas of:** Computer Hardware/Software; Design; Engineering; Manufacturing. **Positions commonly filled include:** Aerospace Engineer; Architect; Biological Scientist/Biochemist; Chemist; Civil Engineer; Commercial Artist; Designer; Draftsperson; Electrical/Electronics Engineer; Industrial Designer; Industrial Engineer; Light Industrial Worker; Mechanical Engineer; Physicist/Astronomer; Quality Control Supervisor; Technical Writer/Editor; Technician. **Number of placements per year:** 1000+.

VOLT TEMPORARY SERVICES INC.
6140 Stoneridge Mall Road, Suite 145, Pleasanton CA 94588. 510/463-2800. **Contact:** Lisa Wilson, Sales Representative. **Description:** A temporary agency. Company pays fee. **Specializes in the areas of:** Accounting/Auditing; Clerical; Secretarial. **Positions commonly filled include:** Administrative Assistant; Bookkeeper; Clerk; Customer Service Representative; Data Entry Clerk; Driver; Factory Worker; Legal Secretary; Light Industrial Worker; Medical Secretary; Receptionist; Secretary; Typist/Word Processor. **Number of placements per year:** 1000+.

WESTERN STAFF SERVICES OF WALNUT CREEK
P.O. Box 9280, Walnut Creek CA 94598. 510/930-5300. **Contact:** Janet Bowman, Vice President/National Training Director. **Description:** A temporary agency. **Specializes in the areas of:** Accounting/Auditing; Banking; Clerical; Computer Hardware/Software; Health/Medical; MIS/EDP; Sales and Marketing; Secretarial; Technical and Scientific. **Positions commonly filled include:** Accountant/Auditor; Actuary; Administrative Assistant; Aerospace Engineer; Agricultural Engineer; Architect; Attorney; Bank Teller; Biological Scientist/Biochemist; Biomedical Engineer; Bookkeeper; Ceramics Engineer; Civil Engineer; Claim Representative; Clerk; Commercial Artist; Computer Programmer; Customer Service Representative; Data Entry Clerk; Dietician/Nutritionist; Draftsperson; Economist/Market Research Analyst; EDP Specialist; Electrical/Electronics Engineer; Electronics Technician; Factory Worker; Financial Analyst; Industrial Designer; Industrial Engineer; Interior Designer; Legal Assistant; Light Industrial Worker; Marketing Specialist; Mechanical Engineer; Medical Secretary; Metallurgical Engineer; Mining Engineer; Nurse; Petroleum Engineer; Pharmacist; Physicist/Astronomer; Public Relations Specialist; Purchasing Agent and Manager; Receptionist; Reporter; Sales Representative; Secretary; Security Officer; Statistician; Stenographer; Systems Analyst; Technical Writer/Editor; Technician; Typist/Word Processor; Underwriter/Assistant Underwriter. **Number of placements per year:** 1000+.

PERMANENT EMPLOYMENT AGENCIES

ACCRO PERSONNEL SERVICES
1654 Foothill Park Circle, Lafayette CA 94549. 510/937-3387. **Contact:** Harry B. Coyle, Owner. **Description:** An employment agency. Company pays fee. **Number of placements per year:** 1 - 49.

APPLE ONE SERVICES
1970 Broadway, Suite 110, Oakland CA 94612. 510/835-0217. **Contact:** General Manager. **Description:** An employment agency. Company pays fee. **Specializes in the**

areas of: Accounting/Auditing; Clerical; Finance. **Positions commonly filled include:** Accountant/Auditor; Administrative Assistant; Aerospace Engineer; Bank Officer/ Manager; Bookkeeper; Buyer; Civil Engineer; Claim Representative; Clerk; Computer Operator; Computer Programmer; Credit Manager; Customer Service Representative; Data Entry Clerk; Draftsperson; Economist/Market Research Analyst; Electrical/ Electronics Engineer; Factory Worker; Financial Analyst; Human Resources Specialist; Industrial Engineer; Legal Secretary; Marketing Specialist; Mechanical Engineer; Medical Secretary; Operations/Production Manager; Quality Control Supervisor; Receptionist; Sales Representative; Secretary; Stenographer; Typist/Word Processor. **Number of placements per year:** 1000+.

THE COMPUTER RESOURCES GROUP, INC.
275 Battery Street, Suite 800, San Francisco CA 94111. 415/398-3535. **Contact:** Jackie Autry, Vice President. **Description:** An employment agency. **Specializes in the areas of:** Computer Hardware/Software; MIS/EDP. **Positions commonly filled include:** Computer Programmer; EDP Specialist; MIS Specialist; Systems Analyst. **Number of placements per year:** 1000+.

CORPORATE SOLUTIONS
1173 Ninth Street, Monterey CA 93940. 408/646-0779. **Contact:** Judy Marra, CPC, Owner. **Description:** An employment agency. Company pays fee. **Specializes in the areas of:** Accounting/Auditing; Finance. **Positions commonly filled include:** Accountant/Auditor; Budget Analyst; Financial Analyst. **Number of placements per year:** 1 - 49.

MARLENE CRITCHFIELD COMPANY
150 West Gabilan, Suite 2, Salinas CA 93901. 408/753-2466. **Fax:** 408/753-2467. **Contact:** Marlene Critchfield, Owner. **Description:** An employment agency. Company pays fee. **Specializes in the areas of:** Accounting/Auditing; Food Industry; General Management; Manufacturing; Sales and Marketing. **Positions commonly filled include:** Accountant/Auditor; Aerospace Engineer; Agricultural Scientist; Budget Analyst; Financial Analyst; Food Scientist/Technologist; General Manager; Human Resources Specialist; Industrial Engineer; Mechanical Engineer; Operations/Production Manager; Quality Control Supervisor; Transportation/Traffic Specialist. **Number of placements per year:** 1 - 49.

CULVER PERSONNEL SERVICE
1555 Old Bayshore Highway, Suite 100, Burlingame CA 94010. 415/692-9090. **Fax:** 415/692-6618. **Contact:** Paul Revetti, Branch Manager. **Description:** An employment agency. Company pays fee. **Specializes in the areas of:** Advertising; Banking; Computer Science/Software; Finance; General Management; Health/Medical; Retail; Sales and Marketing; Transportation. **Positions commonly filled include:** Bank Officer/ Manager; Branch Manager; Claim Representative; Customer Service Representative; General Manager; Hotel Manager/Assistant Manager; Management Trainee; Manufacturer's/Wholesaler's Sales Rep.; Operations/Production Manager; Real Estate Appraiser; Restaurant/Food Service Manager; Services Sales Representative; Underwriter/Assistant Underwriter; Wholesale and Retail Buyer. **Number of placements per year:** 500 - 999.

DATA SYSTEMS SEARCH CONSULTANTS
1756 Lacassie Avenue, Suite 202, Walnut Creek CA 94596. 510/256-0635. **Contact:**

John R. Martinez, President. **Description:** An employment agency. Company pays fee. **Specializes in the areas of:** Computer Hardware/Software. **Positions commonly filled include:** Computer Operator; Computer Programmer; EDP Specialist; MIS Specialist; Operations/Production Manager; Systems Analyst.

DENT-ASSIST PERSONNEL SERVICE
725 30th Street, Suite 206, Sacramento CA 95816. 916/443-1113. **Contact:** Lisa Saiia, Director. **Description:** An employment agency. Company pays fee.

DRUMMER PERSONNEL, INC.
2121 South El Camino, Suite 515B, San Mateo CA 94403. 415/345-7691. **Fax:** 415/345-8496. **Contact:** Geri Geller, Sole Proprietor. **Description:** An employment agency. Company pays fee. **Specializes in the areas of:** Business Services; Finance; Sales and Marketing. **Positions commonly filled include:** Customer Service Representative; Management Trainee; Manufacturer's/Wholesaler's Sales Rep. **Number of placements per year:** 50 - 99.

DUNHILL PROFESSIONAL SEARCH OF OAKLAND, INC.
3732 Mount Diablo Boulevard, Suite 375, Lafayette CA 94549. 510/283-5300. **Fax:** 510/283-5310. **Contact:** John F. Tierney, President. **Description:** An employment agency. Company pays fee. **Specializes in the areas of:** Engineering; Food Industry; Industrial Sales and Marketing; Manufacturing. **Positions commonly filled include:** Biomedical Engineer; Chemical Engineer; Civil Engineer; Electrical/Electronics Engineer; Food Scientist/Technologist; Industrial Engineer; Mechanical Engineer; Metallurgical Engineer; Nuclear Engineer; Petroleum Engineer; Software Engineer; Stationary Engineer. **Number of placements per year:** 50 - 99.

EXECUTIVE SEARCH CONSULTANTS
2108 Appaloosa Circle, Petaluma CA 94954. 707/763-0100. **Fax:** 707/765-6983. **Contact:** Peg Iversen, Principal. **Description:** An employment agency. Company pays fee. **Specializes in the areas of:** Engineering; Technical and Scientific. **Positions commonly filled include:** Electrical/Electronics Engineer; Software Engineer. **Number of placements per year:** 1 - 49.

FASTEK TECHNICAL SERVICES
4479 Stoneridge Drive, Pleasanton CA 94588. 510/462-1050. **Fax:** 510/462-1139. **Contact:** Holly Quisenberry, Technical Recruiter. **Description:** An employment agency. **Specializes in the areas of:** Accounting/Auditing; Computer Science/Software; Engineering; Technical and Scientific. **Positions commonly filled include:** Accountant/Auditor; Aerospace Engineer; Agricultural Engineer; Agricultural Scientist; Architect; Biological Scientist/Biochemist; Biomedical Engineer; Broadcast Technician; Buyer; Chemical Engineer; Chemist; Civil Engineer; Clinical Lab Technician; Computer Programmer; Computer Systems Analyst; Cost Estimator; Designer; Draftsperson; Editor; Electrical/Electronics Engineer; Electrician; Geographer; Geologist/Geophysicist; Human Resources Specialist; Industrial Engineer; Landscape Architect; Mathematician; Mechanical Engineer; Metallurgical Engineer; Mining Engineer; Petroleum Engineer; Physicist/Astronomer; Purchasing Agent and Manager; Quality Control Supervisor; Science Technologist; Software Engineer; Stationary Engineer; Structural Engineer; Technical Writer/Editor; Transportation/Traffic Specialist. **Number of placements per year:** 500 - 999.

GPL ENGINEERING
3031 Tisch Way, Suite 810, San Jose CA 95128. 408/243-1077. **Fax:** 408/241-2652. **Contact:** Guy Leo, Owner. **Description:** An employment agency. Company pays fee. **Specializes in the areas of:** Computer Science/Software; Electrical; Engineering. **Positions commonly filled include:** Electrical/Electronics Engineer; Software Engineer. **Number of placements per year:** 1 - 49.

GARNETT EMPLOYMENT SERVICE
17190 Monterey Road, Morgan Hill CA 95037. 408/778-0729. **Fax:** 408/779-9154. **Contact:** Linda Wright, President. **Description:** An employment agency. Company pays fee. **Specializes in the areas of:** Engineering; Food Industry; General Management; Manufacturing; Sales and Marketing; Secretarial; Technical and Scientific; Transportation. **Positions commonly filled include:** Administrative Services Manager; Blue-Collar Worker Supervisor; Clerical Supervisor; Customer Service Representative; General Manager; Industrial Production Manager; Restaurant/Food Service Manager; Services Sales Representative; Transportation/Traffic Specialist; Truck Driver. **Number of placements per year:** 500 - 999.

INTERIM PERSONNEL
160 Pine Street, Suite 300, San Francisco CA 94111. 415/391-5965. **Contact:** Jan Van Amburg, Branch Manager. **Description:** An employment agency. Company pays fee. **Specializes in the areas of:** Accounting/Auditing; Clerical; MIS/EDP; Sales and Marketing; Secretarial; Temporary Assignments. **Positions commonly filled include:** Administrative Assistant; Clerk; Human Resources Specialist; Legal Secretary; Receptionist; Secretary; Stenographer; Typist/Word Processor. **Number of placements per year:** 200 - 499.

MARK ASSOCIATES
300 Montgomery Street, Suite 860, San Francisco CA 94104. 415/392-1835. **Contact:** Judy Steinmetz, Vice President. **Description:** An employment agency. Company pays fee. **Specializes in the areas of:** Legal. **Positions commonly filled include:** Legal Secretary; Paralegal; Typist/Word Processor. **Number of placements per year:** 100 - 199.

McCALL STAFFING SERVICES
351 California Street, Suite 1200, San Francisco CA 94104. 415/981-3400. **Contact:** Pegi White, Owner. **Description:** An employment agency. Company pays fee. **Specializes in the areas of:** Clerical; Secretarial. **Positions commonly filled include:** Administrative Assistant; Bookkeeper; Clerk; Data Entry Clerk; Legal Secretary; Receptionist; Secretary; Typist/Word Processor. **Number of placements per year:** 200 - 499.

JOSEPH MICHAELS
1440 Broadway, Suite 506, Oakland CA 94612. 510/832-1090. **Fax:** 510/832-1099. **Contact:** Joe M. Pelayo, President. **Description:** An employment agency. Company pays fee. **Specializes in the areas of:** Accounting/Auditing; Finance. **Positions commonly filled include:** Accountant/Auditor; Bookkeeper. **Number of placements per year:** 100 - 199.

MONROE PERSONNEL SERVICES/TEMPTIME
333 Market Street, Suite 3320, San Francisco CA 94105. 415/882-7100. **Fax:** 415/882-7145. **Contact:** Debra Monroe, Owner. **Description:** An employment agency. Company

pays fee. **Specializes in the areas of:** Accounting/Auditing; Secretarial; Temporary Assignments. **Positions commonly filled include:** Administrative Assistant; Bookkeeper; Clerk; Data Entry Clerk; Legal Secretary; Receptionist; Secretary; Typist/Word Processor. **Number of placements per year:** 50 - 99.

MOTHERS-IN-DEED, INC.
425 Sherman Avenue, Suite 130, Palo Alto CA 94306. 415/326-8570. **Fax:** 415/326-1556. **Contact:** Caitlin Field, Recruiter. **Description:** An employment agency. Company pays fee. **Specializes in the areas of:** Childcare, In-Home. **Positions commonly filled include:** Nanny. **Number of placements per year:** 200 - 499.

OFFICEMATES 5
DAYSTAR TEMPORARY SERVICES
3031 Tisch Way, Suite 606, San Jose CA 95128. 408/246-9696. **Fax:** 408/246-9696. **Contact:** Verna File, Manager. **Description:** An employment agency. Company pays fee. **Specializes in the areas of:** Accounting/Auditing; Computer Science/Software; Finance; Secretarial. **Positions commonly filled include:** Administrative Assistant; Administrative Services Manager; Advertising Clerk; Branch Manager; Credit Manager; Customer Service Representative; Financial Analyst; Property and Real Estate Manager; Purchasing Agent and Manager; Secretary; Services Sales Representative; Underwriter/Assistant Underwriter. **Number of placements per year:** 100 - 199.

OMNI SEARCH INC.
1875 South Grant Street, Suite 530, San Mateo CA 94402. 415/574-6090. **Fax:** 415/574-4109. **Contact:** David Scardifield, President/Owner. **Description:** An employment agency. **Specializes in the areas of:** Computer Science/Software; Datacommunications; Engineering; Sales and Marketing; Technical and Scientific; Telecommunications. **Positions commonly filled include:** Computer Programmer; Computer Systems Analyst; Electrical/Electronics Engineer; Services Sales Representative; Software Engineer. **Number of placements per year:** 50 - 99.

PRYOR & ASSOCIATES
100 Pine Street, Suite 1660, San Francisco CA 94111. 415/989-9890. **Fax:** 415/989-8013. **Contact:** Jo-Ann Pryor, Managing Partner. **Description:** An employment agency. Company pays fee. **Specializes in the areas of:** Insurance. **Positions commonly filled include:** Accountant/Auditor; Actuary; Adjuster; Administrative Services Manager; Claim Representative; Insurance Agent/Broker; Underwriter/Assistant Underwriter. **Number of placements per year:** 50 - 99.

RILEY COLE PROFESSIONAL RECRUITERS
P.O. Box 10635, Oakland CA 94610. 510/428-2022. **Fax:** 510/428-2072. **Contact:** Jim Riley or Don Cole, Partners. **Description:** An employment agency. Company pays fee. **Specializes in the areas of:** Accounting/Auditing; Engineering; Finance; General Management; Industrial; Manufacturing; Personnel/Labor Relations; Retail; Sales and Marketing; Technical and Scientific; Transportation. **Positions commonly filled include:** Agricultural Engineer; Buyer; Chemist; Customer Service Representative; Electrical/Electronics Engineer; Financial Analyst; Food Scientist/Technologist; General Manager; Human Resources Specialist; Industrial Engineer; Management Analyst/Consultant; Manufacturer's/Wholesaler's Sales Rep.; Mechanical Engineer; Purchasing Agent and Manager; Quality Control Supervisor; Transportation/Traffic Specialist; Wholesale and Retail Buyer. **Number of placements per year:** 1 - 49.

SAFECARE
Seven Mount Lassen Drive, San Raphael CA 94903. 415/472-4457. **Fax:** 415/472-4458. **Contact:** Kimberley Altmann, Owner/Operator. **Description:** An employment agency. **Specializes in the areas of:** Childcare, In-Home. **Positions commonly filled include:** Domestic Help. **Number of placements per year:** 50 - 99.

SAN PABLO PERSONNEL AGENCY
629 El Portal Circle, San Pablo CA 94806. 510/233-7363. **Contact:** Ed Lane, Owner. **Description:** An employment agency. Company pays fee. **Specializes in the areas of:** Non-Specialized. **Positions commonly filled include:** Accountant/Auditor; Administrative Assistant; Agricultural Engineer; Biological Scientist/Biochemist; Biomedical Engineer; Bookkeeper; Civil Engineer; Claim Representative; Clerk; Computer Programmer; Construction Trade Worker; Credit Manager; Customer Service Representative; Data Entry Clerk; Draftsperson; EDP Specialist; Electrical/Electronics Engineer; Factory Worker; Hotel Manager/Assistant Manager; Human Resources Specialist; Industrial Designer; Industrial Engineer; Legal Secretary; Mechanical Engineer; Medical Secretary; Metallurgical Engineer; Petroleum Engineer; Purchasing Agent and Manager; Receptionist; Secretary; Statistician; Stenographer; Systems Analyst; Technical Writer/Editor; Technician; Typist/Word Processor. **Number of placements per year:** 200 - 499.

SNELLING PERSONNEL SERVICES
26229 Eden Landing Road, Suite 3, Hayward CA 94545. 510/538-3750. **Contact:** Gloria S. Capron, CEO. **Description:** An employment agency. Company pays fee. **Specializes in the areas of:** Accounting/Auditing; Advertising; Banking; Clerical; Computer Hardware/Software; Construction; Food Industry; Legal; Manufacturing; Printing/Publishing; Real Estate; Secretarial; Technical and Scientific. **Positions commonly filled include:** Accountant/Auditor; Administrative Assistant; Bookkeeper; Credit Manager; Customer Service Representative; Data Entry Clerk; Legal Secretary; Receptionist; Secretary; Typist/Word Processor. **Number of placements per year:** 200 - 499.

SOURCE ENGINEERING
1290 Oakmead Parkway, Suite 318, Sunnyvale CA 94086. 408/738-8440. **Fax:** 408/730-1042. **Contact:** Jeff Block, Managing Director. **Description:** An employment agency. Company pays fee. **Specializes in the areas of:** Computer Science/Software; Engineering; Sales and Marketing; Technical and Scientific. **Positions commonly filled include:** Branch Manager; Computer Programmer; Computer Systems Analyst; Customer Service Representative; Electrical/Electronics Engineer; General Manager; Management Analyst/Consultant; Software Engineer. **Number of placements per year:** 50 - 99.

SUNDAY & ASSOCIATES, INC.
P.O. Box 21122, Piedmont CA 94620-1122. 510/644-0440. **Contact:** Michael Sunday, Owner. **Description:** An employment agency. **Specializes in the areas of:** Computer Hardware/Software; Technical and Scientific. **Positions commonly filled include:** Computer Programmer; Software Engineer; Systems Analyst; Technical Writer/Editor.

SYSTEM ONE
3021 Citrus Circle, Suite 230, Walnut Creek CA 94598. 510/932-8801. **Contact:** Dave Doyle, Owner. **Description:** An employment agency. **Specializes in the areas of:**

Clerical; Engineering. **Positions commonly filled include:** Bookkeeper; Chemical Engineer; Electrical/Electronics Engineer; Industrial Engineer; Legal Secretary; Manufacturing Engineer; Mechanical Engineer; Secretary; Typist/Word Processor.

SYSTEMS CAREERS
211 Sutter Street, Suite 607, San Francisco CA 94104. 415/434-4770. **Contact:** Wayne Sarchett, Principal. **Description:** An employment agency. Company pays fee. **Specializes in the areas of:** Banking; Computer Hardware/Software; Food Industry; Manufacturing; MIS/EDP; Sales and Marketing; Transportation. **Positions commonly filled include:** Computer Programmer; EDP Specialist; Industrial Engineer; Management Analyst/Consultant; Software Engineer.

TECH SEARCH
2015 Bridgeway, Suite 301, Sausalito CA 94965. 415/332-1282. **Fax:** 415/332-1285. **Contact:** Roger M. King, President. **Description:** An employment agency. Company pays fee. **Specializes in the areas of:** Computer Science/Software. **Positions commonly filled include:** Computer Programmer; Computer Systems Analyst; Software Engineer; Technical Writer/Editor. **Number of placements per year:** 200 - 499.

TOD PERSONNEL
690 Market Street, Suite 100, San Francisco CA 94104. 415/392-0700. **Fax:** 415/392-0752. **Contact:** Branch Manager. **Description:** An employment agency. **Specializes in the areas of:** Legal. **Positions commonly filled include:** Accountant/Auditor; Administrative Services Manager; Advertising Clerk; Branch Manager; Budget Analyst; Buyer; Claim Representative; Clerical Supervisor; Computer Programmer; Computer Systems Analyst; Cost Estimator; Credit Manager; Customer Service Representative; Financial Analyst; Management Trainee; Paralegal; Purchasing Agent and Manager; Services Sales Representative; Statistician; Technical Writer/Editor. **Other area locations:** 20 East 20th Avenue, San Mateo CA. **Number of placements per year:** 500 - 999.

TOD PERSONNEL
20 East 20th Avenue, San Mateo CA 94403. 415/574-8900. **Fax:** 415/574-2636. **Contact:** Branch Manager. **Description:** An employment agency. **Specializes in the areas of:** Legal. **Positions commonly filled include:** Accountant/Auditor; Administrative Services Manager; Advertising Clerk; Branch Manager; Budget Analyst; Buyer; Claim Representative; Clerical Supervisor; Computer Programmer; Computer Systems Analyst; Cost Estimator; Credit Manager; Customer Service Representative; Financial Analyst; Management Trainee; Paralegal; Purchasing Agent and Manager; Services Sales Representative; Statistician; Technical Writer/Editor. **Other area locations:** 690 Market Street, San Francisco CA. **Number of placements per year:** 500 - 999.

WOLBERG MICHELSON PERSONNEL SERVICE
3480 Buskirk, Suite 100, Pleasant Hill CA 94523. 510/946-0200. **Contact:** Jackie Abrams, Branch Manager. **Description:** An employment agency. Company pays fee. **Specializes in the areas of:** Clerical; General Labor. **Positions commonly filled include:** Administrative Worker/Clerk; Bookkeeper; Clerk; Data Entry Clerk; Receptionist; Sales Representative; Secretary; Stenographer; Typist/Word Processor.

EXECUTIVE SEARCH FIRMS

ADVANCED TECHNOLOGY CONSULTANTS, INC.
536 Weddell Drive, Suite 7, Sunnyvale CA 94089. 408/734-0635. **Fax:** 408/734-5833. **Contact:** Mr. Reza Vakili, Staffing Manager. **Description:** An executive search firm. **Specializes in the areas of:** Computer Science/Software; Engineering. **Positions commonly filled include:** Computer Programmer; Electrical/Electronics Engineer; Software Engineer; Technical Writer/Editor.

AGRI SEARCH INTERNATIONAL AND AG CHEM SEARCH
P.O. Box 775, Elk Grove CA 95759-0775. 916/689-6400. **Contact:** Ken Yelle, Director. **Description:** An executive search firm. **Specializes in the areas of:** Agri-Business. **Positions commonly filled include:** Agricultural Engineer; Agricultural Scientist; Veterinarian. Company pays fee.

ALLARD ASSOCIATES
44 Montgomery Street, Suite 500, San Francisco CA 94104. 415/433-0500. **Toll-free fax:** 800/526-7791. **Contact:** Susan Allard, Partner. **Description:** An executive search firm. Company pays fee. **Specializes in the areas of:** Banking; Retail. **Positions commonly filled include:** Credit Manager; Customer Service Manager; Database Management Specialist; Economist/Market Research Analyst; Marketing/Advertising/PR Manager; Mathematician; Operations/Production Manager; Product Manager; Statistician. **Number of placements per year:** 50 - 99.

AMATO & ASSOCIATES OF CALIFORNIA, INC.
388 Market Street, San Francisco CA 94111. 415/781-7664. **Contact:** Joe Amato, President. **Description:** An executive search firm. **Specializes in the areas of:** Insurance. **Number of placements per year:** 100 - 199.

ANDREW SEARCH ASSOCIATES
2005 De La Cruz Boulevard, Suite 180, Santa Clara CA 95050. 408/986-8989. **Fax:** 408/986-1493. **Contact:** Andrew B. Leach, President. **Description:** An executive search firm. **Specializes in the areas of:** Computer Hardware/Software; Engineering; Manufacturing; Technical and Scientific. **Positions commonly filled include:** Biological Scientist/Biochemist; Biomedical Engineer; Ceramics Engineer; Chemical Engineer; Chemist; Computer Programmer; Industrial Designer; Industrial Engineer; Manufacturing Engineer; Marketing Specialist; Mechanical Engineer; Metallurgical Engineer; Software Engineer. **Number of placements per year:** 50 - 99.

BAY RESOURCES INC.
519 17th Street, Suite 510, Oakland CA 94612. 510/465-2781. **Contact:** Sandra Adams, President. **Description:** An executive search firm. **Specializes in the areas of:** Accounting/Auditing; Banking; Finance. **Number of placements per year:** 100 - 199.

THOMAS BECK INC.
P.O. Box 789, Sausalito CA 94966-0789. 415/331-1555. **Fax:** 415/381-1608. **Contact:** Thomas Beck, CEO. **Description:** An executive search firm. Company pays fee. **Specializes in the areas of:** Electronics; Engineering; Sales and Marketing. **Number of placements per year:** 1 - 49.

EDWARD BELL ASSOCIATES
50 First Street, Suite 410, San Francisco CA 94105. 415/442-0270. **Fax:** 415/442-1862. **Contact:** Professional Recruiter. **Description:** An executive search firm. Company pays fee. **Specializes in the areas of:** Accounting/Auditing; Administration/MIS/EDP; Computer Science/Software; Finance; Secretarial. **Positions commonly filled include:** Accountant/Auditor; Computer Programmer; Computer Systems Analyst; Paralegal; Software Engineer. **Number of placements per year:** 100 - 199.

HARVEY BELL & ASSOCIATES
700 Lindsay Avenue, Rohnert Park CA 94928. 707/795-0650. **Contact:** Harvey Bell, Owner. **Description:** An executive search firm. Company pays fee. **Specializes in the areas of:** Administration/MIS/EDP; Architecture/Construction/Real Estate; Banking; Computer Science/Software; Education; Engineering; Finance; General Management; Health/Medical; Insurance; Legal; Sales and Marketing. **Positions commonly filled include:** Attorney; Bank Officer/Manager; Biomedical Engineer; Branch Manager; Chiropractor; Computer Programmer; Computer Systems Analyst; Dentist; Economist/ Market Research Analyst; Education Administrator; Electrical/Electronics Engineer; General Manager; Geographer; Geologist/Geophysicist; Health Services Manager; Instrument Engineer; Licensed Practical Nurse; Management Analyst/Consultant; Manufacturer's/Wholesaler's Sales Rep.; Operations/Production Manager; Paralegal; Physician; Quality Control Supervisor; Real Estate Agent; Registered Nurse; Securities Sales Representative; Services Sales Representative; Software Engineer; Teacher; Travel Agent; Veterinarian.

BIALLA AND ASSOCIATES, INC.
4000 Bridgeway, Suite 201, Sausalito CA 94965. 415/332-7111. **Fax:** 415/332-3964. **Contact:** H. Scott Thomson, Partner and General Manager. **Description:** An executive search firm. Company pays fee. **Specializes in the areas of:** Advertising; General Management; Sales and Marketing. **Number of placements per year:** 50 - 99.

BRYSON MYERS COMPANY
1101 San Antonio Road, Suite 308, Mountain View CA 94043. 415/964-7600. **Fax:** 415/964-7655. **Contact:** Chris Myers, Partner. **Description:** An executive search firm. Company pays fee. **Specializes in the areas of:** Computer Hardware/Software; Engineering; Health/Medical; Technical and Scientific. **Positions commonly filled include:** Biomedical Engineer; Ceramics Engineer; Computer Programmer; Electrical/ Electronics Engineer; Industrial Designer; Industrial Engineer; Manufacturing Engineer; MIS Specialist; Software Engineer; Technical Writer/Editor. **Number of placements per year:** 50 - 99.

CN ASSOCIATES
100 Smith Ranch Road, Suite 301, San Raphael CA 94903. 415/883-1114. **Fax:** 415/883-3321. **Contact:** Professional Placement. **Description:** An executive search firm. **Specializes in the areas of:** Computer Science/Software; Engineering. **Positions commonly filled include:** Branch Manager; Computer Programmer; Computer Systems Analyst; Software Engineer. **Number of placements per year:** 1 - 49.

CR ASSOCIATES
P.O. Box 60998, Palo Alto CA 94306. 415/324-9000. **Contact:** Harold Stephenson, Owner. **Description:** An executive search firm. **Specializes in the areas of:** Banking; Finance.

CALIFORNIA MANAGEMENT SEARCH (CMS)
881 11th Street, Suite 117, Lakeport CA 95453. 707/263-6000. **Fax:** 707/263-6800. **Contact:** Manager/Owner. **Description:** An executive search firm. Company pays fee. **Specializes in the areas of:** Insurance. **Number of placements per year:** 1 - 49.

CONSULTANT REGISTRY INTERNATIONAL (CRI)
1784 Leimert Boulevard, Oakland CA 94602. 510/531-1681. **Contact:** Chuck Acridge, Owner. **Description:** An executive search firm. **Specializes in the areas of:** Health/Medical. **Positions commonly filled include:** Nurse; Physician. **Number of placements per year:** 1 - 49.

CORPORATE SEARCH
6457 Edgemoor Way, San Jose CA 95129. 408/996-3000. **Contact:** Hal Wilson, President. **Description:** An executive search firm. Company pays fee. **Specializes in the areas of:** Computer Science/Software; Design; Engineering; Personnel/Labor Relations. **Positions commonly filled include:** Accountant/Auditor; Aerospace Engineer; Biomedical Engineer; Chemical Engineer; Computer Programmer; Computer Systems Analyst; Electrical/Electronics Engineer; Financial Analyst; Industrial Engineer; Management Analyst/Consultant; Mechanical Engineer; Metallurgical Engineer; Nuclear Engineer; Technical Writer/Editor; Travel Agent. **Number of placements per year:** 1 - 49.

CORPORATE TECHNOLOGY INC.
P.O. Box 70310, Sunnyvale CA 94086. 408/735-1690. **Contact:** John Reinhardt, President. **Description:** An executive search firm. Company pays fee. **Specializes in the areas of:** Engineering; Manufacturing; Technical and Scientific. **Positions commonly filled include:** Ceramics Engineer; Computer Programmer; Electrical/Electronics Engineer; Mechanical Engineer. **Number of placements per year:** 1 - 49.

DALEY CONSULTING & SEARCH
1866 Clayton Road, Suite 211, Concord CA 94520. 510/798-3866. **Fax:** 510/798-4475. **Contact:** Mike Daley, Senior Recruiting Consultant. **Description:** An executive search firm. Company pays fee. **Specializes in the areas of:** Administration/MIS/EDP; Computer Science/Software; Information Systems. **Positions commonly filled include:** Computer Programmer; Computer Systems Analyst; Data Entry Clerk; MIS Specialist. **Number of placements per year:** 1 - 49.

DUNHILL PROFESSIONAL SEARCH OF SAN FRANCISCO
220 Montgomery Street, Box 2909, San Francisco CA 94104. 415/956-3700. **Contact:** George Curtiss, President. **Description:** An executive search firm. **Specializes in the areas of:** Banking; Computer Hardware/Software; Electronics; Health/Medical; Paper; Sales and Marketing.

DUNHILL PROFESSIONAL SEARCH OF SAN JOSE
1190 Saratoga Avenue, Suite 210, San Jose CA 95129. 408/236-3262. **Fax:** 408/296-7866. **Contact:** Kevin A. P. Keifer, President. **Description:** An executive search firm. Company pays fee. **Specializes in the areas of:** Computer Science/Software; Engineering; Industrial; Manufacturing; Sales and Marketing; Secretarial; Technical and Scientific. **Positions commonly filled include:** Chemical Engineer; Computer Programmer; Customer Service Representative; Electrical/Electronics Engineer; Manufacturer's/Wholesaler's Sales Rep.; Mechanical Engineer; Operations/Production

Manager; Quality Control Supervisor; Software Engineer. **Number of placements per year:** 1 - 49.

EAGLE SEARCH ASSOCIATES
410 Pacific, San Francisco CA 94133. 415/398-6066. **Fax:** 415/398-0858. **Contact:** Mark Gideon, Executive Director. **Description:** An executive search firm. Company pays fee. **Specializes in the areas of:** Computer Science/Software; Sales and Marketing. **Positions commonly filled include:** Computer Systems Analyst. **Number of placements per year:** 1 - 49.

ETHOS CONSULTING, INC.
100 Pine Street, Suite 2750, San Francisco CA 94111-5208. 415/397-2211. **Fax:** 415/397-0856. **Contact:** Conrad E. Prusak, Managing Partner. **Description:** An executive search firm. Company pays fee. **Specializes in the areas of:** Food Industry; General Management. **Positions commonly filled include:** Bank Officer/Manager; General Manager; Management Analyst/Consultant. **Number of placements per year:** 1 - 49.

FISHER & ASSOCIATES
1063 Lenor Way, San Jose CA 95128. 408/554-0156. **Contact:** Gary Fisher, Owner. **Description:** An executive search firm. Company pays fee. **Specializes in the areas of:** Administration/MIS/EDP; Computer Science/Software; Engineering; General Management; Sales and Marketing. **Positions commonly filled include:** General Manager; Software Engineer. **Number of placements per year:** 1 - 49.

GM ASSOCIATES
1500 Golden Rain Road, Suite One, Walnut Creek CA 94595. 510/256-6513. **Contact:** Proprietor. **Description:** An executive search firm. **Specializes in the areas of:** Engineering. **Number of placements per year:** 200 - 499.

THE GOODMAN GROUP
P.O. Box 150960, San Rafael CA 94915. 415/455-1500. **Contact:** Recruitment. **Description:** An executive search firm. Company pays fee. **Specializes in the areas of:** Computer Hardware/Software; Engineering; Health/Medical; Insurance; MIS/EDP; Sales and Marketing. **Positions commonly filled include:** Aerospace Engineer; Biomedical Engineer; Civil Engineer; Computer Programmer; EDP Specialist; Electrical/ Electronics Engineer; General Manager; Management Analyst/Consultant; Physician; Sales Representative; Systems Analyst. **Number of placements per year:** 50 - 99.

INSURANCE STAFFERS
5435 Madison Avenue, Sacramento CA 95841. 916/349-1221. **Fax:** 916/332-4166. **Contact:** Bruce Marx, Recruiter. **Description:** An executive search firm. **Specializes in the areas of:** Insurance. **Positions commonly filled include:** Claim Representative; Insurance Agent/Broker; Underwriter/Assistant Underwriter.

MAJOR, WILSON & AFRICA
655 Commercial Street, San Francisco CA 94111. 415/956-1010. **Fax:** 415/398-2425. **Contact:** Robert A. Major, Partner. **Description:** An executive search firm. Company pays fee. **Specializes in the areas of:** Legal. **Positions commonly filled include:** Attorney. **Number of placements per year:** 50 - 99.

MANAGEMENT RECRUITERS INTERNATIONAL
2316 Bell Executive Lane, Suite 100, Sacramento CA 95825. 916/920-0441. **Contact:** Ken McCollum, Manager. **Description:** An executive search firm. **Specializes in the areas of:** Accounting/Auditing; Administration/MIS/EDP; Advertising; Architecture/Construction/Real Estate; Banking; Communications; Computer Hardware/Software; Construction; Electrical; Engineering; Finance; Food Industry; General Management; Health/Medical; Insurance; Legal; Manufacturing; Operations Management; Personnel/Labor Relations; Pharmaceutical; Printing/Publishing; Procurement; Retail; Sales and Marketing; Technical and Scientific; Textiles; Transportation.

MANAGEMENT RECRUITERS OF BURLINGAME
111 Anza Boulevard, Suite 109, Burlingame CA 94010. 415/548-4800. **Contact:** Office Manager. **Description:** An executive search firm. **Specializes in the areas of:** Accounting/Auditing; Administration/MIS/EDP; Advertising; Architecture/Construction/Real Estate; Banking; Communications; Computer Hardware/Software; Construction; Electrical; Engineering; Finance; Food Industry; General Management; Health/Medical; Insurance; Legal; Manufacturing; Operations Management; Personnel/Labor Relations; Pharmaceutical; Printing/Publishing; Procurement; Retail; Sales and Marketing; Technical and Scientific; Textiles; Transportation.

MANAGEMENT RECRUITERS OF CLOVIS
150 Clovis Avenue, Suite 205, Clovis CA 93612-1152. 209/299-7992. **Fax:** 209/299-2167. **Contact:** Gary Hendrickson, General Manager and Owner. **Description:** An executive search firm. Company pays fee. **Specializes in the areas of:** Chemical; Engineering; Food Industry; Industrial; Manufacturing; Personnel/Labor Relations; Plastics; Sales and Marketing; Technical and Scientific; Transportation. **Positions commonly filled include:** Agricultural Engineer; Biological Scientist/Biochemist; Chemical Engineer; Designer; Electrical/Electronics Engineer; Food Scientist/Technologist; General Manager; Human Resources Specialist; Industrial Engineer; Industrial Production Manager; Mechanical Engineer; Metallurgical Engineer; Operations/Production Manager; Quality Control Supervisor; Restaurant/Food Service Manager; Transportation/Traffic Specialist. **Number of placements per year:** 1 - 49.

MANAGEMENT RECRUITERS OF EMERYVILLE
2000 Powell Street, Suite 1200, Emeryville CA 94608. 707/746-6944. **Contact:** Mark Hoffman, Manager. **Description:** An executive search firm. **Specializes in the areas of:** Accounting/Auditing; Administration/MIS/EDP; Advertising; Architecture/Construction/Real Estate; Banking; Communications; Computer Hardware/Software; Construction; Engineering; Finance; Food Industry; General Management; Health/Medical; Insurance; Legal; Manufacturing; Operations Management; Personnel/Labor Relations; Pharmaceutical; Printing/Publishing; Procurement; Retail; Sales and Marketing; Technical and Scientific; Textiles; Transportation.

MANAGEMENT RECRUITERS OF PLEASANTON
4125 Mohr Avenue, Suite M, Pleasanton CA 94566-4740. 510/462-8579. **Contact:** Mike Machi, Co-Manager. **Description:** An executive search firm. **Specializes in the areas of:** Accounting/Auditing; Administration/MIS/EDP; Architecture/Construction/Real Estate; Banking; Communications; Computer Hardware/Software; Construction; Electrical; Engineering; Finance; Food Industry; General Management; Health/Medical; Personnel/Labor Relations; Pharmaceutical; Printing/Publishing; Procurement; Retail; Sales and Marketing; Technical and Scientific; Textiles; Transportation.

MANAGEMENT RECRUITERS OF SAN FRANCISCO
591 Redwood Highway, Suite 2225, Mill Valley CA 94941. 415/981-5950. **Contact:** Eric Wheel, Manager. **Description:** An executive search firm. **Specializes in the areas of:** Accounting/Auditing; Administration/MIS/EDP; Advertising; Architecture/Construction/Real Estate; Banking; Communications; Computer Hardware/Software; Construction; Electrical; Engineering; Finance; Food Industry; General Management; Health/Medical; Insurance; Legal; Manufacturing; Operations Management; Personnel/Labor Relations; Pharmaceutical; Printing/Publishing; Procurement; Retail; Sales and Marketing; Technical and Scientific; Textiles; Transportation.

MASTER SEARCH
P.O. Box 9070, Santa Rosa CA 95405. 707/538-4000. **Contact:** Gregory Masters, President. **Description:** An executive search firm. Company pays fee. **Specializes in the areas of:** Computer Science/Software; Engineering; Food Industry; General Management; Industrial; Manufacturing; Technical and Scientific; Transportation. **Positions commonly filled include:** Biological Scientist/Biochemist; Biomedical Engineer; Chemical Engineer; Electrical/Electronics Engineer; Food Scientist/Technologist; General Manager; Manufacturing Engineer; Mechanical Engineer; Operations/Production Manager; Quality Control Supervisor; Science Technologist; Software Engineer; Transportation/Traffic Specialist. **Number of placements per year:** 1 - 49.

MEDICAL EXECUTIVE RECRUITERS
1220 Melody Lane, Suite 106, Roseville CA 95678. 916/786-8615. **Fax:** 916/786-8609. **Contact:** John Cunningham, CEO/President. **Description:** An executive search firm. Company pays fee. **Specializes in the areas of:** Biology; Biotechnology; Computer Science/Software; General Management; Health/Medical; Pharmaceutical; Sales and Marketing; Technical and Scientific. **Positions commonly filled include:** Biological Scientist/Biochemist; Biomedical Engineer; Branch Manager; Clinical Lab Technician; Dietician/Nutritionist; Economist/Market Research Analyst; EEG Technologist; EKG Technician; Electrical/Electronics Engineer; Emergency Medical Technician; General Manager; Health Services Manager; Management Analyst/Consultant; Manufacturer's/Wholesaler's Sales Rep.; Medical Records Technician; Nuclear Engineer; Nuclear Medicine Technologist; Occupational Therapist; Operations/Production Manager; Pharmacist; Physician; Public Relations Specialist; Quality Control Supervisor; Radiologic Technologist; Registered Nurse; Respiratory Therapist; Science Technologist; Services Sales Representative; Surgical Technician. **Number of placements per year:** 100 - 199.

MULTISEARCH RECRUITERS
P.O. Box 309, Ballico CA 95303. 209/634-5814. **Fax:** 209/634-2648. **Contact:** Dennis Gallagher, President. **Description:.** An executive search firm.

NATIONAL HOSPITALITY RECRUITERS
1465 Enea Circle, Suite E-960, Concord CA 94520. 510/825-5400. **Fax:** 510/825-5525. **Contact:** Mike Blanchard, Owner. **Description:** An executive search firm. Company pays fee. **Specializes in the areas of:** Food Industry. **Positions commonly filled include:** Dietician/Nutritionist; Food Scientist/Technologist; Hotel Manager/Assistant Manager; Restaurant/Food Service Manager. **Number of placements per year:** 200 - 499.

NETWORK RESOURCE GROUPS
P.O. Box 25253, San Mateo CA 94402. 415/344-5550. **Fax:** 415/365-8065. **Contact:** Bob Read, Manager. **Description:** An executive search firm. Company pays fee. **Number of placements per year:** 1 - 49.

NORSELL & ASSOCIATES, INC.
P.O. Box 6686, Auburn CA 95604-6686. 916/269-0121. **Fax:** 916/268-3202. **Contact:** Paul Norsell, President. **Description:** An executive search firm. **Specializes in the areas of:** Biotechnology; General Management; Manufacturing; Pharmaceutical; Sales and Marketing; Technical and Scientific. **Positions commonly filled include:** Attorney; Biological Scientist/Biochemist; Biomedical Engineer; Chemical Engineer; Chemist; Electrical/Electronics Engineer; General Manager; Geologist/Geophysicist; Industrial Production Manager; Management Analyst/Consultant; Mechanical Engineer; Operations/Production Manager; Petroleum Engineer; Physician; Science Technologist; Software Engineer.

NYBORG-DOW ASSOCIATES
12781 Woodlake Road, Grass Valley CA 95949. 916/477-7817. **Fax:** 916/477-0475. **Contact:** Marilyn Nyborg, Manager. **Description:** An executive search firm. Company pays fee. **Specializes in the areas of:** Engineering. **Positions commonly filled include:** Electrical/Electronics Engineer; Marketing Specialist; Software Engineer. **Number of placements per year:** 1 - 49.

PEDEN & ASSOCIATES
2000 Broadway Street, Redwood City CA 94063. 415/367-1181. **Fax:** 415/367-7525. **Contact:** Ann Peden, President. **Description:** An executive search firm. Company pays fee. **Positions commonly filled include:** Electrical/Electronics Engineer; Software Engineer.

EDWARD RAST AND COMPANY
235 Montgomery Street, Suite 901, San Francisco CA 94104. 415/986-1710. **Contact:** Edward Rast, Managing Director. **Description:** An executive search firm. Company pays fee. **Specializes in the areas of:** Accounting/Auditing; Administration/MIS/EDP; Biology; Biotechnology; Computer Science/Software; Finance; General Management; Health/Medical; Nonprofit; Retail; Sales and Marketing; Technical and Scientific; Transportation. **Positions commonly filled include:** Accountant/Auditor; Biological Scientist/Biochemist; Biomedical Engineer; Budget Analyst; Buyer; Clinical Lab Technician; Computer Programmer; Computer Systems Analyst; Credit Manager; Economist/Market Research Analyst; Financial Analyst; General Manager; Health Services Manager; Human Resources Specialist; Management Analyst/Consultant; Operations/Production Manager; Public Relations Specialist; Software Engineer; Technical Writer/Editor; Wholesale and Retail Buyer. **Number of placements per year:** 50 - 99.

RITTER ASSOCIATES
4010 Moorpark Avenue, Suite 105D, San Jose CA 95117. 408/244-9900. **Fax:** 408/244-9903. **Contact:** Willis Ritter, President. **Description:** An executive search firm. **Specializes in the areas of:** Accounting/Auditing; Administration/MIS/EDP; Computer Science/Software; Engineering; Finance; General Management; Legal; Manufacturing; Sales and Marketing. **Positions commonly filled include:** Accountant/Auditor; Administrative Services Manager; Aerospace Engineer; Attorney; Branch Manager; Computer Systems Analyst; Electrical/Electronics Engineer; Financial Analyst; General

Manager; Human Resources Specialist; Industrial Engineer; Management Analyst/ Consultant; Manufacturer's/Wholesaler's Sales Rep.; Property and Real Estate Manager; Real Estate Agent; Science Technologist; Software Engineer. **Number of placements per year:** 1 - 49.

SAI
2855 Mitchell Drive, Suite 117, Walnut Creek CA 94598. 510/932-3000. **Fax:** 510/932-3857. **Contact:** Steve Sloan, President. **Description:** An executive search firm. Company pays fee. **Specializes in the areas of:** Computer Science/Software. **Positions commonly filled include:** Branch Manager; Computer Systems Analyst. **Number of placements per year:** 50 - 99.

SALES CONSULTANTS
1101 Sylvan Avenue, Building B, Suite B20, Modesto CA 95350. 209/529-5051. **Fax:** 209/529-5054. **Contact:** Jim Ortman, General Manager. **Description:** An executive search firm. Company pays fee. **Specializes in the areas of:** Engineering; Food Industry; Industrial; Manufacturing; Sales and Marketing; Technical and Scientific. **Positions commonly filled include:** Biological Scientist/Biochemist; Biomedical Engineer; Branch Manager; Chemical Engineer; Chemist; Electrical/Electronics Engineer; Food Scientist/Technologist; Industrial Engineer; Nuclear Engineer; Wastewater Specialist. **Number of placements per year:** 50 - 99.

SALES CONSULTANTS OF BURLINGAME
111 Anza Boulevard, Suite 109, Burlingame CA 94010. 415/548-4800. **Contact:** Don Hirschbein, Manager. **Description:** An executive search firm. **Specializes in the areas of:** Accounting/Auditing; Administration/MIS/EDP; Advertising; Architecture/ Construction/Real Estate; Banking; Communications; Computer Hardware/Software; Construction; Electrical; Engineering; Finance; Food Industry; General Management; Health/Medical; Insurance; Legal; Manufacturing; Operations Management; Personnel/ Labor Relations; Pharmaceutical; Printing/Publishing; Procurement; Retail; Sales and Marketing; Technical and Scientific; Textiles; Transportation.

SALES CONSULTANTS OF OAKLAND
480 Roland Way, Suite 103, Oakland CA 94621. 510/569-6231. **Fax:** 510/562-7237. **Contact:** Tom Thrower, Manager. **Description:** An executive search firm. **Specializes in the areas of:** Accounting/Auditing; Administration/MIS/EDP; Architecture/ Construction/Real Estate; Banking; Communications; Computer Hardware/Software; Electrical; Engineering; Finance; Food Industry; General Management; Health/Medical; Insurance; Legal; Manufacturing; Operations Management; Personnel/Labor Relations; Pharmaceutical; Printing/Publishing; Procurement; Retail; Sales and Marketing; Technical and Scientific; Transportation.

SALES CONSULTANTS OF SACRAMENTO
4811 Chippendale Drive, Suite 701, Sacramento CA 95841. 916/344-3737. **Contact:** Ron Whitney, Manager. **Description:** An executive search firm. **Specializes in the areas of:** Accounting/Auditing; Administration/MIS/EDP; Advertising; Architecture/ Construction/Real Estate; Banking; Communications; Computer Hardware/Software; Construction; Electrical; Engineering; Finance; Food Industry; General Management; Health/Medical; Insurance; Legal; Manufacturing; Operations Management; Personnel/ Labor Relations; Pharmaceutical; Printing/Publishing; Procurement; Retail; Sales and Marketing; Technical and Scientific; Textiles; Transportation.

SALES PROFESSIONALS PERSONNEL SERVICES
595 Market Street, Suite 2500, San Francisco CA 94105. 415/543-2828. **Contact:** Sheldon Israel, President. **Description:** An executive search firm. **Specializes in the areas of:** Sales and Marketing. **Number of placements per year:** 50 - 99.

SCHLATTER & ASSOCIATES
388 Market Street, Suite 400, San Francisco CA 94111. 415/433-8100. **Contact:** Craig Schlatter, President. **Description:** An executive search firm. **Specializes in the areas of:** Accounting/Auditing; Finance; MIS/EDP. **Number of placements per year:** 100 - 199.

SEARCH RESOURCES
P.O. Box 708, Lockeford CA 95237. 209/931-0102. **Fax:** 209/931-0154. **Contact:** Charles Blackburn, President. **Description:** An executive search firm. Company pays fee. **Specializes in the areas of:** Food Industry. **Positions commonly filled include:** Agricultural Engineer; Blue-Collar Worker Supervisor; Customer Service Representative; General Manager; Human Resources Specialist; Industrial Engineer; Industrial Production Manager; Mechanical Engineer; Quality Control Supervisor; Transportation/Traffic Specialist. **Number of placements per year:** 50 - 99.

SEITCHIK, CORWIN AND SEITCHIK, INC.
1830 Jackson Street, San Francisco CA 94109. 415/928-5717. **Contact:** Bill Seitchik, Vice President. **Description:** An executive search firm. **Specializes in the areas of:** Fashion; Manufacturing.

SINGER STROUSE
235 Montgomery Street, Suite 615, San Francisco CA 94104. 415/781-6444. **Contact:** Pamela Singer, Owner. **Description:** An executive search firm. **Specializes in the areas of:** Accounting/Auditing. **Number of placements per year:** 1 - 49.

SPECTRAWEST
39899 Balentine Drive, Suite 218, Newark CA 94560. 510/490-4500. **Fax:** 510/490-6877. **Contact:** Fred Arredondo, Director. **Description:** An executive search firm. Company pays fee. **Specializes in the areas of:** Computer Science/Software; Engineering. **Positions commonly filled include:** Chemical Engineer; Electrical/ Electronics Engineer; Metallurgical Engineer; Software Engineer. **Number of placements per year:** 1 - 49.

K.K. WALKER PROFESSIONAL RECRUITMENT
7803 Madison Avenue, Suite 712, Citrus Heights CA 95610. 916/863-6363. **Fax:** 916/863-3224. **Contact:** Karen Walker, Owner. **Description:** An executive search firm. Company pays fee. **Specializes in the areas of:** Health/Medical. **Positions commonly filled include:** Branch Manager; Clinical Lab Technician; Health Services Manager; Occupational Therapist; Pharmacist; Physical Therapist; Physician; Psychologist; Registered Nurse; Respiratory Therapist; Science Technologist. **Number of placements per year:** 1 - 49.

WENDELL ASSOCIATES
P.O. Box 7376, San Jose CA 95150-7376. 408/725-1345. **Contact:** Oliver Peeler, Owner. **Description:** An executive search firm. Company pays fee. **Specializes in the areas of:** Computer Hardware/Software; Health/Medical; Sales and Marketing. **Positions commonly filled include:** Biomedical Engineer; Computer Programmer; Electrical/ Electronics Engineer; Mechanical Engineer; Software Engineer.

S.R. WILSON
520 Mendicino Avenue, Suite 200, Santa Rosa CA 95401. 707/571-5990. **Contact:** Stoney Wilson, President. **Description:** An executive search firm. **Specializes in the areas of:** Engineering; Legal.

RESUME/CAREER COUNSELING SERVICES

CONTINENTAL TRAINING CENTER
1333 Willow Pass Road, Suite 203, Concord CA 94520. 510/680-2875. **Fax:** 510/680-1514. **Contact:** Bruce Klimoski, Owner. **Description:.** A career/outplacement counseling firm.

TONIK PERSONNEL AGENCY
2235 Park Towne Circle, Sacramento CA 95825. 916/488-5300. **Contact:** Peggy Ragland, Director. **Description:.** A career/outplacement counseling firm.

INDEX OF PRIMARY EMPLOYERS

NOTE: *Below is an alphabetical index of primary employer listings included in this book. Those employers in each industry that fall under the headings "Additional employers" are not indexed here.*

A

B

C

D

E

F

N

O

P

Q, R

S

X, Y, Z

Your Job Hunt
Your Feedback

Comments, questions, or suggestions? We want to hear from you. Please complete this questionnaire and mail it to:

The JobBank Staff
Adams Media Corporation
260 Center Street
Holbrook, MA 02343

Did this book provide helpful advice and valuable information which you used in your job search? Was the information easy to access?

Recommendations for improvements. How could we improve this book to help in your job search? No suggestion is too small or too large.

Would you recommend this book to a friend beginning a job hunt?

Name: ______________________________

Occupation: ______________________________

Which JobBank did you use? ______________________________

Address: ______________________________

Daytime phone: ______________________________